Cisco Data Center
Fundamentals

T0073685

)o

CCIE No. 28603, CCDE No. 20170002

Iskren Nikolov

CCIE No. 20164, CCSI No. 32481

Cisco Press

Cisco Data Center Fundamentals

Somit Maloo and Iskren Nikolov

Copyright© 2023 Cisco Systems, Inc.

Published by: Cisco Press

All rights reserved. This publication is protected by copyright, and permission must be obtained from the publisher prior to any prohibited reproduction, storage in a retrieval system, or transmission in any form or by any means, electronic, mechanical, photocopying, recording, or likewise. For information regarding permissions, request forms, and the appropriate contacts within the Pearson Education Global Rights & Permissions Department, please visit www.pearson.com/permissions.

No patent liability is assumed with respect to the use of the information contained herein. Although every precaution has been taken in the preparation of this book, the publisher and author assume no responsibility for errors or omissions. Nor is any liability assumed for damages resulting from the use of the information contained herein.

ScoutAutomatedPrintCode

Library of Congress Control Number: 2022909825

ISBN-13: 978-0-13763824-6
ISBN-10: 0-13-763824-8

Warning and Disclaimer

This book is designed to provide information about Cisco Data Center Fundamentals. Every effort has been made to make this book as complete and as accurate as possible, but no warranty or fitness is implied.

The information is provided on an "as is" basis. The authors, Cisco Press, and Cisco Systems, Inc. shall have neither liability nor responsibility to any person or entity with respect to any loss or damages arising from the information contained in this book or from the use of the discs or programs that may accompany it.

The opinions expressed in this book belong to the author and are not necessarily those of Cisco Systems, Inc.

Trademark Acknowledgments

All terms mentioned in this book that are known to be trademarks or service marks have been appropriately capitalized. Cisco Press or Cisco Systems, Inc., cannot attest to the accuracy of this information. Use of a term in this book should not be regarded as affecting the validity of any trademark or service mark.

Special Sales

For information about buying this title in bulk quantities, or for special sales opportunities (which may include electronic versions; custom cover designs; and content particular to your business, training goals, marketing focus, or branding interests), please contact our corporate sales department at corpsales@pearsoned.com or (800) 382-3419.

For government sales inquiries, please contact governmentsales@pearsoned.com.

For questions about sales outside the U.S., please contact intlcs@pearson.com.

Feedback Information

At Cisco Press, our goal is to create in-depth technical books of the highest quality and value. Each book is crafted with care and precision, undergoing rigorous development that involves the unique expertise of members from the professional technical community.

Readers' feedback is a natural continuation of this process. If you have any comments regarding how we could improve the quality of this book, or otherwise alter it to better suit your needs, you can contact us through email at feedback@ciscopress.com. Please make sure to include the book title and ISBN in your message.

We greatly appreciate your assistance.

Editor-in-Chief: Mark Taub	**Copy Editor:** Bart Reed
Alliances Manager, Cisco Press: Arezou Gol	**Technical Editor:** Ozden Karakok, CCIE No. 6331
Director, ITP Product Management: Brett Bartow	**Editorial Assistant:** Cindy Teeters
Executive Editor: James Manly	**Designer:** Chuti Prasertsith
Managing Editor: Sandra Schroeder	**Composition:** codeMantra
Development Editor: Ellie Bru	**Indexer:** Ken Johnson
Project Editor: Mandie Frank	**Proofreader:** Barbara Mack

CISCO.

Americas Headquarters	Asia Pacific Headquarters	Europe Headquarters
Cisco Systems, Inc.	Cisco Systems (USA) Pte. Ltd.	Cisco Systems International BV Amsterdam,
San Jose, CA	Singapore	The Netherlands

Cisco has more than 200 offices worldwide. Addresses, phone numbers, and fax numbers are listed on the Cisco Website at **www.cisco.com/go/offices.**

Cisco and the Cisco logo are trademarks or registered trademarks of Cisco and/or its affiliates in the U.S. and other countries. To view a list of Cisco trademarks, go to this URL: www.cisco.com/go/trademarks. Third party trademarks mentioned are the property of their respective owners. The use of the word partner does not imply a partnership relationship between Cisco and any other company. (1110R)

Pearson's Commitment to Diversity, Equity, and Inclusion

Pearson is dedicated to creating bias-free content that reflects the diversity of all learners. We embrace the many dimensions of diversity, including but not limited to race, ethnicity, gender, socioeconomic status, ability, age, sexual orientation, and religious or political beliefs.

Education is a powerful force for equity and change in our world. It has the potential to deliver opportunities that improve lives and enable economic mobility. As we work with authors to create content for every product and service, we acknowledge our responsibility to demonstrate inclusivity and incorporate diverse scholarship so that everyone can achieve their potential through learning. As the world's leading learning company, we have a duty to help drive change and live up to our purpose to help more people create a better life for themselves and to create a better world.

Our ambition is to purposefully contribute to a world where

- Everyone has an equitable and lifelong opportunity to succeed through learning

- Our educational products and services are inclusive and represent the rich diversity of learners

- Our educational content accurately reflects the histories and experiences of the learners we serve

- Our educational content prompts deeper discussions with learners and motivates them to expand their own learning (and worldview)

While we work hard to present unbiased content, we want to hear from you about any concerns or needs with this Pearson product so that we can investigate and address them.

Please contact us with concerns about any potential bias at https://www.pearson.com/report-bias.html.

About the Authors

Somit Maloo, CCIE No. 28603, CCDE No. 20170002, is a content architect from the data center team at Learning@Cisco. He holds a master's degree in telecommunication networks and a bachelor's degree in electronics and telecommunication engineering. He is also a penta-CCIE in enterprise infrastructure, service provider, enterprise wireless, security, and data center technologies. Somit holds various industry-leading certifications, including CCDE, PMP, RHCSA, and VMware VCIX6 in Data Center and Network Virtualization. Somit has extensive experience in designing and developing various data center courses for the official Cisco curriculum. He started his career as a Cisco TAC engineer. Somit has more than 12 years of experience in the networking industry, working mostly with data center networks. You can reach Somit on Twitter: @somitmaloo.

Iskren Nikolov, CCIE No.20164, CCSI No.32481, MCT Alumni, Content architect, engineer, and developer with the Cisco Learning & Certifications Data Center and Cloud team. He is responsible for designing, developing, reviewing Data Center Official Learning Cisco courses, including lab infrastructures and exercises. He holds a master's degree in computer systems and management from the Technical University-Sofia, Bulgaria. Iskren has more than 26 years of experience in designing, implementing, and supporting solutions based on technologies such as data center, security, storage, wide area network, software-defined network, cloud, hybrid, and multicloud, including 11 years of teaching and developing Cisco Data Center and Cloud courses and Microsoft Azure courses. Because of his vast experience across technologies from multiple vendors, such as Cisco Systems, VMware, Microsoft, and Barracuda, combined with the different perspectives he has gained from his different work roles and working with customers from different industries, Iskren has a unique view of the current data center technologies and future trends. You can reach Iskren on LinkedIn: https://www.linkedin.com/in/iskrennikolov.

About the Technical Reviewers

Ozden Karakok, CCIE No. 6331, is a technical consultant on data center technologies and solutions at Flint Consulting. She worked at Cisco for 19 years as a technical leader supporting data center solutions. Prior to joining Cisco, Ozden spent five years working for a number of Cisco's large customers in various telecommunication roles. She is a Cisco Certified Internetwork Expert in routing and switching, SNA/IP, and storage. She has co-authored three Cisco Press books: *CCNA Data Center DCICN 200-150*, *CCNA Data Center DCICT 200-155*, and *Data Center Technologies DCICT 640-916*. Ozden holds a degree in computer engineering from Istanbul Bogazici University. You can reach Ozden on Twitter: @okarakok.

Dedications

Somit Maloo:

To AUM.

To Rehmat Baba, the guiding angel in my life.

To my loving wife, Renuka, for her unending love and support.

To my wonderful kids, Navya and Namit.

Iskren Nikolov:

To my loving family—my wife Petya and my kids Diana and Valentin—for their unlimited support!

To my parents, for teaching me values and responsibility!

Acknowledgments

Somit Maloo:

I would like to thank my co-author, Iskren Nikolov, for teaming up with me to complete this book. Without his support, it would not have been possible. I am thankful to the professional editors and the whole production team at Cisco Press, especially James Manly and Ellie Bru, for their patience and guidance at every step of the book publishing process. I would also like to thank our technical editor, Ozden Karakok, for her keen attention to detail and for taking time out of her busy schedule to review the book.

Iskren Nikolov:

I would like to thank my co-author, Somit Maloo. He not only worked with me as a team on this book but guided me through the process of being a Cisco Press author. I am thankful to the whole production team, especially James Manly and Ellie Bru, for their professionalism and endless patience with me! Also, special thanks to our technical editor, Ozden Karakok, for providing another valuable perspective on how we can tell a better story about this technology!

Contents at a Glance

Reader Services

Register your copy at www.ciscopress.com/title/ISBN for convenient access to downloads, updates, and corrections as they become available. To start the registration process, go to www.ciscopress.com/register and log in or create an account*. Enter the product ISBN 9780137638246 and click Submit. When the process is complete, you will find any available bonus content under Registered Products.

*Be sure to check the box that you would like to hear from us to receive exclusive discounts on future editions of this product.

Contents

Icons Used in This Book

User	Clock	Database	Router	Virtual Router
API Controller	Cisco Nexus 9000 in NX-OS Mode	Virtual Machine	Fibre Channel Disk Subsystem	Building
Camera	Cisco Nexus 5000	Cloud	Fibre Channel Storage	Hub
Route Switch Processor	Cisco Nexus 7000	Cisco Nexus 9500	Server	Cisco MDS Multilayer Director
ATM/FastGb Etherswitch	File Server	Laptop	Storage Array	Fibre Channel Director

Command Syntax Conventions

The conventions used to present command syntax in this book are the same conventions used in the IOS Command Reference. The Command Reference describes these conventions as follows:

- **Boldface** indicates commands and keywords that are entered literally as shown. In actual configuration examples and output (not general command syntax), boldface indicates commands that are manually input by the user (such as a **show** command).

- *Italic* indicates arguments for which you supply actual values.

- Vertical bars (|) separate alternative, mutually exclusive elements.

- Square brackets ([ ]) indicate an optional element.

- Braces ({ }) indicate a required choice.

- Braces within brackets ([{ }]) indicate a required choice within an optional element.

Introduction

This book is intended to give you an understanding of Cisco data center products and data center–related protocols. This book is for those who are new to the data center technologies, such as computer networking students, systems engineers, and server administrators, as well as network engineers with many years of experience administering larger data center networks. The only prerequisite is a basic understanding of networking protocols.

This book is written as a self-study guide for learning data center technologies. The information has been organized to help those who want to read the book from cover to cover and also for those looking for specific information. A brief look at the contents of this book will give you an idea of what is covered and what is needed to have a good understanding of data center technologies.

Our approach for writing this book was to do our best to explain each concept in a simple, step-by-step approach, as well as to include the critical details. It was challenging to balance between providing as much information as possible and not overwhelming you, the reader. Data center technologies are not difficult to learn, but they involve multiple protocols and processes that might be new to some.

RFCs and Cisco's official configuration guides are cited throughout the book. It was important to include these references, as we wanted to give you the authoritative source for the material in this book so that you have resources for more information. If you are not familiar with reading RFCs, don't be intimidated. Most of them are not difficult to read, and they do their best to explain their topic clearly.

At times in this book, we introduce a technology or concept but state that it is covered in more detail in a later chapter. We do this to explain the concept as it relates to the topic being discussed without getting lost in the details. The details are covered where appropriate.

The objective of this book is to explain data center technologies as clearly as possible. At times, it was like herding cats, trying to decide which topic to cover first. The first chapter covers various data center architectures, including data center basics, and is designed to give you an overview of the main topics. Having this overview will make it easier as you progress through the rest of the book.

Goals and Methods

The most important and somewhat obvious goal of this book is to acquaint readers with not only the Cisco Data Center products but also the technologies involved, their interdependencies, and how to configure them. A book covering fundamentals generally struggles to cover as many subjects as possible with just enough detail. The fine balance between breadth and depth is challenging, but this book handles this challenge very well.

The book provides much more than a simple overview of the various data center product architectures, protocols, and features. This information helps you understand the various pieces involved in setting up and managing a data center.

The book has been organized such that you might begin with little or no knowledge of Cisco Data Center products. The book discusses installation and deployment of the data center technologies, and some possible applications are also discussed to show some basic capabilities of these products. It is largely up to you to decide how to best utilize these technologies within your organization.

Who Should Read This Book?

Cisco Data Center Fundamentals is intended for beginner and intermediate engineers looking to understand the architecture, configuration, and operation of Cisco Data Center products, including but not limited to Cisco Nexus switches, Cisco MDS switches, Cisco Application Centric Infrastructure (ACI), and Cisco Unified Computing System (UCS).

The reader should be familiar with networking protocols, because having a basic understanding of them is a prerequisite for this book.

Finally, this book is especially useful to people who are preparing for the CCNP DCCOR exam. This book acts as a bridge between CCNA and CCNP DCCOR concepts and introduces Cisco Data Center products and technologies related to the CCNP DCCOR exam.

How This Book Is Organized

If you are new to Cisco Data Center products and technologies, you should read this book from cover to cover. However, if you have some knowledge of Cisco Data Center products and technologies, this book is designed to be flexible and allow you to easily move between chapters and sections of chapters to cover just the material you want to review.

The book is divided into five parts:

- Part I consists of Chapters 1 to 9 and covers Cisco's data center switches along with basic networking concepts related to the data center.

- Part II consists of Chapters 10 to 15 and covers Cisco's data center storage products and storage concepts related to the data center.

- Part III consists of Chapters 16 to 18 and covers Cisco's compute products and concepts related to data center compute.

- Part IV consists of Chapters 19 and 20 and covers basic automation concepts related to data center products.

- Part V consists of Chapter 21 and covers basic cloud concepts.

The following list highlights the topics covered in each chapter and the book's organization:

- **Chapter 1, "Data Center Architectures":** This chapter discusses data center basics and analyzes the Data Center Architecture from a holistic point of view, which is Cisco's unique approach to the creation of a unified data center. It also discusses different core components of a data center—network infrastructure, storage infrastructure, and computing infrastructure.

- **Chapter 2, "Describing the Cisco Nexus Family and Cisco NX-OS Software":** This chapter discusses Cisco Nexus Data Center products, Cisco Fabric Extenders (FEXs), and Cisco NX-OS Software Architecture and concludes by exploring the Cisco NX-OS CLI.

- **Chapter 3, "Describing Layer 3 First-Hop Redundancy":** This chapter discusses the challenges presented by single default gateway configuration on end hosts along with its solutions using Hot Standby Router Protocol (HSRP), Virtual Router Redundancy Protocol (VRRP), and Gateway Load Balancing Protocol (GLBP) as Layer 3 redundancy protocols.

- **Chapter 4, "Port Channels and vPCs":** This chapter discusses Ethernet port channels including port channel modes, port channel compatibility requirements, and port channel load balancing. It also discusses virtual port channels (vPCs), including various vPC topology implementations, vPC components, vPC control plane and data plane, vPC failure scenarios, and vPC configuration and verification.

- **Chapter 5, "Switch Virtualization":** This chapter discusses Cisco Nexus switch functional planes, Cisco Nexus switch process separation and restartability, and virtual routing and forwarding (VRF) configuration and verification on NX-OS. It also discusses Cisco Nexus 7000 switch VDCs, including VDC architecture, VDC types, VDC resources, VDC fault isolation, VDC high availability, VDC management, along with VDC configuration and verification.

- **Chapter 6, "Nexus Switch Routing":** This chapter discusses the underlying concepts along with the configuration and verification for the Layer 3 unicast routing protocols in Cisco NX-OS, including RIPv2, EIGRP, and OSPFv2. It also discusses the multicast fundamentals, including PIM configuration and verification in Cisco NX-OS.

- **Chapter 7, "Network Virtualization":** This chapter discusses overlay network protocols such as Network Virtualization using GRE (NVGRE), Cisco Overlay Transport Virtualization (OTV), and VXLAN Overlay. It also discusses network interface virtualization using FEX technology and VMware vSphere virtual switches.

- **Chapter 8, "Describing Cisco ACI":** This chapter provides an overview of Cisco ACI and discusses building blocks, deployment models, hardware components, and fabric startup discovery, along with Cisco ACI policy model, including logical constructs, fabric policies, and access policies. It also briefly discusses packet forwarding within the ACI fabric.

- **Chapter 9, "Operating Cisco ACI":** This chapter discusses Cisco ACI external connectivity options, including L2Out and L3Out, Cisco ACI and VMM integration, Cisco ACI and L4–L7 integration, Cisco ACI management options, Cisco ACI Anywhere, and Cisco Nexus Dashboard.

- **Chapter 10, "Data Center Storage Concepts":** This chapter discusses the data center storage protocols and design, including block-based and file-based storage protocols, NAS, DA, SAN, the Fibre Channel protocol and topologies, and also makes an overview of the Cisco MDS family of Fibre Channel switches.

- **Chapter 11, "Fibre Channel Protocol Fundamentals":** This chapter discusses in more depth the Fibre Channel protocol, starting from the Fibre Channel layered model, going through the building of the switched fabric, and finishing with the flow control and routing.

- **Chapter 12, "Describing VSANs and Fibre Channel Zoning":** This chapter describes the vSANs and Fibre Channel zoning and the implementation of these features on the Cisco MDS switches.

- **Chapter 13, "Storage Virtualization":** This chapter describes the storage virtualization features supported on the Cisco Data Center switches, including the NPV and NPIV.

- **Chapter 14, "Describing Data Center Ethernet Enhancements":** This chapter discusses the data center bridging enhancements such as priority flow control, enhanced transmission selection, and the DCBX protocol, which make it possible for FCoE protocol communication.

- **Chapter 15, "Describing FCoE":** This chapter discusses the FCoE protocol, including the FCoE architecture, FCIP, and FCoE configuration on Cisco Data Center switches.

- **Chapter 16, "Describing Cisco UCS Components":** This chapter describes the Cisco UCS components of the Cisco compute solution, including the Cisco UCS Fabric Interconnects, blade chassis, B- and C-series servers, as well as the Cisco HyperFlex platform and the latest generation of the Cisco UCS X-series modular system.

- **Chapter 17, "Describing Cisco UCS Abstraction":** This chapter discusses the hardware abstraction approach used on the Cisco UCS, and what basic configuration is needed, including the Cisco UCS service profiles, templates, policies, and an overview of the Cisco UCS Central.

- **Chapter 18, "Server Virtualization":** This chapter discusses key server virtualization components, including the virtual machine and its components, types of hypervisors, VMware vSphere architecture, VMware ESXi, and the VMware vCenter Server appliance installation procedure.

- **Chapter 19, "Using APIs":** This chapter starts the discussion about automation in the data center by introducing the APIs and the data model–based framework, including the YANG data models; the NETCONF, RESTCONF, and gRPC configuration protocols; and the JSON, XML, and YAML data formats. This chapter also provides an overview of the APIs supported on the Cisco NX-OS and the Cisco UCS.

- **Chapter 20, "Automating the Data Center":** This chapter discusses the data center automation, orchestration, management, and toolsets.

- **Chapter 21, "Cloud Computing":** This chapter discusses cloud computing, looking at its definition, characteristics, services, and deployment models. This chapter also provides an overview of the Cisco Intersight hybrid cloud platform.

Figure Credits

Figure 18-6	Oracle
Figure 18-32–Figure 18-66	VMware, Inc
Figure 21-19A	HashiCorp

Chapter 1

Data Center Architectures

A data center is home to the computational power, storage, and applications necessary to support an enterprise business. The data center infrastructure is central to the IT architecture from which all content is sourced or through which all content passes. Proper planning of the data center infrastructure design is required, considering performance, resiliency, and scalability needs. Also, the data center design should be flexible in quickly deploying and supporting new services. Such a design requires solid initial planning and thoughtful consideration in the areas of port density, access layer uplink bandwidth, true server capacity, and oversubscription, to name just a few.

In this chapter, we will discuss the data center basics and analyze the data center architecture from a holistic point of view that is Cisco's unique approach to creating a unified data center. We will also discuss different core components of a data center: the network infrastructure, storage infrastructure, and computing infrastructure.

Data Center Basics

Before we dig deep into what the different architectures of a data center are, let's first discuss what a data center is, what its core components are, and what the different types of data centers are.

At its simplest, a data center is a physical facility that organizations use to house their critical applications and data. A data center's design is based on a network of computing and storage resources that enable the delivery of shared applications and data. The key components of a data center design include routers, switches, firewalls, storage systems, servers, and application-delivery controllers.

Modern data centers are very different from what they were just a short time ago. Infrastructure has shifted from traditional on-premises physical servers to virtual networks that support applications and workloads across pools of physical infrastructure and into a multicloud environment. In this era, data exists and is connected across multiple data centers, the edge, and public and private clouds. The data center must be able to communicate across these multiple sites—both on-premises and in the cloud. Even the public cloud is a collection of data centers. When applications are hosted in the cloud, they use data center resources from the cloud provider.

In the world of enterprise IT, data centers are designed to support the following business applications and activities:

- Email and file sharing

- Productivity applications

- Customer relationship management (CRM)

- Enterprise resource planning (ERP) and databases

- Big data, artificial intelligence, and machine learning

- Virtual desktops, communications, and collaboration services

A data center consists of the following core infrastructure components:

- **Network infrastructure:** This connects servers (physical and virtualized), data center services, storage, and external connectivity to end-user locations.

- **Storage infrastructure:** Data is the fuel of the modern data center. Storage systems are used to hold this valuable commodity.

- **Computing infrastructure:** Applications are the engines of a data center. Computing infrastructure consists of servers, which provide the processing, memory, local storage, and network connectivity that drive applications. Computing infrastructure has experienced three macro waves of evolution over the last 65 years:

  - The first wave saw the shift from proprietary mainframes to x86-based servers, based on-premises and managed by internal IT teams.

  - A second wave saw widespread virtualization of the infrastructure that supported applications. This allowed for improved use of resources and mobility of workloads across pools of physical infrastructure.

  - The third wave finds us in the present, where we are seeing the move to cloud, hybrid cloud, and cloud-native (that is, applications born in the cloud).

This evolution has given rise to distributed computing. This is where data and applications are distributed among disparate systems, connected and integrated by network services and interoperability standards to function as a single environment. It has meant the term *data center* is now used to refer to the department that has responsibility for these systems irrespective of where they are located.

Since data center components store and manage business-critical data and applications, data center security is critical in the data center design. The following data center services are typically deployed to protect the performance and integrity of the core data center components:

- **Network security appliances:** These include firewall and intrusion protection to safeguard the data center.

- **Application delivery assurance:** To maintain application performance, these mechanisms provide application resiliency and availability via automatic failover and load balancing.

Data center components require significant infrastructure to support the center's hardware and software. This includes power subsystems, uninterruptible power supplies (UPSs), ventilation, cooling systems, fire suppression, backup generators, and connections to external networks.

Standards for Data Center Infrastructure

The most widely adopted standard for data center design and data center infrastructure is ANSI/TIA-942. It includes standards for ANSI/TIA-942-ready certification, which ensures compliance with one of four categories of data center tiers rated for levels of redundancy and fault tolerance:

- **Tier 1:** Basic site infrastructure. A tier 1 data center offers limited protection against physical events. It has single-capacity components and a single, nonredundant distribution path.

- **Tier 2:** Redundant-capacity component site infrastructure. This data center offers improved protection against physical events. It has redundant-capacity components and a single, nonredundant distribution path.

- **Tier 3:** Concurrently maintainable site infrastructure. This data center protects against virtually all physical events, providing redundant-capacity components and multiple independent distribution paths. Each component can be removed or replaced without disrupting services to end users.

- **Tier 4:** Fault-tolerant site infrastructure. This data center provides the highest levels of fault tolerance and redundancy. Redundant-capacity components and multiple independent distribution paths enable concurrent maintainability, and one fault anywhere in the installation doesn't cause downtime.

Types of Data Centers

Many types of data centers and service models are available. Their classification depends on whether they are owned by one or many organizations, how they fit (if they fit) into the topology of other data centers, what technologies they use for computing and storage, and even their energy efficiency. There are four main types of data centers:

- **Enterprise data centers:** These are built, owned, and operated by companies and are optimized for their end users. Most often they are housed on the corporate campus.

- **Managed services data centers:** These data centers are managed by a third party (or a managed services provider) on behalf of a company. The company leases the equipment and infrastructure instead of buying it.

- **Colocation data centers:** In colocation ("colo") data centers, a company rents space within a data center owned by others and located off company premises. The colocation data center hosts the infrastructure (building, cooling, bandwidth, security, and so on), while the company provides and manages the components, including servers, storage, and firewalls.

- **Cloud data centers:** In this off-premises form of data center, data and applications are hosted by a cloud services provider such as Amazon Web Services (AWS), Microsoft Azure, or IBM Cloud, or other public cloud provider.

Organizations can choose to build and maintain their own hybrid cloud data centers, lease space within colocation facilities (colos), consume shared compute and storage services, or use public cloud-based services. The net effect is that applications today no longer reside in just one place. They operate in multiple public and private clouds, managed offerings, and traditional environments. In this multicloud era, the data center has become vast and complex, geared to drive the ultimate user experience.

Cisco Unified Data Center Platform

A variety of virtualization, computing, storage, and cloud technologies have entered the market to help increase scalability and flexibility in the data center, but each new technology layer introduced makes the data center more complex and less agile.

The Cisco Unified Data Center is a comprehensive, fabric-based platform that integrates computing, networking, security, virtualization, and management solutions into a single, highly efficient, and simplified architecture. The platform does not just accommodate virtualization; it was designed to build on the advantages of virtualization, increasing the density, performance, mobility, and security of data center resources. The result is a platform that is significantly easier to scale than other solutions, whether you are adding processing power within the data center, expanding geographic coverage by linking multiple data centers, or securely connecting additional users and devices.

This less complex, unified approach also facilitates the introduction of automation, which can dramatically increase data center efficiency, productivity, and agility, including the capability to manage deployment and operations across physical and virtual resources, which is critical to the delivery of IT as a Service (ITaaS). Less complexity means faster time to value—a significant advantage over other data center architectures.

The Cisco Unified Data Center is based on three pillars of Cisco innovation: Unified Fabric, Unified Computing, and Unified Management, as shown in Figure 1-1.

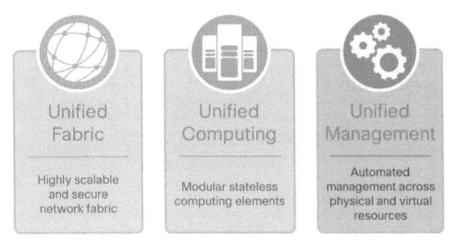

Figure 1-1   *Cisco Unified Data Center*

Unified Fabric

Cisco's fabric-based approach to data center infrastructure eliminates the tiered silos and inefficiencies of multiple network domains, instead offering a flatter, unified fabric that allows consolidation of local area network (LAN), storage area network (SAN), and network-attached storage (NAS) over one high-performance and fault-tolerant network. Cisco Unified Fabric delivers massive scalability and resiliency to the data center by creating large pools of virtualized network resources that can be easily moved and rapidly reprovisioned. This approach reduces complexity and enables automated deployment of new virtual machines and applications. Deep integration between the architecture of the server and the network enables delivery of secure IT services within the data center, between data centers, or beyond the data center to users from any device. Cisco Unified Fabric is based on the Cisco Nexus family of switches, which runs on a common operating system named Cisco NX-OS.

Unified Computing

This highly scalable computing solution integrates servers, flash-memory acceleration, and networking with embedded management and automation to simplify operations for physical, virtual, and cloud workloads. Cisco Unified Computing solution is based on the Cisco Unified Computing System (UCS). Cisco UCS integrates industry-standard x86-architecture servers, access and storage networking, and enterprise-class management into a single system for greater speed, simplicity, and scalability. Cisco UCS eliminates the multiple redundant devices that populate traditional blade servers and add layers of management complexity. When used within the high-bandwidth, low-latency Cisco Unified Fabric framework, Cisco UCS gives IT managers a wire-once platform for providing highly elastic and agile pools of virtualized resources.

Cisco UCS is massively scalable to hundreds of blades and thousands of virtual machines, all with a single point of connectivity and management. Every aspect of the system's configuration can be programmed through an intuitive GUI using automated rules and policies and operating across bare-metal, virtualized, and cloud computing environments. Open standards-based application programming interfaces (APIs) offer exceptional flexibility for integration of diverse application, virtualization, storage, and system management solutions.

Unified Management

Automation, orchestration, and lifecycle management tools simplify deployment and operation of physical and bare-metal environments, virtual environments, and private, public, and hybrid cloud environments. Most organizations have dozens of different management solutions that do not necessarily work all that well together. Cisco offers the open platform for centrally managing all data center resources across physical, virtual, and cloud environments. The flexible automation of Cisco Unified Management solutions reduces the time and cost of setting up and provisioning infrastructure. Role- and policy-based provisioning using service profiles and templates simplifies operations. By providing lifecycle management and process automation, Cisco Unified Management solutions deliver greater agility and scalability for the data center while reducing complexity and risk. The Cisco Unified Management solution includes Cisco UCS Manager, Cisco UCS Central, Cisco Intersight, Cisco Nexus Dashboard, Cisco Nexus Insights, Cisco Network Assurance Engine (NAE), and more.

Data Center Network Infrastructure

In the previous section, we saw the data center architecture from a holistic point of view. Cisco Unified Fabric consists of LAN and SAN networks, which will be discussed in the sections "Data Center Network Infrastructure" and "Data Center Storage Infrastructure." Data center network infrastructure can be classified into two major design options: three-tier network and spine-leaf network.

Three-Tier Network: Core, Aggregation, and Access

The data center is at the foundation of modern software technology, serving a critical role in expanding capabilities for enterprises. The traditional data center uses a three-tier architecture, with servers segmented into pods based on location, as shown in Figure 1-2.

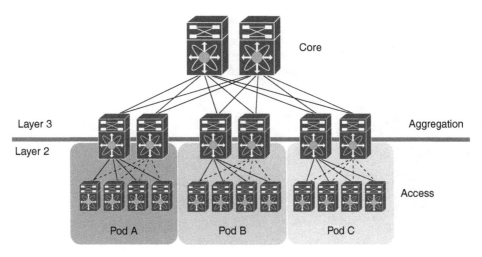

Figure 1-2 *Traditional Three-Tier Data Center Design*

The architecture consists of core routers, aggregation routers (sometimes called distribution routers), and access switches. Between the aggregation routers and access switches, Spanning Tree Protocol is used to build a loop-free topology for the Layer 2 part of the network. Spanning Tree Protocol provides several benefits. For example, it is simple, and it is a plug-and-play technology requiring little configuration. VLANs are extended within each pod, and servers can move freely within a pod without the need to change IP address and default gateway configurations. However, Spanning Tree Protocol cannot use parallel forwarding paths, and it always blocks redundant paths in a VLAN.

In 2010, Cisco introduced virtual port channel (vPC) technology to overcome the limitations of Spanning Tree Protocol. vPC eliminates spanning tree's blocked ports, provides active-active uplink from the access switches to the aggregation routers, and makes full use of the available bandwidth, as shown in Figure 1-3. With vPC technology, Spanning Tree Protocol is still used as a failsafe mechanism.

vPC technology works well in a relatively small data center environment where most traffic consists of northbound and southbound communication between clients and servers. We will discuss vPCs in detail in Chapter 4, "Port Channels and vPCs."

Since 2003, with the introduction of virtual technology, the computing, networking, and storage resources that were segregated in pods in Layer 2 in the three-tier data center design can be pooled. This revolutionary technology created a need for a larger Layer 2 domain, from the access layer to the core layer, as shown in Figure 1-4.

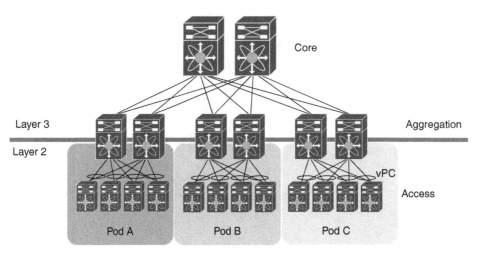

Figure 1-3 *Data Center Design Using vPC*

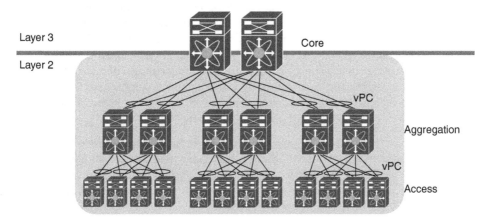

Figure 1-4 *Data Center Design with Extended Layer 2 Domain*

With Layer 2 segments extended across all the pods, the data center administrator can create a central, more flexible resource pool that can be reallocated based on needs. Servers are virtualized into sets of virtual machines that can move freely from server to server without the need to change their operating parameters.

With virtualized servers, applications are increasingly deployed in a distributed fashion, which leads to increased east-west traffic. This traffic needs to be handled efficiently, with low and predictable latency. However, vPC can provide only two active parallel uplinks; therefore, bandwidth becomes a bottleneck in a three-tier data center architecture. Another challenge in a three-tier architecture is that server-to-server latency varies depending on the traffic path used.

A new data center design called the Clos network–based spine-leaf architecture was developed to overcome these limitations. This architecture has been proven to deliver the high-bandwidth, low-latency, nonblocking server-to-server connectivity.

Spine-Leaf Network

In this two-tier Clos architecture, every lower-tier switch (leaf layer) is connected to each of the top-tier switches (spine layer) in a full-mesh topology. The leaf layer consists of access switches that connect to devices such as servers. The spine layer is the backbone of the network and is responsible for interconnecting all leaf switches. Every leaf switch connects to every spine switch in the fabric. The path is randomly chosen so that the traffic load is evenly distributed among the top-tier switches. If one of the top tier switches were to fail, it would only slightly degrade performance throughout the data center.

Figure 1-5 shows a typical two-tiered spine-leaf topology.

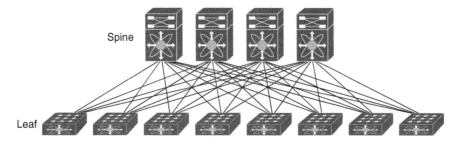

Figure 1-5   *Typical Spine-and-Leaf Topology*

If oversubscription of a link occurs (that is, if more traffic is generated than can be aggregated on the active link at one time), the process for expanding capacity is straight-forward. An additional spine switch can be added, and uplinks can be extended to every leaf switch, resulting in the addition of interlayer bandwidth and the reduction of the oversubscription. If device port capacity becomes a concern, a new leaf switch can be added by connecting it to every spine switch and adding the network configuration to the switch. The ease of expansion optimizes the IT department's process of scaling the network. If no oversubscription occurs between the lower-tier switches and their uplinks, a nonblocking architecture can be achieved.

With a spine-and-leaf architecture, no matter which leaf switch a server is connected to, its traffic always has to cross the same number of devices to get to another server (unless the other server is located on the same leaf). This approach keeps latency at a predictable level because a payload only has to hop to a spine switch and another leaf switch to reach its destination.

Data Center Storage Infrastructure

Data center storage infrastructure consists of a dedicated storage area network (SAN), which provides high-speed network connectivity between servers and a shared pool of storage devices. The connectivity between server and storage device can be provided using various physical media; for example, fiber-optic cable uses light waves to transmit data with a connection protocol known as Fibre Channel protocol, and Ethernet cables use a storage connection protocol such as iSCSI (Internet Small Computer Systems Interface) to move and store data.

There are various benefits of using a SAN. It allows the storage disks to be connected to servers over large distances, making it ideal for enterprise data center networks. The same physical disk can be connected to more than one server, allowing for effective disk utilization. A SAN provides high availability using multiple physical paths from server to storage. SAN supports nondisruptive scalability (that is, additional storage can be added to the storage network without affecting the device currently using the network).

There are three types of SAN topologies: single-tier, two-tier, and three-tier topology.

Single-Tier Topology

In single-tier topology, also called collapsed-core topology, servers connect to the core switches, which provide storage services. Storage devices connect to one or more core switches, as shown in Figure 1-6. Core devices have a large number of blades to support initiator (host) and target (storage) ports. High availability is achieved using two physically separate, but identical, redundant SAN fabrics. This topology has single management per fabric and is suitable for small SAN environments.

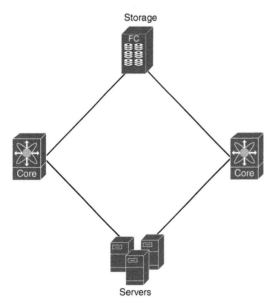

Figure 1-6 *Collapsed-Core Topology for SAN Networks*

Two-Tier Topology

Two-tier topology, also called core-edge topology, is the most common SAN network topology. In this topology, servers connect to the edge switches, whereas storage devices connect to one or more core switches, as shown in Figure 1-7. Core switches provide storage services to one or more edge switches, thus servicing more servers in the fabric. Inter-Switch Links (ISLs) have to be designed in such a way that enough links/bandwidth are available between the switches to avoid congestion when servers communicate with storage devices. High availability is achieved using two physically separate, but identical, redundant SAN fabrics. This topology guarantees a single switch hop (edge to core) reachability from servers to storage. The key drawback of this topology is that core connections and the storage are in contention for extension. This topology provides room for minimal growth.

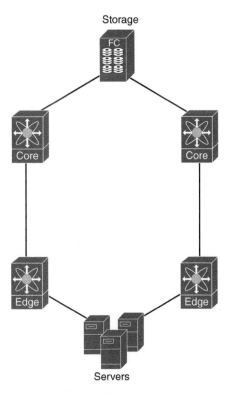

Figure 1-7   *Core-Edge Topology for SAN Networks*

Three-Tier Topology

In three-tier topology, also called edge-core-edge topology, servers connect to the edge switches. Storage devices connect to one or more edge switches, as shown in Figure 1-8. Core switches provide storage services to one or more edge switches, thus servicing more servers and storage in the fabric. ISLs have to be designed in such a way that enough links/bandwidth are available between the switches to avoid congestion when servers communicate with storage devices. High availability is achieved using two physically separate, but identical, redundant SAN fabrics. In this topology, a core switch is used exclusively for edge switch interconnections, allowing easy SAN expansion by storage size (adding more edge switches connected to storage) or by computing power (adding more edge switches connected to servers) independently.

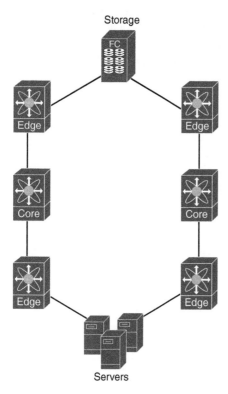

Figure 1-8 *Edge-Core-Edge Topology for SAN Networks*

Data Center Computing Infrastructure

Computing infrastructure consists of servers that provide the processing, memory, local storage, and network connectivity that drive applications. We will discuss Cisco Unified Computing System (UCS) along with Converged Infrastructure and Hyperconverged Infrastructure products under the data center computing infrastructure. Computing infrastructure corresponds to the Unified Computing pillar of the Cisco Unified Data Center platform.

Cisco Unified Computing System (UCS)

Cisco UCS combines industry-standard, x86-architecture servers with networking and storage access into a single unified system. The system is flexible, agile, and adaptable, and the portfolio of products supported by Cisco UCS includes blade, rack, multinode, and storage-intensive servers; Converged Infrastructure; Hyperconverged Infrastructure (Cisco HyperFlex systems); and solutions for the network edge such as Cisco UCS Mini and Cisco HyperFlex Edge.

We will discuss Cisco UCS in detail in Chapter 16, "Describing Cisco UCS Components." However, Figure 1-9 provides a sneak peek at the Cisco UCS anatomy. Cisco UCS is built using the hierarchy of components illustrated in Figure 1-9.

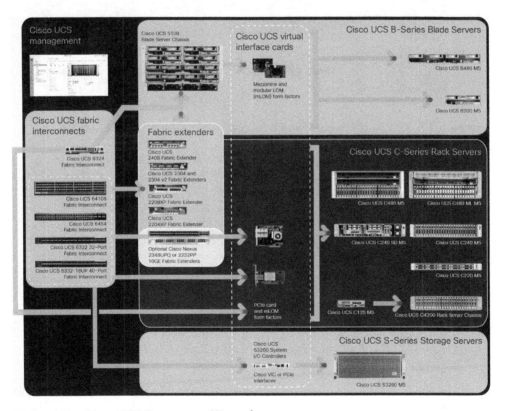

Figure 1-9   *Cisco UCS Component Hierarchy*

Each Cisco UCS domain is established with a pair of Cisco UCS fabric interconnects, with a comprehensive set of options for connecting blade, rack, multinode, and storage servers to them either directly or indirectly. Cisco UCS fabric interconnects provide a single point of connectivity and management for an entire Cisco UCS system. Deployed as an active-active pair, the system's fabric interconnects integrate all components into a single, highly available management domain. Cisco fabric interconnects support low-latency, line-rate, lossless Ethernet and Fibre Channel over Ethernet (FCoE) connectivity. A pair of Cisco UCS fabric interconnects forms the single point of connectivity for a Cisco UCS domain. Blade servers connect through fabric extenders, most rack servers can connect through optional fabric extenders, and rack servers, multinode rack servers, and storage servers can connect directly to the fabric interconnects, as illustrated in Figure 1-10.

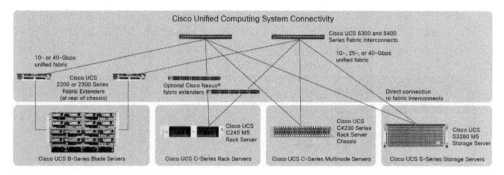

Figure 1-10   *Cisco UCS Connectivity Options for Blade, Rack, and Storage Servers*

Cisco fabric extenders are zero-management, low-cost, low-power-consuming devices that distribute the system's connectivity and management planes to rack servers and blade chassis to scale the system without adding complex switches or management points. Cisco fabric extenders eliminate the need for top-of-rack switches and blade-server-resident Ethernet and Fibre Channel switches and management modules, dramatically reducing the infrastructure cost per server. Rack and storage servers can be connected directly to Cisco fabric interconnects for outstanding dedicated network bandwidth.

Cisco UCS virtual interface cards (VICs) extend the network fabric directly to both servers and virtual switches so that a single connectivity mechanism can be used to connect both physical and virtual servers with the same level of visibility and control.

Cisco UCS B-Series blade servers provide massive amounts of computing power in a compact form factor, helping increase density in computation-intensive and enterprise application environments.

Cisco UCS C-Series rack servers can integrate into Cisco UCS through Cisco UCS fabric interconnects or be used as standalone servers with Cisco or third-party switches. These servers provide a wide range of I/O, memory, internal disk, solid-state disk (SSD) drive and Non-Volatile Memory Express (NVMe) storage device capacity, enabling you to easily match servers to workloads. Cisco UCS C4200 Series multinode rack servers are designed for clustered workloads where high core density is essential.

Cisco UCS S-Series storage servers are modular servers that support up to 60 large-form-factor internal drives to support storage-intensive workloads, including big data, content streaming, online backup, and Storage as a Service applications. The servers support one or two computing nodes with up to two CPUs each, connected to a system I/O controller that links the server to the network. These servers offer the flexibility of compute processing to balance the needed storage for workloads like big data, data protections, and software-defined storage.

Multiple management tools are available that use Cisco UCS Unified API to manage Cisco UCS. Cisco UCS Manager and Cisco Intersight are two of the most widely used management tools.

Cisco UCS Manager is embedded in each fabric interconnect. Running in a redundant, high-availability configuration, it creates a single, self-aware, self-integrating unified system that recognizes and integrates components as they are added to the system. It quickly and accurately configures computing, network, storage, and storage-access resources to reduce the chance of errors that can cause downtime. Its role- and policy-based approach helps organizations more easily align policies and configurations with workloads. Cisco UCS Manager requires an "always-on" connection.

Cisco Intersight Software as a Service provides a consistent management interface for all your Cisco UCS instances, Cisco HyperFlex clusters, edge deployments, and standalone rack servers, regardless of their location. You can access the Intersight platform through the cloud or through an optional management appliance. Intersight is designed to integrate management capabilities with a broader set of features, including a recommendation engine, integration with Cisco Technical Assistance Center (TAC), contract management, inventory management, and alerts.

Converged Infrastructure

Rapidly changing demand and workload diversity have forced the IT organizations to create large sets of hardware and software components—and spend time integrating them into a workable solution. Cisco Converged Infrastructure is a powerful and unique integration of high-performance computing, networking, and storage coupled with resource and performance management software, multicloud orchestration, and support for multiple deployment models.

Cisco's Converged Infrastructure core components are built using Cisco Unified Computing System (Cisco UCS), Cisco Nexus switches, and Cisco Intersight Software as a Service management and enterprise-approved storage systems to offer a range of converged solutions to meet an enterprise's needs. Figure 1-11 shows the Cisco Converged Infrastructure portfolio, including solutions for FlexPod with NetApp, FlashStack with Pure Storage, Cisco and Hitachi Adaptive Solutions, VersaStack with IBM, and VxBlock Systems with Dell EMC.

Figure 1-11   *Cisco Converged Infrastructure Solutions*

The following list provides some of the many benefits of Converged Infrastructure:

■ **Operational efficiency:** Component solutions or partially integrated infrastructure from different vendors can cause delays in development and deployment schedules. Component solutions force the staff to spend time making everything work together to perform as expected. The Converged Infrastructure solutions let you move from technology silos to a holistic approach that transforms the data center into pools of resources that can be easily allocated and repurposed.

■ **Lower total cost of ownership:** The management teams recognize that operations—including people, management, software, and facilities—are the largest cost in the data center, far greater than the cost of underlying hardware. Cisco Converged Infrastructure solutions help to get more work done with the same resources and enable the staff to reduce the amount of time they spend "keeping the lights on." With these innovative solutions, the IT staff can consolidate more workloads onto fewer servers so there are fewer components to buy and manage. All components are connected through a unified fabric that delivers high-performance data and storage networking to simplify deployment, help ensure the quality of the user experience, and reduce operating costs. These solutions also reduce cabling, power, and cooling requirements and automate routine tasks to increase productivity.

■ **Reduced risk:** Deployment delays and service disruptions affect the company's profitability. That's why it is important to deploy infrastructure correctly the first time. Converged Infrastructure reduces risk and guesswork by giving the architects and administrators a guidebook for implementing solutions. Converged Infrastructure solutions are pre-validated and documented so that you can get environments up and running quickly and with confidence.

■ **More choice and flexibility:** There's no perfect solution or one-size-fits-all approach that can support every nuance of every business application situation. Converged Infrastructure pre-validated solutions let you choose from a family of solutions that are designed to work together for your organization. It helps the IT staff reduce the risk of transitioning the existing data center environments to deliver a better digital experience.

Hyperconverged Infrastructure (HCI)

Current IT infrastructure weighs data centers down with sluggish arrays of hard-to-manage components, preventing them from keeping up with the quick-turnaround demands of business and the cloud. Hyperconverged Infrastructure (HCI) comes to the rescue here. HCI combines compute, virtualization, storage, and networking in a single cluster. Starting with as few as three nodes, users can easily scale out to match computing and storage resource needs. Hyperconvergence brings cloudlike simplicity on-premises and within a single, easily managed platform.

Before we discuss HCI in detail, let's first see what the difference is between Converged and Hyperconverged Infrastructures. Converged and hyperconverged systems both aim to simplify data center management. Converged Infrastructure has the same components, but they're discrete, separable, and cumbersome to manage compared with HCI. Hyperconverged Infrastructure fully integrates all components and is software-defined. In essence, HCI is designed to work as one system with software-managed storage, as opposed to converged solutions and their separate components. HCI delivers deeper abstraction and higher automation and scalability than Converged Infrastructure. HCI simplifies administration by providing a single point of management. HCI fully integrates with the entire data center, eliminating the need for separate servers and network storage and delivering on-demand infrastructure for data-centric workloads.

Cisco HyperFlex engineered on the Cisco UCS is an HCI solution. Cisco HyperFlex systems with Intel Xeon Scalable Processors deliver hyperconvergence with power and simplicity for any application, on any cloud, anywhere. Cisco HyperFlex includes hybrid, all-flash, all-NVMe, and edge configurations, an integrated network fabric, and powerful data optimization features that bring the full potential of hyperconvergence to a wide range of workloads and use cases. Cisco UCS fabric interconnects provide a single point of connectivity integrating Cisco HyperFlex HX-Series all-flash, all-NVMe, or hybrid nodes and other Cisco UCS servers into a single unified cluster. More on Cisco HyperFlex can be found in Chapter 16.

Figure 1-12 shows a typical Cisco HyperFlex system with virtualized and containerized applications support.

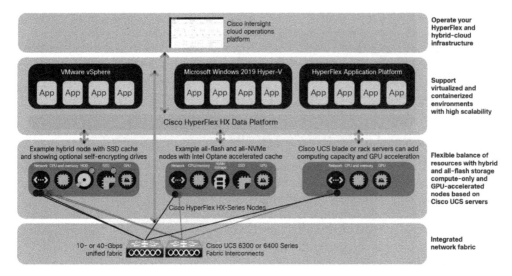

Figure 1-12   *Cisco HyperFlex Systems*

The following list provides some of the many benefits of hyperconverged infrastructure:

- **Lower cost:** Integrating components into one platform reduces storage footprint, power use, maintenance costs, and total cost of ownership (TCO). Hyperconverged systems eliminate the need to overprovision to accommodate growth and help enable data centers to scale in small, easily managed steps.

- **Simplicity and agility:** Hyperconverged systems can deploy in a fraction of the time of traditional IT infrastructure. And there is no need for IT specialists for each resource area. Plus, automation makes management simple, giving staff and administrators more time to focus on strategic initiatives.

- **Performance:** Hyperconvergence helps organizations deploy any workload and enjoy high levels of performance. Many organizations use hyperconverged solutions for the most intensive workloads, including enterprise apps and SQL Server.

- **Flexible scaling:** Hyperconverged infrastructure scales easily. Additional resources can be added by simply connecting a new node to the cluster. Plus, with some hyperconverged systems, you can scale compute and storage separately. New resources are automatically identified and integrated into the cluster.

- **Multicloud support:** Hyperconvergence dramatically simplifies hybrid cloud environments and reduces the time and cost of transitioning to a hybrid cloud. It also makes it easy to move data and applications back and forth between on-premises servers and the public cloud.

- **Security and data protection:** On-premises IT infrastructure is more secure than other options. Security is baked into hyperconverged systems, with features including self-encrypting drives and tools that provide high levels of visibility. Backup and disaster recovery are also built in.

Different products corresponding to the Unified Management pillar of the Cisco Unified Data Center platform, such as Cisco UCS Manager, Cisco UCS Central, and so on, will be discussed in detail in Chapter 17, "Describing Cisco UCS Abstraction." Cisco Intersight will be discussed in Chapter 21, "Cloud Computing," and Cisco Nexus Dashboard in Chapter 9, "Operating ACI."

Summary

This chapter discusses data center basics, Cisco's Unified Data Center platform architecture, and core components of data center infrastructure, including the following points:

- A data center is a physical facility that organizations use to house their critical applications and data.

- A data center consists of three core infrastructure components: network infrastructure, storage infrastructure, and computing infrastructure.

- As per the ANSI/TIA-942 standard, data centers are categorized into four tiers, depending on the levels of redundancy and fault tolerance.

- There are four main types of data centers, depending on whether they are owned by one or many organizations, how they fit (if they fit) into the topology of other data centers, and what technologies they use for computing and storage. These are enterprise data centers, managed services data centers, colocation data centers, and cloud data centers.

- The Cisco Unified Data Center is a comprehensive, fabric-based platform that integrates computing, networking, security, virtualization, and management solutions in a single, highly efficient, and simplified architecture.

- The Cisco Unified Data Center is based on three pillars: Unified Fabric, Unified Computing, and Unified Management

- A data center network infrastructure can be built using traditional three-tier network architecture or two-tier Clos architecture.

- A data center storage infrastructure can be built using single-tier, two-tier, or three-tier architecture, depending on the size of the organization and taking into account future growth consideration.

- A data center computing infrastructure is built using Cisco UCS as its core component.

- A converged infrastructure use enterprise-approved storage systems along with Cisco UCS, Cisco Nexus switches, and Cisco Intersight Software as a Service management.

- Hyperconverged infrastructure, such as Cisco HyperFlex engineered on Cisco UCS, fully integrates compute, virtualization, storage, and networking components in a single cluster and is software-defined.

References

"Cisco Unified Data Center: Simplified, Efficient, and Agile Infrastructure for the Data Center," https://www.cisco.com/c/dam/global/en_in/solutions/collateral/ns340/ns517/ns224/solution_overview_c22-700817.pdf

"Cisco Data Center Spine-and-Leaf Architecture: Design Overview White Paper," https://www.cisco.com/c/en/us/products/collateral/switches/nexne-7000-series-switches/white-paper-c11-737022.html

"Cisco Unified Computing System Solution Overview," https://www.cisco.com/c/en/us/products/collateral/servers-unified-computing/solution-overview-c22-744677.html

"Cisco HyperFlex Systems Solution Overview," https://www.cisco.com/c/en/us/products/collateral/hyperconverged-infrastructure/hyperflex-hx-series/solution-overview-c22-744674.html

Relevant Cisco Live sessions: http://www.ciscolive.com

Chapter 2

Describing the Cisco Nexus Family and Cisco NX-OS Software

Cisco NX-OS software is an extensible, open, and programmable network operating system for next-generation data centers and cloud networks. It is the most deployed data center operating system, based on a highly resilient, Linux-based software architecture, built to enable the most performance-demanding cloud environments. Cisco NX-OS runs on the Cisco Nexus family of network switches, which include Cisco Nexus 9000, 7000, 3000 series switches, Cisco Nexus 2000 Series fabric extenders, and the Cisco MDS family of storage network switches.

In this chapter, we will discuss the Cisco Nexus Data Center product, Cisco Fabric Extender (FEX), and Cisco NX-OS software architecture, and we will conclude by exploring the Cisco NX-OS CLI.

Cisco Nexus Data Center Product Overview

The Cisco Nexus switches are a foundational component of the Cisco data center and are well-suited for both traditional and fully automated software-defined data center deployments. Cisco Nexus switches offer an exceptional portfolio of networking solutions and integrated, converged, and hyperconverged platforms.

Cisco Nexus 9000 Series Switches

The Cisco Nexus 9000 Series switches operate in one of two modes: Cisco Application Centric Infrastructure (Cisco ACI) or Cisco NX-OS. In Cisco ACI mode, these switches provide a turnkey, fully automated, policy-based architecture to design and manage data center fabrics. In Cisco NX-OS mode, these switches provide the capability to use foundational Layer 2/3 technologies, as well as modern technologies such as VXLAN, with a Border Gateway Protocol–Ethernet VPN (BGP-EVPN) control plane, segment routing, Multiprotocol Label Switching (MPLS), and automation via NX-APIs.

The Cisco Nexus 9000 Series switches include the Nexus 9500 Series modular switches and the Nexus 9200/9300 Series fixed switches, as shown in Figure 2-1.

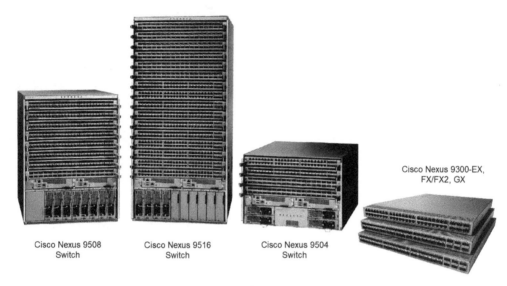

Figure 2-1   *Cisco Nexus 9000 Series Switches*

Cisco Nexus 9500 Platform Switches

The Cisco Nexus 9500 platform modular switches support a comprehensive selection of line cards and fabric modules that provide 1-, 10-, 25-, 40-, 50-, 100-, 200-, and 400-Gigabit Ethernet interfaces. The supervisor, system controller, power supplies, and line cards are common across all three switches. Each switch, however, has unique fabric modules and fan trays that plug in vertically into the rear of the chassis.

The Cisco Nexus 9500 Series modular switch includes the components shown in Figure 2-2.

The Cisco Nexus 9500 Series modular switches support several line cards and fabric modules. A pair of redundant supervisor modules manage all switch operations using a state-synchronized, active-standby model. The supervisor accepts an external clock and supports management through multiple ports: two USB ports, a serial port, and a 10/100/1000Mbps Ethernet port. All supervisors support Cisco ACI or NX-OS deployments. Redundant supervisors should be of the same type within a chassis.

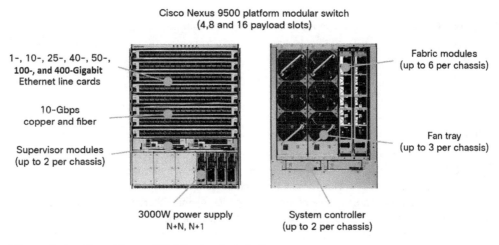

Cisco Nexus 9500 platform modular switch
(4,8 and 16 payload slots)

1-, 10-, 25-, 40-, 50-, 100-, and 400-Gigabit Ethernet line cards

10-Gbps copper and fiber

Supervisor modules (up to 2 per chassis)

Fabric modules (up to 6 per chassis)

Fan tray (up to 3 per chassis)

3000W power supply N+N, N+1

System controller (up to 2 per chassis)

Figure 2-2   *Cisco Nexus 9500 Series Switch Components*

A pair of redundant system controllers offload chassis management functions from the supervisor modules. The controllers are responsible for managing the power supplies and fan trays; they are also the central point for the Gigabit Ethernet Out-of-Band Channel (EOBC) between the supervisors, fabric modules, and line cards.

Each Cisco Nexus 9500 Series chassis supports up to six fabric modules, which plug in vertically at the back of the chassis behind the fan trays.

The Cisco Nexus 9500 chassis supports two versions of hot-swappable fan trays that are compatible with specific fabric modules. Each fan tray covers two fabric module slots and enables front-to-back airflow for the entire chassis. An appropriate fabric module blank card should be installed in all empty fabric module slots to ensure proper airflow and cooling of the chassis.

The Cisco Nexus 9500 platform supports hot-swappable, front-panel-accessible AC, DC, and universal high-voltage AC/DC power supplies. The total power budget required for the mix and number of line cards and fabric modules installed in the chassis determines the ability to support power supply redundancy modes (combined, n + 1, n + n, or input-source redundancy).

Note   Cisco introduces new models of line cards and fabric modules with enhanced capacity and feature set from time to time. For the latest supported line cards and fabric modules in 9500 Series modular chassis, refer to the datasheet located at https://www.cisco.com/c/en/us/products/switches/nexus-9000-series-switches/datasheet-listing.html.

Cisco Nexus 9300 Platform Switches

The Cisco Nexus 9300 platform consists of fixed-port switches designed for top-of-rack (ToR) and middle-of-row (MoR) deployments in data centers that support enterprise applications, service provider hosting, and cloud computing environments. Cisco Nexus 9300-GX switches are capable of supporting 400-Gigabit Ethernet (GE). Cisco Nexus 9300-EX and 9300-FX series switches offer a variety of interface options to transparently migrate existing data centers from 100Mbps, 1Gbps, and 10Gbps speeds to 25Gbps at the server, and from 10Gbps and 40Gbps speeds to 50Gbps and 100Gbps at the aggregation layer. The Cisco Nexus 93120TX is a line-rate Layer 2 and Layer 3 10- and 40-Gigabit Ethernet switch for both three-tier and spine-leaf architectures.

Table 2-1 summarizes the Cisco Nexus 9300 platform switch models.

Table 2-1   *Cisco Nexus 9300 Platform Switches*

Model	Description
Cisco Nexus 9316D-GX	16 x 400/100Gbps QSFP-DD ports
Cisco Nexus 93600CD-GX	28 x 100/40Gbps QSFP28 and 8 x 400/100Gbps QSFP-DD ports
Cisco Nexus 9332D-GX2B	32 x 400Gbps QSFP-DD and 2x 1/10Gbps SFP+ ports
Cisco Nexus 9364D-GX2A	64 x 400Gbps QSFP-DD and 2x 1/10Gbps SFP+ ports
Cisco Nexus 93120TX	96 x 100M/1/10-GBASE-T ports and 6 x 40Gbps QSFP+ ports
Cisco Nexus 93108TC-EX	48 x 100M/1/10GBASE-T ports and 6 x 40/100Gbps QSFP28 ports
Cisco Nexus 9348GC-FXP	48 x 100M/1G BASE-T ports, 4 x 1/10/25Gbps SFP28 ports and 2 x 40/100Gbps QSFP28 ports
Cisco Nexus 93108TC-FX	48 x 100M/1/10GBASE-T ports and 6 x 40/100Gbps QSFP28 ports
Cisco Nexus 93108TC-FX3P	48 x 100M/1/2.5/5/10G BASE-T ports and 6 x 40/100Gbps QSFP28 ports
Cisco Nexus 93216TC-FX2	96 x 100M/1/10GBASE-T ports and 12 x 40/100-Gigabit QSFP28 ports

Model	Description
Cisco Nexus 93180YC-EX	48 x 1/10/25Gbps fiber ports and 6 x 40/100Gbps QSFP28 ports
Cisco Nexus 93180YC-FX	48 x 1/10/25Gbps fiber ports and 6 x 40/100Gbps QSFP28 ports
Cisco Nexus 93180YC-FX3	48 x 1/10/25Gbps fiber ports and 6 x 40/100Gbps QSFP28 ports
Cisco Nexus 93180YC-FX3S	48 x 1/10/25Gbps fiber ports and 6 x 40/100Gbps QSFP28 ports
Cisco Nexus 93240YC-FX2	48 x 1/10/25Gbps fiber ports and 12 x 40/100Gbps QSFP28 ports
Cisco Nexus 93360YC-FX2	96 x 1/10/25Gbps fiber ports and 12 x 40/100Gbps QSFP28 ports
Cisco Nexus 9364C	64 x 40/100G QSFP28 ports and 2-port 1/10G SFP+ ports
Cisco Nexus 9336C-FX2	36 x 40/100Gbps QSFP28 ports
Cisco Nexus 9336C-FX2-E	36 x 40/100Gbps QSFP28 ports
Cisco Nexus 9332C	32 x 40/100G QSFP28 ports and 2-port 1/10G SFP+ ports
Cisco Nexus 9364C-GX	64 x 100/40Gbps QSFP28 ports

Note Quad Small Form Factor Pluggable Double Density (QSFP-DD) transceivers can support up to 400Gbps bandwidth, whereas QSFP+ and QSFP28 support a maximum bandwidth of 40Gbps and 100Gbps, respectively.

Cisco Nexus 9200 Platform Switches

Built on the latest Cisco Cloud Scale technology, the Cisco Nexus 9200 platform consists of ultra-high-density fixed-configuration data center switches with line-rate Layer 2 and 3 features that support enterprise and commercial applications, service provider hosting, and cloud computing environments. These switches support a wide range of port speeds with flexible combinations of 1/10/25/40/50/100Gbps connectivity in compact form factors.

Table 2-2 summarizes the Cisco Nexus 9200 platform switch models.

Table 2-2   *Cisco Nexus 9200 Platform Switches*

Model	Description
Cisco Nexus 92160YC-X	48 x 1/10/25Gbps SFP+ ports and 6 x QSFP28 ports (4 of the 6 QSFP+ ports are 100Gbps capable ports)
Cisco Nexus 9272Q	72 x 40Gbps QSFP+ ports
Cisco Nexus 92304QC	56 x 40Gbps QSFP+ ports and 8 x 40/100Gbps QSFP28 ports
Cisco Nexus 9236C	36 x 40/100Gbps QSFP28 ports
Cisco Nexus 92300YC	48 x 1/10/25Gbps SFP+ ports and 18 x 40/100Gbps QSFP28 ports
Cisco Nexus 92348GC-X	48 x 100M/1G Base-T ports + 4 x 1/10/25G SPF28,+ 2 x 40/100G QSFP28 ports

Note   Refer to the following link for comparing hardware capabilities of various Nexus 9000 Series switches: https://www.cisco.com/c/en/us/products/switches/nexus-9000-se-ries-switches/models-comparison.html

Cisco Nexus 7000 Series Switches

Cisco Nexus 7000 Series switches provide the foundation for Cisco Unified Fabric. These switches were designed to meet the requirements of mission-critical data centers as well as deliver exceptional availability, outstanding scalability, and a comprehensive Cisco NX-OS software data center switching feature set. They are a modular data center–class product line designed for highly scalable 1/10/40/100 Gigabit Ethernet networks. These switches deliver continuous system operation and virtualized, pervasive services. Cisco Nexus 7000 series switches consist of modular Cisco Nexus 7000 and 7700 platform switches and support supervisor modules, fabric modules, and input/output (I/O) modules.

The supervisor module delivers control-plane and management functions. The supervisor controls the Layer 2 and Layer 3 services, redundancy capabilities, configuration management, status monitoring, power and environmental management, and more. It provides centralized arbitration to the system fabric for all line cards. The fully distributed forwarding architecture allows the supervisor to support transparent upgrades to I/O and fabric modules with greater forwarding capacity. Two supervisors are required for a fully redundant system, with one supervisor module running as the active device and the other in hot-standby mode, providing exceptional high-availability features such as stateful switchover and In-Service Software Upgrade (ISSU) on mission-critical data center–class products.

The fabric modules provide parallel fabric channels to each I/O and supervisor module slot. All fabric modules connect to all module slots. The addition of each fabric module increases the bandwidth to all module slots up to the system limit of five fabric modules for 7000 platform switches and six fabric modules for 7700 platform switches. The architecture supports lossless fabric failover, with the remaining fabric modules load-balancing the bandwidth to all the I/O module slots, helping ensure graceful removal and insertion.

Cisco Nexus 7000 Platform Switches

Coupled with Cisco NX-OS, the Cisco Nexus 7000 platform switches deliver a comprehensive set of features with nonstop operation in four chassis form factors, as shown in Figure 2-3:

- Eighteen-slot chassis with 18 front-accessible module slots and side-to-side airflow in a compact horizontal form factor with purpose-built integrated cable management.

- Ten-slot chassis with ten front-accessible vertical module slots and front-to-back airflow and an integrated cable management system.

- Nine-slot with nine front-accessible module slots and side-to-side airflow in a compact horizontal form factor with purpose-built integrated cable management.

- Four-slot chassis with all front-accessible module slots and side-to-back airflow in a small form factor with purpose-built integrated cable management.

Figure 2-3 *Cisco Nexus 7000 Series*

All Cisco Nexus 7000 Series chassis use a passive mid-plane architecture, providing physical connectors and copper traces for interconnecting the fabric modules and the I/O modules for direct data transfer. All intermodule switching is performed via the crossbar fabric ASICs on the individual I/O modules and fabric modules. In the case of Cisco Nexus 7004 chassis, since there are no fabric modules, the mid-plane provides the connectors and traces to interconnect the fabric ASICs on the I/O modules directly.

A scalable, fully distributed fabric architecture composed of up to five fabric modules combined with the chassis midplane delivers up to 550Gbps per slot for 8.8Tbps, 9.9Tbps, and 18.7Tbps (terabits per second) of forwarding capacity in the 9-slot, 10-slot, and 18-slot switches, respectively. The 4-slot chassis delivers up to 1.92Tbps of forwarding capacity in combination with the built-in fabric system.

The midplane design on the 9-slot, 10-slot, and 18-slot chassis and the backplane design on the 4-slot chassis support flexible technology upgrades as your needs change, providing ongoing investment protection.

Cisco Nexus 7700 Platform Switches

The Cisco Nexus 7700 platform switches have operational and feature consistency with the existing Cisco Nexus 7000 platform switches, using common system architecture, the same Application-Specific Integrated Circuit (ASIC) technology, and the same Cisco NX-OS software releases.

With more than 83Tbps of overall switching capacity, the Cisco Nexus 7700 switches deliver the highest-capacity 10-, 40-, and 100-Gigabit Ethernet ports, with up to 768 native 10Gbps ports, 384 40Gbps ports, or 192 100Gbps ports. This high system capacity is designed to meet the scalability requirements of the largest cloud environments.

Powered by Cisco NX-OS, the Cisco Nexus 7700 switches deliver a comprehensive set of features with nonstop operations in four chassis form factors (that is, 2-, 6-, 10-, and 18-slot), as shown in Figure 2-4. All 7700 chassis have front-accessible module slots with front-to-back airflow and an integrated cable management system.

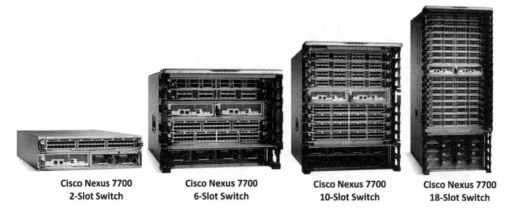

Cisco Nexus 7700
2-Slot Switch

Cisco Nexus 7700
6-Slot Switch

Cisco Nexus 7700
10-Slot Switch

Cisco Nexus 7700
18-Slot Switch

Figure 2-4 *Cisco Nexus 7700 Switches*

A scalable, fully distributed fabric architecture uses up to six fabric modules to deliver up to 1.32Tbps per slot of bandwidth in the Cisco Nexus 7700 6-, 10-, and 18-slot switches on day one. In the case of the Cisco Nexus 7700 2-slot chassis, the fabric modules are not required since it uses a single I/O module. The midplane design on the 2-, 6-, 10-, and 18-slot chassis supports flexible technology upgrades as your needs change, providing ongoing investment protection.

Note   Cisco introduces new supervisor modules, I/O modules, and fabric modules with enhanced capacity and feature sets from time to time. For the latest supported line cards and fabric modules in 7000 Series modular chassis, refer to the datasheet located at https://www.cisco.com/c/en/us/products/switches/nexus-7000-series-switches/datasheet-listing.html.

Cisco Nexus 3000 Series Switches

The Cisco Nexus 3000 Series switches are a comprehensive portfolio of 1-, 10-, 40-, 100- and 400-Gigabit Ethernet switches built from a switch-on-a-chip (SoC) architecture. This series of switches provides line-rate Layer 2 and 3 performance and is suitable for ToR architecture. This series of switches has established itself as a leader in high-frequency trading (HFT), high-performance computing (HPC), and big data environments by pairing high performance and low latency with innovations in performance visibility, automation, and time synchronization. Cisco Nexus 3000 Series provides 24 to 256 ports, offering flexible connectivity, high performance, and a comprehensive feature set to meet various data center requirements.

The Cisco Nexus 3000 Series switches include the Nexus 3100/3200/3400/3500 and 3600 platform fixed switches.

Figure 2-5 shows Cisco Nexus 3000 Series switches.

Cisco Nexus 31108PC-V

Cisco Nexus 3432D-S

Cisco Nexus 3636C-R

Figure 2-5   *Cisco Nexus 3000 Series Switches*

Table 2-3 summarizes the Cisco Nexus 3000 series switch models.

Table 2-3 *Cisco Nexus 3000 Series Switches*

Model	Description
Cisco Nexus 3172PQ/PQ-XL	72 x 1/10Gbps SFP+ ports, or 48 x 1/10Gbps SFP+ and 6 x 40Gbps QSFP+ ports
Cisco Nexus 3172TQ/TQ-XL	72 x 1/10Gbps SFP+ ports, or 48 x RJ-45 and 6 x 40Gbps QSFP+ ports
Cisco Nexus 31128PQ	96 x 1/10Gbps SFP+ ports and 8 x 40Gbps QSFP+ ports
Cisco Nexus 31108PC-V	48 x 1/10Gbps SFP+ ports and 6 x 40/100Gbps QSFP28 ports
Cisco Nexus 31108TC-V	48 x 100M/1G/10Gbps RJ-45 ports and 6 x 40/100Gbps QSFP28 ports
Cisco Nexus 3132Q-V	32 x 10/40Gbps QSFP+ ports
Cisco Nexus 3132C-Z	32 x 10/25/40/50/100Gbps QSFP28 ports
Cisco Nexus 3232C	32 x 10/25/40/50/100Gbps QSFP28 ports
Cisco Nexus 3264C-E	64 x 10/25/40/50/100Gbps QSFP28 ports
Cisco Nexus 3432D-S	32 x 40/100/200/400Gbps QSFP-DD ports
Cisco Nexus 3408-S	32 x 400Gbps QSFP-DD ports or 128 x 100Gbps QSFP28 ports
Cisco Nexus 3524-X/XL	24 x 1/10Gbps SFP+ ports
Cisco Nexus 3548-X/XL	48 x 1/10Gbps SFP+ ports
Cisco Nexus 36180YC-R	48 x 1/10/25Gbps SFP28 ports + 6 x 40/100Gbps QSFP28 ports
Cisco Nexus 3636C-R	36 x 10/25/40/100Gbps QSFP28 ports

Cisco Fabric Extenders

Cisco Fabric Extender (FEX) technology comprises technologies that enable fabric extensibility with simplified management enabling the switching access layer to extend and expand all the way to the server hypervisor as the customer's business grows. Based on the emerging standard IEEE 802.1BR, the Cisco FEX technology solution is composed of a parent switch that can be a Nexus 7000 Series Switch, Nexus 9000 Series Switch, or a Cisco UCS Fabric Interconnect. The parent switch is then extended to connect to the server either as a remote line card with Nexus 2200/2300 Series fabric extenders or logically partitioned or virtualized adapter ports to connect to any type of server (rack and/or blades) with Cisco Adapter FEX and Cisco Data Center VM-FEX technologies. Although this chapter is for the Cisco Nexus family of products, we will also introduce the fabric extender products used on the Unified Compute side so that you know what fabric extender products exist today.

Cisco Nexus 2200 Platform Fabric Extenders

The Cisco Nexus 2200 platform fabric extenders comprise a category of data center products designed to simplify data center access architecture and operations. The Cisco Nexus 2200 platform fabric extenders use the Cisco fabric extender architecture to provide a highly scalable unified server-access platform across a range of 100-Megabit Ethernet, 1- and 10-Gigabit Ethernet, Unified Fabric, copper and fiber connectivity, and rack and blade server environments. The platform is well-suited to support today's traditional 1-Gigabit Ethernet environments while allowing transparent migration to 10-Gigabit Ethernet, virtual machine-aware, Unified Fabric technologies.

The Cisco Nexus 2200 platform fabric extenders behave like remote line cards for a parent Cisco Nexus switch. The fabric extenders are essentially extensions of the parent Cisco Nexus switch fabric, with the fabric extenders and the parent switch together forming a distributed modular system. This architecture enables physical topologies with the flexibility and benefits of both ToR and EoR (end-of-row) deployments.

The Cisco Nexus 2200 platform fabric extenders provide two types of ports: ports for end-host attachment (host interfaces) and uplink ports (fabric interfaces). Fabric interfaces, differentiated with a yellow color, are for connectivity to the upstream parent Cisco Nexus switch.

Figure 2-6 shows various Cisco Nexus 2200 platform fabric extenders.

Figure 2-6 *Cisco Nexus 2200 Platform Fabric Extenders: Cisco Nexus 2232TM-E (Top Left), Cisco Nexus 2248TP-E (Top Right), and Cisco Nexus Cisco Nexus 2232PP (Bottom)*

Table 2-4 summarizes the Cisco Nexus 2200 platform fabric extender models.

Table 2-4   *Cisco Nexus 2200 Platform Fabric Extenders*

Model	Description
Cisco Nexus 2232PP 10GE	32 x 1/10-Gigabit Ethernet and Fibre Channel over Ethernet (FCoE) host interfaces (SFP+) and 8 x 10-Gigabit Ethernet and FCoE fabric interfaces (SFP+)
Cisco Nexus 2232TM-E 10GE	32 x 100M, 1/10GBASE-T host interfaces and uplink modules (8 x 10-Gigabit Ethernet fabric interfaces [SFP+]); FCoE support for up to 30m with Category 6a and 7 cables
Cisco Nexus 2248TP-E	48 x 100/1000BASE-T host interfaces and 4 x 10 Gigabit Ethernet fabric interfaces (SFP+)

Cisco Nexus 2300 Platform Fabric Extenders

Cisco Nexus 2300 platform fabric extenders are the successors to the Cisco Nexus 2200 Series fabric extenders. The Cisco Nexus 2300 platform with its Cisco fabric extender architecture provides a highly scalable unified server-access platform across a range of connectivity options, such as 100-Megabit Ethernet; 1-, 10-, and 40-Gigabit Ethernet; Unified Fabric; copper and fiber connectivity; and rack and blade server environments. The platform offers excellent support for migration from traditional 1-Gigabit Ethernet to 10- and 40-Gigabit Ethernet and virtual machine–aware Unified Fabric technologies.

The Cisco Nexus 2300 platform maintains all the existing Cisco Nexus 2200 Series features, including a single point of management, high availability with virtual port channels (vPC), vPC+, Enhanced vPC, and LAN and SAN convergence using Fibre Channel over Ethernet (FCoE).

Figure 2-7 shows various Cisco Nexus 2300 platform fabric extenders.

Figure 2-7   *Cisco Nexus 2300 Platform Fabric Extenders: Cisco Nexus 2332TQ (Top Left), Cisco Nexus 2348UPQ (Middle Left), Cisco Nexus 2348TQ (Bottom Left), and Cisco Nexus 2348TQ-E (Right)*

Table 2-5 summarizes the Cisco Nexus 2300 platform fabric extender models.

Table 2-5 *Cisco Nexus 2300 Platform Fabric Extenders*

Model	Description
Cisco Nexus 2348UPQ 10GE	48 x 1/10-Gigabit Ethernet and Unified Port host interfaces (SFP+) and up to 6 QSFP+ 10/40-Gigabit Ethernet fabric interfaces
Cisco Nexus 2348TQ 10GE	48 x 100MBASE-T and 1/10GBASE-T port host interfaces (RJ-45) and up to 6 QSFP+ 10/40-Gigabit Ethernet fabric interfaces; FCoE support for up to 30m with Category 6a and 7 cables
Cisco Nexus 2332TQ 10GE	32 x 100MBASE-T and 1/10GBASE-T port host interfaces (RJ-45) and up to 4 QSFP+ 10/40-Gigabit Ethernet fabric interfaces; FCoE support for up to 30m with Category 6a and 7 cables
Cisco Nexus 2348TQ-E 10GE	48 x 100MBASE-T and 1/10GBASE-T port host interfaces (RJ-45) and up to 6 QSFP+ 10/40-Gigabit Ethernet fabric interfaces; FCoE support for up to 30m with Category 6a and 7 cables

Cisco Nexus B22 Blade Fabric Extender

The Cisco Nexus B22 blade fabric extender is designed to simplify data center server-access architecture and operations in environments in which third-party blade servers are used. The platform offers excellent support for the integration of third-party blade chassis into a Cisco Unified Fabric.

The Cisco Nexus B22 blade fabric extender behaves like a remote line card for a parent Cisco Nexus switch, together forming a distributed modular system. This architecture simplifies data center access operations and architecture by combining the management simplicity of a single high-density access switch with the cabling simplicity of integrated blade switches and ToR access switches.

The Cisco Nexus B22 provides two types of ports: ports for blade server attachment (host interfaces) and uplink ports (fabric interfaces). Fabric interfaces, located on the front of the Cisco Nexus B22 module, are for connectivity to the upstream parent Cisco Nexus switch.

The Cisco Nexus B22 comes in four models, as shown in Figure 2-8.

Figure 2-8   *Cisco Nexus B22 Blade Fabric Extender for Dell (Left), IBM (Middle), HP (Top Right), and Fujitsu (Bottom Right)*

Table 2-6 summarizes the Cisco Nexus B22 fabric extender models.

Table 2-6   *Cisco Nexus B22 Fabric Extenders*

Model	Description
Cisco Nexus B22HP fabric extender (blade fabric extender for HP)	16 x 1/10GBASE-KR internal host interfaces and 8 x 10-Gigabit Ethernet fabric interfaces (Enhanced Small Form-Factor Pluggable [SFP+])
Cisco Nexus B22IBM fabric extender (blade fabric extender for IBM)	14 x 1/10GBASE-KR internal host interfaces and 8 x 10-Gigabit Ethernet fabric interfaces (SFP+)
Cisco Nexus B22F fabric extender (blade fabric extender for Fujitsu)	16 x 10GBASE-KR internal host interfaces and 8 x 10-Gigabit Ethernet fabric interfaces (SFP+)
Cisco Nexus B22DELL fabric extender (blade fabric extender for Dell)	16 x 1/10GBASE-KR internal host interfaces and 8 x 10-Gigabit Ethernet fabric interfaces (SFP+)

Cisco Adapter FEX

Cisco Adapter FEX extends the Cisco FEX technology into traditional rack servers. Cisco Adapter FEX enables the server adapter to be logically partitioned into multiple virtual network interface cards (vNICs). Each vNIC behaves like a physical NIC port and meets the network connectivity needs for each application so that security and quality of service (QoS) policies can be applied for each vNIC and application. Cisco has partnered with server adapter vendors including Emulex, Broadcom, and QLogic to deliver this capability.

Cisco Data Center VM-FEX

Cisco Data Center VM-FEX extends the Cisco FEX technology to virtualized servers. Cisco Data Center VM-FEX partitions the server adapter into multiple vNICs, and each vNIC is assigned to individual virtual machines. Because the switching of VM traffic is provided in hardware switches instead of a software switch within the hypervisor, greater performance is achieved through the consolidation of the virtual and physical access layers.

Cisco UCS Fabric Extenders

The Cisco UCS 2200/2300/2400 Series fabric extenders extend the Cisco FEX technology to Cisco Unified Computing System blade servers. The Cisco UCS fabric extenders together with the Cisco UCS fabric interconnects form a parent switch and line card architecture to deliver scalability. More on Cisco UCS fabric extenders in Chapter 16.

Cisco FEX Overview

Today's data center networks require higher port density at the access layer to accommodate more servers, which in turn requires more switches to be added to the network at the access layer. This has increased the complexity of the infrastructure and cost associated with the higher number of switches. Cisco introduced Cisco FEX product family to solve this problem by pushing the logic and complexity up to the core and distribution layer but at the same time obtaining port density at the access layer.

Cisco FEX technology offers a flexible solution for adding access port connectivity to the data center network as well as simplifying migration from 100Mbps or 1Gbps to 10Gbps at the server access layer. Cisco FEX provides flexibility and simplified cabling of ToR designs as well as simplified management of EoR designs. Finally, unified ports support flexible LAN and SAN deployments via Ethernet, Fibre Channel, and FCoE connectivity.

The fabric extender integrates with its parent switch, which is a Cisco Nexus Series device, to allow automatic provisioning and configuration taken from the settings on the parent device. This integration allows large numbers of servers and hosts to be supported by using the same feature set as the parent device with a single management domain. The fabric extender and its parent switch enable a large multipath, loop-free data center topology without the use of the Spanning Tree Protocol (STP).

The Cisco Nexus 2000 Series fabric extender forwards all traffic to its parent Cisco Nexus Series device over 10-Gigabit Ethernet fabric uplinks, which allows all traffic to be inspected by policies established on the Cisco Nexus Series device. No software is included with the fabric extender. The software is automatically downloaded and upgraded from its parent device.

Server Deployment Models

Most data centers are deployed according to two design philosophies: end of row (EoR) and top of rack (ToR). These two models impact the cost of cabling, the number of switches required, the power and cooling strategy, and the sizing of the data center facility. With the introduction of Cisco FEX, a new FEX deployment model came into existence, which uses the benefits of both EoR and ToR models.

End-of-Row (EoR) Deployment Model

This topology consists of large, director-class switching devices at the end of each row of servers. End-of-the-row topologies require significant cabling bulk to be carried from all server racks to the network rack. The main advantage of end-of-the-row topologies is the fact that fewer configuration points (switches) control a large number of server ports.

Figure 2-9 illustrates a typical EoR deployment model.

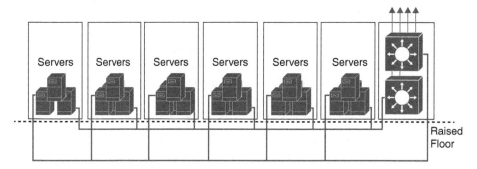

Figure 2-9   *End-of-Row Deployment Model*

EoR benefits include the following:

- Fewer configuration and management points in the network

- Fewer devices, so less power required

- Lower CapEx and OpEx

- Ease in rolling out services and software upgrades

- Feature consistency (security, QoS, multicast, and so on)

- High-density server aggregation allowed at access layer

- Greater control on oversubscription

However, the EoR deployment model has the following disadvantages:

- An expensive, bulky, rigid, copper cabling infrastructure with increased cable complexity is required.

- Additional infrastructure is required for patching and cable management.

- Long twisted-pair copper cabling limits the adoption of lower-power higher-speed server I/O.

- Less flexible "per row" architecture. Platform upgrades/changes affect entire row.

- Addition of racks is limited by aggregation switch capacity.

Top-of-Rack (ToR) Deployment Model

This topology consists of one-rack unit (1RU) or 2RU devices at the top or bottom of each server rack, providing server (or blade server) connectivity within each rack that's aggregated by a switch at the aggregation layer. ToR topologies are more efficient in terms of cabling because fewer cables are required from each rack to the EoR switch. On the other hand, ToR topologies require more switches than EoR topologies require for the same number of switch ports, which increases the management burden.

Figure 2-10 illustrates a typical ToR deployment model.

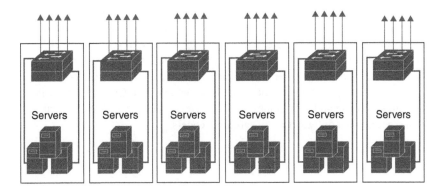

Figure 2-10 *Top-of-Rack Deployment Model*

ToR benefits include the following:

- Flexible and scalable POD design

- Ease in replication of racks

- Shorter server-to-access switch cabling

- Fewer across-rack cables

- Lower cabling costs

However, the ToR deployment model has the following disadvantages:

- More switches to manage. More ports are required in the aggregation switches.

- ToR switches may be underutilized, resulting in unnecessary power usage and increased cooling without direct benefit to performance.

- Potential scalability concerns (STP logical ports, aggregation switch capacity).

- If the ToR switch fails, the entire rack goes offline.

- More Layer 2 server-to-server traffic in the aggregation.

- More STP instances to manage as racks are connected at Layer 2.

- Unique control plane per switch. Higher skill set needed for switch replacement.

FEX Deployment Model

The FEX deployment model enables physical topologies with the flexibility and benefits of both ToR and EoR deployments. It uses the pod approach of a ToR deployment and the management simplicity of the EoR deployment model. Pods are retained, but they are connected into a single management domain. Together, the Cisco Nexus 2000 Series fabric extenders and the parent Cisco Nexus switch (such as a Cisco Nexus 9000 or 7000 Series switch) form a distributed modular system. The distributed modular system forms one network component from the parent switch at the EoR to the FEX at the ToR. One single point of management and policy enforcement using upstream Cisco Nexus switches eases the commissioning and decommissioning of server racks through zero-touch installation and automatic configuration of fabric extenders.

Figure 2-11 illustrates a typical FEX deployment model.

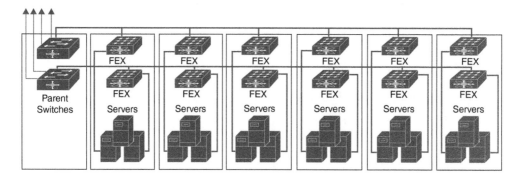

Figure 2-11   *FEX Deployment Model*

The FEX deployment model benefits include the following:

- Combines the benefits of both ToR and EoR architectures: high-density server aggregation switch that physically resides on the top of each rack but logically acts like an end-of-row access switch

- Reduces management devices

- Ensures feature consistency across hundreds of servers

- Reduces cable runs

- Reduces management point

- Lower total cost of ownership (TCO)

FEX Forwarding

The Cisco Nexus 2000 (that is, the 2200 or 2300 platform) Series fabric extender does not perform any local switching. All traffic is sent to the parent switch, which provides central forwarding and policy enforcement, including host-to-host communications between two systems that are connected to the same fabric extender, as shown in Figure 2-12.

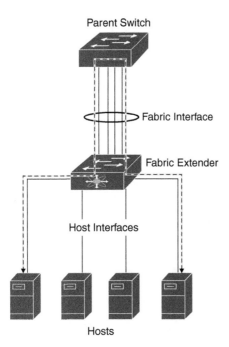

Figure 2-12 *FEX Forwarding*

The forwarding model facilitates feature consistency between the fabric extender and its parent Cisco Nexus device. The fabric extender provides end-host connectivity into the network fabric. As a result, BPDU Guard is enabled on all its host interfaces. If you connect a bridge or switch to a host interface, that interface is placed in an error-disabled state when a BPDU is received. You cannot disable BPDU Guard on the host interfaces of the fabric extender.

The fabric extender supports egress multicast replication from the network to the host. Packets sent from the parent switch for multicast addresses attached to the fabric extender are replicated by the fabric extender ASICs and then sent to corresponding hosts.

Two methods (the static pinning fabric interface connection and the dynamic fabric interface connection) allow the traffic from an end host to the parent switch to be distributed when going through the Cisco Nexus 2000 Series fabric extender.

Static Pinning

Static pinning provides a deterministic relationship between the host interfaces and the parent switch. You configure the fabric extender to use individual fabric interface connections. In this configuration, the 10-Gigabit Ethernet fabric interfaces connect to the parent switch, as shown in Figure 2-13. You can use any number of fabric interfaces, up to the maximum available on the model of the fabric extender.

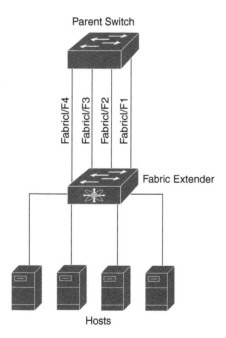

Figure 2-13 *Static Pinning Fabric Interface Connections*

When the fabric extender is brought up, its host interfaces are distributed equally among the available fabric interfaces. As a result, the bandwidth that is dedicated to each end host toward the parent switch is never changed by the switch but instead is always specified by you.

> **Note**   The FEX static pinning fabric interface connection is not supported on Nexus 7000 and 9000 Series switches. Static pinning was supported on Nexus 5000 and 6000 Series switches, which are end-of-life/end-of-sale at the time of this writing. We have covered it here, as Nexus 5000 and 6000 Series switches are still deployed at scale at various data centers.

Dynamic Pinning

Dynamic pinning provides load balancing between the host interfaces and the parent switch. You configure the fabric extender to use a port channel fabric interface connection. This connection bundles 10-Gigabit Ethernet fabric interfaces into a single logical channel, as shown in Figure 2-14.

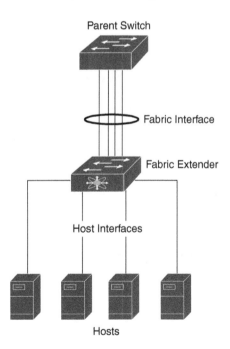

Figure 2-14   *Dynamic Pinning Fabric Interface Connections*

When you configure the fabric extender to use a port channel fabric interface connection to its parent switch, the switch load balances the traffic from the hosts that are connected to the host interface ports by using the following load-balancing criteria to select the link:

- For a Layer 2 frame, the switch uses the source and destination MAC addresses.

- For a Layer 3 frame, the switch uses the source and destination MAC addresses and the source and destination IP addresses.

A fabric interface that fails in the port channel does not trigger a change to the host interfaces. Traffic is automatically redistributed across the remaining links in the port channel fabric interface. If all links in the fabric port channel go down, all host interfaces on the FEX are set to the down state.

Note   Nexus 2000 Series fabric extenders support various topologies using dynamic pinning. Although covering all the supported/unsupported topologies is beyond the scope of this chapter, it is highly recommended that you refer to the following link to know more about them: https://www.cisco.com/c/en/us/support/docs/switches/nexus-2000-series-fabric-extenders/200363-nexus-2000-fabric-extenders-supported-un.html.

Virtual Network Tag (VN-Tag)

Cisco FEX uses VN-Tag technology based on the IEEE 802.1Qbh Bridge Port Extension standard, which allows virtualization of the port extender host interface. VN-Tag provides the capability to differentiate traffic between different host interfaces traversing the fabric uplinks. The VN-Tag is inserted between the source MAC address and the IEEE 802.1Q fields from the original Ethernet frame, as shown in Figure 2-15.

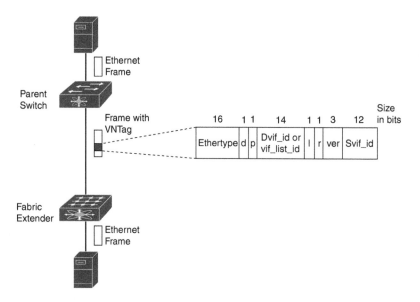

Figure 2-15   *FEX VN-Tag*

The VN-Tag fields are as follows:

- **Ethertype:** This field identifies a VN-Tag frame. IEEE reserved the value 0x8926 for Cisco VN-Tag.

- **Direction bit (d):** A 0 indicates that the frame is traveling from the FEX to the parent switch. A 1 means that the frame is traveling from the parent switch to the FEX.

- **Pointer bit (p):** A 1 indicates that a Vif_list_id is included in the tag. A 0 signals that a Dvif_id is included in the frame.

- **Virtual Interface List Identifier (Vif_list_id):** This is a 14-bit value mapped to a list of host interfaces to which this frame must be forwarded.

- **Destination Virtual Interface Identifier (Dvif_id):** This is a 12-bit value mapped to a single host interface to which an Ethernet frame will be forwarded.

- **Looped bit (l):** This field indicates a multicast frame that was forwarded out the switch port and later received. In this case, the FEX checks the Svif_id and filters the frame from the corresponding port.

- **Reserved bit (r):** This bit is reserved for future use.

- **Source Virtual Interface Identifier (Svif_id):** This is a 12-bit value mapped to the host interface that received this frame (if it is going from the FEX to the parent switch).

FEX includes the following physical and logical interfaces:

- **NIF (Network Interface)/Fabric Interface (FIF):** These are physical uplink interfaces on the FEX. These interfaces can only connect back to the parent switch and carry only VN-Tagged traffic.

- **Host Interfaces (HIFs):** These are physical user/host interfaces on the FEX. These interfaces receive normal Ethernet traffic before it is encapsulated with the VN-Tag header. Each HIF interface is assigned a unique VN-Tag ID that is used with the encapsulation.

- **Logical Interface (LIF):** This is a logical interface representation of a HIF and its configuration on the parent switch. Forwarding decisions are based on the LIF.

- **Virtual Interface (VIF):** This is a logical interface on the FEX. The parent switch assigns/pushes the config of an LIF to the VIF of an associated FEX, which is mapped to a physical HIF. This is why replacing an FEX becomes trivial in that the broken FEX is unplugged and the replacement is plugged in.

Figure 2-16 shows various FEX interfaces.

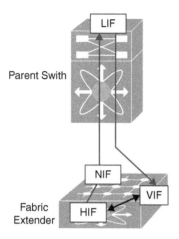

Figure 2-16   *FEX Interfaces*

Cisco NX-OS Software Architecture

Cisco NX-OS software is a data center–class operating system built with modularity, resiliency, and serviceability at its foundation. Cisco NX-OS helps ensure continuous availability for mission-critical data center environments. The self-healing and highly modular design of Cisco NX-OS ensures zero-impact operations and enables exceptional operational flexibility.

Cisco NX-OS provides a robust and comprehensive feature set that fulfills the switching and storage networking needs of present and future data centers. Cisco NX-OS runs on the Cisco Nexus family of network switches, which include Cisco Nexus 9000, 7000, and 3000 Series switches, Cisco Nexus 2000 Series fabric extenders, and the Cisco MDS family of storage network switches. A single Cisco NX-OS image runs on Cisco Nexus switching platforms—Nexus 9000 and Nexus 3000 series switches based on Cisco Cloud Scale ASICs and merchant silicon ASICs.

Cisco NX-OS Modular Architecture

Cisco NX-OS modular architecture has several components, as shown in Figure 2-17.

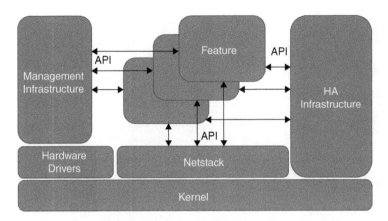

Figure 2-17 *NX-OS Modular Architecture*

- The Linux kernel brings the benefits of Linux to NX-OS, such as preemptive multi-tasking and multithreading, and is the foundation on which all other processes run on NX-OS. It has multi-CPU/core support.

- Hardware drivers are chipset-specific code and provide a hardware abstraction layer (HAL).

- A complete network stack is implemented in user space: L2 packet management, IPv4/v6, ICMPv4/v6, VRFs, TCP/UDP, and socket library.

- Management infrastructure provides an SNMP agent, NETCONF/XML interface, CLI, and configuration interfaces.

- NX-OS features provide a highly granular implementation of individual services, as shown in Figure 2-18. Each service is an individual memory-protected process with support for multiple instances of a particular service. This provides effective fault isolation between services, and each service can be individually monitored and managed. Also, each service can be explicitly enabled or disabled. Disabling a service releases associated resources and removes the associated CLI and configuration.

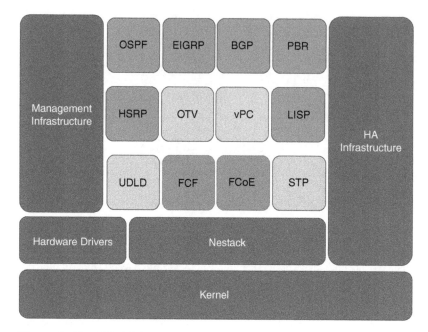

Figure 2-18   *NX-OS Feature/Service Granularity*

- The NX-OS high-availability infrastructure is composed of three subservices:

  - **System manager (sysmgr):** System manager is at the center of service management and fault recovery. It starts up configured features/services and receives heartbeats from services to detect service freeze-ups.

  - **Message & Transaction Service (MTS):** MTS is the message relay system for inter-process communication (IPC) and provides reliable unicast and multicast delivery. MTS is used for service-to-service and module-to-module messaging.

  - **Persistent Storage Service (PSS):** PSS is a lightweight key/value database and provides store options for DRAM or NVRAM. It also provides an API for services to store data and is used to maintain runtime data/state.

Cisco NX-OS Capabilities

The Cisco NX-OS network operating system's key capabilities include the following:

- **Architectural flexibility**

  - Support for Layer 3 (v4/v6) unicast and multicast routing protocol suites such as BGP, OSPF, EIGRP, PIM-SM, SSM, and MDSP.

  - Support for VXLAN EVPN overlay fabrics, including VXLAN EVPN vPC fabric peering for an enhanced dual-homing access solution.

- **Extensive programmability**

  - Support for day-zero automation through Power-On Auto Provisioning (POAP), which streamlines the deployment of production fabrics down to minutes.

  - Support for DevOps configuration-management applications, including Ansible, Chef, Puppet, and SaltStack.

  - Pervasive APIs for all-switch CLI functions with NX-API (JSON-based RPC over HTTP/HTTPs).

  - Comprehensive software development kit for custom Cisco NX-OS applications with NX-SDK in Python, Go, and C++.

  - Support for modular and secure application integration architecture such as Secure LXC and Docker application-hosting options natively on Cisco NX-OS.

- **Pervasive visibility**

  - Support for a flexible NetFlow feature that enables enhanced network anomalies and security detection.

  - Support for monitoring real-time flows, flow paths, and latency, which allows organizations to gain invaluable visibility into their fabrics with Cisco Nexus Insights.

- **Modularity, network resiliency, and high availability**

  - Enables service-level high availability with (a) process isolation and (b) process restartability. Process isolation provides a highly fault-tolerant software infrastructure and fault isolation between the services. Cisco NX-OS processes run in protected memory spaces that are independent of each other and the kernel. Process restartability ensures that process-level failures do not cause system-level failure.

  - Enables system-level high availability by supporting physical redundancy (power, fan, system controller, supervisor, and fabric).

  - Supports nondisruptive, zero-packet-loss upgrades using In-Service Software Upgrade (ISSU), enhanced ISSU, graceful insertion and removal (GIR), and Software Maintenance Upgrade (SMU) packages or RPM patches.

  - Support for Cisco vPC and equal-cost multipath (ECMP).

- **Security and services**

  - Strong line-rate encryption capability and secure communication on Ethernet links with MACsec (hop-by-hop encryption).

  - MAC Authentication Bypass (MAB) to authorize a supplicant based on the supplicant MAC address.

- **Network modeling**

  - Cisco Nexus 9000v switch (virtual NX-OS), with both 9300 and 9500 form factors, extends automation and operational models for DevOps and NetOps integration, with images built for Vagrant, VMware ESXi, KVM, and Fusion.

  - Extensive support for Nexus 9000v is available in Cisco Virtual Internet and Routing Lab (Cisco VIRL) and Cisco Modeling Labs (CML).

- **Closed-loop automation with Cisco DCNM**

  - Accelerates provisioning from days to minutes and simplifies deployments from day zero through day *N* using Cisco DCNM, the network management platform for all Cisco NX-OS-enabled deployments.

  - Reduces troubleshooting cycles with real-time graphical operational visibility for topology, network fabric, and infrastructure.

  - Eliminates configuration errors and automates ongoing changes in a closed loop, with templated deployment models and configuration-compliance alerts with automatic remediation.

Note   The Cisco NX-OS naming convention differs among the various Nexus product family. For example, Nexus 7000 and MDS switches follow one naming convention, whereas Nexus 9000 and Nexus 3000 switches follow another. Refer to the following links for naming conventions of NX-OS for different Nexus products:

- Nexus 7000 and MDS switches: https://tools.cisco.com/security/center/resources/ios_nx_os_reference_guide as part of hyperlink.

- Nexus 9000 and Nexus 3000 switches: https://www.cisco.com/c/en/us/products/collateral/ios-nx-os-software/nx-os-software/guide_c07-658595.html

---

Exploring Cisco NX-OS CLI

Although the graphical user interface is visually intuitive and easier to understand for beginners, the device command-line interface (CLI) is still the most reliable configuration interface available. It can work on slow and erratic connections, uses simple protocols that are easy to establish, and provides clear and reliable feedback on actions taken. It is the essential tool in data center configuration regardless of whether or not a graphical interface is available.

Exploring NX-OS Command Modes

Once you first access an NX-OS device using either console port or vty lines via telnet or ssh, the Cisco NX-OS software places you in EXEC mode, as shown in Example 2-1. The commands available in EXEC mode include the **show** commands, which display the device status and configuration information, the **clear** commands, and other commands that perform actions you do not save in the device configuration.

Example 2-1 *EXEC Mode*

```
login as: admin
Password:******

Cisco Nexus Operating System (NX-OS) Software
TAC support: http://www.cisco.com/tac
Copyright (C) 2002-2020, Cisco and/or its affiliates.
All rights reserved.
The copyrights to certain works contained in this software are
owned by other third parties and used and distributed under their own
licenses, such as open source.  This software is provided "as is," and unless
otherwise stated, there is no warranty, express or implied, including but not
limited to warranties of merchantability and fitness for a particular purpose.
Certain components of this software are licensed under
the GNU General Public License (GPL) version 2.0 or
GNU General Public License (GPL) version 3.0  or the GNU
Lesser General Public License (LGPL) Version 2.1 or
Lesser General Public License (LGPL) Version 2.0.
A copy of each such license is available at
http://www.opensource.org/licenses/gpl-2.0.php and
http://opensource.org/licenses/gpl-3.0.html and
http://www.opensource.org/licenses/lgpl-2.1.php and
http://www.gnu.org/licenses/old-licenses/library.txt.
N9K#
```

Global configuration mode provides access to the broadest range of commands. The term indicates characteristics or features that affect the device as a whole. You can enter commands in global configuration mode to configure your device globally or to enter more specific configuration modes to configure specific elements such as interfaces or protocols.

Example 2-2 illustrates global configuration mode. The global configuration mode can be enabled using the command **configure terminal**.

Example 2-2 *Global Configuration Mode*

```
N9K# configure terminal
Enter configuration commands, one per line. End with CNTL/Z.
N9K(config)#
```

To configure interfaces on your device, you must specify the interface and enter interface configuration mode from global configuration mode, as shown in Example 2-3. You can enable many features on a per-interface basis. *Interface configuration* commands modify the operation of the interfaces on the device, such as Ethernet interfaces or management interfaces (mgmt0).

Example 2-3   *Interface Configuration Mode*

```
N9K(config)# interface Ethernet 1/3
N9K(config-if)#
```

From global configuration mode, you can access a configuration submode for configuring VLAN interfaces called subinterfaces. In subinterface configuration mode, you can configure multiple virtual interfaces on a single physical interface. Subinterfaces appear to a protocol as distinct physical interfaces. Subinterfaces also allow multiple encapsulations for a protocol on a single interface. For example, you can configure IEEE 802.1Q encapsulation to associate a subinterface with a VLAN.

Example 2-4 illustrates subinterface configuration mode, which is enabled by specifying a subinterface from global configuration mode.

Example 2-4   *Subinterface Configuration Mode*

```
N9K(config)# interface Ethernet 1/2.1
N9K(config-subif)#
```

The Cisco NX-OS software allows you to save the current command mode, configure a feature, and then restore the previous command mode. The **push** command saves the command mode, and the **pop** command restores the command mode.

Example 2-5 shows how to save and restore a command mode using the **push** and **pop** commands.

Example 2-5   *The push and pop Commands*

```
N9K# configure terminal
Enter configuration commands, one per line. End with CNTL/Z.
N9K(config)# interface Ethernet 1/2.1
N9K(config-subif)# push
N9K(config-subif)# end
N9K# pop
Enter configuration commands, one per line. End with CNTL/Z.
N9K(config-subif)#
```

To exit a configuration command mode, you can use either the **exit** or **end** command. The **exit** command exits from the current configuration command mode and returns to the previous configuration command mode, as shown in Example 2-6.

Example 2-6 *The exit Command*

```
N9K (config-if)# exit
N9K (config)#
```

The **end** command exits from the current configuration command mode and returns to EXEC mode, as shown in Example 2-7.

Example 2-7 *The end Command*

```
N9K (config-if)# end
N9K #
```

Exploring Special Characters and Keystroke Shortcuts

Table 2-7 lists the characters that have special meaning in Cisco NX-OS text strings and should be used only in regular expressions or other special contexts.

Table 2-7 *Special Characters*

Character	Description
%	Percent
#	Pound, hash, or number
...	Ellipsis
|	Vertical bar
< >	Less than or greater than
[ ]	Brackets
{ }	Braces

The output from **show** commands can be lengthy and cumbersome. The Cisco NX-OS software provides the means to search and filter the output so that you can easily locate information. The searching and filtering options follow a pipe character (|) at the end of the **show** command, as shown in Example 2-8.

Example 2-8   *Pipe (|) Character Filtering*

```
N9K# show running-config | include management
vrf context management
  vrf member management
N9K#
```

Table 2-8 lists command key combinations that can be used in both EXEC and configuration modes.

Table 2-8   *Keystroke Shortcuts*

Keystrokes	Description
Ctrl-A	Moves the cursor to the beginning of the line.
Ctrl-B	Moves the cursor one character to the left. When you enter a command that extends beyond a single line, you can press the left arrow key or the Ctrl-B key combination repeatedly to scroll back toward the system prompt and verify the beginning of the command entry, or you can press the Ctrl-A key combination.
Ctrl-C	Cancels the command and returns to the command prompt.
Ctrl-D	Deletes the character at the cursor.
Ctrl-E	Moves the cursor to the end of the line.
Ctrl-F	Moves the cursor one character to the right.
Ctrl-G	Exits to the previous command mode without removing the command string.
Ctrl-K	Deletes all characters from the cursor to the end of the command line.
Ctrl-L	Redisplays the current command line.
Ctrl-N	Displays the next command in the command history.
Ctrl-O	Clears the terminal screen.
Ctrl-P	Displays the previous command in the command history.
Ctrl-R	Redisplays the current command line.
Ctrl-T	Transposes the character under the cursor with the character located to the right of the cursor. The cursor is then moved to the right one character.

Keystrokes	Description
Ctrl-U	Deletes all characters from the cursor to the beginning of the command line.
Ctrl-V	Removes any special meaning for the following keystroke. For example, press Ctrl-V before entering a question mark (?) in a regular expression.
Ctrl-W	Deletes the word to the left of the cursor.
Ctrl-X, H	Lists the history of commands you have entered. When using this key combination, press and release the Ctrl and X keys together before pressing H.
Ctrl-Y	Recalls the most recent entry in the buffer (press keys simultaneously).
Ctrl-Z	Ends a configuration session and returns you to EXEC mode. When used at the end of a command line in which a valid command has been typed, the resulting configuration is first added to the running configuration file.
Up arrow key	Displays the previous command in the command history.
Down arrow key	Displays the next command in the command history.
Right arrow key Left arrow key	Moves your cursor through the command string, either forward or backward, allowing you to edit the current command.
?	Displays a list of available commands.
Tab	Completes the word for you after you enter the first characters of the word and then press the Tab key. All options that match are presented. Use tabs to complete the following items: ■ Command names ■ Scheme names in the file system ■ Server names in the file system ■ Filenames in the file system

You can display all the options following a pipe character using the CLI context-sensitive help (?) facility, as shown in Example 2-9.

Example 2-9   *Pipe and Context-Sensitive Help*

```
N9K# show running-config | ?
  awk          Mini AWK
  cut          Print selected parts of lines.
  diff         Show difference between current and previous invocation (creates
               temp files: remove them with 'diff-clean' command and dont use it on
               commands
               with big outputs, like 'show tech'!)
  egrep        Egrep - print lines matching a pattern
  email        Email command output
  grep         Grep - print lines matching a pattern
  head         Display first lines
  human        Output in human format
  json         Output in json format
  json-pretty  Output in json pretty print format
  last         Display last lines
  less         Filter for paging
  no-more      Turn-off pagination for command output
  section      Show lines that include the pattern as well as the subsequent lines
               that are more indented than matching line
  sed          Stream Editor
  sort         Stream Sorter
  tr           Translate, squeeze, and/or delete characters
  uniq         Discard all but one of successive identical lines
  vsh          The shell that understands cli command
  wc           Count words, lines, characters
  xml          Output in xml format (according to .xsd definitions)
  xmlin        Convert CLI show commands to their XML formats
  xmlout       Output in xml format (according to the latest .xsd version)
  begin        Begin with the line that matches
  count        Count number of lines
  end          End with the line that matches
  exclude      Exclude lines that match
  include      Include lines that match

N9K#
```

Pressing the Tab key completes the word for you. If there is ambiguity and there are multiple commands possible, the Tab key lists all the possible options that match, as shown in Example 2-10.

Example 2-10   *The Tab Key*

```
N9K# show interface s<Tab>
server-info    snmp-ifindex   status         switchport
N9K#


N9K# conf<Tab>
N9K# configure
```

Exploring Command Abbreviations

You can abbreviate commands and keywords by entering the first few characters of a command. The abbreviation must include sufficient characters to make it unique from other commands or keywords. If you are having trouble entering a command, check the system prompt and enter the question mark (?) for a list of available commands. You might be in the wrong command mode or using incorrect syntax.

Example 2-11 illustrates various command abbreviations.

Example 2-11   *Command Abbreviations*

```
! sh run translates to show running-config, int e 1/2 translates to interface
ethernet 1/2, and conf t translates configure terminal.


N9K# sh run

!Command: show running-config
!Running configuration last done at: Mon Nov  8 09:57:14 2021
!Time: Tue Nov  9 08:42:28 2021

version 9.3(5) Bios:version 05.45
hostname N9K
vdc N9K id 1
  limit-resource vlan minimum 16 maximum 4094
  limit-resource vrf minimum 2 maximum 4096
  limit-resource port-channel minimum 0 maximum 511
  limit-resource u4route-mem minimum 248 maximum 248
  limit-resource u6route-mem minimum 96 maximum 96
  limit-resource m4route-mem minimum 58 maximum 58
  limit-resource m6route-mem minimum 8 maximum 8
  limit-resource vni_bd minimum 4096 maximum 4096
```

```
feature interface-vlan
feature lldp
<output omitted>

N9K# conf t
Enter configuration commands, one per line. End with CNTL/Z.
N9K(config)# int e 1/2
N9K(config-if)#
```

Exploring the no Form of a Command

Almost every configuration command has a "no" form that can be used to disable a feature, revert to a default value, or remove a configuration. Example 2-12 illustrates the no form of the **feature** command.

Example 2-12   *The no Form of a Command*

```
N9K# configure terminal
Enter configuration commands, one per line. End with CNTL/Z.
N9K(config)# feature tacacs+
N9K(config)# show feature | include tacacs
tacacs                  1            enabled
N9K(config)# no feature tacacs+
N9K(config)# show feature | include tacacs
tacacs                  1            disabled
N9K(config)#
```

Exploring Cisco Nexus Device Configuration

The Cisco NX-OS software has two types of configuration files: running configuration and startup configuration. The device uses the startup configuration (**startup-config**) during device startup to configure the software features. The running configuration (**running-config**) contains the current changes you make to the startup configuration file. The two configuration files can be different. You might want to change the device configuration for a short time period rather than permanently. In this case, you would change the running configuration by using commands in global configuration mode but not save the changes to the startup configuration.

To change the running configuration, use the **configure terminal** command to enter global configuration mode. As you use the Cisco NX-OS configuration modes, commands generally are executed immediately and are saved to the running configuration file either immediately after you enter them or when you exit a configuration mode.

To change the startup configuration file, you can either save the running configuration file to the startup configuration using the **copy running-config startup-config** command or copy a configuration file from a file server to the startup configuration.

Example 2-13 illustrates various Nexus device configurations and their impact on running configuration and startup configuration files.

Example 2-13 *Nexus Device Configuration*

```
! Currently running-config and startup-config doesn't have any description config-
  ured under interface Ethernet 1/5

N9K# show running-config interface Ethernet 1/5

interface Ethernet1/5

N9K# show startup-config interface Ethernet 1/5

interface Ethernet1/5

! Configuring description TEST for interface Ethernet 1/5

N9K# configure terminal
Enter configuration commands, one per line. End with CNTL/Z.
N9K(config)# interface Ethernet 1/5
N9K(config-if)# description TEST
N9K(config-if)# end

! Once the description is configured, only running-config reflects the description
  under interface Ethernet 1/5

N9K# show running-config interface Ethernet 1/5

interface Ethernet1/5
  description TEST

N9K# show startup-config interface Ethernet 1/5

interface Ethernet1/5

! Once the configuration is saved on startup-config using copy running-config
  startup-config command, the description is reflected under interface Ethernet 1/5
  in startup-config also.
```

```
N9K# copy running-config startup-config
[########################################] 100%
Copy complete, now saving to disk (please wait)...
Copy complete.
N9K# show startup-config interface Ethernet 1/5


interface Ethernet1/5
  description TEST


N9K#
```

The **write erase** command erases the entire startup configuration, except for the following:

- Boot variable definitions
- The IPv4 and IPv6 configuration on the mgmt0 interface, including the following:
  - Address
  - Subnet mask
  - Default gateway/route in the management VRF

To remove the boot variable definitions and the IPv4/IPv6 configuration on the mgmt0 interface, use the **write erase boot** command. To remove all application persistency files (such as patch rpms, third party rpms, and application configuration) in the /etc directory other than configuration, use 'install reset'.

Exploring Command Aliases

You can define command aliases to replace frequently used commands. The command aliases can represent all or part of the command syntax. Command aliases are global and enabled for all user sessions on an NX-OS device and persist across reboots if you save them to the startup configuration. You can define command aliases for commands in any command mode. Command alias translation always takes precedence over any keyword in any configuration mode or submode.

Example 2-14 illustrates command alias configuration and verification.

Example 2-14   *Command Alias*

```
! Configuring wr as alias for copy running-config startup-config command.


N9K# configure terminal
Enter configuration commands, one per line. End with CNTL/Z.
N9K(config)# cli alias name wr copy running-config startup-config
N9K(config)# exit
N9K# show running-config | include alias
cli alias name wr copy running-config startup-config

! Using alias wr to save running config to starup-config


N9K# wr
[#########################################] 100%
Copy complete, now saving to disk (please wait)...
Copy complete.
N9K# show startup-config | include alias
cli alias name wr copy running-config startup-config
N9K#
```

Exploring Device Hardware and Software

You can use the **show version** command to determine the software version and device model number, as shown in Example 2-15.

Example 2-15   *Show Version Command*

```
! Under the software section of show version command, you can see that the software
  version of NX-OS installed is 9.3(5) version and under the hardware section of the
  output, you can see that the device model is C93180YC-FX.


N9K# show version
Cisco Nexus Operating System (NX-OS) Software
TAC support: http://www.cisco.com/tac
Copyright (C) 2002-2020, Cisco and/or its affiliates.
All rights reserved.
The copyrights to certain works contained in this software are
owned by other third parties and used and distributed under their own
licenses, such as open source.  This software is provided "as is," and unless
otherwise stated, there is no warranty, express or implied, including but not
```

```
limited to warranties of merchantability and fitness for a particular purpose.
Certain components of this software are licensed under
the GNU General Public License (GPL) version 2.0 or
GNU General Public License (GPL) version 3.0  or the GNU
Lesser General Public License (LGPL) Version 2.1 or
Lesser General Public License (LGPL) Version 2.0.
A copy of each such license is available at
http://www.opensource.org/licenses/gpl-2.0.php and
http://opensource.org/licenses/gpl-3.0.html and
http://www.opensource.org/licenses/lgpl-2.1.php and
http://www.gnu.org/licenses/old-licenses/library.txt.


Software
  BIOS: version 05.45
 NXOS: version 9.3(5)
  BIOS compile time:  07/05/2021
  NXOS image file is: bootflash:///nxos.9.3.5.bin
  NXOS compile time:  7/20/2020 20:00:00 [07/21/2020 06:30:11]



Hardware
  cisco Nexus9000 C93180YC-FX Chassis
   Intel(R) Xeon(R) CPU D-1528 @ 1.90GHz with 24569356 kB of memory.
   Processor Board ID FDO23510ELW

   Device name: N9K
   bootflash:  115805708 kB
Kernel uptime is 1 day(s), 1 hour(s), 44 minute(s), 43 second(s)

Last reset at 298285 usecs after Mon Nov  8 08:55:23 2021
   Reason: Reset Requested by CLI command reload
   System version: 9.3(5)
   Service:

plugin
  Core Plugin, Ethernet Plugin

Active Package(s):

N9K#
```

The **show module** command displays all the hardware modules installed in a modular chassis. For fixed models, the **show module** command displays the preinstalled modules, as illustrated in Example 2-16.

Example 2-16 *Show Module Command*

```
N9K# show module
Mod Ports               Module-Type                      Model              Status
--- ----- ------------------------------------ --------------------- ---------
1    54    48x10/25G/32G + 6x40/100G Ethernet/FC N9K-C93180YC-FX       active *


Mod  Sw                    Hw     Slot
---  --------------------- ------ ----
1    9.3(5)                1.2    NA


Mod  MAC-Address(es)                        Serial-Num
---  -------------------------------------- ----------
1    c4-b2-39-93-8f-e0 to c4-b2-39-93-90-3f  FDO23510ELW


Mod  Online Diag Status
---  ------------------
1    Pass


* this terminal session
N9K#
```

Summary

This chapter discusses Cisco Nexus Data Center, Cisco Fabric Extender (FEX), Cisco NX-OS software architecture, and the Cisco NX-OS CLI, including the following points:

- The Cisco Nexus switches are a foundational component of the Cisco Data Center and are well-suited for both traditional and fully automated software-defined data center deployments.

- The Cisco Nexus 9000 Series switches operate in one of two modes: Cisco Application Centric Infrastructure (Cisco ACI) or Cisco NX-OS. The Cisco Nexus 9000 Series switches include the Nexus 9500 Series modular switches and the Nexus 9200/9300 Series fixed switches.

- Cisco Nexus 7000 Series switches are a modular data center–class product line designed for highly scalable 1/10/40/100-Gigabit Ethernet networks. The Cisco Nexus 7000 Series switches include the Nexus 7000 and 7700 platform modular switches.

- The Cisco Nexus 3000 Series switches are a comprehensive portfolio of 1-, 10-, 40-, 100-, and 400-Gigabit Ethernet switches built from a switch-on-a-chip (SoC) architecture.

- The Cisco FEX technology solution is based on Standard IEEE 802.1BR and includes a parent switch that can be a Nexus 7000 Series switch, Nexus 9000 Series switch, or a Cisco UCS Fabric Interconnect. The parent switch is then extended to connect to the server either as a remote line card with Nexus 2200/2300 Series fabric extenders or logically partitioned or virtualized adapter ports to connect to any type of server (rack and/or blades) with Cisco Adapter FEX and Cisco Data Center VM-FEX technologies.

- There are three major server deployment models: end-of-row (EoR) deployment model, top-of-rack (ToR) deployment model, and Fabric Extender (FEX) deployment model. The FEX deployment model enables physical topologies with the flexibility and benefits of both ToR and EoR deployments.

- FEX supports two forwarding models: static pinning, which provides a deterministic relationship between the host interfaces and the parent switch, and dynamic pinning, which provides load balancing between the host interfaces and the parent switch.

- Cisco NX-OS software is a data center–class operating system built with modularity, resiliency, and serviceability at its foundation and runs on the Cisco Nexus family of network switches, which include Cisco Nexus 9000, 7000, 3000 Series switches, Cisco Nexus 2000 Series fabric extenders, and the Cisco MDS family of storage network switches.

- Cisco NX-OS CLI supports various configuration modes such as EXEC mode, global configuration mode, and subinterface configuration mode to configure specific elements.

- Cisco NX-OS CLI supports various features, such as command abbreviations and command aliases, that help an administrator to configure and deploy the device quickly with less effort.

References

Relevant Cisco Nexus Switches Data Sheets: https://www.cisco.com/c/en/us/products/switches/nexus-9000-series-switches/datasheet-listing.html

"Cisco Nexus 9000 NX-OS Fundamentals Configuration Guide, Release 10.2(x)," https://www.cisco.com/c/en/us/td/docs/dcn/nx-os/nexus9000/102x/configuration/fundamentals/cisco-nexus-9000-nx-os-fundamentals-configuration-guide-102x.html

Relevant Cisco Live sessions: http://www.ciscolive.com

"Cisco Nexus 2000 Series NX-OS Fabric Extender Configuration Guide for Cisco Nexus 9000 Series Switches, Release 10.2(x)," https://www.cisco.com/c/en/us/td/docs/dcn/nx-os/nexus9000/102x/configuration/fex/cisco-nexus-2000-series-nx-os-fabric-extender-configuration-guide-for-cisco-nexus-9000-series-switches-release-102x.html

"Cisco Nexus 2000 Series Fabric Extender Software Configuration Guide for Cisco Nexus 7000 Series Switches, Release 8.x," https://www.cisco.com/c/en/us/td/docs/switches/datacenter/nexus2000/sw/configuration/guide/b_Configuring_the_Cisco_Nexus_2000_Series_Fabric_Extender_rel_8_x.html

"Cisco Adapter Fabric Extender: Solution Overview," https://www.cisco.com/c/en/us/products/collateral/switches/nexus-5000-series-switches/data_sheet_c78-657397.html

Chapter 3

Describing Layer 3 First-Hop Redundancy

First-hop redundancy protocols (FHRPs) consist of networking protocols that provide an active default IP gateway at all times. FHRPs use two or more routers or Layer 3 switches to transparently fail over at the first-hop IP router.

In this chapter, we will discuss the challenges presented by single default gateway configuration on end hosts, along with its solutions using Hot Standby Router Protocol (HSRP), Virtual Router Redundancy Protocol (VRRP), and Gateway Load Balancing Protocol (GLBP) as Layer 3 redundancy protocols.

Default Gateway Redundancy

The default gateway facilitates communication between hosts on different networks. The source host sends the data to its default gateway. The default gateway is an IP address on a router (or Layer 3 switch), connected to the same subnet the source host is on, that forwards the data to the destination host. End hosts are typically configured with a single default gateway IP address that does not change when the network topology changes. If the default gateway cannot be reached, the local device is unable to send packets off the local network segment. Even if a redundant router exists that could serve as a default gateway for that segment, there is no dynamic method by which end hosts can determine the address of a new default gateway.

Figure 3-1 illustrates the default gateway's limitations. Router A is configured as the default gateway for Host A. If Router A becomes unavailable, the routing protocols can quickly and dynamically converge and determine that Router B can transfer packets to the destination server that would otherwise have gone through Router A. However, most workstations, servers, and printers do not receive this dynamic routing information.

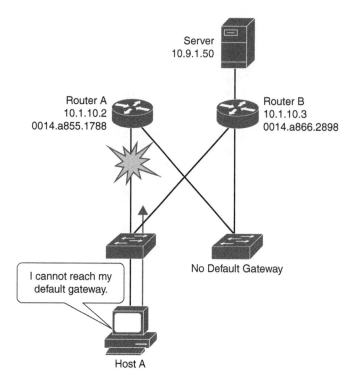

Figure 3-1   *Default Gateway Limitations*

The default gateway limitation discussed earlier can be resolved by using router redundancy. In router redundancy, multiple routers are configured to work together to present the illusion of a single virtual router to the hosts on a particular IP segment. This is achieved by sharing a virtual IP (Layer 3) address and a virtual MAC (Layer 2) address between multiple routers. The IP address of the virtual router is configured as the default gateway for the hosts on that particular IP segment.

In the beginning, before the end host can send any packets to a different network than its own, the end host uses Address Resolution Protocol (ARP) to resolve the MAC address that is associated with the IP address of the default gateway. The ARP resolution returns the MAC address of the virtual router. Frames that are sent to the MAC address of the virtual router can be physically processed by an active router or standby router that is part of that virtual router group, depending on the first-hop redundancy protocol used.

Figure 3-2 illustrates the router redundancy concept.

Host devices send traffic to the address of the virtual router. The physical router that forwards this traffic is transparent to the end stations. The redundancy protocol provides the mechanism for determining which router should take the active role in forwarding traffic and determining when a standby router must assume that role. In short, first-hop redundancy provides a network the ability to dynamically recover from the failure of a device acting as a default gateway.

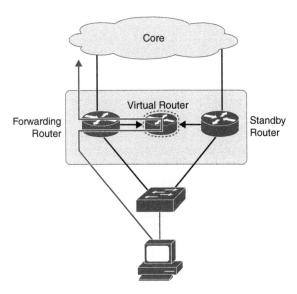

Figure 3-2 *Router Redundancy*

In Figure 3-3, when the forwarding router fails, the standby router stops receiving hello messages from the forwarding router. We will discuss the concept of hello messages in router redundancy protocols later in this chapter. The standby router assumes the role of the forwarding router and assumes the IP address and the MAC address of the virtual router. During this failover, the end hosts see no disruption in service, as the end hosts are still sending the data packets to the same virtual IP and MAC address of the default gateway configured on them.

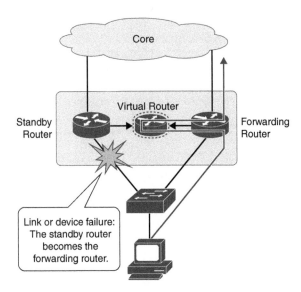

Figure 3-3 *Router Failover*

Hot Standby Router Protocol

Hot Standby Router Protocol (HSRP) is a Cisco proprietary first-hop redundancy protocol (FHRP) for establishing a fault-tolerant default gateway for IP hosts on Ethernet networks. When you use HSRP, you configure the HSRP *virtual IP address* and *virtual MAC address*. The HSRP virtual IP address is used as the host's default router (instead of the IP address of the actual router). The virtual IP address is an IPv4 or IPv6 address that is shared among a group of routers that run HSRP. You configure the same virtual IP address on each HSRP-enabled interface in the group. You also configure a unique IP address and MAC address on each interface that acts as the real address. HSRP selects one of these interfaces to be the *active router*, which receives and routes packets destined for the virtual MAC address of the group. When the designated active router fails, a selected *standby router* assumes control of the virtual MAC and IP addresses of the HSRP group. HSRP also selects a new standby router at that time.

Because hosts are configured with their default router as the HSRP virtual IP address, hosts must communicate with the MAC address associated with the HSRP virtual IP address. This MAC address is a virtual MAC address, 0000.0C07.ACxy, where xy is the HSRP group number in hexadecimal based on the respective interface. For example, HSRP group 1 uses the HSRP virtual MAC address 0000.0C07.AC01. Hosts on the adjoining LAN segment use the normal Address Resolution Protocol (ARP) process to resolve the associated MAC addresses.

Interfaces that run HSRP send and receive multicast User Datagram Protocol–based hello messages to detect a failure and to designate active and standby routers. When the active router fails to send a hello message within a configurable period of time, the standby router with the highest priority becomes the active router. The transition of packet-for-warding functions between the active and standby routers is completely transparent to all hosts on the network.

HSRP hello packets are sent to the destination IP multicast address 224.0.0.2 (reserved multicast address used to communicate to all routers) on User Datagram Protocol (UDP) port 1985. The active router sources hello packets from its configured IP address and the HSRP virtual MAC address, while the standby router sources hellos from its configured IP address and the interface MAC address, which might be the burned-in address (BIA). The BIA is the last 6 bytes of the MAC address assigned by the manufacturer of the network interface card (NIC).

A priority mechanism is used to determine which HSRP-configured interface becomes the default active router. To configure an interface as the active router, you assign it with a priority that is higher than the priority of all the other HSRP-configured interfaces in the group. The default priority is 100, so if you configure just one interface with a higher priority, that interface becomes the default active router.

HSRP Object Tracking

HSRP object tracking allows you to modify the priority of an HSRP interface based on the operational state of another interface. The tracking process periodically polls the tracked objects and notes any value change. The value change triggers HSRP to recalculate the priority. The HSRP interface with the higher priority becomes the active router if you configure the HSRP interface for preemption.

Two objects you can track are the line protocol state of an interface and the reachability of an IP route. If the specified object goes down, Cisco NX-OS reduces the HSRP priority by the configured amount. Object tracking allows you to route to a standby router if the interface to the main network fails.

Figure 3-4 illustrates the HSRP object-tracking feature. In the left diagram, uplinks from Router A and Router B were tracked by HSRP. Router A was the HSRP standby router and Router B was the HSRP active router. When the uplink from Router B fails, HSRP decreases the HSRP priority on Router B, making Router A the active router to process the traffic.

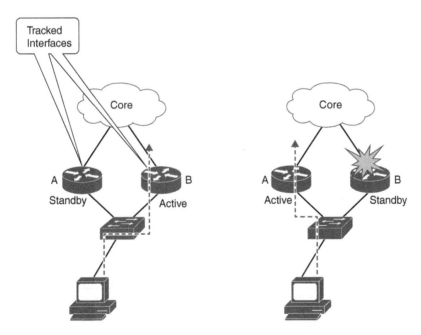

Figure 3-4   *HSRP Object (Interface) Tracking*

HSRP Load Balancing

HSRP allows you to configure multiple groups on an interface. You can configure two overlapping IPv4 HSRP groups to load share the traffic from the connected hosts while providing the default router redundancy expected from HSRP.

Figure 3-5 illustrates HSRP load balancing.

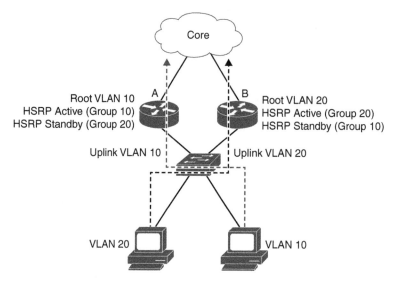

Figure 3-5   *HSRP Load Balancing*

Figure 3-5 shows two routers (A and B) and two HSRP groups (10 and 20). Router A is the active router for group 10 but is the standby router for group 20. Similarly, Router B is the active router for group 20 and the standby router for group 10. If both routers remain active, HSRP load-balances the traffic from the hosts across both routers. If either router fails, the remaining router continues to process traffic for both hosts.

HSRP States

Each HSRP router will go through a number of states before it ends up as an active or standby router. Table 3-1 describes the various HSRP states.

Table 3-1   *HSRP States*

State	Definition
Initial	This is the state at the start. This state indicates that HSRP does not run. This state is entered through a configuration change or when an interface first becomes available.
Learn	The router has not determined the virtual IP address and has not yet seen an authenticated hello message from the active router. In this state, the router still waits to hear from the active router.
Listen	The router knows the virtual IP address, but the router is neither the active router nor the standby router. It listens for hello messages from those routers.

State	Definition
Speak	The router sends periodic hello messages and actively participates in the election of the active and/or standby router. A router cannot enter speak state unless the router has the virtual IP address.
Standby	The router is a candidate to become the next active router and sends periodic hello messages. With the exclusion of transient conditions, there is, at most, one router in the group in standby state.
Active	The router currently forwards packets that are sent to the group virtual MAC address. The router sends periodic hello messages. With the exclusion of transient conditions, there must be, at most, one router in active state in the group.

Note   The terminology *router/switch* might be a little confusing in Table 3-1. Cisco Nexus devices are Layer 3 switches, meaning they are capable of both switching and routing. The naming *switch* or *router* is applied depending on the OSI protocol layer the configuration applies to. HSRP is a Layer 3 redundancy protocol. Therefore, the Nexus devices act as routers in this case.

HSRP Versions

Cisco NX-OS supports HSRP version 1 by default. You can configure an interface to use HSRP version 2. With HSRP version 2, you gain the following enhancements:

- **Expanded group number range:** HSRP version 1 supports group numbers from 0 to 255. HSRP version 2 supports group numbers from 0 to 4095.

- **Use of the new IP multicast address:** HSRP version 2 uses the IPv4 multicast address 224.0.0.102 to send hello packets instead of the multicast address of 224.0.0.2, which is used by HSRP version 1.

- **Use of the new MAC address range:** HSRP version 2 uses the MAC address range from 0000.0C9F.F000 to 0000.0C9F.FFFF. HSRP version 1 uses the MAC address range 0000.0C07.AC00 to 0000.0C07.ACFF.

- **Support for MD5 authentication:** HSRP version 2 supports MD5 authentication. HSRP Message Digest 5 (MD5) algorithm authentication protects against HSRP-spoofing software and uses the industry-standard MD5 algorithm for improved reliability and security.

- **Type-Length-Value Packet format:** HSRP version 2 has a different packet format than HSRP version 1. The packet format uses a type-length-value (TLV) format. HSRP version 2 packets received by an HSRP version 1 router are ignored.

When you change the HSRP version, Cisco NX-OS reinitializes the HSRP group because it now has a new virtual MAC address. Since the interface is reset during the reinitialization of the HSRP group, the version change process is disruptive in nature.

HSRP Configuration

Configuring basic HSRP is a multistep process. The following are the steps to configure a basic HSRP configuration on the Cisco Nexus 7000 or 9000 Series switch:

Step 1.   Enable the HSRP feature.

Step 2.   Configure the HSRP version.

Step 3.   Configure the HSRP group.

Step 4.   Configure the virtual IP of the HSRP group.

Step 5.   Configure the HSRP interface priority and preemption.

Step 6.   (Optional) Configure HSRP authentication.

Step 7.   (Optional) Configure HSRP object tracking.

First, you must globally enable the HSRP feature. Next, you configure the HSRP version on the interface supporting HSRP configuration. Then, you configure an HSRP group on the same interface and configure the virtual IP address. Next, you configure the HSRP priority on an interface along with preemption feature, if required. Optionally, you can configure HSRP authentication using either a plaintext password or MD5 authentication. Also, you can optionally configure the HSRP group to adjust its priority based on the availability of an interface.

Table 3-2 summarizes the NX-OS CLI commands related to basic HSRP configuration and verification.

Table 3-2 *Summary of NX-OS CLI Commands for HSRP Configuration and Verification*

Command	Purpose
configure terminal	Enters global configuration mode.
[no] feature hsrp	Enables the HSRP feature. Use the **no** form of this command to disable HSRP for all groups.
interface vlan *number*	Creates a VLAN interface. The number range is from 1 to 4094.
hsrp version {1 | 2}	Confirms the HSRP version. Version 1 is the default.
hsrp *group-number* [ipv4 | ipv6]	Creates an HSRP group and enters HSRP configuration mode.
ip [*ip-address* [secondary]]	Configures the virtual IP address for the HSRP group and enables the group. This address should be in the same subnet as the IPv4 address of the interface.

Command	Purpose
priority [*value*]	Sets the priority level used to select the active router in an HSRP group. The range is from 0 to 255. The default is 100.
preempt [delay [minimum *seconds*] **[reload** *seconds*] **[sync** *seconds*]]	Configures the router to take over as the active router for an HSRP group if it has a higher priority than the current active router. This command is disabled by default. Optionally, you configure a delay of the HSRP group preemption by the configured time. The range is from 0 to 3600 seconds.
show hsrp [group *group-number*] **[ipv4]**	Displays HSRP information.
show hsrp brief	Displays a brief summary of the HSRP status for all groups in the device.

Examples 3-1 to 3-3 show the basic HSRP configuration and verification on the sample topology shown in Figure 3-6. The base IP addresses have already been configured in VLAN 100 on the sample topology. Here, we will focus on HSRP-specific configuration. N7K-A and N7K-B will act as redundant gateways using HSRP.

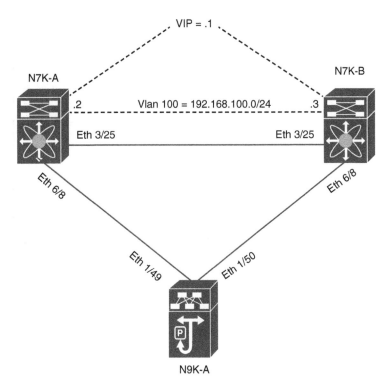

Figure 3-6 *Sample Topology for HSRP Configuration and Verification*

In Example 3-1, we will see the basic HSRP configuration on N7K-A and N7K-B.

Example 3-1   *HSRP Configuration*

```
! Enabling HSRP feature on N7K-A and N7K-B.

N7K-A

N7K-A# configure terminal
Enter configuration commands, one per line.  End with CNTL/Z.
N7K-A(config)# feature hsrp
N7K-A(config)#


N7K-B

N7K-B# configure terminal
Enter configuration commands, one per line.  End with CNTL/Z.
N7K-B(config)# feature hsrp
N7K-B(config)#


! Configuring HSRP version 2 for interface Vlan 100. HSRP version 1 is the default.

N7K-A

N7K-A(config)# interface vlan 100
N7K-A(config-if)# hsrp version 2


N7K-B

N7K-B(config)# interface vlan 100
N7K-B(config-if)# hsrp version 2



! Configuring the HSRP group 100 for interface vlan 100 with 192.168.100.1 as the
virtual IP.

N7K-A

N7K-A(config-if)# hsrp 100
N7K-A(config-if-hsrp)# ip 192.168.100.1
N7K-A(config-if-hsrp)#
```

```
N7K-B
N7K-B(config-if)# hsrp 100
N7K-B(config-if-hsrp)# ip 192.168.100.1
N7K-B(config-if-hsrp)#


! Setting higher priority for N7K-A with preemption feature. The default priority
is 100. Preempt setting only applies to the router with higher priority if a router
with lower priority is in active state. This usually means that there was a fail-
ure of the router with higher priority. Below configuration will assure that N7K-A
becomes HSRP active router.


N7K-A

N7K-A(config-if-hsrp)# priority 120
N7K-A(config-if-hsrp)# preempt
N7K-A(config-if-hsrp)# end
N7K-A#
```

In Example 3-2, we see the HSRP verification commands.

Example 3-2   *HSRP Verification*

```
! Verifying HSRP group 100 and hsrp configuration in brief format.

N7K-A

N7K-A# show hsrp group 100
Vlan100 - Group 100 (HSRP-V2) (IPv4)
  Local state is Active, priority 120 (Cfged 120), may preempt
    Forwarding threshold(for vPC), lower: 1 upper: 120
  Hellotime 3 sec, holdtime 10 sec
  Next hello sent in 0.687000 sec(s)
  Virtual IP address is 192.168.100.1 (Cfged)
  Active router is local
  Standby router is 192.168.100.3 , priority 100 expires in 9.771000 sec(s)
  Authentication text "cisco"
  Virtual mac address is 0000.0c9f.f064 (Default MAC)
  7 state changes, last state change 00:21:48
  IP redundancy name is hsrp-Vlan100-100 (default)

N7K-A# show hsrp brief
*:IPv6 group    #:group belongs to a bundle
                      P indicates configured to preempt.
                     |
```

```
Interface   Grp  Prio  P State   Active addr      Standby addr     Group addr
Vlan100     100  120   P Active  local            192.168.100.3    192.168.100.1
  (conf)
N7K-A#




N7K-B


N7K-B# show hsrp group 100
Vlan100 - Group 100 (HSRP-V2) (IPv4)
  Local state is Standby, priority 100 (Cfged 100)
    Forwarding threshold(for vPC), lower: 1 upper: 100
  Hellotime 3 sec, holdtime 10 sec
  Next hello sent in 1.945000 sec(s)
  Virtual IP address is 192.168.100.1 (Cfged)
  Active router is 192.168.100.2, priority 120 expires in 9.040000 sec(s)
  Standby router is local
  Authentication text "cisco"
  Virtual mac address is 0000.0c9f.f064 (Default MAC)
  6 state changes, last state change 00:22:48
  IP redundancy name is hsrp-Vlan100-100 (default)

N7K-B# show hsrp brief
*:IPv6 group   #:group belongs to a bundle
                   P indicates configured to preempt.
                   |
Interface   Grp  Prio  P State   Active addr      Standby addr     Group addr
Vlan100     100  100     Standby 192.168.100.2    local            192.168.100.1
  (conf)
N7K-B#
```

In Example 3-3, we see the impact of the HSRP preempt configuration on HSRP operation.

Example 3-3 *Preempt Feature Verification*

```
! Shutting down interface vlan 100 on N7K-A HSRP active router. N7K-B takes over
the active role. HSRP on N7K-A will be stuck in initial state.


N7K-A


N7K-A# configure terminal
Enter configuration commands, one per line.  End with CNTL/Z.
N7K-A(config)# interface vlan 100
N7K-A(config-if)# shutdown
```

```
N7K-A(config-if)# show hsrp brief
*:IPv6 group   #:group belongs to a bundle
                       P indicates configured to preempt.
                       |

Interface   Grp  Prio P State   Active addr     Standby addr    Group addr
Vlan100     100  120  P Initial unknown         unknown         192.168.100.1
  (conf)
```

N7K-B

```
N7K-B# show hsrp brief
*:IPv6 group   #:group belongs to a bundle
                       P indicates configured to preempt.
                       |

Interface   Grp  Prio P State   Active addr     Standby addr    Group addr
Vlan100     100  100    Active  local           unknown         192.168.100.1
  (conf)
N7K-B#
```

! Bringing the interface vlan 100 up on N7K-A. Preempt feature kicks in because
N7K-A has higher priority and N7K-A takes over the active role once again.

N7K-A

```
N7K-A(config-if)# no shutdown
N7K-A(config-if)# show hsrp brief
*:IPv6 group   #:group belongs to a bundle
                       P indicates configured to preempt.
                       |

Interface   Grp  Prio P State   Active addr     Standby addr    Group addr
Vlan100     100  120  P Active  local           unknown         192.168.100.1
  (conf)
N7K-A(config-if)#
```

N7K-B

```
N7K-B# show hsrp brief
*:IPv6 group   #:group belongs to a bundle
                       P indicates configured to preempt.
                       |

Interface   Grp  Prio P State   Active addr     Standby addr    Group addr
Vlan100     100  100    Standby 192.168.100.2   local           192.168.100.1
  (conf)
N7K-B#
```

Virtual Router Redundancy Protocol

Virtual Router Redundancy Protocol (VRRP) allows for a transparent failover at the first-hop IP router by configuring a group of routers (a VRRP group) to share a single virtual IP address. VRRP selects an allowed router in that group to handle all packets for the virtual IP address. The remaining routers are in standby mode and take over if the allowed router fails. In a VRRP setup, the LAN clients are configured with the virtual IP address as their default gateway.

Figure 3-7 shows a basic VLAN topology. In this example, Routers A, B, and C form a VRRP group. The IP address of the group is the same address that was configured for the Ethernet interface of Router A (10.0.0.1).

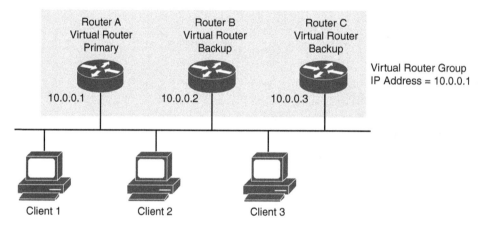

Figure 3-7   *Basic VRRP Topology*

Because the virtual IP address uses the IP address of the physical Ethernet interface of Router A, Router A is the primary router (also known as the IP address owner). As the primary, Router A owns the virtual IP address of the VRRP group and forwards packets sent to this IP address. Clients 1 through 3 are configured with the default gateway IP address of 10.0.0.1. Routers B and C function as backups. If the primary fails, the backup router with the highest priority becomes the primary and takes over the virtual IP address to provide uninterrupted service for the LAN hosts. When Router A recovers, it becomes the primary again.

The VRRP primary sends VRRP advertisements to other VRRP routers in the same group. The advertisements communicate the priority and state of the primary. Cisco NX-OS encapsulates the VRRP advertisements in IP packets and sends them to the IP multicast address 224.0.0.18, assigned to the VRRP group. Cisco NX-OS sends the advertisements once every second, by default, but you can configure a different advertisement interval.

VRRP Tracking

VRRP supports the following options for tracking:

■ **Native interface tracking:** Tracks the state of an interface and uses that state to determine the priority of the VRRP router in a VRRP group. The tracked state is down if the interface is down or if the interface does not have a primary IP address.

■ **Object tracking:** Tracks the state of a configured object and uses that state to determine the priority of the VRRP router in a VRRP group. The tracked object can be an interface IP routing state or IP route reachability.

If the tracked state (interface or object) goes down, VRRP updates the priority based on what you have configured the new priority to be for the tracked state. When the tracked state comes up, VRRP restores the original priority for the virtual router group. For example, you might want to lower the priority of a VRRP group member if its uplink to the network goes down so that another group member can take over as primary for the VRRP group.

VRRP Router Priority and Preemption

VRRP router priority determines the role each VRRP router plays (that is, primary or backup) and the order of ascendancy for backup routers to become a primary if the primary fails. The priority of the primary router is 255, and the priorities of the backups are lower.

In Figure 3-8, if Router A (the primary in a LAN topology) fails, VRRP must determine if one of the backups (B or C) should take over. If you configure Router B with priority 101 and Router C with the default priority of 100, VRRP selects Router B to become the primary because it has the higher priority. If you configure both Routers B and C with the default priority of 100, VRRP selects the backup with the higher IP address to become the primary. In this case, Router C will become the primary, as it has a higher IP address.

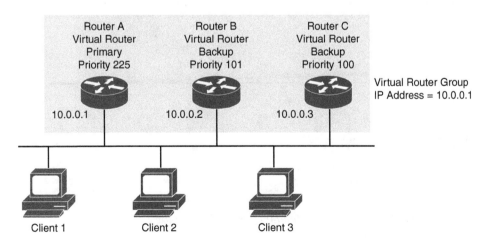

Figure 3-8 *VRRP Router Priority*

VRRP uses preemption to determine what happens after a VRRP backup router becomes the primary. With preemption enabled by default, VRRP switches to a backup if that backup comes online with a priority higher than the new primary. In the previous example, if Router A is the primary and fails, VRRP selects Router B (next in order of priority). If Router C comes online with a higher priority than Router B, VRRP selects Router C as the new primary, even though Router B has not failed. If you disable preemption, VRRP switches only if the original primary recovers (that is, Router A) or the new primary fails.

VRRP Load Balancing

You can configure multiple VRRP groups on a physical interface. The number of VRRP groups that a router interface can support depends on the router processing capability and memory capabilities. A single physical interface can support up to 255 VRRP groups. In a topology where multiple VRRP groups are configured on a router interface, the interface can act as a primary for one VRRP group and as a backup for one or more other VRRP groups.

Figure 3-9 shows a LAN topology in which VRRP is configured so that Routers A and B share the traffic to and from Clients 1 through 4. Routers A and B act as backups to each other if either router fails. The topology contains two virtual IP addresses for two VRRP groups that overlap. For VRRP group 1, Router A is the owner of IP address 10.0.0.1 and is the primary. Router B is the backup to Router A. Clients 1 and 2 are configured with the default gateway IP address of 10.0.0.1. For VRRP group 2, Router B is the owner of IP address 10.0.0.2 and is the primary. Router A is the backup to Router B. Clients 3 and 4 are configured with the default gateway IP address of 10.0.0.2. If Router A fails, Router B takes the role of the primary router and forwards the traffic from all the clients until Router A becomes available again.

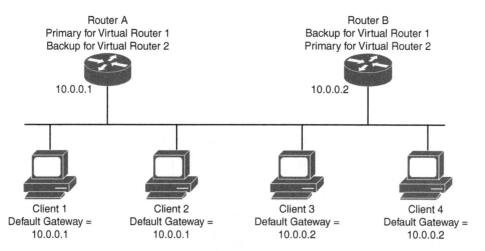

Figure 3-9   *Load Balancing and Redundancy in VRRP Topology*

Table 3-3 lists various differences and similarities between VRRP and HSRP.

Table 3-3 *VRRP vs. HSRP*

VRRP	HSRP
Open standard.	Cisco proprietary.
RFC 3768.	RFC 2281.
IP encapsulation: IP Protocol number 112.	UDP encapsulation: Port number 1985.
One primary router and multiple backup routers.	One active router, one standby router, and other listening routers.
Uses the router interface IP address or virtual IP address.	Uses a virtual IP address.
Primary router election is based on the highest priority or highest IP address.	Active router election is based on the highest priority or highest IP address.
Default priority is 100.	Default priority is 100.
Supports tracking, preemption, and timers.	Supports tracking, preemption, and timers.
Advertisements at 1-second intervals.	Hello at 3-second intervals.
Support for load balancing.	Support for load balancing.
Advertisement propagation using multicast IP address 224.0.0.18.	Hello propagation using multicast IP address 224.0.0.2 (version 1) and 224.0.0.102 (version 2).
Virtual MAC address is 0000.5E00.01XX, where XX is the Virtual Router Identifier (255 total).	Virtual MAC address is 0000.0C07.ACXX, where the XX is the HSRP group number.
Preemption enabled by default.	Preemption disabled by default.

VRRP Configuration

Configuring basic VRRP is a multistep process. The following are the steps to configure a basic VRRP configuration on the Cisco Nexus 7000 or 9000 Series switch:

Step 1.   Enable the VRRP feature.

Step 2.   Configure the VRRP group.

Step 3.   Configure the virtual IP of the VRRP group.

Step 4.   Configure the VRRP interface priority.

Step 5.   (Optional) Configure VRRP authentication.

Step 6.   (Optional) Configure VRRP object tracking.

First, you must globally enable the VRRP feature before you can configure VRRP groups. Next, you configure a VRRP group on an interface and configure the virtual IP address of the VRRP group. The virtual IP address should be in the same subnet as the IPv4 address of the interface. Next, you configure the VRRP priority on the interface. The priority range for a virtual router is from 1 to 254 (1 is the lowest priority and 254 is the highest). The default is 100 for backups and 255 for a primary router. Optionally, you can configure simple text authentication for the VRRP group. Also, you can optionally configure the VRRP group to adjust its priority based on the availability of an interface.

Gateway Load Balancing Protocol

Gateway Load Balancing Protocol (GLBP) is a Cisco-proprietary gateway resiliency solution. GLBP allows a group of Layer 3 routers to share the load of the default gateway on a LAN, and the traffic is routed to single gateway distributed across routers. Multiple routers on the LAN combine to offer a single virtual first-hop IP gateway while sharing the IP packet-forwarding load. GLBP allows full use of resources on all devices without the administrative burden of creating multiple groups. Other routers on the LAN might act as redundant GLBP gateways that become active if any of the existing forwarding gateways fail.

GLBP performs a similar function to the Hot Standby Redundancy Protocol (HSRP) and the Virtual Router Redundancy Protocol (VRRP). In HSRP and VRRP, multiple routers participate in a virtual group configured with a virtual IP address. These protocols elect one member as the active router to forward packets sent to the virtual IP address for the group. The other routers in the group are redundant until the active router fails. GLBP performs an additional load-balancing function that the other protocols do not provide. GLBP load-balances over multiple routers (gateways) using a single virtual IP address and multiple virtual MAC addresses. GLBP shares the forwarding load among all routers in a GLBP group instead of allowing a single router to handle the whole load while the other routers remain idle. You configure each host with the same virtual IP address, and all routers in the virtual group participate in forwarding packets. GLBP members communicate between each other using periodic hello messages.

Figure 3-10 illustrates GLBP forwarding.

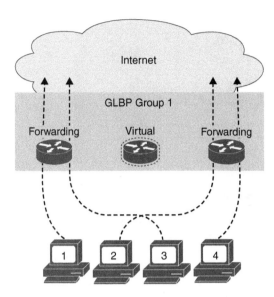

Figure 3-10   *GLBP Forwarding*

GLBP Operation

GLBP prioritizes gateways to elect an active virtual gateway (AVG). Other group members provide backup for the AVG if that AVG becomes unavailable. If multiple gateways have the same priority, the gateway with the highest real IP address becomes the AVG. The group members request a virtual MAC address after they discover the AVG through hello messages. The AVG assigns a virtual MAC address to each member of the GLBP group. Each member is the active virtual forwarder (AVF) for its assigned virtual MAC address, forwarding packets sent to its assigned virtual MAC address. The AVG also answers Address Resolution Protocol (ARP) requests for the virtual IP address. Load sharing is achieved when the AVG replies to the ARP requests with different virtual MAC addresses.

Figure 3-11 illustrates the GLBP ARP resolution process. Router R1 is the AVG for a GLBP group, and it is responsible for the virtual IP (vIP in the figure) address 10.88.1.10. Router R1 is responsible for responding to ARP requests for default gateway (10.88.1.10) and handing out a MAC address of an AVF. Router R1 is also an AVF for the virtual MAC address 0000.0000.0001. Router R2 is a member of the same GLBP group and is designated as the AVF for the virtual MAC address 0000.0000.0002. Client A has a default gateway IP address of 10.88.1.10 and, during initial ARP resolution for the default gateway IP address, receives a gateway MAC address of 0000.0000.0001. Client B shares the same default gateway IP address but receives the gateway MAC address 0000.0000.0002 because R2 is sharing the traffic load with R1.

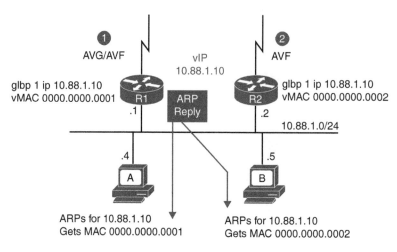

Figure 3-11   *GLBP ARP*

Figure 3-12 illustrates the traffic forwarding in the GLBP environment. Clients A and B send their off-network traffic to separate next-hop routers because each has cached a different MAC address for the single virtual gateway IP address (in this case, 10.88.1.10). Each GLBP router is an AVF for the MAC address it has been assigned.

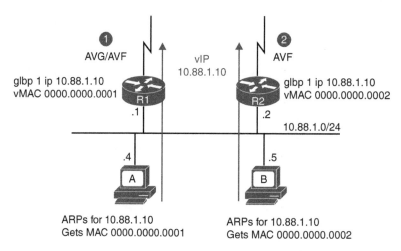

Figure 3-12   *GLBP Traffic Forwarding*

GLBP Interface Tracking

You can configure GLBP to track an interface or routes and enable the secondary virtual forwarder to take over if the tracked object goes down. GLBP tracking uses weighted load balancing to determine whether a GLBP group member acts as an AVF. You must configure the initial weighting values and optional thresholds to enable or disable this group member as an AVF. You can also configure the interface to track and the value that reduces the interface's weighting if the interface goes down. When the GLBP group weighting drops below the lower threshold, the member is no longer an AVF and a secondary virtual forwarder takes over. When the weighting rises above the upper threshold, the member can resume its role as an AVF.

Figure 3-13 illustrates the GLBP interface-tracking feature. Router R2 is the secondary virtual forwarder for Client A and is configured for preemption. If Router R1 becomes unavailable, the weight of the interface connecting Client A to R1 drops below the lower threshold configured, and Router R2 preempts and takes over as AVF for vMAC 0000.0000.0001. Client A will not lose access to the outside network because R2 will assume responsibility for forwarding packets sent to the virtual MAC address of R1 and for responding to packets sent to its own virtual MAC address. R2 will also assume the role of the AVG for the entire GLBP group. Communication for the GLBP members continues despite the failure of a router in the GLBP group.

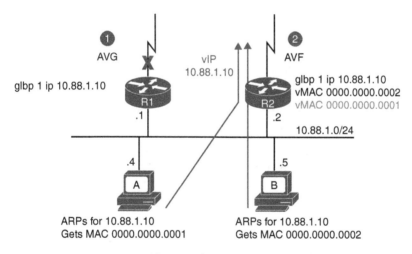

Figure 3-13 *GLBP Interface Tracking*

Note   At the time of this writing, GLBP is not supported on Nexus 9000 Series switches. Nexus 7000 Series switches support GLBP.

Summary

This chapter discusses the challenges of single default gateway configuration on end hosts along with the solutions using default gateway redundancy, including Hot Standby Router Protocol (HSRP), Virtual Router Redundancy Protocol (VRRP), and Gateway Load Balancing Protocol (GLBP). The following points were discussed:

■ End hosts are typically configured with a single default gateway IP address that does not change when the network topology changes.

■ In router redundancy, multiple routers are configured to work together to present the illusion of a single virtual router to the hosts on a particular IP segment. The IP address of the virtual router is configured as the default gateway for the hosts on that particular IP segment.

■ HSRP, VRRP, and GLBP are first-hop redundancy protocols (FHRPs) for establishing a fault-tolerant default gateway for IP hosts on Ethernet networks.

■ HSRP selects one active router (responsible for forwarding traffic destined to the HSRP virtual IP address) and one standby router, and the remaining routers are in the listening state.

■ VRRP selects one primary router (responsible for forwarding traffic destined to the VRRP virtual IP address) and multiple backup routers.

■ GLBP selects one active virtual gateway (AVG) and up to four active virtual forwarders (AVFs). AVG itself can act as AVF. All AVFs can forward traffic at the same time, resulting in in-built load balancing.

■ HSRP and VRRP use one virtual IP and one virtual MAC, whereas GLBP uses one virtual IP with multiple virtual MACs.

References

"Cisco Nexus 9000 Series NX-OS Unicast Routing Configuration Guide, Release 10.2(x)," https://www.cisco.com/c/en/us/td/docs/dcn/nx-os/nexus9000/102x/configuration/ Unicast-routing/cisco-nexus-9000-series-nx-os-unicast-routing-configuration-guide-release-102x.html

"Cisco Nexus 7000 Series NX-OS Unicast Routing Configuration Guide, Release 8.x," https://www.cisco.com/c/en/us/td/docs/switches/datacenter/nexus7000/sw/unicast/ config/cisco_nexus7000_unicast_routing_config_guide_8x.html

"Cisco Nexus 7000 Series NX-OS High Availability and Redundancy Guide, Release 8.x," https://www.cisco.com/c/en/us/td/docs/switches/datacenter/nexus7000/sw/high-availability/config/cisco_nexus7000_high_availability_config_guide_8x.html

Relevant Cisco Live sessions: http://www.ciscolive.com

Chapter 4

Port Channels and vPCs

In early Layer 2 Ethernet network environments, Spanning Tree Protocol (STP) was the primary solution to limit the disastrous effects of a topology loop in the network. STP has one suboptimal principle: to break loops in a network, only one active path is allowed from one device to another, regardless of how many actual connections might exist in the network. The single logical link creates two problems: one problem is that half (or more) of the available system bandwidth is off limits to data traffic, and the other problem is that a failure of the active link tends to cause multiple seconds of systemwide data loss while the network re-evaluates the new "best" solution for network forwarding in the Layer 2 network. In addition, no efficient dynamic mechanism exists for using all the available bandwidth in a robust network with STP loop management. To overcome these challenges, enhancements to Layer 2 Ethernet networks were made in the form of port channel and virtual port channel (vPC) technologies. Port Channel technology allows multiple links between two participating devices to be used to forward traffic by using a load-balancing algorithm that equally balances traffic across the available Inter-Switch Links (ISLs) while also managing the loop problem by bundling the links as one logical link. vPC technology allows multiple devices to form a port channel. In vPC, a pair of switches acting as a vPC peer endpoint looks like a single logical entity to port channel–attached devices; the two devices that act as the logical port channel endpoint are still two separate devices. The vPC environment combines the benefits of hardware redundancy with the benefits of port channel loop management.

In this chapter, we will discuss Ethernet port channels, including port channel modes, port channel compatibility requirements, and port channel load balancing. We will also discuss virtual port channels, including various vPC topology implementations, vPC components, vPC control and data planes, vPC failure scenarios, and vPC configuration and verification.

Ethernet Port Channels

A port channel bundles physical links into a channel group to create a single logical link that provides the aggregate bandwidth of up to 32 physical links. A port channel logically bonds several physical connections into one logical connection. Port channeling also load-balances traffic across these physical interfaces. From the perspective of a Nexus switch, the data plane of the receiving Cisco Nexus device, in a port channel setup, treats packets that travel through physical links as coming through several links, while the management plane treats the packets as a single data flow. If a member port within a port channel fails, the traffic previously carried over the failed link switches to the remaining member ports within the port channel, and the port channel stays operational as long as at least one physical interface within the port channel is operational. Each port can be in only one port channel.

Figure 4-1 illustrates port channel physical and logical views.

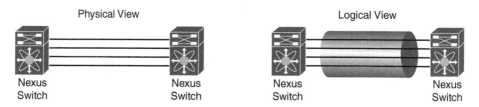

Figure 4-1   *Port Channel Physical and Logical Views*

You can create a Layer 2 port channel by bundling compatible Layer 2 interfaces, or you can create Layer 3 port channels by bundling compatible Layer 3 interfaces. You cannot combine Layer 2 and Layer 3 interfaces in the same port channel. You can also change the port channel from Layer 3 to Layer 2. You can create port channels directly by creating the port channel interface, or you can create a channel group that acts to aggregate individual ports into a bundle. When you associate an interface with a channel group, the Cisco NX-OS software creates a matching port channel automatically if the port channel does not already exist. In this instance, the port channel assumes the Layer 2 or Layer 3 configuration of the first interface. You can also create the port channel first. In this instance, the Cisco NX-OS software creates an empty channel group with the same channel number as the port channel and takes the default Layer 2 or Layer 3 configuration as well as the compatibility configuration.

You can configure Layer 2 port channels in either access or trunk mode. A Layer 2 port channel interface and its member ports can have different STP parameters. Changing the STP parameters of the port channel does not impact the STP parameters of the member ports because a port channel interface takes precedence if the member ports are bundled. After a Layer 2 port becomes part of a port channel, all switchport configurations must be done on the port channel; you can no longer apply switchport configurations to individual port channel members. Layer 3 port channel interfaces have routed ports as channel members. You cannot apply Layer 3 configurations to an individual port channel member either; you must apply the configuration to the entire port channel. You can configure a Layer 3 port channel with a static MAC address. If you do not configure this value, the Layer 3 port channel uses the router MAC of the first channel member to come up.

Figure 4-2 illustrates Layer 2 (access and trunk) and Layer 3 (routed) port channel interfaces. Port channel 20 is the L2 access port channel, with only VLAN 1 allowed on the port channel. Port channel 21 is the L2 trunk port channel, with VLAN 1 and VLAN 2 allowed on the port channel. Port channel 22 is the L3 routed port channel, whereas Eth 2/3 is the regular Ethernet routed interface.

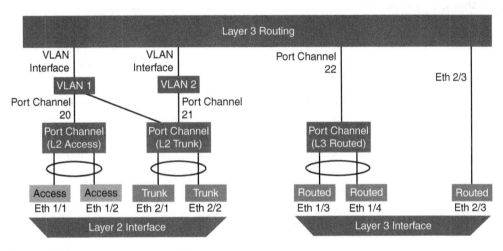

Figure 4-2 *Port Channel Interfaces*

For simplified port channel configuration, you can use static port channels with no associated aggregation protocol. For more flexibility, you can use the Link Aggregation Control Protocol (LACP), which is defined in the IEEE 802.1AX and IEEE 802.3ad standards. LACP controls how physical ports are bundled together to form one logical channel; for example, you can control the maximum number of bundled ports allowed. You cannot configure LACP on shared interfaces.

The port channel is operationally up when at least one of the member ports is up and that port's status is channeling. The port channel is operationally down when all member ports are operationally down. On Cisco Nexus 7000 Series switches, all ports in a port channel must be in the same virtual device context (VDC).

Port Channel Modes

Individual interfaces in port channels are configured with channel modes. When you run static port channels with no aggregation protocol, the channel mode is always set to on. When you run LACP as the aggregation protocol, you must first enable the LACP feature. By default, LACP is disabled. The system automatically takes a checkpoint before disabling the feature, and you can roll back to this checkpoint. You cannot disable LACP while any LACP configurations are present. After you enable LACP globally on the device, you enable LACP for each channel by setting the channel mode for each interface to either active or passive. You can configure channel mode for individual links in the LACP channel group when you are adding the links to the channel group. When you delete the port channel, the software automatically deletes the associated channel group. All member interfaces revert to their original configuration.

Table 4-1 describes the channel modes.

Table 4-1 *Channel Modes*

Channel Mode	Description
Passive	The LACP is enabled on this port channel, and the ports are in a passive negotiating state. Ports respond to the LACP packets they receive but do not initiate LACP negotiation.
Active	The LACP is enabled on this port channel, and the ports are in an active negotiating state. Ports initiate negotiations with other ports by sending LACP packets.
On	The LACP is disabled on this port channel, and the ports are in a non-negotiating state. The "on" state of the port channel represents the static mode.
	The port will not verify or negotiate port channel memberships. When an LACP attempts to negotiate with an interface in the on state, it does not receive any LACP packets and becomes an individual link with that interface. The link with the on state configured does not join the LACP channel group. The on state is the default port channel mode.

Both the passive and active modes allow LACP to negotiate between ports to determine if they can form a port channel based on criteria such as the port speed and the trunking state. The passive mode is useful when you do not know whether the remote system, or partner, supports LACP.

Two devices can form an LACP port channel, even when their ports are in different LACP modes, if the modes are compatible.

Table 4-2 shows various compatible channel modes for port channels.

Table 4-2 *Channel Modes Compatibility*

Device 1 > Port-1	Device 2 > Port-2	Result
Active	Active	Can form a port channel.
Active	Passive	Can form a port channel.

Device 1 > Port-1	Device 2 > Port-2	Result
Passive	Passive	Cannot form a port channel because no ports can initiate negotiation.
On	Active	Cannot form a port channel because LACP is enabled only on one side.
On	Passive	Cannot form a port channel because LACP is not enabled.

Port Channel Compatibility Requirements

When you add an interface to a channel group, the NX-OS software checks certain interface and operational attributes to ensure that the interface is compatible with the channel group. If you configure a member port with an incompatible attribute, the software suspends that port in the port channel. You can use the **show port-channel compatibility-parameters** command to see the full list of compatibility checks that Cisco NX-OS uses. You can force ports with incompatible parameters to join the port channel if the following parameters are the same:

- (Link) Speed capability and speed configuration

- Duplex capability and duplex configuration

- Flow-control capability and flow-control configuration

When the interface joins a port channel, some of its individual parameters are removed and replaced with the values on the port channel. The following list provides some of these individual parameters:

- Bandwidth

- Delay

- VRF

- IP address

- MAC address

- Spanning Tree Protocol (STP)

- Service policy

- Access control lists (ACLs)

All the QoS service policies on the port channel are implicitly applied on the member ports when they join the port channel. You will not see QoS service policies in the running-config of the member ports. When you delete the port channel, the software sets all member interfaces as if they were removed from the port channel.

Many interface parameters remain unaffected when the interface joins or leaves a port channel, including those in the following list:

- Description
- CDP
- LACP port priority
- UDLD
- Rate mode
- Shutdown
- SNMP trap

Each port that is configured to use LACP has an LACP port priority. LACP uses the port priority to decide which ports should be put in standby mode when there is a limitation that prevents all compatible ports from aggregating and which ports should be put into active mode. You can accept the default value of 32768 for the LACP port priority, or you can configure a value between 1 and 65535. A higher port priority value means a lower priority for LACP. You can configure the port priority so that specified ports have a lower priority for LACP and are most likely to be chosen as active links rather than as hot-standby links.

Port Channel Load Balancing

Because a port channel uses several links to transport packets through physical infrastructure, the packets must be distributed between the physical links through some load-balancing algorithm. The Cisco NX-OS software load-balances traffic across all operational interfaces in a port channel by hashing the addresses in the frame to a numerical value that selects one of the links in the channel.

You can configure the load-balancing mode to apply to all port channels that are configured on the entire device or on specified modules. The per-module configuration takes precedence over the load-balancing configuration for the entire device. You cannot configure the load-balancing method per port channel. The default load-balancing method for Layer 2 packets is src-dst-mac. The default method for Layer 3 packets is src-dst ip-l4port.

You can configure the device to use one of the following methods to load-balance across the port channel:

- Destination MAC address
- Source MAC address
- Source and destination MAC address
- Destination IP address

- Source IP address

- Source and destination IP address

- Source TCP/UDP port number

- Destination TCP/UDP port number

- Source and destination TCP/UDP port number

- GRE inner IP headers with source, destination, and source-destination

Virtual Port Channels

A virtual port channel (vPC) allows links that are physically connected to two different Cisco Nexus 7000 or 9000 Series devices to appear as a single port channel by a third device. The third device can be a switch, server, or any other networking device that supports port channels. A vPC can provide Layer 2 multipathing, which allows you to create redundancy and increase the bisectional bandwidth by enabling multiple parallel paths between nodes and allowing load-balancing traffic. You can use only Layer 2 port channels in the vPC. You configure the port channels by using LACP or static no protocol configuration.

Figure 4-3 shows the vPC physical and logical topology.

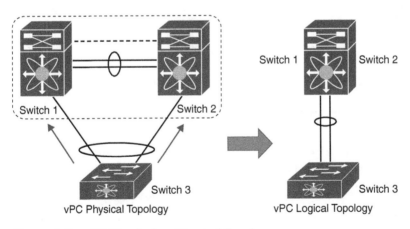

Figure 4-3 *vPC Physical and Logical Topology*

vPC provides the following technical benefits:

- Allows a single device to use a port channel across two upstream devices

- Eliminates Spanning Tree Protocol (STP) blocked ports

- Provides a loop-free topology

- Uses all available uplink bandwidth

- Provides fast convergence if either the link or a device fails
- Provides link-level resiliency
- Ensures high availability

vPC Topology Implementations

vPC supports various topology implementation, as follows:

A. **Dual-uplink Layer 2 access:** In this topology, an access switch such as a Cisco Nexus 9000 Series switch is dual-homed to a pair of distribution switches, such as Cisco Nexus 7000 Series switches, as shown in Figure 4-4(A).

B. **Server dual-homing:** In this topology, a server is connected via two interfaces to two access switches, as shown in Figure 4-4(B).

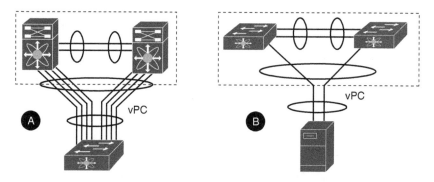

Figure 4-4   *(A) Dual-Uplink Layer 2 Access and (B) Server Dual-Homing*

C. **FEX supported topologies:** FEX supports various vPC topologies with Cisco Nexus 7000 and 9000 Series as their parent switches.

- **Host vPC (single link or dual links) and FEX single-homed (port channel mode) straight-through design:** In this topology, you connect a server with dual or quad network adapters that are configured in a vPC to a pair of FEXs that are connected straight through to the Cisco Nexus 9000 or Cisco Nexus 7000 Series switches. The link between the server and FEXs can be single link, as shown in Figure 4-5(1), or Dual Links, as shown in Figure 4-5(2).

- **Single-homed host and active-active (dual-homed) FEX (vPC) design:** In this topology, you connect the FEX to two upstream Cisco Nexus 9000 or Cisco Nexus 7000 Series switches and downstream to several single-homed servers, as shown in Figure 4-6(1).

- **Host port channel and active-active (dual-homed) FEX (vPC) design:** In this topology, you connect the FEX to two upstream Cisco Nexus 9000 or Cisco Nexus 7000 Series switches in vPC fashion and downstream to several single-homed servers using port channel, as shown in Figure 4-6(2).

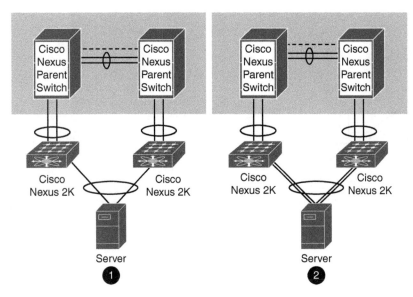

Figure 4-5   *Single-Link (1) or Dual-Link (2) Connected Host vPC with Single-Homed FEX*

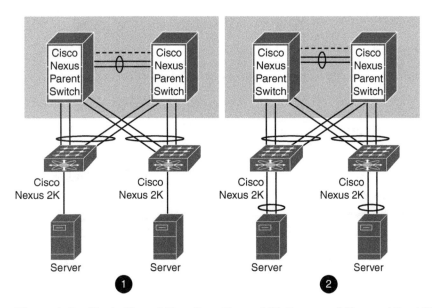

Figure 4-6   *Single-Homed (1) or Port Channel (2) Connected Host and Dual-Homed FEX vPC*

■ **Dual-homed host (active/standby) and active-active (dual-homed) FEX (vPC) design:** In this topology, you have host-side NIC in active/standby teaming and connected to two FEX devices as shown in Figure 4-7.

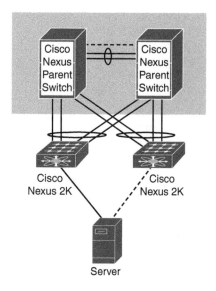

Figure 4-7   *Dual-Homed Host (Active/Standby) and Dual-Homed FEX vPC*

Note   FEX vPC is not supported between any model of FEX and the Cisco Nexus 9500 platform switches as the parent switches.

vPC Components

Figure 4-8 shows the components of vPC along with their naming conventions.

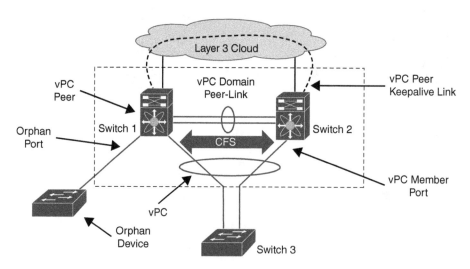

Figure 4-8   *vPC Components*

The components used in vPCs are as follows:

- **vPC:** The combined port channel between the vPC peer devices and the downstream device.

- **vPC peer device:** One of a pair of devices connected with the special port channel known as the vPC peer-link. You can have only two devices as vPC peers; each device can serve as a vPC peer to only one other vPC peer. The vPC peer devices can also have non-vPC links to other devices.

- **vPC peer-keepalive link:** The peer-keepalive link monitors the vitality of vPC peer devices. The peer-keepalive link sends configurable, periodic keepalive messages between vPC peer devices. It is highly recommended to associate a peer-keepalive link to a separate virtual routing and forwarding (VRF) instance that is mapped to a Layer 3 interface in each vPC peer device. If you do not configure a separate VRF, the system uses the management VRF by default. However, if you use the management interfaces for the peer-keepalive link, you must put a management switch connected to both the active and standby management ports on each vPC peer device. Do not use Ethernet crossover cables to connect the management ports on the vPC peers to each other back-to-back because the peer-keepalive link will fail on supervisor switchover. No data or synchronization traffic moves over the vPC peer-keepalive link; the only traffic on this link is a message that indicates that the originating switch is operating and running a vPC.

- **vPC peer-link:** The vPC peer-link carries essential vPC traffic between the vPC peer switches and is used to synchronize state between the vPC peer devices. The vPC peer-link is a port channel and should consist of at least two dedicated 10-Gigabit Ethernet links terminated on two different I/O modules, if at all possible, for high availability. Higher-bandwidth interfaces (such as 25-Gigabit Ethernet, 40-Gigabit Ethernet, 100-Gigabit Ethernet, and so on) may also be used to form the port channel. The peer-link should only allow traffic that is part of the vPC domain. If other traffic is also allowed, it could overload the link during failures. The system cannot bring up the vPC peer-link unless the peer-keepalive link is already up and running.

- **vPC member port:** A port that is assigned to a vPC channel group. These ports form the virtual port channel and are split between the vPC peers.

- **Host vPC port:** A fabric extender host interface that belongs to a vPC.

- **Orphan port:** A non-vPC port, also known as an orphaned port, is a port that is not part of a vPC.

- **Orphan device:** An orphan device is a device connected to a vPC domain using regular links instead of connecting through a vPC.

- **vPC domain:** The vPC domain includes both vPC peer devices, the vPC peer-keepalive link, and all of the port channels in the vPC connected to the downstream devices. It is also associated to the configuration mode you must use to assign vPC global parameters. Each vPC domain has a vPC instance number that is shared between two devices. Only two devices can be part of the same vPC domain, but you can have many vPC domains on a single device. The domain ID can be any value between 1 and 1000, and the same value must be configured on both switches that form the vPC pair. The vPC peer devices use the vPC domain ID to automatically assign a unique vPC system MAC address. Each vPC domain has a unique MAC address that is used as a unique identifier for the specific vPC-related operation. Although the devices use the vPC system MAC addresses only for link-scope operations such as LACP, it is recommended that you create each vPC domain within the contiguous Layer 2 network with a unique domain ID. You can also configure a specific MAC address for the vPC domain rather than having Cisco NX-OS software assign the address.

■ **Cisco Fabric Services:** The Cisco Fabric Services (CFS) is a reliable state transport mechanism used to synchronize the actions of the vPC peer devices. CFS carries messages and packets for many features linked with vPC, such as STP and IGMP. Information is carried in CFS/CFS over Ethernet (CFSoE) protocol data units (PDUs). When you enable the vPC feature, the device automatically enables CFSoE, and you do not have to configure anything. CFSoE distributions for vPCs do not need the capabilities to distribute over IP or the CFS regions. CFS messages provide a copy of the configuration on the local vPC peer device to the remote vPC peer device. All MAC addresses for those VLANs configured on both devices are synchronized between vPC peer devices using the CFSoE protocol. The primary vPC device synchronizes the STP state on the vPC secondary peer device using Cisco Fabric Services over Ethernet (CFSoE).

■ **vPC VLANs:** The VLANs allowed on the vPC are called vPC VLANs. These VLANs must also be allowed on the vPC peer-link.

■ **Non-vPC VLANs:** Any of the STP VLANs that are not carried over the vPC peer-link.

vPC Control Plane

A vPC uses CFSoE as the primary control plane protocol for vPC. The CFSoE protocol runs on vPC peer-link and performs the following control plane operations:

■ Validation and comparison for consistency check

■ Synchronization of MAC addresses for member ports

■ Status of member ports advertisement

■ Primary and secondary vPC devices election

■ STP management

■ Synchronization of IGMP snooping

■ Synchronization of Address Resolution Protocol (ARP) table

Figure 4-9 illustrates the functions performed by vPC control plane.

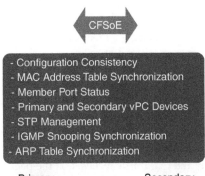

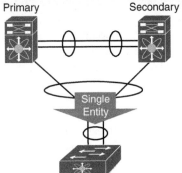

Figure 4-9   *vPC Control Plane*

Similar to regular port channels, virtual port channels are subject to consistency checks and compatibility checks. CFSoE protocol communicates essential configuration information to ensure configuration consistency between peer switches. During a compatibility check, one vPC peer conveys configuration information to the other vPC peer to verify that vPC member ports can actually form a port channel. For example, if two ports that are going to join the channel carry a different set of VLANs, this is a misconfiguration. Depending on the severity of the misconfiguration, vPC may either warn the user (Type-2 misconfiguration) or suspend the port channel (Type-1 misconfiguration). In the specific case of a VLAN mismatch, only the VLAN that differs between the vPC member ports will be suspended on all the vPC port channels. You can verify the consistency between vPC peers by using the command **show vpc consistency-parameter.** In addition to compatibility checks for the individual vPCs, CFSoE also performs consistency checks for a set of switch-wide parameters that must be configured consistently on the two peer switches.

The vPC peers must synchronize the Layer 2 forwarding table (that is, the MAC address information between the vPC peers). If one vPC peer learns a new MAC address, that MAC address is also communicated to the other vPC peer using the CFSoE protocol. The other vPC peer then programs the new MAC address information into the Layer 2 forwarding table. This MAC address learning mechanism replaces the regular switch MAC address learning mechanism and prevents traffic from being forwarded across the vPC peer-link unnecessarily.

If one vPC member port goes down on a vPC peer (for instance, if a link from a NIC goes down), the member is removed from the port channel without bringing down the vPC entirely. The vPC peer where the member port went down informs the other vPC peer using the CFSoE protocol. The vPC peer on which the remaining port is located will allow frames to be sent from the peer-link to the vPC orphan port. The Layer 2 forwarding table for the switch that detected the failure is also updated to point the MAC addresses that were associated with the vPC port to the peer-link. When all vPC member ports on one of the vPC peer switches go down, Cisco Fabric Services notifies the other vPC peer switch that its ports are now orphan ports and that traffic received on the peer-link for that vPC should now be forwarded to the vPC.

When you configure the vPC peer-link, the vPC peer devices negotiate using the CFSoE protocol and perform an election to determine the primary and secondary role of peer switches. The Cisco NX-OS software uses the lowest MAC address to elect the primary device. The software takes different actions on each device (that is, the primary and secondary) only in certain failover conditions. We will look at different failure scenarios later in this chapter. vPCs do not support role preemption. If the primary vPC peer device fails, the secondary vPC peer device takes over to become operationally the vPC primary device. However, the original operational roles are not restored if the formerly primary vPC comes up again.

Although vPCs provide a loop-free Layer 2 topology, STP is still required to provide a fail-safe mechanism to protect against any incorrect or defective cabling or possible misconfiguration. When you first bring up a vPC, STP reconverges. STP treats the vPC peer-link as a special link and always includes the vPC peer-link in the STP active topology. STP is distributed; that is, the protocol continues running on both vPC peer devices. However, the configuration on the vPC peer device elected as the primary device controls the STP process for the vPC interfaces on the secondary vPC peer device. The primary vPC device synchronizes the STP state on the vPC secondary peer device using CFSoE. The STP process for vPC also relies on the periodic keepalive messages to determine when one of the connected devices on the vPC peer-link fails. It is recommended to configure the primary vPC peer device as the STP primary root device and configure the secondary VPC device to be the STP secondary root device. If the primary vPC peer device fails over to the secondary vPC peer device, there is no change in the STP topology. The vPC primary device sends and processes BPDUs on the vPC interfaces and uses its own bridge ID. The secondary switch only relays BPDUs and does not generate any BPDU. The vPC peer switch feature allows a pair of vPC peers to appear as a single STP root in the Layer 2 topology. In vPC peer switch mode, STP BPDUs are sent from both vPC peer devices, and both primary and secondary switches use the same bridge ID to present themselves as a single switch. This improves vPC convergence. You must configure both ends of vPC peer-link with the identical STP configuration.

The IGMP snooping process on a vPC peer device shares the learned group information with the other vPC peer device through the vPC peer-link using the CFSoE protocol. When IGMP traffic enters a vPC peer switch through a vPC port channel, it triggers hardware programming for the multicast entry on both vPC member devices. Multicast traffic is copied over the peer-link to help ensure that orphan ports get the multicast stream and to help with failure scenarios. This happens regardless of the presence of receivers on the vPC peer.

The ARP table synchronization across vPC peers uses CFSoE. The ARP table synchronization feature enables faster convergence of address tables between the vPC peers. This convergence overcomes the delay that occurs in ARP table restoration for IPv4 or ND table restoration for IPv6 when the vPC peer-link port channel flaps or when a vPC peer comes back online. This feature is disabled by default and can be enabled using the **ip arp synchronize** or **ipv6 nd synchronize** command.

vPC Data Plane Traffic Flow

vPC performs loop avoidance at the data plane by implementing certain forwarding rules. The most important forwarding rule for a vPC is that a frame that enters the vPC peer switch from the peer-link cannot exit the switch from a vPC member port. This packet can exit on any other type of port, such as an L3 port or an orphan port. This rule prevents the packets received on a vPC from being flooded back onto the same vPC by the other peer switch.

When communicating with external networks, the vPC domain prioritizes forwarding through local ports, except in certain situations such as traffic forwarding to orphan devices and flooding traffic (broadcast, multicast, and unknown unicast traffic), which uses the vPC peer-link. For forwarding regular vPC traffic, vPC peer-link is not used to forward data packets. An exception to this rule is when a vPC peer switch has lost all its member ports, resulting in orphan ports on other peer switch. In this case, the vPC peer switch, where the member ports are up, will be allowed to forward the traffic received on the peer-link to one of the remaining active vPC member ports.

Figure 4-10 illustrates the vPC loop avoidance mechanism.

Switch 3 and Switch 4 are connected to Switch 1 and 2 with vPCs Po51 and Po52. A host connected to Switch 4 sends either an unknown unicast or a broadcast that gets hashed to port Ethernet2/2 on Switch 4 on port channel 52. Switch 2 receives the broadcast and will correctly forward it to Po51 on port 2/9 and place it on the peer-link for the potential orphan ports on Switch 1 to receive it. Upon receiving the broadcast, Switch 1 detects that this frame is coming from a vPC peer-link. Therefore, it does not forward it to port 2/9 or 2/10; otherwise, a duplicate frame on Switch 3 or Switch 4 would be created. If port Ethernet2/2 on Switch 3 goes down, port 2/9 on Switch 1 would become an orphan port and, as a result, will receive traffic that traverses the peer-link.

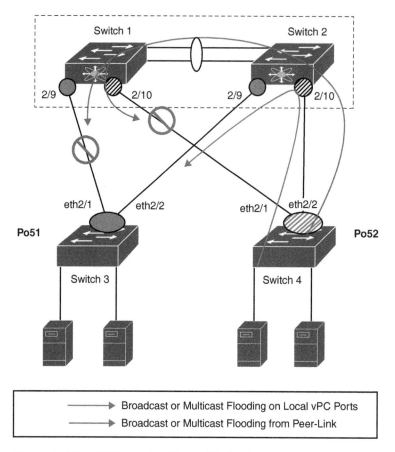

Figure 4-10 *vPC Loop Avoidance Mechanism*

vPC peer switches commonly use an FHRP, such as HSRP, GLBP, or VRRP, for default gateway redundancy. You can configure vPC peer devices to act as the gateway even for packets destined to the vPC peer device's MAC address using the peer-gateway feature. The vPC peer-gateway capability allows a vPC switch to act as the active gateway for packets that are addressed to the router MAC address of the vPC peer. This feature enables local forwarding of packets without the need to cross the vPC peer-link. Configuring the peer-gateway feature must be done on both primary and secondary vPC peers and is nondisruptive to the operations of the device or to the vPC traffic. VRRP acts similarly to HSRP when running on vPC peer devices. When the primary vPC peer device fails over to the secondary vPC peer device, the FHRP traffic continues to flow seamlessly.

Figure 4-11 illustrates the traffic forwarding in a vPC environment. In the left diagram, the data traffic reaching Cisco Nexus switches Agg1 and Agg2 from the core is forwarded toward the access switches acc1, acc2, and acc3 without traversing the peer Cisco Nexus switch device using the vPC peer-link. Similarly, traffic from the server directed to the core reaches Cisco Nexus switches Agg1 and Agg 2, and the receiving Cisco Nexus switch routes it directly to the core without unnecessarily passing it to the peer Cisco Nexus device using the peer-link. This happens regardless of which Cisco Nexus device is the primary HSRP device for a given VLAN.

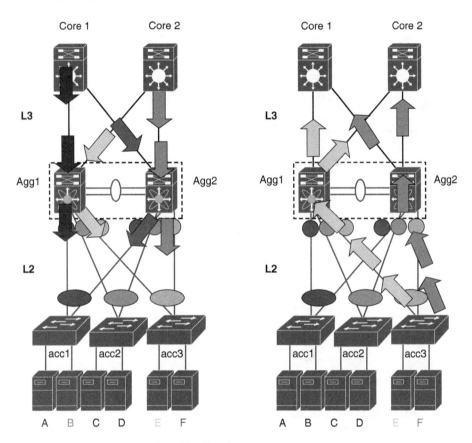

Figure 4-11   *vPC Data Plane Traffic Flow*

vPC Failure Scenarios

The following describes how vPC Nexus switches interact with events triggered by failure of a vPC peer-keepalive link, vPC peer-link, and so on:

- **vPC member port failure:** When one vPC member port fails, the host MAC detects a link failure on one of the port channel members and redistributes the affected flows to the remaining port channel members. Before the failure, the MAC pointed to primary port, and after the failure, it points to secondary port. This is one of the scenarios where a vPC peer-link is used to carry data traffic.

■ **vPC peer-link failure:** In a vPC topology, one vPC peer switch is elected as the vPC primary switch and the other switch is elected as the vPC secondary switch, based on the configured role priority for the switch. In a scenario where the vPC peer-link goes down, the vPC secondary switch shuts down all of its vPC member ports if it can still receive keepalive messages from the vPC primary switch (which indicates that the vPC primary switch is still alive). The vPC primary switch keeps all of its interfaces up, as shown in Figure 4-12.

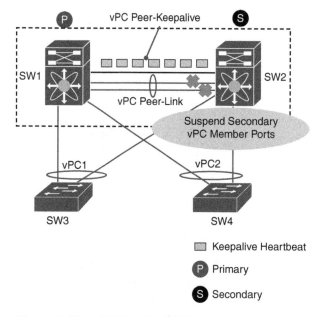

Figure 4-12 *vPC Peer-Link Failure Scenario*

■ **vPC peer-keepalive link failure:** During a vPC peer-keepalive link failure, there is no impact on traffic flow.

■ **vPC primary switch failure:** In a vPC topology, if a failure occurs on a primary switch, the secondary switch becomes the operational primary switch. If the primary switch comes back again, it will take the role of vPC operational secondary.

■ **vPC keepalive-link failure followed by a peer-link failure:** If the vPC keepalive link fails first and then a peer-link fails, the vPC primary switch continues to be primary but the vPC secondary switch becomes the operational primary switch and keeps its vPC member ports up (this is also known as a dual active scenario). This can occur when both the vPC switches are healthy but the failure has occurred because of a connectivity issue between the switches. This situation is known as a split-brain scenario. There is no loss of traffic for existing flows, but new flows can be affected as the peer-link is not available. The two vPC switches cannot synchronize the unicast MAC address and the IGMP groups and therefore cannot maintain the complete unicast and multicast forwarding table. Also, there may be some duplicate packet forwarding, as shown in Figure 4-13.

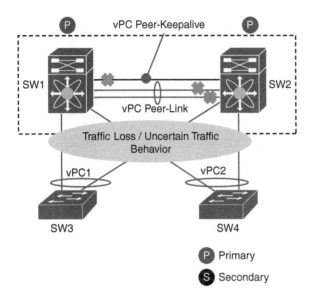

Figure 4-13 *vPC Keepalive Link Failure Followed by a Peer-Link Failure Scenario*

- **vPC peer-link and keepalive both fail but only keepalive returns:** Initially a dual active state will exist. When the keepalive link is restored, we can expect that the configured primary will become the operational primary.

vPC Guidelines

vPCs have the following configuration guidelines and limitations:

- A vPC can be deployed on two identical Cisco Nexus 9300 Series switches or two identical Cisco Nexus 9500 Series switches. Both switches must be the exact same model and both switches must consist of the same models of line cards, fabric modules, supervisor modules, and system controllers inserted in the same slots of the chassis.

- A vPC peer-link must consist of Ethernet ports with an interface speed of 10Gbps or higher. It is recommended to use at least two 10-Gigabit Ethernet ports in dedicated mode on two different I/O modules.

- A vPC keepalive must not run across a vPC peer-link.

- A vPC is a per-VDC function on the Cisco Nexus 7000 Series switches. A vPC can be configured in multiple VDCs, but the configuration is entirely independent. Each VDC requires an independent vPC peer-link and vPC peer-keepalive link. vPC domains cannot be stretched across multiple VDCs on the same switch, and all ports for a given vPC must be in the same VDC.

■ By definition, a vPC domain consists of a pair of switches that are identified by a shared vPC domain ID. It is not possible for a switch or VDC to participate in more than one vPC domain.

■ A vPC is a Layer 2 port channel. A vPC does not support the configuration of Layer 3 port channels. Dynamic routing from the vPC peers to routers connected on a vPC is not supported. It is recommended that routing adjacencies be established on separate routed links.

■ A vPC can be used as a Layer 2 link to establish a routing adjacency between two external routers. The routing restrictions for vPCs only apply to routing adjacencies between the vPC peer switches and routers that are connected on a vPC.

■ A vPC has support for static routing to FHRP addresses. The FHRP enhancements for vPCs enable routing to a virtual FHRP address across a vPC.

vPC Configuration

Configuring a basic vPC is a multistep process. The following are the steps to enable a basic vPC configuration on the Cisco Nexus 7000 or 9000 Series switch:

Step 1.   Enter the global configuration mode.

Step 2.   Enable the vPC feature.

Step 3.   Create a vPC domain and enter the vPC domain mode.

Step 4.   Configure the vPC peer-keepalive link.

Step 5.   Create the vPC peer-link.

Step 6.   Create a port channel and configure it as a vPC.

From the global configuration mode, you must enable the vPC feature before you can configure and use vPCs. The next step is to create a vPC domain. Use a unique vPC domain number throughout a single vPC domain. This domain ID is used to automatically form the vPC system MAC address. You can then configure the destination IP for the peer-keepalive link that carries the keepalive messages. Once the vPC peer-keepalive link is configured, you can create the vPC peer-link by designating the port channel you want on each device as the vPC peer-link for the specified vPC domain. Once the vPC peer-link is configured, you can connect the downstream device. You create a port channel from the downstream device to the primary and secondary vPC peer devices. On each vPC peer device, you assign a vPC number to the port channel that connects to the downstream device.

Table 4-3 summarizes the NX-OS CLI commands related to basic vPC configuration and verification.

Table 4-3 *Summary of NX-OS CLI Commands for vPC Configuration and Verification*

Command	Purpose
configure terminal	Enters global configuration mode.
[no] feature vpc	Enables vPCs on the device.
[no] feature lacp	Enables LACP on the device.
vrf context *vrf-name*	Creates a new VRF and enters VRF configuration mode. The *vrf-name* can be any case-sensitive, alphanumeric string up to 32 characters.
interface *interface-type slot/port*	Enters interface configuration mode.
no switchport	Configures the interface as a Layer 3 interface.
vrf member *vrf-name*	Adds this interface to a VRF.
ip address *ip-prefix/length*	Configures an IP address for this interface. You must do this step after you assign this interface to a VRF.
switchport mode trunk	Sets the interface as a Layer 2 trunk port. A trunk port can carry traffic in one or more VLANs on the same physical link.
channel-group *channel-number* [force] [mode {on | active | passive}]	Configures the port in a channel group and sets the mode. The *channel-number* range is from 1 to 4096. This command creates the port channel associated with this channel group, if the port channel does not already exist. All static port channel interfaces are set to mode on. You must set all LACP-enabled port channel interfaces to active or passive. The default mode is on.
vpc domain *domain-id*	Creates a vPC domain if it does not already exist, and enters the **vpc domain** configuration mode. There is no default; the range is from 1 to 1000.
peer-keepalive destination *ipaddress* source *ipaddress* | vrf {*name* | management vpc-keepalive}	Configures the IPv4 and IPv6 addresses for the remote end of the vPC peer-keepalive link.
interface port-channel *channel-number*	Selects the port channel and enters interface configuration mode.
vpc peer-link	Configures the selected port channel as the vPC peer-link.

Command	Purpose
vpc *number*	Configures the selected port channel into the vPC to connect to the downstream device. The range is from 1 and 4096.
	Note The vPC number you assign to the port channel connecting to the downstream device from the vPC peer device must be identical on both vPC peer devices.
show cdp neighbors {device-id | interface *interface-type slot/port*} [detail]	Displays the CDP neighbor status.
show port-channel summary	Displays information about the port channel.
show vpc	Displays information about each vPC domain.
show vpc brief	Displays brief information about each vPC domain.
show vpc role	Displays the peer status, role of the local device, vPC system MAC address and system priority, and MAC address and priority for the local vPC device.
show vpc peer-keepalive	Displays information about the peer-keepalive messages.
show vpc statistics	Displays statistics about the vPCs.
show vpc consistency-parameters	Displays the status of those parameters that must be consistent across all vPC interfaces.
show running-config vpc	Displays running configuration information for vPCs.

Examples 4-1 to 4-3 show the basic vPC configuration and verification on the sample topology shown in Figure 4-14. Layer 3 connectivity between N7K-A and N7K-B and N9K-A is established in the backend. In this example, we will focus only on vPC configuration and verification. We will configure N7K-A and N7K-B as vPC peers in vPC domain 11. We will configure the link connecting the interface Ethernet 3/25 on both vPC peers as a vPC peer-keepalive link. We will also configure the link connecting the interfaces Ethernet 3/26 and Ethernet 3/31 in the port channel on both vPC peers and configure it as vPC peer-link. vPC 10 will be set up toward N9K-A on the interfaces shown in Figure 4-14.

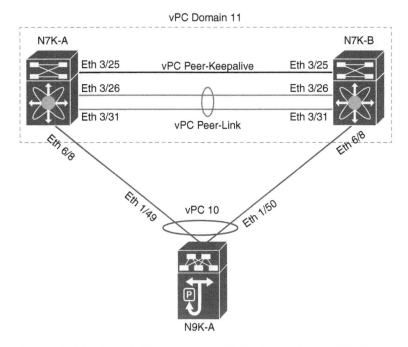

Figure 4-14 *Sample Topology for vPC Configuration and Verification*

In Example 4-1, we will do some pre-configuration, such as setting up the Layer 3 link between vPC peers to be later utilized as a vPC keepalive link and setting up a port channel between vPC peers to be later utilized as a vPC peer-link during vPC configuration.

Example 4-1 *Preparing for vPC*

```
! Verifying the physical connectivity between N7K-A, N7K-B and N9K-A.


N7K-A

N7K-A# show cdp neighbors
Capability Codes: R - Router, T - Trans-Bridge, B - Source-Route-Bridge
                  S - Switch, H - Host, I - IGMP, r - Repeater,
                  V - VoIP-Phone, D - Remotely-Managed-Device,
                  s - Supports-STP-Dispute


Device-ID        Local Intrfce  Hldtme Capability  Platform      Port ID
N7K-B(JAF1752AKJA)
                 Eth3/25         171    R S I s    N7K-C7009     Eth3/25
N7K-B(JAF1752AKJA)
                 Eth3/26         172    R S I s    N7K-C7009     Eth3/26
```

```
N7K-B(JAF1752AKJA)
                    Eth3/31        173    R S I s    N7K-C7009       Eth3/31
N9K-A(FDO241519JZ)
                    Eth6/8         176    R S I s    N9K-C93180YC-FX Eth1/49

Total entries displayed: 4
```

N7K-B

```
N7K-B# show cdp neighbors
Capability Codes: R - Router, T - Trans-Bridge, B - Source-Route-Bridge
                  S - Switch, H - Host, I - IGMP, r - Repeater,
                  V - VoIP-Phone, D - Remotely-Managed-Device,
                  s - Supports-STP-Dispute

Device-ID          Local Intrfce Hldtme Capability  Platform      Port ID
N7K-A(JAF1752AKGC)
                    Eth3/25        174    R S I s    N7K-C7009       Eth3/25
N7K-A(JAF1752AKGC)
                    Eth3/26        174    R S I s    N7K-C7009       Eth3/26
N7K-A(JAF1752AKGC)
                    Eth3/31        175    R S I s    N7K-C7009       Eth3/31
N9K-A(FDO241519JZ)
                    Eth6/8         154    R S I s    N9K-C93180YC-FX Eth1/50

Total entries displayed: 4
```

N9K-A

```
N9K-A# show cdp neighbors
Capability Codes: R - Router, T - Trans-Bridge, B - Source-Route-Bridge
                  S - Switch, H - Host, I - IGMP, r - Repeater,
                  V - VoIP-Phone, D - Remotely-Managed-Device,
                  s - Supports-STP-Dispute

Device-ID          Local Intrfce Hldtme Capability  Platform      Port ID
N7K-A(JAF1752AKGC)
                    Eth1/49        138    R S I s    N7K-C7009       Eth6/8
```

```
N7K-B(JAF1752AKJA)
                      Eth1/50        174    R S I s   N7K-C7009    Eth6/8

Total entries displayed: 2
```

! Configuring the Layer 3 link between N7K-A and N7K-B and making it ready to be later used as vPC Peer-Keepalive link. We will configure this link in vrf VPC-KEE-PALIVE and make sure the end-to-end connectivity between vPC peers N7K-A and N7K-B is established via this link.

N7K-A

```
N7K-A# configure terminal
Enter configuration commands, one per line.  End with CNTL/Z.
N7K-A(config)# vrf context VPC-KEEPALIVE
N7K-A(config-vrf)# interface Ethernet 3/25
N7K-A(config-if)# no switchport
N7K-A(config-if)# vrf member VPC-KEEPALIVE
Warning: Deleted all L3 config on interface Ethernet3/25
N7K-A(config-if)# ip address 10.1.1.10/24
N7K-A(config-if)# end
N7K-A#
```

N7K-B

```
N7K-B# configure terminal
Enter configuration commands, one per line.  End with CNTL/Z.
N7K-B(config)# vrf context VPC-KEEPALIVE
N7K-B(config-vrf)# interface Ethernet 3/25
N7K-B(config-if)# no switchport
N7K-B(config-if)# vrf member VPC-KEEPALIVE
Warning: Deleted all L3 config on interface Ethernet3/25
N7K-B(config-if)# ip address 10.1.1.20/24
N7K-B(config-if)# end
N7K-B#
```

! Verifying end-to-end connectivity across newly created Layer 3 link.

N7K-A

```
N7K-A# ping 10.1.1.20 vrf VPC-KEEPALIVE
PING 10.1.1.20 (10.1.1.20): 56 data bytes
64 bytes from 10.1.1.20: icmp_seq=0 ttl=254 time=1.349 ms
64 bytes from 10.1.1.20: icmp_seq=1 ttl=254 time=0.916 ms
64 bytes from 10.1.1.20: icmp_seq=2 ttl=254 time=0.923 ms
64 bytes from 10.1.1.20: icmp_seq=3 ttl=254 time=0.866 ms
64 bytes from 10.1.1.20: icmp_seq=4 ttl=254 time=0.91 ms

--- 10.1.1.20 ping statistics ---
5 packets transmitted, 5 packets received, 0.00% packet loss
round-trip min/avg/max = 0.866/0.992/1.349 ms
```

N7K-B

```
N7K-B# ping 10.1.1.10 vrf VPC-KEEPALIVE
PING 10.1.1.10 (10.1.1.10): 56 data bytes
64 bytes from 10.1.1.10: icmp_seq=0 ttl=254 time=1.334 ms
64 bytes from 10.1.1.10: icmp_seq=1 ttl=254 time=0.902 ms
64 bytes from 10.1.1.10: icmp_seq=2 ttl=254 time=0.876 ms
64 bytes from 10.1.1.10: icmp_seq=3 ttl=254 time=0.903 ms
64 bytes from 10.1.1.10: icmp_seq=4 ttl=254 time=0.858 ms

--- 10.1.1.10 ping statistics ---
5 packets transmitted, 5 packets received, 0.00% packet loss
round-trip min/avg/max = 0.858/0.974/1.334 ms
```

Configuring Port-Channel 1 between N7K-A and N7K-B using links Ethernet 3/26 and Ethernet 3/31 and making it ready to be later used as vPC Peer-Link. Although the channel group number can be any value between 1 and 4096, matching the port channel number of vPC Peer-Link with the vPC domain number may help with troubleshooting. In this exercise, the same number is not used to demonstrate that it is not required for configuring the vPC domain.

N7K-A

```
N7K-A(config)# interface Ethernet 3/26, Ethernet 3/31
N7K-A(config-if-range)# switchport
```

```
N7K-A(config-if-range)# switchport mode trunk
N7K-A(config-if-range)# channel-group 1
N7K-A(config-if-range)# end
```

N7K-B

```
N7K-B(config)# interface Ethernet 3/26, Ethernet 3/31
N7K-B(config-if-range)# switchport
N7K-B(config-if-range)# switchport mode trunk
N7K-B(config-if-range)# channel-group 1
N7K-B(config-if-range)# end
```

```
! Verifying the newly created Layer 2 Port-Channel. The flags next to the interfaces
are described by the legend at the beginning of the command output. The interface
port-channel 1 is switched port (S) and is up (U), its member ports are flagged
with (P).
```

N7K-A

```
N7K-A# show port-channel summary
Flags:  D - Down         P - Up in port-channel (members)
        I - Individual   H - Hot-standby (LACP only)
        s - Suspended    r - Module-removed
        b - BFD Session Wait
        S - Switched     R - Routed
        U - Up (port-channel)
        M - Not in use. Min-links not met
--------------------------------------------------------------------------------
Group Port-       Type    Protocol  Member Ports
      Channel
--------------------------------------------------------------------------------
1     Po1(SU)     Eth     NONE      Eth3/26(P)   Eth3/31(P)
```

N7K-B

```
N7K-B# show port-channel summary
Flags:  D - Down         P - Up in port-channel (members)
        I - Individual   H - Hot-standby (LACP only)
        s - Suspended    r - Module-removed
        b - BFD Session Wait
        S - Switched     R - Routed
```

```
          U - Up (port-channel)
          M - Not in use. Min-links not met
--------------------------------------------------------------------------------
Group Port-        Type    Protocol  Member Ports
      Channel
--------------------------------------------------------------------------------
1     Po1(SU)      Eth     NONE      Eth3/26(P)   Eth3/31(P)
```

In Example 4-2, we configure vPC 10 toward the N9K-A switch.

Example 4-2 *vPC Configuration*

```
! Entering global configuration and enabling the vPC feature.


N7K-A

N7K-A# configure terminal
Enter configuration commands, one per line.  End with CNTL/Z.
N7K-A(config)# feature vpc
N7K-A(config)#



N7K-B

N7K-B# configure terminal
Enter configuration commands, one per line.  End with CNTL/Z.
N7K-B(config)# feature vpc
N7K-B(config)#



! Configuring the vPC domain 11 for the vPC and configuring the vPC peer-keepalive
link.


N7K-A

N7K-A(config)# vpc domain 11
N7K-A(config-vpc-domain)# peer-keepalive destination 10.1.1.20 source 10.1.1.10 vrf
  VPC-KEEPALIVE
N7K-A(config-vpc-domain)# exit
N7K-A(config)#

N7K-B
```

```
N7K-B(config)# vpc domain 11
N7K-B(config-vpc-domain)# peer-keepalive destination 10.1.1.10 source 10.1.1.20 vrf
  VPC-KEEPALIVE
N7K-B(config-vpc-domain)# exit
N7K-B(config)#
```

! Configuring the vPC Peer-Link

N7K-A

```
N7K-A(config)# interface port-channel 1
N7K-A(config-if)# vpc peer-link
Warning:
Ensure that VPC peer-link member ports on both peers use identical VDC types (limit-
resource module-type VDC config command).

Please note that spanning tree port type is changed to "network" port type on vPC
peer-link.

This will enable spanning tree Bridge Assurance on vPC peer-link provided the STP
Bridge Assurance (which is enabled by default) is not disabled.
N7K-A(config-if)# exit
N7K-A(config)#
```

N7K-B

```
N7K-B(config)# interface port-channel 1
N7K-B(config-if)# vpc peer-link
Warning:
Ensure that VPC peer-link member ports on both peers use identical VDC types (limit-
resource module-type VDC config command).

Please note that spanning tree port type is changed to "network" port type on vPC
peer-link.

This will enable spanning tree Bridge Assurance on vPC peer-link provided the STP
Bridge Assurance (which is enabled by default) is not disabled.
N7K-B(config-if)# exit
N7K-B(config)#
```

! Configuring vPC Member Ports on vPC peers N7K-A and N7K-B. First, we will enable
LACP feature and configure the member ports on Port-Channel 10.

N7K-A

```
N7K-A(config)# feature lacp
N7K-A(config)# interface Ethernet 6/8
N7K-A(config-if)# channel-group 10 mode active
N7K-A(config-if)# interface port-channel 10
N7K-A(config-if)# vpc 10
N7K-A(config-if)# end
N7K-A#
```

N7K-B

```
N7K-B(config)# feature lacp
N7K-B(config)# interface Ethernet 6/8
N7K-B(config-if)# channel-group 10 mode active
N7K-B(config-if)# interface port-channel 10
N7K-B(config-if)# vpc 10
N7K-B(config-if)# end
N7K-B#
```

l Configuring upstream port-channel 15 on N9K-A and verifying that the port-channel is UP and working. Although the channel group number can be any value between 1 and 4096, matching the downstream device port channel number with the vPC number may help with troubleshooting. In this exercise, the same number is not used to demonstrate that it is not a requirement.

N9K-A

```
N9K-A# configure terminal
Enter configuration commands, one per line. End with CNTL/Z.
N9K-A(config)# feature lacp
N9K-A(config)# interface Ethernet 1/49-50
N9K-A(config-if-range)# channel-group 15 mode active
N9K-A(config-if-range)# end

N9K-A# show port-channel summary
Flags:  D - Down        P - Up in port-channel (members)
        I - Individual  H - Hot-standby (LACP only)
        s - Suspended   r - Module-removed
        b - BFD Session Wait
        S - Switched    R - Routed
        U - Up (port-channel)
        p - Up in delay-lacp mode (member)
        M - Not in use. Min-links not met
```

```
--------------------------------------------------------------------------------
Group Port-        Type     Protocol  Member Ports
      Channel
--------------------------------------------------------------------------------
15    Po15(SU)    Eth      LACP      Eth1/49(P)   Eth1/50(P)
N9K-A#
```

In Example 4-3, we perform vPC verification on N7K-A.

Example 4-3 *vPC Verification on N7K-A*

```
! Verifying the vPC.


N7K-A# show vpc
Legend:
                (*) - local vPC is down, forwarding via vPC peer-link


vPC domain id                     : 11
Peer status                       : peer adjacency formed ok
vPC keep-alive status             : peer is alive
Configuration consistency status  : success
Per-vlan consistency status       : success
Type-2 consistency status         : success
vPC role                          : primary
Number of vPCs configured         : 1
Peer Gateway                      : Disabled
Dual-active excluded VLANs and BDs : -
Graceful Consistency Check        : Enabled
Auto-recovery status              : Enabled, timer is off.(timeout = 240s)
Delay-restore orphan ports status : Timer is off.(timeout = 0s)
Operational Layer3 Peer-router    : Disabled
Self-isolation                    : Disabled


vPC Peer-link status
--------------------------------------------------------------------------------
id   Port   Status Active vlans              Active BDs
--   ----   ------ -------------------------------------------------------------
1    Po1    up     1,200                     -


vPC status
Id              : 10
```

```
Port              : Po10
Status            : up
Consistency       : success
Reason            : success
Active Vlans      : 1,200


! Verifying vPC details in brief format.


N7K-A# show vpc brief
Legend:
                    (*) - local vPC is down, forwarding via vPC peer-link


vPC domain id                             : 11
Peer status                               : peer adjacency formed ok
vPC keep-alive status                     : peer is alive
Configuration consistency status          : success
Per-vlan consistency status               : success
Type-2 consistency status                 : success
vPC role                                  : primary
Number of vPCs configured                 : 1
Peer Gateway                              : Disabled
Dual-active excluded VLANs and BDs        : -
Graceful Consistency Check                : Enabled
Auto-recovery status                      : Enabled, timer is off.(timeout = 240s)
Delay-restore status                      : Timer is off.(timeout = 30s)
Delay-restore SVI status                  : Timer is off.(timeout = 10s)
Delay-restore orphan ports status         : Timer is off.(timeout = 0s)
Operational Layer3 Peer-router            : Disabled
Self-isolation                            : Disabled


vPC Peer-link status
---------------------------------------------------------------------------
id    Port    Status Active vlans                    Active BDs
--    ----    ------ ----------------------------------------------------------
1     Po1     up     1,200                           -


vPC status
------------------------------------------------------------
id    Port          Status Consistency Active VLANs
----- ------------- ------ ----------- ----------------
10    Po10          up     success     1,200
```

```
! Verifying vPC role of vPC peers. The show vpc role command also shows the vPC
system-mac created from vPC domain ID. The last octet (0b, or decimal 11) is
derived from the vPC domain ID 11.


N7K-A# show vpc role

vPC Role status
---------------------------------------------------
vPC role                       : primary
vPC system-mac                 : 00:23:04:ee:be:0b
vPC system-priority            : 32667
vPC local system-mac           : e4:c7:22:15:2c:45
vPC local role-priority        : 32667
vPC peer system-mac            : e4:c7:22:15:33:c5
vPC peer role-priority         : 32667


! Verifying vPC peer-keepalive link details.


N7K-A# show vpc peer-keepalive

vPC keep-alive status          : peer is alive
--Peer is alive for            : (2658) seconds, (484) msec
--Send status                  : Success
--Last send at                 : 2022.02.17 20:18:33 495 ms
--Sent on interface            : Eth3/25
--Receive status               : Success
--Last receive at              : 2022.02.17 20:18:33 495 ms
--Received on interface        : Eth3/25
--Last update from peer        : (0) seconds, (854) msec

vPC Keep-alive parameters
--Destination                  : 10.1.1.20
--Keepalive interval           : 1000 msec
--Keepalive timeout            : 5 seconds
--Keepalive hold timeout       : 3 seconds
--Keepalive vrf                : VPC-KEEPALIVE
--Keepalive udp port           : 3200
--Keepalive tos                : 192



! Verifying vPC peer keepalive statistics.


N7K-A# show vpc statistics peer-keepalive
```

```
vPC keep-alive statistics
-------------------------------------------------
peer-keepalive tx count:         2888
peer-keepalive rx count:         2843
average interval for peer rx:    992
Count of peer state changes:     0


! Verifying vPC Peer-Link statistics.

N7K-A# show vpc statistics peer-link
port-channel1 is up
admin state is up
  Hardware: Port-Channel, address: b0aa.771c.c991 (bia b0aa.771c.c991)
  MTU 9216 bytes, BW 20000000 Kbit, DLY 10 usec
  reliability 255/255, txload 1/255, rxload 1/255
  Encapsulation ARPA, medium is broadcast
  Port mode is trunk
  full-duplex, 10 Gb/s
  Input flow-control is off, output flow-control is off
  Auto-mdix is turned off
  Switchport monitor is off
  EtherType is 0x8100
  Members in this channel: Eth3/26, Eth3/31
  Last clearing of "show interface" counters never
  4 interface resets
  Load-Interval #1: 30 seconds
    30 seconds input rate 2192 bits/sec, 2 packets/sec
    30 seconds output rate 904 bits/sec, 1 packets/sec
    input rate 2.19 Kbps, 2 pps; output rate 904 bps, 1 pps
  Load-Interval #2: 5 minute (300 seconds)
    300 seconds input rate 2184 bits/sec, 1 packets/sec
    300 seconds output rate 920 bits/sec, 1 packets/sec
    input rate 2.18 Kbps, 1 pps; output rate 920 bps, 1 pps
  RX
    48 unicast packets  3192 multicast packets  0 broadcast packets
    3208 input packets  2850183 bytes
    23 jumbo packets  0 storm suppression packets
    0 runts  0 giants  14 CRC/FCS  0 no buffer
    14 input error  0 short frame  0 overrun  0 underrun  0 ignored
    0 watchdog  0 bad etype drop  0 bad proto drop  0 if down drop
    0 input with dribble  0 input discard
    0 Rx pause
```

```
TX
    48 unicast packets  3587 multicast packets  2 broadcast packets
    3587 output packets  364772 bytes
    7 jumbo packets
    0 output error  0 collision  0 deferred  0 late collision
    0 lost carrier  0 no carrier  0 babble  0 output discard
    0 Tx pause

! Verifying newly created vPC 10 statistics.

N7K-A# show vpc statistics vpc 10
port-channel10 is up
admin state is up
 vPC Status: Up, vPC number: 10
  Hardware: Port-Channel, address: 308b.b2d8.432c (bia 308b.b2d8.432c)
  MTU 1500 bytes, BW 40000000 Kbit, DLY 10 usec
  reliability 255/255, txload 1/255, rxload 1/255
  Encapsulation ARPA, medium is broadcast
  Port mode is trunk
  full-duplex, 40 Gb/s
  Input flow-control is off, output flow-control is off
  Auto-mdix is turned off
  Switchport monitor is off
  EtherType is 0x8100
  Members in this channel: Eth6/8
  Last clearing of "show interface" counters never
  1 interface resets
  Load-Interval #1: 30 seconds
    30 seconds input rate 80 bits/sec, 0 packets/sec
    30 seconds output rate 16 bits/sec, 0 packets/sec
    input rate 80 bps, 0 pps; output rate 16 bps, 0 pps
  Load-Interval #2: 5 minute (300 seconds)
    300 seconds input rate 136 bits/sec, 0 packets/sec
    300 seconds output rate 144 bits/sec, 0 packets/sec
    input rate 136 bps, 0 pps; output rate 144 bps, 0 pps
RX
    292 unicast packets  741 multicast packets  4 broadcast packets
    745 input packets  70652 bytes
    0 jumbo packets  0 storm suppression packets
    0 runts  0 giants  0 CRC/FCS  0 no buffer
    0 input error  0 short frame  0 overrun  0 underrun  0 ignored
    0 watchdog  0 bad etype drop  0 bad proto drop  0 if down drop
```

```
      0 input with dribble  0 input discard
      0 Rx pause
    TX
      292 unicast packets  145 multicast packets  0 broadcast packets
      145 output packets  32776 bytes
      0 jumbo packets
      0 output error  0 collision  0 deferred  0 late collision
      0 lost carrier  0 no carrier  0 babble  0 output discard
      0 Tx pause



! Verifying vPC global consistency parameters.


N7K-A# show vpc consistency-parameters global


    Legend:
        Type 1 : vPC will be suspended in case of mismatch


Name                           Type  Local Value            Peer Value
-------------                  ----  ---------------------  -----------------------
STP MST Simulate PVST          1     Enabled                Enabled
STP Port Type, Edge            1     Normal, Disabled,      Normal, Disabled,
BPDUFilter, Edge BPDUGuard           Disabled               Disabled
STP MST Region Name            1     ""                     ""
STP Disabled                   1     None                   None
STP Mode                       1     Rapid-PVST             Rapid-PVST
STP Bridge Assurance           1     Enabled                Enabled
STP Loopguard                  1     Disabled               Disabled
STP MST Region Instance to     1
 VLAN Mapping
STP MST Region Revision        1     0                      0
Interface-vlan admin up        2     200                    200
Interface-vlan routing         2     1,200                  1,200
capability
Allowed VLANs                  -     1,200                  1,200
Local error VLANs              -     -                      -

! Verifying newly created vPC 10 consistency parameters.


N7K-A# show vpc consistency-parameters vpc 10


    Legend:
        Type 1 : vPC will be suspended in case of mismatch
```

```
Name                   Type  Local Value           Peer Value
-------------          ----  --------------------  ---------------------
Interface type         1     port-channel          port-channel
LACP Mode              1     on                    on
STP Port Guard         1     Default               Default
STP Port Type          1     Default               Default
Speed                  1     40 Gb/s               40 Gb/s
Duplex                 1     full                  full
MTU                    1     1500                  1500
Vlan xlt mapping       1     Enabled               Enabled
Port Mode              1     trunk                 trunk
STP MST Simulate PVST  1     Default               Default
Native Vlan            1     1                     1
Admin port mode        1     trunk                 trunk
lag-id                 1     [(7f9b,               [(7f9b,
                             0-23-4-ee-be-b, 800a, 0-23-4-ee-be-b, 800a,
                             0, 0), (8000,         0, 0), (8000,
                             ac-4a-67-43-15-a7, e, ac-4a-67-43-15-a7, e,
                             0, 0)]                0, 0)]
mode                   1     active                active
vPC card type          1     F3                    F3
Allowed VLANs          -     1,200                 1,200
Local error VLANs      -     -                     -
```

! Verifying vPC related running-configuration on the device.

```
N7K-A# show running-config vpc

!Command: show running-config vpc
!Running configuration last done at: Thu Feb 17 20:09:58 2022
!Time: Thu Feb 17 20:22:41 2022

version 8.4(2)
feature vpc

vpc domain 113
  peer-keepalive destination 10.1.1.20 source 10.1.1.10 vrf VPC-KEEPALIVE

interface port-channel1
  vpc peer-link

interface port-channel10
  vpc 10

N7K-A#
```

Similar verification can be done on N7K-B.

Summary

This chapter discusses Ethernet port channels, virtual port channels (vPCs), and vPC configuration and verification, including the following points:

- A port channel bundles physical links into a channel group to create a single logical link that provides an aggregate bandwidth of up to 32 physical links.

- You can configure Layer 2 port channels in either access or trunk mode. Layer 3 port channel interfaces have routed ports as channel members. You cannot combine Layer 2 and Layer 3 interfaces in the same port channel.

- Individual interfaces in port channels are configured with channel modes. When you run static port channels with no aggregation protocol, the channel mode is always set to on. When you configure LACP port channels, the channel mode is set to either active or passive.

- In active mode, ports initiate negotiations with other ports by sending LACP packets. In passive mode, ports respond to LACP packets they receive but do not initiate LACP negotiation.

- When you add an interface to a channel group, the NX-OS software checks certain interface and operational attributes to ensure that the interface is compatible with the channel group. If you configure a member port with an incompatible attribute, the software suspends that port in the port channel.

- The Cisco NX-OS software load-balances traffic across all operational interfaces in a port channel by hashing the addresses in the frame to a numerical value that selects one of the links in the channel.

- A vPC allows links that are physically connected to two different Cisco Nexus 7000 or 9000 Series devices to appear as a single port channel by a third device. You can use only Layer 2 port channels in the vPC.

- vPC supports various topology implementations, including dual-uplink Layer 2 access, server dual-homing, and FEX dual-homed (active-active) vPC designs.

- A vPC uses CFSoE as the primary control plane protocol for vPC.

- vPC forwarding rule: a frame that enters the vPC peer switch from the peer-link cannot exit the switch from a vPC member port.

- vPC interacts differently with events triggered by failure of vPC peer-keepalive link, vPC peer-link, and so on.

References

"Cisco Nexus 9000 NX-OS Interfaces Configuration Guide, Release 10.2(x)," https://www.cisco.cSom/c/en/us/td/docs/dcn/nx-os/nexus9000/102x/configuration/interfaces/cisco-nexus-9000-nx-os-interfaces-configuration-guide-102x.html

"Cisco Nexus 7000 Series NX-OS Interfaces Configuration Guide 8.x," https://www.cisco.com/c/en/us/td/docs/switches/datacenter/nexus7000/sw/interfaces/config/cisco_nexus7000_interfaces_config_guide_8x.html

"Understand Virtual Port Channel (vPC) Enhancements," https://www.cisco.com/c/en/us/support/docs/ios-nx-os-software/nx-os-software/217274-understand-virtual-port-channel-vpc-en.html

"Supported Topologies for Routing over Virtual Port Channel on Nexus Platforms," https://www.cisco.com/c/en/us/support/docs/ip/ip-routing/118997-technote-nexus-00.html

"Best Practices for Virtual Port Channels (vPC) on Cisco Nexus 7000 Series Switches," https://www.cisco.com/c/dam/en/us/td/docs/switches/datacenter/sw/design/vpc_design/vpc_best_practices_design_guide.pdf

"Nexus 2000 Fabric Extenders Supported/Unsupported Topologies," https://www.cisco.com/c/en/us/support/docs/switches/nexus-2000-series-fabric-extenders/200363-nexus-2000-fabric-extenders-supported-un.html

Relevant Cisco Live sessions: http://www.ciscolive.com

Chapter 5

Switch Virtualization

Cisco Nexus Series switches support many virtualization options, including Layer 3 virtual routing and forwarding (VRF) instances and virtual device contexts (VDCs). A VRF can be used to virtualize the Layer 3 forwarding and routing tables. VDCs allow the Cisco Nexus 7000 Series switches to be virtualized at the device level. Cisco Nexus Series switches also provide operational segmentation into functional planes to segment the functions of the switch into functional layers. This segmentation enables features such as control plane policing (CoPP) that prevent operational disruptions. All these functionalities allow you to establish a stable data center environment with high performance and easy management.

In this chapter, we discuss Cisco Nexus switch functional planes, Cisco Nexus switch process separation and restartability, and VRF configuration and verification on Cisco NX-OS. We will also discuss Cisco Nexus 7000 switch VDCs, including VDC architecture, VDC types, VDC resources, VDC fault isolation, VDC high availability, VDC management, along with VDC configuration and verification.

Cisco Nexus Switch Functional Planes

The Cisco Nexus switch by design divides the traffic it manages into three functional components or planes:

- **Data plane:** Handles all the data traffic. The basic functionality of a Cisco NX-OS device is to forward packets from one interface to another. The packets that are not meant for the switch itself are called the *transit packets*. These packets are handled by the data plane.

- **Control plane:** Handles all routing protocol control traffic. These protocols, such as the Border Gateway Protocol (BGP) and the Open Shortest Path First (OSPF) protocol, send control packets between devices. These packets are destined to router addresses and are called *control plane packets*.

■ **Management plane:** Runs the components meant for Cisco NX-OS device management purposes, such as the command-line interface (CLI) and Simple Network Management Protocol (SNMP).

The Cisco NX-OS device provides control plane policing (CoPP), which protects the control plane and separates it from the data plane, thus ensuring network stability, reachability, and packet delivery. The CoPP feature allows a policy map to be applied to the control plane. This policy map looks like a normal quality of service (QoS) policy and is applied to all traffic entering the switch from a non-management port.

The Cisco Nexus switch supervisor module has both the management plane and control plane and is critical to the operation of the network. Any disruption to or attacks against the supervisor module will result in serious network outages. For example, excessive traffic to the supervisor module could overload and slow down the performance of the entire Cisco NX-OS device. To protect the control plane, the Cisco NX-OS device segregates different packets destined for the control plane into different classes. Once these classes are identified, the Cisco NX-OS device polices the packets, which ensures that the supervisor module is not overwhelmed.

The following types of packets can reach the control plane:

■ **Receive packets:** Packets that have the destination address of a router. The destination address can be a Layer 2 address (such as a router MAC address) or a Layer 3 address (such as the IP address of a router interface). These packets include router updates and keepalive messages. Multicast packets can also be in this category, where packets are sent to multicast addresses used by a router.

■ **Exception packets:** Packets that need special handling by the supervisor module. For example, if a destination address is not present in the Forwarding Information Base (FIB) and results in a miss, the supervisor module sends an ICMP unreachable packet back to the sender. Another example is a packet with IP options set.

■ **Redirected packets:** Packets that are redirected to the supervisor module.

■ **Glean packets:** If a Layer 2 MAC address for a destination IP address is not present in the FIB, the supervisor module receives the packet and sends an ARP request to the host.

All of these different packets could be maliciously used to attack the control plane and overwhelm the Cisco NX-OS device. CoPP classifies these packets to different classes and provides a mechanism to individually control the rate at which the supervisor module receives these packets. For example, you might want to be less strict with a protocol packet such as Hello messages but more strict with a packet that is sent to the supervisor module because the IP option is set. You configure packet classifications and rate-controlling policies using class maps and policy maps.

Table 5-1 summarizes the NX-OS CLI commands related to CoPP verification.

Table 5-1 *Summary of NX-OS CLI Commands for CoPP Verification*

Command	Purpose
show copp status	Displays the CoPP status, including the last configuration operation and its status
show copp profile {strict | moderate | lenient | dense}	Displays the details of the CoPP best practice policy, along with the classes and policer values
show policy-map interface control-plane	Displays the policy values with associated class maps and drops per policy or class map
show copp diff profile {strict | moderate | lenient | dense} [prior-ver] profile {strict | moderate | lenient | dense}	Displays the difference between two CoPP best practice policies

Example 5-1 shows the CoPP verification on a standalone Nexus 9000 switch.

Example 5-1 *CoPP Verification on a Standalone Nexus 9000 Switch*

```
! Reviewing CoPP profile options.
N9K# show copp profile ?
  dense     Display dense profile
  lenient   Display lenient profile
  moderate  Display moderate profile
  strict    Display strict profile

! Reviewing CoPP status. In this output N9K is using strict profile for the CoPP.
N9K# show copp status
Last Config Operation: copp profile strict
Last Config Operation Timestamp: 13:12:26 UTC Dec 12 2021
Last Config Operation Status: Success
Policy-map attached to the control-plane: copp-system-p-policy-strict

! Listing the details of the strict CoPP profile.
N9K# show copp profile strict

ip access-list copp-system-p-acl-auto-rp
  permit ip any 224.0.1.39/32
  permit ip any 224.0.1.40/32
ip access-list copp-system-p-acl-bgp
  permit tcp any gt 1023 any eq bgp
  permit tcp any eq bgp any gt 1023
ipv6 access-list copp-system-p-acl-bgp6
  permit tcp any gt 1023 any eq bgp
```

```
  permit tcp any eq bgp any gt 1023
ip access-list copp-system-p-acl-dhcp
  permit udp any eq bootpc any
  permit udp any neq bootps any eq bootps
ip access-list copp-system-p-acl-dhcp-relay-response
  permit udp any eq bootps any
  permit udp any any eq bootpc
<output omitted>

! Viewing the statistics that are compiled for the CoPP class-maps.
N9K# show policy-map interface control-plane
Control Plane

  Service-policy  input: copp-system-p-policy-strict

    class-map copp-system-p-class-l3uc-data (match-any)
      match exception glean
      set cos 1
      police cir 800 kbps , bc 32000 bytes
      module 1 :
        transmitted 146 bytes;
        5-minute offered rate 0 bytes/sec
        conformed 0 peak-rate bytes/sec

        dropped 0 bytes;
        5-min violate rate 0 byte/sec
        violated 0 peak-rate byte/sec

    class-map copp-system-p-class-critical (match-any)
      match access-group name copp-system-p-acl-bgp
      match access-group name copp-system-p-acl-rip
      match access-group name copp-system-p-acl-vpc
      match access-group name copp-system-p-acl-bgp6
      match access-group name copp-system-p-acl-ospf
      match access-group name copp-system-p-acl-rip6
      match access-group name copp-system-p-acl-eigrp
      match access-group name copp-system-p-acl-ospf6
      match access-group name copp-system-p-acl-eigrp6
      match access-group name copp-system-p-acl-auto-rp
      match access-group name copp-system-p-acl-mac-l3-isis
      set cos 7
      police cir 36000 kbps , bc 1280000 bytes
```

```
    module 1 :
      transmitted 100947782 bytes;
      5-minute offered rate 15 bytes/sec
      conformed 51 peak-rate bytes/sec
        at Wed Dec 22 08:22:02 2021

      dropped 0 bytes;
      5-min violate rate 0 byte/sec
      violated 0 peak-rate byte/sec
<output omitted>
```

! Filtering the CoPP statistics to obtain an aggregate view of conformed and vio-
lated counters for all the CoPP class-maps.
```
N9K# show policy-map interface control-plane | include
class|conform|violated
    class-map copp-system-p-class-l3uc-data (match-any)
      conformed 0 peak-rate bytes/sec
      violated 0 peak-rate byte/sec
    class-map copp-system-p-class-critical (match-any)
      conformed 51 peak-rate bytes/sec
      violated 0 peak-rate byte/sec
    class-map copp-system-p-class-important (match-any)
      conformed 66 peak-rate bytes/sec
      violated 0 peak-rate byte/sec
    class-map copp-system-p-class-openflow (match-any)
      conformed 0 peak-rate bytes/sec
      violated 0 peak-rate byte/sec
    class-map copp-system-p-class-multicast-router (match-any)
      conformed 19 peak-rate bytes/sec
      violated 0 peak-rate byte/sec
    class-map copp-system-p-class-multicast-host (match-any)
      conformed 0 peak-rate bytes/sec
      violated 0 peak-rate byte/sec
<output omitted>
```

! Comparing CoPP profiles. In this output we are comparing dense and strict CoPP
profiles.
```
N9K# show copp diff profile dense profile strict
Prior Profile Doesn't Exist.
```

'+' Line presents only in profile dense(ver: 10.2(1)I9(1))
'-' Line presents only in profile strict(ver: 10.2(1)I9(1))
```
    -policy-map type control-plane copp-system-p-policy-strict
```

```
- class copp-system-p-class-l3uc-data
-   set cos 1
-   police cir 800 kbps bc 32000 bytes conform transmit violate drop
- class copp-system-p-class-critical
-   set cos 7
-   police cir 36000 kbps bc 1280000 bytes conform transmit violate drop
- class copp-system-p-class-important
-   set cos 6
-   police cir 2500 kbps bc 1280000 bytes conform transmit violate drop
- class copp-system-p-class-openflow
-   set cos 5
-   police cir 1000 kbps bc 32000 bytes conform transmit violate drop
- class copp-system-p-class-multicast-router
-   set cos 6
-   police cir 2600 kbps bc 128000 bytes conform transmit violate drop
<output omitted>
```

Cisco Nexus Switch Process Separation and Restartability

Cisco NX-OS provides isolation between software components so that a failure within one process does not disrupt others. In the Cisco NX-OS software, independent processes, known as *services*, perform a function or set of functions for a subsystem or feature set. Each service and service instance runs as an independent, protected process. This approach provides a highly fault-tolerant software infrastructure and fault isolation between services. A failure in a service instance (such as BGP) does not affect any other services running at that time, such as the Link Aggregation Control Protocol (LACP). In addition, each instance of a service can run as an independent process, which means that two instances of a routing protocol (for example, two instances of the OSPF protocol) can run as separate processes.

The Cisco NX-OS service restart features allow you to restart a faulty service without restarting the supervisor to prevent process-level failures from causing system-level failures. You can restart a service depending on current errors, failure circumstances, and the high-availability policy for the service. A service can undergo either a stateful or stateless restart. Cisco NX-OS allows services to store runtime state information and messages for a stateful restart. In a stateful restart, the service can retrieve this stored state information and resume operations from the last checkpoint service state. In a stateless restart, the service can initialize and run as if it had just been started with no prior state.

Not all services are designed for a stateful restart. For example, Cisco NX-OS does not store runtime state information for Layer 3 routing protocols such as Open Shortest Path

First (OSPF) and Routing Information Protocol (RIP). Their configuration settings are preserved across a restart, but these protocols are designed to rebuild their operational state using information obtained from neighbor routers.

Backend management and orchestration of processes and services supporting stateful restarts are handled by a set of high-level system-control services:

- **System Manager:** The system manager directs overall system function, service management, and system health monitoring and enforces high-availability policies. The system manager is responsible for launching, stopping, monitoring, and restarting services as well as initiating and managing the synchronization of service states and supervisor states for a stateful switchover.

- **Persistent storage service:** Cisco NX-OS services use the persistent storage service (PSS) to store and manage operational runtime information. The PSS component works with system services to recover states in the event of a service restart. PSS functions as a database of state and runtime information that allows services to make a checkpoint of their state information whenever needed. A restarting service can recover the last-known operating state that preceded a failure, which allows for a stateful restart. Each service that uses PSS can define its stored information as private (it can be read only by that service) or shared (the information can be read by other services). If the information is shared, the service can specify that it is local (the information can be read only by services on the same supervisor) or global (it can be read by services on either supervisor or on modules). For example, if the PSS information of a service is defined as shared and global, services on other modules can synchronize with the PSS information of the service that runs on the active supervisor.

- **Message and transaction service:** The message and transaction service (MTS) is a high-performance interprocess communications (IPC) message broker. MTS handles message routing and queuing between services on and across modules and between supervisors. MTS facilitates the exchange of messages such as event notification, synchronization, and message persistency between system services and system components. MTS can maintain persistent messages and logged messages in queues for access even after a service restart.

- **High Availability (HA) policies:** Cisco NX-OS allows each service to have an associated set of internal HA policies that define how a failed service is restarted. Each service can have four defined policies—a primary policy and secondary policy when two supervisors are present and a primary policy and secondary policy when only one supervisor is present. If no HA policy is defined for a service, the default HA policy to be performed upon a service failure is a switchover (if two supervisors are present) or a supervisor reset (if only one supervisor is present).

Virtual Routing and Forwarding (VRF)

Cisco NX-OS supports multiple virtual routing and forwarding instances (VRFs). Each VRF contains a separate address space with unicast and multicast route tables for IPv4 and IPv6 and makes routing decisions independent of any other VRF. Each NX-OS device has a default VRF and a management VRF. All Layer 3 interfaces and routing protocols exist in the default VRF until you assign them to another VRF. The mgmt0 interface exists in the management VRF. You can create additional VRFs as needed.

Figure 5-1 shows Cisco NX-OS VRF instances.

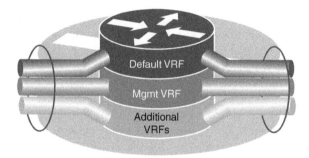

Figure 5-1   *Cisco NX-OS VRF Instances*

Following are the characteristics of the management VRF:

- The management VRF is for management purposes only.

- Only the mgmt0 interface can be in the management VRF.

- The mgmt0 interface cannot be assigned to another VRF.

- No routing protocols can run in the management VRF (static only).

Following are the characteristics of the default VRF:

- All Layer 3 interfaces exist in the default VRF until they are assigned to another VRF.

- Routing protocols run in the default VRF context unless another VRF context is specified.

- The default VRF uses the default routing context for all **show** commands.

- The default VRF is similar to the global routing table concept in Cisco IOS.

All unicast and multicast routing protocols support VRFs. When you configure a routing protocol in a VRF, you set routing parameters for the VRF that are independent of routing parameters in another VRF for the same routing protocol instance. You can assign interfaces and route protocols to a VRF to create virtual Layer 3 networks. An interface exists in only one VRF.

By default, Cisco NX-OS uses the VRF of the incoming interface to select which routing table to use for a route lookup. You can configure a route policy to modify this behavior and set the VRF that Cisco NX-OS uses for incoming packets.

A fundamental feature of the Cisco NX-OS architecture is that every IP-based feature is "VRF aware." Table 5-2 shows VRF-aware services that can select a particular VRF to reach a remote server or to filter information based on the selected VRF.

Table 5-2 *VRF-Aware Services*

Authentication, Authorization, and Accounting (AAA)	Open Shortest Path First (OSPF)
Bidirectional Forwarding Detection (BFD)	Ping and traceroute
Border Gateway Protocol (BGP)	Remote Authentication Dial-In User Service (RADIUS)
Call Home	Simple Network Management Protocol (SNMP)
Domain Name System (DNS)	Secure Shell (SSH)
Enhanced Interior Gateway Routing Protocol (EIGRP)	Syslog
Hot Standby Router Protocol (HSRP)	Terminal Access Controller Access Control System Plus (TACACS+)
Hypertext Transfer Protocol (HTTP)	Trivial File Transfer Protocol (TFTP)
Intermediate System-to-Intermediate System (IS-IS)	Virtual Port Channel (vPC)
Locator/ID Separation Protocol (LISP)	Virtual Private Networks (VPN)
NetFlow	Virtual Router Redundancy Protocol (VRRP)
Network Time Protocol (NTP)	

VRFs have the following configuration guidelines and limitations:

- When you make an interface a member of an existing VRF, Cisco NX-OS removes all Layer 3 configurations. You should configure all Layer 3 parameters after adding an interface to a VRF.

- If you configure an interface for a VRF before the VRF exists, the interface is operationally down until you create the VRF.

- Cisco NX-OS creates the default and management VRFs by default. You should add the mgmt0 interface to the management VRF and configure the mgmt0 IP address and other parameters after you add it to the management VRF.

■ The **write erase boot** command does not remove the management VRF
configurations. You must use the **write erase** command and then the **write erase
boot** command to remove the management VRF configurations.

Table 5-3 summarizes the NX-OS CLI commands that are related to basic VRF configuration and verification.

Table 5-3 *Summary of NX-OS CLI Commands for VRF Configuration and Verification*

Command	Purpose
configure terminal	Enters global configuration mode.
[**no**] **vrf context** *name*	Creates a new VRF and enters VRF configuration mode. The *name* can be any case-sensitive, alphanumeric string up to 32 characters.
	Using the **no** option with this command deletes the VRF and all associated configurations.
interface *interface-type slot/ port*	Enters interface configuration mode.
vrf member *vrf-name*	Adds this interface to a VRF.
show vrf [*vrf-name*]	Displays VRF information.

Examples 5-2 to 5-6 show the basic VRF configuration and verification on the sample
topology shown in Figure 5-2. OSPF area 0 is preconfigured on the topology, and OSPF
neighborship is already fully functional. We will concentrate only on the VRF configuration and its impact on the OSPF routing in this example.

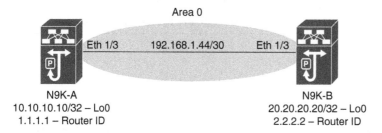

Figure 5-2 *Sample Topology for VRF Configuration and Verification*

> **Note** OSPF fundamentals, along with configuration and verification, are covered
> in detail in Chapter 6, "Nexus Switch Routing."

In Example 5-2, we verify the management VRF on N9K-A.

Example 5-2   *Management VRF Verification on N9K-A*

```
! Verifying the VRFs configured on N9K-A
N9K-A# show vrf
VRF-Name                        VRF-ID State  Reason
default                              1 Up     --
management                           2 Up     --


! Verifying configuration of management interface mgmt 0. Management interface is
under vrf management and have IP address 10.10.1.6.
N9K-A# show run interface mgmt 0

!Command: show running-config interface mgmt0
!Running configuration last done at: Tue Jan  4 15:36:03 2022
!Time: Wed Jan  5 06:31:13 2022


version 10.2(1) Bios:version 05.45


interface mgmt0
  vrf member management
  ip address 10.10.1.6/24

! If you don't specify the vrf, a simple ping to the management interface will ini-
tiate the ping from the default vrf. Since the interface is under vrf management,
the ping will fail as default vrf is not aware of the management vrf interfaces.
N9K-A# ping 10.10.1.6
PING 10.10.1.6 (10.10.1.6): 56 data bytes
ping: sendto 10.10.1.6 64 chars, No route to host
Request 0 timed out
ping: sendto 10.10.1.6 64 chars, No route to host
Request 1 timed out
ping: sendto 10.10.1.6 64 chars, No route to host
Request 2 timed out
ping: sendto 10.10.1.6 64 chars, No route to host
Request 3 timed out
ping: sendto 10.10.1.6 64 chars, No route to host
Request 4 timed out


--- 10.10.1.6 ping statistics ---
5 packets transmitted, 0 packets received, 100.00% packet loss


! Default vrf routing table is not aware of the management interface IP address.
N9K-A# show ip route
IP Route Table for VRF "default"
'*' denotes best ucast next-hop
```

```
'**' denotes best mcast next-hop
'[x/y]' denotes [preference/metric]
'%<string>' in via output denotes VRF <string>


10.10.10.10/32, ubest/mbest: 2/0, attached
    *via 10.10.10.10, Lo0, [0/0], 15:08:39, local
    *via 10.10.10.10, Lo0, [0/0], 15:08:39, direct
192.168.1.44/30, ubest/mbest: 1/0, attached
    *via 192.168.1.45, Eth1/3, [0/0], 15:07:27, direct
192.168.1.45/32, ubest/mbest: 1/0, attached
    *via 192.168.1.45, Eth1/3, [0/0], 15:07:27, local


! Pinging the management interface specifying the correct vrf. This time, the ping
will succeed as management vrf routing table have reachability information for
all the IP addresses in the management vrf.
N9K-A# ping 10.10.1.6 vrf management
PING 10.10.1.6 (10.10.1.6): 56 data bytes
64 bytes from 10.10.1.6: icmp_seq=0 ttl=255 time=0.295 ms
64 bytes from 10.10.1.6: icmp_seq=1 ttl=255 time=0.178 ms
64 bytes from 10.10.1.6: icmp_seq=2 ttl=255 time=0.172 ms
64 bytes from 10.10.1.6: icmp_seq=3 ttl=255 time=0.169 ms
64 bytes from 10.10.1.6: icmp_seq=4 ttl=255 time=0.258 ms


--- 10.10.1.6 ping statistics ---
5 packets transmitted, 5 packets received, 0.00% packet loss
round-trip min/avg/max = 0.169/0.214/0.295 ms


N9K-A# show ip route vrf management
IP Route Table for VRF "management"
'*' denotes best ucast next-hop
'**' denotes best mcast next-hop
'[x/y]' denotes [preference/metric]
'%<string>' in via output denotes VRF <string>


0.0.0.0/0, ubest/mbest: 1/0
    *via 10.10.1.254, [1/0], 3w2d, static
10.10.1.0/24, ubest/mbest: 1/0, attached
    *via 10.10.1.6, mgmt0, [0/0], 3w2d, direct
10.10.1.6/32, ubest/mbest: 1/0, attached
    *via 10.10.1.6, mgmt0, [0/0], 3w2d, local


N9K-A#
```

In Examples 5-3 and 5-4, we verify the OSPF configuration and end-to-end connectivity.

Example 5-3 *Verification of OSPF Configuration and End-to-End Connectivity on N9K-A*

```
! Verifying if the interfaces are configured correctly. Note that all interfaces
are in vrf default.
N9K-A# show ip interface brief
IP Interface Status for VRF "default"(1)
Interface          IP Address       Interface Status
Lo0                10.10.10.10      protocol-up/link-up/admin-up
Eth1/3             192.168.1.45     protocol-up/link-up/admin-up


! Verifying pre-configured OSPF configuration.
N9K-A# show running-config ospf
!Command: show running-config ospf
!Running configuration last done at: Wed Jan  5 07:44:58 2022
!Time: Wed Jan  5 09:22:03 2022

version 10.2(1) Bios:version 05.45
feature ospf

router ospf 1
  router-id 1.1.1.1

interface loopback0
  ip router ospf 1 area 0.0.0.0

interface Ethernet1/3
  ip router ospf 1 area 0.0.0.0


! Verifying OSPF neighbors. Note that the OSPF neighborship is formed under vrf
default.
N9K-A# show ip ospf neighbors
OSPF Process ID 1 VRF default
Total number of neighbors: 1
Neighbor ID     Pri State        Up Time  Address        Interface
2.2.2.2           1 FULL/BDR      01:36:30 192.168.1.46   Eth1/3

! Verifying OSPF routing table under vrf default.
N9K-A# show ip route ospf
IP Route Table for VRF "default"
```

```
'*' denotes best ucast next-hop
'**' denotes best mcast next-hop
'[x/y]' denotes [preference/metric]
'%<string>' in via output denotes VRF <string>


20.20.20.20/32, ubest/mbest: 1/0
    *via 192.168.1.46, Eth1/3, [110/5], 01:36:57, ospf-1, intra


! End-to-End connectivity between Loopback interfaces of N9K-A and N9K-B is
achieved using OSPF routing under vrf default.
N9K-A# ping 20.20.20.20 source 10.10.10.10
PING 20.20.20.20 (20.20.20.20) from 10.10.10.10: 56 data bytes
64 bytes from 20.20.20.20: icmp_seq=0 ttl=254 time=0.894 ms
64 bytes from 20.20.20.20: icmp_seq=1 ttl=254 time=0.459 ms
64 bytes from 20.20.20.20: icmp_seq=2 ttl=254 time=0.474 ms
64 bytes from 20.20.20.20: icmp_seq=3 ttl=254 time=0.454 ms
64 bytes from 20.20.20.20: icmp_seq=4 ttl=254 time=0.51 ms


--- 20.20.20.20 ping statistics ---
5 packets transmitted, 5 packets received, 0.00% packet loss
round-trip min/avg/max = 0.454/0.558/0.894 ms
N9K-A#
```

Example 5-4 *Verification of OSPF Configuration and End-to-End Connectivity on N9K-B*

```
! Verifying if the interfaces are configured correctly. Note that all interfaces
are in vrf default.
N9K-B# show ip interface brief
IP Interface Status for VRF "default"(1)
Interface            IP Address         Interface Status
Lo0                  20.20.20.20        protocol-up/link-up/admin-up
Eth1/3               192.168.1.46       protocol-up/link-up/admin-up


! Verifying pre-configured OSPF configuration.
N9K-B# show running-config ospf
!Command: show running-config ospf
!Running configuration last done at: Wed Jan  5 07:46:27 2022
!Time: Wed Jan  5 09:25:05 2022


version 10.2(1) Bios:version 05.45
feature ospf
```

```
router ospf 1
  router-id 2.2.2.2

interface loopback0
  ip router ospf 1 area 0.0.0.0

interface Ethernet1/3
  ip router ospf 1 area 0.0.0.0

! Verifying OSPF neighbors. Note that the OSPF neighborship is formed under vrf
default.
N9K-B# show ip ospf neighbors
OSPF Process ID 1 VRF default
Total number of neighbors: 1
Neighbor ID     Pri State          Up Time  Address       Interface
1.1.1.1           1 FULL/DR         01:38:43 192.168.1.45  Eth1/3

! Verifying OSPF routing table under vrf default.
N9K-B# show ip route ospf
IP Route Table for VRF "default"
'*' denotes best ucast next-hop
'**' denotes best mcast next-hop
'[x/y]' denotes [preference/metric]
'%<string>' in via output denotes VRF <string>

10.10.10.10/32, ubest/mbest: 1/0
    *via 192.168.1.45, Eth1/3, [110/5], 01:38:49, ospf-1, intra

! End-to-End connectivity between Loopback interfaces of N9K-A and N9K-B is achieved
using OSPF routing under vrf default.
N9K-B# ping 10.10.10.10 source 20.20.20.20
PING 10.10.10.10 (10.10.10.10) from 20.20.20.20: 56 data bytes
64 bytes from 10.10.10.10: icmp_seq=0 ttl=254 time=1.001 ms
64 bytes from 10.10.10.10: icmp_seq=1 ttl=254 time=0.751 ms
64 bytes from 10.10.10.10: icmp_seq=2 ttl=254 time=0.674 ms
64 bytes from 10.10.10.10: icmp_seq=3 ttl=254 time=0.665 ms
64 bytes from 10.10.10.10: icmp_seq=4 ttl=254 time=0.967 ms

--- 10.10.10.10 ping statistics ---
5 packets transmitted, 5 packets received, 0.00% packet loss
round-trip min/avg/max = 0.665/0.811/1.001 ms
N9K-B#
```

In Examples 5-5 and 5-6, we configure the nondefault VRF DCFNDU on the Loopback 0 and Ethernet 1/3 interfaces on N9K-A and N9K-B and verify its impact on OSPFv2 routing. Since adding an interface to a VRF wipes its configuration, we need to reconfigure the IP address and the OSPF configuration.

Example 5-5   *Nondefault VRF Configuration on N9K-A and N9K-B*

```
N9K-A

! Creating vrf DCFNDU.
N9K-A# configure terminal
Enter configuration commands, one per line. End with CNTL/Z.
N9K-A(config)# vrf context DCFNDU
N9K-A(config-vrf)# exit

! Verifying the new non-default vrf DCFNDU creation.
N9K-A(config)# show vrf
VRF-Name                        VRF-ID State   Reason
DCFNDU                               3 Up      --
default                              1 Up      --
management                           2 Up      --

! Placing the Loopback 0 and Ethernet 1/3 interface into vrf instance DCFNDU.
N9K-A(config)# interface Loopback 0
N9K-A(config-if)# vrf member DCFNDU
Warning: Deleted all L3 config on interface loopback0
N9K-A(config-if)# ip address 10.10.10.10/32
N9K-A(config-if)# ip router ospf 1 area 0
N9K-A(config-if)# interface Ethernet 1/3
N9K-A(config-if)# vrf member DCFNDU
Warning: Deleted all L3 config on interface Ethernet1/3
N9K-A(config-if)# ip address 192.168.1.45/30
N9K-A(config-if)# ip router ospf 1 area 0
N9K-A(config-if)# end
N9K-A#


N9K-B

! Creating vrf DCFNDU.
N9K-B# configure terminal
Enter configuration commands, one per line. End with CNTL/Z.
N9K-B(config)# vrf context DCFNDU
N9K-B(config-vrf)# exit
```

```
! Verifying the new non-default vrf DCFNDU creation.
N9K-B(config)# show vrf
VRF-Name                        VRF-ID State   Reason
DCFNDU                               3 Up      --
default                              1 Up      --
management                           2 Up      --


! Placing the Loopback 0 and Ethernet 1/3 interface into vrf instance DCFNDU.
N9K-B(config)# interface Loopback 0
N9K-B(config-if)# vrf member DCFNDU
Warning: Deleted all L3 config on interface loopback0
N9K-B(config-if)# ip address 20.20.20.20/32
N9K-B(config-if)# ip router ospf 1 area 0
N9K-B(config-if)# interface Ethernet 1/3
N9K-B(config-if)# vrf member DCFNDU
Warning: Deleted all L3 config on interface Ethernet1/3
N9K-B(config-if)# ip address 192.168.1.46/30
N9K-B(config-if)# ip router ospf 1 area 0
N9K-B(config-if)# end
N9K-B#
```

Example 5-6   *Verification of Impact of Nondefault VRF Configuration on N9K-A*

```
! Once the interfaces are moved under vrf instance DCFNDU, the ospf neighborship is
formed under vrf DCFNDU and not under default vrf.
N9K-A# show ip ospf neighbors
N9K-A# show ip ospf neighbors vrf DCFNDU
 OSPF Process ID 1 VRF DCFNDU
 Total number of neighbors: 1
 Neighbor ID      Pri State           Up Time  Address        Interface
 192.168.1.46       1 FULL/BDR         00:15:55 192.168.1.46   Eth1/3


! OSPF routing table under vrf default don't show any routes as there is no neigh-
borship formed under vrf instance default. All OSPF routes are showing up under vrf
instance DCFNDU.
N9K-A# show ip route ospf
IP Route Table for VRF "default"
'*' denotes best ucast next-hop
'**' denotes best mcast next-hop
'[x/y]' denotes [preference/metric]
'%<string>' in via output denotes VRF <string>
```

```
N9K-A# show ip route ospf vrf DCFNDU
IP Route Table for VRF "DCFNDU"
'*' denotes best ucast next-hop
'**' denotes best mcast next-hop
'[x/y]' denotes [preference/metric]
'%<string>' in via output denotes VRF <string>


20.20.20.20/32, ubest/mbest: 1/0
    *via 192.168.1.46, Eth1/3, [110/5], 00:00:07, ospf-1, intra


! Ping between Loopback interfaces of N9K-A and N9K-B fails under vrf instance
default. End-to-End reachability between Loopback interfaces of N9K-A and N9K-B is
achieved only under vrf instance DCFNDU.
N9K-A# ping 20.20.20.20 source 10.10.10.10
ping: can't bind to address 10.10.10.10


N9K-A# ping 20.20.20.20 source 10.10.10.10 vrf DCFNDU
PING 20.20.20.20 (20.20.20.20) from 10.10.10.10: 56 data bytes
64 bytes from 20.20.20.20: icmp_seq=0 ttl=254 time=0.947 ms
64 bytes from 20.20.20.20: icmp_seq=1 ttl=254 time=0.497 ms
64 bytes from 20.20.20.20: icmp_seq=2 ttl=254 time=0.732 ms
64 bytes from 20.20.20.20: icmp_seq=3 ttl=254 time=0.612 ms
64 bytes from 20.20.20.20: icmp_seq=4 ttl=254 time=0.447 ms


--- 20.20.20.20 ping statistics ---
5 packets transmitted, 5 packets received, 0.00% packet loss
round-trip min/avg/max = 0.447/0.647/0.947 ms
N9K-A#

! Note that similar verification can be done on N9K-B.
```

Cisco Nexus 7000 VDCs

VDCs partition a single physical device into multiple logical devices that provide fault isolation, management isolation, address allocation isolation, service differentiation domains, and adaptive resource management. In simple terms, VDCs enable the virtualization of the control plane, data plane, and management plane of a switch, along with its hardware resource virtualization. You can manage a VDC instance within a physical device independently. Each VDC appears as a unique device to the connected users. A VDC runs as a separate logical entity within the physical device, maintains its own unique set of running software processes, has its own configuration, and can be managed by a separate administrator.

VDCs virtualize the control plane, which includes all those software functions processed by the CPU on the active supervisor module. A VDC contains its own unique and independent set of VLANs and VRFs. Each VDC can have assigned to it physical ports, thus allowing for the hardware data plane to be virtualized as well. Within each VDC, a separate management domain can manage the VDC itself, thus allowing the management plane itself to also be virtualized.

In its default state, the switch control plane runs a single device context (called VDC 1) within which it will run approximately 80 processes. Some of these processes can have other threads spawned, resulting in as many as 250 processes actively running on the system at a time depending on the services configured. This single device context also has a number of Layer 2 and 3 services running on top of the infrastructure and kernel components of the OS, as shown in Figure 5-3.

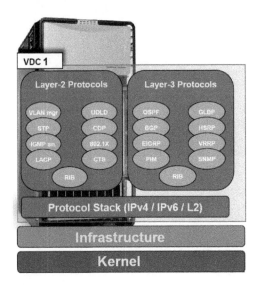

Figure 5-3   *Default Operating Mode with Single Default VDC*

This collection of processes constitutes what is seen as the control plane for a single physical device (that being with no other virtual device contexts enabled). VDC 1 is always active, always enabled, and can never be deleted. When you create a subsequent (additional) VDC, the Cisco NX-OS software takes several of the control plane processes and replicates it for each device context that exists in the switch. When this occurs, duplication of VRF names and VLAN IDs is possible. For example, you could have a VRF called "sales" in one device context and the same "sales" name applied to a VRF in another virtual device context. Hence, each VDC administrator essentially interfaces with its own set of processes and its own set of VRFs and VLANs, which in turn, represents its own logical (or virtual) switch context. This provides a clear delineation of management contexts and forms the basis for configuration separation and independence between VDCs.

Each VDC has a minimum of two VRF instances- a default VRF instance and a management VRF instance. All Layer 3 interfaces and routing protocols exist in the default VRF instance until they are assigned to another VRF instance. The mgmt0 interface exists in the management VRF instance and is accessible from any VDC. Up to 4000 VRF instances per system are permitted. With each new VDC configured, the number of configurable VRF instances per system is reduced by two because each VDC has a default VRF instance and a management VRF instance that are not removable.

Figure 5-4 represents VDC service and protocol separation.

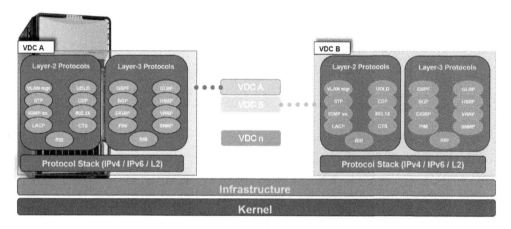

Figure 5-4   *VDC Service and Protocol Separation*

VDC Architecture

The Cisco NX-OS software provides the base upon which the VDCs are supported. Figure 5-5 shows NX-OS in VDC mode.

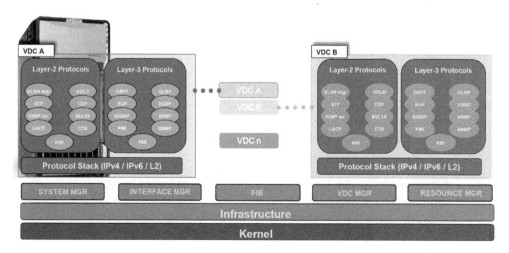

Figure 5-5   *NX-OS in VDC Mode*

At the heart of the NX-OS, are the kernel and infrastructure layer. The kernel supports all processes and all VDCs that run on the switch, but only a single instance of the kernel exists at any one point in time. The infrastructure layer provides an interface between the higher layer processes and the hardware resources of the physical switch (TCAM and so on). Having a single instance of this layer reduces complexity (when managing the hardware resources). Having a single infrastructure layer also helps scale performance by avoiding duplication of this system's management process.

Working under control of the infrastructure layer are a number of other important system processes that also exist as unique entities. Of these, the VDC manager is a key process when it comes to supporting VDCs. The VDC manager is responsible for the creation and deletion of VDCs. More importantly, it provides VDC-related APIs for other infrastructure components, such as the system manager and resource manager, to perform their own related functions.

When a VDC is created, the system manager is responsible for launching all services required for VDC startup that run on a per-VDC basis. As new services are configured, the system manager will launch the appropriate process. For example, if OSPF were enabled in a VDC named Marketing, the system manager would launch an OSPF process for that VDC. If a VDC is deleted, the system manager is responsible for tearing down all related processes for that VDC.

The resources manager is responsible for managing the allocation and distribution of resources between VDCs. Resources such as VLANs, VRFs, port channels, and physical ports are examples of resources managed by the resource manager.

Sitting above the infrastructure layer and its associated managers are processes that run on a per-VDC basis. All the Layer 2 and Layer 3 protocol services run within a VDC. Each protocol service started within a VDC runs independently of the protocol services in other VDCs. The infrastructure layer protects the protocol services within a VDC so that a fault or other problem in a service in one VDC does not impact other VDCs. The Cisco NX-OS software creates these virtualized services only when a VDC is created. Each VDC has its own instance of each service. These virtualized services are unaware of other VDCs and only work on resources assigned to that VDC. Only a user with the network-admin role can control the resources available to these virtualized services. (You can find more on the network-admin role later in this chapter in the "VDC Management" section.) The Cisco NX-OS software also creates a virtualized control plane for each VDC that processes all the protocol-related events.

VDC Types

The use of VDCs with the Cisco Nexus 7000 Series Supervisor 2E or 3E modules allows a single Cisco Nexus 7000 Series switch to be partitioned into up to eight VDCs: the default VDC and seven additional VDCs. Another available choice is to create one admin VDC and eight additional VDCs. More than four VDCs require additional licenses. The VDC types are discussed in the sections that follow.

Default VDC

The physical device always has at least one VDC, the default VDC (VDC 1). When you first log in to a new Cisco NX-OS device, you begin in the default VDC. Initially, all hardware resources of the switch belong to the default VDC. The default VDC is a fully functional VDC with all the capabilities and can be used for production traffic with no issues. Some customers may choose to reserve it for administrative functions.

Figure 5-6 illustrates Default VDC.

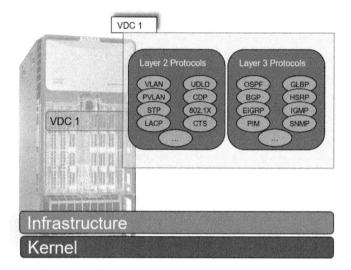

Figure 5-6   *Default VDC*

Some tasks can only be performed in the default VDC, including the following:

- VDC creation/deletion/suspend

- Resource allocation (interfaces and memory)

- NX-OS upgrade across all VDCs

- EPLD upgrade, as directed by TAC or to enable new features

- Ethanalyzer captures for control/data plane traffic

- Feature set installation for Nexus 2000, FabricPath, and FCoE

- Control plane policing (CoPP) configuration

- Systemwide QoS and port channel load-balancing configuration

- Hardware IDS checks control

- Licensing operations

- Reload of the entire switch

The default VDC has a special role: it controls all hardware resources and can access all other VDCs. VDCs are always created from the default VDC. Hardware resources, such as interfaces and memory, are also allocated to other VDCs from the default VDC. Other VDCs only have access to the resources allocated to them and cannot access any other VDCs.

VDCs are separated on the data plane, control plane, and management plane. The only exception to this rule is the default VDC, which can interact with the other VDCs on the management plane. Control plane and data plane functions of the default VDC are still separated from the other VDCs.

Admin VDC

You can enable an admin VDC at the initial system bootup through a setup script. It is an optional step, and the creation of an admin VDC is not required. When an admin VDC is enabled at bootup, it replaces the default VDC. An admin VDC is used for administrative functions only and is not a fully functional VDC like the default VDC. If an admin VDC is created, it does not count toward the maximum of eight VDCs on Cisco Nexus 7000 Series switches.

You can also change the default VDC to admin VDC using the following methods.

- When you enter the **system admin-vdc** command after bootup, the default VDC becomes the admin VDC. The nonglobal configuration in the default VDC is lost after you enter this command. This option is recommended for existing deployments where the default VDC is used only for administration and does not pass any traffic.

- You can change the default VDC to the admin VDC with the **system admin-vdc migrate** *new vdc name* command. After you enter this command, the nonglobal configuration on a default VDC is migrated to the new migrated VDC. This option is recommended for existing deployments where the default VDC is used for production traffic whose downtime must be minimized.

Once an admin VDC is created, it cannot be deleted and it cannot be changed back to the default VDC without erasing the configuration and performing a fresh bootup.

Admin VDCs are supported on Supervisor 1 and Supervisor 2/2e/3e modules. When an admin VDC is enabled, only the mgmt0 port can be allocated to the admin VDC, which means that for an admin VDC, only out-of-band management is possible through the mgmt0 interface and console port. No other physical Ethernet or logical interfaces are associated with the admin VDC.

Figure 5-7 shows the admin VDC.

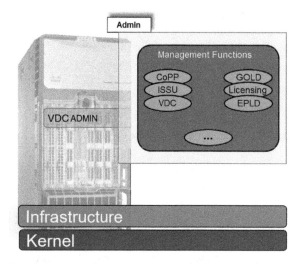

Figure 5-7 *Admin VDC*

The admin VDC provides access only to pure system administration tasks, including the following:

- Create, change attributes for, or delete a nondefault VDC

- In Service Software Upgrade/Downgrade (ISSU/ISSD)

- Erasable Programmable Logic Device (EPLD) upgrades

- Control plane policing (CoPP) configuration

- Reload of the entire switch

- Collection of show tech-support, **tac-pac** commands, run **debug** commands, and Cisco Generic Online Diagnostics (GOLD)

- Systemwide QoS and port channel load-balancing configuration

- Feature set installation for Nexus 2000 and FCoE

- Licensing operations

Nondefault VDC

Nondefault VDCs are created by the default VDC and are fully functional VDCs with all capabilities. Changes done in a nondefault VDC only affect that particular VDC. Nondefault VDCs have discrete configuration file and checkpoints per VDC. Nondefault VDCs run independent processes for each protocol per VDC and thus provide fault isolation. Nondefault VDCs can be of the Ethernet type or Storage type. VDCs that only have Ethernet interfaces allocated to them are called Ethernet VDCs. Ethernet VDCs don't have any storage ports such as FCoE ports allocated to them.

Figure 5-8 shows a nondefault VDC.

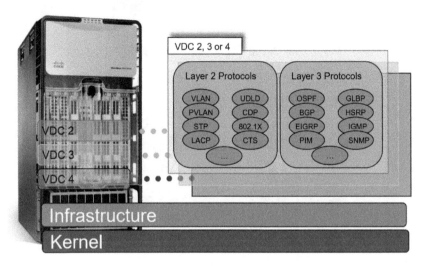

Figure 5-8 *Nondefault VDC*

Storage VDC

Beginning with Cisco NX-OS Release 5.2(1), Nexus 7000 Series devices support Fibre Channel over Ethernet (FCoE). To run FCoE, a dedicated storage VDC should be configured on the Cisco Nexus 7000 Series devices. The storage VDC is one type of nondefault VDC. Storage virtual device context (VDC) separates LAN and SAN traffic on the same switch and maintains one physical infrastructure, but with separate logical data paths. A storage VDC creates a virtual MDS switch within the Nexus 7000 chassis and participates as a full Fibre Channel forwarder (FCF) in the network. A storage VDC can be configured with zoning, a Fibre Channel alias, Fibre Channel domains, fabric binding, and so on. After the storage VDC is created, FCoE VLANs can be configured, and interfaces are specified as dedicated FCoE interfaces or shared interfaces. A shared interface can carry both Ethernet and FCoE traffic, however; storage traffic is processed in the storage VDC, while Ethernet traffic is processed in another Ethernet VDC. Traffic is split based on Ethertype. Traffic from the storage protocol is sent to the storage VDC, while the rest is sent to the Ethernet VDC, as you can see in Figure 5-9.

The Ethernet VDC administratively "owns" the interface. The shared port must be configured as an 802.1Q trunk in the Ethernet VDC. All ports on the ASIC (port group) must be configured for sharing. Shutting down a shared interface in the Ethernet VDC shuts down both Ethernet and storage VDC interfaces. However, shutting down a shared interface in the storage VDC only shuts down the FCoE interface, not the Ethernet interface.

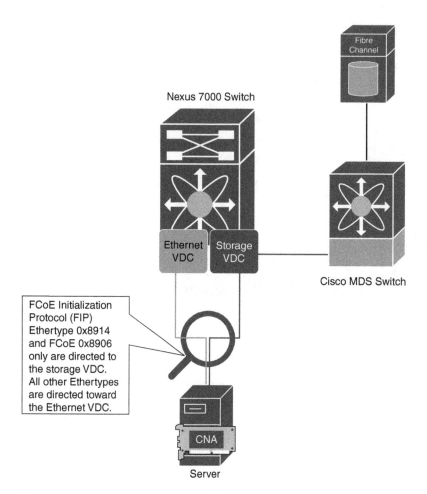

Figure 5-9 *Storage VDC*

Although a storage VDC does not require an advanced license (VDCs), it requires the FCoE license to enable the FCoE function on the modules. There can be only one storage VDC on the Cisco Nexus 7000 Series device. A default VDC cannot be configured as the storage VDC. Only the Cisco Nexus 7000 F-series module supports the storage VDC. The M-series I/O modules do not support storage VDCs. F1 and F2/F2e Series modules cannot be intermixed in the storage VDC.

VDC Module Type Modes

Not all line card modules support all Cisco NX-OS features and can cause problems when improperly assigned to a VDC. For example, OTV is not supported on the F1 or F2 module. To prevent widespread disruption within a VDC, you can restrict certain line cards from being assigned to a VDC by using the system **limit-resource module-type** command. For example, the **limit-resource module-type f1 m1 m1-xl m2-xl** command allows a mix of M1, M1-XL, M2-XL, and F1 modules in the same VDC.

Figure 5-10 shows three VDCs configured on the same physical Nexus 7000 Switch: M1-F1 mixed VDC, M1-XL only VDC, and F2 only VDC.

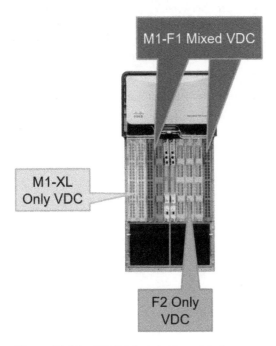

Figure 5-10 *VDC Module Type Modes*

Table 5-4 shows the VDC module type compatibilities for Cisco NX-OS Release 8.x, the latest version at the time of this writing.

Table 5-4 *VDC Module Type Compatibility for Release 8.x*

	F1	F2	M2XL	F2e(F2CR)	F3	M3
F1	True	False	True	False	False	False
F2	False	True	False	True	True	False
M2XL	True	False	True	True	True	True
F2e(F2CR)	False	True	True	True	True	False
F3	False	True	True	True	True	True
M3	False	False	True	False	True	True

Communicating Between VDCs

Cisco NX-OS software does not support direct communication between VDCs on a single physical device. You must make a physical connection from a port that is allocated to one VDC to a port that is allocated to another VDC to allow the VDCs to communicate. You must use the front panel port to connect between VDCs; soft cross-connect on backplane inter-VDC communications does not exist. Storage shared ports can communicate with each other within their respective VDC. There is no restriction on L2/L3 or line card models. When using vPC or vPC+ between VDCs, you have to ensure domain IDs are unique. (More on vPCs can be found in Chapter 4, "Port Channels and vPCs.")

Figure 5-11 shows two VDCs that are connected externally but not connected internally.

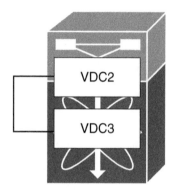

Figure 5-11 *Communicating Between VDCs*

VDC Resources

When you're creating VDCs, certain resources are shared across VDCs while others must be dedicated to a VDC. Three types of VDC resources can be defined:

- **Global resources:** These resources can only be allocated, set, or configured globally for all VDCs. These resources include boot image configuration, Ethanalyzer session, NTP servers, CoPP configuration, and in-band SPAN sessions. For example, boot string specifies the version of software that should be used upon booting up the switch. It is not possible to run different versions of the Cisco NX-OS software in different VDCs.

- **Dedicated resources:** These resources are allocated to a particular VDC, such as Ethernet interfaces.

- **Shared resources:** These resources are shared between VDCs, such as the OOB Ethernet management port on the supervisor. For example, if multiple VDCs are configured and accessible from the management interface, they must share it, and the OOB management interface cannot be allocated to a VDC like other regular switch ports. The management interfaces of the VDCs should be configured with IP addresses on the same IP subnet as the management VRF instance.

Types of Resources

VDC resources can also be classified into two broad categories: physical and logical.

Physical Resources

Network admins can allocate physical device resources exclusively for the use of a VDC. Once a resource is assigned to a specific VDC, you can manage it only from that VDC. Users logging directly into the VDC can only see this limited view of the device and can manage only those resources that the network administrator explicitly assigns to that VDC. Users within a VDC cannot view or modify resources in other VDCs.

The only physical resources that you can allocate to a VDC are the Ethernet interfaces. For the Ethernet VDCs, each physical Ethernet interface can belong to only one VDC, including the default VDC, at any given time. When you are working with shared interfaces in the storage VDC, the physical interface can belong to both one Ethernet VDC and one storage VDC simultaneously, but to no more than one of each.

Initially, all physical interfaces belong to the default VDC (VDC 1). When you create a new VDC, the Cisco NX-OS software creates the virtualized services for the VDC without allocating any physical interfaces to it. After you create a new VDC, you can allocate a set of physical interfaces from the default VDC to the new VDC. When you allocate an interface to a VDC, all configuration for that interface is erased. The VDC administrator must configure the interface from within the VDC. Only the interfaces allocated to the VDC are visible for configuration. On many I/O modules, any port can be individually assigned to a VDC. The exceptions to this rule include modules whose architecture uses port groups that consist of two, four, or eight ports each, where the ports within the same port group share some common hardware elements. In this case, ports in the same group must be assigned to the same VDC. For example, the N7K-M132XP-12 line card has eight port groups of four interfaces each, so in total 32 interfaces. Hence all N7K-M132XP-12 line cards require allocation in groups of four ports. Interfaces belonging to the same port group must belong to the same VDC.

Figure 5-12 illustrates the interface allocation for port groups on a Cisco N7K-M132XP-12 line card.

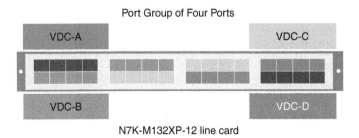

Figure 5-12 *Interface Allocation for Port Groups on Cisco N7K-M132XP-12 Line Card*

Note   Beginning with Cisco NX-OS Release 5.2(1) for Cisco Nexus 7000 Series devices, all members of a port group are automatically allocated to the VDC when you allocate an interface.

Logical Resources

Each VDC acts as a separate logical device within a single physical device, which means that all the namespaces are unique within a VDC. However, you cannot use an identical namespace within a storage VDC and an Ethernet VDC.

When you create a VDC, it has its own default VLAN and VRF that are not shared with other VDCs. You can also create other logical entities within a VDC for the exclusive use of that VDC. These logical entities, which include SPAN monitoring sessions, port channels, VLANs, and VRFs, are for Ethernet VDCs. When you create a logical entity in a VDC, only users in that VDC can use it even when it has the same identifier as another logical entity in another VDC. A VDC administrator can configure VLAN IDs independently of the VLAN IDs used in other Ethernet VDCs on the same physical device. For example, if VDC administrators for Ethernet VDC A and Ethernet VDC B both create VLAN 10, these VLANs are internally mapped to separate unique identifiers as shown in Figure 5-13. But remember, when you are working with both storage VDCs and Ethernet VDCs, the VLAN ID and logical entity must be entirely separate for the storage VDCs.

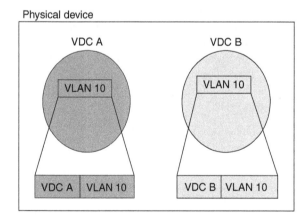

Figure 5-13   *VLAN Configuration for Ethernet VDCs*

VDC CPU Shares

Beginning with Cisco NX-OS Release 6.1, you can use CPU shares to control the CPU resources among the VDCs allowing you to prioritize VDC access to the CPU during CPU contention. The number of shares assigned to a VDC determine the priority of the VDC compared to other VDCs within the same Cisco Nexus 7000 Series switch. CPU shares are supported on Supervisor 2/2e/3e modules. You can also configure the number of CPU shares on a VDC. For example, a VDC with 10 CPU shares gets twice the CPU time compared to a VDC that has five CPU shares, as shown in Figure 5-14.

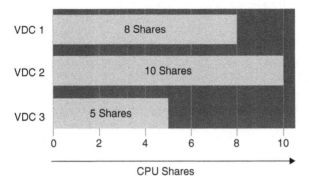

Figure 5-14 *VDC CPU Shares*

CPU shares are not used to limit the CPU that is available to a VDC but to allocate CPU cycles to a VDC with a higher priority during times of congestion. CPU shares' configuration takes effect immediately, and there is no need to restart/reload the switch. The CPU time a process receives is as follows:

cpu.share / (sum of cpu.share of all processes that want CPU time)

VDC Resource Templates

A network administrator can allocate resources to VDCs using resource templates. Each resource template describes how a set of resources is allocated to a VDC. When you create a VDC, you use a VDC resource template to set the minimum and maximum limits on the number of certain logical entities you can create in the VDC. These logical entities include port channels, SPAN monitor sessions, VLANs, IPv4 and IPv6 route memory, and VRFs. You can explicitly specify a VDC resource template, or you can use the default VDC template provided by the Cisco NX-OS software. If you do not set limits for a resource in a VDC resource template, the default limits are the limits for that resource in the default VDC resource template You cannot change the configuration of the default resource templates. You can set only one value for the multicast and unicast route memory resources' maximum and minimum limits. If you specify a minimum limit, that is the value for both the minimum and maximum limits, and the maximum limit is ignored. If you specify only a maximum limit, that is the value for both the minimum and maximum limits. The changes that you make to a VDC resource template do not affect any VDCs you created by using that VDC resource template. To update a VDC with the new limits in the VDC resource, you must explicitly reapply the template to the VDC.

Note   You cannot change the limits in the default VDC resource template.

Scaling Resources Using VDCs

Each line card uses a local hardware-forwarding engine to perform Layer 2 and Layer 3 forwarding in hardware. The use of VDCs enables this local forwarding engine to optimize the use of its resources for both Layer 2 and Layer 3 operations.

Layer 2 Address Learning with VDCs

The forwarding engine on each line card is responsible for Layer 2 address learning and will maintain a local copy of the Layer 2 forwarding table. The MAC address table on each line card supports 128,000 MAC addresses. When a new MAC address is learned by a line card, it will forward a copy of that MAC address to other line cards. This enables the Layer 2 address learning process to be synchronized across line cards. Layer 2 learning is a VDC local process and, as such, has a direct effect on what addresses are placed into each line card. Forwarding engines on the line cards only contain MAC address entries for VDCs that have a port on the line cards.

Figure 5-15 shows how the distributed Layer 2 learning process is affected by the presence of VDCs. On line card 1, MAC address A is learned from port 1/2 in VDC 10. This address is installed in the local Layer 2 forwarding table of line card 1. The MAC address is then forwarded to both line cards 2 and 3. As line card 3 has no ports that belong to VDC 10, it will not install any MAC addresses learned from that VDC. Line card 2, however, does have a local port in VDC 10, so it will install MAC address A into its local forwarding tables.

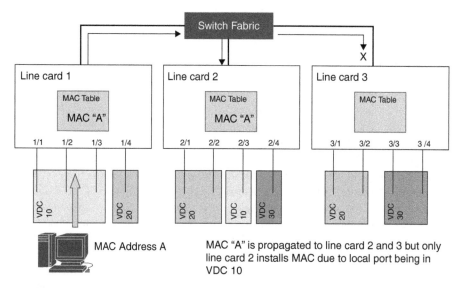

Figure 5-15 *MAC Address Learning*

With this implementation of Layer 2 learning, the Cisco Nexus 7000 Series switch offers a way to scale the use of the Layer 2 MAC address table more efficiently when VDCs are unique to line cards.

Layer 3 Resources and VDCs

The forwarding engine on each line card supports 128,000 entries in the forwarding information base (used to store forwarding prefixes), 64,000 access control lists, and 512,000 ingress and 512,000 egress NetFlow entries.

When the default VDC is the only active VDC, learned routes and ACLs are loaded into each line card TCAM table so that each line card has the necessary information local to it to make an informed forwarding decision. Figure 5-16 illustrates this process, where the routes for the default "red" VDC are present in the FIB and ACL TCAMs.

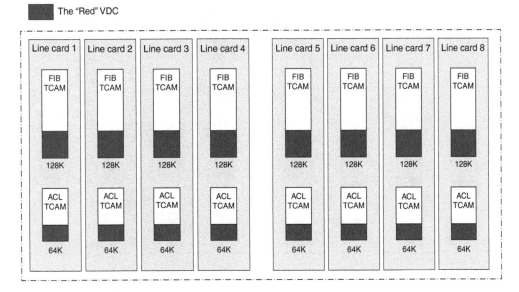

Figure 5-16 *Default Resource Allocation*

When physical port resources are split between VDCs, only the line cards associated with that VDC are required to store forwarding information and associated ACLs. In this way, the resources can be scaled beyond the default system limits seen in the preceding example. Table 5-5 illustrates a resource separation example.

Table 5-5 *Resource Separation Example*

VDC	Number of Routes	Number of Access Control Entries (ACE)	Allocated Line Cards
10	90,000	40,000	LC 1, LC 2
20	18,000	10,000	LC 1, LC 2, LC 3, LC 5
30	80,000	30,000	LC 3, LC 5

Figure 5-17 show the resource allocation/split as per Table 5-5.

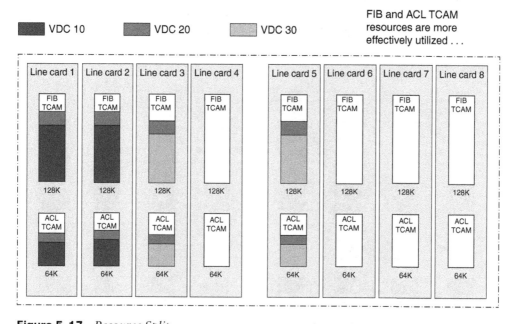

Figure 5-17 *Resource Split*

The effect of allocating a subset of ports to a given VDC results in the FIB and ACL TCAM for the respective line cards being primed with the forwarding information and ACLs for that VDC. This extends the use of those TCAM resources beyond the simple system limit described earlier. In the preceding example, a total of 188,000 forwarding entries have been installed in a switch that, without VDCs, would have a system limit of 128,000 forwarding entries. Likewise, a total of 80,000 ACEs have been installed, where a single VDC would only allow 64,000 access control entries. More important, FIB and ACL TCAM space on line cards 4, 6, 7, and 8 is free for use by additional VDCs that might be created. This further extends the use of those resources well beyond the defined system limits noted here.

VDC Fault Isolation

When multiple VDCs are created in a physical switch, inherently the architecture of the VDC provides a means to prevent failures within that VDC from affecting other VDCs. So, for instance, a spanning tree recalculation that might be started in one VDC is not going to affect the spanning tree domains of other VDCs in the same physical chassis. An OSPF process crash is another example where the fault is isolated locally to that VDC. Process isolation within a VDC thus plays an important role in fault isolation and serves as a major benefit for organizations that embrace the VDC concept.

Figure 5-18 shows that a fault in a process running in VDC 1 does not impact any of the running processes in the other VDCs. Other equivalent processes will continue to run uninhibited by any problems associated with the faulty running process.

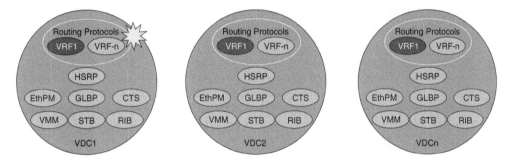

Figure 5-18 *Per-VDC Fault Isolation*

Fault isolation is enhanced with the ability to provide per-VDC **debug** commands. Per-VDC logging of messages via syslog is also another important characteristic of the VDC fault isolation capabilities. When combined, these two features provide a powerful tool for administrators to locate problems.

The creation of multiple VDCs also permits configuration isolation. Each VDC has its own unique configuration file that is stored separately in NVRAM. There are a number of resources in each VDC whose associated numbers and IDs can overlap between multiple VDCs without having an effect on another VDC's configuration. For example, the same VRF IDs, port channel numbers, VLAN IDs, and management IP address can exist on multiple VDCs. More important, configuration separation in this manner not only secures configurations between VDCs but also isolates a VDC from being affected by an erroneous configuration change in another VDC.

VDC High Availability

The Cisco NX-OS software platform incorporates a high-availability feature set that helps ensure minimal or no effect on the data plane should the control plane fail. Different high-availability service levels are provided, from service restart to stateful supervisor switchover to ISSU without affecting data traffic.

Should a control plane failure occur, the administrator has a set of options that can be configured on a per-VDC basis defining what action will be taken regarding that VDC. Three actions can be configured: restart, bringdown, and reset. The restart option will delete the VDC and then re-create it with the running configuration. This configured action will occur regardless of whether there are dual supervisors or a single supervisor present in the chassis. The bringdown option will simply delete the VDC. The reset option will issue a reset for the active supervisor when there is only a single supervisor in the chassis. If dual supervisors are present, the reset option will force a supervisor switchover.

The default VDC always has a high-availability option of reset assigned to it. Subsequent VDCs created will have a default value of bringdown assigned to them. This value can be changed under configuration control.

Stateful switchover is supported with dual supervisors in the chassis. During the course of normal operation, the primary supervisor will constantly exchange and synchronize its state with the redundant supervisor. A software process (watchdog) is used to monitor the responsiveness of the active (primary) supervisor. Should the primary supervisor fail, a fast switchover is enacted by the system. Failover occurs at both the control plane and data plane layers. At supervisor switchover, the data plane continues to use the Layer 2– and Layer 3–derived forwarding entries simply by maintaining the state written into the hardware. For the control plane, the graceful restart process that is part of nonstop forwarding (NSF) is used to provide failover for Layer 3. For Layer 2, the control plane is maintained by locally stateful PSS mechanisms. This process provides for the following:

- Uninterrupted forwarding during a failover

- Rapid recovery from the failure to a stable operating state

- A nondisruptive recovery mechanism that will not render the network unstable during the recovery process

Table 5-6 shows the result of various policy configurations, depending on single-supervisor or dual-supervisor module configuration.

Table 5-6   *Single-Supervisor vs. Dual-Supervisor Policy Implications*

Module Configuration	Policy	Result
Single supervisor	Bringdown	This policy puts the VDC in the failed state.
	Restart	This policy takes down the VDC processes and interfaces and restarts them using the startup configuration (default policy for nondefault VDC).
	Reload	This policy reloads the supervisor module (default policy for default VDC).

Module Configuration	Policy	Result
Dual supervisor	**Bringdown**	This policy puts the VDC in the failed state.
	Restart	This policy takes down the VDC processes and interfaces and restarts them using the startup configuration.
	Switchover	This policy initiates a supervisor module switchover (default policy for default and nondefault VDC).

ISSU is another important aspect of high availability that has a direct effect on VDCs. ISSU allows the administrator to install and activate a new version of software in a chassis that is running two supervisors. The software upgrade can be applied to the backup supervisor, and then a switchover to that upgraded supervisor is invoked. The other supervisor is then upgraded with the same new set of software; all the while the system maintains data flow without interruption. ISSU cannot be applied on a per-VDC basis. The installed software on the chassis is applicable for all active VDCs.

VDC Management

When several departments share a single physical device and each department has its own administrator, it presents a security concern to share one administrator account with every department admin. VDC user roles comes to the rescue here. Using VDC user roles, each VDC can be managed by a different VDC administrator. An action taken by a VDC administrator in one VDC does not impact users in other VDCs. A VDC administrator within a VDC can create, modify, and delete the configuration for resources allocated to VDC with no impact to other VDCs.

The Cisco NX-OS software has default user roles that the network administrator can assign to the user accounts that administer VDCs. These user roles make available a set of commands the user can execute after logging into the device. All commands the user is not allowed to execute are hidden from the user or return an error. You must have the network-admin or vdc-admin role to create user accounts in a VDC.

The Cisco NX-OS software provides default user roles with different levels of authority for VDC administration as follows:

- **network-admin:** The first user account created on a Cisco Nexus 7000 Series switch in the default VDC is the user "admin." This user is automatically assigned the network-admin role. The network-admin role, which exists only in the default VDC, allows access to all the global configuration commands (such as **reload** and **install**) and all the features on the physical device. A custom user role is not granted access to these network-admin-only commands or to other commands that are scoped admin-only. Only the network administrator can access all the commands related to the physical state of the device. This role can perform system-impacting functions such as upgrading software and running an Ethernet analyzer on the traffic. Network administrators can create and delete VDCs, allocate resources for these VDCs, manage device resources reserved for the VDCs, and configure features within any VDC. Network administrators can also access nondefault VDCs using the **switchto vdc** command from the default VDC. When network administrators switch to a nondefault VDC, they acquire vdc-admin permissions, which are the highest permissions available in a nondefault VDC.

■ **network-operator:** The second default role that exists on Cisco Nexus 7000 Series switches is the network-operator role. This role gives a user read-only rights in the default VDC. The network-operator role, which exists only in the default VDC, allows users to display information for all VDCs on the physical device. Users with network-operator roles can access nondefault VDCs using the **switchto vdc** command from the default VDC. By default, there are no users assigned to this role. The role must be specifically assigned to a user by a user who has network-admin rights.

■ **vdc-admin:** When a VDC is created, the first user account created on that VDC is the user "admin," similar to the way the admin user was created for the whole physical switch in default VDC. The admin user on a nondefault VDC is automatically assigned the vdc-admin role. Users who have the vdc-admin role can configure all features within a VDC. Users with either the network-admin or vdc-admin role can create, modify, or remove user accounts within the VDC. All configurations for the interfaces allocated to a VDC must be performed within the VDC. Users with the vdc-admin role are not allowed to execute any configuration commands related to the physical device.

■ **vdc-operator:** The vdc-operator role has read-only rights for a specific VDC. This role has no rights to any of the other VDCs. Users assigned the vdc-operator role can display information only for the VDC. Users with either the network-admin or vdc-admin role can assign the vdc-operator role to user accounts within the VDC. The vdc-operator role does not allow the user to change the configuration of the VDC. When a user who has the network-admin or network-operator role accesses a nondefault VDC using the **switchto** command, that user will be mapped to a role of the same level in that VDC. A user with the network-admin role will get the VDC-admin role in the nondefault VDCs. A user with the network-operator role will get the VDC-operator role in the nondefault VDCs.

Figure 5-19 shows various default user roles available for VDC administration.

Default VDC access is restricted to a select few administrators who are allowed to modify the global configuration (network-admin role). Few features (such as CoPP and rate limits) can only be configured in the default VDC. If the default VDC is used for data plane traffic, administrators who require default VDC configuration access but not global configuration access should be assigned with the vdc-admin role. This role restricts administrative functions to the default VDC exclusively and prevents access to global VDC configuration commands.

Figure 5-19 *Default User Roles for VDC Administration*

Out-of-Band VDC Management

The Cisco NX-OS software provides a virtual management (mgmt0) interface for out-of-band management for each VDC so that VDCs can be individually managed. You can configure a separate IP address of the virtual management interface from within each VDC by entering the VDC with VDC-admin privileges and assigning an IP address to the virtual mgmt0 interface that is accessed through the physical mgmt0 interface on the supervisor. Because the virtual management interface allows the use of only one management network, the AAA servers and syslog servers can be shared among the VDCs.

Figure 5-20 illustrates that all the VDCs share the management network, but their virtual management interface IP addresses are unique. Also, the services are using shared or separate external services, such as syslog.

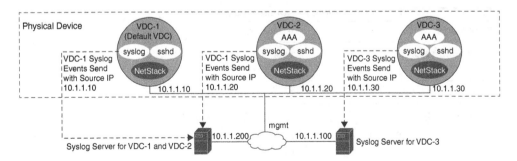

Figure 5-20 *Out-of-Band VDC Management Example*

In-Band VDC Management

VDCs also support in-band management, which allows a VDC to be managed within its specific network. In this case, they function as if they were managed as separate physical devices. You can access the VDC using one of the Ethernet interfaces allocated to the VDC. Because the in-band management allows the use of only separate management networks, separate AAA servers and syslog servers can be used among the VDCs.

Figure 5-21 illustrates how each VDC has management access from its own unique network, and external services such as RADIUS and syslog are unique to each VDC.

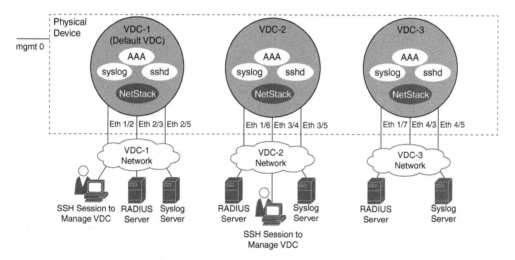

Figure 5-21 *In-Band VDC Management Example*

VDC Configuration

Table 5-7 summarizes the NX-OS CLI commands related to basic VDC configuration and verification.

Table 5-7 *Summary of NX-OS CLI Commands for VDC Configuration and Verification*

Command	Purpose
show resource	Displays the VDC resource configuration for the current VDC.
show vdc [*vdc-name*]	Displays the VDC configuration information.
show vdc detail	Displays the VDC status information.
show running-config {vdc | vdc-all}	Displays the VDC information in the running configuration.
show module	Displays module information.

Command	Purpose
configure terminal	Enters global configuration mode.
vdc {switch | *vdc-name*} **[ha-policy {dual-sup {bringdown	restart	switchover} [single-sup {bringdown	reload	restart}] [id** *vdc-number*] **[template** *template-name*] **[template** *template-name*] **[type storage]**	Creates a VDC and enters the VDC configuration mode. The keywords and arguments are as follows: ■ **switch:** Specifies the default VDC. VDC number 1 is reserved for the default VDC. ■ *vdc-name*: Specifies a nondefault VDC. The VDC name can be a maximum of 32 characters. The VDC name cannot begin with a number. Nondefault VDC numbers are from 2 to 9. The next available number is assigned when a nondefault VDC is created. ■ **id:** Specifies the VDC ID. ■ **template:** Specifies the VDC resource template. The default resource template is used if you do not specify one. ■ **type storage:** Specifies a nondefault VDC as a storage VDC.
limit-resource module-type *module type*	Configures the specified line card type. VDCs support the F1, F2, F2e, M1, M1XL, and M2XL Series module types. **Note** F2e Series modules cannot exist in the same VDC with F1 Series modules. F2 Series modules cannot exist in the same VDC with F1, M1, M1XL, and M2XL Series modules.
[no] allocate interface ethernet *slot/port - last-port*	Allocates a range of interfaces on the same module to the VDC. The *slot* argument specifies the slot, the *port* argument specifies the first interface in the range, and the *last-port* argument specifies the last interface in the range you are allocating.

Command	Purpose
limit-resource vrf minimum *min-value* maximum {*max-value* | equal-to-min}	Specifies the limits for VRF. The **equal-to-min** keyword automatically sets the maximum limit equal to the minimum limit.
show vdc membership [status]	Displays the status of VDC interface membership.
switchto vdc *vdc-name*	Switches to the nondefault VDC.
show user-account	Displays the role configuration.

Examples 5-7 and 5-8 show the basic VDC configuration and verification on a standalone Nexus 7000 Series switch. In Example 5-7, we create a nondefault VDC named Pod8 from the admin VDC and allocate interfaces to it. In Example 5-8, we set up the newly created nondefault VDC and do the final verification from the newly created nondefault VDC Pod8 itself.

Example 5-7   *Creation and Verification of a Nondefault VDC Pod8*

```
! Checking currently configured VDCs. N7K-A with vdc_id 1 is configured as Admin
VDC. Currently 1 Admin and 7 non-default VDCs are configured.
N7K-A# show vdc


Switchwide mode is m1 f1 m1xl f2 m2xl f2e f3 m3s


vdc_id  vdc_name            state          mac               type          lc
------  --------            -----          ----------        ---------     ------
1       N7K-A               active         e4:c7:22:15:2c:41 Admin         None
2       Pod1                active         e4:c7:22:15:2c:42 Ethernet      f3
3       Pod2                active         e4:c7:22:15:2c:43 Ethernet      f3
4       Pod3                active         e4:c7:22:15:2c:44 Ethernet      f3
5       Pod4                active         e4:c7:22:15:2c:45 Ethernet      f3
6       Pod5                active         e4:c7:22:15:2c:46 Ethernet      f3
7       Pod6                active         e4:c7:22:15:2c:47 Ethernet      f3
8       Pod7                active         e4:c7:22:15:2c:48 Ethernet      f3


! Checking configured resources for Admin VDC. In Admin VDC, no of vrfs are limited
to 2048.
N7K-A# show resource

    Resource                Min     Max     Used    Unused   Avail
    --------                ---     ---     ----    ------   -----
    vlan                    16      4094    24      0        4070
    monitor-session         0       2       0       0        2
```

```
    monitor-session-erspan-dst 0        23        0        0        23
    vrf                         2        2048      2        0        2046
    port-channel                0        768       0        0        767
    u4route-mem                 96       96        1        95       95
    u6route-mem                 24       24        1        23       23
    m4route-mem                 58       58        0        58       58
    m6route-mem                 8        8         0        8        8
    monitor-session-inband-src 0        1         0        0        1
    anycast_bundleid            0        16        0        0        16
    monitor-session-mx-excepti 0        1         0        0        1
    monitor-session-extended    0        12        0        0        12
    monitor-rbs-filter          0        12        0        0        12
    monitor-rbs-product         0        12        0        0        12
```

```
! Checking running-config of Admin VDC. Note that the Default VDC was converted to
Admin VDC using the command system admin-vdc.
N7K-A# show running-config vdc | begin admin
system admin-vdc
vdc N7K-A id 1
  cpu-share 5
  limit-resource vlan minimum 16 maximum 4094
  limit-resource monitor-session minimum 0 maximum 2
  limit-resource monitor-session-erspan-dst minimum 0 maximum 23
  limit-resource vrf minimum 2 maximum 2048
  limit-resource port-channel minimum 0 maximum 768
  limit-resource u4route-mem minimum 96 maximum 96
  limit-resource u6route-mem minimum 24 maximum 24
  limit-resource m4route-mem minimum 58 maximum 58
  limit-resource m6route-mem minimum 8 maximum 8
  limit-resource monitor-session-inband-src minimum 0 maximum 1
  limit-resource anycast_bundleid minimum 0 maximum 16
  limit-resource monitor-session-mx-exception-src minimum 0 maximum 1
  limit-resource monitor-session-extended minimum 0 maximum 12
  limit-resource monitor-rbs-filter minimum 0 maximum 12
  limit-resource monitor-rbs-product minimum 0 maximum 12
<output omitted>
```

```
! Checking modules installed on the Nexus 7000 Switch Chassis. All line cards
installed are F3 modules. Since the switch has Sup2E supervisor module, it supports
Admin + 8 Non-default VDCs, so in total 9 VDCs. Currently only Admin + 7 Non-default
VDCs are configured.
N7K-A# show module
```

```
Mod   Ports  Module-Type                           Model               Status
---   -----  ------------------------------------  ------------------  ----------
1     0      Supervisor Module-2                   N7K-SUP2E           active *
3     48     1/10 Gbps Ethernet Module             N7K-F348XP-25       ok
4     48     1/10 Gbps Ethernet Module             N7K-F348XP-25       ok
5     12     10/40 Gbps Ethernet Module            N7K-F312FQ-25       ok
6     12     10/40 Gbps Ethernet Module            N7K-F312FQ-25       ok
7     12     10/40 Gbps Ethernet Module            N7K-F312FQ-25       ok
8     12     10/40 Gbps Ethernet Module            N7K-F312FQ-25       ok


Mod   Sw              Hw
---   --------------  ------
1     8.4(2)          6.1
3     8.4(2)          1.0
4     8.4(2)          1.0
5     8.4(2)          1.1
6     8.4(2)          1.1
7     8.4(2)          1.1
8     8.4(2)          1.1
<output omitted>



! Configuring a new non-default VDC named Pod8.
N7K-A# configure terminal
Enter configuration commands, one per line.  End with CNTL/Z.
N7K-A(config)# vdc Pod8
Note:  Creating VDC, one moment please ...
2022 Jan 21 17:15:03  %$ VDC-9 %$ %SYSLOG-2-SYSTEM_MSG : logflash ONLINE


! Pod8 VDC was automatically assigned vdc_id 9 and supported linecards as m1 m1xl
m2xl and f2e by default.
N7K-A(config-vdc)# show vdc

Switchwide mode is m1 f1 m1xl f2 m2xl f2e f3 m3

vdc_id  vdc_name   state    mac                 type        lc
------  --------   -----    ----------          ---------   ------
1       N7K-A      active   e4:c7:22:15:2c:41   Admin       None
2       Pod1       active   e4:c7:22:15:2c:42   Ethernet    f3
3       Pod2       active   e4:c7:22:15:2c:43   Ethernet    f3
4       Pod3       active   e4:c7:22:15:2c:44   Ethernet    f3
5       Pod4       active   e4:c7:22:15:2c:45   Ethernet    f3
6       Pod5       active   e4:c7:22:15:2c:46   Ethernet    f3
```

```
7         Pod6         active       e4:c7:22:15:2c:47    Ethernet    f3
8         Pod7         active       e4:c7:22:15:2c:48    Ethernet    f3
9         Pod8         active       e4:c7:22:15:2c:49    Ethernet    m1 m1xl m2xl f2e
```

! Since we are having only F3 line cards in the chassis, we will limit the module-
type resource to f3 type modules and allocate ports from module 4 and 8 to the
newly created non-default VDC Pod8.

N7K-A(config-vdc)# **limit-resource module-type f3**

This will cause all ports of unallowed types to be removed from this vdc. Continue
(y/n)? [yes] y

N7K-A(config-vdc)# **allocate interface Ethernet4/25-32**

Moving ports will cause all config associated to them in source vdc to be removed.
Are you sure you want to move the ports (y/n)? [yes] **y**

N7K-A(config-vdc)# **allocate interface Ethernet8/7-12**

Moving ports will cause all config associated to them in source vdc to be removed.
Are you sure you want to move the ports (y/n)? [yes] **y**

! Verifying the module-type resource limitations on the newly created VDC. It is
now correctly reflecting the F3 module-type line card limitation.

N7K-A(config-vdc)# **show vdc**

Switchwide mode is m1 f1 m1xl f2 m2xl f2e f3 m3


```
vdc_id  vdc_name        state        mac               type        lc
------  ---------       -----        ----------        ---------   ------
1       N7K-A           active       e4:c7:22:15:2c:41 Admin       None
2       Pod1            active       e4:c7:22:15:2c:42 Ethernet    f3
3       Pod2            active       e4:c7:22:15:2c:43 Ethernet    f3
4       Pod3            active       e4:c7:22:15:2c:44 Ethernet    f3
5       Pod4            active       e4:c7:22:15:2c:45 Ethernet    f3
6       Pod5            active       e4:c7:22:15:2c:46 Ethernet    f3
7       Pod6            active       e4:c7:22:15:2c:47 Ethernet    f3
8       Pod7            active       e4:c7:22:15:2c:48 Ethernet    f3
9       Pod8            active       e4:c7:22:15:2c:49 Ethernet    f3
```

! Verifying the running-config of the newly created non-default VDC Pod8. Note that
the maximum number of vrf that can be configured on Pod8 VDC is 4096.

N7K-A(config-vdc)# **show running-config vdc | begin Pod8**

vdc Pod8 id 9
  limit-resource module-type f3
  allow feature-set fabricpath
  allow feature-set fabric

```
    cpu-share 5
    allocate interface Ethernet4/25-32
    allocate interface Ethernet8/7-12
    boot-order 1
    limit-resource vlan minimum 16 maximum 4094
    limit-resource monitor-session minimum 0 maximum 2
    limit-resource monitor-session-erspan-dst minimum 0 maximum 23
    limit-resource vrf minimum 2 maximum 4096
    limit-resource port-channel minimum 0 maximum 768
    limit-resource u4route-mem minimum 8 maximum 8
    limit-resource u6route-mem minimum 4 maximum 4
    limit-resource m4route-mem minimum 8 maximum 8
    limit-resource m6route-mem minimum 5 maximum 5
    limit-resource monitor-session-inband-src minimum 0 maximum 1
    limit-resource anycast_bundleid minimum 0 maximum 16
    limit-resource monitor-session-mx-exception-src minimum 0 maximum 1
    limit-resource monitor-session-extended minimum 0 maximum 12
    limit-resource monitor-rbs-filter minimum 0 maximum 12
    limit-resource monitor-rbs-product minimum 0 maximum 12
<output omitted>


! Limiting the maximum vrf numbers to 2048 and verifying the same.
N7K-A(config-vdc)# limit-resource vrf minimum 2 maximum 2048
N7K-A(config-vdc)# show running-config vdc | begin Pod8 | include Pod8|vrf
vdc Pod8 id 9
    limit-resource vrf minimum 2 maximum 2048


! Verifying the unallocated interfaces on the Nexus 7000 Switch Chassis. Note that
unallocated interfaces are assigned to vdc_id 0 and not Admin VDC (vdc_id 1). Pod8
VDC is showing correctly the allocated interfaces in previous steps.
N7K-A(config-vdc)# show vdc membership
Flags : b - breakout port
--------------------------------


vdc_id: 0 vdc_name: Unallocated interfaces:
        Ethernet3/33          Ethernet3/34          Ethernet3/35
        Ethernet3/36          Ethernet3/37          Ethernet3/38
        Ethernet3/39          Ethernet3/40          Ethernet3/41
        Ethernet3/42          Ethernet3/43          Ethernet3/44
        Ethernet3/45          Ethernet3/46          Ethernet3/47
        Ethernet3/48


        Ethernet4/33          Ethernet4/34          Ethernet4/35
        Ethernet4/36          Ethernet4/37          Ethernet4/38
```

```
              Ethernet4/39          Ethernet4/40          Ethernet4/41
              Ethernet4/42          Ethernet4/43          Ethernet4/44
              Ethernet4/45          Ethernet4/46          Ethernet4/47
              Ethernet4/48

<output omitted>


vdc_id: 9 vdc_name: Pod8 interfaces:
              Ethernet4/25          Ethernet4/26          Ethernet4/27
              Ethernet4/28          Ethernet4/29          Ethernet4/30
              Ethernet4/31          Ethernet4/32


              Ethernet8/7           Ethernet8/8           Ethernet8/9
              Ethernet8/10          Ethernet8/11          Ethernet8/12

N7K-A(config-vdc)# end
N7K-A#
```

Example 5-8 *Setup and Verification of the Newly Created Nondefault VDC Pod8*

```
! Switching to newly created non-default VDC Pod8 and doing initial set-up of the
Pod8 VDC. The options are self-explanatory.
N7K-A# switchto vdc Pod8



        ---- System Admin Account Setup ----



Do you want to enforce secure password standard (yes/no) [y]: y

  Enter the password for "admin": erQW4321
  Confirm the password for "admin": erQW4321
WARNING: DES is a weak encryption algorithm and currently the default. This will be
deprecated and AES128 will be made default in an upcoming release.



        ---- Basic System Configuration Dialog VDC: 9 ----


This setup utility will guide you through the basic configuration of
the system. Setup configures only enough connectivity for management
of the system.
```

```
Please register Cisco Nexus7000 Family devices promptly with your
supplier. Failure to register may affect response times for initial
service calls. Nexus7000 devices must be registered to receive
entitled support services.

Press Enter at anytime to skip a dialog. Use ctrl-c at anytime
to skip the remaining dialogs.

Would you like to enter the basic configuration dialog (yes/no): yes


  Create another login account (yes/no) [n]: n

  Configure read-only SNMP community string (yes/no) [n]: n

  Configure read-write SNMP community string (yes/no) [n]: n

  Enter the switch name : Pod8

  Continue with Out-of-band (mgmt0) management configuration? (yes/no) [y]: y

    Mgmt0 IPv4 address : 192.168.10.185

    Mgmt0 IPv4 netmask : 255.255.255.0

  Configure the default gateway? (yes/no) [y]: y

    IPv4 address of the default gateway : 192.168.10.254

  Configure advanced IP options? (yes/no) [n]: n

  Enable the telnet service? (yes/no) [n]: n

  Enable the ssh service? (yes/no) [y]: y

    Type of ssh key you would like to generate (dsa/rsa) [rsa]: rsa

    Number of rsa key bits <1024-4096> [1024]: <Enter>

  Configure default interface layer (L3/L2) [L3]: <Enter>

  Configure default switchport interface state (shut/noshut) [shut]: <Enter>
```

```
The following configuration will be applied:
  password strength-check
  switchname Pod8
vrf context management
ip route 0.0.0.0/0 192.168.10.254
exit
  no feature telnet
  ssh key rsa 1024 force
  feature ssh
  no system default switchport
  system default switchport shutdown
interface mgmt0
ip address 192.168.10.185 255.255.255.0
no shutdown


Would you like to edit the configuration? (yes/no) [n]: n


Use this configuration and save it? (yes/no) [y]: y


Configuration update aborted: This vdc has had a global configuration change since
the last saved config. Please save config in default vdc before proceeding


Cisco Nexus Operating System (NX-OS) Software
TAC support: http://www.cisco.com/tac
Copyright (c) 2002-2020, Cisco Systems, Inc. All rights reserved.
The copyrights to certain works contained in this software are
owned by other third parties and used and distributed under
license. Certain components of this software are licensed under
the GNU General Public License (GPL) version 2.0 or the GNU
Lesser General Public License (LGPL) Version 2.1. A copy of each
such license is available at
http://www.opensource.org/licenses/gpl-2.0.php and
http://www.opensource.org/licenses/lgpl-2.1.php
N7K-A-Pod8#
```

I **show vdc** command from within a non-default VDC displays only the information
about the non-default VDC you are logged in.

```
N7K-A-Pod8# show vdc


Switchwide mode is m1 f1 m1xl f2 m2xl f2e f3 m3


vdc_id   vdc_name      state      mac               type       lc
------   --------      -----      ----------        ---------  ------
9        Pod8          active     e4:c7:22:15:2c:49 Ethernet   f3
```

```
! Verifying detailed vdc configuration of the non-default VDC Pod8. Note the config-
ured vdc ha policy of RESTART and dual-sup ha policy of SWITCHOVER. These are the
defaults for single sup and dual sup module configuration.
N7K-A-Pod8# show vdc detail

Switchwide mode is m1 f1 m1xl f2 m2xl f2e f3 m3

vdc id: 9
vdc name: Pod8
vdc state: active
vdc mac address: e4:c7:22:15:2c:49
vdc ha policy: RESTART
vdc dual-sup ha policy: SWITCHOVER
vdc boot Order: 1
CPU Share: 5
CPU Share Percentage: 11%
vdc create time: Fri Jan 21 17:15:31 2022
vdc reload count: 0
vdc uptime: 0 day(s), 0 hour(s), 39 minute(s), 45 second(s)
vdc restart count: 1
vdc restart time: Fri Jan 21 17:15:31 2022
vdc type: Ethernet
vdc supported linecards: f3


! Verifying interfaces allocated to the VDC.
N7K-A-Pod8# show vdc membership
Flags : b - breakout port
--------------------------------


vdc_id: 9 vdc_name: Pod8 interfaces:
        Ethernet4/25            Ethernet4/26            Ethernet4/27
        Ethernet4/28            Ethernet4/29            Ethernet4/30
        Ethernet4/31            Ethernet4/32


        Ethernet8/7             Ethernet8/8             Ethernet8/9
        Ethernet8/10            Ethernet8/11            Ethernet8/12



! Verifying role assigned to the user configured.
N7K-A-Pod8# show user-account
user:admin
        this user account has no expiry date
        roles:vdc-admin
N7K-A-Pod8#
```

Summary

This chapter discusses Cisco Nexus switch functional planes, Cisco Nexus switch process separation and restartability, virtual routing and forwarding (VRFs) instances, and Cisco Nexus 7000 switch VDC configuration and verification on NX-OS, including the following points:

- Cisco Nexus switch divides the traffic it manages into three functional components or planes: data plane, control plane, and management plane.

- Cisco NX-OS provides isolation between software components so that a failure within one process does not disrupt other processes.

- The Cisco NX-OS service restart feature restarts a faulty service without restarting the supervisor to prevent process-level failures from causing system-level failures.

- A VRF virtualizes the Layer 3 forwarding and routing tables. Each VRF makes routing decisions independent of any other VRFs. Each NX-OS device has a default VRF and a management VRF.

- VDCs partition a single physical device into multiple logical devices that provide fault isolation, management isolation, address allocation isolation, service differentiation domains, and adaptive resource management.

- There are three types of VDCs: default VDC, admin VDC, and nondefault VDC. Nondefault VDCs are further classified as Ethernet VDCs and storage VDCs.

- There are three types of VDC resources: global resources, dedicated resources, and shared resources. VDC resources can also be classified as physical resources and logical resources.

- CPU shares are used to control the CPU resources among the VDCs to prioritize VDC access to the CPU during CPU contention.

- A resource template describes how a set of resources is allocated to a VDC.

- VDCs provide different high-availability features, from service restart to stateful supervisor switchover to ISSU, that help ensure minimal or no effect on the data plane during control plane failures.

- The Cisco NX-OS software provides four default user roles with different levels of authority for VDC administration: network-admin, network-operator, vdc-admin, and vdc-operator.

References

"Cisco Nexus 9000 Series NX-OS Security Configuration Guide, Release 10.2(x)," https://www.cisco.com/c/en/us/td/docs/dcn/nx-os/nexus9000/102x/configuration/Security/cisco-nexus-9000-nx-os-security-configuration-guide-102x.html

"Cisco Nexus 7000 Series NX-OS Security Configuration Guide, Release 8.x," https://www.cisco.com/c/en/us/td/docs/switches/datacenter/nexus7000/sw/security/config/cisco_nexus7000_security_config_guide_8x.html

"Cisco Nexus 9000 Series NX-OS High Availability and Redundancy Guide, Release 10.1(x)," https://www.cisco.com/c/en/us/td/docs/dcn/nx-os/nexus9000/101x/configuration/high-availability-and-redundancy/cisco-nexus-9000-series-nx-os-high-availability-and-redundancy-guide-101x.html

"Cisco Nexus 7000 Series NX-OS High Availability and Redundancy Guide, Release 8.x," https://www.cisco.com/c/en/us/td/docs/switches/datacenter/nexus7000/sw/high-availability/config/cisco_nexus7000_high_availability_config_guide_8x.html

"Cisco Nexus 9000 Series NX-OS Unicast Routing Configuration Guide, Release 10.2(x)," https://www.cisco.com/c/en/us/td/docs/dcn/nx-os/nexus9000/102x/configuration/Unicast-routing/cisco-nexus-9000-series-nx-os-unicast-routing-configuration-guide-release-102x.html

"Cisco Nexus 7000 Series NX-OS Unicast Routing Configuration Guide, Release 8.x," https://www.cisco.com/c/en/us/td/docs/switches/datacenter/nexus7000/sw/unicast/config/cisco_nexus7000_unicast_routing_config_guide_8x.html

"Cisco Nexus 7000 Series Virtual Device Context Configuration Guide, Release 8.x," https://www.cisco.com/c/en/us/td/docs/switches/datacenter/nexus7000/sw/vdc/config/cisco_nexus7000_vdc_config_guide_8x.html

Relevant Cisco Live sessions: http://www.ciscolive.com

Chapter 6

Nexus Switch Routing

Modern-day data centers have rapidly evolving trends and technologies that underscore the need for scale and fast convergence. In order to efficiently route traffic within the data center, Interior Gateway Protocols (IGPs) are deployed either in the network core or within the underlay network. The IGPs commonly used today are Open Shortest Path First Protocol (OSPF) and Enhanced Interior Gateway Routing Protocol (EIGRP). In addition, traditional IP communication allows a host to send packets to a single host (unicast transmission) or to all hosts (broadcast transmission). IP multicast provides a third possibility: allowing a host to send packets to a subset of all hosts as a group transmission. Protocol-Independent Multicast (PIM) is the routing protocol for multicast forwarding.

In this chapter, we will discuss the underlying concepts along with the configuration and verification for the Layer 3 unicast routing protocols in Cisco NX-OS, including RIPv2, EIGRP, and OSPFv2. We will also discuss the multicast fundamentals, including PIM configuration and verification in Cisco NX-OS.

Routing Fundamentals

Layer 3 unicast routing involves two basic activities: determining optimal routing paths and packet switching. You can use routing algorithms to calculate the optimal path from the router to a destination. This calculation depends on the algorithm selected, route metrics, and other considerations such as load balancing and alternate path discovery.

Optimal Path Determination

Routing protocols use a metric to evaluate the best path to the destination. A metric is a standard of measurement, such as a path bandwidth, that routing algorithms use to determine the optimal path to a destination. To aid path determination, routing algorithms initialize and maintain routing tables that contain route information such as the IP destination address, the address of the next router, or the next hop. Destination and next-hop associations tell a router that an IP destination can be reached optimally by sending the packet to a particular router that represents the next hop on the way to the final destination. When a router receives an incoming packet, it checks the destination address and attempts to associate this address with the next hop.

Routing tables can contain other information, such as the data about the desirability of a path. Routers compare metrics to determine optimal routes, and these metrics differ depending on the design of the routing algorithm used.

Routers communicate with one another and maintain their routing tables by transmitting a variety of messages. The routing update message is one such message that consists of all or a portion of a routing table. By analyzing routing updates from all other routers, a router can build a detailed picture of the network topology. A link-state advertisement, which is another example of a message sent between routers, informs other routers of the link state of the sending router. You can also use link information to enable routers to determine optimal routes to network destinations.

A key aspect to measure for any routing algorithm is how much time a router takes to react to network topology changes. When a part of the network changes for any reason, such as a link failure, the routing information in different routers might not match. Some routers will have updated information about the changed topology, while others will still have the old information. The convergence is the amount of time before all routers in the network have updated, matching routing information. The convergence time varies depending on the routing algorithm. Fast convergence minimizes the chance of lost packets caused by inaccurate routing information.

Packet Switching

In packet switching, a host determines that it must send a packet to another host. Having acquired a router address by some means, the source host sends a packet addressed specifically to the router physical (Media Access Control [MAC] layer) address but with the IP (network layer) address of the destination host.

The router examines the destination IP address and tries to find the IP address in the routing table. If the router does not know how to forward the packet, it typically drops the packet. If the router knows how to forward the packet, it changes the destination MAC address to the MAC address of the next-hop router and transmits the packet.

The next hop might be the ultimate destination host or another router that executes the same switching decision process. As the packet moves through the internetwork, its physical address changes but its protocol address remains constant, as shown in Figure 6-1.

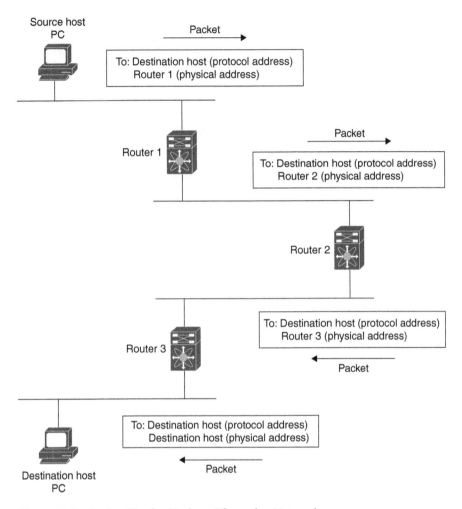

Figure 6-1 *Packet Header Updates Through a Network*

Routing Metrics

Routing algorithms use many different metrics to determine the best route. Sophisticated routing algorithms can base route selection on multiple metrics.

Path Length

The path length is the most common routing metric. Some routing protocols allow you to assign arbitrary costs to each network link. In this case, the path length is the sum of the costs associated with each link traversed. Other routing protocols define the hop count, which is a metric that specifies the number of passes through internetworking products, such as routers, that a packet must take from a source to a destination.

Reliability

The reliability, in the context of routing algorithms, is the dependability (in terms of the bit-error rate) of each network link. Some network links might go down more often than others. After a network fails, certain network links might be repaired more easily or more quickly than other links. The reliability factors you can take into account when assigning the reliability rating are arbitrary numeric values you usually assign to network links.

Routing Delay

The routing delay is the length of time required to move a packet from a source to a destination through the internetwork. The delay depends on many factors, including the bandwidth of intermediate network links, the port queues at each router along the way, the network congestion on all intermediate network links, and the physical distance the packet must travel. Because the routing delay is a combination of several important variables, it is a common and useful metric.

Bandwidth

The bandwidth is the available traffic capacity of a link. For example, a 10-Gigabit Ethernet link is preferable to a 1-Gigabit Ethernet link. Although the bandwidth is the maximum attainable throughput on a link, routes through links with greater bandwidth do not necessarily provide better routes than routes through slower links. For example, if a faster link is busier, the actual time required to send a packet to the destination could be greater.

Load

The load is the degree to which a network resource, such as a router, is busy. You can calculate the load in a variety of ways, including CPU usage and packets processed per second. Monitoring these parameters on a continual basis can be resource intensive.

Communication Cost

The communication cost is a measure of the operating cost to route over a link. The communication cost is another important metric, especially if you do not care about performance as much as operating expenditures. For example, the line delay for a private line might be longer than a public line, but you can send packets over your private line rather than through the public lines, which cost money for usage time.

Router IDs

Each routing process has an associated router ID. You can configure the router ID to any interface in the system. If you do not configure the router ID, Cisco NX-OS selects the router ID based on the following criteria:

- Cisco NX-OS prefers loopback0 over any other interface. If loopback0 does not exist, Cisco NX-OS prefers the first loopback interface over any other interface type.

- If you have not configured a loopback interface, Cisco NX-OS uses the first interface in the configuration file as the router ID. If you configure any loopback interface after Cisco NX-OS selects the router ID, the loopback interface becomes the router ID. If the loopback interface is not loopback0 and you configure loopback0 with an IP address, the router ID changes to the IP address of loopback0.

- If the IP address of the interface the router ID is based on changes, that new IP address becomes the router ID. If any other interface changes its IP address, there is no router ID change.

Autonomous Systems

An autonomous system (AS) is a portion of an internetwork under common administrative authority that is regulated by a particular set of administrative guidelines. Autonomous systems divide global external networks into individual routing domains, where local routing policies are applied. This organization simplifies routing domain administration and simplifies consistent policy configuration. Each autonomous system can support multiple interior routing protocols that dynamically exchange routing information through route redistribution.

The autonomous system number assignment for public and private networks is governed by the Internet Assigned Number Authority (IANA). A public autonomous system can be directly connected to the Internet. This autonomous system number (AS number) identifies both the routing process and the autonomous system. Private autonomous system numbers are used for internal routing domains but must be translated by the router for traffic that is routed out to the Internet. You should not configure routing protocols to advertise private autonomous system numbers to external networks. By default, Cisco NX-OS does not remove private autonomous system numbers from routing updates.

Administrative Distance

An administrative distance is a rating of the trustworthiness of a routing information source. A higher value indicates a lower trust rating. Typically, a route can be learned through more than one protocol. Administrative distance is used to distinguish between routes learned from more than one protocol. The route with the lowest administrative distance is installed in the IP routing table.

Table 6-1 shows the default administrative distance for selected routing information sources.

Table 6-1 *Default Administrative Distance*

Route Source	Default Administrative Distance
Connected network	0
Static route	1
EIGRP	90
OSPF	110
RIPv2	120
External EIGRP	170
Unknown or unbelievable	255 (will not be used to pass traffic)

Routing protocols can use load balancing or equal-cost multipath (ECMP) to share traffic across multiple paths. If the router receives and installs multiple paths with the same administrative distance and cost to a destination, load balancing can occur. Load balancing distributes the traffic across all the paths, sharing the load. The number of paths used is limited by the number of entries the routing protocol puts in the routing table. ECMP does not guarantee equal load balancing across all links. It guarantees only that a particular flow will choose one particular next hop at any point in time.

If you have multiple routing protocols configured in your network, you can configure these protocols to share routing information by configuring route redistribution in each protocol. The router that is redistributing routes from another protocol sets a fixed route metric for those redistributed routes, which prevents incompatible route metrics between the different routing protocols. For example, routes redistributed from EIGRP into OSPF are assigned a fixed link cost metric that OSPF understands. Route redistribution also uses an administrative distance to distinguish between routes learned from two different routing protocols. The preferred routing protocol is given a lower administrative distance so that its routes are picked over routes from another protocol with a higher administrative distance assigned.

Routing Algorithms

Routing algorithms determine how a router gathers and reports reachability information, how it deals with topology changes, and how it determines the optimal route to a destination. Various types of routing algorithms exist, and each algorithm has a different impact on network and router resources. Routing algorithms use a variety of metrics that affect calculation of optimal routes. You can classify routing algorithms in the following major categories.

Static Routes and Dynamic Routing Protocols

Static routes are route table entries that you manually configure. These static routes do not change unless you reconfigure them. Static routes are simple to design and work well in environments where network traffic is relatively predictable and where network design is relatively simple.

Because static routing systems cannot react to network changes, you should not use them for large, constantly changing networks. Most routing protocols today use dynamic routing algorithms that adjust to changing network circumstances by analyzing incoming routing update messages. If the message indicates that a network change has occurred, the routing software recalculates routes and sends out new routing update messages. These messages permeate the network, triggering routers to rerun their algorithms and change their routing tables accordingly.

Interior and Exterior Gateway Protocols

You can separate networks into unique routing domains or autonomous systems. Routing protocols that route between autonomous systems are called exterior gateway protocols (EGPs) or interdomain protocols. The Border Gateway Protocol (BGP) is an example of an exterior gateway protocol (IGPs). Routing protocols used within an autonomous system are called interior gateway protocols or intradomain protocols. RIPv2, EIGRP, and OSPF are examples of interior gateway protocols.

Figure 6-2 shows various interior and exterior gateway protocols.

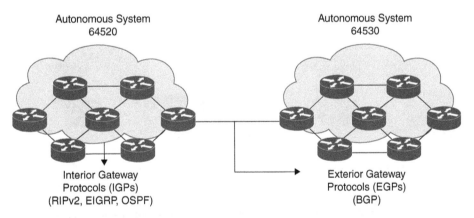

Figure 6-2 *Interior and Exterior Gateway Protocols*

Distance Vector and Link-State Protocols

Distance vector protocols use distance vector algorithms (also known as Bellman-Ford algorithms) that call for each router to send all or some portion of its routing table to its neighbors. Distance vector algorithms define routes by distance (for example, the number of hops to the destination) and direction (for example, the next-hop router). These routes are then broadcast to the directly connected neighbor routers. Each router uses these updates to verify and update the routing tables.

Figure 6-3 shows a routing table example for a distance vector protocol.

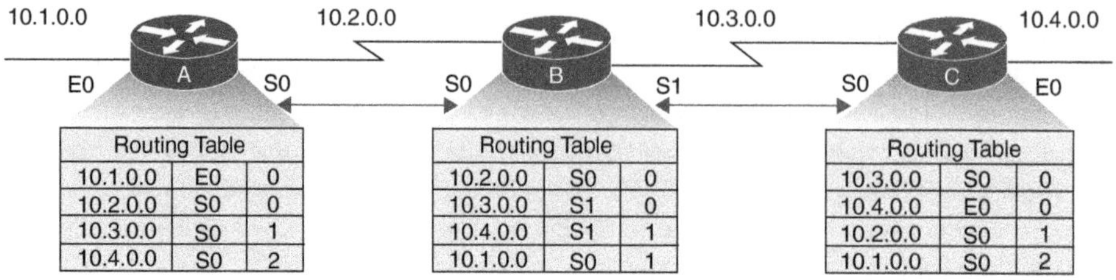

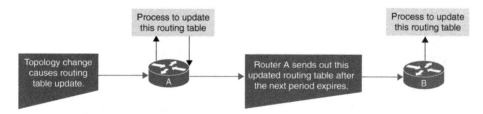

Figure 6-3   *Distance Vector Protocol—Routing Table Example*

To prevent routing loops, most distance vector algorithms use split horizon with poison reverse, which means that the routes learned from an interface are set as unreachable and advertised back along the interface that they were learned on during the next periodic update. This process prevents the router from seeing its own route updates coming back.

Distance vector algorithms send updates at fixed intervals but can also send updates in response to changes in route metric values. These triggered updates can speed up the route convergence time. The Routing Information Protocol (RIP) is a distance vector protocol.

Figure 6-4 illustrates a distance vector protocol update mechanism.

Figure 6-4   *Distance Vector Protocol—Update Mechanism*

The link-state protocols, also known as shortest path first (SPF), use the Dijkstra algorithm to find the shortest path between two nodes in the network. Each router shares information with neighboring routers and builds a link-state advertisement (LSA) that contains information about each link and directly connected neighbor routers. Each LSA has a sequence number. When a router receives an LSA and updates its link-state database, the LSA is flooded to all adjacent neighbors. If a router receives two LSAs with the same sequence number (from the same router), the router does not flood the last LSA it received to its neighbors because it wants to prevent an LSA update loop. Because the router floods the LSAs immediately after it receives them, the convergence time for link-state protocols is minimized.

Figure 6-5 illustrates the link-state protocol update and convergence mechanism.

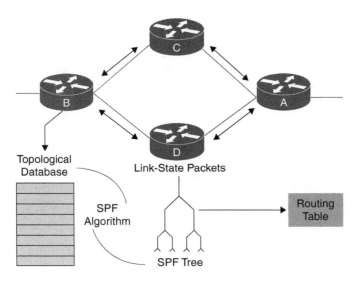

Figure 6-5 *Link-State Protocol—Update and Convergence Mechanism*

Discovering neighbors and establishing adjacency is an important part of a link-state protocol. Neighbors are discovered using special Hello packets that also serve as keepalive notifications to each neighbor router. Adjacency is the establishment of a common set of operating parameters for the link-state protocol between neighbor routers.

The LSAs received by a router are added to the router's link-state database. Each entry consists of the following parameters:

■ Router ID (for the router that originated the LSA)

■ Neighbor ID

■ Link cost

■ Sequence number of the LSA

■ Age of the LSA entry

The router runs the SPF algorithm on the link-state database, building the shortest path tree for that router. This SPF tree is used to populate the routing table. In link-state algorithms, each router builds a picture of the entire network in its routing tables. The link-state algorithms send small updates everywhere, while distance vector algorithms send larger updates only to neighboring routers. Because they converge more quickly, link-state algorithms are less likely to cause routing loops than distance vector algorithms. However, link-state algorithms require more CPU power and memory than distance vector algorithms, and they can be more expensive to implement and support. Link-state protocols are generally more scalable than distance vector protocols. OSPF is an example of a link-state protocol.

Table 6-2 compares a distance vector protocol with a link-state protocol.

Table 6-2 *Distance Vector vs. Link-State Protocol*

Distance Vector Protocol	Link-State Protocol
Routers communicate with neighbor routers, advertising networks as a measure of distance and direction/vector.	Routers communicate with all other routers, exchanging link-state information to build a topology of the entire network.
Each router is aware only of its immediate neighbors.	Each router is aware of all other routers in the area.
Uses Bellman-Ford algorithm to calculate the shortest path.	Uses Dijkstra algorithm to calculate the shortest path.
Frequent updates of entire routing table.	Event-triggered partial updates.
Convergence is slow.	Convergence is fast.
Examples include RIPv2 and EIGRP.	Examples include OSPF and IS-IS.

Cisco NX-OS Forwarding Architecture

The Cisco NX-OS forwarding architecture is responsible for processing all routing updates and populating the forwarding information to all modules in the chassis. The Cisco NX-OS forwarding architecture consists of multiple components, as shown in Figure 6-6.

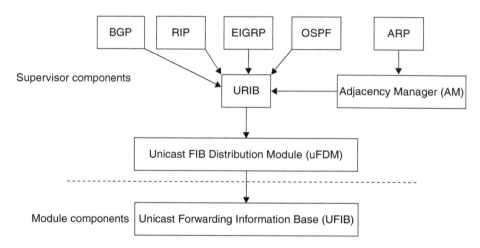

Figure 6-6 *Cisco NX-OS Forwarding Architecture*

The unicast routing information base (URIB) exists on the active supervisor. It maintains the routing table with directly connected routes, static routes, and routes learned from dynamic unicast routing protocols. The unicast RIB also collects adjacency information from sources such as the Address Resolution Protocol (ARP). The unicast RIB determines the best next hop for a given route and populates the FIB by using the services of the unicast forwarding information base (FIB) distribution module (uFDM). Each dynamic routing protocol must update the unicast RIB for any route that has timed out. The unicast RIB then deletes that route and recalculates the best next hop for that route (if an alternate path is available).

The adjacency manager (AM) exists on the active supervisor and maintains adjacency information for different protocols, including ARP, Neighbor Discovery Protocol (NDP), and static configuration. The most basic adjacency information is the Layer 3 to Layer 2 address mapping discovered by these protocols. Outgoing Layer 2 packets use the adjacency information to complete the Layer 2 header. The adjacency manager can trigger ARP requests to find a particular Layer 3 to Layer 2 mapping. The new mapping becomes available when the corresponding ARP reply is received and processed. For IPv6, the adjacency manager finds the Layer 3 to Layer 2 mapping information from NDP.

The unicast FIB distribution module (uFDM) exists on the active supervisor and distributes the forwarding path information from the unicast RIB and other sources. The unicast RIB generates forwarding information that the unicast FIB (UFIB) programs into the hardware forwarding tables on the standby supervisor and the modules. The unicast FDM also downloads the FIB information to newly inserted modules. The unicast FDM gathers adjacency information, rewrite information, and other platform-dependent information when updating routes in the unicast FIB. The adjacency and rewrite information consists of interface, next hop, and Layer 3 to Layer 2 mapping information. The interface and next-hop information is received in route updates from the unicast RIB. The Layer 3 to Layer 2 mapping is received from the adjacency manager.

The UFIB exists on supervisors and switching modules and builds the information used for the hardware forwarding engine. The UFIB receives route updates from the uFDM and sends the information to be programmed in the hardware forwarding engine. The UFIB controls the addition, deletion, and modification of routes, paths, and adjacencies. The unicast FIBs are maintained on a per-VRF and per-address-family basis (that is, one for IPv4 and one for IPv6 for each configured VRF; for more about VRFs, refer to Chapter 5, "Switch Virtualization"). Based on route update messages, the UFIB maintains a per-VRF prefix and next-hop adjacency information database. The next-hop adjacency data structure contains the next-hop IP address and the Layer 2 rewrite information. Multiple prefixes could share a next-hop adjacency information structure.

Hardware Forwarding and Software Forwarding

Cisco NX-OS supports distributed packet forwarding. The ingress port takes relevant information from the packet header and passes the information to the local switching engine. The local switching engine does the Layer 3 lookup and uses this information to rewrite the packet header. The ingress module forwards the packet to the egress port. If the egress port is on a different module, the packet is forwarded using the switch fabric to the egress module. The egress module does not participate in the Layer 3 forwarding decision.

The software forwarding path in Cisco NX-OS is used mainly to handle features that are not supported in the hardware or to handle errors encountered during the hardware processing. Typically, packets with IP options or packets that need fragmentation are passed to the CPU on the active supervisor. All packets that should be switched in the software or terminated go to the supervisor. The supervisor uses the information provided by the unicast RIB and the adjacency manager to make the forwarding decisions. The module is not involved in the software forwarding path. Software forwarding is controlled by control plane policies and rate limiters.

RIPv2 on NX-OS

The Routing Information Protocol (RIP) is a distance vector protocol that uses a hop count as its metric. The hop count is the number of routers a packet can traverse before reaching its destination. A directly connected network has a metric of 1; an unreachable network has a metric of 16. This small range of metrics makes RIP an unsuitable routing protocol for large networks. RIP is an Interior Gateway Protocol (IGP), which means that it performs routing within a single autonomous system. RIP uses User Datagram Protocol (UDP) data packets to exchange routing information. RIPv2 supports IPv4.

RIP uses the following two message types:

■ **Request:** Sent to the multicast address 224.0.0.9 to request route updates from other RIP-enabled routers.

■ **Response:** Sent every 30 seconds by default. The router also sends response messages after it receives a request message. The response message contains the entire RIP route table. RIP sends multiple response packets for a request if the RIP routing table cannot fit in one response packet.

RIP uses an optional authentication feature supported by the RIPv2 protocol. You can configure authentication on RIP messages to prevent unauthorized or invalid routing updates in your network. Cisco NX-OS supports a simple password or an MD5 authentication digest. RIPv2 supports key-based authentication using keychains for password management. Keychains are nothing but a sequence of keys.

You can use split horizon to ensure that RIP never advertises a route out of the interface where it was learned. Split horizon is a method that controls the sending of RIP update and query packets. When you enable split horizon on an interface, Cisco NX-OS does not send update packets for destinations that were learned from this interface. Controlling update packets in this manner reduces the possibility of routing loops. You can use split horizon with poison reverse to configure an interface to advertise routes learned by RIP as unreachable over the interface that learned the routes. By default, split horizon is enabled on all interfaces.

You can configure a route policy on a RIP-enabled interface to filter the RIP updates. Cisco NX-OS updates the route table with only those routes that the route policy allows.

You can configure multiple summary aggregate addresses for a specified interface. Route summarization simplifies route tables by replacing a number of more-specific addresses with an address that represents all the specific addresses. For example, you can replace 10.1.1.0/24, 10.1.2.0/24, and 10.1.3.0/24 with one summary address, 10.1.0.0/16. If more specific routes are in the routing table, RIP advertises the summary address from the interface with a metric equal to the maximum metric of the more specific routes.

You can use RIP to redistribute static routes or routes from other protocols. You must configure a route map with the redistribution to control which routes are passed into RIP. A route policy allows you to filter routes based on attributes such as the destination, origination protocol, route type, route tag, and so on. Whenever you redistribute routes into a RIP routing domain, Cisco NX-OS does not, by default, redistribute the default route into the RIP routing domain. You can generate a default route into RIP, which can be controlled by a route policy. You also configure the default metric that is used for all imported routes into RIP.

You can use load balancing to allow a router to distribute traffic over all the router network ports that are the same distance from the destination address. Load balancing increases the usage of network segments and increases effective network bandwidth. Cisco NX-OS supports the Equal-Cost Multipath (ECMP) feature with up to 16 equal-cost paths in the RIP route table and the unicast RIB. You can configure RIP to load-balance traffic across some or all of those paths.

Cisco NX-OS supports stateless restarts for RIP. After a reboot or supervisor switcho-ver, Cisco NX-OS applies the running configuration, and RIP immediately sends request packets to repopulate its routing table.

Cisco NX-OS supports multiple instances of RIP that run on the same system. RIP sup-ports virtual routing and forwarding (VRF) instances. VRFs exist within virtual device contexts (VDCs). You can configure up to four RIP instances on a VDC. By default, Cisco NX-OS places you in the default VDC and default VRF unless you specifically configure another VDC and VRF.

Note   Cisco NX-OS does not support RIPv1. If Cisco NX-OS receives a RIPv1 packet, it logs a message and drops the packet. In this chapter, RIP and RIPv2 are used interchangeably.

Configuring basic RIP is a multistep process. The following are the steps to enable a basic configuration of RIP:

Step 1.   Enable RIP.

Step 2.   Configure an RIP instance.

Step 3.   Assign interfaces to the RIP instance.

Step 4.   Configure authentication in RIP (optional).

Step 5.   Verify the RIP operation.

Table 6-3 summarizes the NX-OS CLI commands that are related to basic RIPv2 configuration and verification.

Table 6-3   *Summary of NX-OS CLI Commands for RIPv2 Configuration and Verification*

Command	Purpose
configure terminal	Enters global configuration mode.
[no] feature rip	Enables the RIP feature.
	The **no** option disables the RIP feature and removes all associated configurations.
[no] router rip *instance-tag*	Creates a new RIP instance with the configured *instance-tag*.
interface *interface-type slot/port*	Enters interface configuration mode.
ip router rip *instance-tag*	Associates this interface with an RIP instance.
key chain *name*	Creates the keychain and enters keychain configuration mode.
key *key-ID*	Enters key configuration mode for the key that you specified. The *key-ID* argument must be a whole number between 0 and 65535.
key-string [*encryption-type*] *text-string*	Configures the text string for the key. The *text-string* argument is alphanumeric, case-sensitive, and supports special characters. The *encryption-type* argument can be one of the following values: ■ **0:** The *text-string* argument you enter is unencrypted text. This is the default. ■ **7:** The *text-string* argument you enter is encrypted. The encryption method is a Cisco proprietary method. This option is useful when you are entering a text string based on the encrypted output of a **show key chain** command that you ran on another Cisco NX-OS device.
ip rip authentication mode {text | md5}	Sets the authentication type for RIP on this interface as cleartext or MD5 authentication digest.
ip rip authentication key-chain *key*	Configures the authentication key used for RIP on this interface.
show feature	Displays enabled and disabled features.

Command	Purpose
show ip rip [instance *instance-tag*] neighbor [*interface-type number*] [vrf *vrf-name*]	Displays the RIP neighbor table.
show ip route	Displays routes from the unicast routing information base (URIB).
show ip rip [instance *instance-tag*] route [*ip-prefix/length* [longer-prefixes | shorter-prefixes]] [summary] [vrf *vrf-name*]	Displays the RIP route table.
show ip rip [instance *instance-tag*] interface [*interface-type slot/port*] [vrf *vrf-name*] [detail]	Displays RIP information for an interface.

Examples 6-1 through 6-4 show the basic RIPv2 configuration and verification on the sample topology shown in Figure 6-7. In this example, we will configure the MD5 authentication on the interface connecting the two Nexus switches.

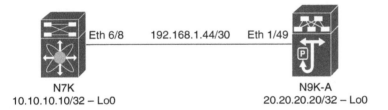

Eth 6/8   192.168.1.44/30   Eth 1/49

N7K   N9K-A
10.10.10.10/32 – Lo0   20.20.20.20/32 – Lo0

Figure 6-7   *Sample Topology for RIPv2 Configuration and Verification*

Example 6-1   *RIPv2 Configuration on N7K*

```
! Verifying if the interfaces are configured correctly.
N7K# show ip interface brief
IP Interface Status for VRF "default"(1)
Interface         IP Address       Interface Status
Lo0               10.10.10.10      protocol-up/link-up/admin-up
Eth6/8            192.168.1.45     protocol-up/link-up/admin-up


! Verifying if the RIP feature is enabled or not.
N7K# configure terminal
Enter configuration commands, one per line.  End with CNTL/Z.
```

```
N7K(config)# show feature | in rip
rip               1        disabled
rip               2        disabled
rip               3        disabled
rip               4        disabled


! Since RIP feature was not enabled, Enabling RIP feature, and confirming the same.
N7K(config)# feature rip
N7K(config)# show feature | in rip
rip               1        enabled(not-running)
rip               2        enabled(not-running)
rip               3        enabled(not-running)
rip               4        enabled(not-running)


! Configuring RIP instance and keychain named MYKEYS having only one key with key-
string cisco.
N7K(config)# router rip DCFNDU
N7K(config-router)# key chain MYKEYS
N7K(config-keychain)# key 1
N7K(config-keychain-key)# key-string cisco
N7K(config-keychain-key)# end


! Enabling RIP and configuring MD5 authentication using keychain MYKEYS on interface
connected to N9K-A.
N7K# configure terminal
Enter configuration commands, one per line.  End with CNTL/Z.
N7K(config)# interface Ethernet 6/8
N7K(config-if)# ip router rip DCFNDU
N7K(config-if)# ip rip authentication mode md5
N7K(config-if)# ip rip authentication key-chain MYKEYS


! Enabling RIP on Loopback interface.
N7K(config-if)# interface Loopback 0
N7K(config-if)# ip router rip DCFNDU
N7K(config-if)# end
N7K#
```

Example 6-2   *RIPv2 Configuration on N9K-A*

```
! Verifying if the interfaces are configured correctly.
N9K-A# show ip interface brief

IP Interface Status for VRF "default"(1)
Interface         IP Address      Interface Status
```

```
Lo0                     20.20.20.20    protocol-up/link-up/admin-up
Eth1/49                 192.168.1.46   protocol-up/link-up/admin-up
```

! Verifying if the RIP feature is enabled or not.
```
N9K-A# configure terminal
Enter configuration commands, one per line. End with CNTL/Z.
N9K-A(config)# show feature | in rip
rip                  1             disabled
rip                  2             disabled
rip                  3             disabled
rip                  4             disabled
```

! Since RIP feature was not enabled, Enabling RIP feature, and confirming the same.
```
N9K-A(config)# feature rip
N9K-A(config)# show feature | in rip
rip                  1             enabled(not-running)
rip                  2             enabled(not-running)
rip                  3             enabled(not-running)
rip                  4             enabled(not-running)
```

! Configuring RIP instance and keychain named MYKEYS having only one key with key-string cisco.
```
N9K-A(config)# router rip DCFNDU
N9K-A(config-router)# key chain MYKEYS
N9K-A(config-keychain)# key 1
N9K-A(config-keychain-key)# key-string cisco
N9K-A(config-keychain-key)# end
```

! Enabling RIP and configuring MD5 authentication using keychain MYKEYS on interface connected to N7K.
```
N9K-A# configure terminal
Enter configuration commands, one per line. End with CNTL/Z.
N9K-A(config)# interface Ethernet 1/49
N9K-A(config-if)# ip router rip DCFNDU
N9K-A(config-if)# ip rip authentication mode md5
N9K-A(config-if)# ip rip authentication key-chain MYKEYS
```

! Enabling RIP on Loopback interface.
```
N9K-A(config-if)# interface Loopback 0
N9K-A(config-if)# ip router rip DCFNDU
N9K-A(config-if)# end
N9K-A#
```

Example 6-3   *RIPv2 Verification on N7K*

```
! Verifying RIP neighbor.
N7K# show ip rip neighbor
Process Name "rip-DCFNDU" VRF "default"
RIP Neighbor Information (number of neighbors = 1)
('dead' means more than 300 seconds ago)

192.168.1.46, Ethernet6/8
    Last Response sent/received: 00:00:17/00:00:23
    Last Request  sent/received: dead/dead
    Bad Pkts Received: 0
    Bad Routes Received: 0

! Verifying unicast routing table. N9K-A Loopback 0 interface is learned via RIP.
N7K# show ip route
IP Route Table for VRF "default"
'*' denotes best ucast next-hop
'**' denotes best mcast next-hop
'[x/y]' denotes [preference/metric]
'%<string>' in via output denotes VRF <string>

10.10.10.0/24, ubest/mbest: 1/0 time, attached
    *via 10.10.10.10, Lo0, [0/0], 6d00h, direct
10.10.10.10/32, ubest/mbest: 1/0 time, attached
    *via 10.10.10.10, Lo0, [0/0], 6d00h, local
20.20.20.20/32, ubest/mbest: 1/0 time
    *via 192.168.1.46, Eth6/8, [120/2], 00:07:56, rip-DCFNDU, rip
192.168.1.44/30, ubest/mbest: 1/0 time, attached
    *via 192.168.1.45, Eth6/8, [0/0], 6d00h, direct
192.168.1.45/32, ubest/mbest: 1/0 time, attached
    *via 192.168.1.45, Eth6/8, [0/0], 6d00h, local

! Verifying interfaces configured for RIP.
N7K# show ip rip interface
Process Name "rip-DCFNDU" VRF "default"
RIP-configured interface information

Ethernet6/8, protocol-up/link-up/admin-up, RIP state : up
  address/mask 192.168.1.45/30, metric 1, split-horizon
  Authentication Mode: md5  Keychain: MYKEYS
```

```
loopback0, protocol-up/link-up/admin-up, RIP state : up
  address/mask 10.10.10.10/24, metric 1, split-horizon

! Verifying end-to-end connectivity from N7K to N9K-A.
N7K# ping 20.20.20.20 source 10.10.10.10
PING 20.20.20.20 (20.20.20.20) from 10.10.10.10: 56 data bytes
64 bytes from 20.20.20.20: icmp_seq=0 ttl=254 time=1.003 ms
64 bytes from 20.20.20.20: icmp_seq=1 ttl=254 time=0.782 ms
64 bytes from 20.20.20.20: icmp_seq=2 ttl=254 time=0.797 ms
64 bytes from 20.20.20.20: icmp_seq=3 ttl=254 time=0.79 ms
64 bytes from 20.20.20.20: icmp_seq=4 ttl=254 time=0.752 ms

--- 20.20.20.20 ping statistics ---
5 packets transmitted, 5 packets received, 0.00% packet loss
round-trip min/avg/max = 0.752/0.824/1.003 ms
N7K#
```

Example 6-4 *RIPv2 Verification on N9K-A*

```
! Verifying RIP neighbor.
N9K-A# show ip rip neighbor
Process Name "rip-DCFNDU" VRF "default"
RIP Neighbor Information (number of neighbors = 1)
('dead' means more than 300 seconds ago)

192.168.1.45, Ethernet1/49
    Last Response sent/received: 00:00:22/00:00:18
    Last Request  sent/received: dead/never
    Bad Pkts Received: 0
    Bad Routes Received: 0
! Verifying unicast routing table. N7K Loopback 0 interface is learned via RIP.
N9K-A# show ip route
IP Route Table for VRF "default"
'*' denotes best ucast next-hop
'**' denotes best mcast next-hop
'[x/y]' denotes [preference/metric]
'%<string>' in via output denotes VRF <string>

10.10.10.0/24, ubest/mbest: 1/0
    *via 192.168.1.45, Eth1/49, [120/2], 00:09:07, rip-DCFNDU, rip
20.20.20.20/32, ubest/mbest: 2/0, attached
    *via 20.20.20.20, Lo0, [0/0], 6d00h, local
```

```
    *via 20.20.20.20, Lo0, [0/0], 6d00h, direct
192.168.1.44/30, ubest/mbest: 1/0, attached
    *via 192.168.1.46, Eth1/49, [0/0], 6d00h, direct
192.168.1.46/32, ubest/mbest: 1/0, attached
    *via 192.168.1.46, Eth1/49, [0/0], 6d00h, local

! Verifying interfaces configured for RIP.
N9K-A# show ip rip interface
Process Name "rip-DCFNDU" VRF "default"
RIP-configured interface information

Ethernet1/49, protocol-up/link-up/admin-up, RIP state : up
  address/mask 192.168.1.46/30, metric 1, split-horizon
  Authentication Mode: md5  Keychain: MYKEYS
loopback0, protocol-up/link-up/admin-up, RIP state : up
  address/mask 20.20.20.20/32, metric 1, split-horizon

! Verifying end-to-end connectivity from N9K-A to N7K.
N9K-A# ping 10.10.10.10 source 20.20.20.20
PING 10.10.10.10 (10.10.10.10) from 20.20.20.20: 56 data bytes
64 bytes from 10.10.10.10: icmp_seq=0 ttl=254 time=0.997 ms
64 bytes from 10.10.10.10: icmp_seq=1 ttl=254 time=0.666 ms
64 bytes from 10.10.10.10: icmp_seq=2 ttl=254 time=0.639 ms
64 bytes from 10.10.10.10: icmp_seq=3 ttl=254 time=0.613 ms
64 bytes from 10.10.10.10: icmp_seq=4 ttl=254 time=0.632 ms

--- 10.10.10.10 ping statistics ---
```

EIGRP on NX-OS

The Enhanced Interior Gateway Routing Protocol (EIGRP) is a unicast routing protocol that has the characteristics of both distance vector and link-state routing protocols. EIGRP relies on its neighbors to provide the routes. It constructs the network topology from the routes advertised by its neighbors, similar to a link-state protocol, and uses this information to select loop-free paths to destinations.

EIGRP sends out periodic Hello messages for neighbor discovery. Once EIGRP learns a new neighbor, it sends a one-time update of all the local EIGRP routes and route metrics. The receiving EIGRP router calculates the route distance based on the received metrics and the locally assigned cost of the link to that neighbor. After this initial full route table update, EIGRP sends incremental updates to only those neighbors affected by the route change. This process speeds convergence and minimizes the bandwidth used by EIGRP.

EIGRP uses Reliable Transport Protocol, which includes the following message types:

- **Hello:** Used for neighbor discovery and recovery. By default, EIGRP sends a periodic multicast Hello message on the local network at the configured hello interval. By default, the hello interval is 5 seconds.

- **Acknowledgment:** Used to verify reliable reception of updates, queries, and replies.

- **Updates:** Sent to affected neighbors when routing information changes. Updates include the route destination, address mask, and route metrics such as delay and bandwidth. The update information is stored in the EIGRP topology table.

- **Queries and replies:** Sent as part of the Diffusing Update Algorithm (DUAL) used by EIGRP.

DUAL calculates the routing information based on the destination networks in the topology table. The topology table includes the following information:

- **IPv4 address/mask:** The network address and network mask for this destination.

- **Successors:** The IP address and local interface connection for all feasible successors or neighbors that advertise a shorter distance to the destination than the current feasible distance.

- **Feasibility distance (FD):** The lowest calculated distance to the destination. The feasibility distance is the sum of the advertised distance from a neighbor plus the cost of the link to that neighbor.

DUAL uses the distance metric to select efficient, loop-free paths. DUAL selects routes to insert into the unicast RIB based on feasible successors. When a topology change occurs, DUAL looks for feasible successors in the topology table. If there are feasible successors, DUAL selects the feasible successor with the lowest feasible distance and inserts that into the unicast RIB, thus avoiding unnecessary recomputation. When there are no feasible successors but there are neighbors advertising the destination, DUAL transitions from the passive state to the active state and triggers a recomputation to determine a new successor or next-hop router to the destination. The amount of time required to recompute the route affects the convergence time. EIGRP sends Query messages to all neighbors, searching for feasible successors. Neighbors that have a feasible successor send a Reply message with that information. Neighbors that do not have feasible successors trigger a DUAL recomputation.

When a topology change occurs, EIGRP sends an Update message with only the changed routing information to affected neighbors. This Update message includes the distance information to the new or updated network destination. The distance information in EIGRP is represented as a composite of available route metrics, including bandwidth, delay, load utilization, and link reliability. Each metric has an associated weight that determines if the metric is included in the distance calculation. You can configure these metric weights. You can fine-tune link characteristics to achieve optimal paths, but using the default settings for configurable metrics is recommended.

Internal routes are routes that occur between neighbors within the same EIGRP autonomous system. These routes have the following metrics:

- **Next hop:** The IP address of the next-hop router.

- **Delay:** The sum of the delays configured on the interfaces that make up the route to the destination network. The delay is configured in tens of microseconds.

- **Bandwidth:** The calculation from the lowest configured bandwidth on an interface that is part of the route to the destination.

- **MTU:** The smallest maximum transmission unit value along the route to the destination.

- **Hop count:** The number of hops or routers that the route passes through to the destination. This metric is not directly used in the DUAL computation.

- **Reliability:** An indication of the reliability of the links to the destination.

- **Load:** An indication of how much traffic is on the links to the destination.

By default, EIGRP uses the bandwidth and delay metrics to calculate the distance to the destination. You can modify the metric weights to include the other metrics in the calculation.

External routes are routes that occur between neighbors in different EIGRP autonomous systems. These routes have the following metrics:

- **Next hop:** The IP address of the next-hop router.

- **Router ID:** The ID of the router that redistributed this route into EIGRP.

- **AS number:** The autonomous system number of the destination.

- **Protocol ID:** A code that represents the routing protocol that learned the destination route.

- **Tag:** An arbitrary tag that can be used for route maps.

- **Metric:** The route metric for this route from the external routing protocol.

EIGRP adds all learned routes to the EIGRP topology table and the unicast RIB. When a topology change occurs, EIGRP uses these routes to search for a feasible successor. EIGRP also listens for notifications from the unicast RIB for changes in any routes redistributed to EIGRP from another routing protocol. You can also configure an interface as a passive interface for EIGRP. A passive interface does not participate in EIGRP adjacency, but the network address for the interface remains in the EIGRP topology table.

You can configure authentication on EIGRP messages to prevent unauthorized or invalid routing updates in your network. EIGRP authentication supports MD5 authentication digest. You can configure the EIGRP authentication using keychain management for the authentication keys. Keychain management allows you to control changes to the authentication keys used by MD5 authentication digest. For MD5 authentication, you configure a password that is shared at the local router and all remote EIGRP neighbors. When an EIGRP message is created, Cisco NX-OS creates an MD5 one-way message digest based on the message itself and the encrypted password and sends this digest along with the EIGRP message. The receiving EIGRP neighbor validates the digest using the same encrypted password. If the message has not changed, the calculation is identical, and the EIGRP message is considered valid. MD5 authentication also includes a sequence number with each EIGRP message that is used to ensure no message is replayed in the network.

You can use the EIGRP stub routing feature to improve network stability, reduce resource usage, and simplify stub router configuration. Stub routers connect to the EIGRP network through a remote router. When using EIGRP stub routing, you need to configure the distribution and remote routers to use EIGRP and configure only the remote router as a stub. EIGRP stub routing does not automatically enable summarization on the distribution router. In most cases, you need to configure summarization on the distribution routers. EIGRP stub routing allows you to prevent queries to the remote router.

You can configure a summary aggregate address for a specified interface. Route summarization simplifies route tables by replacing a number of more-specific addresses with an address that represents all the specific addresses. For example, you can replace 10.1.1.0/24, 10.1.2.0/24, and 10.1.3.0/24 with one summary address, 10.1.0.0/16. If more specific routes are in the routing table, EIGRP advertises the summary address from the interface with a metric equal to the minimum metric of the more specific routes.

You can use EIGRP to redistribute static routes, routes learned by other EIGRP autonomous systems, or routes from other protocols. You must configure a route map with the redistribution to control which routes are passed into EIGRP. A route map allows you to filter routes based on attributes such as the destination, origination protocol, route type, route tag, and so on. You also configure the default metric that is used for all imported routes into EIGRP. You use distribute lists to filter routes from routing updates.

You can use load balancing to allow a router to distribute traffic over all the router network ports that are the same distance from the destination address. Load balancing increases the usage of network segments, which increases effective network bandwidth. Cisco NX-OS supports the equal-cost multipath (ECMP) feature with up to 16 equal-cost paths in the EIGRP route table and the unicast RIB. You can configure EIGRP to load-balance traffic across some or all of those paths.

You can use split horizon to ensure that EIGRP never advertises a route out of the interface where it was learned. Split horizon is a method that controls the sending of EIGRP update and query packets. When you enable split horizon on an interface, Cisco NX-OS does not send update and query packets for destinations that were learned from this interface. Controlling update and query packets in this manner reduces the possibility of routing loops. Split horizon with poison reverse configures EIGRP to advertise a learned route as unreachable back through the interface from which EIGRP learned the route. By default, the split horizon feature is enabled on all interfaces.

EIGRP supports virtual routing and forwarding (VRF) instances. Cisco NX-OS supports multiple instances of EIGRP that run on the same system. Every instance uses the same system router ID. You can optionally configure a unique router ID for each instance.

Configuring basic EIGRP is a multistep process. The following are the steps to enable a basic configuration of EIGRP:

Step 1.   Enable EIGRP.

Step 2.   Configure an EIGRP instance.

Step 3.   Configure an autonomous system (optional).

Step 4.   Assign interfaces to the EIGRP instance.

Step 5.   Configure authentication in EIGRP (optional).

Step 6.   Verify the EIGRP operation.

Table 6-4 summarizes the NX-OS CLI commands related to basic EIGRP configuration and verification.

Table 6-4   *Summary of NX-OS CLI Commands for EIGRP Configuration and Verification*

Command	Purpose
configure terminal	Enters global configuration mode.
[no] feature eigrp	Enables the EIGRP feature. The **no** option disables the EIGRP feature and removes all associated configurations.
[no] router eigrp *instance-tag*	Creates a new EIGRP process with the configured instance tag. The instance tag can be any case-sensitive, alphanumeric string up to 20 characters. If you configure an *instance-tag* that does not qualify as an AS number, you must use the **autonomous-system** command to configure the AS number explicitly; otherwise, this EIGRP instance will remain in the shutdown state.
autonomous-system *as-number*	Configures a unique AS number for this EIGRP instance. The range is from 1 to 65535.
interface *interface-type slot/port*	Enters interface configuration mode.
ip router eigrp *instance-tag*	Associates this interface with the configured EIGRP process.
key chain *name*	Creates the keychain and enters keychain configuration mode.
key *key-ID*	Enters key configuration mode for the key you specified. The *key-ID* argument must be a whole number between 0 and 65535.

Command	Purpose
key-string [*encryption-type*] *text-string*	Configures the text string for the key. The *text-string* argument is alphanumeric, case-sensitive, and supports special characters.
	The *encryption-type* argument can be one of the following values:
	■ **0:** The *text-string* argument you enter is unencrypted text. This is the default.
	■ **7:** The *text-string* argument you enter is encrypted. The encryption method is a Cisco proprietary method. This option is useful when you are entering a text string based on the encrypted output of a **show key chain** command you ran on another Cisco NX-OS device.
ip authentication key-chain eigrp *instance-tag keychain*	Associates a keychain with this EIGRP process for this interface. This configuration overrides the authentication configuration set in the router VRF mode.
ip authentication mode eigrp *instance-tag* **md5**	Configures the MD5 message digest authentication mode for this interface. This configuration overrides the authentication configuration set in the router VRF mode.
show feature	Displays enabled and disabled features.
show ip eigrp *instance-tag* **neighbors** [*type number*] [**detail**]	Displays information about all the EIGRP neighbors. Use this command to verify the EIGRP neighbor configuration.
show ip route	Displays routes from the unicast routing information base (URIB).
show ip eigrp [*instance-tag*] **route** [*ip-prefix/length*] [**active**] [**all-links**] [**detail-links**] [**pending**] [**summary**] [**zero-successors**] [**vrf** *vrf-name*]	Displays information about all the EIGRP routes.
show ip eigrp [*instance-tag*] **topology** [*ip-prefix/length*] [**active**] [**all-links**] [**detail-links**] [**pending**] [**summary**] [**zero-successors**] [**vrf** *vrf-name*]	Displays information about the EIGRP topology table.
show ip eigrp [*instance-tag*] **interfaces** [*type number*] [**brief**] [**detail**]	Displays information about all configured EIGRP interfaces.

Examples 6-5 through 6-8 show the basic EIGRP configuration and verification on the sample topology shown in Figure 6-8. In this example, we will configure the MD5 authentication on the interface connecting the two Nexus switches.

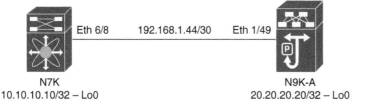

Figure 6-8   *Sample Topology for EIGRP Configuration and Verification*

Example 6-5   *EIGRP Configuration on N7K*

```
! Verifying if the interfaces are configured correctly.
N7K# show ip interface brief
IP Interface Status for VRF "default"(1)
Interface          IP Address       Interface Status
Lo0                10.10.10.10      protocol-up/link-up/admin-up
Eth6/8             192.168.1.45     protocol-up/link-up/admin-up


! Verifying if the EIGRP feature is enabled or not.
N7K# configure terminal
Enter configuration commands, one per line.  End with CNTL/Z.
N7K(config)# show feature | in eigrp
eigrp              1             disabled
eigrp              2             disabled
eigrp              3             disabled
<output omitted>


! Since EIGRP feature was not enabled, Enabling EIGRP feature, and confirming the
same.
N7K(config)# feature eigrp
N7K(config)# show feature | in eigrp
eigrp              1             enabled(not-running)
eigrp              2             enabled(not-running)
eigrp              3             enabled(not-running)
<output omitted>


! Configuring EIGRP instance with autonomous-system number 100
N7K(config)# router eigrp DCFNDU
N7K(config-router)# autonomous-system 100
N7K(config-router)# exit
```

```
! Configuring keychain named MYKEYS having only one key with key-string cisco.
N7K(config)# key chain MYKEYS
N7K(config-keychain)# key 1
N7K(config-keychain-key)# key-string cisco
N7K(config-keychain-key)# end


! Enabling EIGRP and configuring MD5 authentication using keychain MYKEYS on inter-
face connected to N9K-A.
N7K# configure terminal
Enter configuration commands, one per line.   End with CNTL/Z.
N7K(config)# interface Ethernet 6/8
N7K(config-if)# ip router eigrp DCFNDU
N7K(config-if)# ip authentication key-chain eigrp DCFNDU MYKEYS
N7K(config-if)# ip authentication mode eigrp DCFNDU md5


! Enabling EIGRP on Loopback interface.
N7K(config-if)# interface Loopback 0
N7K(config-if)# ip router eigrp DCFNDU
N7K(config-if)# end
```

Example 6-6   *EIGRP Configuration on N9K-A*

```
! Verifying if the interfaces are configured correctly.
N9K-A# show ip interface brief
IP Interface Status for VRF "default"(1)

Interface          IP Address       Interface Status
Lo0                20.20.20.20      protocol-up/link-up/admin-up
Eth1/49            192.168.1.46     protocol-up/link-up/admin-up


! Enabling EIGRP feature and configuring EIGRP instance with autonomous-system
number 100
N9K-A# configure terminal
Enter configuration commands, one per line. End with CNTL/Z.
N9K-A(config)# feature eigrp
N9K-A(config)# router eigrp DCFNDU
N9K-A(config-router)# autonomous-system 100
N9K-A(config-router)# exit


! Configuring keychain named MYKEYS having only one key with key-string cisco.
N9K-A(config)# key chain MYKEYS
N9K-A(config-keychain)# key 1
```

```
N9K-A(config-keychain-key)# key-string cisco
N9K-A(config-keychain-key)# end

! Enabling EIGRP and configuring MD5 authentication using keychain MYKEYS on inter-
face connected to N7K.
N9K-A# configure terminal
Enter configuration commands, one per line. End with CNTL/Z.
N9K-A(config)# interface Ethernet 1/49
N9K-A(config-if)# ip router eigrp DCFNDU
N9K-A(config-if)# ip authentication key-chain eigrp DCFNDU MYKEYS
N9K-A(config-if)# ip authentication mode eigrp DCFNDU md5

! Enabling EIGRP on Loopback interface.
N9K-A(config-if)# interface Loopback 0
N9K-A(config-if)# ip router eigrp DCFNDU
N9K-A(config-if)# end
```

Example 6-7 *EIGRP Verification on N7K*

```
! Verifying EIGRP neighbor.
N7K# show ip eigrp neighbors
IP-EIGRP neighbors for process 100 VRF default
H   Address              Interface     Hold  Uptime   SRTT   RTO   Q    Seq
                                       (sec)          (ms)         Cnt  Num
0   192.168.1.46         Eth6/8        10    00:07:02  1     50    0    8

! Verifying unicast routing table. N9K-A Loopback 0 interface is learned via EIGRP.
N7K# show ip route
IP Route Table for VRF "default"
'*' denotes best ucast next-hop
'**' denotes best mcast next-hop
'[x/y]' denotes [preference/metric]
'%<string>' in via output denotes VRF <string>

10.10.10.0/24, ubest/mbest: 1/0 time, attached
    *via 10.10.10.10, Lo0, [0/0], 21:47:22, direct
10.10.10.10/32, ubest/mbest: 1/0 time, attached
    *via 10.10.10.10, Lo0, [0/0], 21:47:22, local
20.20.20.20/32, ubest/mbest: 1/0 time
    *via 192.168.1.46, Eth6/8, [90/128576], 00:07:09, eigrp-DCFNDU, internal
192.168.1.44/30, ubest/mbest: 1/0 time, attached
    *via 192.168.1.45, Eth6/8, [0/0], 21:05:51, direct
```

```
192.168.1.45/32, ubest/mbest: 1/0 time, attached
    *via 192.168.1.45, Eth6/8, [0/0], 21:05:51, local
```

```
! Verifying EIGRP Topology table.
N7K# show ip eigrp topology
IP-EIGRP Topology Table for AS(100)/ID(10.10.10.10) VRF default

Codes: P - Passive, A - Active, U - Update, Q - Query, R - Reply,
       r - reply Status, s - sia Status

P 10.10.10.0/24, 1 successors, FD is 128320
        , via Connected, loopback0
P 20.20.20.20/32, 1 successors, FD is 128576
        , via 192.168.1.46 (128576/128320), Ethernet6/8
P 192.168.1.44/30, 1 successors, FD is 320
        , via Connected, Ethernet6/8
```

```
! Verifying interfaces configured for EIGRP.
N7K# show ip eigrp interfaces
IP-EIGRP interfaces for process 100 VRF default

                      Xmit Queue   Mean   Pacing Time   Multicast   Pending
Interface      Peers  Un/Reliable  SRTT   Un/Reliable   Flow Timer  Routes
Eth6/8           1       0/0         1        0/0           50          0
  Hello interval is 5 sec
  Holdtime interval is 15 sec
  Next xmit serial <none>
  Un/reliable mcasts: 0/4  Un/reliable ucasts: 9/5
  Mcast exceptions: 0  CR packets: 0  ACKs suppressed: 2
  Retransmissions sent: 0  Out-of-sequence rcvd: 0
  Authentication mode is md5,   key-chain is "MYKEYS"
  Use multicast
  Classic/wide metric peers: 1/0
Lo0              0       0/0         0        0/0           0           0
  Hello interval is 5 sec
  Holdtime interval is 15 sec
  Next xmit serial <none>
  Un/reliable mcasts: 0/0  Un/reliable ucasts: 0/0
  Mcast exceptions: 0  CR packets: 0  ACKs suppressed: 0
  Retransmissions sent: 0  Out-of-sequence rcvd: 0
  Authentication mode is not set
  Use multicast
  Classic/wide metric peers: 0/0
```

```
! Verifying end-to-end connectivity from N7K to N9K-A.
N7K# ping 20.20.20.20 source 10.10.10.10
PING 20.20.20.20 (20.20.20.20) from 10.10.10.10: 56 data bytes
64 bytes from 20.20.20.20: icmp_seq=0 ttl=254 time=0.96 ms
64 bytes from 20.20.20.20: icmp_seq=1 ttl=254 time=0.649 ms
64 bytes from 20.20.20.20: icmp_seq=2 ttl=254 time=0.706 ms
64 bytes from 20.20.20.20: icmp_seq=3 ttl=254 time=0.659 ms
64 bytes from 20.20.20.20: icmp_seq=4 ttl=254 time=0.645 ms

--- 20.20.20.20 ping statistics ---
5 packets transmitted, 5 packets received, 0.00% packet loss
round-trip min/avg/max = 0.645/0.723/0.96 ms
N7K#
```

Example 6-8   *EIGRP Verification on N9K-A*

```
! Verifying EIGRP neighbor.
N9K-A# show ip eigrp neighbors
IP-EIGRP neighbors for process 100 VRF default
H   Address               Interface       Hold Uptime   SRTT   RTO  Q  Seq
                                          (sec)         (ms)       Cnt Num
0   192.168.1.45          Eth1/49         14   00:08:10 1      50   0  9

! Verifying unicast routing table. N7K Loopback 0 interface is learned via EIGRP.
N9K-A# show ip route
IP Route Table for VRF "default"
'*' denotes best ucast next-hop
'**' denotes best mcast next-hop
'[x/y]' denotes [preference/metric]
'%<string>' in via output denotes VRF <string>

10.10.10.0/24, ubest/mbest: 1/0
    *via 192.168.1.45, Eth1/49, [90/128576], 00:08:17, eigrp-DCFNDU, internal
20.20.20.20/32, ubest/mbest: 2/0, attached
    *via 20.20.20.20, Lo0, [0/0], 21:06:20, local
    *via 20.20.20.20, Lo0, [0/0], 21:06:20, direct
192.168.1.44/30, ubest/mbest: 1/0, attached
    *via 192.168.1.46, Eth1/49, [0/0], 21:06:39, direct
192.168.1.46/32, ubest/mbest: 1/0, attached
    *via 192.168.1.46, Eth1/49, [0/0], 21:06:39, local
```

! Verifying EIGRP Topology table.

```
N9K-A# show ip eigrp topology
IP-EIGRP Topology Table for AS(100)/ID(20.20.20.20) VRF default

Codes: P - Passive, A - Active, U - Update, Q - Query, R - Reply,
       r - reply Status, s - sia Status

P 10.10.10.0/24, 1 successors, FD is 128576
        via 192.168.1.45 (128576/128320), Ethernet1/49
P 20.20.20.20/32, 1 successors, FD is 128320
        via Connected, loopback0
P 192.168.1.44/30, 1 successors, FD is 320
        via Connected, Ethernet1/49
```

! Verifying interfaces configured for EIGRP.

```
N9K-A# show ip eigrp interface
IP-EIGRP interfaces for process 100 VRF default

                     Xmit Queue  Mean   Pacing Time  Multicast   Pending
Interface    Peers   Un/Reliable SRTT   Un/Reliable  Flow Timer  Routes
Eth1/49        1        0/0        1        0/0           50         0
  Hello interval is 5 sec
  Holdtime interval is 15 sec
  Next xmit serial <none>
  Un/reliable mcasts: 0/4  Un/reliable ucasts: 3/13
  Mcast exceptions: 0  CR packets: 0  ACKs suppressed: 0
  Retransmissions sent: 9  Out-of-sequence rcvd: 0
  Authentication mode is md5,  key-chain is "MYKEYS"
  Use multicast
  Classic/wide metric peers: 1/0
Lo0            0        0/0        0        0/0           0          0
  Hello interval is 5 sec
  Holdtime interval is 15 sec
  Next xmit serial <none>
  Un/reliable mcasts: 0/0  Un/reliable ucasts: 0/0
  Mcast exceptions: 0  CR packets: 0  ACKs suppressed: 0
  Retransmissions sent: 0  Out-of-sequence rcvd: 0
  Authentication mode is not set
  Use multicast
  Classic/wide metric peers: 0/0
```

```
! Verifying end-to-end connectivity from N9K-A to N7K.
N9K-A# ping 10.10.10.10 source 20.20.20.20
PING 10.10.10.10 (10.10.10.10) from 20.20.20.20: 56 data bytes
64 bytes from 10.10.10.10: icmp_seq=0 ttl=254 time=0.941 ms
64 bytes from 10.10.10.10: icmp_seq=1 ttl=254 time=0.648 ms
64 bytes from 10.10.10.10: icmp_seq=2 ttl=254 time=0.625 ms
64 bytes from 10.10.10.10: icmp_seq=3 ttl=254 time=0.64 ms
64 bytes from 10.10.10.10: icmp_seq=4 ttl=254 time=0.619 ms

--- 10.10.10.10 ping statistics ---
5 packets transmitted, 5 packets received, 0.00% packet loss
round-trip min/avg/max = 0.619/0.694/0.941 ms
N9K-A#
```

OSPFv2 on NX-OS

OSPFv2 is a link-state protocol for IPv4 networks. An OSPFv2 router sends a special message, called a hello packet, out each OSPF-enabled interface to discover other OSPFv2 neighbor routers. Once a neighbor is discovered, the two routers compare information in the Hello packet to determine if the routers have compatible configurations. The neighbor routers try to establish adjacency, which means that the routers synchronize their link-state databases to ensure they have identical OSPFv2 routing information. Adjacent routers share link-state advertisements (LSAs) that include information about the operational state of each link, the cost of the link, and any other neighbor information. The routers then flood these received LSAs out every OSPF-enabled interface so that all OSPFv2 routers eventually have identical link-state databases. When all OSPFv2 routers have identical link-state databases, the network is converged. Each router then uses Dijkstra's Shortest Path First (SPF) algorithm to build its route table.

OSPFv2 routers periodically send Hello packets on every OSPF-enabled interface. The hello interval determines how frequently the router sends these Hello packets and is configured per interface. OSPFv2 uses Hello packets for the following tasks:

- **Neighbor discovery:** The Hello packet contains information about the originating OSPFv2 interface and router, including the assigned OSPFv2 cost of the link, the hello interval, and optional capabilities of the originating router. An OSPFv2 interface that receives these Hello packets determines if the settings are compatible with the receiving interface settings. Compatible interfaces are considered neighbors and are added to the neighbor table.

- **Keepalives:** OSPFv2 uses Hello packets as a keepalive message to determine if a neighbor is still communicating. If a router does not receive a Hello packet by the configured dead interval (usually a multiple of the hello interval), the neighbor is removed from the local neighbor table.

■ **Bidirectional communications:** Hello packets also include a list of router IDs for the routers that the originating interface has communicated with. If the receiving interface sees its own router ID in this list, bidirectional communication has been established between the two interfaces.

■ **Designated router election:** Networks with multiple routers present a unique situation for OSPF. If every router floods the network with LSAs, the same link-state information is sent from multiple sources. Depending on the type of network, OSPFv2 might use a single router, the designated router (DR), to control the LSA floods and represent the network to the rest of the OSPFv2 area. If the DR fails, OSPFv2 selects a backup designated router (BDR) and uses the BDR. The DR and BDR are selected based on the information in the Hello packet. When an interface sends a Hello packet, it sets the priority field and the DR and BDR field if it knows who the DR and BDR are. The routers follow an election procedure based on which routers declare themselves in the DR and BDR fields and the priority field in the Hello packet. As a final tie breaker, OSPFv2 chooses the highest router IDs as the DR and BDR. All other routers establish adjacency with the DR and the BDR and use the IPv4 multicast address 224.0.0.6 to send LSA updates to the DR and BDR. DRs are based on a router interface. A router might be the DR for one network and not for another network on a different interface.

OSPF network types are as follows:

■ **Point-to-point:** A network that exists only between two routers. All neighbors on a point-to-point network establish adjacency, and there is no DR.

■ **Broadcast:** A network with multiple routers that can communicate over a shared medium that allows broadcast traffic, such as Ethernet. OSPFv2 routers establish a DR and a BDR that controls LSA flooding on the network. OSPFv2 uses the well-known IPv4 multicast addresses 224.0.0.5 and the MAC address 0100.5e00.0005 to communicate with neighbors.

An OSPFv2 interface must have a compatible configuration with a remote interface before the two can be considered neighbors. The two OSPFv2 interfaces must match the following criteria:

■ Hello interval

■ Dead interval

■ Area ID

■ Authentication

■ Optional capabilities

If there is a match, the following information is entered into the neighbor table:

- **Neighbor ID:** The router ID of the neighbor.

- **Priority:** Priority of the neighbor. The priority is used for designated router election.

- **State:** Indication of whether the neighbor has just been heard from, is in the process of setting up bidirectional communications, is sharing the link-state information, or has achieved full adjacency.

- **Dead time:** Indication of the time since the last Hello packet was received from this neighbor.

- **IP address:** The IP address of the neighbor.

- **Designated router:** Indication of whether the neighbor has been declared as the designated router or as the backup designated router.

- **Local interface:** The local interface that received the Hello packet for this neighbor.

Adjacency is established using Database Description (DD) packets, Link-State Request (LSR) packets, and Link-State Update (LSU) packets in OSPF. The Database Description packet includes just the LSA headers from the link-state database (LSDB) of the neighbor. The local router compares these headers with its own link-state database and determines which LSAs are new or updated. The local router sends an LSR packet for each LSA for which it needs new or updated information. The neighbor responds with an LSU packet. This exchange continues until both routers have the same link-state information.

You can divide OSPFv2 networks into areas. Routers send most LSAs only within one area, which reduces the CPU and memory requirements for an OSPF-enabled router. An area is a logical division of routers and links within an OSPFv2 domain that creates separate subdomains. LSA flooding is contained within an area, and the link-state database is limited to links within the area. You can assign an area ID to the interfaces within the defined area. The area ID is a 32-bit value that you can enter as a number or in dotted decimal notation, such as 10.2.3.1. Cisco NX-OS always displays the area in dotted decimal notation. If you define more than one area in an OSPFv2 network, you must also define the backbone area, which has the reserved area ID of 0. If you have more than one area, then one or more routers become area border routers (ABRs).

Figure 6-9 shows how an ABR connects to both the backbone area and at least one other defined area.

The ABR has a separate link-state database for each area to which it connects. The ABR sends Network Summary (type 3) LSAs from one connected area to the backbone area. The backbone area sends summarized information about one area to another area. In Figure 6-9, Area 0 sends summarized information about Area 5 to Area 3.

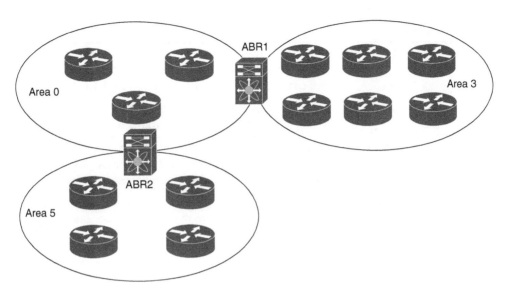

Figure 6-9 *OSPFv2 Areas*

OSPFv2 defines one other router type: the autonomous system boundary router (ASBR). This router connects an OSPFv2 area to another autonomous system. An autonomous system is a network controlled by a single technical administration entity. OSPFv2 can redistribute its routing information into another autonomous system or receive redistributed routes from another autonomous system.

Each OSPFv2 interface is assigned a link cost. The cost is an arbitrary number. By default, Cisco NX-OS assigns a cost that is the configured reference bandwidth divided by the interface bandwidth. By default, the reference bandwidth is 40Gbps. The link cost is carried in the LSA updates for each link.

OSPFv2 uses link-state advertisements (LSAs) to build its routing table. When an OSPFv2 router receives an LSA, it forwards that LSA out every OSPF-enabled interface, flooding the OSPFv2 area with this information. This LSA flooding guarantees that all routers in the network have identical routing information.

Table 6-5 shows the LSA types supported by Cisco NX-OS.

Table 6-5 *LSA Types*

Type	Name	Description
1	Router LSA	LSA sent by every router. This LSA includes the state and the cost of all links and a list of all OSPFv2 neighbors on the link. Router LSAs trigger an SPF recalculation. Router LSAs are flooded to the local OSPFv2 area.
2	Network LSA	LSA sent by the DR. This LSA lists all routers in the multi-access network. Network LSAs trigger an SPF recalculation.

Type	Name	Description
3	Network Summary LSA	LSA sent by the area border router (ABR) to an external area for each destination in the local area. This LSA includes the link cost from the area border router to the local destination.
4	ASBR Summary LSA	LSA sent by the area border router (ABR) to an external area. This LSA advertises the link cost to the ASBR only.
5	AS External LSA	LSA generated by the ASBR. This LSA includes the link cost to an external autonomous system destination. AS External LSAs are flooded throughout the autonomous system.
7	NSSA External LSA	LSA generated by the ASBR within a not-so-stubby area (NSSA). This LSA includes the link cost to an external autonomous system destination. NSSA External LSAs are flooded only within the local NSSA.
9-11	Opaque LSAs	LSA used to extend OSPF.

Opaque LSAs allow you to extend OSPF functionality. Opaque LSAs consist of a standard LSA header followed by application-specific information. This information might be used by OSPFv2 or by other applications. The three Opaque LSA types are defined as follows:

- **LSA type 9**: Flooded to the local network

- **LSA type 10**: Flooded to the local area

- **LSA type 11**: Flooded to the local autonomous system

Each router maintains a link-state database for the OSPFv2 network. This database contains all the collected LSAs and includes information on all the routes through the network. OSPFv2 uses this information to calculate the best path to each destination and populates the routing table with these best paths. LSAs are removed from the link-state database if no LSA update has been received within a set interval, called the MaxAge. Routers flood a repeat of the LSA every 30 minutes to prevent accurate link-state information from being aged out.

OSPFv2 runs the Dijkstra shortest path first algorithm on the link-state database. This algorithm selects the best path to each destination based on the sum of all the link costs for each link in the path. The resultant shortest path for each destination is then put in the OSPFv2 route table. When the OSPFv2 network is converged, this route table feeds into the unicast RIB.

You can configure authentication on OSPFv2 messages to prevent unauthorized or invalid routing updates in your network. Cisco NX-OS supports two authentication methods:

- **Simple password authentication:** Simple password authentication uses a simple cleartext password that is sent as part of the OSPFv2 message. The receiving OSPFv2 router must be configured with the same cleartext password to accept the OSPFv2 message as a valid route update. Because the password is in cleartext, anyone who can watch traffic on the network can learn the password.

- **Cryptographic authentication:** Cryptographic authentication uses an encrypted password for OSPFv2 authentication. The transmitter computes a code using the packet to be transmitted and the key string, inserts the code and the key ID in the packet, and transmits the packet. The receiver validates the code in the packet by computing the code locally using the received packet and the key string (corresponding to the key ID in the packet) configured locally. Both Message Digest 5 (MD5) and Hash-based Message Authentication Code Secure Hash Algorithm (HMAC-SHA) cryptographic authentication are supported.

In OSPFv2, you can limit the amount of external routing information that floods an area by making it a stub area. A stub area is an area that does not allow AS External (type 5) LSAs. These LSAs are usually flooded throughout the local autonomous system to propagate external route information. Stub areas use a default route for all traffic that needs to go through the backbone area to the external autonomous system.

A not-so-stubby area (NSSA) is similar to a stub area, except that an NSSA allows you to import autonomous system external routes within an NSSA using redistribution. The NSSA ASBR redistributes these routes and generates NSSA External (type 7) LSAs that it floods throughout the NSSA. You can optionally configure the ABR that connects the NSSA to other areas to translate this NSSA External LSA to AS External (type 5) LSAs. The ABR then floods these AS External LSAs throughout the OSPFv2 autonomous system. Summarization and filtering are supported during the translation. The backbone Area 0 cannot be an NSSA. You can, for example, use NSSA to simplify administration if you are connecting a central site using OSPFv2 to a remote site that is using a different routing protocol. Before NSSA, the connection between the corporate site border router and a remote router could not be run as an OSPFv2 stub area because routes for the remote site could not be redistributed into a stub area. With NSSA, you can extend OSPFv2 to cover the remote connection by defining the area between the corporate router and remote router as an NSSA.

Virtual links allow you to connect an OSPFv2 area ABR to a backbone area ABR when a direct physical connection is not available. You can also use virtual links to temporarily recover from a partitioned area, which occurs when a link within the area fails, isolating part of the area from reaching the designated ABR to the backbone area.

OSPFv2 can learn routes from other routing protocols by using route redistribution. You configure OSPFv2 to assign a link cost for these redistributed routes or a default link cost for all redistributed routes. Route redistribution uses route maps to control which external routes are redistributed. You must configure a route map with the redistribution to control which routes are passed into OSPFv2. A route map allows you to filter routes based on attributes such as the destination, origination protocol, route type, route tag, and so on. You can use route maps to modify parameters in the AS External (type 5) and NSSA External (type 7) LSAs before these external routes are advertised in the local OSPFv2 autonomous system.

Because OSPFv2 shares all learned routes with every OSPF-enabled router, you can use route summarization to reduce the number of unique routes that are flooded to every OSPF-enabled router. Route summarization simplifies route tables by replacing more-specific addresses with an address that represents all the specific addresses. For example, you can replace 10.1.1.0/24, 10.1.2.0/24, and 10.1.3.0/24 with one summary address, 10.1.0.0/16. Typically, you would summarize at the boundaries of area border routers (ABRs). Although you could configure summarization between any two areas, it is better to summarize in the direction of the backbone so that the backbone receives all the aggregate addresses and injects them, already summarized, into other areas. The two types of summarization are as follows:

■ **Inter-area route summarization:** Inter-area route summarization is configured on ABRs, summarizing routes between areas in the autonomous system.

■ **External route summarization:** External route summarization is specific to external routes that are injected into OSPFv2 using route redistribution.

When you configure a summary address, Cisco NX-OS automatically configures a discard route for the summary address to prevent routing black holes and route loops.

Cisco NX-OS supports multiple instances of the OSPFv2 protocol that run on the same node. You cannot configure multiple instances over the same interface. By default, every instance uses the same system router ID. You must manually configure the router ID for each instance if the instances are in the same OSPFv2 autonomous system.

Configuring basic OSPFv2 is a multistep process. The following are the steps to enable a basic configuration of OSPFv2:

Step 1.   Enable OSPFv2.

Step 2.   Configure an OSPFv2 instance.

Step 3.   Configure the router ID (optional).

Step 4.   Assign interfaces to the OSPFv2 instance.

Step 5.   Configure authentication for an area/interface (optional).

Step 6.   Verify the OSPFv2 operation.

Table 6-6 summarizes the NX-OS CLI commands related to basic OSPFv2 configuration and verification.

Table 6-6 *Summary of NX-OS CLI Commands for OSPFv2 Configuration and Verification*

Command	Purpose
configure terminal	Enters global configuration mode.
[no] feature ospf	Enables the OSPFv2 feature.
[no]router ospf *instance-tag*	Creates a new OSPFv2 instance with the configured instance tag.
(Optional) **router-id** *ip-address*	Configures the OSPFv2 router ID. This IP address identifies this OSPFv2 instance and must exist on a configured interface in the system.
interface *interface-type slot/port*	Enters interface configuration mode.
ip router ospf *instance-tag* area *area-id* [secondaries none]	Adds the interface to the OSPFv2 instance and area.
ip ospf network { broadcast | point-to-point }	Sets the network type.
ip ospf authentication [message-digest]	Enables interface authentication mode for OSPFv2 for either cleartext or message digest type. Overrides area-based authentication for this interface. All neighbors must share this authentication type.
ip ospf message-digest-key *key-id* md5 [0 | 3 | 7] *key*	Configures message digest authentication for this interface. Use this command if the authentication is set to message digest. The *key-id* range is from 1 to 255. The MD5 options are as follows: ■ **0:** Configures the password in cleartext ■ **3:** Configures the pass key as 3DES encrypted ■ **7:** Configures the key as Cisco type 7 encrypted
show ip ospf neighbors [*neighbor-id*] [detail] [*interface - type number*] [vrf { *vrf-name* | all | default | management }] [summary]	Displays the list of OSPFv2 neighbors.
show ip ospf database [vrf { *vrf-name* | all | default | management}]	Displays the OSPFv2 link-state database summary.
show ip ospf interface *number* [vrf { *vrf-name* | all | default | management }]	Displays OSPFv2-related interface information.

Command	Purpose
show ip route	Displays routes from the unicast routing information base (URIB).
show ip ospf route [*ospf-route*] [**summary**] [**vrf** { *vrf-name* | **all** | **default** | **management** }]	Displays the internal OSPFv2 routes.

Examples 6-9 through 6-14 show the basic OSPFv2 configuration and verification on the sample topology shown in Figure 6-10. The link between N7K and N9K-A is configured as a point-to-point network in Area 0, and the link between N7K and N9K-B is configured as a broadcast network in Area 1. In this example, we will configure the MD5 authentication on the interfaces. Router N7K will act as an area border router.

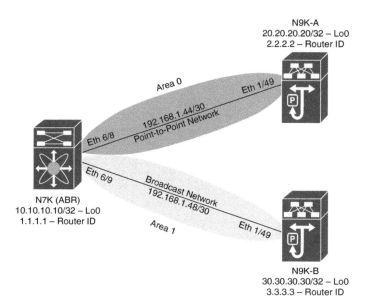

Figure 6-10   *Sample Topology for OSPFv2 Configuration and Verification*

Example 6-9   *OSPFv2 Configuration on N7K*

```
! Verifying if the interfaces are configured correctly.
N7K# show ip interface brief
IP Interface Status for VRF "default"(1)
Interface           IP Address         Interface Status
Lo0                 10.10.10.10        protocol-up/link-up/admin-up
Eth6/8              192.168.1.45       protocol-up/link-up/admin-up
Eth6/9              192.168.1.49       protocol-up/link-up/admin-up
```

```
! Verifying if the OSPF feature is enabled or not.
N7K# configure terminal
Enter configuration commands, one per line.  End with CNTL/Z.
N7K(config)# show feature | in ospf
ospf                  1           disabled
ospf                  2           disabled
ospf                  3           disabled
<output omitted>


! Since OSPF feature was not enabled, Enabling OSPF feature, and confirming the
same.
N7K(config)# feature ospf
N7K(config)# show feature | in ospf
ospf                  1           enabled(not-running)
ospf                  2           enabled(not-running)
ospf                  3           enabled(not-running)
<output omitted>


! Configuring OSPF instance with router-id 1.1.1.1.
N7K(config)# router ospf 1
N7K(config-router)# router-id 1.1.1.1


! Configuring Loopback 0 and Ethernet 6/8 in ospf area 0 and Ethernet 6/9 in ospf
area 1. Interface Ethernet 6/8 is configured as ospf point-to-point network and
Ethernet 6/9 is configured as ospf broadcast network.
N7K(config-router)# interface loopback 0
N7K(config-if)# ip router ospf 1 area 0
N7K(config-if)# exit
N7K(config)# interface Ethernet 6/8
N7K(config-if)# ip ospf network point-to-point
N7K(config-if)# ip router ospf 1 area 0
N7K(config-if)# int eth 6/9
N7K(config-if)# ip ospf network broadcast
N7K(config-if)# ip router ospf 1 area 1


! Configuring md5 authentication on Ethernet 6/8 and Ethernet 6/9 interface with
message-digest-key as cisco.
N7K(config-if)# interface Ethernet 6/8, Ethernet 6/9
N7K(config-if-range)# ip ospf authentication message-digest
N7K(config-if-range)# ip ospf message-digest-key 1 md5 cisco
N7K(config-if-range)# end
N7K#
```

Example 6-10 *OSPFv2 Configuration on N9K-A*

```
! Verifying if the interfaces are configured correctly.
N9K-A# show ip interface brief
IP Interface Status for VRF "default"(1)
Interface            IP Address       Interface Status
Lo0                  20.20.20.20      protocol-up/link-up/admin-up
Eth1/49              192.168.1.46     protocol-up/link-up/admin-up

! Enabling OSPF feature.
N9K-A# configure terminal
Enter configuration commands, one per line. End with CNTL/Z.
N9K-A(config)# feature ospf

! Configuring OSPF instance with router-id 2.2.2.2.
N9K-A(config)# router ospf 1
N9K-A(config-router)# router-id 2.2.2.2

! Configuring Loopback 0 and Ethernet 1/49 in ospf area 0. Interface Ethernet 1/49
is configured as ospf point-to-point network with cisco as message-digest key for
md5 authentication.
N9K-A(config-router)# interface loopback 0
N9K-A(config-if)# ip router ospf 1 area 0
N9K-A(config-if)# interface Ethernet 1/49
N9K-A(config-if)# ip ospf network point-to-point
N9K-A(config-if)# ip router ospf 1 area 0
N9K-A(config-if)# ip ospf authentication message-digest
N9K-A(config-if)# ip ospf message-digest-key 1 md5 cisco
N9K-A(config-if)# end
N9K-A#
```

Example 6-11 *OSPFv2 Configuration on N9K-B*

```
! Verifying if the interfaces are configured correctly.
N9K-B# show ip interface brief
IP Interface Status for VRF "default"(1)
Interface            IP Address       Interface Status
Lo0                  30.30.30.30      protocol-up/link-up/admin-up
Eth1/49              192.168.1.50     protocol-up/link-up/admin-up

! Enabling OSPF feature.
N9K-B# configure terminal
Enter configuration commands, one per line. End with CNTL/Z.
N9K-B(config)# feature ospf
```

```
! Configuring OSPF instance with router-id 3.3.3.3.
N9K-B(config)# router ospf 1
N9K-B(config-router)# router-id 3.3.3.3


! Configuring Loopback 0 and Ethernet 1/49 in ospf area 1. Interface Ethernet 1/49
is configured as ospf broadcast network with cisco as message-digest key for md5
authentication.
N9K-B(config-router)# interface loopback 0
N9K-B(config-if)# ip router ospf 1 area 1
N9K-B(config-if)# interface Ethernet 1/49
N9K-B(config-if)# ip ospf network broadcast
N9K-B(config-if)# ip router ospf 1 area 1
N9K-A(config-if)# ip ospf authentication message-digest
N9K-A(config-if)# ip ospf message-digest-key 1 md5 cisco
N9K-B(config-if)# end
N9K-B#
```

Example 6-12   *OSPFv2 Verification on N7K*

```
! Verifying OSPF neighbors.
N7K# show ip ospf neighbors
 OSPF Process ID 1 VRF default
 Total number of neighbors: 2
 Neighbor ID     Pri State          Up Time  Address        Interface
 2.2.2.2           1 FULL/ -        15:01:45 192.168.1.46   Eth6/8
 3.3.3.3           1 FULL/DR        00:12:01 192.168.1.50   Eth6/9


! Verifying unicast routing table. N9K-A and N9K-B Loopback 0 interfaces are learned
via OSPF.
N7K# show ip route
IP Route Table for VRF "default"
'*' denotes best ucast next-hop
'**' denotes best mcast next-hop
'[x/y]' denotes [preference/metric]
'%<string>' in via output denotes VRF <string>

10.10.10.0/24, ubest/mbest: 1/0 time, attached
    *via 10.10.10.10, Lo0, [0/0], 16:02:44, direct
10.10.10.10/32, ubest/mbest: 1/0 time, attached
    *via 10.10.10.10, Lo0, [0/0], 16:02:44, local
20.20.20.20/32, ubest/mbest: 1/0 time
    *via 192.168.1.46, Eth6/8, [110/2], 15:01:47, ospf-1, intra
30.30.30.30/32, ubest/mbest: 1/0 time
    *via 192.168.1.50, Eth6/9, [110/2], 00:12:02, ospf-1, intra
```

```
192.168.1.44/30, ubest/mbest: 1/0 time, attached
    *via 192.168.1.45, Eth6/8, [0/0], 15:21:13, direct
192.168.1.45/32, ubest/mbest: 1/0 time, attached
    *via 192.168.1.45, Eth6/8, [0/0], 15:21:13, local
192.168.1.48/30, ubest/mbest: 1/0 time, attached
    *via 192.168.1.49, Eth6/9, [0/0], 00:13:39, direct
192.168.1.49/32, ubest/mbest: 1/0 time, attached
    *via 192.168.1.49, Eth6/9, [0/0], 00:13:39, local
```

```
! Verifying OSPF database.
N7K# show ip ospf database
        OSPF Router with ID (1.1.1.1) (Process ID 1 VRF default)

                Router Link States (Area 0.0.0.0)

Link ID         ADV Router      Age       Seq#       Checksum Link Count
1.1.1.1         1.1.1.1         779       0x8000002f 0x108f   3
2.2.2.2         2.2.2.2         1356      0x80000023 0xf589   3


                Summary Network Link States (Area 0.0.0.0)

Link ID         ADV Router      Age       Seq#       Checksum
30.30.30.30     1.1.1.1         738       0x80000002 0xf5e7
192.168.1.48    1.1.1.1         779       0x80000002 0xa41b


                Router Link States (Area 0.0.0.1)

Link ID         ADV Router      Age       Seq#       Checksum Link Count
1.1.1.1         1.1.1.1         744       0x80000021 0xbb36   1
3.3.3.3         3.3.3.3         745       0x80000024 0x58fc   2


                Network Link States (Area 0.0.0.1)

Link ID         ADV Router      Age       Seq#       Checksum
192.168.1.50    3.3.3.3         745       0x80000002 0xf8aa


                Summary Network Link States (Area 0.0.0.1)

Link ID         ADV Router      Age       Seq#       Checksum
10.10.10.10     1.1.1.1         744       0x8000001f 0x4dc4
20.20.20.20     1.1.1.1         744       0x8000001f 0x895f
192.168.1.44    1.1.1.1         744       0x8000001f 0x9214
```

```
! Verifying end-to-end connectivity from N7K to N9K-A and N9K-B.
N7K# ping 20.20.20.20 source 10.10.10.10
PING 20.20.20.20 (20.20.20.20) from 10.10.10.10: 56 data bytes
64 bytes from 20.20.20.20: icmp_seq=0 ttl=254 time=1.309 ms
64 bytes from 20.20.20.20: icmp_seq=1 ttl=254 time=0.792 ms
64 bytes from 20.20.20.20: icmp_seq=2 ttl=254 time=0.835 ms
64 bytes from 20.20.20.20: icmp_seq=3 ttl=254 time=0.761 ms
64 bytes from 20.20.20.20: icmp_seq=4 ttl=254 time=0.828 ms


--- 20.20.20.20 ping statistics ---
5 packets transmitted, 5 packets received, 0.00% packet loss
round-trip min/avg/max = 0.761/0.905/1.309 ms


N7K# ping 30.30.30.30 source 10.10.10.10
PING 30.30.30.30 (30.30.30.30) from 10.10.10.10: 56 data bytes
64 bytes from 30.30.30.30: icmp_seq=0 ttl=254 time=1.869 ms
64 bytes from 30.30.30.30: icmp_seq=1 ttl=254 time=1.448 ms
64 bytes from 30.30.30.30: icmp_seq=2 ttl=254 time=1.438 ms
64 bytes from 30.30.30.30: icmp_seq=3 ttl=254 time=1.442 ms
64 bytes from 30.30.30.30: icmp_seq=4 ttl=254 time=1.401 ms


--- 30.30.30.30 ping statistics ---
5 packets transmitted, 5 packets received, 0.00% packet loss
round-trip min/avg/max = 1.401/1.519/1.869 ms
```

Example 6-13 *OSPFv2 Verification on N9K-A*

```
! Verifying OSPF neighbors.
N9K-A# show ip ospf neighbors
 OSPF Process ID 1 VRF default
 Total number of neighbors: 1
 Neighbor ID     Pri State        Up Time  Address        Interface
 1.1.1.1           1 FULL/ -      15:04:15 192.168.1.45   Eth1/49


! Verifying unicast routing table. N7K and N9K-B Loopback 0 interfaces are learned
via OSPF.
N9K-A# show ip route
IP Route Table for VRF "default"
'*' denotes best ucast next-hop
'**' denotes best mcast next-hop
'[x/y]' denotes [preference/metric]
'%<string>' in via output denotes VRF <string>
```

```
10.10.10.10/32, ubest/mbest: 1/0
    *via 192.168.1.45, Eth1/49, [110/2], 15:04:14, ospf-1, intra
20.20.20.20/32, ubest/mbest: 2/0, attached
    *via 20.20.20.20, Lo0, [0/0], 15:23:00, local
    *via 20.20.20.20, Lo0, [0/0], 15:23:00, direct
30.30.30.30/32, ubest/mbest: 1/0
    *via 192.168.1.45, Eth1/49, [110/3], 00:14:28, ospf-1, inter
192.168.1.44/30, ubest/mbest: 1/0, attached
    *via 192.168.1.46, Eth1/49, [0/0], 15:23:19, direct
192.168.1.46/32, ubest/mbest: 1/0, attached
    *via 192.168.1.46, Eth1/49, [0/0], 15:23:19, local
192.168.1.48/30, ubest/mbest: 1/0
    *via 192.168.1.45, Eth1/49, [110/2], 00:15:08, ospf-1, inter


! Verifying OSPF database.
N9K-A# show ip ospf database
        OSPF Router with ID (2.2.2.2) (Process ID 1 VRF default)

                Router Link States (Area 0.0.0.0)

Link ID         ADV Router      Age       Seq#        Checksum Link Count
1.1.1.1         1.1.1.1         928       0x8000002f 0x108f    3
2.2.2.2         2.2.2.2         1503      0x80000023 0xf589    3


                Summary Network Link States (Area 0.0.0.0)

Link ID         ADV Router      Age       Seq#        Checksum
30.30.30.30     1.1.1.1         887       0x80000002 0xf5e7
192.168.1.48    1.1.1.1         928       0x80000002 0xa41b


! Verifying end-to-end connectivity from N9K-A to N7K and N9K-B.
N9K-A# ping 10.10.10.10 source 20.20.20.20
PING 10.10.10.10 (10.10.10.10) from 20.20.20.20: 56 data bytes
64 bytes from 10.10.10.10: icmp_seq=0 ttl=254 time=1.037 ms
64 bytes from 10.10.10.10: icmp_seq=1 ttl=254 time=0.639 ms
64 bytes from 10.10.10.10: icmp_seq=2 ttl=254 time=0.676 ms
64 bytes from 10.10.10.10: icmp_seq=3 ttl=254 time=2.237 ms
64 bytes from 10.10.10.10: icmp_seq=4 ttl=254 time=0.663 ms

--- 10.10.10.10 ping statistics ---
5 packets transmitted, 5 packets received, 0.00% packet loss
round-trip min/avg/max = 0.639/1.05/2.237 ms
```

```
N9K-A# ping 30.30.30.30 source 20.20.20.20
PING 30.30.30.30 (30.30.30.30) from 20.20.20.20: 56 data bytes
64 bytes from 30.30.30.30: icmp_seq=0 ttl=253 time=1.229 ms
64 bytes from 30.30.30.30: icmp_seq=1 ttl=253 time=0.688 ms
64 bytes from 30.30.30.30: icmp_seq=2 ttl=253 time=0.517 ms
64 bytes from 30.30.30.30: icmp_seq=3 ttl=253 time=0.704 ms
64 bytes from 30.30.30.30: icmp_seq=4 ttl=253 time=0.699 ms

--- 30.30.30.30 ping statistics ---
5 packets transmitted, 5 packets received, 0.00% packet loss
round-trip min/avg/max = 0.517/0.767/1.229 ms
```

Example 6-14   *OSPFv2 Verification on N9K-B*

```
! Verifying OSPF neighbors.
N9K-B# show ip ospf neighbors
 OSPF Process ID 1 VRF default
 Total number of neighbors: 1
 Neighbor ID     Pri State        Up Time  Address       Interface
 1.1.1.1           1 FULL/BDR      00:16:13 192.168.1.49  Eth1/49


! Verifying unicast routing table. N7K and N9K-A Loopback 0 interfaces are learned
via OSPF.
N9K-B# show ip route
IP Route Table for VRF "default"
'*' denotes best ucast next-hop
'**' denotes best mcast next-hop
'[x/y]' denotes [preference/metric]
'%<string>' in via output denotes VRF <string>


10.10.10.10/32, ubest/mbest: 1/0
    *via 192.168.1.49, Eth1/49, [110/2], 00:16:11, ospf-1, inter
20.20.20.20/32, ubest/mbest: 1/0
    *via 192.168.1.49, Eth1/49, [110/3], 00:16:11, ospf-1, inter
30.30.30.30/32, ubest/mbest: 2/0, attached
    *via 30.30.30.30, Lo0, [0/0], 15:19:04, local
    *via 30.30.30.30, Lo0, [0/0], 15:19:04, direct
192.168.1.44/30, ubest/mbest: 1/0
    *via 192.168.1.49, Eth1/49, [110/2], 00:16:11, ospf-1, inter
192.168.1.48/30, ubest/mbest: 1/0, attached
    *via 192.168.1.50, Eth1/49, [0/0], 00:17:48, direct
```

```
192.168.1.50/32, ubest/mbest: 1/0, attached
    *via 192.168.1.50, Eth1/49, [0/0], 00:17:48, local
```

! Verifying OSPF database.

```
N9K-B# show ip ospf database
        OSPF Router with ID (3.3.3.3) (Process ID 1 VRF default)

                Router Link States (Area 0.0.0.1)

Link ID         ADV Router      Age     Seq#        Checksum Link Count
1.1.1.1         1.1.1.1         984     0x80000021 0xbb36    1
3.3.3.3         3.3.3.3         984     0x80000024 0x58fc    2

                Network Link States (Area 0.0.0.1)

Link ID         ADV Router      Age     Seq#        Checksum
192.168.1.50    3.3.3.3         984     0x80000002 0xf8aa

                Summary Network Link States (Area 0.0.0.1)

Link ID         ADV Router      Age     Seq#        Checksum
10.10.10.10     1.1.1.1         985     0x8000001f 0x4dc4
20.20.20.20     1.1.1.1         985     0x8000001f 0x895f
192.168.1.44    1.1.1.1         985     0x8000001f 0x9214


N9K-B#
```

! Verifying end-to-end connectivity from N9K-B to N7K and N9K-A.

```
N9K-B# ping 10.10.10.10 source 30.30.30.30
PING 10.10.10.10 (10.10.10.10) from 30.30.30.30: 56 data bytes
64 bytes from 10.10.10.10: icmp_seq=0 ttl=254 time=1.878 ms
64 bytes from 10.10.10.10: icmp_seq=1 ttl=254 time=1.39 ms
64 bytes from 10.10.10.10: icmp_seq=2 ttl=254 time=1.386 ms
64 bytes from 10.10.10.10: icmp_seq=3 ttl=254 time=1.437 ms
64 bytes from 10.10.10.10: icmp_seq=4 ttl=254 time=1.479 ms

--- 10.10.10.10 ping statistics ---
5 packets transmitted, 5 packets received, 0.00% packet loss
round-trip min/avg/max = 1.386/1.514/1.878 ms

N9K-B# ping 20.20.20.20 source 30.30.30.30
PING 20.20.20.20 (20.20.20.20) from 30.30.30.30: 56 data bytes
64 bytes from 20.20.20.20: icmp_seq=0 ttl=253 time=1.199 ms
```

```
64 bytes from 20.20.20.20: icmp_seq=1 ttl=253 time=0.587 ms
64 bytes from 20.20.20.20: icmp_seq=2 ttl=253 time=0.462 ms
64 bytes from 20.20.20.20: icmp_seq=3 ttl=253 time=0.565 ms
64 bytes from 20.20.20.20: icmp_seq=4 ttl=253 time=0.584 ms

--- 20.20.20.20 ping statistics ---
5 packets transmitted, 5 packets received, 0.00% packet loss
round-trip min/avg/max = 0.462/0.679/1.199 ms
N9K-B#
```

Note   There are a few more commands you can use to verify OSPF configuration, including **show ip ospf**, **show ip ospf neighbors detail**, and **show ip ospf interface**.

Multicast Fundamentals

IP multicast is a method of forwarding the same set of IP packets to a number of hosts within a network. You can use multicast in IPv4 networks to provide efficient delivery of data to multiple destinations. Multicast involves both a method of delivery and discovery of senders and receivers of multicast data, which is transmitted on IP multicast addresses called groups. A multicast address that includes a group and source IP address is often referred to as a channel. The Internet Assigned Number Authority (IANA) has assigned 224.0.0.0 through 239.255.255.255 as IPv4 multicast addresses.

The routers in the network listen for receivers to advertise their interest in receiving multicast data from selected groups. The routers then replicate and forward the data from sources to the interested receivers. Multicast data for a group is transmitted only to those LAN segments with receivers that requested it.

Multicast Distribution Trees

A multicast distribution tree represents the path that multicast data takes between the routers that connect sources and receivers. The multicast software builds different types of trees to support different multicast methods.

Source Trees

A source tree represents the shortest path that the multicast traffic takes through the network from the sources that transmit to a particular multicast group to receivers that requested traffic from that same group. Because of the shortest path characteristic of a source tree, this tree is often referred to as a shortest path tree (SPT). Figure 6-11 shows a source tree for group 224.1.1.1 that begins at host A and connects to hosts B and C.

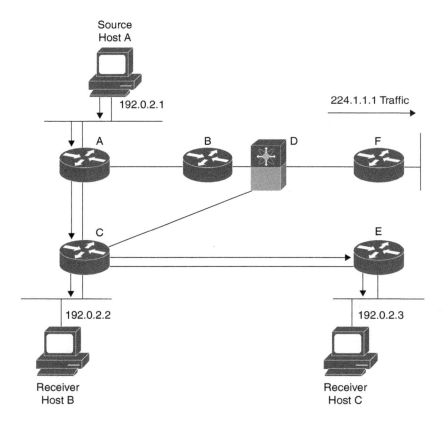

Figure 6-11 *Source Tree*

The notation (S, G) represents the multicast traffic from source S on group G. The SPT in this figure is written (192.0.2.1, 224.1.1.1). Multiple sources can be transmitting on the same group.

Shared Trees

A shared tree represents the shared distribution path that the multicast traffic takes through the network from a shared root or rendezvous point (RP) to each receiver. The RP creates an SPT to each source. A shared tree is also called an RP tree (RPT). Figure 6-12 shows a shared tree for group 224.2.2.2 with the RP at router D. Source hosts A and D send their data to router D, the RP, which then forwards the traffic to receiver hosts B and C.

The notation (*, G) represents the multicast traffic from any source on group G. The shared tree in this figure is written (*, 224.2.2.2).

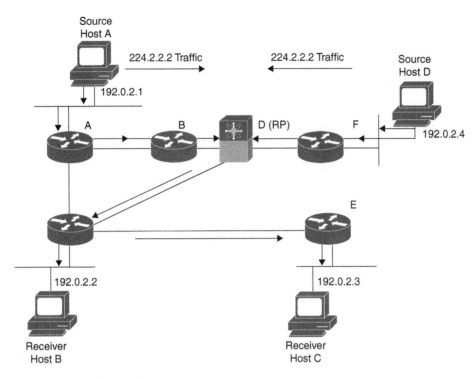

Figure 6-12   *Shared Tree*

Bidirectional Shared Trees

A bidirectional shared tree represents the shared distribution path that the multicast traffic takes through the network from a shared root, or rendezvous point (RP), to each receiver. With Bidirectional PIM (BIDIR-PIM), traffic from the source is forwarded toward the RP by the designated forwarder (DF). On each point-to-point link and every network segment, one DF is elected for every RP of the bidirectional group, and the DF will also be responsible for forwarding multicast traffic received from the source on that network. In BIDIR-PIM, the traffic from the source can be forwarded directly on the branch toward the interesting receivers without first reaching the RP. From the perspective of the receiver, there are no significant changes compared to the regular PIM-SM. The last-hop designated routers will forward (*, G) joins toward the RP serving the group. The only difference is that the DF performs the tasks of the designated router. (More on the designated router and designated forwarder can be found in the "PIM Sparse Mode" and "BIDIR-PIM" sections, later in this chapter.) The advantage of the bidirectional shared tree is shown in Figure 6-13.

Multicast traffic flows directly from source host A to receiver host B through routers B and C by designated forwarder B, because the receiver can be reached by DF without reaching RP on the shared tree. In a shared tree scenario, the data from source host A is first sent to the RP (router D) and then forwarded to router B for delivery to host B.

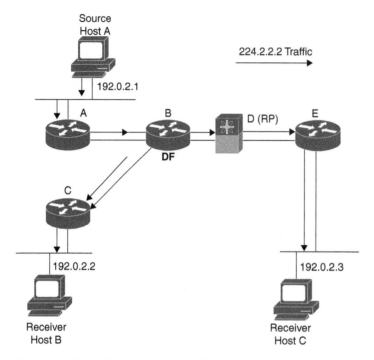

Figure 6-13   *Bidirectional Shared Tree*

The notation (*, G) represents the multicast traffic from any source on group G. The bidirectional tree in the figure is written as (*, 224.2.2.2).

The forwarding and tree building process in bidirectional shared trees consists of three main stages:

1. The DF is responsible for sending (*, G) joins toward the RP for the active bidirectional group. Downstream routers address their (*, G) joins to upstream DFs. This is accomplished by putting the IP address of the upstream DF in the upstream router field of a PIM join message.

2. When the DF receives an (*, G) join, it adds the link to the OIL of the (*, G) entry and joins toward the RP. If the interface exists in the OIL, the interface timer is refreshed.

3. The DF also has the responsibility of forwarding multicast traffic in BIDIR-PIM. When multicast traffic is received from the source on a link for which the router is the DF, the router must forward that traffic via its RPF interface toward the RP. Furthermore, the DF must forward the received traffic out all other interfaces in the (*, G) OIL, excluding the interface on which the traffic was received.

Note   Steps 1 and 2 describe the bidirectional shared tree building process and step 3 describes the multicast forwarding process in BIDIR-PIM.

Multicast Forwarding

In unicast routing, traffic is routed through the network along a single path from the source to the destination host. A unicast router does not consider the source address; it considers only the destination address and how to forward the traffic toward that destination. The router scans through its routing table for the destination address and then forwards a single copy of the unicast packet out the correct interface in the direction of the destination.

In multicast forwarding, the source is sending traffic to an arbitrary group of hosts that are represented by a multicast group address. The multicast router must determine which direction is the upstream direction (toward the source) and which is the downstream direction (or directions). If there are multiple downstream paths, the router replicates the packet and forwards it down the appropriate downstream paths (best unicast route metric), which is not necessarily all paths. Forwarding multicast traffic away from the source, rather than to the receiver, is called reverse path forwarding (RPF).

PIM uses the unicast routing information to create a distribution tree along the reverse path from the receivers toward the source. The multicast routers then forward packets along the distribution tree from the source to the receivers. RPF is a key concept in multicast forwarding. It enables routers to correctly forward multicast traffic down the distribution tree. RPF makes use of the existing unicast routing table to determine the upstream and downstream neighbors. A router will forward a multicast packet only if it is received on the upstream interface. This RPF check helps to guarantee that the distribution tree will be loop-free.

Because multicast traffic is destined for an arbitrary group of hosts, the router uses reverse path forwarding (RPF) to route data to active receivers for the group. When receivers join a group, a path is formed toward the RP (ASM mode). The path from a source to a receiver flows in the reverse direction from the path that was created when the receiver joined the group.

For each incoming multicast packet, the router performs an RPF check. If the packet arrives on the interface leading to the source, the packet is forwarded out each interface in the outgoing interface (OIF) list for the group. Otherwise, the router drops the packet.

Figure 6-14 shows an example of RPF checks on packets coming in from different interfaces. The packet that arrives on E0 fails the RPF check because the unicast route table lists the source of the network on interface E1. The packet that arrives on E1 passes the RPF check because the unicast route table lists the source of that network on interface E1.

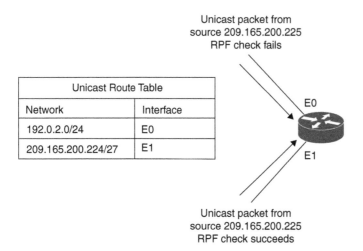

Figure 6-14 *RPF Check Example*

Multicast Control Protocols

The NX-OS software supports the following protocols to implement IP multicast routing:

■ Internet Group Management Protocol (IGMP) is used between hosts on a LAN and the routers on that LAN to track the multicast groups of which hosts are members.

■ Protocol-Independent Multicast (PIM) is used between routers so that they can track which multicast packets to forward to each other and to their directly connected LANs.

Internet Group Management Protocol (IGMP)

IGMP is used to dynamically register individual hosts in a multicast group on a particular LAN. Hosts identify group memberships by sending IGMP messages to their local multicast router. Under IGMP, routers listen to IGMP messages and periodically send out queries to discover which groups are active or inactive on a particular subnet. There are three versions of IGMP: IGMP version 1, IGMP version 2, and IGMP version 3.

IGMP Version 1

In Version 1, only the following two types of IGMP messages exist:

■ Membership query

■ Membership report

Hosts send out IGMP membership reports corresponding to a particular multicast group to indicate that they are interested in joining that group. The TCP/IP stack running on a host automatically sends the IGMP membership report when an application opens a multicast socket. The router periodically sends out an IGMP membership query to verify that at least one host on the subnet is still interested in receiving traffic directed to that group. When there is no reply to three consecutive IGMP membership queries, the router times out the group and stops forwarding traffic directed toward that group. IGMPv1 supports membership report suppression, which means that if two hosts on the same subnet want to receive multicast data for the same group, the host that receives a member report from the other host suppresses sending its report. Membership report suppression occurs for hosts that share a port.

IGMP Version 2

IGMPv1 has been superseded by IGMP Version 2 (IGMPv2). IGMPv2 is backward compatible with IGMPv1. In Version 2, the following four types of IGMP messages exist:

- Membership query

- Version 1 membership report

- Version 2 membership report

- Leave group

IGMP Version 2 works basically the same way as Version 1 and supports membership report suppression. The main difference is that there is a leave group message. With this message, the hosts can actively communicate to the local multicast router that they intend to leave the group. The router then sends out a group-specific query and determines if any remaining hosts are interested in receiving the traffic. If there are no replies, the router times out the group and stops forwarding the traffic. The addition of the leave group message in IGMP Version 2 greatly reduces the leave latency compared to IGMP Version 1. Unwanted and unnecessary traffic can be stopped much sooner.

IGMP Version 3

IGMPv3 adds support for "source filtering," which enables a multicast receiver host to signal to a router the groups from which it wants to receive multicast traffic as well as from which sources this traffic is expected. This membership information enables Cisco NX-OS software to forward traffic from only those sources from which receivers requested the traffic.

In IGMPv3, the following types of IGMP messages exist:

- Version 3 membership query

- Version 3 membership report

IGMPv3 supports applications that explicitly signal sources from which they want to receive traffic.

Note   The NX-OS device supports IGMPv2 and IGMPv3 as well as IGMPv1 report reception.

The MLD protocol is equivalent to IGMP in the IPv6 domain and is used by a host to request multicast data for a particular group. MLDv1 is derived from IGMPv2, and MLDv2 is derived from IGMPv3. Also, IGMP uses IP Protocol 2 message types, while MLD uses IP Protocol 58 message types, which is a subset of the ICMPv6 messages. In this chapter, we cover only IGMP for IPv4. To know more about MLD, refer to "Cisco Nexus 9000 Series NX-OS Multicast Routing Configuration Guide" for the latest version of NX-OS code.

Protocol-Independent Multicast (PIM)

Once the clients signal their interest in certain multicast groups, the routers are responsible for building a distribution tree to forward the data from the sources to the receivers. The protocol commonly used in this case is Protocol-Independent Multicast version 2 (PIMv2). In NX-OS devices, PIM can be deployed in the following distribution modes for connecting sources and receivers.

PIM Sparse Mode

PIM sparse mode is commonly used in Any Source Multicast (ASM) deployments. ASM is a PIM tree building mode that uses shared trees to discover new sources and receivers as well as source trees to form shortest paths from receivers to sources. The shared tree uses a network node as the root, called the rendezvous point (RP). The source tree is rooted at first-hop routers, directly attached to each source that is an active sender. The ASM mode requires an RP for a group range. An RP can be configured statically or learned dynamically by the Auto-RP or BSR group-to-RP discovery protocols. If an RP is learned, the group operates in ASM mode. The ASM mode is the default mode when you configure RPs.

In PIM ASM mode, the NX-OS software chooses a designated router (DR) from the routers on each network segment. The DR is responsible for forwarding multicast data for specified groups and sources on that segment. The DR for each LAN segment is determined as described in the Hello messages. In ASM mode, the DR is responsible for unicasting PIM register packets to the RP. When a DR receives an IGMP membership report from a directly connected receiver, the shortest path is formed to the RP, which may or may not go through the DR. The result is a shared tree that connects all sources transmitting on the same multicast group to all receivers of that group.

PIM-SSM

Source-Specific Multicast (SSM) is an extension of the PIM protocol that allows for an efficient data delivery mechanism in one-to-many communications. SSM enables a receiving client once it has learned about a particular multicast source and receives content directly from the source, rather than receiving it using a shared RP. Source-Specific Multicast (SSM) is a PIM mode that builds a source tree that originates at the designated router on the LAN segment that receives a request to join a multicast source. Source trees are built by sending PIM join messages in the direction of the source. The SSM mode does not require any RP configuration. The SSM mode allows receivers to connect to sources outside the PIM domain.

BIDIR-PIM

Bidirectional PIM (BIDIR-PIM) is an enhancement of the PIM protocol that was designed for efficient many-to-many communications, where each participant is a receiver as well as a sender. Multicast groups in bidirectional mode can scale to an arbitrary number of sources.

The shared trees created in PIM sparse mode are unidirectional. This means that a source tree must be created to bring the data stream to the RP (the root of the shared tree) and then it can be forwarded down the branches to the receivers. The traffic from sources to the RP initially flows encapsulated in register messages. This activity presents a significant burden because of the encapsulation and de-encapsulation mechanisms. Additionally, an SPT is built between the RP and the source, which results in (S,G) entries being created between the RP and the source.

In a many-to-many multicast model, where each participant is a receiver as well as a sender, the (*, G) and (S, G) entries appear at points along the path from participants and the associated RP. Additional entries in the multicast routing table increase memory and CPU utilization. An increase of the overhead may become a significant issue in networks where the number of participants in the multicast group grows quite large.

BIDIR-PIM eliminates the registration/encapsulation process and the (S,G) state. Packets are natively forwarded from a source to the RP using the (*, G) state only. This capability ensures that only (*, G) entries appear in multicast forwarding tables. The path that is taken by packets flowing from the participant (source or receiver) to the RP and from the RP to the participant will be the same by using a bidirectional shared tree.

In BIDIR-PIM, the packet-forwarding rules have been improved over PIM SM, allowing traffic to be passed up the shared tree toward the RP. To avoid multicast packet looping, BIDIR-PIM introduces a new mechanism called the designated forwarder (DF), which establishes a loop-free SPT rooted at the RP. A single DF for a particular BIDIR-PIM group exists on every link within a PIM domain. Elected on both multi-access and point-to-point links, the DF is the router on the link with the best unicast route to the RP.

A DF for a given RP is in charge of forwarding the following:

- Downstream traffic that flows down the shared tree onto the link

- Upstream traffic that flows from the link toward the RP

The DF does this for all the bidirectional groups served by the RP. The election mechanism for the DF must ensure that all the routers on the link have a consistent view of the path toward the RP.

On every link in the network, the BIDIR-PIM routers participate in a procedure called DF election. The procedure selects one router as the DF for every RP of bidirectional groups. The router with the best unicast route to the RP is elected as a DF. There is also an election tie-breaking process if there are parallel equal-cost paths to the RP. If the elected DF fails, it is detected via the normal PIM hello mechanism, and a new DF election process will be initiated.

Note   There are various ways of configuring and selecting the RP in a PIM-SM network, such as static-RP, BSRs, Auto-RP, Anycast-RP, and so on, depending on if we have a single or multiple RPs in a PIM domain. Covering all the RP configuration methods is beyond the scope of this book. For simplicity, we will stick to static-RP configuration in multicast configuration examples.

Multicast Source Discovery Protocol (MSDP)

In the PIM sparse mode model, the router that's closest to the sources or receivers registers with the RP. The RP knows about all the sources and receivers for any particular group. Network administrators may want to configure several RPs and create several PIM-SM domains. In each domain, RPs have no way of knowing about sources located in other domains. MSDP is an elegant way to solve this problem.

MSDP was developed for peering between Internet service providers (ISPs). ISPs did not want to rely on an RP maintained by a competing ISP to provide service to their customers. MSDP allows each ISP to have its own local RP and still forward and receive multicast traffic to the Internet.

MSDP enables RPs to share information about active sources. RPs know about the receivers in their local domain. When RPs in remote domains hear about the active sources, they can pass on that information to their local receivers and multicast data can then be forwarded between the domains. A useful feature of MSDP is that it allows each domain to maintain an independent RP that does not rely on other domains. MSDP gives the network administrators the option of selectively forwarding multicast traffic between domains or blocking particular groups or sources. PIM-SM is used to forward the traffic between the multicast domains.

The RP in each domain establishes an MSDP peering session using a TCP connection with the RPs in other domains or with border routers leading to the other domains. When the RP learns about a new multicast source within its own domain (through the normal PIM register mechanism), the RP encapsulates the first data packet in a Source-Active (SA) message and sends the SA to all MSDP peers. MSDP uses a modified RPF check in determining which peers should be forwarded the SA messages. This modified RPF check is done at an AS level instead of a hop-by-hop metric. The SA is forwarded by each receiving peer, also using the same modified RPF check, until the SA reaches every MSDP router in the internetwork—theoretically, the entire multicast Internet. If the receiving MSDP peer is an RP, and the RP has an (*, G) entry for the group in the SA (that is, there is an interested receiver), the RP creates the (S, G) state for the source and joins the shortest path tree for the source. The encapsulated data is decapsulated and forwarded down the shared tree of that RP. When the packet is received by the last-hop router of the receiver, the last-hop router also may join the shortest path tree to the source. The MSDP speaker periodically sends SAs that include all sources within the domain of the RP.

When a receiver joins a group that is transmitted by a source in another domain, the RP sends PIM join messages in the direction of the source to build a shortest path tree. The DR sends packets on the source tree within the source domain, which can travel through the RP in the source domain and along the branches of the source tree to other domains. In domains where there are receivers, RPs in those domains can be on the source tree. The peering relationship is conducted over a TCP connection.

Figure 6-15 shows four PIM domains. The connected RPs (routers) are called MSDP peers because they are exchanging active source information with each other. Each MSDP peer advertises its own set of multicast source information to the other peers. Source host 2 sends the multicast data to group 224.1.1.1. On RP 6, the MSDP process learns about the source through PIM register messages and generates Source-Active (SA) messages to its MSDP peers that contain information about the sources in its domain. When RP 3 and RP 5 receive the SA messages, they forward these messages to their MSDP peers. When RP 5 receives the request from host 1 for the multicast data on group 224.1.1.1, it builds a shortest path tree to the source by sending a PIM join message in the direction of host 2 at 192.1.1.1.

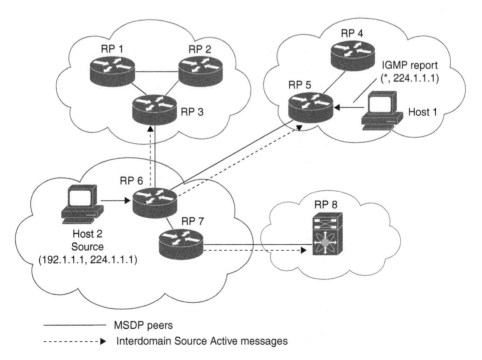

Figure 6-15 *MSDP Peering Between RPs in Different PIM Domains*

IGMP Snooping

The default behavior for a Layer 2 switch is to forward all multicast traffic to every port that belongs to the destination LAN on the switch. This behavior reduces the efficiency of the switch, whose purpose is to limit traffic to the ports that need to receive the data. IGMP snooping efficiently handles IP multicast in a Layer 2 environment; in other words, IGMP snooping makes Layer 2 switches IGMP-aware. IGMP snooping is used on subnets that include end users or receiver clients.

IGMP snooping is an IP multicast constraining mechanism that runs on a Layer 2 LAN switch. IGMP snooping requires the LAN switch to examine, or "snoop," some Layer 3 information (IGMP join/leave messages) in the IGMP packets sent between the hosts and the router. When the switch hears the IGMP host report from a host for a particular multicast group, the switch adds the port number of the host to the associated multi-cast table entry. When the switch hears the IGMP leave group message from a host, the switch removes the table entry of the host. Because IGMP control messages are sent as multicast packets, they are indistinguishable from multicast data at Layer 2. A switch run-ning IGMP snooping examines every multicast data packet to determine if it contains any pertinent IGMP control information.

IGMP snooping configured on Nexus switches examines Layer 2 IP multicast traffic within a VLAN to discover the ports where interested receivers reside. Using the port information, IGMP snooping can reduce bandwidth consumption in a multi-access LAN environment to avoid flooding the entire VLAN. IGMP snooping tracks which ports are attached to multicast-capable routers to help the routers forward IGMP membership reports. The IGMP snooping responds to topology change notifications. By default, IGMP snooping is enabled on the NX-OS device.

Figure 6-16 shows an IGMP snooping switch that sits between the host and the IGMP router. The IGMP snooping switch snoops the IGMP membership reports and the Leave messages and then forwards them only when necessary to the connected IGMP routers.

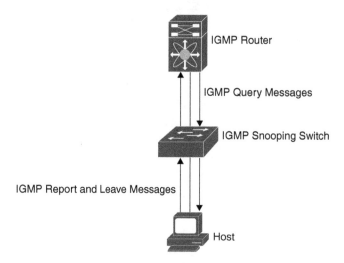

Figure 6-16 *IGMP Snooping Switch*

The IGMP snooping feature operates on IGMPv1, IGMPv2, and IGMPv3 control plane packets where Layer 3 control plane packets are intercepted and influence the Layer 2 forwarding behavior.

With IGMP snooping, the switch learns about connected receivers of a multicast group. The switch can use this information to forward corresponding multicast frames only to the interested receivers. The forwarding decision is based on the destination MAC address. The switch uses the IP-to-MAC address mapping to decide which frames go to which IP multicast receivers (or destination MAC).

The IANA owns a block of Ethernet MAC addresses that start with 01:00:5E in hexadecimal format. Half of this block is allocated for multicast addresses. The range from 0100.5e00.0000 through 0100.5e7f.ffff is the available range of Ethernet MAC addresses for IP multicast.

For IPv4, mapping of the IP multicast group address to a Layer 2 multicast address happens by taking the 23 low-order bits from the IPv4 address and adding them to the 01:00:5e prefix, as shown in Figure 6-17. By the standard, the upper 9 bits of the IP address are ignored, and any IP addresses that only differ in the value of these upper bits are mapped to the same Layer 2 address, since the lower 23 bits used are identical. For example, 239.255.0.1 is mapped to the MAC multicast group address 01:00:5e:7f:00:01. Up to 32 IP multicast group addresses can be mapped to the same Layer 2 address.

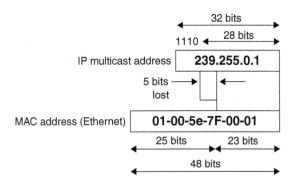

Figure 6-17 *IP Multicast to Ethernet MAC Address Mapping*

Because the upper 5 bits of the IP multicast address are dropped in this mapping, the resulting address is not unique. In fact, 32 different multicast group IDs map to the same Ethernet address, as shown in Figure 6-18. Network administrators should consider this fact when assigning IP multicast addresses. For example, 224.1.1.1 and 225.1.1.1 map to the same multicast MAC address on a Layer 2 switch. If one user subscribes to Group A (as designated by 224.1.1.1) and the other users subscribe to Group B (as designated by 225.1.1.1), they would both receive both A and B streams. This situation limits the effectiveness of this multicast deployment.

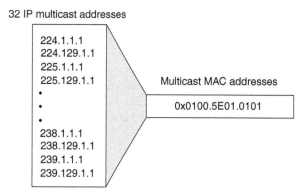

32 IP multicast addresses

224.1.1.1
224.129.1.1
225.1.1.1
225.129.1.1
•
•
•
238.1.1.1
238.129.1.1
239.1.1.1
239.129.1.1

Multicast MAC addresses

0x0100.5E01.0101

Figure 6-18 *MAC Address Ambiguities*

Multicast Configuration on NX-OS

In Cisco NX-OS, multicast is enabled only after you enable the PIM feature on each router and then enable PIM sparse mode on each interface you want to participate in multicast. If you have not already enabled IGMP on the router, PIM enables it automatically.

The PIM process begins when the router establishes PIM neighbor adjacencies by sending PIM hello messages to the multicast IPv4 address 224.0.0.13. Hello messages are sent periodically at the interval of 30 seconds. When all neighbors have replied, the PIM software chooses the router with the highest priority in each LAN segment as the designated router (DR). The DR priority is based on a value in the PIM hello message. If the DR priority value is not supplied by all routers, or if the priorities match, the highest IP address is used to elect the DR.

The hello message also contains a hold-time value, which is typically 3.5 times the hello interval. If this hold time expires without a subsequent hello message from its neighbor, the device detects a PIM failure on that link.

When the DR receives an IGMP membership report message from a receiver for a new group or source, the DR creates a tree to connect the receiver to the source by sending a PIM join message out the interface toward the rendezvous point (ASM mode). The rendezvous point (RP) is the root of a shared tree, which is used by all sources and hosts in the PIM domain in the ASM mode.

When the DR determines that the last host has left a group or source, it sends a PIM prune message to remove the path from the distribution tree. The routers forward the join or prune action hop by hop up the multicast distribution tree to create (join) or tear down (prune) the path.

PIM requires that multicast entries are refreshed within a 3.5-minute timeout interval. The state refresh ensures that traffic is delivered only to active listeners, and it keeps routers from using unnecessary resources.

To maintain the PIM state, the last-hop DR sends join-prune messages once per minute. State creation applies to both (*, G) and (S, G) states as follows:

- **(*, G) state creation example:** An IGMP (*, G) report triggers the DR to send an (*, G) PIM join message toward the RP.

- **(S, G) state creation example:** An IGMP (S, G) report triggers the DR to send an (S, G) PIM join message toward the source.

If the state is not refreshed, the PIM software tears down the distribution tree by removing the forwarding paths in the multicast outgoing interface list of the upstream routers.

PIM register messages are unicast to the RP by DRs that are directly connected to multicast sources. The PIM register message has the following functions:

- To notify the RP that a source is actively sending to a multicast group

- To deliver multicast packets sent by the source to the RP for delivery down the shared tree

The DR continues to send PIM register messages to the RP until it receives a Register-Stop message from the RP. The RP sends a Register-Stop message in either of the following cases:

- The RP has no receivers for the multicast group being transmitted.

- The RP has joined the SPT to the source but has not started receiving traffic from the source.

The PIM triggered register is enabled by default.

Configuring basic PIM sparse mode is a multistep process. The following are the steps to enable a basic configuration of PIM sparse mode:

Step 1. Select the range of multicast groups that you want to configure in the multicast distribution mode.

Step 2. Enable PIM.

Step 3. Configure PIM sparse mode on interfaces.

Step 4. Configure authentication in PIM (optional).

Step 5. Configure RP.

Step 6. Verify the PIM operation.

Table 6-7 summarizes the NX-OS CLI commands related to basic PIM configuration and verification.

Table 6-7   *Summary of NX-OS CLI Commands for PIM Configuration and Verification*

Command	Purpose
configure terminal	Enters global configuration mode.
[no] feature pim	Enables PIM. By default, PIM is disabled.
interface *interface-type slot/port*	Enters interface configuration mode.
ip pim sparse-mode	Enables PIM sparse mode on this interface. The default is disabled.
ip pim hello-authentication ah-md5 *auth-key*	Enables an MD5 hash authentication key in PIM hello messages. You can enter an unencrypted (cleartext) key or one of these values followed by a space and the MD5 authentication key: ■ **0**: Specifies an unencrypted (cleartext) key ■ **3**: Specifies a 3-DES encrypted key ■ **7**: Specifies a Cisco type 7 encrypted key The key can be up to 16 characters. The default is disabled.
ip igmp version *value*	Sets the IGMP version to the value specified. Values can be 2 or 3. The default is 2. The **no** form of the command sets the version to 2.
ip igmp join-group {*group* [source *source*] | route-map *policy-name*}	Configures an interface on the device to join the specified group or channel. The device accepts the multicast packets for CPU consumption only.
ip pim rp-address *rp-address* [group-list *ip-prefix* | prefix-list *name* |override |route-map *policy-name*] [bidir]	Configures a PIM static RP address for a multicast group range. You can specify a **prefix-list** policy name for the static RP address or a **route-map** policy name that lists the group prefixes to use with the **match ip multicast** command. The mode is ASM unless you specify the **bidir** keyword. The **override** option causes the RP address to override the dynamically learned RP addresses for specified groups in **route-map**.

Command	Purpose
show ip pim neighbor [interface *interface* | *ip-prefix*] [vrf *vrf-name* | all]	Displays neighbors by the interface.
show ip pim interface [*interface* | brief] [vrf *vrf-name* | all]	Displays information by the interface.
show ip pim rp [*ip-prefix*] [vrf *vrf-name* | all]	Displays rendezvous points known to the software, how they were learned, and their group ranges.
show ip pim group-range [*ip-prefix*] [vrf *vrf-name* | all]	Displays the learned or configured group ranges and modes.
show ip mroute *ip-address*	Displays the **mroute** entries.

Examples 6-15 through 6-24 show the basic PIM and IGMP configuration and verification on the sample topology shown in Figure 6-19. In this example, we will configure the MD5 authentication on the interfaces connecting the Nexus switches. We will configure Loopback 0 on N9K-B as the multicast receiver for the multicast group 230.0.0.0. Source is connected to the Eth 1/50 interface on N9K-A. OSPFv2 is already configured for the topology in the background for the multicast RPF check to pass.

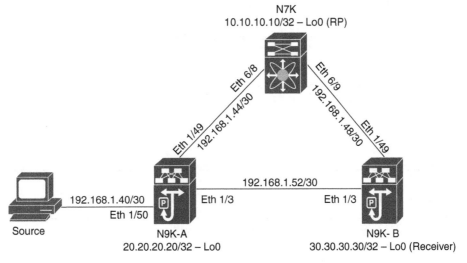

Figure 6-19 *Sample Topology for PIM Configuration and Verification*

Example 6-15   *PIM Configuration on N7K*

```
! Verifying if the interfaces are configured correctly.
N7K# show ip interface brief
IP Interface Status for VRF "default"(1)
Interface          IP Address      Interface Status
Lo0                10.10.10.10     protocol-up/link-up/admin-up
Eth6/8             192.168.1.45    protocol-up/link-up/admin-up
Eth6/9             192.168.1.49    protocol-up/link-up/admin-up


! Enabling PIM feature.
N7K# configure terminal
Enter configuration commands, one per line.  End with CNTL/Z.
N7K(config)# feature pim

! Enabling Loopback 0, Ethernet 6/8 and Ethernet 6/9 for pim sparse-mode and config-
uring md5 authentication with authentication key cisco on interface Ethernet 6/8
and Ethernet 6/9.
N7K(config)# interface Loopback 0
N7K(config-if)# ip pim sparse-mode
N7K(config-if)# interface Ethernet 6/8
N7K(config-if)# ip pim sparse-mode
N7K(config-if)# ip pim hello-authentication ah-md5 cisco
N7K(config-if)# interface Ethernet 6/9
N7K(config-if)# ip pim sparse-mode
N7K(config-if)# ip pim hello-authentication ah-md5 cisco
N7K(config-if)# exit


! Configuring Loopback 0 interface of N7K as static RP. Since we are not specifying
the group for the RP, it will act as RP for whole multicast range i.e. 224.0.0.0/4.
N7K(config)# ip pim rp-address 10.10.10.10
N7K(config)# exit
N7K#
```

Example 6-16   *PIM Configuration on N9K-A*

```
! Verifying if the interfaces are configured correctly.
N9K-A# show ip interface brief
IP Interface Status for VRF "default"(1)
Interface          IP Address      Interface Status
Lo0                20.20.20.20     protocol-up/link-up/admin-up
Eth1/3             192.168.1.53    protocol-up/link-up/admin-up
Eth1/49            192.168.1.46    protocol-up/link-up/admin-up
```

```
Eth1/50              192.168.1.42    protocol-up/link-up/admin-up

! Enabling PIM feature.
N9K-A# configure terminal
Enter configuration commands, one per line. End with CNTL/Z.
N9K-A(config)# feature pim


! Enabling Loopback 0, Ethernet 1/49 and Ethernet 1/3 for pim sparse-mode and con-
figuring md5 authentication with authentication key cisco on interface Ethernet
1/49 and Ethernet 1/3.
N9K-A(config)# interface Loopback 0
N9K-A(config-if)# ip pim sparse-mode
N9K-A(config-if)# interface Ethernet 1/49
N9K-A(config-if)# ip pim sparse-mode
N9K-A(config-if)# ip pim hello-authentication ah-md5 cisco
N9K-A(config-if)# interface Ethernet 1/3
N9K-A(config-if)# ip pim sparse-mode
N9K-A(config-if)# ip pim hello-authentication ah-md5 cisco
N9K-A(config-if)# exit


! Configuring Loopback 0 interface of N7K as static RP. Since we are not specifying
the group for the RP, it will act as RP for whole multicast range i.e. 224.0.0.0/4.
N9K-A(config)# ip pim rp-address 10.10.10.10
N9K-A(config)# exit
N9K-A#
```

Example 6-17 *PIM Configuration on N9K-B*

```
! Verifying if the interfaces are configured correctly.
N9K-B# show ip interface brief
IP Interface Status for VRF "default"(1)
Interface         IP Address      Interface Status
Lo0               30.30.30.30     protocol-up/link-up/admin-up
Eth1/3            192.168.1.54    protocol-up/link-up/admin-up
Eth1/49           192.168.1.50    protocol-up/link-up/admin-up


! Enabling PIM feature.
N9K-B# configure terminal
Enter configuration commands, one per line. End with CNTL/Z.
N9K-B(config)# feature pim
```

```
! Enabling Loopback 0, Ethernet 1/49 and Ethernet 1/3 for pim sparse-mode and con-
figuring md5 authentication with authentication key cisco on interface Ethernet
1/49 and Ethernet 1/3.
N9K-B(config)# interface Loopback 0
N9K-B(config-if)# ip pim sparse-mode
N9K-B(config-if)# interface Ethernet 1/49
N9K-B(config-if)# ip pim sparse-mode
N9K-B(config-if)# ip pim hello-authentication ah-md5 cisco
N9K-B(config-if)# interface Ethernet 1/3
N9K-B(config-if)# ip pim sparse-mode
N9K-B(config-if)# ip pim hello-authentication ah-md5 cisco
N9K-B(config-if)# exit

! Configuring Loopback 0 interface of N7K as static RP. Since we are not specifying
the group for the RP, it will act as RP for whole multicast range i.e. 224.0.0.0/4.
N9K-B(config)# ip pim rp-address 10.10.10.10
N9K-B(config)# exit
N9K-B#
```

Example 6-18 *PIM Verification on N7K*

```
! Verifying PIM neighbors.
N7K# show ip pim neighbor
PIM Neighbor Status for VRF "default"
Neighbor        Interface           Uptime    Expires   DR      Bidir- BFD
ECMP Redirect
                                                        Priority Capable State
Capable
192.168.1.46    Ethernet6/8         00:05:44  00:01:43  1        yes    n/a
no
192.168.1.50    Ethernet6/9         00:01:38  00:01:34  1        yes    n/a
no


! Verifying interfaces configured for PIM.
N7K# show ip pim interface brief
PIM Interface Status for VRF "default"
Interface          IP Address       PIM DR Address    Neighbor  Border
                                                      Count     Interface
Ethernet6/8        192.168.1.45     192.168.1.46      1         no
Ethernet6/9        192.168.1.49     192.168.1.50      1         no
loopback0          10.10.10.10      10.10.10.10       0         no


! Verifying RP configured for PIM.
N7K# show ip pim rp
```

```
PIM RP Status Information for VRF "default"
BSR disabled
Auto-RP disabled
BSR RP Candidate policy: None
BSR RP policy: None
Auto-RP Announce policy: None
Auto-RP Discovery policy: None

RP: 10.10.10.10*, (0),
 uptime: 00:08:46   priority: 255,
 RP-source: (local),
 group ranges:
 224.0.0.0/4


! Verifying current multicast groups configured for PIM.
N7K# show ip pim group-range
PIM Group-Range Configuration for VRF "default"
Group-range       Action Mode  RP-address      Shrd-tree-range   Origin
232.0.0.0/8       Accept SSM   -               -                 Local
224.0.0.0/4       -      ASM   10.10.10.10     -                 Static

! Verifying multicast routing table.
N7K# show ip mroute
IP Multicast Routing Table for VRF "default"

(*, 232.0.0.0/8), uptime: 00:20:58, pim ip
  Incoming interface: Null, RPF nbr: 0.0.0.0
  Outgoing interface list: (count: 0)
```

Example 6-19 *PIM Verification on N9K-A*

```
! Verifying PIM neighbors.
N9K-A# show ip pim neighbor
PIM Neighbor Status for VRF "default"
Neighbor        Interface        Uptime    Expires   DR    Bidir-  BFD
ECMP Redirect
                                                     Priority Capable State
Capable
192.168.1.54    Ethernet1/3      00:01:06  00:01:36  1     yes     n/a
no
192.168.1.45    Ethernet1/49     00:05:28  00:01:44  1     yes     n/a
no


! Verifying interfaces configured for PIM.
```

```
N9K-A# show ip pim interface brief
PIM Interface Status for VRF "default"
Interface          IP Address      PIM DR Address   Neighbor  Border
                                                    Count     Interface

Ethernet1/3        192.168.1.53    192.168.1.54     1         no
Ethernet1/49       192.168.1.46    192.168.1.46     1         no
loopback0          20.20.20.20     20.20.20.20      0         no


! Verifying RP configured for PIM.
N9K-A# show ip pim rp
PIM RP Status Information for VRF "default"
BSR disabled
Auto-RP disabled
BSR RP Candidate policy: None
BSR RP policy: None
Auto-RP Announce policy: None
Auto-RP Discovery policy: None

RP: 10.10.10.10, (0),
 uptime: 00:11:05   priority: 255,
 RP-source: (local),
 group ranges:
 224.0.0.0/4


! Verifying current multicast groups configured for PIM.
N9K-A# show ip pim group-range
PIM Group-Range Configuration for VRF "default"
Group-range        Action Mode  RP-address      Shared-tree-range Origin
232.0.0.0/8        Accept SSM   -               -                 Local
224.0.0.0/4        -      ASM   10.10.10.10     -                 Static


! Verifying multicast routing table.
N9K-A# show ip mroute
IP Multicast Routing Table for VRF "default"

(*, 232.0.0.0/8), uptime: 00:12:38, pim ip
  Incoming interface: Null, RPF nbr: 0.0.0.0
  Outgoing interface list: (count: 0)
```

Example 6-20   *PIM Verification on N9K-B*

```
! Verifying PIM neighbors.
N9K-B# show ip pim neighbor
PIM Neighbor Status for VRF "default"
Neighbor        Interface         Uptime    Expires   DR        Bidir- BFD
ECMP Redirect
                                                      Priority Capable State
Capable
192.168.1.53    Ethernet1/3       00:00:46  00:01:31  1         yes    n/a
no
192.168.1.49    Ethernet1/49      00:01:02  00:01:30  1         yes    n/a
no


! Verifying interfaces configured for PIM.
N9K-B# show ip pim interface brief
PIM Interface Status for VRF "default"
Interface         IP Address      PIM DR Address  Neighbor  Border
                                                  Count     Interface
Ethernet1/3       192.168.1.54    192.168.1.54    1         no
Ethernet1/49      192.168.1.50    192.168.1.50    1         no
loopback0         30.30.30.30     30.30.30.30     0         no


! Verifying RP configured for PIM.
N9K-B# show ip pim rp
PIM RP Status Information for VRF "default"
BSR disabled
Auto-RP disabled
BSR RP Candidate policy: None
BSR RP policy: None
Auto-RP Announce policy: None
Auto-RP Discovery policy: None


RP: 10.10.10.10, (0),
 uptime: 00:08:13   priority: 255,
 RP-source: (local),
 group ranges:
 224.0.0.0/4


! Verifying current multicast groups configured for PIM.
N9K-B# show ip pim group-range
PIM Group-Range Configuration for VRF "default"
Group-range       Action Mode  RP-address      Shared-tree-range Origin
232.0.0.0/8       Accept SSM   -               -                 Local
224.0.0.0/4       -      ASM   10.10.10.10     -                 Static
```

```
! Verifying multicast routing table.
N9K-B# show ip mroute
IP Multicast Routing Table for VRF "default"

(*, 232.0.0.0/8), uptime: 00:11:35, pim ip
  Incoming interface: Null, RPF nbr: 0.0.0.0
  Outgoing interface list: (count: 0)
```

Example 6-21   *IGMP Configuration on N9K-B*

```
! Configuring Loopback 0 on N9K-B to join the 230.0.0.0 group and act as receiver
for the group.
N9K-B# configure terminal
Enter configuration commands, one per line. End with CNTL/Z.
N9K-B(config)# interface Loopback 0
N9K-B(config-if)# ip igmp version 3
N9K-B(config-if)# ip igmp join-group 230.0.0.0
Note: IGMP join-group disrupts forwarding on the outgoing interface list

N9K-B(config-if)# end
N9K-B#
```

Once we configure the receiver, a shared tree is formed from the RP to the receiver represented by the (*, G) entry, as shown in Figure 6-20. When the receiver sends the IGMP report to the RP, you will see an (*, G) entry on the shared tree path from RP to receiver (that is, N7K and N9K-B switches). The shared tree path can be verified by checking the incoming interface and outgoing interface list in the multicast routing table, as shown in Example 6-22.

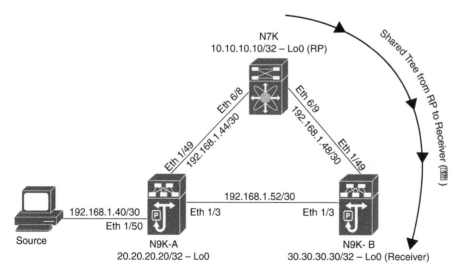

Figure 6-20   *Shared Tree (*, G) from RP to Receiver*

Example 6-22   *The mroute Verification on N7K, N9K-A, and N9K-B After Configuring IGMP*

```
! Verifying the multicast routing table on N7K, N9K-A and N9K-B to trace the shared
tree path from RP(N7K) to Receiver(N9K-B).


N7K


N7K# show ip mroute
IP Multicast Routing Table for VRF "default"

(*, 230.0.0.0/32), uptime: 00:01:20, pim ip
  Incoming interface: loopback0, RPF nbr: 10.10.10.10
  Outgoing interface list: (count: 1)
    Ethernet6/9, uptime: 00:01:20, pim



(*, 232.0.0.0/8), uptime: 00:03:10, pim ip
  Incoming interface: Null, RPF nbr: 0.0.0.0
  Outgoing interface list: (count: 0)


N9K-A


N9K-A# show ip mroute
IP Multicast Routing Table for VRF "default"

(*, 232.0.0.0/8), uptime: 00:03:51, pim ip
  Incoming interface: Null, RPF nbr: 0.0.0.0
  Outgoing interface list: (count: 0)


N9K-B


N9K-B# show ip mroute
IP Multicast Routing Table for VRF "default"

(*, 230.0.0.0/32), uptime: 00:00:38, igmp ip pim
  Incoming interface: Ethernet1/49, RPF nbr: 192.168.1.49
  Outgoing interface list: (count: 1)
    loopback0, uptime: 00:00:38, igmp



(*, 232.0.0.0/8), uptime: 00:02:33, pim ip
  Incoming interface: Null, RPF nbr: 0.0.0.0
  Outgoing interface list: (count: 0)
```

Before the source generates any traffic, we have to enable PIM sparse mode on the Ethernet 1/50 interface on N9K-A, as shown in Example 6-23, to make it multicast capable.

Example 6-23   *Enabling the Interface Connected to the Source with PIM*

```
N9K-A(config-if)# interface Ethernet 1/50
N9K-A(config-if)# ip pim sparse-mode
```

Once the source generates some multicast traffic for the receivers, you will see an (S, G) entry on the path from the source to the receiver (that is, N9K-A, N7K, and N9K-B switch). The shortest path tree can be verified by checking the incoming interface and outgoing interface list in the multicast routing table, as shown in Example 6-24.

Example 6-24   *The mroute Verification on N7K, N9K-A, and N9K-B with Multicast Traffic from Source to Receiver*

```
! Verifying the multicast routing table on N7K, N9K-A and N9K-B to trace the Short-
est Path Tree (SPT) from the Source to the Receiver(N9K-B).


N7K


N7K# show ip mroute
IP Multicast Routing Table for VRF "default"

(*, 230.0.0.0/32), uptime: 00:00:39, pim ip
  Incoming interface: loopback0, RPF nbr: 10.10.10.10
  Outgoing interface list: (count: 1)
    Ethernet6/9, uptime: 00:00:39, pim


(192.168.1.41/32, 230.0.0.0/32), uptime: 00:00:08, pim mrib ip
  Incoming interface: Ethernet6/8, RPF nbr: 192.168.1.46, internal
  Outgoing interface list: (count: 1)
    Ethernet6/9, uptime: 00:00:08, pim


(*, 232.0.0.0/8), uptime: 00:00:42, pim ip
  Incoming interface: Null, RPF nbr: 0.0.0.0
  Outgoing interface list: (count: 0)
```

```
N9K-A


N9K-A# show ip mroute
IP Multicast Routing Table for VRF "default"


(192.168.1.41/32, 230.0.0.0/32), uptime: 00:00:39, ip pim
  Incoming interface: Ethernet1/50, RPF nbr: 192.168.1.41
  Outgoing interface list: (count: 1)
    Ethernet1/49, uptime: 00:00:39, pim



(*, 232.0.0.0/8), uptime: 00:01:08, pim ip
  Incoming interface: Null, RPF nbr: 0.0.0.0
  Outgoing interface list: (count: 0)


N9K-B



N9K-B# show ip mroute
IP Multicast Routing Table for VRF "default"

(*, 230.0.0.0/32), uptime: 00:01:28, igmp ip pim
  Incoming interface: Ethernet1/49, RPF nbr: 192.168.1.49
  Outgoing interface list: (count: 1)
    loopback0, uptime: 00:01:28, igmp



(192.168.1.41/32, 230.0.0.0/32), uptime: 00:00:57, ip mrib pim
  Incoming interface: Ethernet1/49, RPF nbr: 192.168.1.49
  Outgoing interface list: (count: 1)
    loopback0, uptime: 00:00:57, mrib



(*, 232.0.0.0/8), uptime: 00:01:28, pim ip
  Incoming interface: Null, RPF nbr: 0.0.0.0
  Outgoing interface list: (count: 0)
```

Figure 6-21 illustrates the shortest path tree (SPT) from the source to the receiver (N9K-B).

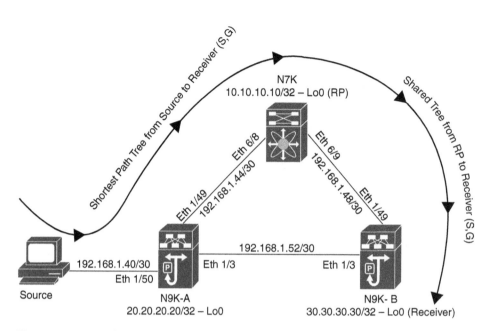

Figure 6-21   *Multicast Packet Flow from Source to Receiver*

Summary

This chapter discusses routing fundamentals, configuration and verification of RIPv2, EIGRP, and OSPFv2 unicast routing protocols on NX-OS, multicast fundamentals, and PIMv2 configuration and verification on NX-OS, including the following points:

■ Layer 3 unicast routing involves two basic activities: determining optimal routing paths and packet switching.

■ Routing algorithms use many different metrics to determine the best path to the destination.

■ An autonomous system (AS) is a portion of an internetwork under common administrative authority that is regulated by a particular set of administrative guidelines.

■ An administrative distance is a rating of the trustworthiness of a routing information source. A higher value indicates a lower trust rating.

■ Routing protocols that route packets between autonomous systems are called exterior gateway protocols or interdomain protocols. Routing protocols used within an autonomous system are called interior gateway protocols or intradomain protocols.

■ Distance vector protocols use distance vector algorithms (also known as Bellman-Ford algorithms) that call for each router to send all or some portion of its routing table to its neighbors.

In link-state protocols, also known as shortest path first (SPF), each router builds a link-state advertisement (LSA) that contains information about each link and directly connected neighbor router and shares the information with its neighboring routers.

The Routing Information Protocol (RIP) is a distance vector protocol that uses a hop count as its metric.

The Enhanced Interior Gateway Routing Protocol (EIGRP) is a unicast routing protocol that has the characteristics of both distance vector and link-state routing protocols. By default, EIGRP uses the bandwidth and delay as its metrics.

- OSPFv2 is a link-state protocol that uses a link cost as its metric and uses link-state advertisements (LSAs) to build its routing table.

- Multicast involves both a method of delivery and discovery of senders and receivers of multicast data, which is transmitted on IP multicast addresses called groups.

- A multicast distribution tree represents the path that multicast data takes between the routers that connect sources and receivers. Protocol-Independent Multicast (PIM) is used to dynamically create a multicast distribution tree.

- IGMP is used to dynamically register individual hosts in a multicast group on a particular LAN. IGMP snooping allows switches to examine IGMP packets and make forwarding decisions based on their content.

- MSDP enables RPs to share information about active sources across PIM-SM domains.

References

"Cisco Nexus 9000 Series NX-OS Unicast Configuration Guide, Release 10.2(x),": https://www.cisco.com/c/en/us/td/docs/dcn/nx-os/nexus9000/102x/configuration/Unicast-routing/cisco-nexus-9000-series-nx-os-unicast-configuration-guide-release-102x.html

"Cisco Nexus 7000 Series NX-OS Unicast Routing Configuration Guide, Release 8.x," https://www.cisco.com/c/en/us/td/docs/switches/datacenter/nexus7000/sw/unicast/config/cisco_nexus7000_unicast_routing_config_guide_8x.html

"Cisco Nexus 9000 Series NX-OS Multicast Routing Configuration Guide, Release 10.2(x)," https://www.cisco.com/c/en/us/td/docs/dcn/nx-os/nexus9000/102x/configuration/multicast-routing/cisco-nexus-9000-series-nx-os-multicast-routing-configuration-guide-release-102x.html

"Cisco Nexus 7000 Series NX-OS Multicast Routing Configuration Guide, Release 8.x," https://www.cisco.com/c/en/us/td/docs/switches/datacenter/nexus7000/sw/multicast/config/cisco_nexus7000_multicast_routing_config_guide_8x.html

Relevant Cisco Live sessions: http://www.ciscolive.com

Chapter 7

Network Virtualization

Network virtualization is a method of combining the available resources in a network to consolidate multiple physical networks and making them operate as single or multiple independent networks called virtual networks. Once the virtual networks are created, the hardware-based physical network is then only responsible for forwarding packets while the virtual network is used to deploy and manage network services. In other words, network virtualization is the abstraction of network resources that were traditionally delivered in hardware to software.

In this chapter, we will discuss overlay network protocols such as Network Virtualization using GRE (NVGRE), Cisco Overlay Transport Virtualization (OTV), and VXLAN Overlay. We will also discuss network interface virtualization using FEX technology and VMware vSphere virtual switches.

Overlay Network Protocols

Modern virtualized data center fabrics must meet certain requirements to accelerate application deployment and support DevOps needs. For example, fabrics need to support scaling of forwarding tables, scaling of network segments, Layer 2 segment extension, virtual device mobility, forwarding path optimization, and virtualized networks for multitenant support on shared physical infrastructure. Overlay network protocols such as NVGRE, Cisco OTV, VXLAN, and so on help to achieve these requirements. Before we discuss various overlay network protocols, let's first make sure you understand the concepts of underlay and overlay.

An underlay network is the physical infrastructure above which an overlay network is built. It is the underlying network responsible for the delivery of packets across networks. In data center environments, the role of the physical underlay network is to provide unicast IP connectivity from any physical device (server, storage device, router, or switch) to any other physical device. Underlay networks are less scalable due to technology limitations.

Network overlays are virtual networks of interconnected nodes that share an underlying physical network, allowing deployment of applications that require specific network topologies without the need to modify the underlying network. Multiple overlay networks can coexist at the same time.

Figure 7-1 illustrates underlay and overlay network concepts.

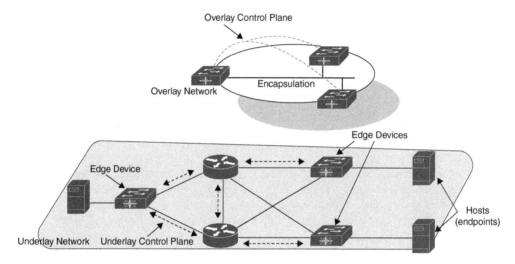

Figure 7-1   *Underlay and Overlay Networks*

There are two types of overlay networks:

■ **Layer 2 overlays:** Layer 2 overlays emulate a LAN segment and transport both IP and non-IP packets, and forwarding is based on Ethernet frame headers. Mobility is restricted to a single subnet (that is, a single L2 domain). Since it's a single L2 domain, Layer 2 floods are not uncommon. Layer 2 overlays are useful in emulating physical topologies.

■ **Layer 3 overlays:** Layer 3 overlays abstract IP-based connectivity and transport IP packets. They provide full mobility regardless of subnets. Flooding is contained to network-related failures. Layer 3 overlays are useful in abstracting connectivity and policy.

Figure 7-2 illustrates Layer 2 and Layer 3 overlays.

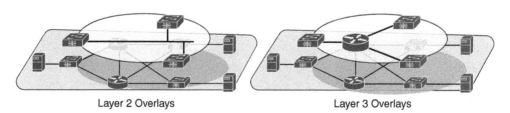

Figure 7-2   *Layer 2 and Layer 3 Overlays*

Depending on the types of overlay edge devices (that is, where the virtualized network is terminated), overlays are classified into three categories.

■ **Network-based overlays:** In network-based overlays, edge routers/switches act as endpoints. Encapsulation and forwarding are performed at the edge router/switch. Tunneling is initiated at the edge router/switch, and control is distributed. Traditional VPNs and OTV are examples of network-based overlays.

■ **Host-based overlays:** In host-based overlays, the endpoints are virtual. Encapsulation and forwarding are performed at the server. Tunneling is initiated at the server, and control is centralized. NVGRE and VXLAN are examples of host-based overlays.

■ **Hybrid overlays:** Hybrid overlays are a combination of network-based and host-based overlay types, where the endpoints can be either physical (routers/switches) or virtual (virtual machines). VXLAN is an example of a hybrid overlay and can have either physical or virtual endpoints.

Figure 7-3 illustrates network-based and host-based overlays.

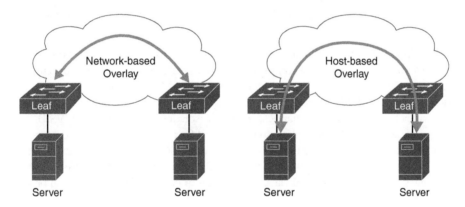

Figure 7-3 *Network-Based vs. Host-Based Overlays*

Overlay technologies allow the network to scale by focusing scaling on the network overlay edge devices. With overlays used at the fabric edge, the core devices are freed from the need to add end-host information to their forwarding tables. Most overlay technologies used in the data center allow virtual network IDs to uniquely scope and identify individual private networks. This scoping allows potential overlap in MAC and IP addresses between tenants. The overlay encapsulation also allows the underlying infrastructure address space to be administered separately from the tenant address space.

Network Virtualization Using GRE

NVGRE (Network Virtualization using Generic Routing Encapsulation) is a network virtualization method that creates virtual Layer 2 topologies on top of a physical Layer 3 network. Connectivity in the virtual topology is provided by tunneling Ethernet frames in GRE over IP over the physical network. The purpose is to enable multitenant and load-balanced networks that can be shared across on-premises and cloud environments. NVGRE protocol was proposed by Microsoft and its partners as part of the Hyper-V solution. Hyper-V is Microsoft's hardware virtualization solution, similar to VMWare's ESXi solution.

In NVGRE, every virtual Layer 2 network is associated with a 24-bit identifier, called a virtual subnet identifier (VSID). A 24-bit VSID supports up to 16 million virtual sub-nets in the same management domain, in contrast to only 4094 achievable with VLANs. Thus, NVGRE solves the problems caused by the limited number of VLANs the IEEE 802.1Q specification enables, which is inadequate for complex virtualized environments and makes it difficult to stretch network segments over the long distances required for dispersed data centers. To support a multi-subnet virtual topology, data center admin-istrators can configure routes to facilitate communication between virtual subnets of the same tenant. NVGRE leverages the GRE header to carry VSID information in each packet.

NVGRE endpoints (NVEs) are the ingress/egress points between the virtual and the physical networks. Any physical server or network device can be an NVGRE endpoint. One common deployment is for the endpoint to be part of a hypervisor. The primary function of this endpoint is to encapsulate/decapsulate Ethernet data frames to and from the GRE tunnel, ensure Layer 2 semantics, and apply isolation policy scoped on VSID. The endpoint can optionally participate in routing and function as a gateway in the vir-tual topology. To encapsulate an Ethernet frame, the endpoint needs to know the location information for the destination address in the frame. This information can be provisioned via a management plane or obtained via a combination of control-plane distribution or data-plane learning approaches.

Figure 7-4 shows the NVGRE frame format.

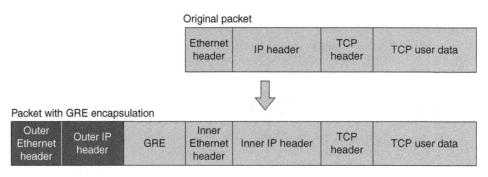

Figure 7-4 *NVGRE Frame Format*

- **Outer Ethernet header:** The source Ethernet address in the outer frame is set to the MAC address associated with the NVGRE endpoint. The destination endpoint may or may not be on the same physical subnet. The destination Ethernet address is set to the MAC address of the next-hop IP address for the destination NVE.

- **Outer IP header:** The IP address in the outer frame is referred to as the Provider Address (PA). There can be one or more PAs associated with an NVGRE endpoint, with policy controlling the choice of which PA to use for a given Customer Address (CA) for a customer VM.

- **GRE header:** In the GRE header, the C (Checksum Present) and S (Sequence Number Present) bits must be 0 and the K (Key Present) bit must be set to 1. The 32-bit Key field in the GRE header is used to carry the VSID and the Flow ID. Flow ID is an 8-bit value that is used to provide per-flow entropy for flows in the same VSID and must not be modified by transit devices. If FlowID is not generated, it must be set to all zeros. The protocol field in the GRE header is set to 0x6558.

- **Inner Ethernet and IP header:** The inner Ethernet frame is composed of an inner Ethernet header followed by *optional* inner IP header, followed by the IP payload. The inner frame could be any Ethernet data frame, not just IP. The IP address contained in the inner frame is referred to as the Customer Address (CA).

Figure 7-5 shows a typical NVGRE communication. The traffic is transported from VM1 (10.0.0.5) to VM2 (10.0.0.7). Two VM1s with the same IP address are representing two different customers using the same IP address space. The original IP packet is encapsulated with the MAC header containing MAC addresses of the source and destination VMs of specific customer VMs that are communicating. On top of that, a GRE header is added that contains a VSID used to identify each virtual network. The outer IP header contains the source and destination IP address of the tunnel endpoints (that is, the provider address).

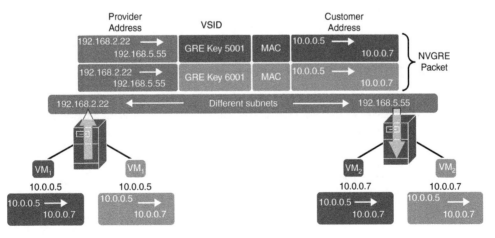

Figure 7-5 *NVGRE Communication*

Cisco Overlay Transport Virtualization

Cisco Overlay Transport Virtualization (OTV) is a MAC-in-IP method that provides a Layer 2 LAN extension over Layer 2, Layer 3, or label-switched Multiprotocol Label Switching–based networks. OTV provides Layer 2 connectivity between remote network sites by using MAC address-based routing and IP-encapsulated forwarding across a transport network to provide support for applications that require Layer 2 adjacency, such as clusters and virtualization. OTV is deployed on the edge devices in each site. OTV requires no other changes to the sites or the transport network.

OTV uses the following terms:

- **Edge device:** An edge device performs typical Layer 2 learning and forwarding on the site-facing interfaces (internal interfaces) and performs IP-based virtualization on the transport-facing interfaces. The edge device capability can be colocated in a device that performs Layer 2 and Layer 3 functionality. OTV functionality only occurs in an edge device. A given edge device can have multiple overlay interfaces. You can also configure multiple edge devices on a site.

- **Authoritative edge device:** OTV provides loop-free multihoming by electing a designated forwarding device per site for each VLAN. This forwarder is known as an authoritative edge device (AED). The edge devices at the site communicate with each other on the internal interfaces to elect the AED.

- **Transport network:** The network that connects OTV sites. This network can be customer managed, provided by a service provider, or a mix of both.

- **Join interface:** One of the uplink interfaces of the edge device. The join interface is a point-to-point routed interface. The edge device joins an overlay network through this interface. The IP address of this interface is used to advertise reachability of a MAC address present in this site.

- **Internal interface:** The Layer 2 interface on the edge device that connects to the VLANs that are to be extended. These VLANs typically form a Layer 2 domain known as a site and can contain site-based switches or site-based routers. The internal interface is a Layer 2 access or trunk interface regardless of whether the internal interface connects to a switch or a router.

- **MAC routing:** Associates the destination MAC address of the Layer 2 traffic with an edge device IP address. The MAC-to-IP association is advertised to the edge devices through the OTV control-plane protocol. In MAC routing, MAC addresses are reachable through the IP address of a remote edge device on the overlay network. Layer 2 traffic destined to a MAC address is encapsulated in an IP packet based on the MAC-to-IP mapping in the MAC table.

- **Overlay interface:** A logical multi-access, multicast-capable interface. The overlay interface encapsulates Layer 2 frames in IP unicast or multicast headers.

- **Overlay network:** A logical network that interconnects remote sites for MAC routing of Layer 2 traffic. The overlay network is composed of multiple edge devices.

- **Site:** A Layer 2 network that may be single-homed or multihomed to the transport network and the OTV overlay network. Layer 2 connectivity between sites is provided by edge devices that operate in an overlay network. Layer 2 sites are physically separated from each other by the transport network.

- **Site VLAN:** OTV sends local hello messages on the site VLAN to detect other OTV edge devices in the site and uses the site VLAN to determine the authoritative edge device for the OTV-extended VLANs. VLAN 1 is the default site VLAN. It is recommended to use a dedicated VLAN as a site VLAN. You should ensure that the site VLAN is active on at least one of the edge device ports and that the site VLAN is not extended across the overlay.

Figure 7-6 shows various OTV interfaces.

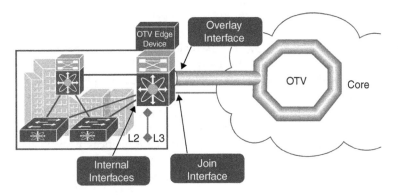

Figure 7-6 *OTV Interfaces*

OTV builds Layer 2 reachability information by communicating between edge devices with the overlay protocol. The overlay protocol forms adjacencies with all edge devices. Once each edge device is adjacent with all its peers on the overlay, the edge devices share MAC address reachability information with other edge devices that participate in the same overlay network.

OTV offers unicast and multicast as transports between sites. For a small number of sites such as two or three sites, unicast works just fine without losing any features or functions. In unicast-only transport, edge devices register with an adjacency server (AS) edge device and receive a full list of neighbors (oNL) from the AS. An edge device can be manually configured to act as an AS edge device. OTV hellos and updates are encapsulated in IP and unicast to each neighbor. Figure 7-7 illustrates the neighbor discovery process over unicast-only transport.

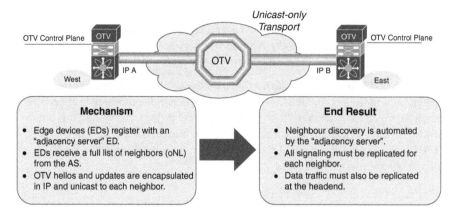

Figure 7-7   *Neighbor Discovery (over Unicast-only Transport)*

Multicast is the preferred transport because of its flexibility and smaller overhead when communicating with multiple sites. In multicast transport, one multicast address (the control-group address) is used to encapsulate and exchange OTV control-plane protocol updates. Each edge device that participates in the particular overlay network shares the same control-group address with all the other edge devices. As soon as the control-group address and the join interface are configured, the edge device sends an IGMP report message to join the control group. The edge devices act as hosts in the multicast network and send multicast IGMP report messages to the assigned multicast group address. Figure 7-8 illustrates the neighbor discovery process over multicast transport.

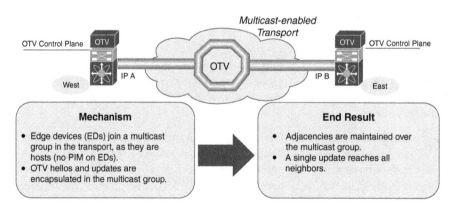

Figure 7-8   *Neighbor Discovery (over Multicast Transport)*

As in traditional link-state routing protocols, edge devices exchange OTV control-plane hellos to build adjacencies with other edge devices in the overlay network. Once the adjacencies are established, OTV control-plane link-state packets (LSPs) communicate MAC-to-IP mappings to the adjacent devices. These LSPs contain the IP address of the remote edge device, the VLAN IDs, and the learned MAC addresses that are reachable through that edge device.

Edge devices participate in data-plane learning on internal interfaces to build up the list of MAC addresses that are reachable within a site. OTV sends these locally learned MAC addresses in the OTV control-plane updates to remote sites.

When an edge device receives a Layer 2 frame on an internal interface, OTV performs the MAC table lookup based on the destination address of the Layer 2 frame. If the frame is destined to a MAC address that is reachable through another internal interface, the frame is forwarded out on that internal interface. OTV performs no other actions, and the processing of the frame is complete.

If the frame is destined to a MAC address that was learned over an overlay interface, OTV performs the following tasks, as illustrated in Figure 7-9:

1. Strips off the preamble and frame check sequence (FCS) from the Layer 2 frame.

2. Adds an OTV shim header to the Layer 2 frame and copies the 802.1Q information into the OTV shim header. The outer OTV shim header contains the VLAN, overlay number, and so on.

3. Adds the IP address to the packet, based on the initial MAC address table lookup. This IP address is used as a destination address for the IP packet that is sent into the core switch. In the process, 42 bytes of overhead to the packet IP MTU size is added for IPv4 packet.

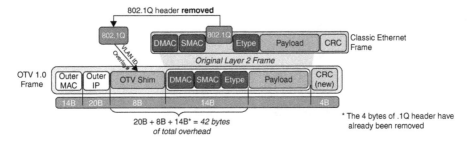

Figure 7-9 *OTV Encapsulation*

OTV traffic appears as IP traffic to the network core. At the destination site, the edge device performs the reverse operation and presents the original Layer 2 frame to the local site. That edge device determines the correct internal interface to forward the frame on, based on the local MAC address table.

In Figure 7-10, the west site communicates with the east site over the overlay network. Edge Device 1 receives the Layer 2 frame from MAC1, which belongs to Server 1, and looks up the destination MAC address, MAC3, in the MAC table. The edge device encapsulates the Layer 2 frame in an IP packet with the IP destination address set for Edge Device 3 (IP B). When Edge Device 3 receives the IP packet, it strips off the IP header and sends the original Layer 2 frame onto the VLAN and port that MAC3 is connected to.

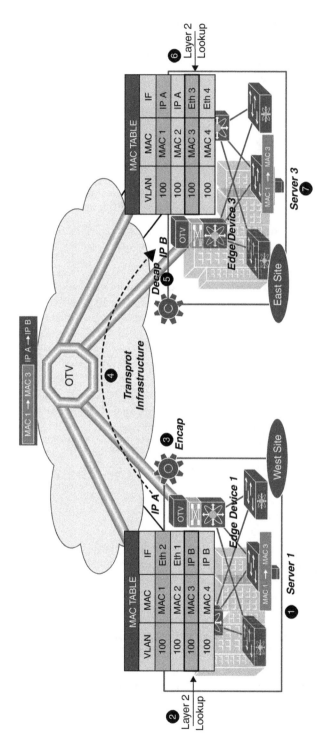

Figure 7-10   *MAC Routing*

VXLAN Overlay

Traditional network segmentation has been provided by VLANs that are standardized under the IEEE 802.1Q group. VLANs provide logical segmentation of Layer 2 boundaries or broadcast domains. However, due to the inefficient use of available network links with VLAN use, the rigid requirements on device placement in the data center network, and the limited scalability to a maximum of 4094 VLANs, using VLANs has become a limiting factor for IT departments and cloud providers as they build large multitenant data centers. Virtual Extensible LAN (VXLAN) provides the solution to the data center network challenges posed by traditional VLAN technology by providing elastic workload placement and the higher scalability of Layer2 segmentation required by today's application demands.

Virtual Extensible LAN (VXLAN) is a Layer 2 overlay scheme over a Layer 3 network and provides a means to extend Layer 2 segments across a Layer 3 infrastructure using MAC-in-UDP encapsulation and tunneling. VXLAN supports a flexible, large-scale multitenant environment over a shared common physical infrastructure. The transport protocol over the physical data center network is IP plus UDP.

VXLAN has the following benefits:

- **Flexible placement of workloads across the data center fabric:** VXLAN provides a way to extend Layer 2 segments over the underlying shared Layer 3 network infrastructure so that tenant workloads can be placed across physical pods in a single data center—or even across several geographically diverse data centers.

- **Higher scalability to allow more Layer 2 segments:** VXLAN uses a 24-bit segment ID, the VXLAN network identifier (VNID). This allows a maximum of 16 million VXLAN segments to coexist in the same administrative domain. In comparison, traditional VLANs use a 12-bit segment ID that can support a maximum of 4096 VLANs.

- **Optimized utilization of available network paths in the underlying infrastructure:** VXLAN packets are transferred through the underlying network based on their Layer 3 headers. They use equal-cost multipath (ECMP) routing and link aggregation protocols to use all available paths. In contrast, a Layer 2 network might block valid forwarding paths to avoid loops.

Before understanding the VXLAN operation, let's first discuss a few important terms:

- **VXLAN tunnel:** VXLAN encapsulated communication between two devices, where they encapsulate and decapsulate an inner Ethernet frame, is called a VXLAN tunnel. VXLAN tunnels are stateless since they are UDP-encapsulated.

- **Virtual network instance (VNI):** Each VNI identifies a specific virtual network in the data plane and provides traffic isolation. VLANs are mapped to a VNI to extend a VLAN across a Layer 3 infrastructure.

■ **VXLAN network identifier (VNID):** This is a unique 24-bit identifier added to an original L2 frame during VXLAN encapsulation. It can be compared to a VLAN identifier field and is used to provide a unique identifier for the individual VXLAN segment (VNI). With all 24 bits in VNID, VXLAN can support 16 million LAN segments.

■ **VXLAN tunnel endpoint (VTEP):** VXLAN tunnel endpoints (VTEPs) are devices, either physical or virtual, that terminate VXLAN tunnels. They perform VXLAN encapsulation and de-encapsulation. Each VTEP has two interfaces. One is a Layer 2 interface on the local LAN segment to support a local endpoint communication through bridging. The other is a Layer 3 interface on the IP transport network. The IP interface has a unique address that identifies the VTEP device in the transport network. The VTEP device uses this IP address to encapsulate Ethernet frames and transmit the packets on the transport network. A VTEP discovers other VTEP devices that share the same VNIs it has locally connected. It advertises the locally connected MAC addresses to its peers. It also learns remote MAC address to VTEP mappings through its IP interface.

VXLAN Frame Format

Figure 7-11 shows the VXLAN frame format.

A VXLAN frame adds 50 bytes to the original Layer 2 frame after encapsulation. This overhead includes the outer MAC header, outer IP header, outer UDP header, and VXLAN header. If the optional VLAN Type and VLAN ID Tag fields are used on the Outer MAC header, the overhead will be 54 bytes.

In the VXLAN header:

■ The "I" flag in the VXLAN Flags field must be set to 1 for a valid VXLAN network ID (VNI). The other 7 bits (designated "R") are reserved fields and must be set to 0.

■ The VNI field has a 24-bit value that is used to identify an individual VXLAN overlay network on which the communicating VMs are situated. VMs in different VXLAN overlay networks cannot communicate with each other.

■ Reserved fields (24 bits and 8 bits) must be set to 0.

In the Outer UDP header:

■ The source port is calculated using a hash of fields from the inner Ethernet frame's headers. This enables a level of entropy for the ECMP/load balancing of the VM-to-VM traffic across the VXLAN overlay.

■ The VXLAN port uses well-known destination UDP port 4789.

■ The UDP checksum should be transmitted as 0. If the encapsulating endpoint includes a nonzero UDP checksum, it must be correctly calculated across the entire packet, including the IP header, UDP header, VXLAN header, and encapsulated Layer 2 frame; otherwise, the receiver may discard the packet during verification while decapsulating the packet.

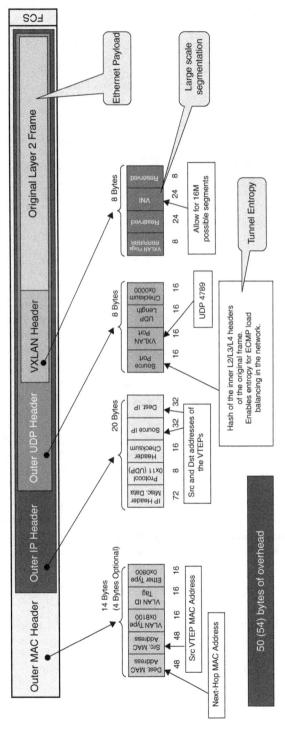

Figure 7-11 *VXLAN Frame Format*

In the Outer IP header:

- The source IP is the IP address of the source VTEP.

- The destination IP address can be a unicast or multicast IP address. If it's unicast, it represents the IP address of the destination VTEP.

In the Outer MAC header:

- The source MAC address is the source VTEP MAC address.

- The destination MAC address can be either the MAC address of the target VTEP or of an intermediate Layer 3 router.

- The VLAN Type (2 bytes) and VLAN ID Tag (2 bytes) are optional. If present, they may be used for delineating VXLAN traffic on the LAN.

VXLAN Control Plane

The initial IETF VXLAN standard (RFC 7348) defined a multicast-based flood-and-learn VXLAN without a control plane. It relies on data-driven flood-and-learn behavior for remote VXLAN tunnel endpoint (VTEP) peer discovery and remote end-host learning. The overlay broadcast, unknown unicast, and multicast traffic are encapsulated into multicast VXLAN packets and transported to remote VTEP switches through the underlay multicast forwarding. Flooding in such a deployment can present a challenge for the scalability of the solution. The requirement to enable multicast capabilities in the underlay network also presents a challenge because some organizations do not want to enable multicast in their data centers or WAN networks.

To overcome the limitations of the flood-and-learn VXLAN, organizations can use Multiprotocol Border Gateway Protocol Ethernet Virtual Private Network (MP-BGP EVPN) as the control plane for VXLAN. MP-BGP EVPN has been defined by IETF as the standards-based control plane for VXLAN overlays. The MP-BGP EVPN control plane provides protocol-based VTEP peer discovery and end-host reachability information distribution that allows more scalable VXLAN overlay network designs. The MP-BGP EVPN control plane introduces a set of features that reduces or eliminates traffic flooding in the overlay network and enables optimal forwarding for both west-east and south-north traffic.

Flood-and-Learn

In the flood-and-learn method, VXLAN uses existing Layer 2 mechanisms (flooding and dynamic MAC address learning) to do the following:

- Transport broadcast, unknown unicast, and multicast traffic

- Discover remote VTEPs

- Learn remote host MAC addresses and MAC-to-VTEP mappings for each VXLAN segment

For the three traffic types, IP multicast is used to reduce the flooding scope of the set of hosts participating in the VXLAN segment. Each VXLAN segment, or VNID, is mapped to an IP multicast group in the transport IP network. Each VTEP device is independently configured and joins this multicast group as an IP host through the Internet Group Management Protocol (IGMP). The IGMP joins trigger Protocol-Independent Multicast (PIM) joins and signaling through the transport network for the particular multicast group. The multicast distribution tree for this group is built through the transport network based on the locations of participating VTEPs. This multicast group is used to transmit VXLAN broadcast, unknown unicast, and multicast traffic through the IP network, limiting Layer 2 flooding to those devices that have end systems participating in the same VXLAN segment. VTEPs communicate with one another through the flooded or multicast traffic in this multicast group.

The Flood-and-Learn VXLAN implementation uses the classic Layer 2 data plane flooding and learning mechanisms for remote VTEP discovery and tenant address learning. Figure 7-12 shows the remote VTEP discovery and end-host address learning process.

The tenant VXLAN segment has VNID 10 and uses the multicast group 239.1.1.1 over the transport network. It has three participating VTEPs in the data center. Assume that no address learning has been performed between locations. End System A (with IP-A, MAC-A) starts IP communication with End System B (with IP-B, MAC-B). The sequence of steps is as follows:

1. End System A sends out an Address Resolution Protocol (ARP) request for IP-B on its Layer 2 VXLAN network.

2. VTEP-1 receives the ARP request. It does not yet have a mapping for IP-B. VTEP-1 encapsulates the ARP request in an IP multicast packet and forwards it to the VXLAN multicast group. The encapsulated multicast packet has the IP address of VTEP-1 as the source IP address and the VXLAN multicast group address as the destination IP address.

3. The IP multicast packet is distributed to all members in the tree. VTEP-2 and VTEP-3 receive the encapsulated multicast packet because they've joined the VXLAN multicast group. They de-encapsulate the packet and check its VNID in the VXLAN header. If it matches their configured VXLAN segment VNID, they forward the ARP request to their local VXLAN network. They also learn the IP address of VTEP-1 from the outer IP address header and inspect the packet to learn the MAC address of End System A, placing this mapping in the local table.

4. End System B receives the ARP request forwarded by VTEP-2. It responds with its own MAC address (MAC-B) and learns the IP-A-to-MAC-A mapping.

5. VTEP-2 receives the ARP reply of End System B with MAC-A as the destination MAC address. It now knows about MAC-A-to-IP-1 mapping. It can use the unicast tunnel to forward the ARP reply back to VTEP-1. In the encapsulated unicast packet, the source IP address is IP-2 and the destination IP address is IP-1. The ARP reply is encapsulated in the UDP payload.

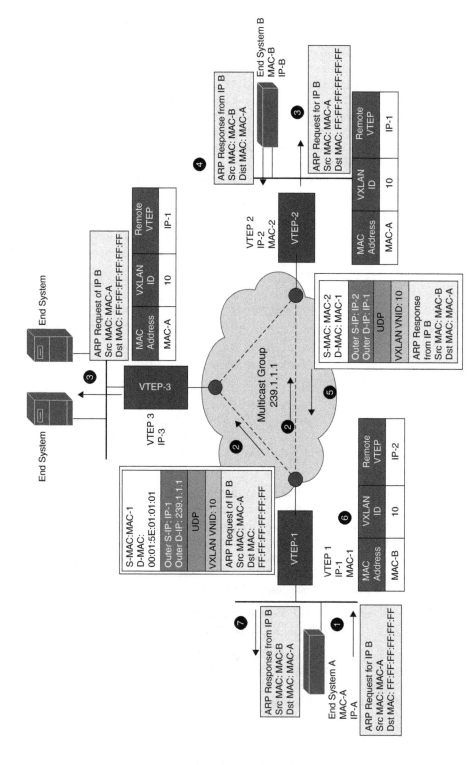

Figure 7-12   *VXLAN Remote VTEP Discovery and End-Host Address Learning*

6. VTEP-1 receives the encapsulated ARP reply from VTEP-2. It de-encapsulates and forwards the ARP reply to End System A. It also learns the IP address of VTEP-2 from the outer IP address header and inspects the original packet to learn the MAC-B-to-IP-2 mapping.

7. End System A receives the ARP reply sent from End System B. Subsequent IP packets between End Systems A and B are unicast forwarded, based on the mapping information on VTEP-1 and VTEP-2, using the VXLAN tunnel between them.

8. VTEP-1 can optionally perform proxy ARPs for subsequent ARP requests for IP-B to reduce the flooding over the transport network.

VXLAN MP-BGP EVPN

MP-BGP EVPN is a control protocol for VXLAN overlay networks. Prior to EVPN, VXLAN overlay networks operated in the flood-and-learn mode, where end-host information learning and VTEP discovery are both data plane driven, with no control protocol to distribute end-host reachability information among VTEPs. MP-BGP EVPN changes this model. It introduces control-plane learning for end hosts behind remote VTEPs. It provides control-plane and data-plane separation and a unified control plane for both Layer 2 and Layer 3 forwarding in a VXLAN overlay network.

The MP-BGP EVPN control plane offers the following main benefits:

- The MP-BGP EVPN protocol is based on industry standards, allowing multivendor interoperability.

- It enables control-plane learning of end-host Layer 2 and Layer 3 reachability information, enabling organizations to build more robust and scalable VXLAN overlay networks.

- It uses the decade-old MP-BGP VPN technology to support scalable multitenant VXLAN overlay networks.

- The EVPN address family carries both Layer 2 and Layer 3 reachability information, thus providing integrated bridging and routing in VXLAN overlay networks.

- It minimizes network flooding through protocol-based host MAC/IP route distribution and Address Resolution Protocol (ARP) suppression on the local VTEPs.

- It provides optimal forwarding for east-west and north-south traffic and supports workload mobility with the distributed anycast function.

- It provides VTEP peer discovery and authentication, mitigating the risk of rogue VTEPs in the VXLAN overlay network.

- It provides mechanisms for building active-active multihoming at Layer 2.

IP transport devices provide IP routing in the underlay network. By running the MP-BGP EVPN protocol, they become part of the VXLAN control plane and distribute the MP-BGP EVPN routes among their MP-BGP EVPN peers. Devices might be MP-iBGP

EVPN peers or route reflectors, or MP External BGP (MP-eBGP) EVPN peers. Their operating system software needs to support MP-BGP EVPN so that it can understand the MP-BGP EVPN updates and distribute them to other MP-BGP EVPN peers using the standards-defined constructs. For data forwarding, IP transport devices perform IP routing based only on the outer IP address of a VXLAN encapsulated packet. They don't need to support the VXLAN data encapsulation and decapsulation functions.

VTEPs running MP-BGP EVPN need to support both the control-plane and data-plane functions. In the control plane, they initiate MP-BGP EVPN routes to advertise their local hosts. They receive MP-BGP EVPN updates from their peers and install the EVPN routes in their forwarding tables. For data forwarding, they encapsulate user traffic in VXLAN and send it over the IP underlay network. In the reverse direction, they receive VXLAN encapsulated traffic from other VTEPs, decapsulate it, and forward the traffic with native Ethernet encapsulation toward the host.

The correct switch platforms need to be selected for the different network roles. For IP transport devices, the software needs to support the MP-EVPN control plane, but the hardware doesn't need to support VXLAN data-plane functions. For VTEP, the switch needs to support both the control-plane and data-plane functions.

The MP-BGP EVPN control plane provides integrated routing and bridging by distributing both the Layer 2 and Layer 3 reachability information for end hosts on VXLAN overlay networks. Communication between hosts in different subnets requires inter-VXLAN routing. BGP EVPN enables this communication by distributing Layer 3 reachability information in either a host IP address route or an IP address prefix. In the data plane, the VTEP needs to support IP address route lookup and perform VXLAN encapsulation based on the lookup result. This capability is referred to as the VXLAN routing function.

Like other network routing control protocols, MP-BGP EVPN is designed to distribute network layer reachability information (NLRI) for the network. A unique feature of EVPN NLRI is that it includes both the Layer 2 and Layer 3 reachability information for end hosts that reside in the EVPN VXLAN overlay network. In other words, it advertises both MAC and IP addresses of EVPN VXLAN end hosts. This capability forms the basis for VXLAN integrated routing and bridging support.

Traffic between end hosts in the same VNI needs to be bridged in the overlay network, which means that VTEP devices in a given VNI need to know about other MAC addresses of end hosts in this VNI. Distribution of MAC addresses through BGP EVPN allows unknown unicast flooding in the VXLAN to be reduced or eliminated. Layer 3 host IP addresses are advertised through MP-BGP EVPN so that inter-VXLAN traffic can be routed to the destination end host through an optimal path. For inter-VXLAN traffic that needs to be routed to the destination end host, host-based IP routing can provide the optimal forwarding path to the exact location of the destination host.

Local and Remote End-Host Learning

The MP-BGP EVPN control plane provides integrated routing and bridging by distributing both Layer 2 and Layer 3 reachability information for the end host residing in the

VXLAN overlay networks. Each VTEP performs local learning to obtain MAC and IP address information from its locally attached hosts and then distributes this information through the MP-BGP EVPN control plane. Hosts attached to remote VTEPs are learned remotely through the MP-BGP control plane. This approach reduces network flooding for end-host learning and provides better control over end-host reachability information distribution.

A VTEP in MP-BGP EVPN learns the MAC addresses and IP addresses of locally attached end hosts through local learning. This learning can be local data plane based using the standard Ethernet and IP learning procedures, such as source MAC address learning from the incoming Ethernet frames and IP address learning when the hosts send Gratuitous ARP (GARP) and Reverse ARP (RARP) packets or ARP requests for the gateway IP address on the VTEP.

After learning the localhost MAC and IP addresses, a VTEP advertises the host information in the MP-BGP EVPN control plane so that this information can be distributed to other VTEPs. This approach enables EVPN VTEPs to learn the remote end hosts in the MP-BGP EVPN control plane. The EVPN routes are advertised through the L2VPN EVPN address family. The BGP L2VPN EVPN routes include the following information:

- **Route distinguisher (RD):** A route distinguisher is an 8-bit octet number used to distinguish one set of routes (one VRF instance) from another. It is a unique number prepended to each route so that if the same route is used in several different VRF instances, BGP can treat them as distinct routes. The route distinguisher is transmitted along with the route through MP-BGP when EVPN routes are exchanged with MP-BGP peers.

- **MAC address length:** 6 bytes

- **MAC address:** Host MAC address

- **IP address length:** 32 or 128

- **IP address:** Host IP address (IPv4 or IPv6)

- **L2 VNI:** VNI of the bridge domain to which the end host belongs

- **L3 VNI:** VNI associated with the tenant VRF routing instance

MP-BGP EVPN uses the BGP extended community attribute to transmit the exported route targets in an EVPN route. When an EVPN VTEP receives an EVPN route, it compares the route target attributes in the received route to its locally configured route target import policy to decide whether to import or ignore the route. This approach uses the decade-old MP-BGP VPN technology (RFC 4364) and provides scalable multitenancy in which a node that does not have a VRF locally does not import the corresponding routes. Route target is an extended-community attribute to filter appropriate VPN routes into the correct VRFs.

When a VTEP switch originates MP-BGP EVPN routes for its locally learned end hosts, it uses its own VTEP address as the BGP next hop. This BGP next hop must remain unchanged through the route distribution across the network because the remote VTEP must learn the originating VTEP address as the next hop for VXLAN encapsulation when forwarding packets for the overlay network.

Figure 7-13 shows local and remote end-host address learning and distribution in an MP-iBGP EVPN using route reflectors.

In Figure 7-13, VTEP-1 learns the MAC addresses and IP addresses of locally attached end hosts through local learning. VTEP-1 then sends a BGP update to the route-reflector in the transit network, informing about the host IP (H-IP-1) and MAC (H-MAC-1) address along with the L2-VNI information. The next-hop in the MP-BGP EVPN route update is set to VTEP-1. When remote VTEP-2 and VTEP-3 receive the route update from the route reflector, they install the host information in their routing information base (RIB) and forwarding information base (FIB).

VTEP Peer Discovery and Authentication

Prior to MP-BGP EVPN, VXLAN didn't have a control-protocol-based VTEP peer-discovery mechanism or a method for authenticating VTEP peers. These limitations present major security risks in real-world VXLAN deployments because they allow easy insertion of a rogue VTEP into a VNI segment to send or receive VXLAN traffic.

With the MP-BGP EVPN control plane, a VTEP device first needs to establish BGP neighbor adjacency with other VTEPs or with Internal BGP (iBGP) route reflectors. In addition to the BGP updates for end-host NLRI, VTEPs exchange the following information about themselves through BGP:

- Layer 3 VNI
- VTEP address
- Router MAC address

As soon as a VTEP receives BGP EVPN route updates from a remote VTEP BGP neighbor, it adds the VTEP address from that route advertisement to the VTEP peer list. This VTEP peer list is then used as an allowed list of valid VTEP peers. VTEPs that are not on this allowed list are considered invalid or unauthorized sources. VXLAN encapsulated traffic from these invalid VTEPs will be discarded by other VTEPs.

Along with the VTEP address that promotes VTEP peer learning, BGP EVPN routes carry VTEP router MAC addresses. Each VTEP has a router MAC address. Once a VTEP's router MAC address is distributed via MP-BGP and learned by other VTEPs, the other VTEPs use it as an attribute of the VTEP peer to encapsulate inter-VXLAN routed packets to that VTEP peer. The router MAC address is programmed as the inner destination MAC address for routed VXLAN.

For additional security, the existing BGP Message Digest 5 (MD5) authentication can be conveniently applied to the BGP neighbor sessions so that switches can't become BGP neighbors to exchange MP-BGP EVPN routes until they successfully authenticate each other with a preconfigured MD5 Triple Data Encryption Standard (3DES) key.

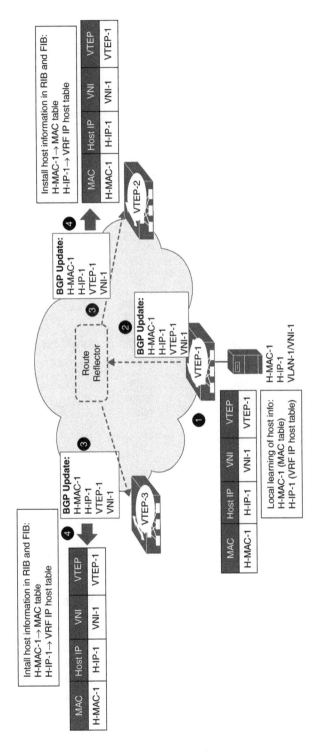

Figure 7-13 *Local and Remote Host Address Learning*

Distributed Anycast Gateway in MP-BGP EVPN

In MP-BGP EVPN, any VTEP in a VNI can be the distributed anycast gateway for end hosts in its IP subnet by supporting the same virtual gateway IP address and the virtual gateway MAC address, as illustrated in Figure 7-14. With the anycast gateway function in EVPN, end hosts in a VNI can always use their local VTEPs for this VNI as their default gateway to send traffic to outside of their IP subnet. This capability enables optimal forwarding for northbound traffic from end hosts in the VXLAN overlay network. A distributed anycast gateway also offers the benefit of seamless host mobility in the VXLAN overlay network. Because the gateway IP and virtual MAC address are identically provisioned on all VTEPs within a VNI, when an end host moves from one VTEP to another VTEP, it doesn't need to send another ARP request to relearn the gateway MAC address.

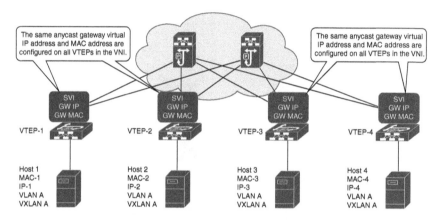

Figure 7-14   *Distributed Anycast Gateway in MP-BGP EVPN*

ARP Suppression in MP-BGP EVPN

The ARP suppression feature provided by the MP-BGP EVPN control plane reduces network flooding caused by broadcast traffic from ARP requests. When ARP suppression is enabled for a VNI, each of its VTEPs maintain an ARP suppression cache table for known IP hosts and their associated MAC addresses in the VNI segment. When an end host in the VNI sends an ARP request for another end host IP address, its local VTEP intercepts the ARP request and checks for the ARP'ed IP address in its ARP suppression cache table. If it finds a match, the local VTEP sends an ARP response on behalf of the remote end host. The local host learns the MAC address of the remote host in the ARP response. If the local VTEP doesn't have the ARP'ed IP address in its ARP suppression table, it floods the ARP request to the other VTEPs in the VNI. This ARP flooding can occur for the initial ARP request to a silent host in the network. The VTEPs in the network don't see any traffic from the silent host until another host sends an ARP request for its IP address and it sends an ARP response back. After the local VTEP learns about the MAC and IP addresses of the silent host, the information is distributed through the MP-BGP EVPN control plane to all other VTEPs. Any subsequent ARP requests do not need to be flooded.

Figure 7-15 illustrates the ARP suppression feature in MP-BGP EVPN.

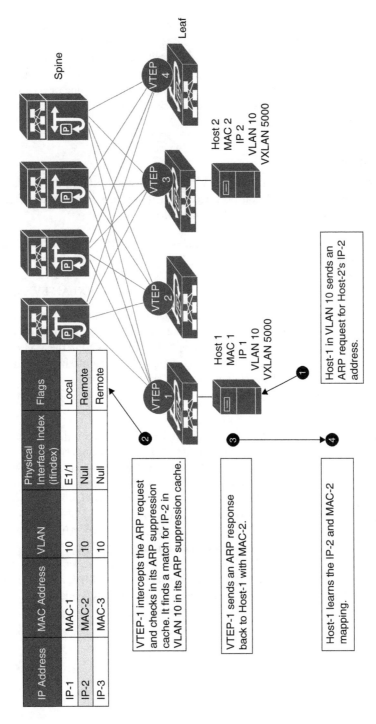

Figure 7-15 *ARP Suppression in MP-BGP EVPN*

Because most end hosts send GARP or RARP requests to announce themselves to the network right after they come online, the local VTEP will immediately have the opportunity to learn their MAC and IP addresses and distribute this information to other VTEPs through the MP-BGP EVPN control plane. Therefore, most active IP hosts in VXLAN EVPN should be learned by the VTEPs either through local learning or control-plane-based remote learning. As a result, ARP suppression reduces the network flooding caused by host ARP learning behavior.

VXLAN Data Plane

VXLAN uses stateless tunnels between VTEPs to transmit traffic of the overlay Layer 2 network through the Layer 3 transport network. Let's discuss a few terms before we look at the actual packet walk for the VXLAN data plane:

- **Layer 2 VNI:** An EVPN VXLAN tenant can have multiple Layer 2 networks, each with a corresponding VNI. These Layer 2 networks are bridge domains in the overlay network. The VNIs associated with them are often referred to as Layer 2 (L2) VNIs. A VTEP can have all or a subset of the Layer 2 VNIs in a VXLAN EVPN.

- **Layer 3 VNI:** Each tenant VRF instance is mapped to a unique Layer 3 VNI in the network. This mapping needs to be consistent on all the VTEPs in network. All inter-VXLAN routed traffic is encapsulated with the Layer 3 VNI in the VXLAN header and provides the VRF context for the receiving VTEP. The receiving VTEP uses this VNI to determine the VRF context in which the inner IP packet needs to be forwarded. This VNI also provides the basis for enforcing Layer 3 segmentation in the data plane.

- **VTEP router MAC address:** Each VTEP has a unique system MAC address that other VTEPs can use for inter-VNI routing. This MAC address is referred to as the router MAC address. The router MAC address is used as the inner destination MAC address for the routed VXLAN packet. As shown in Figure 7-16, when a packet is sent from VNI A to VNI B, the ingress VTEP routes the packet to the Layer 3 VNI. It rewrites the inner destination MAC address to the egress VTEP's router MAC address and encodes the Layer 3 VNI in the VXLAN header. After the egress VTEP receives the encapsulated VXLAN packet, it first decapsulates the packet by removing the VXLAN header. Then it looks at the inner packet header. Because the destination MAC address in the inner packet header is its own MAC address, it performs a Layer 3 routing lookup. The Layer 3 VNI in the VXLAN header provides the VRF context in which this routing lookup is performed.

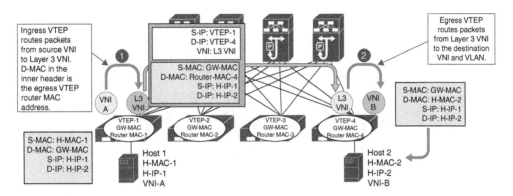

Figure 7-16 *VXLAN Routing*

When an EVPN VTEP performs forwarding lookup and VXLAN encapsulation for the packets it receives from its local end hosts, it uses either a Layer 2 VNI or the Layer 3 VNI in the VXLAN header, depending on whether the packets need to be bridged or routed. If the destination MAC address in the original packet header does not belong to the local VTEP, the local VTEP performs a Layer 2 lookup and bridges the packet to the destination end host located in the same Layer 2 VNI as the source host. The local VTEP embeds this Layer 2 VNI in the VXLAN header. In this case, both the source and destination hosts are in the same Layer 2 broadcast domain. If the destination MAC address belongs to the local VTEP switch (that is, if the local VTEP is the IP gateway for the source host, and the source and destination hosts are in different IP subnets), the packet will be routed by the local VTEP. In this case, it performs Layer 3 routing lookup. It then encapsulates the packets with the Layer 3 VNI in the VXLAN header and rewrites the inner destination MAC address to the remote VTEP's router MAC address. Upon receipt of the encapsulated VXLAN packet, the remote VTEP performs another routing lookup based on the inner IP header because the inner destination MAC address in the received packet belongs to the remote VTEP itself.

The destination VTEP address in the outer IP header of a VXLAN packet identifies the location of the destination host in the underlay network. VXLAN packets are routed toward the egress VTEP through the underlay network based on the outer destination IP address. After the packet arrives at the egress VTEP, the VNI in the VXLAN header is examined to determine the VLAN in which the packet should be bridged or the tenant VRF instance to which it should be routed. In the latter case, the VXLAN header is encoded with a Layer 3 VNI. A Layer 3 VNI is associated with a tenant VRF routing instance, so the egress VTEP can directly map the routed VXLAN packets to the appropriate tenant routing instance. This approach makes multitenancy easier to support for both Layer 2 and Layer 3 segmentation. The following two VXLAN data plane packet walk examples illustrate the VXLAN bridging and routing concept.

Communication Between Hosts in Same VLAN/VNI

An example of a VXLAN packet-forwarding flow between hosts in the same VLAN/VNI is shown in Figure 7-17.

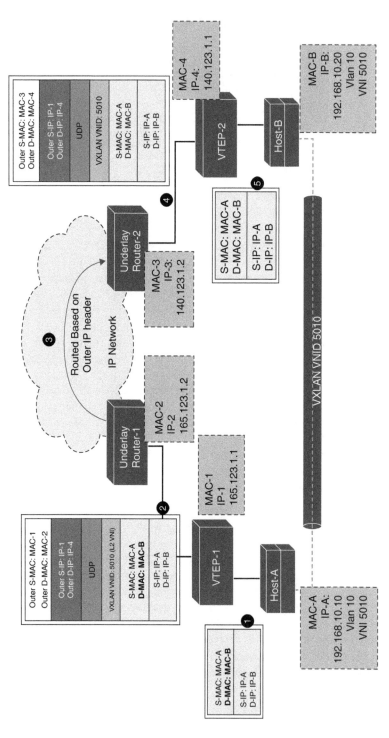

Figure 7-17 *Communication Between Hosts in Same VLAN/VNI*

In Figure 7-17, Host-A and Host-B in VXLAN segment 5010 communicate with each other through the VXLAN tunnel between VTEP-1 and VTEP-2. This example assumes that address learning has been done on both sides and that corresponding MAC-to-VTEP mappings exist on both VTEPs.

When Host-A sends traffic to Host-B, it forms Ethernet frames with the MAC-B address of Host-B as the destination MAC address and sends them out to VTEP-1. VTEP-1, with a mapping of MAC-B to VTEP-2 in its mapping table, performs VXLAN encapsulation on the packets by adding VXLAN, UDP, and outer IP address headers to them. In the outer IP address header, the source IP address is the IP address of VTEP-1, and the destination IP address is the IP address of VTEP-2. VTEP-1 then performs an IP address lookup for the IP address of VTEP-2 to resolve the next hop in the transit network and subsequently uses the MAC address of the next-hop device to further encapsulate the packets in an Ethernet frame to send to the next-hop device.

The packets are routed toward VTEP-2 through the transport network based on their outer IP address header, which has the IP address of VTEP-2 as the destination address. After VTEP-2 receives the packets, it strips off the outer Ethernet, IP, UDP, and VXLAN headers and then forwards the packets to Host-B, based on the original destination MAC address in the Ethernet frame.

Communication Between Hosts in Different VLANs/VNIs

An example of a VXLAN packet-forwarding flow between hosts in different VLANs/VNIs is shown in Figure 7-18.

In Figure 7-18, Host-A belongs to VNI 5010 and Host-B belongs to VNI 5020, and both belong to the same tenant with VRF A. Since intra-VRF communication is allowed, Host-A can communicate with Host-B through the VXLAN tunnel in VRF A with L3 VNID 9999 between VTEP-1 and VTEP-2. Since the communication between Host-A and Host-B is inter-VLAN/VNI, L3 VNI will be used instead of L2 VNI during VXLAN encapsulation at the source VTEP. This example assumes that address learning has been done on both sides using the MP-BGP EVPN control plane and that corresponding IP-to-VTEP mappings exist on both VTEPs.

When Host-A sends traffic to Host-B, it forms Ethernet frames with an anycast default gateway MAC GW-MAC address of VTEP-1 as the destination MAC address and sends them out to VTEP-1. Since the destination MAC is the anycast gateway MAC, VTEP-1 does an L3 lookup and finds a mapping of IP-B to VTEP-2 in its routing table; it then performs VXLAN encapsulation on the packets by adding VXLAN, UDP, and outer IP address headers to them. This time, VTEP-1 uses Layer 3 VNI 9999 for the encapsulation since the communication is between hosts in different VLAN/VNI. In the outer IP address header, the source IP address is the IP address of VTEP-1, and the destination IP address is the IP address of VTEP-2. VTEP-1 then performs an IP address lookup for the IP address of VTEP-2 to resolve the next hop in the transit network and subsequently uses the MAC address of the next-hop device to further encapsulate the packets in an Ethernet frame to send to the next-hop device. Since the packet is routed, VTEP-1 will rewrite the source MAC to VTEP-1 and destination MAC to VTEP-2 in the inner Ethernet frame L2 header.

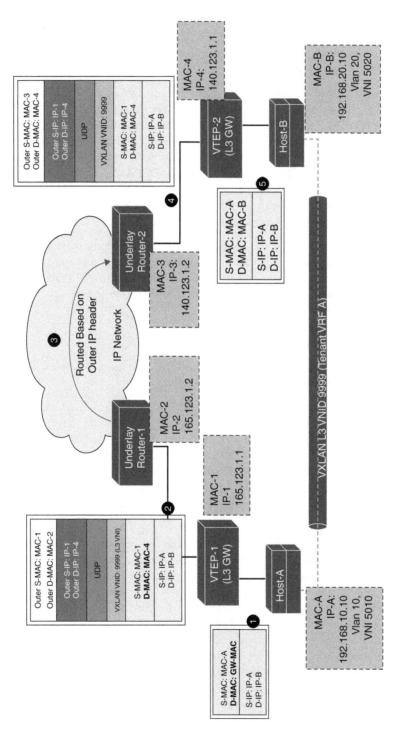

Figure 7-18 *Communication Between Hosts in Different VLANs/VNIs*

The packets are routed toward VTEP-2 through the transport network based on their outer IP address header, which has the IP address of VTEP-2 as the destination address. After VTEP-2 receives the packets, it strips off the outer Ethernet, IP, UDP, and VXLAN headers. VTEP-2 finds that the inner packet has a destination IP address of Host-B and does the routing lookup, rewrites the packet with the source MAC of VTEP-2 and destination MAC of Host-B, and then forwards the packets to Host-B.

VXLAN Forwarding with vPC

Virtual port channel (vPC) VTEP combines the two technologies, vPC and VXLAN, to provide device-level redundancy for VTEPs. A pair of vPC switches share the same VTEP address, referred to as the anycast VTEP address, and function as a logical VTEP. The other VTEPs in the network see the two switches as a single VTEP with the anycast VTEP address. When both the vPC VTEP switches are up and running, they load share in an active-active configuration. If one vPC switch goes down, the other switch takes over the entire traffic load so that the failure event doesn't cause the loss of connectivity for the devices connected to the vPC pair.

The MP-BGP EVPN control plane works transparently with the vPC VTEP. With an MP-BGP EVPN control plane, vPC VTEPs continue to function as a single logical VTEP with the anycast VTEP address for VTEP functions, but they operate as two separate entities from the perspective of MP-BGP. They have different router IDs for BGP, form BGP neighbor adjacency with the BGP peers separately, and advertise EVPN routes independently, as illustrated in Figure 7-19. In the EVPN routes, they both use the anycast VTEP address as the next hop so that the remote VTEPs can use the learned EVPN routes and encapsulate packets using the anycast VTEP address as the destination in the outer IP header of encapsulated packets.

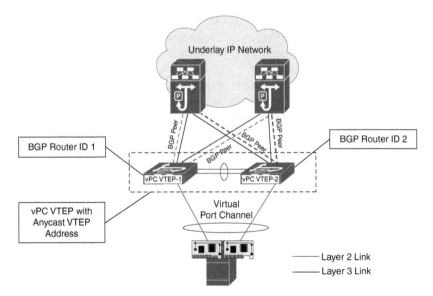

Figure 7-19 *vPC VTEPs*

Network Interface Virtualization Using FEX

Cisco FEX technology is based on the IEEE 802.1BR standard. The Cisco FEX technology solution is composed of a parent switch that can be a Cisco Nexus 5000 Series switch, Nexus 6000 Series switch, Nexus 7000 Series switch, Nexus 9000 Series switch, or a Cisco UCS fabric interconnect. The parent switch is then extended to connect to the server either as a remote line card with Nexus 2000 Series fabric extenders or logically partitioned or virtualized adapter ports to connect to any type of servers (racks and/or blades), with Cisco Adapter FEX and VM-FEX technologies. FEX technology has been discussed in detail in Chapter 2, "Describing the Cisco Nexus Family and Cisco NX-OS Software." Here, we will discuss the network adapter virtualization using adapter FEX and VM-FEX technology.

- **Cisco Adapter FEX:** Typical deployments of virtual machines have an extra layer of switching in the hypervisor. The software switches in the hypervisor emulate hardware at the expense of application performance. Cisco virtual interface cards (VICs) solve this problem by acting as adapter fabric extenders and bringing the network to virtual machines (VMs) using Cisco Adapter FEX technology. Cisco Adapter FEX enables the server adapter to be logically partitioned into multiple virtual network interface cards (vNICs). Each vNIC behaves like a physical NIC port and meets the network connectivity needs for each application so that security and quality of service (QoS) policies can be applied for each vNIC and application.

- **Cisco Data Center VM-FEX:** Network administrators have no control on the software switches in the hypervisor, which makes monitoring of network traffic to individual VMs very cumbersome. Cisco VICs use the VN-Tag standard in IEEE 802.1 BR standard to manage each link from the VM as if it were a physical link. The VICs can provide dynamic interfaces to virtual machines, allowing the network to bypass the hypervisor and directly connect to the VM using VM-FEX technology. Cisco Data Center VM-FEX partitions the server adapter into multiple vNICs, and each vNIC is assigned to individual virtual machines, allowing network administrators to monitor the ports easily. Additionally, the VMs can move from one server to another with the same security policies and no compromises on the overall network security to allow the move. Switching of VM traffic happens in hardware switches instead of using a software switch within the hypervisor.

Figure 7-20 illustrates the difference in the implementation of Adapter FEX and VM-FEX technology using Cisco VIC card.

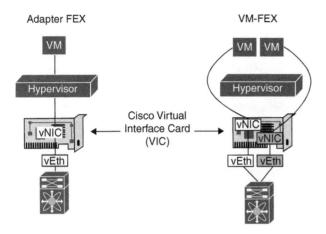

Figure 7-20 *Adapter FEX vs VM-FEX*

VMware vSphere Virtual Switches

Virtual switches are the key networking components in the VMware infrastructure. VMware vSphere virtual switches provide network connectivity to hosts and virtual machines and support VLANs that are compatible with standard VLAN implementations.

VMware vSphere Standard Switch

A VMware vSphere standard switch works like a physical Ethernet switch. It bridges traffic internally between virtual machines in the same VLAN and provides network connectivity to external networks. A single ESXi host can have multiple vSwitches configured and segregated from each other, in a manner similar to VMs.

Physical NICs of the host are connected to the uplink ports on the standard switch. Uplink ports connect the virtual switch to the physical world. A virtual switch can have one or more uplinks. Virtual machines' network adapters (vNICs) are connected to the port groups on the standard switch. Port groups are groups of virtual ports with similar configurations. Each logical port on the standard switch is a member of a single port group. Every port group can use one or more physical NICs to handle its network traffic. If a port group does not have a physical NIC connected to it, virtual machines on the same port group can only communicate with each other but not with the external network.

The standard switch also handles VMkernel traffic. A VMkernel port (or the VMkernel adapter or interface) is used by the hypervisor for VMkernel services when we need to connect to the physical network. Every VMkernel adapter has an IP address by which this service is accessible. VMkernel NICs support services such as management traffic, vMotion traffic, IP storage traffic and discovery, fault tolerance traffic, vSphere replication traffic, vSAN traffic, and more. Note that a port group can either be used for VMs or VMkernel ports, not both simultaneously. You can create two port groups with the same VLAN ID: one for VMs and one for VMkernel ports. A VLAN ID, which restricts port group traffic to a logical Ethernet segment within the physical network, is optional.

Figure 7-21 illustrates the VMware vSphere standard switch architecture.

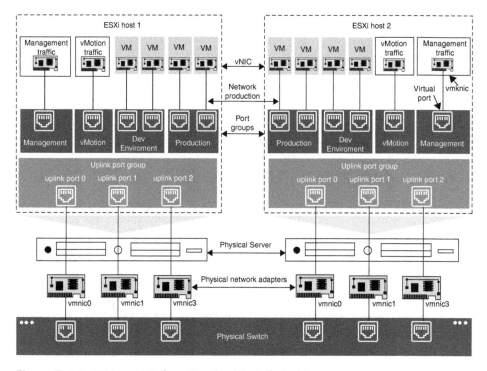

Figure 7-21   *VMware vSphere Standard Switch Architecture*

Each port group on a standard switch is identified by a network label, which must be unique to the current host. You can use network labels to make the networking configuration of virtual machines portable across hosts. You should give the same label to the port groups in a data center that use physical NICs connected to one broadcast domain on the physical network. Likewise, if two port groups are connected to physical NICs on different broadcast domains, the port groups should have distinct labels. For example, you can create Production and Dev environment port groups as virtual machine networks on the hosts that share the same broadcast domain on the physical network, as shown in Figure 7-21.

A standard switch supports the following features:

■ Forwarding of L2 frames

■ VLAN segmentation

- 802.1q encapsulation support

- Outbound (Tx) traffic shaping

- NIC teaming (support for more than one uplink)

- Cisco Discovery Protocol (CDP) support

VMware vSphere Distributed Switch

A vSphere distributed switch (VDS) is a virtual switch that provides centralized management and monitoring of the networking configuration of all hosts associated with the switch. A distributed switch is set up on a vCenter Server system, and its settings are propagated to all hosts associated with the switch.

A network switch in vSphere consists of two logical sections: the data plane and the management plane. The data plane implements the packet switching, filtering, tagging, and so on. The management plane is the control structure you use to configure the data plane functionality. A vSphere standard switch contains both data and management planes, and the standard switch is configured and maintained individually. A vSphere distributed switch separates the data plane and the management plane, as shown in Figure 7-22. The management functionality of the distributed switch resides on the vCenter Server system, which lets you administer the networking configuration of your environment on a data center level. The data plane remains locally on every host associated with the distributed switch. The data plane section of the distributed switch is called a host proxy switch. The networking configuration you create on vCenter Server (the management plane) is automatically pushed down to all host proxy switches (the data plane).

Figure 7-22 illustrates the VMware vSphere distributed switch architecture.

The vSphere distributed switch introduces two abstractions, the uplink port group and the distributed port group, that create a consistent networking configuration for physical NICs, virtual machines, and VMkernel services.

An uplink port group or dvuplink port group is defined during the creation of the distributed switch and can have one or more uplinks. An uplink is a template you use to configure physical connections of hosts as well as failover and load-balancing policies. Physical NICs of hosts are mapped to uplinks on the distributed switch. At the host level, each physical NIC is connected to an uplink port with a particular ID. Once the policies such as failover and load balancing are configured over uplinks, the policies are automatically propagated to the host proxy switches, or the data plane. The automatic propagation of policies ensures consistent failover and load-balancing configuration for the physical NICs of all hosts associated with the distributed switch.

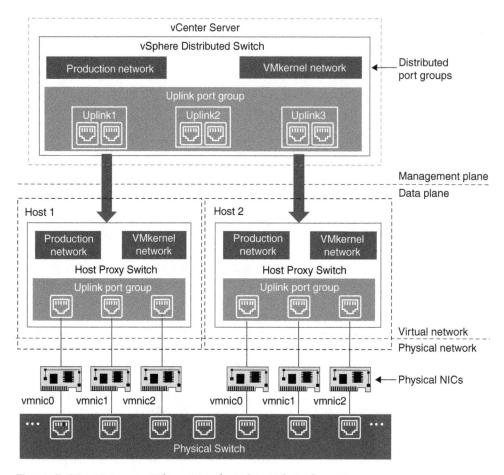

Figure 7-22   *VMware vSphere Distributed Switch Architecture*

Distributed port groups provide network connectivity to virtual machines and accommodate VMkernel traffic. Each distributed port group is identified by using a network label,
which must be unique to the current data center. Policies such as NIC teaming, failover,
load balancing, VLAN, security, traffic shaping, and other policies are configured on the
distributed port groups. The virtual ports connected to a distributed port group share the
same properties configured for the distributed port group. As with uplink port groups,
the configuration you set on distributed port groups on vCenter Server (the management
plane) is automatically propagated to all hosts on the distributed switch through the host
proxy switches (the data plane). A group of virtual machines associated to the same distributed port group share the same networking configuration.

A vSphere distributed switch supports all the features of a standard switch. In addition,
the vSphere distributed switch supports the following features:

■ Data-center-level management

- Network I/O control

- Traffic filtering and marking

- Inbound (Rx) traffic shaping

- Configuration backup and restore

- Private VLANs

- Link aggregation control support

- Port state monitoring

- Port mirroring

- NetFlow

Summary

This chapter discusses overlay network protocols such as NVGRE, Cisco OTV, VXLAN Overlay, along with network interface virtualization using FEX and VMware vSphere virtual switches, including the following points:

- An underlay network is the physical infrastructure above which an overlay network is built. It is the underlying network responsible for the delivery of packets across networks.

- Network overlays are virtual networks of interconnected nodes that share an underlying physical network, allowing deployment of applications that require specific network topologies without the need to modify the underlying network.

- NVGRE (Network Virtualization using Generic Routing Encapsulation) is a network virtualization method that creates virtual Layer 2 topologies on top of a physical Layer 3 network. Connectivity in the virtual topology is provided by tunneling Ethernet frames in GRE over IP over the physical network.

- Cisco Overlay Transport Virtualization (OTV) is a MAC-in-IP overlay method that provides Layer 2 LAN extension over Layer 2, Layer 3, or label-switched Multiprotocol Label Switching–based networks.

- Virtual Extensible LAN (VXLAN) is a Layer 2 overlay scheme over a Layer 3 network that provides a means to extend Layer 2 segments across a Layer 3 infrastructure using MAC-in-UDP encapsulation and tunneling.

- The VXLAN control plane can use one of two methods: flood-and-learn or MP-BGP EVPN.

- The VXLAN data plane uses stateless tunnels between VTEPs to transmit traffic of the overlay Layer 2 network through the Layer 3 transport network.

- Cisco Adapter FEX enables the server adapter to be logically partitioned into multiple virtual network interface cards (vNICs). Cisco Data Center VM-FEX provides dynamic vNIC interfaces to virtual machines, bypassing the hypervisor and directly connecting to the VM.

- VMware vSphere virtual switches provide network connectivity to hosts and virtual machines and support VLANs that are compatible with standard VLAN implementations.

References

"Cisco Data Center Spine-and-Leaf Architecture: Design Overview White Paper," https://www.cisco.com/c/en/us/products/collateral/switches/nexus-7000-series-switches/white-paper-c11-737022.html

"Cisco Overlay Transport Virtualization Technology Introduction and Deployment Considerations," https://www.cisco.com/c/en/us/td/docs/solutions/Enterprise/Data_Center/DCI/whitepaper/DCI3_OTV_Intro.html

"Cisco Nexus 7000 Series NX-OS OTV Configuration Guide, Release 8.x," https://www.cisco.com/c/en/us/td/docs/switches/datacenter/nexus7000/sw/otv/config/cisco_nexus7000_otv_config_guide_8x.html

"Overlay Transport Virtualization Best Practices Guide," https://www.cisco.com/c/dam/en/us/products/collateral/switches/nexus-7000-series-switches/guide_c07-728315.pdf

"Cisco Nexus 9000 Series NX-OS VXLAN Configuration Guide, Release 10.1(x)," https://www.cisco.com/c/en/us/td/docs/dcn/nx-os/nexus9000/101x/configuration/vxlan/cisco-nexus-9000-series-nx-os-vxlan-configuration-guide-release-101x.html

"Cisco Nexus 7000 Series NX-OS VXLAN Configuration Guide, Release 8.x," https://www.cisco.com/c/en/us/td/docs/switches/datacenter/nexus7000/sw/vxlan/config/cisco_nexus7000_vxlan_config_guide_8x.html

"VXLAN EVPN Multi-Site Design and Deployment White Paper," https://www.cisco.com/c/en/us/products/collateral/switches/nexus-9000-series-switches/white-paper-c11-739942.html

"VXLAN Network with MP-BGP EVPN Control Plane Design Guide," https://www.cisco.com/c/en/us/products/collateral/switches/nexus-9000-series-switches/guide-c07-734107.html

"VXLAN Overview: Cisco Nexus 9000 Series Switches," https://www.cisco.com/c/en/us/products/collateral/switches/nexus-9000-series-switches/white-paper-c11-729383.html

"Cisco Nexus 2000 Series NX-OS Fabric Extender Configuration Guide for Cisco Nexus 9000 Series Switches, Release 9.2(x)," https://www.cisco.com/c/en/us/td/docs/switches/datacenter/nexus9000/sw/92x/fex/configuration/guide/b-cisco-nexus-2000-nx-os-fabric-extender-configuration-guide-for-nexus-9000-switches-92x.html

"Cisco Programmable Fabric with VXLAN BGP EVPN Configuration Guide,"
   https://www.cisco.com/c/en/us/td/docs/switches/datacenter/pf/configuration/
   guide/b-pf-configuration.html

"VMware vSphere Documentation," https://docs.vmware.com/en/VMware-vSphere/
   index.html

Relevant Cisco Live sessions: http://www.ciscolive.com

IETF NVGRE RFC: https://datatracker.ietf.org/doc/html/rfc7637

IETF MP-BGP VPN RFC: https://datatracker.ietf.org/doc/html/rfc4364

IETF MP-BGP EVPN RFC: https://datatracker.ietf.org/doc/html/rfc7432

IETF VXLAN RFC: https://datatracker.ietf.org/doc/html/rfc7348

Chapter 8

Describing Cisco ACI

Organizations today are challenged to keep pace with everchanging customer demands and ever-present competitive threats. To succeed, organizations need to be much more agile and focused on delivering a superior customer experience. This requires fine-tuning and in many cases upgrading processes, culture, and technology; this is commonly referred to as a digital transformation. Applications are at the center of the drive to modernize traditional businesses and the foundation of their digital transformation. It is critical to ensure that all applications are deployed rapidly, perform optimally, remain highly available, and are secure. Technologies using software-defined capabilities are key enablers of digital transformation. Cisco Application-Centric Infrastructure (ACI) is a software-defined networking (SDN) solution designed for data centers. Cisco ACI allows application requirements to define the network. The Cisco ACI architecture simplifies, optimizes, and accelerates the entire application deployment lifecycle.

In this chapter, we will discuss Cisco ACI overview, building blocks, deployment models, hardware components, fabric startup discovery, along with the Cisco ACI policy model, including logical constructs, fabric policies, and access policies. We will also discuss in brief about the packet forwarding within the ACI fabric.

Cisco ACI Overview

Cisco ACI is a spine/leaf network of Nexus 9k switches using the ACI operating system with a management platform. The network management platform called APIC provides a single place from which the network can be managed.

Cisco ACI solutions have the following building blocks:

- **Cisco Application Policy Infrastructure Controller (APIC):** The infrastructure controller is the main architectural component of the Cisco ACI solution. It is the unified point of automation and management for the Cisco ACI fabric, policy enforcement, and health monitoring. The APIC is not involved in data plane forwarding.

- **Cisco Nexus 9000 Series leaf switches:** Represent connection points for end devices, including APIC, and are connected to spine switches.

- **Cisco Nexus 9000 Series spine switches:** Represent the backbone of the ACI fabric and are connected to leaf switches.

Cisco ACI resolves the following challenges of traditional networks:

- **Complicated topology:** Usually, traditional networks use core distribution access layers. When you add more devices, this topology can be complicated to manage. Cisco ACI uses a simple spine-leaf topology wherein all the connections within the Cisco ACI fabric are from leaf-to-spine switches, and a mesh topology is between them. There is no leaf-to-leaf and no spine-to-spine connectivity.

Figure 8-1 shows a traditional network versus a Cisco ACI spine/leaf architecture.

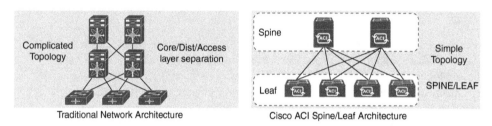

Figure 8-1   *Traditional Network vs. Cisco ACI Spine/Leaf Architecture*

- **Layer 2 loops:** Traditional networks rely on the Spanning Tree Protocol (STP) for loop-free topology. Cisco ACI use equal-cost multipath (ECMP), and since there is IP reachability between leaf and spine switches, there is no need for STP, and you do not have to block any port to avoid the Layer 2 loops.

Figure 8-2 shows a traditional network versus Cisco ACI loop avoidance.

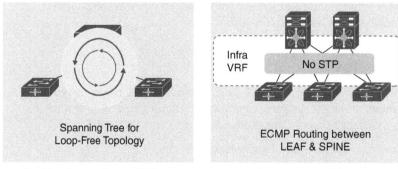

Figure 8-2   *Traditional Network vs. Cisco ACI Loop Avoidance*

■ **Security:** From the security perspective, in a traditional network device, all the traffic is allowed by default, and you need to explicitly configure the device to block the traffic. However, in Cisco ACI, an allow-list model is used. By default, everything is blocked, unless you explicitly allow the traffic.

Figure 8-3 shows a traditional network versus the Cisco ACI security model.

No default
security isolation

Traditional network security model

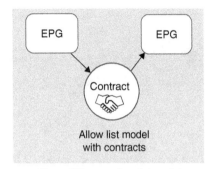

EPG   EPG

Contract

Allow list model
with contracts

Cisco ACI uses allow list model

Figure 8-3 *Traditional Network vs. Cisco ACI Security Model*

■ **Device management:** In a traditional network, hardware devices are configured using CLI by doing SSH to every device. A lot of copying/pasting is required during the configuration, and it's harder to scale as the number of devices increases. In a leaf-and-spine topology, there can be tens or hundreds of devices. Instead of using SSH for each and every device to configure and build the Cisco ACI fabric, you can use the centralized controller, called APIC. You can still directly access the leaf-and-spine switches, but you cannot configure anything directly on them. You always configure the Cisco ACI fabric from the Cisco APIC. Cisco APIC enables access to all devices in the fabric via Cisco API. In Cisco ACI, all configurations can be represented by policies and objects. These policies and objects can be stored in XML or JavaScript Object Notation (JSON) format. Policies and objects can be easily accessed via APIs or configured via APIs.

Figure 8-4 shows a traditional network versus Cisco ACI device management.

■ **Automation:** In a traditional network, usually there is no automation, and configuration is done manually and statically. In Cisco ACI, by using REST API calls, it is easy to automate configuration. It is also possible to provide dynamic integrations, where you can dynamically communicate and push the configuration to another vendor's controller (VMware vCenter server, for example).

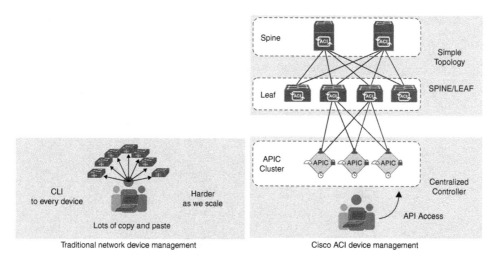

Figure 8-4   *Traditional Network vs. Cisco ACI Device Management*

Figure 8-5 shows a traditional network versus Cisco ACI automation.

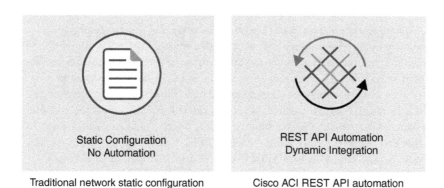

Figure 8-5   *Traditional Network vs. Cisco ACI Automation*

■ **Coordination between the network and server team:** Typically, the network and server teams are two different teams. They need to cooperate to make sure that, for example, the new service has correct security rules, the correct VLAN, and that the correct VLAN is deployed in the correct place. Sometimes, that communication is not an easy task. By using the dynamic integration, for example, VMware integration, you can dynamically push the configuration to the vCenter Server. Then you can verify that the network (ACI) side has the configuration deployed and also that the server side has the mapped configuration.

Figure 8-6 shows a traditional network versus Cisco ACI coordination between network and server teams.

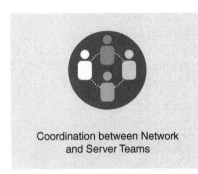

Coordination between Network
and Server Teams

Traditional network manual coordination between server and
network team

VMware Integration
and so on

Cisco ACI dynamic integration of
server controllers

Figure 8-6   *Traditional Network vs. Cisco ACI Coordination Between the Network and Server Teams*

The main benefits of Cisco ACI include the following:

■ Operational simplicity, with common policy, management, and operation models across application, network, and security resources.

■ Centralized network management and visibility with full automation and real-time network health monitoring.

■ Automation of IT workflows and application deployment agility.

■ A cloud-ready SDN solution—through any hypervisor, for any workload, at any location, using any cloud. Cloud automation enabled by integration with VMware vRealize, Microsoft Azure Pack, OpenStack, Red Hat OpenShift, Kubernetes, and Cisco UCS Director.

■ Common platform for managing physical and virtual environments.

■ Inherent security with a zero-trust allow list model and innovative features in policy enforcement, microsegmentation, and analytics.

■ Open APIs and a programmable SDN fabric, with 65+ ecosystem partners.

Cisco ACI Building Blocks

Prior to Cisco ACI 4.1, the Cisco ACI fabric allowed only the use of a two-tier (spine-and-leaf switch) topology, in which each leaf switch is connected to every spine switch in the network with no interconnection between leaf switches or spine switches. Starting from Cisco ACI 4.1, the Cisco ACI fabric allows a multitier (three-tiers) fabric and the use of two tiers of leaf switches, which provides the capability for vertical expansion of the Cisco ACI fabric. This is useful to migrate a traditional three-tier architecture of core aggregation access that has been a common design model for many enterprise networks and is still required today. The primary reason for this is cable reach, where many hosts are located across floors or across buildings; however, due to the high pricing of fiber cables and the limitations of cable distances, it is not ideal in some situations to build a full-mesh two-tier fabric. In those cases, it is more efficient to build a spine-leaf-leaf topology and continue to benefit from the automation and visibility of Cisco ACI.

Figure 8-7 shows Cisco ACI two-tier and multitier topology.

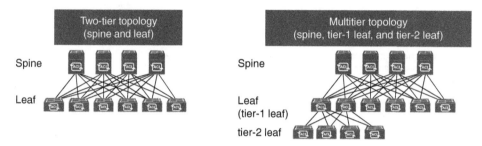

Figure 8-7   *Cisco ACI Two-Tier and Multitier Topology*

Leaf Switches

Leaf switches are the switches to which all endpoints (servers, storage, service nodes, and so on) connect. Leaf switches are available with various port speeds, ranging from 100Mbps to 400Gbps. Leaf switches are at the edge of the fabric and provide the VXLAN tunnel endpoint (VTEP) function. In Cisco ACI terminology, the IP address that represents the leaf VTEP is called the physical tunnel endpoint (PTEP). The leaf switches are responsible for routing or bridging tenant packets and for applying network policies.

In large-scale deployments, leaf switches are often dedicated and categorized by functions:

- **Border leaf:** Leaf switches that provide Layer 2 and Layer 3 connections to outside networks.

- **Services leaf:** Leaf switches that connect to Layer 4–7 service appliances such as load balancers and firewalls.

- **Compute leaf:** Leaf switches that connect to compute resources such as physical and virtualized servers.

- **Storage leaf:** Leaf switches that connect to storage devices for compute resources. This can include iSCSI, NFS, and other Ethernet medium storage devices.

Leaf switches do not need to be delegated to only one category. Depending on the design, the categories can overlap. For example, a leaf switch serving as a border leaf switch can also connect to compute resources.

Spine Switches

Spine switches interconnect leaf switches and provide the backbone of the ACI fabric. Spine switches are available with various port speeds, ranging from 40Gbps to 400Gbps. Within a pod, all tier-1 leaf switches connect to all spine switches, and all spine switches connect to all tier-1 leaf switches, but no direct connectivity is allowed between spine switches, between tier-1 leaf switches, or between tier-2 leaf switches. If you incorrectly cable spine switches to each other or leaf switches in the same tier to each other, the interfaces will be disabled. You may have topologies in which certain leaf switches are not connected to all spine switches, but traffic forwarding may be suboptimal in this scenario. Spine switches can also be used to build a Cisco ACI MultiPod fabric by connecting a Cisco ACI pod to an IP network, or they can connect to a supported WAN device for external Layer 3 connectivity. Spine switches also store all the endpoint-to-VTEP mapping entries (spine switch proxies). Nexus 9000 Series switches used in the ACI fabric run the ACI operating system instead of NX-OS.

Cisco APIC

The Cisco Application Policy Infrastructure Controller (APIC) is the central point of management for the ACI fabric. It is a clustered network control and policy system that provides image management, bootstrapping, and policy configuration for the Cisco ACI fabric. APIC translates a policy created on it into a configuration and pushes it to the right switches. The APIC appliance is deployed as a cluster. A minimum of three infrastructure controllers are configured in a cluster to provide control of the scale-out Cisco ACI fabric. The ultimate size of the controller cluster is directly proportionate to the size of the Cisco ACI deployment and is based on the transaction-rate requirements. Any controller in the cluster can service any user for any operation, and a controller can be transparently added to or removed from the cluster. If you lose one of the controllers, you can still change and add new configurations through the remaining controllers. Since the APIC is not involved in data plane forwarding, even if all the controllers in the fabric go down, the traffic flow is not impacted, and forwarding continues through the leaf and spine switches. If configuration changes need to be made, you must bring the Cisco APIC back up.

Cisco APICs are equipped with two network interface cards (NICs) for fabric connectivity. These NICs should be connected to different leaf switches for redundancy. Cisco APIC connectivity is automatically configured for active-backup teaming, which means that only one interface is active at any given time.

Figure 8-8 shows Cisco APIC fabric connectivity.

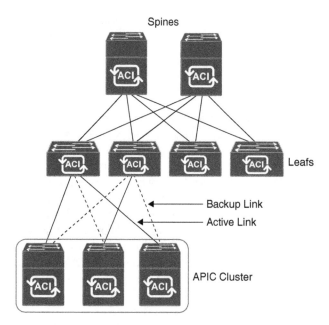

Figure 8-8   *APIC Fabric Connectivity*

The Cisco APIC provides the following control functions:

- **Policy Manager:** Manages the distributed policy repository responsible for the definition and deployment of the policy-based configuration of Cisco ACI.

- **Topology** Manager: Maintains up-to-date Cisco ACI topology and inventory information.

- **Observer:** The monitoring subsystem of the Cisco APIC; serves as a data repository for Cisco ACI operational state, health, and performance information.

- **Boot Director:** Controls the booting and firmware updates of the spine and leaf switches as well as the Cisco APIC elements.

- **Appliance Director:** Manages the formation and control of the Cisco APIC appliance cluster.

- **Virtual Machine Manager (or VMM):** Acts as an agent between the policy repository and a hypervisor and is responsible for interacting with hypervisor management systems such as VMware vCenter.

- **Event Manager:** Manages the repository for all the events and faults initiated from the Cisco APIC and the fabric switches.

- **Appliance element:** Manages the inventory and state of the local Cisco APIC appliance.

Cisco ACI Deployment Models

Cisco ACI consists of the following architectural solutions:

- Cisco ACI MultiPod

- Cisco Nexus Dashboard Orchestrator / Cisco ACI Multi-Site

- Cisco Cloud ACI

- Cisco ACI Physical Remote Leaf

- Cisco ACI vPod

- Cisco ACI Mini Fabric

Cisco ACI MultiPod

Cisco ACI MultiPod is part of the "single APIC cluster/single domain" family of solutions; a single APIC cluster is deployed to manage all the different ACI networks that are interconnected. These separate ACI networks are called "pods," and each of them looks like a regular two-tiers spine-leaf topology. The same APIC cluster can manage several pods, and, to increase the resiliency of the solution, the various controller nodes that make up the cluster can be deployed across different pods, as shown in Figure 8-9.

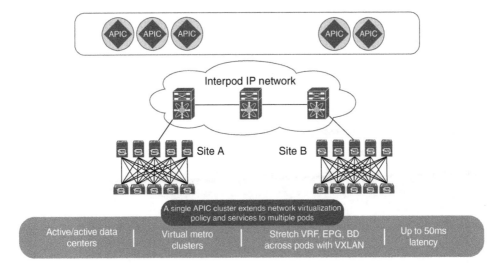

Figure 8-9   *Cisco ACI MultiPod*

Cisco Nexus Dashboard Orchestrator / Cisco Multi-Site

In this deployment mode, multiple Cisco ACI fabrics are connected to the Nexus Dashboard Orchestrator. The Nexus Dashboard Orchestrator provides a single point of provisioning for multiple Cisco ACI fabrics operating in a coordinated way. When this solution is combined with the latest networking enhancements of Cisco ACI, organizations can manage extension network elements such as virtual routing and forwarding (VRF) instances, bridge domains, and subnets across multiple fabrics. (More on VRF, bridge domains, and subnets can be found later in this chapter.) It enables centralized policy and security controls across geographically distributed fabrics and very large scaled-out fabrics with automation and operations from a common point, allowing for a global cloud-scale infrastructure.

The main features of Cisco Nexus Dashboard Orchestrator include the following:

- Single point of administration for multiple Cisco ACI fabrics

- Capability to map tenants, applications, and associated networks to specific availability domains within the Cisco ACI Multi-Site

- Change control across multiple fabrics, allowing staging, testing, and, if required, clean backout of any policy changes

- Automatic configuration and management of fabric network interconnects across an IP backbone

Figure 8-10 shows Cisco Nexus Dashboard Orchestrator deployment mode.

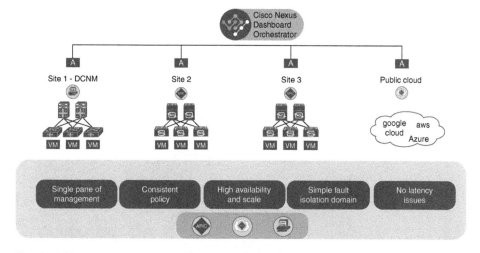

Figure 8-10   *Cisco Nexus Dashboard Orchestrator*

Cisco Cloud ACI

Cisco Cloud Application-Centric Infrastructure (Cisco Cloud ACI) is a comprehensive solution for simplified operations, automated network connectivity, consistent policy management, and visibility for multiple on-premises data centers and public clouds or multicloud environments. The solution captures business and user intents and translates them into native policy constructs for applications deployed across various cloud environments. It uses a holistic approach to enable application availability and segmentation for bare-metal, virtualized, containerized, or microservices-based applications deployed across multiple cloud domains. The common policy and operating model drastically reduce the cost and complexity of managing multicloud deployments. Cisco Cloud ACI provides a single management console to configure, monitor, and operate multiple disjoint environments spread across multiple clouds. It allows you to securely connect and segment workloads, not only in the public cloud, but also across public clouds. Cisco Cloud ACI is available on AWS and Microsoft Azure; future availability for Google Cloud has been announced at the time of this writing.

Cisco Cloud ACI has following components:

- **Cisco Cloud APIC:** Manage multiple cloud regions and the Cisco Cloud Services Routers (CSR) 1000v Series from a single instance of Cisco Cloud APIC and enable consistent policy, security, and operations through secure interconnect for a multicloud environment.

- **Cisco Nexus Dashboard Orchestrator:** Responsible for provisioning, health monitoring, and managing the full lifecycle of Cisco ACI networking policies and stretched tenant policies across Cisco ACI sites around the world, both on-premises and in the cloud. It is the single source of truth for policies.

- **Cisco Cloud Services Router 1000v Series:** Cloud ACI uses the Cisco Cloud Services Router (CSR) 1000v Series as the cloud router for connectivity between on-premises and cloud environments.

Cisco ACI Physical Remote Leaf

With Cisco ACI Physical Remote Leaf, a regular leaf switch is placed in a remote/satellite location and connected back to the spine switch in the main (on-premises) location and, in turn, extends Cisco ACI policy into the remote/satellite location, as shown in Figure 8-11.

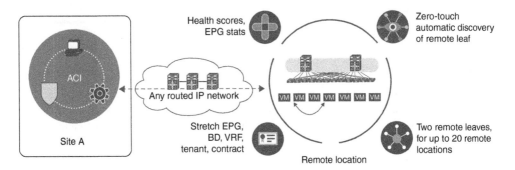

Figure 8-11 *Cisco ACI Physical Remote Leaf*

Cisco ACI vPod

Cisco ACI Virtual Pod (vPod) extends the policy-driven automation to multiple data centers, including satellite data centers with smaller footprints, and extends a common fabric all the way to public clouds that support bare-metal provisioning. The Cisco ACI vPod solution is a software-only extension to the on-premises data center and leverages the common Cisco APIC management to provide centralized policy and management of the data center fabric. A virtual pod consists of virtual spines (vSpines), virtual leafs (vLeafs), and ACI virtual edges (AVEs) that are deployed on a hypervisor infrastructure, as shown in Figure 8-12. Cisco ACI vSpine and vLeaf are deployed in a virtual form factor and emulate the control-plane functionalities of the physical spine and leaf. Packet forwarding, policy enforcement, and all data-plane management are taken care by the Cisco ACI virtual edge running on each host in the Cisco ACI vPod.

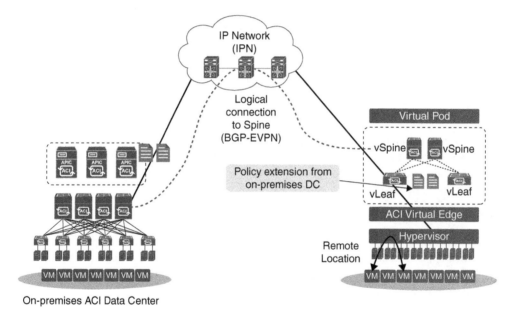

Figure 8-12   *Cisco ACI vPod*

Cisco ACI Mini Fabric

This deployment model expands the data center footprints to smaller remote and satellite locations where power, cooling, space, and cost are challenges. The solution comprises APIC-CLUSTER-XS (one physical and two virtual controllers running in virtual machines) along with two spines and a minimum of two and a maximum of four leafs. This reduces the physical footprint and cost of the APIC cluster, allowing the ACI fabric to be deployed in scenarios with limited rack space or initial budget, such as a colocation facility or a single-room data center, where a full-scale ACI installation may not be practical.

Figure 8-13 shows an example of a mini Cisco ACI fabric with a physical APIC and two virtual APICs (vAPICs).

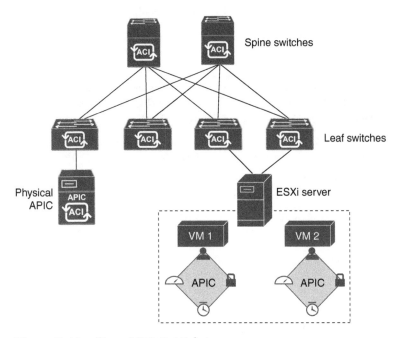

Figure 8-13   *Cisco ACI Mini Fabric*

Cisco ACI Hardware

Cisco APICs can be deployed either as physical or virtual appliances. Physical APICs are Cisco C-Series servers with ACI code installed. The Cisco APIC appliance has two form factors for medium and large configurations. Medium configurations have a medium-size CPU, hard drive, and memory for up to 1000 edge ports. Large configurations have a large-size CPU, hard drive, and memory for more than 1000 edge ports.

Cisco releases new generations of APICs with hardware improvements from time to time. At the time of this writing, Cisco has released three generations of APICs. An APIC appliance is composed of either a cluster of APIC-SERVER-L3 (UCS C220 M5) or APIC-SERVER-M3 (UCS C240 M5) hardware, referred to as third-generation appliances, Cisco UCS 220 M4, referred to as a second-generation appliance, or Cisco UCS 220 M3, referred to as first-generation appliance servers manufactured with an image secured with a Trusted Platform Module (TPM), certificates, and an APIC product ID (PID).

Table 8-1 lists the specifications of the APIC M3 and L3 appliance. Note that at least three appliances need to be configured as a cluster.

Table 8-1 *APIC M3 and L3 Appliance Specifications*

Component	Cisco APIC Appliance Medium Configuration: M3	Cisco APIC ApplianceLarge Configuration: L3
Processor	2 × 1.7GHz Xeon Scalable 3106/85W 8C/11MB Cache/ DDR4 2133M	2 × 2.1GHz Xeon Scalable 4110/85W 8C/11MB Cache/ DDR4 2400MHz
Memory	6 × 16GB DDR4-2666MHz RDIMM/PC4-21300/single rank/x4/1.2v	6 × 16GB DDR4-2666MHz RDIMM/PC4-21300/single rank/x4/1.2v
Hard Drive	2 × 1TB 12G SAS 7.2K RPM SFF HDD	2 × 2.4TB 12G SAS 10K RPM SFF HDD (4K)
PCI Express (PCIe) slots	Cisco UCS VIC 1455 Quad Port 10/25G SFP28 CNA PCIE	Cisco UCS VIC 1455 Quad Port 10/25G SFP28 CNA PCIE
Power supply	770W power supply	770W power supply

Virtual APIC is deployed using two hard disks. Table 8-2 shows the Cisco virtual APIC requirements.

Table 8-2 *Cisco Virtual APIC Requirements*

Component	Virtual APIC
Processor	8 vCPUs
Memory	32GB
Disk space	100G SSD
	300G HDD
ESxi	6.5 or above

The Cisco Nexus 9000 Series switches operate in one of two modes: Cisco ACI or Cisco NX-OS. The Cisco Nexus 9000 Series switches in ACI mode are the spine and leaf switches that build the fabric. Spine switches are available in both modular and fixed variants. Cisco Nexus 9500 Series modular chassis with 4, 8, and 16 slots are used as modular spine switches. The Cisco Nexus 9500 Series modular switches support a comprehensive selection of line cards and fabric modules that provide 1-, 10-, 25-, 40-, 50-, 100-, 200-, and 400-Gigabit Ethernet interfaces. The supervisor, system controller, power supplies, and line cards are common across all three switches. Each switch, however, has unique fabric modules and fan trays that plug in vertically in the rear of the chassis. Cisco Nexus 9300 Series switches are available in both spine and leaf variants.

Figure 8-14 shows Cisco 9500 platform modular switch.

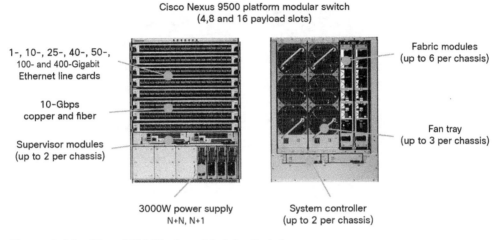

Figure 8-14 *Cisco 9500 Platform Modular Switch*

Table 8-3 shows the various 9500 modular spine switch chassis available at the time of this writing.

Table 8-3 *Cisco Nexus 9500 Modular Spine Switch*

N9K-C9504	Cisco Nexus 9504 switch chassis with four slots
N9K-C9504	Cisco Nexus 9504 switch chassis with four slots
N9K-C9508	Cisco Nexus 9508 switch chassis with eight slots
N9K-C9508-B1	Cisco Nexus 9508 chassis bundle with one supervisor module, three power supplies, two system controllers, three fan trays, and three fabric modules
N9K-C9508-B2	Cisco Nexus 9508 chassis bundle with one supervisor module, three power supplies, two system controllers, three fan trays, and six fabric modules
N9K-C9516	Cisco Nexus 9516 switch chassis with 16 slots

You can easily figure out the capabilities of spine and leaf switches from the product ID of each switch. Try to decode the capabilities of spine and leaf switches from Tables 8-4 through 8-7 from the product ID of each switch using the taxonomy for N9K part numbers, as shown in Figure 8-15.

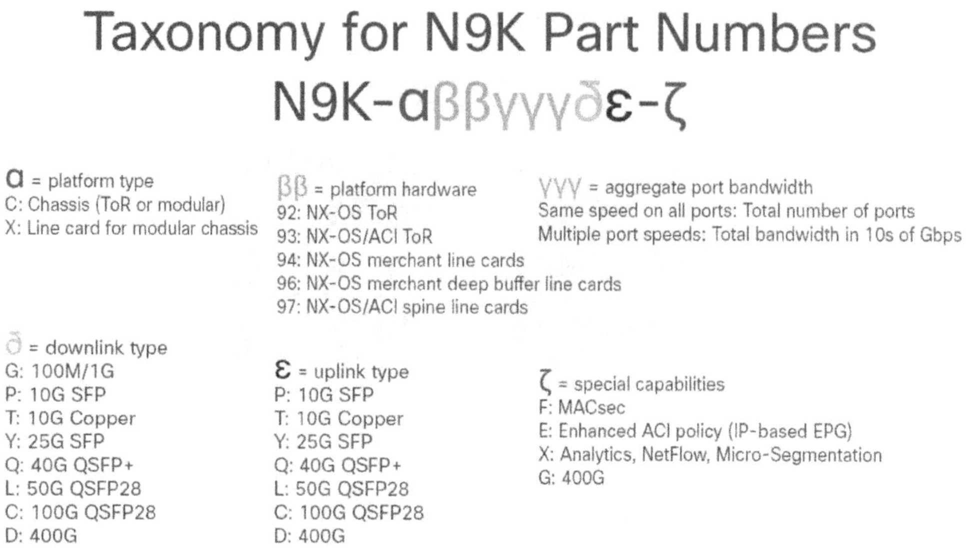

Taxonomy for N9K Part Numbers
N9K-αββγγγðε-ζ

α = platform type
C: Chassis (ToR or modular)
X: Line card for modular chassis

ββ = platform hardware
92: NX-OS ToR
93: NX-OS/ACI ToR
94: NX-OS merchant line cards
96: NX-OS merchant deep buffer line cards
97: NX-OS/ACI spine line cards

γγγ = aggregate port bandwidth
Same speed on all ports: Total number of ports
Multiple port speeds: Total bandwidth in 10s of Gbps

ð = downlink type
G: 100M/1G
P: 10G SFP
T: 10G Copper
Y: 25G SFP
Q: 40G QSFP+
L: 50G QSFP28
C: 100G QSFP28
D: 400G

ε = uplink type
P: 10G SFP
T: 10G Copper
Y: 25G SFP
Q: 40G QSFP+
L: 50G QSFP28
C: 100G QSFP28
D: 400G

ζ = special capabilities
F: MACsec
E: Enhanced ACI policy (IP-based EPG)
X: Analytics, NetFlow, Micro-Segmentation
G: 400G

Figure 8-15 *N9K Part Numbers Taxonomy*

Table 8-4 shows the modular spine switch line cards available at the time of writing.

Table 8-4 *Modular Spine Switch Line Cards*

Product ID	Description
N9K-X9716D-GX	Cisco Nexus 9500 16-port, 400-Gigabit Ethernet QSFP line card
N9K-X9736C-FX	Cisco Nexus 9500 36-port, 40/100-Gigabit Ethernet Cloud Scale line card
N9K-X9736Q-FX	Cisco Nexus 9500 36-port, 40-Gigabit Ethernet Cloud Scale line card
N9K-X9732C-EX	Cisco Nexus 9500 32-port, 40/100 Gigabit Ethernet Cloud Scale line card

Note   Cloud Scale in Table 8-4 refers to line cards using Cisco Cloud Scale ASICs.

Table 8-5 shows the fixed spine switches available at the time of writing.

Table 8-5 *Fixed Spine Switches*

Product ID	Description
N9K-C9332C	Cisco Nexus 9300 platform switch with 32 40/100-Gigabit QSFP28 ports and two SFP ports
N9K-C9364C	Cisco Nexus 9300 platform switch with 64 40/100-Gigabit QSFP28 ports and two 1/10-Gigabit SFP+ ports

Table 8-6 shows the fixed leaf switches available at the time of writing.

Table 8-6 *Fixed Leaf Switches*

Product ID	Description
N9K-C93180YC-FX3	Cisco Nexus 9300 platform switch with 48 100M/1/10/25-Gigabit Ethernet SFP28 ports, six 10/25/40/50/100-Gigabit QSFP28 ports, one management port (10/100/1000BASE-T), one console port (RS-232), and one USB port.
N9K-C93108TC-FX3P	Cisco Nexus 9300 platform switch with 48 100M/1/2.5/5/10-GBASE-T (copper) ports, six 40/100-Gigabit QSFP28 ports, two management ports (one 10/100/1000BASE-T port and one SFP port), one console port (RS-232), and one USB port.
N9K-93240YC-FX2	Cisco Nexus 9300 platform switch with 48 1/10/25-Gigabit Ethernet SFP28 ports and 12 40/100-Gigabit Ethernet QSFP28 ports. The N9K-93240YC-FX2 is a 1.2-RU switch.
N9K-C93216TC-FX2	Cisco Nexus 9300 platform switch with 96 1/10GBASE-T (copper) front-panel ports and 12 40/100-Gigabit Ethernet QSFP28 spine-facing ports.
N9K-C93360YC-FX2	Cisco Nexus 9300 platform switch with 96 1/10/25-Gigabit front-panel ports and 12 40/100-Gigabit Ethernet QSFP spine-facing ports.
N9K-C9336C-FX2	Cisco Nexus C9336C-FX2 top-of-rack (ToR) switch with 36 fixed 40/100-Gigabit Ethernet QSFP28 spine-facing ports.
N9K-C93108TC-FX	Cisco Nexus 9300 platform switch with 48 1/10GBASE-T (copper) front-panel ports and six fixed 40/100-Gigabit Ethernet QSFP28 spine-facing ports.
N9K-C93108TC-FX-24	Cisco Nexus 9300 platform switch with 24 1/10GBASE-T (copper) front-panel ports and six fixed 40/100-Gigabit Ethernet QSFP28 spine-facing ports.
N9K-93240YC-FX2	Cisco Nexus 9300 platform switch with 48 1/10/25-Gigabit Ethernet SFP28 ports and 12 40/100-Gigabit Ethernet QSFP28 ports. The N9K-93240YC-FX2 is a 1.2-RU switch.

Product ID	Description
N9K-C93180YC-FX	Cisco Nexus 9300 platform switch with 48 1/10/25-Gigabit Ethernet SFP28 front-panel ports and six fixed 40/100-Gigabit Ethernet QSFP28 spine-facing ports.
N9K-C93216TC-FX2	Cisco Nexus 9300 platform switch with 96 1/10GBASE-T (copper) front-panel ports and 12 40/100-Gigabit Ethernet QSFP28 spine-facing ports.
N9K-C93180YC-FX-24	Cisco Nexus 9300 platform switch with 24 1/10/25-Gigabit Ethernet SFP28 front-panel ports and six fixed 40/100-Gigabit Ethernet QSFP28 spine-facing ports.
N9K-C9348GC-FXP	Cisco Nexus 9348GC-FXP switch with 48 100/1000-Megabit 1GBASE-T downlink ports, four 10/25-Gigabit SFP28 downlink ports, and two 40/100-Gigabit QSFP28 uplink ports.
N9K-C93108TC-EX	Cisco Nexus 9300 platform switch with 48 1/10GBASE-T (copper) front-panel ports and six 40/100-Gigabit QSFP28 spine-facing ports.
N9K-C93108TC-EX-24	Cisco Nexus 9300 platform switch with 24 1/10GBASE-T (copper) front-panel ports and six 40/100-Gigabit QSFP28 spine-facing ports.
N9K-C93180LC-EX	Cisco Nexus 9300 platform switch with 24 40-Gigabit front-panel ports and six 40/100-Gigabit QSFP28 spine-facing ports.
N9K-C93108TC-FX-24	Cisco Nexus 9300 platform switch with 24 1/10GBASE-T (copper) front-panel ports and six fixed 40/100-Gigabit Ethernet QSFP28 spine-facing ports.
N9K-C93180YC-EX	Cisco Nexus 9300 platform switch with 48 1/10/25-Gigabit front-panel ports and six 40/100 Gigabit QSFP28 spine-facing ports.
N9K-C93180YC-EX-24	Cisco Nexus 9300 platform switch with 24 1/10/25-Gigabit front-panel ports and six 40/100 Gigabit QSFP28 spine-facing ports.
N9K-C93120TX	Cisco Nexus 9300 platform switch with 96 1/10GBASE-T (copper) front-panel ports and six 40-Gigabit Ethernet QSFP spine-facing ports.

Table 8-7 lists the fixed Nexus 9300 series switches at the time of writing. These switches can be used as either spine or leaf switches in an ACI fabric, as per the requirement.

Table 8-7 *Fixed Leaf/Spine Switches*

Product ID	Description
N9K-C9364C-GX	Cisco Nexus 9300 platform switch with 64 100-Gigabit Ethernet QSFP28 ports, two management ports (one RJ-45 port and one SFP port), one console port (RS-232), and one USB port
N9K-C93600CD-GX	Cisco Nexus 9300 platform switch with 28 10/40/100-Gigabit Ethernet QSFP28 ports (ports 1–28) and eight 10/40/100/400-Gigabit QSFP-DD ports (ports 29–36)
N9K-C9316D-GX	Cisco Nexus 9300 platform switch with 16 10/40/100/400-Gigabit QSFP-DD ports (ports 1–16)
N9K-C9332D-GX2B	Cisco Nexus 9300 platform switch with 32 400Gbps QSFP-DD and two 1/10Gbps SFP+ ports
N9K-C9364D-GX2A	Cisco Nexus 9300 platform switch with 64 400Gbps QSFP-DD and two 1/10Gbps SFP+ ports

Note Cisco often launches new leaf/spine switch models with added capabilities. For the most up-to-date information, refer to https://www.cisco.com/c/en/us/products/switches/nexus-9000-series-switches/index.html.

ACI Startup Discovery

The clustered Cisco Application Policy Infrastructure Controller (APIC) provides DHCP, bootstrap configuration, and image management to the fabric for automated startup and upgrades.

The Cisco Nexus ACI fabric software is bundled as an ISO image, which can be installed on the Cisco APIC server through the KVM interface on the Cisco Integrated Management Controller (CIMC). The Cisco Nexus ACI Software ISO contains the Cisco APIC image, the firmware image for the leaf node, the firmware image for the spine node, default fabric infrastructure policies, and the protocols required for operation.

The ACI fabric bootstrap sequence begins when the fabric is booted with factory-installed images on all the switches. The Cisco Nexus 9000 Series switches that run the ACI firmware and APICs use a reserved overlay for the boot process. This infrastructure space is hard-coded on the switches. The APIC can connect to a leaf through the default overlay, or it can use a locally significant identifier.

The ACI fabric uses an infrastructure space, which is securely isolated in the fabric and is where all the topology discovery, fabric management, and infrastructure addressing is performed. ACI fabric management communication within the fabric takes place in the infrastructure space through internal private IP addresses. This addressing scheme allows the APIC to communicate with fabric nodes and other Cisco APICs in the cluster. The APIC discovers the IP address and node information of other Cisco APICs in the cluster using a Link Layer Discovery Protocol–based discovery process.

The following describes the APIC cluster discovery process:

■ Each APIC in the Cisco ACI uses an internal private IP address to communicate with the ACI nodes and other APICs in the cluster. The APIC discovers the IP address of other APICs in the cluster through an LLDP-based discovery process.

■ APICs maintain an appliance vector (AV), which provides a mapping from an APIC ID to an APIC IP address and a universally unique identifier (UUID) of the APIC. Initially, each APIC starts with an AV filled with its local IP address, and all other APIC slots are marked as unknown.

■ When a switch reboots, the policy element (PE) on the leaf gets its AV from the APIC. The switch then advertises this AV to all its neighbors and reports any discrepancies between its local AV and the neighbors' AVs to all the APICs in its local AV.

Using this process, the APIC learns about the other APICs in the ACI through switches. After these newly discovered APICs in the cluster have been validated, they update their local AV and program the switches with the new AV. Switches then start advertising this new AV. This process continues until all the switches have the identical AV and all APICs know the IP address of all the other APICs.

The ACI fabric is brought up in a cascading manner, starting with the leaf nodes directly attached to the APIC. LLDP and control-plane IS-IS convergence occurs in parallel to this boot process. The ACI fabric uses LLDP- and DHCP-based fabric discovery to automatically discover the fabric switch nodes, assign the infrastructure VXLAN tunnel endpoint (VTEP) addresses, and install the firmware on the switches. The fabric uses an IS-IS (Intermediate System to Intermediate System) environment utilizing Level 1 connections within the topology for advertising loopback addresses called the Virtual extensible LAN tunnel endpoints (VTEPs), which are used in the integrated overlay and advertised to all other nodes in the fabric for overlay tunnel use. Prior to this automated process, a minimal bootstrap configuration must be performed on the Cisco APIC. After the APICs are connected and their IP addresses assigned, the APIC GUI can be accessed by entering the address of any APIC into a web browser. The APIC GUI runs HTML5 and eliminates the need for Java to be installed locally.

Cisco ACI Policy Model

The ACI policy model enables the specification of application requirements policies. The APIC automatically renders policies in the fabric infrastructure. When a user or process initiates an administrative change to an object in the fabric, the APIC first applies that change to the policy model. This policy model change then triggers a change to the actual managed endpoint. This approach is called a model-driven framework.

The key characteristics of the policy model include the following:

■ As a model-driven architecture, the software maintains a complete representation of the administrative and operational state of the system (the model). The model applies uniformly to the fabric, services, system behaviors, and virtual and physical devices attached to the network.

■ The logical domain (ACI objects configured by a user in APIC) and concrete domain (ACI objects upon which the switch's operating system acts) are separated; the logical configurations are rendered into concrete configurations by applying the policies in relation to the available physical resources. No configuration is carried out against concrete entities. Concrete entities are configured implicitly as a side effect of the changes to the APIC policy model. Concrete entities can be, but do not have to be, physical (such as a virtual machine or a VLAN).

■ The system prohibits communications with newly connected devices until the policy model is updated to include the new device.

■ Network administrators do not configure logical and physical system resources directly but rather define logical (hardware-independent) configurations and APIC policies that control different aspects of the system behavior.

The Cisco ACI fabric is composed of the physical and logical components recorded in the Management Information Model (MIM), which can be represented in a hierarchical management information tree (MIT). The information model is stored and managed by processes that run on the APIC. The APIC enables the control of managed resources by presenting their manageable characteristics as object properties that can be inherited according to the location of the object within the hierarchical structure of the MIT.

Each node in the tree represents a managed object (MO) or group of objects. MOs are abstractions of fabric resources. An MO can represent a concrete object (such as a switch or adapter) or a logical object (such as an application profile, endpoint group, or fault). Figure 8-16 provides an overview of the MIT.

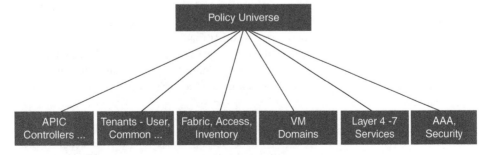

Figure 8-16 *Cisco ACI Policy Management Information Model Overview*

The hierarchical structure starts with the policy universe at the top (root) and contains parent and child nodes. Each node in the tree is an MO, and each object in the fabric has a unique distinguished name (DN) that describes the object and locates its place in the tree. The following managed objects contain the policies that govern the operation of the system:

- APICs comprise a replicated synchronized clustered controller that provides management, policy programming, application deployment, and health monitoring for the multitenant fabric.

- A tenant is a container for policies that enable an administrator to exercise domain-based access control. The system provides the following four kinds of tenants:

  - User tenants are defined by the administrator according to the needs of users. They contain policies that govern the operation of resources such as applications, databases, web servers, network-attached storage, virtual machines, and so on.

  - The common tenant is provided by the system but can be configured by the fabric administrator. It contains policies that govern the operation of resources accessible to all tenants, such as firewalls, load balancers, Layer 4 to Layer 7 services, intrusion detection appliances, and so on.

  - The infrastructure tenant is provided by the system but can be configured by the fabric administrator. It contains policies that govern the operation of infrastructure resources such as the fabric VXLAN overlay. It also enables a fabric provider to selectively deploy resources to one or more user tenants.

  - The management tenant is provided by the system but can be configured by the fabric administrator. It contains policies that govern the operation of fabric management functions used for in-band and out-of-band configuration of fabric nodes. The management tenant contains a private out-of-bound address space for the APIC/fabric internal communications, outside the fabric data path, that provides access through the management port of the switches. The management tenant enables discovery and automation of communications with virtual machine controllers.

- Access policies govern the operation of switch access ports that provide connectivity to resources such as storage, compute, Layer 2 and Layer 3 (bridged and routed) connectivity, virtual machine hypervisors, Layer 4 to Layer 7 devices, and so on. If a tenant requires interface configurations other than those provided in the default link, Cisco Discovery Protocol (CDP), Link Layer Discovery Protocol (LLDP), Link Aggregation Control Protocol (LACP), or Spanning Tree, an administrator must configure access policies to enable such configurations on the access ports of the leaf switches.

- Fabric policies govern the operation of the switch fabric ports, including functions such as Network Time Protocol (NTP) server synchronization, Intermediate System to Intermediate System Protocol (IS-IS), Border Gateway Protocol (BGP) route reflectors, Domain Name System (DNS), and so on. The fabric MO contains objects such as power supplies, fans, chassis, and so on.

- Virtual machine (VM) domains group VM controllers with similar networking policy requirements. VM controllers can share VLAN or Virtual Extensible Local Area Network (VXLAN) space and application endpoint groups (EPGs). The APIC communicates with the VM controller to publish network configurations such as port groups that are then applied to the virtual workloads.

- The Layer 4 to Layer 7 service integration lifecycle automation framework enables the system to dynamically respond when a service comes online or goes offline. Policies provide service device package and inventory management functions.

- Access, authentication, and accounting (AAA) policies govern the user privileges, roles, and security domains of the Cisco ACI fabric.

The hierarchical policy model fits well with the REST API interface. When invoked, the API reads from or writes to objects in the MIT. Any data in the MIT can be described as a self-contained, structured tree text document encoded in XML or JSON.

ACI Logical Constructs

The policy model manages the entire fabric, including the infrastructure, authentication, security, services, applications, and diagnostics. Logical constructs in the policy model define how the fabric meets the needs of any of the functions of the fabric.

Figure 8-17 provides an overview of the ACI policy model logical constructs.

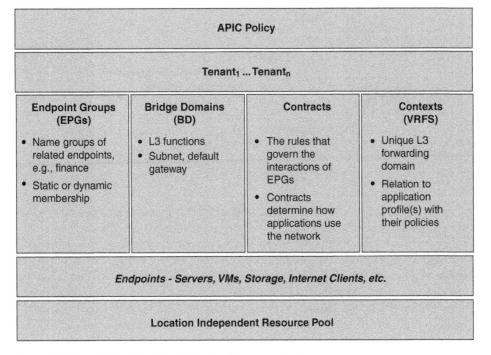

Figure 8-17 *ACI Policy Model Logical Constructs Overview*

Fabric-wide or tenant administrators create predefined policies that contain application or shared resource requirements. These policies automate the provisioning of applications, network-attached services, security policies, and tenant subnets, which puts administrators in the position of approaching the resource pool in terms of applications rather than infrastructure building blocks. The application drives the networking behavior, not the other way around.

Figure 8-18 shows the relationship between different logical constructs.

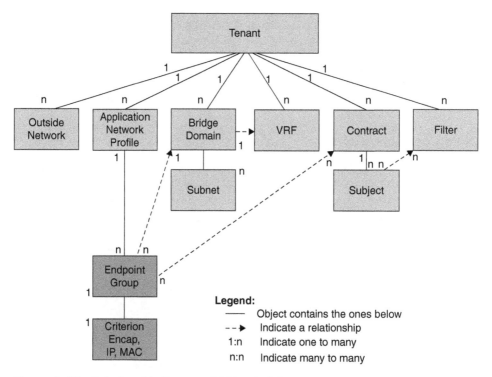

Figure 8-18   *Relationship Between ACI Logical Constructs*

Tenant

A tenant is a logical container for application policies that enable an administrator to exercise domain-based access control. A tenant represents a unit of isolation from a policy perspective, but it does not represent a private network. Tenants can represent a customer in a service provider setting, an organization or domain in an enterprise setting, or just a convenient grouping of policies. Tenants can be isolated from one another or can share resources. The primary elements that the tenant contains are filters, contracts, outside networks, bridge domains, virtual routing and forwarding (VRF) instances, and application profiles that contain endpoint groups (EPGs). Entities in the tenant inherit its policies. VRFs are also known as contexts; each VRF can be associated with multiple bridge domains. Tenants are logical containers for application policies. The fabric can contain multiple tenants. A tenant must be configured before you can deploy any Layer 4 to Layer 7 services. The ACI fabric supports IPv4, IPv6, and dual-stack configurations for tenant networking.

VRFs

A virtual routing and forwarding (VRF), or context, is a tenant network. A tenant can have multiple VRFs. A VRF is a unique Layer 3 forwarding and application policy domain. A VRF defines a Layer 3 address domain. One or more bridge domains are associated with a VRF. All of the endpoints within the Layer 3 domain must have unique IP addresses because it is possible to forward packets directly between these devices if the policy allows it. A tenant can contain multiple VRFs. After an administrator creates a logical device, the administrator can create a VRF for the logical device, which provides a selection criteria policy for a device cluster. A logical device can be selected based on a contract name, a graph name, or the function node name inside the graph.

Application Profiles

An application profile defines the policies, services, and relationships between endpoint groups (EPGs). Application profiles contain one or more EPGs. Modern applications contain multiple components. For example, an e-commerce application could require a web server, a database server, data located in a storage area network, and access to outside resources that enable financial transactions. The application profile contains as many (or as few) EPGs as necessary that are logically related to providing the capabilities of an application.

Endpoint Groups

The endpoint group (EPG) is the most important object in the policy model. An EPG is a managed object that is a named logical entity that contains a collection of endpoints. Endpoints are devices connected to the network directly or indirectly. They have an address (identity), a location, and attributes (such as version or patch level), and they can be physical or virtual. Knowing the address of an endpoint also enables access to all its other identity details. Endpoint examples include servers, virtual machines, network-attached storage, or clients on the Internet. Endpoint membership in an EPG can be dynamic or static. An EPG can be statically configured by an administrator in the APIC, or dynamically configured by an automated system such as vCenter or OpenStack. WAN router connectivity (L3Out) to the fabric is an example of a configuration that uses a static EPG. (More on ACI external connectivity options can be found in Chapter 9, "Operating Cisco ACI.") Virtual machine management connectivity to VMware vCenter is an example of a configuration that uses a dynamic EPG. Once the virtual machine management domain is configured in the fabric, vCenter triggers the dynamic configuration of EPGs that enable virtual machine endpoints to start up, move, and shut down as needed. EPGs contain endpoints that have common policy requirements such as security, virtual machine mobility, QoS, and Layer 4 to Layer 7 services. Rather than endpoints being configured and managed individually, they are placed in an EPG and managed as a group. Policies apply to EPGs, never to individual endpoints.

The ACI fabric can contain the following types of EPGs:

- Application endpoint group

- Layer 2 external outside network instance endpoint group

- Layer 3 external outside network instance endpoint group

- Management endpoint groups for out-of-band or in-band access

Bridge Domains and Subnets

A bridge domain (BD) represents a Layer 2 forwarding construct within the fabric. A BD must be linked to a VRF. With the exception of a Layer 2 VLAN, it must have at least one subnet associated with it. The BD defines the unique Layer 2 MAC address space and a Layer 2 flood domain if flooding is enabled. While a VRF defines a unique IP address space, that address space can consist of multiple subnets. Those subnets are defined in one or more BDs that reference the corresponding VRF. Bridge domains can span multiple switches. A bridge domain can contain multiple subnets, but a subnet is contained within a single bridge domain. Subnets can span multiple EPGs; one or more EPGs can be associated with one bridge domain or subnet.

The options for a subnet under a BD or under an EPG are as follows:

- **Public:** The subnet can be exported to a routed connection.

- **Private:** The subnet applies only within its tenant.

- **Shared:** The subnet can be shared with and exported to multiple VRFs in the same tenant or across tenants as part of a shared service. An example of a shared service is a routed connection to an EPG present in another VRF in a different tenant. This enables traffic to pass in both directions across VRFs. An EPG that provides a shared service must have its subnet configured under that EPG (not under a BD), and its scope must be set to advertised externally and shared between VRFs.

Attachable Entity Profile

An Attachable Entity Profile (AEP) represents a group of external entities with similar infrastructure policy requirements. The infrastructure policies consist of physical interface policies that configure various protocol options, such as Cisco Discovery Protocol (CDP), Link Layer Discovery Protocol (LLDP), or Link Aggregation Control Protocol (LACP). An AEP is required to deploy VLAN pools on leaf switches. Encapsulation blocks (and associated VLANs) are reusable across leaf switches. An AEP implicitly provides the scope of the VLAN pool to the physical infrastructure. The AEP defines the range of allowed VLANs but it does not provision them. No traffic flows unless an EPG is deployed on the port. Without a VLAN pool being defined in an AEP, a VLAN is not enabled on the leaf port even if an EPG is provisioned.

Contracts

In addition to EPGs, contracts are key objects in the policy model. EPGs can only communicate with other EPGs according to contract rules. An administrator uses a contract to select the type(s) of traffic that can pass between EPGs, including the protocols and ports allowed. If there is no contract, inter-EPG communication is disabled by default. There is no contract required for intra-EPG communication; intra-EPG communication is always implicitly allowed. You can also configure contract preferred groups that enable greater control of communication between EPGs in a VRF. If most of the EPGs in the VRF should have open communication, but a few should only have limited communication with the other EPGs, you can configure a combination of a contract preferred group and contracts with filters to control communication precisely. Contracts govern the communication between EPGs that are labeled providers, consumers, or both. EPG providers expose contracts with which a would-be consumer EPG must comply. The relationship between an EPG and a contract can be either a provider or consumer. When an EPG provides a contract, communication with that EPG can be initiated from other EPGs as long as the communication complies with the provided contract. When an EPG consumes a contract, the endpoints in the consuming EPG may initiate communication with any endpoint in an EPG that is providing that contract.

Labels, Filters, and Subjects

Label, filter, and subject managed objects enable mixing and matching among EPGs and contracts so as to satisfy various applications or service delivery requirements. Contracts can contain multiple communication rules, and multiple EPGs can both consume and provide multiple contracts.

Labels control which rules apply when communicating between a specific pair of EPGs. Labels are managed objects with only one property: a name. Labels enable classifying which objects can and cannot communicate with one another. Label matching is done first. If the labels do not match, no other contract or filter information is processed. The label match attribute can be one of these values: at least one (the default), all, none, or exactly one. Labels can be applied to a variety of provider and consumer managed objects, including EPGs, contracts, bridge domains, and so on. Labels do not apply across object types; a label on an application EPG has no relevance to a label on a bridge domain.

Filters are Layer 2 to Layer 4 fields, TCP/IP header fields such as Layer 3 protocol type, Layer 4 ports, and so forth. According to its related contract, an EPG provider dictates the protocols and ports in both the in and out directions. Contract subjects contain associations to the filters (and their directions) that are applied between EPGs that produce and consume the contract.

Subjects are contained in contracts. One or more subjects within a contract use filters to specify the type of traffic that can be communicated and how it occurs. For example, for HTTPS messages, the subject specifies the direction and the filters that specify the IP address type (for example, IPv4), the HTTP protocol, and the ports allowed. Subjects determine if filters are unidirectional or bidirectional.

Outside Networks

Outside network policies control connectivity to the outside. A tenant can contain multiple outside network objects. Outside network policies specify the relevant Layer 2 or Layer 3 properties that control communications between an outside public or private network and the ACI fabric. External devices, such as routers that connect to the WAN and enterprise core, or existing Layer 2 switches, connect to the front panel interface of a leaf switch. The leaf switch that provides such connectivity is known as a border leaf. The border leaf switch interface that connects to an external device can be configured as either a bridged or routed interface. In the case of a routed interface, static or dynamic routing can be used. The border leaf switch can also perform all the functions of a normal leaf switch.

ACI Fabric Policies

Fabric policies govern the operation of internal fabric interfaces and enable the configuration of various functions, protocols, and interfaces that connect spine and leaf switches. Administrators who have fabric administrator privileges can create new fabric policies according to their requirements. The APIC enables administrators to select the pods, switches, and interfaces to which they will apply fabric policies.

Figure 8-19 provides an overview of the fabric policy model.

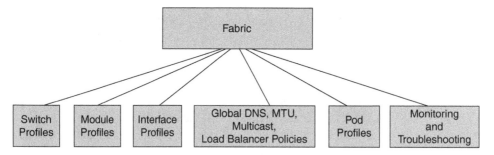

Figure 8-19   *Cisco ACI Fabric Policies Overview*

Fabric policies are grouped into the following categories:

■ Switch profiles specify which switches to configure and the switch configuration policy.

- Module profiles specify which spine switch modules to configure and the spine switch configuration policy.

- Interface profiles specify which fabric interfaces to configure and the interface configuration policy.

- Global policies specify DNS, fabric MTU default, multicast tree, and load balancer configurations to be used throughout the fabric.

- Pod profiles specify date and time, SNMP, Council of Oracle Protocol (COOP), IS-IS, and Border Gateway Protocol (BGP) route reflector policies.

- Monitoring and troubleshooting policies specify what to monitor, thresholds, how to handle faults and logs, and how to perform diagnostics.

Fabric policies configure interfaces that connect spine and leaf switches. Fabric policies can enable features such as monitoring (statistics collection and statistics export), troubleshooting (on-demand diagnostics and SPAN), IS-IS, Council of Oracle Protocol (COOP), SNMP, Border Gateway Protocol (BGP) route reflectors, DNS, and Network Time Protocol (NTP).

To apply a configuration across the fabric, an administrator associates a defined group of policies to interfaces on switches in a single step. In this way, large numbers of interfaces across the fabric can be configured at once; configuring one port at a time is not scalable. Figure 8-20 shows how the process works for configuring the ACI fabric.

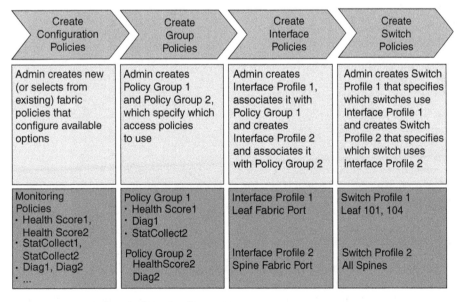

Figure 8-20 *Fabric Policy Configuration Process*

Figure 8-21 shows the result of applying Switch Profile 1 and Switch Profile 2 to the ACI fabric.

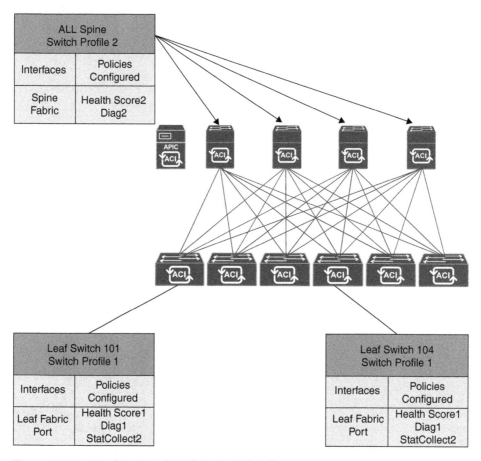

Figure 8-21   *Application of a Fabric Switch Policy*

This combination of infrastructure and scope enables administrators to manage fabric configuration in a scalable fashion. These configurations can be implemented using the REST API, the CLI, or the GUI.

ACI Access Policies

Access policies configure external-facing interfaces that connect to devices such as virtual machine controllers and hypervisors, hosts, network attached storage, routers, or Fabric Extender (FEX) interfaces. Access policies enable the configuration of port channels and virtual port channels, protocols such as Link Layer Discovery Protocol (LLDP), Cisco Discovery Protocol (CDP), and Link Aggregation Control Protocol (LACP), and features such as statistics gathering, monitoring, and diagnostics.

Figure 8-22 provides an overview of the access policy model.

Figure 8-22 *Access Policy Model Overview*

Access policies are grouped into the following categories:

- Switch profiles specify which switches to configure and the switch configuration policy.

- Module profiles specify which leaf switch access cards and access modules to configure and the leaf switch configuration policy.

- Interface profiles specify which access interfaces to configure and the interface configuration policy.

- Global policies enable the configuration of DHCP, QoS, and attachable entity profile (AEP) functions that can be used throughout the fabric. AEP profiles provide a template to deploy hypervisor policies on a large set of leaf ports and associate a Virtual Machine Manager (VMM) domain and the physical network infrastructure. They are also required for Layer 2 and Layer 3 external network connectivity

- Pools specify VLAN, VXLAN, and multicast address pools. A pool is a shared resource that can be consumed by multiple domains such as VMM and Layer 4 to Layer 7 services.

- Physical and external domains policies include the following:

  - External bridged domain Layer 2 domain profiles contain the port and VLAN specifications that a bridged Layer 2 network connected to the fabric uses.

  - External routed domain Layer 3 domain profiles contain the port and VLAN specifications that a routed Layer 3 network connected to the fabric uses.

  - Physical domain policies contain physical infrastructure specifications, such as ports and VLAN, used by a tenant or endpoint group.

- Monitoring and troubleshooting policies specify what to monitor, thresholds, how to handle faults and logs, and how to perform diagnostics.

To apply a configuration across a potentially large number of switches, an administrator defines switch profiles that associate interface configurations in a single policy group. In this way, large numbers of interfaces across the fabric can be configured at once. Switch profiles can contain symmetric configurations for multiple switches or unique special purpose configurations. Figure 8-23 shows the process for configuring access to the ACI fabric.

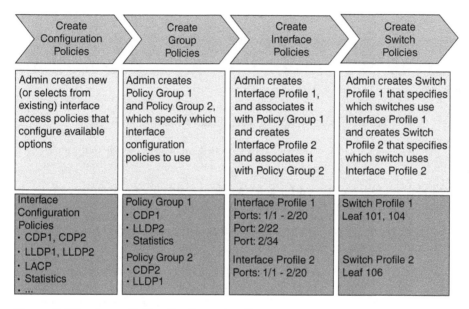

Figure 8-23 *Access Policy Configuration Process*

Figure 8-24 shows the result of applying Switch Profile 1 and Switch Profile 2 to the ACI fabric.

Although configuration steps of each logical construct along with Cisco ACI fabric and access policy components are beyond the scope of this book, I would highly recommend you check out dCloud lab on "Getting Started with Cisco ACI" (https://dcloud2-sng. cisco.com/content/demo/343552?returnPathTitleKey=content-view) to get a feel of the GUI interface and the configuration steps involved in configuring the individual components discussed in this chapter.

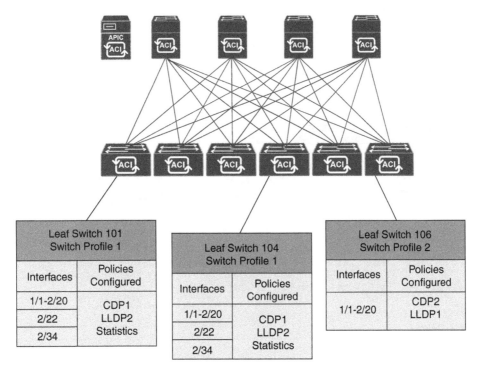

Figure 8-24 *Applying an Access Switch Policy*

Packet Forwarding within the ACI Fabric

The ACI fabric appears as a single switch to the outside world, capable of bridging and routing. As traffic enters the fabric, ACI encapsulates and applies policy to it, forwards it as needed across the fabric through a spine switch (maximum two hops), and de-encapsulates it upon exiting the fabric. All traffic in the ACI fabric is normalized as VXLAN packets. At ingress, ACI encapsulates external VLAN, VXLAN, and NVGRE packets in a VXLAN packet.

Figure 8-25 shows ACI encapsulation normalization.

Within the fabric, ACI uses IS-IS and COOP for all forwarding of endpoint-to-endpoint communications. The forwarding across switch nodes is performed based on the Tunnel Endpoint (TEP) IP in the VXLAN encapsulation. IS-IS provides IP reachability among TEP addresses. In case the ingress leaf is not aware of the destination endpoint location (TEP), ACI has a distributed database called the Council of Oracles Protocol (COOP) on each spine that knows all the mapping of endpoints and TEPs. For propagating routing information between software-defined networks within the fabric and routers external to the fabric, ACI uses the Multiprotocol Border Gateway Protocol (MP-BGP). All ACI links in the fabric are active, equal-cost multipath (ECMP) forwarding, and fast-reconverging.

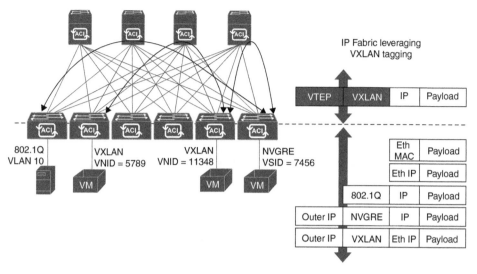

Figure 8-25   *ACI Encapsulation Normalization*

Summary

This chapter discussed Cisco ACI building blocks, deployment models, hardware used in a Cisco ACI solution, Cisco ACI fabric startup discovery, the Cisco ACI policy model, and packet forwarding within the Cisco ACI fabric, including the following points:

- ACI is a spine/leaf network of Nexus 9k switches using the ACI operating system with a management platform called APIC, which provides a single place from which the network can be managed.

- Cisco ACI has many benefits over a traditional network, such as simple spine/leaf architecture, Layer 2 loop avoidance using ECMP, better security using an allow list model, and REST API automation advantage.

- Starting from Cisco ACI 4.1, Cisco ACI supports both two-tier and multitier topologies.

- Leaf switches are the switches to which all endpoints (servers, storage, service nodes, and so on) connect, and they provide the VXLAN tunnel endpoint (VTEP) function. Leaf switches are often categorized by function, such as border leaf, compute leaf, and so on.

- Spine switches interconnect leaf switches and provide the backbone of the ACI fabric.

- The ACI solution supports multiple deployment/architectural models such as Cisco ACI MultiPod, Cisco Nexus Dashboard Orchestrator, Cisco ACI vPod, and so on.

- APICs can be deployed either as physical or virtual appliances.

- The Cisco Nexus 9000 Series switches operate in one of two modes: Cisco Application-Centric Infrastructure (Cisco ACI) or Cisco NX-OS. The Cisco Nexus 9000 Series switches in ACI mode provide the spine and leaf switches that build the fabric.

- During startup discovery, the ACI fabric is brought up in a cascading manner, starting with the leaf nodes that are directly attached to the APIC.

- The ACI policy model enables the specification of application requirements policies. The policy model manages the entire fabric, including the infrastructure, authentication, security, services, applications, and diagnostics.

- A tenant is a container for policies that enable an administrator to exercise domain-based access control. There are four types of tenants: user tenant, common tenant, infrastructure tenant, and management tenant.

- Access policies govern the operation of switch access ports that provide connectivity to resources such as storage, compute, Layer 2 and Layer 3 (bridged and routed) connectivity, virtual machine hypervisors, Layer 4 to Layer 7 devices, and so on.

- Fabric policies govern the operation of the switch fabric ports, including functions such as Network Time Protocol (NTP) server synchronization, Intermediate System to Intermediate System Protocol (IS-IS), Border Gateway Protocol (BGP) route reflectors, Domain Name System (DNS), and so on.

- A tenant is a logical container for application policies that enable an administrator to exercise domain-based access control.

- Virtual routing and forwarding (VRF) is a tenant network and defines a Layer 3 address domain.

- An application profile defines the policies, services, and relationships between endpoint groups (EPGs). An EPG is a managed object that is a named logical entity that contains a collection of endpoints. Endpoints are devices that are connected to the network directly or indirectly.

- A bridge domain represents a Layer 2 forwarding construct within the fabric. While a VRF defines a unique IP address space, that address space can consist of multiple subnets. Those subnets are defined in one or more BDs that reference the corresponding VRF.

- An attachable entity profile (AEP) represents a group of external entities with similar infrastructure policy requirements.

- EPGs can only communicate with other EPGs according to contract rules. Label, filter, and subject managed objects enable mixing and matching among EPGs and contracts so as to satisfy various applications or service delivery requirements.

- All traffic in the ACI fabric is normalized as VXLAN packets. As traffic enters the fabric, ACI encapsulates it in VXLAN packets and applies policy to it, forwards it as needed across the fabric through a spine switch, and de-encapsulates it upon exiting the fabric.

References

"Cisco Application Centric Infrastructure Solution Overview," https://www.cisco.com/c/en/us/solutions/collateral/data-center-virtualization/application-centric-infrastructure/solution-overview-c22-741487.html

"Cisco Application Centric Infrastructure Design Guide," https://www.cisco.com/c/en/us/td/docs/dcn/whitepapers/cisco-application-centric-infrastructure-design-guide.html

"Cisco Application Centric Infrastructure Fundamentals, Release 5.2(x)," https://www.cisco.com/c/en/us/td/docs/dcn/aci/apic/5x/aci-fundamentals/cisco-aci-fundamentals-52x.html

"Cisco APIC Getting Started Guide, Release 5.2(x)," https://www.cisco.com/c/en/us/td/docs/dcn/aci/apic/5x/getting-started/cisco-apic-getting-started-guide-52x.html

"Cisco APIC Basic Configuration Guide, Release 5.2(x)," https://www.cisco.com/c/en/us/td/docs/dcn/aci/apic/5x/basic-configuration/cisco-apic-basic-configuration-guide-52x.html

"Setting Up an ACI Fabric: Initial Setup Configuration Example," https://www.cisco.com/c/en/us/td/docs/switches/datacenter/aci/apic/white_papers/Cisco-ACI-Initial-Deployment-Cookbook.html

"Cisco APIC Layer 2 Networking Configuration Guide, Release 5.2(x)," https://www.cisco.com/c/en/us/td/docs/dcn/aci/apic/5x/layer-2-configuration/cisco-apic-layer-2-networking-configuration-guide-52x.html

"Cisco APIC Layer 3 Networking Configuration Guide, Release 5.2(x)," https://www.cisco.com/c/en/us/td/docs/dcn/aci/apic/5x/l3-configuration/cisco-apic-layer-3-networking-configuration-guide-52x.html

"ACI Fabric Endpoint Learning White Paper," https://www.cisco.com/c/en/us/solutions/collateral/data-center-virtualization/application-centric-infrastructure/white-paper-c11-739989.html

"Cisco Application Centric Infrastructure (ACI) – Endpoint Groups (EPG) Usage and Design," https://www.cisco.com/c/en/us/solutions/collateral/data-center-virtualization/application-centric-infrastructure/white-paper-c11-731630.html

"Cisco Mini ACI Fabric and Virtual APICs," https://www.cisco.com/c/en/us/td/docs/switches/datacenter/aci/apic/sw/kb/Cisco-Mini-ACI-Fabric-and-Virtual-APICs.html

"Cisco ACI Remote Leaf Architecture White Paper," https://www.cisco.com/c/en/us/solutions/collateral/data-center-virtualization/application-centric-infrastructure/white-paper-c11-740861.html

"ACI Multi-Pod White Paper," https://www.cisco.com/c/en/us/solutions/collateral/data-center-virtualization/application-centric-infrastructure/white-paper-c11-737855.html

"Determine Packet Flow Through an ACI Fabric," https://www.cisco.com/c/en/us/support/docs/switches/nexus-9336pq-aci-spine-switch/118930-technote-aci-00.html

"Cisco Cloud Application Centric Infrastructure Solution Overview," https://www.cisco.com/c/en/us/solutions/collateral/data-center-virtualization/application-centric-infrastructure/solution-overview-c22-741802.html

"Cisco Cloud ACI on AWS White Paper," https://www.cisco.com/c/en/us/solutions/collateral/data-center-virtualization/application-centric-infrastructure/white-paper-c11-741998.html

"Cisco Cloud ACI on Microsoft Azure White Paper," https://www.cisco.com/c/en/us/solutions/collateral/data-center-virtualization/application-centric-infrastructure/white-paper-c11-742844.html

Relevant Cisco Nexus switches data sheets: https://www.cisco.com/c/en/us/products/switches/nexus-9000-series-switches/datasheet-listing.html

Relevant Cisco Live sessions: http://www.ciscolive.com

Chapter 9

Operating Cisco ACI

The Cisco Application-Centric Infrastructure (ACI) provides various third-party integrations such AppDynamics, Kubernetes, VMware, and more, along with full-stack observability using Cisco Nexus Dashboard. Cisco ACI also provides various management options such as GUI, CLI, API, and so on, along with external network Layer 2 and Layer 3 connectivity options.

In this chapter, we will discuss Cisco ACI external connectivity options, including L2Out and L3Out, Cisco ACI and VMM integration, Cisco ACI and L4–L7 integration, Cisco ACI management options, Cisco ACI Anywhere, and Cisco Nexus Dashboard.

Cisco ACI External Connectivity Options

Cisco ACI fabric supports a wide range of methods to interconnect the fabric with external networks, data center environments, or segments. Cisco ACI allows you to connect to the outside network using Layer 2 (L2Out) or Layer 3 (L3Out) connections.

The Layer 3 connection between an ACI fabric and an outside network is required in the following scenarios:

- Connecting an existing switch network infrastructure and providing a Layer 3 connection between workloads in the ACI fabric and workloads outside of the ACI fabric.

- Connecting to WAN routers in the data center so that a WAN router provides Layer 3 data center interconnect (DCI) or Internet access for tenants. In some scenarios, a WAN router provides a VPN connection to a tenant's on-premises network.

The Layer 2 connection between an ACI fabric and an outside network is required in the following scenarios:

- In the existing data centers, connecting the existing switching network to an ACI leaf and stretching the same VLAN and subnet across ACI and the existing network.

This allows workloads to be distributed across the existing switching infrastructure and ACI fabric. Customers also have the choice to migrate the workloads from the existing networks to the ACI fabric.

■ Extending the Layer 2 domain from ACI to a DCI platform so that the Layer 2 domain of ACI can be extended to a remote data centers.

Cisco ACI Layer 3 Out (L3Out)

The Layer 3 Out (L3Out) in Cisco ACI is the set of configurations that define connectivity outside of ACI via routing. The ACI fabric is formed from multiple components, including bridge domains (BDs) and endpoint groups (EPGs) to provide L2 connectivity or default gateway functions for a group of endpoints. Another one is the Layer 3 Out (L3Out), which is to provide L3 connectivity between servers connected to ACI and other network domains outside of the ACI fabric through routing protocol or static route.

Cisco ACI was originally built to be a stub network in a data center to manage endpoints. The ACI L3Out was initially designed only as a border between the stub network formed by ACI and the rest of the network, such as intranet, Internet, WAN, and so on, not as a transit network, as shown in Figure 9-1.

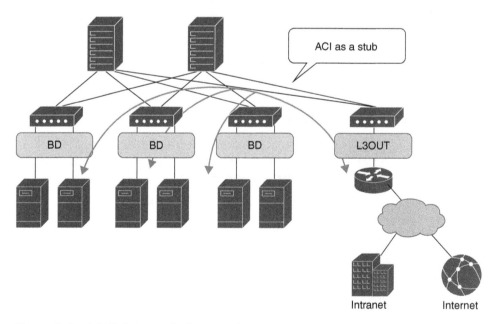

Figure 9-1 *ACI Fabric as a Stub Network*

Due to this stub nature, traffic traversing from one L3Out to another through the ACI network was originally not supported. Beginning with APIC Release 1.1, however, Cisco ACI introduced the Transit Routing feature, which allows the ACI fabric to be a transit network so that traffic can traverse from one L3Out to another L3Out, as shown in Figure 9-2.

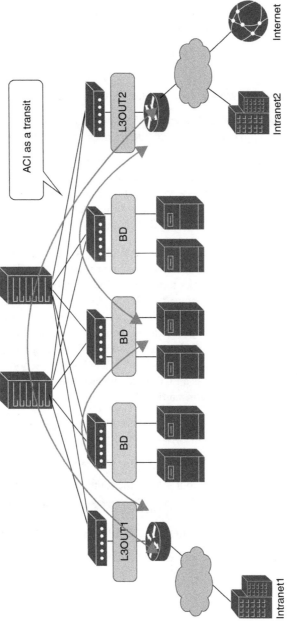

Figure 9-2 *ACI Fabric as a Transit Network*

The border leafs (BLEAFs) are ACI leaves that provide Layer 3 connections to outside networks. Any ACI leaf can be a border leaf. In addition to supporting routing protocols to exchange routes with external routers, the border leaf also applies and enforces policy for traffic between internal and external endpoints.

Three different types of interfaces are supported on a border leaf switch to connect to an external router:

- **Layer 3 interface:** With a physical interface dedicated to a VRF.

- **Sub-interface with 802.1Q tagging:** With sub-interface, the same physical interface can be used to provide multiple outside connections for multiple tenants or VRFs.

- **Switched Virtual Interface (SVI):** With an SVI, the same physical interface that supports Layer 2 and Layer 3 and the same physical interface can be used for a Layer 2 outside connection as well as a Layer 3 outside connection. In addition to supporting routing protocols to exchange routes with external routers, the border leaf also applies and enforces policy for traffic between internal and external endpoints.

Within the ACI fabric, Multiprotocol BGP (MP-BGP) is implemented between leaf and spine switches to propagate external routes within the ACI fabric. The BGP route reflector technology is deployed in order to support a large number of leaf switches within a single fabric. All of the leaf and spine switches are in one single BGP autonomous system (AS). Once the border leaf learns the external routes, it can then redistribute the external routes of a given VRF to an MP-BGP address family VPN version 4 (or VPN version 6 when IPv6 routing is configured). With address family VPN version 4, MP-BGP maintains a separate BGP routing table for each VRF. Within MP-BGP, the border leaf advertises routes to a spine switch, which is a BGP route reflector. The routes are then propagated to all the leafs where the VRFs are instantiated.

The L3Out provides the necessary configuration objects for the following five key functions, which are also displayed in Figure 9-3:

1. Learn external routes via routing protocols (or static routes).

2. Distribute learned external routes (or static routes) to other leaf switches.

3. Advertise ACI internal routes (BD subnets) to outside ACI.

4. Advertise learned external routes to other L3Outs (Transit Routing).

5. Allow traffic to arrive from or be sent to external networks via L3Out by using a contract.

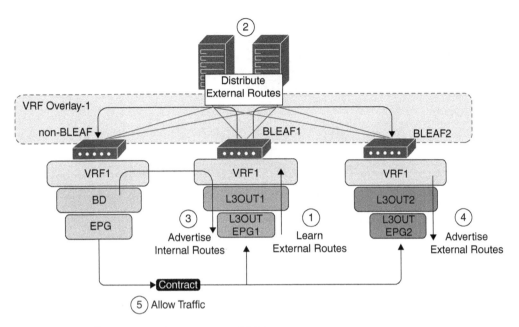

Figure 9-3 *The Five Key Components of L3Out*

Cisco ACI Layer 2 Out (L2Out)

In addition to the Layer 3 outside connection to the outside network, you can also extend a Layer 2 domain beyond the ACI fabric to the existing Layer 2 network, or you can extend the Layer 2 domain to a data center infrastructure (DCI) platform that provides Layer 2 DCI service to a remote site. Sometimes there is a need to assign a port to an EPG in order to connect a switch to the ACI fabric or to connect a hypervisor to the fabric.

There are two common ways of extending a Layer 2 domain outside the Cisco ACI fabric:

■ **Extend the EPG out of the ACI fabric:** You can extend an EPG out of the ACI fabric by statically assigning a port (along with VLAN ID) to an EPG, as shown in Figure 9-4. The leaf will learn the endpoint information, assign the traffic (by matching the port and VLAN ID) to the proper EPG, and then enforce the policy. The endpoint learning, data forwarding, and policy enforcement remain the same whether the endpoint is directly attached to the leaf port or is behind a Layer 2 network (provided the proper VLAN is enabled in the Layer 2 network). This is great for the migration scenario. STP TCNs from the external Layer 2 network may impact ACI internal EPs in the same VLAN. This scenario is avoided by using different VLANs for Layer 2 external network and internal EPs.

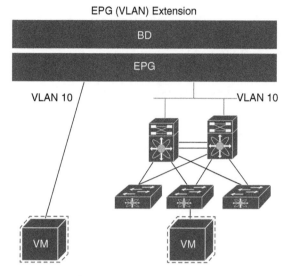

Figure 9-4 *EPG (VLAN) Extension*

- **Extend the bridge domain out of the ACI fabric:** Another option to extend the Layer 2 domain is to create a Layer 2 outside connection (or L2Out, as it's called in the APIC GUI) for a given bridge domain, as shown in Figure 9-5. It effectively extends the bridge domain to the outside network. The external Layer 2 network belongs to its own dedicated EPG. In this scenario, STP TCN from the external Layer 2 network does not affect any internal EPs, which is good for complete separation.

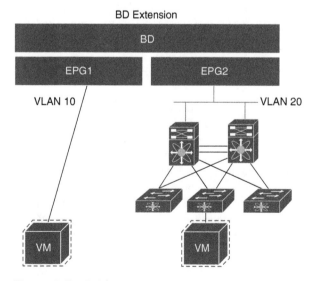

Figure 9-5 *Bridge Domain Extension*

Cisco ACI and VMM Integration

Cisco Application-Centric Infrastructure (ACI) virtual machine (VM) networking supports hypervisors from multiple vendors. It provides the hypervisors programmable and automated access to a high-performance, scalable, virtualized data center infrastructure. The Cisco ACI Open REST API enables virtual machine integration and orchestration of the policy model-based Cisco ACI fabric. Cisco ACI VM networking enables consistent enforcement of policies across both virtual and physical workloads that are managed by hypervisors from multiple vendors.

Cisco ACI supports virtual machine managers (VMMs) from the following products and vendors:

- Cisco Unified Computing System Manager (UCSM)

- Cisco Application-Centric Infrastructure (ACI) Virtual Pod (vPod)

- Cisco ACI Virtual Edge

- Cloud Foundry

- Kubernetes

- Microsoft System Center Virtual Machine Manager (SCVMM)

- OpenShift

- OpenStack

- Red Hat Virtualization (RHV)

- VMware Virtual Distributed Switch (VDS)

VMM domain profiles specify connectivity policies that enable virtual machine controllers to connect to the ACI fabric. Figure 9-6 provides an overview of the VMM domain policy model.

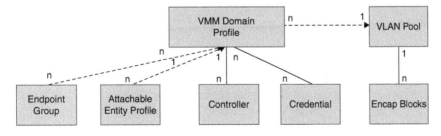

Legend

* Solid lines indicate that objects contain the objects below.
* Dotted lines indicate a relationship
* 1:n indicates one-to-many.
* n:n indicates many-to-many.

Figure 9-6 *VMM Domain Policy Model Overview*

The following are the essential components of an ACI VMM domain policy:

- **Virtual machine manager domain profile:** An APIC VMM domain profile is a policy that defines a VMM domain. It groups VM controllers with similar networking policy requirements. For example, VM controllers can share VLAN pools and application endpoint groups (EPGs). The APIC communicates with the controller to publish network configurations such as port groups that are then applied to the virtual workloads. A VMM domain profile contain VM controllers such as VMware vCenter or Microsoft SCVMM Manager and the credential(s) required for the ACI API to interact with the VM controllers.

- **EPG association:** Endpoint groups regulate connectivity and visibility among the endpoints within the scope of the VMM domain policy. VMM domain EPGs behave as follows:

  - The APIC pushes these EPGs as port groups into the VM controller.

  - An EPG can span multiple VMM domains, and a VMM domain can contain multiple EPGs.

- **Attachable entity profile association:** Associates a VMM domain with the physical network infrastructure. An attachable entity profile (AEP) is a network interface template that enables deploying VM controller policies on a large set of leaf switch ports. An AEP specifies which switches and ports are available as well as how they are configured.

- **VLAN pool association:** A VLAN pool specifies the VLAN IDs or ranges used for VLAN encapsulation that the VMM domain consumes.

The following modes of Cisco ACI and VMware VMM integration are supported:

- **VMware VDS:** When integrated with Cisco ACI, the VMware vSphere distributed switch (VDS) enables you to configure VM networking in the Cisco ACI fabric.

- **Cisco ACI Virtual Edge:** Cisco ACI Virtual Edge is a hypervisor-independent distributed service VM that leverages the native distributed virtual switch that belongs to the hypervisor. Cisco ACI Virtual Edge operates as a virtual leaf.

Figure 9-7 outlines the workflow of how an APIC integrates with VMM domain (VMware vCenter in this case) and pushes policies to the virtual environment.

The APIC administrator configures the vCenter domain policies in the APIC. The APIC administrator provides the following vCenter connectivity information:

- The vCenter IP address, vCenter credentials, and VMM domain policies

- Policies (VLAN pools, domain type such as VMware VDS)

- Connectivity to physical leaf interfaces (using attach entity profiles)

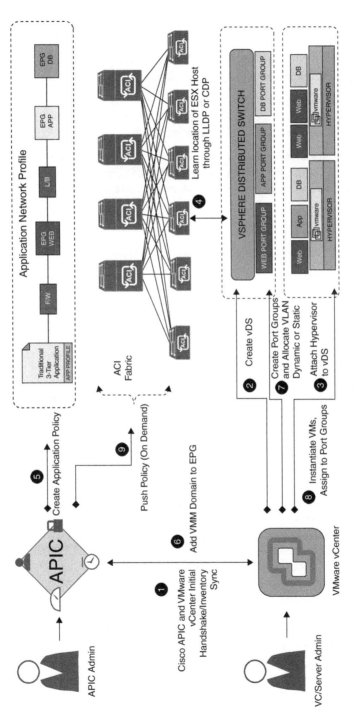

Figure 9-7 *Cisco ACI and VMware VDS Interworking Workflow*

Following outlines the workflow of how a APIC integrates with VMM domain (VMware vCenter in this case) and pushes policies to the virtual environment.

1. The Cisco APIC performs an initial handshake, opens a TCP session with the VMware vCenter specified by a VMM domain, and syncs the inventory.

2. The APIC creates the VDS—or uses an existing VDS if one is already created—matching the name of the VMM domain. If you use an existing VDS, the VDS must be inside a folder on vCenter with the same name.

3. The vCenter administrator or the compute management tool adds the ESXi host or hypervisor to the APIC VDS and assigns the ESXi host hypervisor ports as uplinks on the APIC VDS. These uplinks must connect to the ACI leaf switches.

4. The APIC learns the location of the hypervisor host using the LLDP or CDP information of the hypervisors.

5. The APIC administrator creates application EPG policies.

6. The APIC administrator associates EPG policies to VMM domains.

7. The APIC automatically creates port groups in the VMware vCenter under the VDS. This process provisions the network policy in the VMware vCenter.

8. The vCenter administrator or the compute management tool instantiates and assigns VMs to the port groups.

9. The APIC learns about the VM placements based on the vCenter events. The APIC automatically pushes the application EPG and its associated policy (for example, contracts and filters) to the ACI fabric.

Cisco ACI and L4–L7 Integration

A Layer 4 to Layer 7 (L4–L7) service device is a functional component that is connected to a fabric, such as a firewall, intrusion prevention system (IPS), or load balancer. Traditionally, when you insert services into a network, you must perform a highly manual and complicated VLAN (Layer 2) or VRF instance (Layer 3) stitching between network elements and service appliances. APIC can automate service insertion while acting as a central point of policy control. Cisco ACI enables you to insert L4–L7 functions using a concept called a service graph. Using the service graph, Cisco ACI can redirect traffic between security zones to a firewall or a load balancer, without the need for the firewall or the load balancer to be the default gateway for the servers. Cisco ACI can selectively send traffic to L4–L7 devices based, for instance, on the protocol and the Layer 4 port. Firewall inspection can be transparently inserted in a Layer 2 domain with almost no modification to existing routing and switching configurations. Cisco ACI also allows you to increase the capacity of L4–L7 devices by creating a pool of devices to which Cisco ACI can distribute traffic. The Cisco APIC policies manage both the network fabric and services appliances. The Cisco APIC can configure the network automatically so that traffic flows through the services.

The Cisco ACI allows you to define a sequence of meta-devices, such a firewall of a certain type followed by a load balancer of a certain make and version. This is called a service graph template, also known as an abstract graph. When a service graph template is referenced by a contract, the service graph template is instantiated by being mapped to concrete devices such as the firewall and load balancers present in the fabric. The mapping happens within the concept of a context. The device context is the mapping configuration that allows Cisco ACI to identify which firewalls and which load balancers can be mapped to the service graph template. A logical device represents the cluster of concrete devices. The rendering of the service graph template is based on identifying the suitable logical devices that can be inserted in the path defined by a contract.

The following is the outline of the service graph workflow, as illustrated in Figure 9-8:

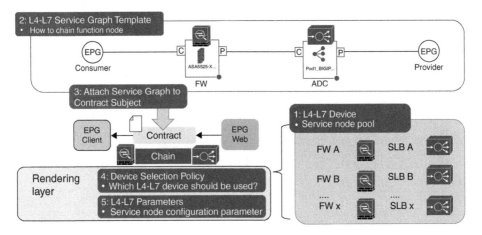

Figure 9-8 *Service Graph Configuration Workflow*

1. Define an L4–L7 device (for example, the ports to which the device is connected).

2. Create a service graph template that defines the flow of the traffic.

3. Apply the service graph template to a contract between two EPGs.

4. Create a device selection policy that ties the intended logical device to a service graph template and contract.

5. Configure the firewall and the load balancers with all the necessary rules for security and load balancing, such as ACL configuration, server farm configuration, and so on.

Cisco ACI Management and Automation

There are a number of fundamental differences between the operations of traditional networking hardware and a Cisco ACI fabric. These differences serve to simplify the management greatly, reduce the number of touch points, and decouple the switching hardware from the desired configuration intent. These changes include the following:

■ Single point of management controller-based architecture

■ Stateless hardware

■ Desired state-driven eventual consistency model

In the ACI architecture, Cisco APIC provides the single point of management and access to all configuration, management, monitoring, and health functions. Cisco APIC can be configured using a graphical user interface (GUI), command-line interface (CLI), and API. The underlying interface for all access methods is provided through a REST-based API, which modifies the contents of a synchronized database that is replicated across APICs in a cluster and provides an abstraction layer between all of the interfaces. This results in a clean and predictable transition between the interfaces with no risk of inconsistency between the various data interfaces.

Figure 9-9 illustrates various ACI fabric management access methods.

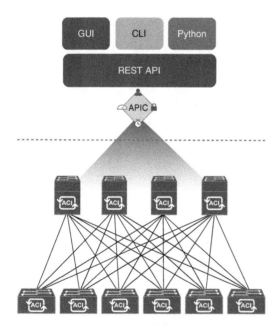

Figure 9-9 *ACI Fabric Management Access Methods*

This controller-based architecture also makes possible a stateless configuration model that decouples the hardware from the configuration running on it. This translates to an APIC cluster that manages individual fabric nodes of leaf and spine switches that derive their identity from what the controller defines as being the desired intent, not from the serial number of the chassis or from a configuration file residing on the devices. Each node receives a unique node identifier, which allows for the device to download the correct configuration attributes from the controller. The device can also be substituted in a stateless fashion, meaning that hardware swaps can be faster, topology changes are less impactful, and network management is simplified.

The desired state model for configuration further complements the concepts of controller-based management and statelessness by taking advantage of a concept known as declarative control-based management, based on a concept known as the promise theory. Declarative control dictates that each object is asked to achieve a desired state and makes a "promise" to reach this state without being told precisely how to do so. This stands in contrast with the traditional model of imperative control, where each managed element must be told precisely what to do, be told how to do it, and take into account the specific situational aspects that will impact its ability to get from its current state to the configured state. A system based on declarative control is able to scale much more efficiently than an imperative-based system, since each entity within the domain is responsible for knowing its current state and the steps required to get to the desired state, as dictated by the managing controller.

Graphical User Interface

The Cisco APIC GUI offers the following features that provide access to the fabric and its components (leafs and spines):

- Based on universal web standards (HTML5). No installers or plugins are required.

- Access to monitoring (statistics, faults, events, audit logs) operational and configuration data.

- Access to the APIC and spine and leaf switches through a single sign-on mechanism.

- Communication with the APIC using the same RESTful APIs available to third parties.

Figure 9-10 shows the management GUI dashboard of Cisco APIC.

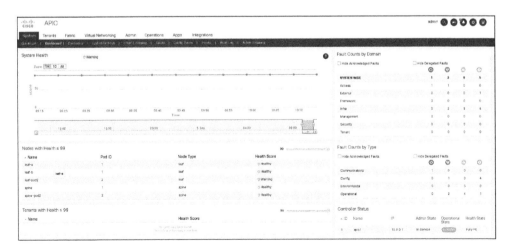

Figure 9-10 *Management GUI Dashboard of Cisco APIC*

Command Line Interface

The CLI features an operational and configuration interface to the APIC, leaf, and spine switches. It offers the following features:

- Implemented from the ground up in Python. You can switch between the Python interpreter and the CLI.

- Plug-in architecture for extensibility.

- VRF-based access to monitoring, operation, and configuration data

- Automation through Python commands or batch scripting

Example 9-1 illustrates an SSH login to the APIC CLI and shows how to view the running configuration.

Example 9-1 *APIC CLI Example*

```
login as: admin
Application Policy Infrastructure Controller
admin@apic's password:
Last login: 2021-09-05T10:16:49.000+00:00 UTC
apic1# show running-config
# Command: show running-config
# Time: Sun Sep  5 10:39:14 2021
  aaa banner 'Application Policy Infrastructure Controller'
  aaa authentication login console
    exit
  aaa authentication login default
    exit
  aaa authentication login domain fallback
    exit
  bgp-fabric
    asn 65001
    route-reflector spine 201
    exit
  <output omitted>
```

Application Programming Interface

ACI is designed as an API first. Everything is built on top of the REST API. The APIC REST API is a programmatic interface that uses the REST architecture. The API accepts and returns HTTP (not enabled by default) or HTTPS messages that contain JavaScript Object Notation (JSON) or Extensible Markup Language (XML) documents. You can use any programming language to generate the messages as well as the JSON or XML documents that contain the API methods or managed object (MO) descriptions.

The REST API is the interface into the management information tree (MIT) and allows manipulation of the object model state. The same REST interface is used by the APIC CLI, GUI, and SDK so that whenever information is displayed, it is read through the REST API, and when configuration changes are made, they are written through the REST API. The REST API also provides an interface through which other information can be retrieved, including statistics, faults, and audit events. It even provides a means of subscribing to push-based event notification so that when a change occurs in the MIT, an event can be sent through a web socket.

Standard REST methods are supported on the API, which includes POST, GET, and DELETE operations through HTTP. The POST and DELETE methods are idempotent, meaning that there is no additional effect if they are called more than once with the same input parameters. The GET method is nullipotent, meaning that it can be called zero or more times without making any changes (or that it is a read-only operation). Payloads to and from the REST interface can be encapsulated through either XML or JSON encoding.

Logical and Concrete Models

The ACI fabric OS renders policies from the APIC into a concrete model that runs in the physical infrastructure. The concrete model is analogous to compiled software; it is the form of the model that the switch operating system can execute. Figure 9-11 shows the relationship of the logical model to the concrete model and the switch OS.

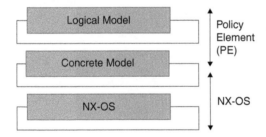

Figure 9-11   *Logical Model Rendered into a Concrete Model*

All the switch nodes contain a complete copy of the concrete model. When an administrator creates a policy in the APIC that represents a configuration, the APIC updates the logical model. The APIC then performs the intermediate step of creating a fully elaborated policy that it pushes into all the switch nodes where the concrete model is updated.

Management Information Tree

All the physical and logical components that comprise the Application-Centric Infrastructure fabric are represented in a hierarchical management information model (MIM), also referred to as the MIT. Each node in the tree represents an MO or group of objects that contains its administrative state and its operational state.

The hierarchical structure starts at the top (root) and contains parent and child nodes. Each node in this tree is an MO, and each object in the ACI fabric has a unique distinguished name (DN) that describes the object and its place in the tree. MOs are abstractions of the fabric resources. An MO can represent a physical object, such as a switch or adapter, or a logical object, such as a policy or fault.

Configuration policies make up the majority of the policies in the system and describe the configurations of different ACI fabric components. Policies determine how the system behaves under specific circumstances. Certain MOs are not created by users but are automatically created by the fabric (for example, power supply objects and fan objects). By invoking the API, you can read and write objects to the MIM.

The information model is centrally stored as a logical model by the APIC, while each switch node contains a complete copy as a concrete model. When a user creates a policy in the APIC that represents a configuration, the APIC updates the logical model. The APIC then performs the intermediate step of creating a fully elaborated policy from the user policy and then pushes the policy into all the switch nodes where the concrete model is updated. The models are managed by multiple data management engine (DME) processes that run in the fabric. When a user or process initiates an administrative change to a fabric component (for example, when you apply a profile to a switch), the DME first applies that change to the information model and then applies the change to the actual managed endpoint. This approach is called a model-driven framework.

Figure 9-12 shows the branch diagram of a leaf switch port that starts at the top root of the ACI fabric MIT and follows a hierarchy that is composed of a chassis with two-line module slots, with a line module in slot 2.

```
|--root--------- (root)
   |--sys-----------(sys)
       |--ch-----------(sys/ch)
          |--lsclot-1------(sys/ch/lcslot-1)
          |--lsclot-2------(sys/ch/lcslot-2)
             |--lc------(sys/ch/lcslot-2/lc)
                |--leafport-1------(sys/ch/lcslot-2/lc/leafport-1)
```

Figure 9-12 *ACI Fabric MIT Branch Diagram of a Leaf Switch Port*

You can identify and access a specific object by its distinguished name (DN) or by its relative name (RN), depending on the current location in the MIT. The RN identifies an object from its siblings within the context of its parent object.

The DN enables you to unambiguously identify a specific target object. The DN consists of a series of RNs:

```
dn = {rn}/{rn}/{rn}/{rn}...
```

For example, following DN contains RNs, as shown in Table 9-1:

```
<dn = "sys/ch/lcslot-1/lc/fabport-1"/>
```

Table 9-1 *Relative Names Example*

Relative Name	Class	Description
sys	top:System	Top level of this system
ch	eqpt:Ch	Hardware chassis container
lcslot-1	eqpt:LCSlot	Line module slot 1
lc	eqpt:LC	Line (I/O) module
fabport-1	eqpt:FabP	Fabric-facing external I/O port 1

Because of the hierarchical nature of the tree and the attribute system used to identify object classes, the tree can be queried in several ways for obtaining managed object information. Queries can be performed on an object itself through its distinguished name, on a class of objects such as a switch chassis, or on the tree level to discover all members of an object:

■ **Tree-level query:** Tree-level queries return the referenced object and its child objects. This approach is useful for discovering the components of a larger system.

■ **Class-level query:** Class-level queries return all the objects of a given class. This approach is useful for discovering all the objects of a certain type that are available in the MIT.

■ **Object-level query:** In an object-level query, a distinguished name is used to return a specific object.

Figure 9-13 illustrates different query levels. The two tree-level queries discover the cards and ports of a given switch chassis. The class-level query used is Cards, which returns all the objects of type Cards. The two object-level queries used are for Node 1 in Chassis 2 and for Node 1 in Chassis 1 in Card 1 in Port 2.

For all MIT queries, an administrator can optionally return the entire subtree or a partial subtree. Additionally, the role-based access control (RBAC) mechanism in the system dictates which objects are returned; only the objects that the user has rights to view will ever be returned.

REST API Request Format

After the object payloads are properly encoded as XML or JSON, they can be used in create, read, update, or delete operations on the REST API. Figure 9-14 shows the syntax for a read operation from the REST API.

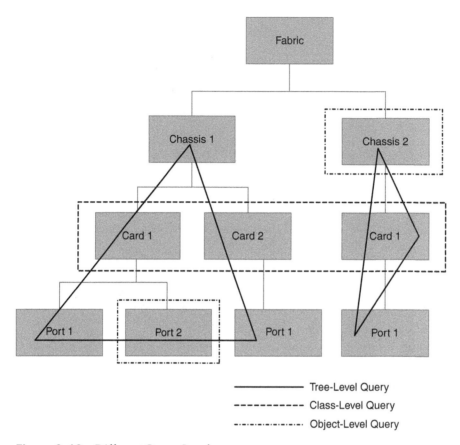

Figure 9-13   *Different Query Levels*

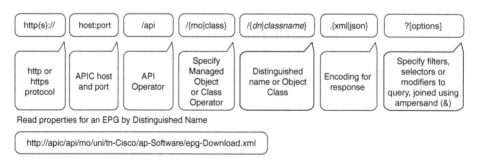

Figure 9-14   *REST Syntax for Read Operation*

Because the REST API is HTTP based, defining the URI to access a certain resource type is important. The first two sections of the request URI simply define the protocol and access details of the APIC. Next in the request URI is the literal string **/api**, indicating that the API will be invoked. Generally, read operations are for an object or class, as discussed earlier, so the next part of the URI specifies whether the operation will be for an MO or class. The next component defines either the fully qualified domain name (FQDN) being queried for object-based queries or the package and class name for class-based queries. The final mandatory part of the request URI is the encoding format: either .xml or .json. The REST API supports a wide range of flexible filters, useful for narrowing the scope of your search to allow information to be located more quickly. The filters themselves are appended as query URI options, starting with a question mark (?) and concatenated with an ampersand (&). Multiple conditions can be joined together to form complex filters.

Both create and update operations in the REST API are implemented using the POST method so that if an object does not already exist, it will be created, and if it does already exist, it will be updated to reflect any changes between its existing state and desired state. Create and update operations use the same syntax as read operations, except that they are always targeted at an object level, because you cannot make changes to every object of a specific class (nor would you want to). The create or update operation should target a specific managed object, so the literal string **/mo** indicates that the DN of the managed object will be provided, followed next by the actual DN. The payload of the POST operation will contain the XML- or JSON-encoded data representing the MO that defines the Cisco API command body. Figure 9-15 shows a sample REST payload.

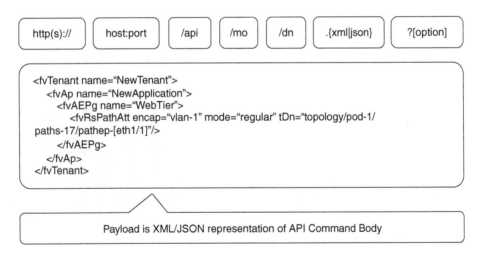

| http(s):// | host:port | /api | /mo | /dn | .{xml\|json} | ?[option] |

```
<fvTenant name="NewTenant">
  <fvAp name="NewApplication">
    <fvAEPg name="WebTier">
      <fvRsPathAtt encap="vlan-1" mode="regular" tDn="topology/pod-1/
paths-17/pathep-[eth1/1]"/>
    </fvAEPg>
  </fvAp>
</fvTenant>
```

Payload is XML/JSON representation of API Command Body

Figure 9-15 *REST Payload*

Cisco ACI Programmability

As discussed in previous sections, ACI uses an advanced object model that represents network configuration with application-based semantics that can be consumed and posted against using a well-documented REST API. In addition to providing this interface into the object model, ACI also provides a number of access methods to read and manipulate this data, at a variety of levels that will cater to the level of comfort the user has with programming, all of which use open standards and open source.

APIC is very flexible in terms of how it can accept configuration and provide administrative and operable states, ~~in addition to~~ and how it extends that configuration into subordinate components. Two primary categories of interfaces facilitate these functions: the northbound REST API and the southbound programmatic interfaces.

The northbound REST API is responsible for accepting configuration as well as providing access to management functions for the controller. This interface is a crucial component for the GUI and CLI and also provides a touch point for automation tools, provisioning scripts and third-party monitoring and management tools. The REST API is a singular entry point to the fabric for making configuration changes, and as such, it is a critical aspect of the architecture for being able to provide a consistent programmatic experience.

Southbound interfaces on APIC allow for the declarative model of intent to be extended beyond the fabric, into subordinate devices. This is a key aspect to the openness of the ACI fabric, in that policy can be programmed once via APIC and then pushed out to hypervisors, L4–L7 devices, and third-party partner devices such as F5, Citrix Embrane, Palo Alto, A10, Sourcefire, and so on, without the need to individually configure those devices.

OpFlex is designed to allow a data exchange of a set of managed objects defined as part of an informational model. OpFlex itself does not dictate the information model and can be used with any tree-based abstract model in which each node in the tree has a universal resource identifier (URI) associated with it. The protocol is designed to support XML and JSON (as well as the binary encoding used in some scenarios) and to use standard remote procedure call (RPC) mechanisms such as JSON-RPC over TCP.

For northbound and southbound API references and tools, Cisco DevNet offers a single central repository. On this site, you can find learning materials for network programmability basics, APIs, tools, a developer sandbox, sample code on GitHub (which includes scripts and libraries for developers of Cisco ACI), and so on. Also, you can use this site to find communities of interest, get access to support, and find more topics on this subject. You can register for Cisco DevNet at https://developer.cisco.com/.

Cisco ACI Anywhere

The data center is no longer a place or a fixed location but instead is defined as wherever the data is created, processed, and used. Cisco ACI Anywhere is a marketing term highlighting unique innovations ACI has gone through to meet customers' different deployment needs: on-premises, remote and satellite locations, bare-metal providers, colocation environments, and public cloud. This term encompasses a host of solutions, including ACI MultiPod, ACI Multi-Site, ACI Multicloud, Remote Leaf, vPod, various ACI integrations, and other future solutions yet to come. Together, ACI Anywhere solutions transform ACI into a true hybrid cloud solution. Cisco ACI Anywhere facilitates application agility and data center automation. It automates management of end-to-end connectivity and enforcement of consistent security policies for applications running throughout the edge-to-cloud continuum.

Figure 9-16 illustrates various ACI Anywhere solutions that facilitate the any workload, any location, any cloud strategy.

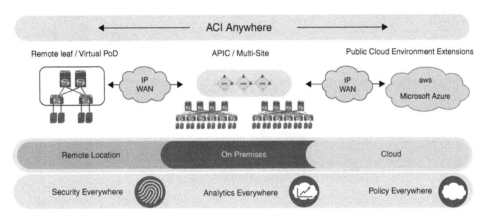

Figure 9-16 *Cisco ACI Anywhere*

In Chapter 8, "Describing Cisco ACI," we discussed various Cisco ACI deployment models that make Cisco ACI Anywhere possible, including ACI MultiPod, Nexus Dashboard Orchestrator, Cloud ACI, Remote Leaf, and so on. Here, we will discuss some of the popular integration solutions for Cisco ACI that are an integral part of Cisco ACI Anywhere.

Cisco ACI and Cisco SD-WAN integration

Cisco offers ACI and SD-WAN integration for branch offices (network edge). This is an integral component of customers' cloud journey that requires secure, policy-driven interconnects between the data center and branch offices that are a cost-efficient alternative to provisioning dedicated connections. Through this integration, you can now automate a WAN path selection between the branch office and the on-premises data center based on application policy.

For example, traffic from a stock trader in a branch office in Chicago can be automatically sent over the fastest possible WAN link to access the trading application hosted in a data center in Germany, based on the application policies and SLAs configured.

Figure 9-17 illustrates Cisco ACI to Cisco SD-WAN integration.

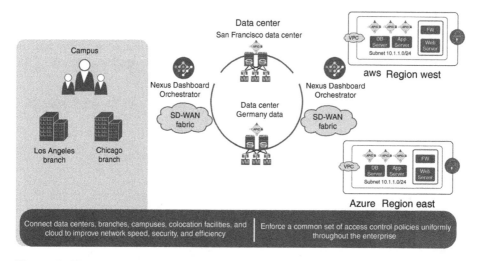

Figure 9-17   *Cisco ACI to Cisco SD-WAN Integration*

Cisco ACI and AppDynamics integration

Digital transformation is a complex team effort across business and IT, requiring end-to-end application management and awareness. AppDynamics provides IT teams the application-layer visibility and monitoring required in an intent-based architecture to validate that IT and business policies are being implemented across the network. Cisco ACI and AppDynamics integration provides dynamic correlation between application and network constructs. This combined solution provides high-quality application performance monitoring, richer diagnostic capability for application and network performance, and faster root-cause analysis of problems, with fast triage, sent quickly to appropriate team members. For example, does a given problem pertain to an application or to the network?

Figure 9-18 illustrates Cisco ACI and AppDynamics integration.

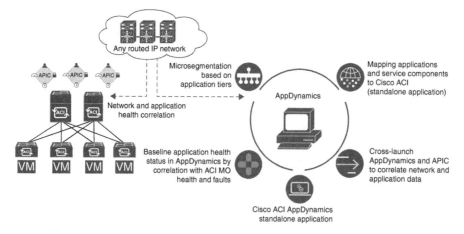

Figure 9-18   *Cisco ACI and AppDynamics Integration*

This integration does the following:

- Dynamically maps the application and service components to the Cisco ACI network elements, thus providing a shared view of the application and infrastructure across teams

- Provides a dynamic view of application use in the infrastructure for the network operations team

- Provides a cross-launch for application teams to correlate network and application fault and performance data

- Baselines application health status in AppDynamics by correlating the Cisco ACI network health and faults

With this integration, you can correlate application service-level management with infrastructure monitoring. This new integration significantly reduces the time it takes to identify and troubleshoot end-to-end application performance issues.

Cisco ACI and Cisco SD-Access Integration

Hyper-distributed applications and highly mobile users, increased cybersecurity threats, and increased regulatory requirements make network segmentation a must for reducing risk and achieving better compliance. Policy integration between Cisco ACI and Cisco SD-Access allows the marrying of Cisco ACI's application-based microsegmentation in the data center with Cisco SD-Access's user-group-based segmentation across the campus and branch. This integration automates the mapping and enforcement of segmentation policy based on the user's security profile as they access resources within the data center. It enables security administrators to manage segmentation seamlessly from end to end, user to application. A common and consistent identity-based microsegmentation capability is provided from the user to the application.

Figure 9-19 illustrates Cisco ACI and Cisco SD-Access integration.

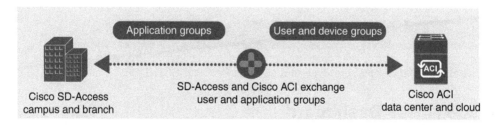

Figure 9-19 *Cisco ACI and Cisco SD-Access Integration*

As a result of this integration, the attack surface is greatly reduced, and any unauthorized or suspicious access to resources and potential threats can quickly be controlled and remediated.

Cisco ACI and Kubernetes Anywhere Integration

Cisco ACI is designed to offer policy-based automation, security, mobility, and visibility for application workloads regardless of whether they run on bare-metal servers, hypervisors, or Linux containers. The Cisco ACI system-level approach extends the support for Linux containers by providing tight integration of Kubernetes, a popular container orchestration platform, and the Cisco ACI platform.

This integration allows Cisco ACI to provide a ready-to-use, secure networking environment for Kubernetes. The integration maintains the simplicity of the user experience in deploying, scaling, and managing containerized applications while still offering the controls, visibility, security, and isolation required by an enterprise.

The Cisco ACI and Kubernetes solution offers the following benefits:

- Flexible approach to policy

- Automated, integrated load-balancing services

- Secure multitenancy

- Visibility and telemetry information

Figure 9-20 illustrates Cisco ACI integration with Kubernetes anywhere.

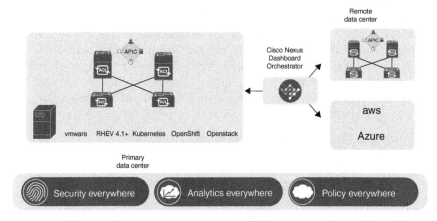

Figure 9-20 *Kubernetes Anywhere Integrated with Cisco ACI*

Cisco Nexus Dashboard

The Cisco Nexus Dashboard offers a centralized management console that allows network operators to easily access applications needed to perform the lifecycle management of their fabric, such as provisioning, troubleshooting, or simply gaining deeper visibility into their network. Using the Cisco Nexus Dashboard platform, you can deploy Cisco Nexus Dashboard Orchestrator (NDO), Cisco Nexus Dashboard Insights, and Cisco Nexus Dashboard Data Broker. The Cisco Nexus Dashboard becomes even more of a collaborative focal point with the inclusion of operations-critical, third-party applications and tools. From the Nexus Dashboard, you can cross-launch any of the sites' controllers, including APIC, Cloud APIC, and Cisco Data Center Network Manager (DCNM) fabrics, which drives the adoption of cloud-native application practices.

Figure 9-21 illustrates the Cisco Nexus Dashboard.

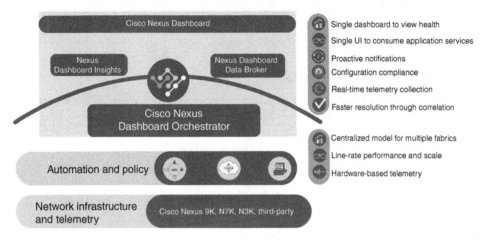

Figure 9-21   *Cisco Nexus Dashboard*

Cisco Nexus Dashboard provides the following benefits:

- Easy to use

  - Customizable role-based UI view to provide a focused view on network operator use cases

  - Single sign-on (SSO) for a seamless user experience across operation services

  - Single console for health monitoring and quick service turnup

- Easy to scale

  - High-availability, scale-out operations from a single dashboard

  - Scale use cases, leveraging flexible deployment options

  - Operations that span across on-premises, multicloud, and edge networks

- Easy to maintain

  - Seamless integration and lifecycle management of operational services

  - Onboarding and managing of operational services across on-premises, cloud, or hybrid environments

  - Single point of integration for critical third-party applications and tools

Cisco Nexus Dashboard Orchestrator

The Cisco Nexus Dashboard Orchestrator, which is hosted on the Cisco Nexus Dashboard, provides policy management, network policy configuration, and application segmentation definition and enforcement policies for multicloud deployments. Using the Cisco Nexus Dashboard Orchestrator, customers get a single view into the Cisco APIC, Cisco DCNM, and Cisco Cloud APIC policies across AWS, Microsoft Azure, and Google Cloud environments.

Cisco Nexus Dashboard Insights

Cisco Nexus Dashboard Insights provides the ability to monitor and analyze the fabric in real time to identify anomalies, to provide root-cause analysis and capacity planning, and to accelerate troubleshooting. By tracking historical context, collecting and processing hardware and software telemetry data, and correlating the designs with Cisco best practices, it provides excellent visibility and awareness of issues affecting the fabric and takes corrective actions. Nexus Dashboard Insights is a microservices-based application designed to be hosted on the Cisco Nexus Dashboard.

Cisco Nexus Dashboard Data Broker

The Cisco Nexus Dashboard Data Broker is a simple, scalable, and cost-effective solution for data center, enterprise, and service provider customers who need to monitor high-volume and business-critical traffic. It replaces traditional purpose-built matrix switches with one or more Cisco Nexus 3000, 9300, or 9500 Series switches that you can interconnect to build a highly scalable TAP-aggregation network that can help copy or mirror the production traffic using Optical TAPs (test access points) and Cisco Switched Port Analyzer (SPAN). The data broker also lets you integrate with Cisco ACI to configure SPAN sessions using the Cisco APIC REST API. It can run as an application on APIC or on Nexus Dashboard.

Summary

This chapter discusses Cisco ACI external connectivity options, various third-party solution integrations with Cisco ACI, Cisco ACI management and automation options, Cisco ACI Anywhere, and Cisco Nexus Dashboard, including the following points:

- The Cisco ACI fabric supports a wide range of methods to interconnect the fabric with external networks, data center environments, or segments, including Layer 2 (L2Out) and Layer 3 (L3Out) connections.

- A Layer 2 domain can be extended beyond the ACI fabric to the existing Layer 2 network via one of two methods: extending the EPG out of the ACI fabric or extending the bridge domain out of the ACI fabric.

- Cisco Application-Centric Infrastructure (ACI) supports virtual machine managers (VMMs) integration with various products and vendors, including VMware VDS, Microsoft SCVMM, and so on.

- Cisco ACI allows you to define a sequence of meta-devices, such a firewall of a certain type followed by a load balancer of a certain make and version, using a service graph template, also known as an abstract graph.

- Cisco APIC can be configured using a graphical user interface (GUI), command-line interface (CLI), and API. The underlying interface for all access methods is provided through a REST-based API.

- All the physical and logical components that comprise the ACI fabric are represented in a hierarchical management information model (MIM), also referred to as the MIT.

- Queries on the MIT can be performed using three levels: tree level, class level, and object level.

- The northbound REST API is responsible for accepting configuration as well as providing access to management functions for the APIC controller. Southbound programmatic interfaces on APIC allow for the declarative model of intent to be extended beyond the fabric, into subordinate devices.

- The Cisco Nexus Dashboard has three main components: Nexus Dashboard Orchestrator, Nexus Dashboard Insights, and Nexus Dashboard Data Broker.

- The Cisco Nexus Dashboard Orchestrator provides policy management, network policy configuration, and application segmentation definition and enforcement policies for multicloud deployments.

- Cisco Nexus Dashboard Insights provides the ability to monitor and analyze the fabric in real time to identify anomalies, to provide root-cause analysis and capacity planning, and to accelerate troubleshooting.

- The Cisco Nexus Dashboard Data Broker is a simple, scalable, and cost-effective solution for data center, enterprise, and service provider customers who need to monitor high-volume and business-critical traffic.

References

"Cisco Application Centric Infrastructure Solution Overview," https://www.cisco.com/c/en/us/solutions/collateral/data-center-virtualization/application-centric-infrastructure/solution-overview-c22-741487.html

"Cisco Application Centric Infrastructure Fundamentals, Release 5.2(x)," https://www.cisco.com/c/en/us/td/docs/dcn/aci/apic/5x/aci-fundamentals/cisco-aci-fundamentals-52x.html

"ACI Fabric L3Out Guide," https://www.cisco.com/c/en/us/solutions/collateral/data-center-virtualization/application-centric-infrastructure/guide-c07-743150.html

"Cisco ACI Virtualization Guide, Release 5.2(x)," https://www.cisco.com/c/en/us/td/docs/dcn/aci/apic/5x/virtualization-guide/cisco-aci-virtualization-guide-52x.html

"Cisco APIC Layer 4 to Layer 7 Services Deployment Guide, Release 5.2(x)," https://www.cisco.com/c/en/us/td/docs/dcn/aci/apic/5x/layer-4-to-layer-7-services-configuration/cisco-apic-layer-4-to-layer-7-services-deployment-guide-52x.html

"Service Graph Design with Cisco ACI White Paper," https://www.cisco.com/c/en/us/solutions/collateral/data-center-virtualization/application-centric-infrastructure/white-paper-c11-2491213.html

Cisco DevNet: https://developer.cisco.com/site/aci/

Relevant Cisco Live sessions: http://www.ciscolive.com

Chapter 10

Data Center Storage Concepts

The data center is the home for applications. The servers provide the computing resources, such as CPU and memory, for the applications to run. The applications consume these resources as they process the requests from users or other applications and they return the needed information. The applications need to be capable of receiving, organizing, structuring, storing, and sending data. This all means that the applications work with data, and this data needs to be not only processed but also stored in a secure and redundant manner.

This chapter discusses the different options for storing data in the data center. You will learn about the different components that make up the storage solutions. There are different ways of transporting data and storing it as well as protocols that communicate with the physical storage devices and the operating systems and applications, and there are transport protocols that allow transporting the data between storage systems and the servers on which the applications are running.

Storage Connectivity Options in the Data Center

The data is stored on different media, which can be electromagnetic, optical, or silicon-based. Examples are the hard disk drives (HDDs), tapes, optical disks such as compact discs (CDs), digital video (versatile) discs (DVDs), Blu-Ray disks, and solid state drives (SSDs). The storage media has evolved during the history of computing, and there are different usages for the different types of media. When it comes to a single computer, such as a laptop or a desktop for personal or office use, usually the applications that run on it are limited and include the operating system and its applications, Internet browsers, and some specialized applications for video editing, word processing, and so on. The storage needs are not big, and usually the internal storage (an HDD or SSD) is more than enough. The real challenge is in the data centers. As already mentioned, the data center servers run the applications that provide the services for companies, organizations, and so on. Some applications process requests; others, such as databases, are responsible for organizing and structuring the data, but all of the applications need a place to store data. As there are multiple applications, the generated amounts of data are usually very large and require storage solutions that can scale up to meet the needs.

Storage solutions always start with two main components: the servers, which need to store or read data and are the active part of such a communication (and are therefore called *initiators*), and the storage systems, which receive and store data from the servers, or read and send data to the servers in response to their requests. The storage systems do not start communication with the servers; they cannot initiate it. They can only wait for communication to start, and because it is intended for them, they are called *targets*.

The storage systems hold multiple storage elements: HDDs or SSDs (we'll call them disks for simplicity). This is the physical storage in a storage system. There are also the controllers that manage these disks and that manage the communication of the storage system. Also, there is the software that manages, abstracts, and virtualizes the underlying hardware. In general, the physical disks are abstracted and virtualized on the storage system by combining the physical drives into a logical unit. From these logical units are created volumes. The volumes are assigned identifiers, which are called Logical Unit Numbers (LUNs). A LUN is the address the initiator will need to access the correct storage resource.

It is important to be in control of what resources are accessed by which server. Also, you do not want to expose the real LUN addressing to the SAN infrastructure; the information is stored in blocks on the storage systems, and if inappropriate or unauthorized access is allowed, the data can be destroyed!

To avoid such situations, two techniques are used at the targets:

- **LUN masking:** The real LUNs are not exposed, visible, to the SAN and the initiators. The exposed LUNs are different, usually a 0 or a 1, and an internal table is used, which maps the correct LUN to the initiator's request, based on the initiator's identity.

- **Initiator groups:** These are similar as in concept to access lists and define which initiators are allowed to access which volume.

Although this book focuses on Cisco data center solutions, the information for the storage systems is very important, because you need to know it when you design a data center storage solution as well as when you need to perform troubleshooting. When troubleshooting the communication between the initiator and the target, you have to follow the whole path of the communication to understand the protocol used, to know which components are configured, and to know where they operate in the storage network system.

The storage systems and the servers can be directly connected or can go through a communication infrastructure. Communication between the initiators and the targets can use different transport protocols. Examples are the Fibre Channel Protocol (FCP) and the Internet Protocol (IP). What transport protocol will be chosen depends on the type of network storage. There are two types: block-based and file-based. The decision of which network storage system type will be used depends on the specific needs of the data center, the requirements, and the infrastructure.

Storage Protocols

With block-based storage, the data is sent to the storage systems and stored in blocks. The data is broken down into blocks of a specific, fixed size. The storage system decides where, physically, each block will be stored. When the initiator requests specific data, the storage system reads the blocks that form the data and return it to the server. The protocols used for the block-based storage communication use unique addressing in order for each block to be able to break down the data in blocks and transport it to the storage system, for the storage system to write the blocks, and to know to which piece of data the blocks belong. The addressing of the blocks is also important for the blocks to be put together in the correct order!

Multiple communication protocols are used in block-based systems, depending on where this communication takes place.

The block-based protocols used with local storage (the storage inside a PC) are as follows:

- Parallel ATA (PATA)

- Serial ATA (SATA)

- Parallel Small Computer Systems Interface (SCSI)

- Serial Attached SCSI (SAS)

The local storage is internal to the computers and uses a bus-based architecture. This means that the communication protocol uses a hardware bus to communicate between the operating system and the storage.

Figure 10-1 illustrates the different protocols using block-based storage and their transport options.

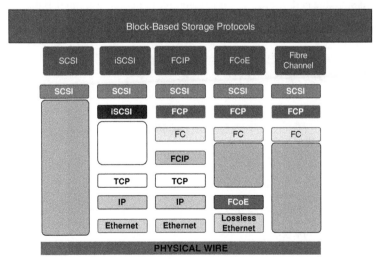

Figure 10-1   *Block-Based Storage Protocols*

When it comes to block-based storage network systems, the communications protocol used is the Small Computer Systems Interface (SCSI) protocol. The SCSI protocol uses different transport protocols and can be transmitted over existing IP networks or over dedicated transport infrastructures, referred to as storage area networks (SANs). The SANs are built from specialized Fibre Channel switches. The Cisco FC switches are the Cisco MDS family of products.

Here are some examples of SCSI transport protocols:

- **FC protocol:** The SCSI commands are encapsulated in FCP frames and transported between the initiators and the targets. The communication takes place in SANs.

- **FC over IP (FCIP):** The SCSI commands are encapsulated in FC frames, but the need to transport these frames over wide area networks, or over long distances, requires the FC frames to be encapsulated in TCP frames and carried over IP environments.

- **FC over Ethernet (FCoE):** The SCSI commands are encapsulated in FC frames, but the infrastructure is an IP environment, built with Ethernet switches that support the FCoE protocol. The FC frames are encapsulated in Ethernet frames and thus transported.

- **Internal Small Computer Systems Interface (iSCSI):** The SCSI commands are encapsulated in TCP packets and transported over an IP network. The Transmission Control Protocol (TCP) provides the security for the transmissions.

A file-based protocol is used to transfer files between a server and a client. The communication happens over a network. Note that with file-based storage, the atomic unit transferred is a file, whereas with the block-based storage, it's a block of data. The protocols used for the file-based storage communication are the Network File System (NFS) on UNIX/Linux systems and Server Message Block (SMB), originally developed by IBM Corporation, but later adopted and enhanced by Microsoft, Intel, IBM, 3Com, and others. The most popular version (dialect) of SMB is the Common Internet File System (CIFS).

Figure 10-2 shows the communication of file-based protocols.

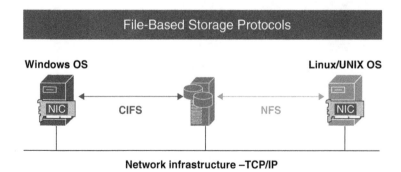

Figure 10-2   *File-Based Storage Protocols*

The CIFS and NFS protocols communicate over TCP/IP. Because of this, latency is high.

Which network storage approach (block- or file-based) is used and which protocols are used depend on the specific storage needs. The block-based storage characteristics are as follows:

- Benefits:

  - **Performance:** Block-based storage uses dedicated, high-capacity hardware in combination with secure and fast protocols, such as FC, which provides a very high number of input/output operations per second (IOPS).

  - **Security and data safety:** The protocols used to transfer data blocks are designed to create secure, reliable, and safe communication between the initiators and the targets.

  - **Scalability and flexibility:** The storage systems' capacities and the SAN infrastructures allow for rapid scaling to keep up with the growth and demands of the organizations.

  - **Easy file modifications:** With block-based storage, when a file is changed, the modifications in the storage system are made at the level where the blocks are changed, not the whole file.

- Drawbacks:

  - **Cost:** Block-based network storage systems require specialized, dedicated infrastructures—the SANs. Also, the initiators and the targets need to have specialized communication adapters, which are called host bus adapters (HBAs), or network adapters with support for iSCSI.

  - **Initiator binding:** The different initiators, depending on their operating system, access the resources of the storage system in different ways.

The file-based storage characteristics are as follows:

- Benefits:

  - **Simplicity:** File-based storage is simpler to implement and does not require specialized hardware.

  - **File sharing:** File-based storage uses sharing to provide access to file resources to multiple users.

  - **Common protocols:** The SMB/CIFS and the NFS are components of the Windows and Linux/Unix operating systems.

  - **Cost:** File-based storage allows for cheaper means to share backup/archive files, as there is no need for specialized infrastructure or communication adapters.

- Drawbacks:

    - **Latency and bandwidth:** The communication is over IP networks in the data center, and the speeds and latency might not be optimal.

    - **Traffic isolation:** Traffic isolation is based on the use of VLANs, which might pose a security issue.

Network File System (NFS)

The NFS was developed in 1984 by Sun Microsystems. It is a file-based storage network solution, using the client/server architecture of communication, and operates at the application layer (Layer 7) of the OSI reference model. The NFS allows a user on the client, which is a computer, to access over the network storage resources on a server, which is called an NFS server. The NFS server has multiple file systems available for the NFS clients to mount and use as if the storage were local. The NFS server can be a computer, or it can be a storage system, such as a NetApp storage system, with the needed software to act as an NFS server.

Currently, there are three versions of the NFS:

- **NFSv2:** Defined in RFC 1094 (March 1989). Originally used the User Datagram Protocol (UDP) for stateless communication. Because it is 32-bit only, the first 2GB of a file can be read.

- **NFSv3:** Defined in RFC 1813 (June 1995). Developed to overcome some of the NFSv2 limitations. It is 64-bit, which allows it to handle files bigger than 2GB. Supports additional file attributes in the replies and asynchronous writes to the NFS server. Added support for TCP-based communication.

- **NFSv4:** First defined in RFC 3010 (December 2000) and revised in RFC 3530 (April 2003). There are additional minor versions, such as NFSv4.1 and NFSv4.2, that add support for clustered server deployments, parallel access to files distributed among different servers, server-side clone and copy, space reservation, application data block (ADP), and session trunking (also known as NFS multipathing). NFSv4 adds support for end-to-end security, such as Kerberos 5. A big advantage is that the NFS server runs the service on a single port (TCP/UDP 2049). The latter makes controlling the NFS communication through firewalls and applying quality of service (QoS) much easier.

As mentioned before, the NFS is supported on Linux/Unix platforms, including the following:

- Solaris

- AIX

- HP-UX

- Apple's macOS

- Different Linux OSs

- FreeBSD

- Microsoft Windows (it's more common to use SMB/CIFS on the Windows OS)

- IBM OS/2

- OpenVMS

The NFS is based on a client/server architecture. This approach is based on the concept that one computer, which will be the server, has resources that are needed by another computer. This other computer is the client. The server will share, or make available, the needed resources to the client. The client and the server communicate with each other through established protocols, which in this case are the protocols defined by the NFS. The client will consume the shared resources as if they were local. The communication takes place in a network environment. If there are multiple servers and multiple clients, or multiple clients and one server, it is a distributed client/server network.

Using the client/server approach is beneficial because of the cost reduction, as there is no need for any additional hardware and there are minimum space requirements. The clients do not need a lot of local disk space because they use storage on the server. Other benefits are the centralized management and maintenance, such as backups, performed on the server.

As the NFS operates at Layer 7, the communication between the client and the server is basically communication between two applications. The applications in a client/server architecture communicate using Remote Procedure Call (RPC), which makes it possible for a client process to call a server process and ask it to execute the call as a local process. The rpcbind, or portmap, is an RPC service that allows clients and servers to communicate with one another by using interprocess communication methods. In other words, the rpcbind (portmap) is a service that takes care of the addressing in the communication between services. It is responsible for mapping the service to a port on which it listens. The RPC services are assigned ports, as long as they are registered with the portmap with a program number, version, and transport protocol. The portmap service is usually running on TCP/UDP port 111, also known as a privileged port in Unix. The NFS servers use the UDP/TCP port 2049 by default.

Based on this information, the NFS flow between the NFS server and client can be described with the following sequence:

1. The NFS server must run the needed services and daemons, such as mountd, nlm_main, NFSD, status monitor, quota daemon, and portmap (also known as rpcbind). These services are required, as each has its own role in that communication. The portmap is responsible for the mapping of the ports to the services and announcing this; the mountd allows the client to mount the storage and so on.

2. The storage that will be shared and available must be exported under the /etc/exports configuration file.

3. The client uses the **mount** command to connect to and use the shared resources (or using the NFS terminology, to mount the shared storage).

    a. The client will call the portmap service on the NFS server to find on which port to communicate.

    b. The client will connect to the NFSD.

    c. The NFSD will proxy the call to the mountd service.

4. The client will be able to access the shared storage.

Figure 10-3 illustrates the NFS client/server architecture and the communication over the network infrastructure.

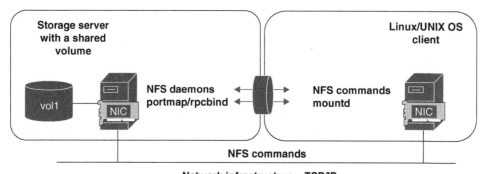

Figure 10-3 *NFS Client/Server Architecture*

Server Message Block (SMB)/Common Internet File System (CIFS)

The Server Message Block (SMB), later renamed and commonly referred to as the Common Internet File System (CIFS), is a file-based protocol that uses the client/server communication architecture. Regarding the naming of the protocol, in this book, SMB and CIFS are used interchangeably. Although there are more details and separation in the components, this discussion is not intended to be a deep dive but rather a high-level overview. The SMB is used to share files, printers, and serial ports among users in a network. Initially developed by Barry Feigenbaum at IBM in 1983, it was later adopted by Microsoft and became a component of the LAN Manager. Microsoft continued to develop the protocol, and it evolved through multiple versions:

- **SMB/CIFX/SMB1:** The SMB/CIFS protocol was created to use NetBIOS over TCP/IP (NBT) communication. Starting with Microsoft Windows 2000 Server operating system, the communication has been changed to use TCP as a transport utilizing TCP port 445. Used natively in Microsoft Windows 2003. In 1996, Microsoft renamed the protocol to Common Internet File System after Sun Microsystems announced the WebNFS initiative.

- **SMB 2.0:** Released in 2006 and supported by Windows 2008 Server and the Windows Vista. Improved the communication by decreasing the handshake messages. Supports symbolic links and the HMAC SHA-256 hashing algorithm for signing. SMB 2.0 uses 32-bit and 64-bit-wide storage fields, and 128 bits for file handles. This allowed for improved performance when copying large files. Fully supported in Samba 3.6.

- **SMB 2.1:** Performance enhancements.

- **SMB 3.0:** Introduced the SMB Direct Protocol, SMB Multichannel, and SMB Transparent Failover. These features provided better support for data centers.

- **SMB 3.1.1:** Released in Windows Server 2016 and Windows 10. Requires secure negotiation and supports AES-128 encryption.

The SMB/CIFS protocol is supported on the Microsoft Windows Server and desktop operating systems, but it can also be used with Linux/Unix and the Apple operating systems. This can be achieved by using the Samba software. The Samba was developed in 1992 by Andrew Tridgell. Here are some of the services and protocols supported:

- NetBIOS over TCP/IP

- SMB/CIFS

- DCE/RPC

- WINS

- Security Account Manager

- NTLM

- AD logon with Kerberos and LDAP

As already mentioned, the CIFS uses the client/server architecture, but in fact it consists of three separate entities:

- **CIFS client:** This piece is on the end-user machine and is capable of communicating with the CIFS server using the CIFS protocol. It is like a driver on your operating system; it has all the needed functionality to communicate using this protocol. The requests to the CIFS server always originate from the CIFS client.

- **CIFS Server:** This entity provides the CIFS functionality. As the CIFS protocol provides access to shared file systems, but also supports the communications between processes on different systems, the CIFS server includes multiple subcomponents and subsystems responsible for the needed functionality. Such components and systems are the SMB Trans, SMB Trans2, and NT Trans, forming the transactions-processing subsystem. There are also the RPC and the user authentication pieces, as well as the Remote Administration Protocol (RAP) and the Distributed File System (DFS).

■ **CIFS Application:** This entity triggers the communication between the CIFS client and the server. The CIFS client and server are the pieces that can communicate with each other, using the CIFS protocol. The application is the piece that actually utilizes the functionality offered by the VIFS server. It cannot natively communicate with the server; that's why it uses the CIFS client.

Small Computer Systems Interface (SCSI)

The Small Computer Systems Interface (SCSI), here referred to as a protocol, is in fact a set of standards that define all the needed components for the communication between an initiator and a storage system. These standards define the physical requirements, such as the electrical and optical, as well as the logical interfaces and the commands and how the negotiation is initiated and performed.

The SCSI protocol was initially implemented for communication between the operating system and the local storage, and later it was used for communication with storage that's reachable over a network.

Initially, the communication took place over a parallel SCSI bus. The parallel SCSI bus is half-duplex, which means at a given moment only a single device can communicate: either a request can be sent or a response can be received. Because commands are exchanged over this channel, data blocks and status messages, being half-duplex, might cause some commands to be dropped while the channel is busy, which creates a multidrop environment. The parallel SCSI bus had limitations such as the following in the latest version:

■ A maximum of 16 devices

■ A maximum of 320Mbps of shared channel bandwidth

■ Half-duplex

■ A maximum length of 25 meters (82 feet)

As already mentioned in the overview of the storage protocols, there are other transports for the SCSI protocol that allow its usage as a block-based protocol over larger distances and bigger infrastructures.

The SCSI protocol itself has the task of performing two major functions:

■ To form and exchange units that contain commands, blocks of data, and status messages

■ To implement a mechanism that allows the blocks of data to be reassembled in the correct order at the destination of the communication

The SCSI protocol sits between the operating system and the peripheral resources. Through the operating system, the applications are capable of using the SCSI protocol for communication with the storage devices and other peripheral units, such as printers.

The architecture of the SCSI protocol is shown on Figure 10-4. The enhanced parallel port (ECP) is a standard signaling method for bidirectional parallel communication between a computer and peripheral devices. The figure illustrates that the communication of the SCSI protocol can happen on different transport mediums, such as ECP and IP networks.

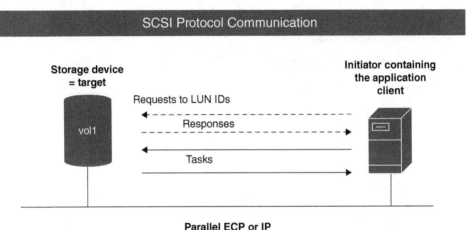

Figure 10-4 *SCSI Protocol Architecture*

The SCSI architecture defines the communication between the initiators and the targets. As initially that communication was taking place over a parallel SCSI bus, the architecture was defined for such a transport. Later, with the use of the iSCSI and FC Protocol, the commands' definition continued to be used with some minimal changes.

The SCSI commands are sent in a Command Descriptor Block (CDB), which consists of an operation code and command-specific parameters. In general, the initiator starts the communication with a request, which is a CDB, to the target. Then the target returns a status message. There are more than 60 SCSI commands, grouped into four types: N (non-data), W (write from initiator to target), R (read data), and B (bidirectional).

The SCSI protocol uses a specific addressing, called a SCSI ID, to support the communication between the different participants. For the purposes of better utilization and flexibility, the physical storage is divided into logical units. Because of this, for the storage systems it is not enough to use only a SCSI ID as a form of identification, as it points to the physical devices only. It also needs to identify a specific logical unit on top of the physical storage. For this, the Logical Unit Numbers (LUNs) are used, which are the numbers that identify the logical units. In this way, the combination between the SCSI ID and the LUN forms the address used in the SCSI communication.

Network Storage Systems Designs

After looking at the different types of storage communication (block-based and the file-based) and understanding the different protocols used in that communication, we need to look at the different designs of storage communication. Depending on the needs of the users, the applications, and the environment in which they exist, different designs can be used:

- Direct-attached storage (DAS)

- Network-attached storage (NAS)

- Storage area network (SAN)

Each of these designs has its advantages and disadvantages, which makes them suitable for different needs and applications.

Direct-Attached Storage (DAS)

Direct-attached storage (DAS) is a storage system that is directly attached to the host, available to it, and the only way of accessing it will be through the operating system/CPU of the host. The communication is based on using different protocols and buses, such as SCSI with Parallel SCSI, Serial Attached SCSI (SAS), NVMe, USB, ATA, SATA, and so on. It is based on host bus adapter, which communicates with the storage system, supporting the appropriate protocol. This means that when DAS is discussed, it does not mean only the local hard drives, but also optical drives, or external enclosures with one or multiple disks that are at the disposal only to that host. One of the characteristics of the DAS is that the relationship between the host and the storage is 1:1. The concept of the DAS is illustrated on Figure 10-5.

Figure 10-5 *Direct-Attached Storage*

On one hand, this is an advantage, as the storage provides all its resources to the host and the access is controlled and secured, which also can be described as captive storage. But, on the other hand, this can be looked at as a disadvantage, as the resources of the storage system are available to and controlled by a single host, which means storage system capacities can be underutilized.

The DAS can also be used by other hosts across a network if it is shared by its host. Still, it's the host that is in control of who uses the resources of the storage system and how they are used. Implementing such a sharing approach can be complex and difficult to monitor and manage.

The resources of the storage system are limited, and even though in certain situations the host might not be able to utilize all of them, there might be situations in which the host will need more resources and the storage system cannot provide more than it has. This means that scalability with the DAS is limited. Using DAS for the purposes of creating and storing backups for multiple hosts is not a good application.

Network-Attached Storage (NAS)

Network-attached storage involves the use of specialized storage devices or servers connected to a network (hence the "network-attached" part of the name). Their resources are shared by and accessible to the other devices and users in the network. NAS is file-based storage, and the protocols used are the NFS and SMB/CIFS, as the underlying transport protocol is usually the TCP.

An NAS device usually has multiple physical hard drives. The storage controllers on that device or server support virtualization technologies, such as RAID, to manage the physical drives, create logical volumes from them, and provide the needed levels of redundancy and data protection.

Figure 10-6 illustrates the concept of the NAS infrastructure.

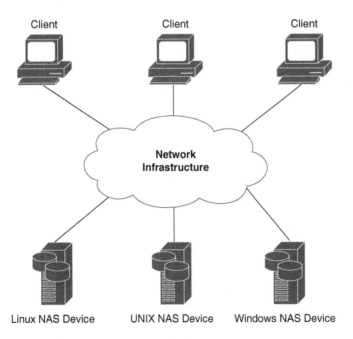

Figure 10-6 *Network-Attached Storage*

On NAS devices is an operating system. It might be a general one, such as a Microsoft Server or Linux/Unix, or a specialized one, but there is always software responsible for the configuration, management, communication, and monitoring of the device. The data on an NAS device is stored as files. It uses the usual hierarchical structure with directories and subdirectories. When there is a request for a file or files to be read, the NAS device must go to the directory, list it, locate the file, check permissions, and then transfer the file. If the file is stored in a directory several levels under the root directory, these operations must be repeated for each of the levels until the file is reached. This can be heavy on the network communication side, and it can be overcome with fine-tuning TCP.

The speed with which the data can be accessed and transferred depends on both the hardware resources and configuration of the physical hard drives on the NAS side as well as the capacities and the speed of the networks.

These characteristics of NAS make it suitable for sharing files and directories with multiple users, where speed is not of critical importance. However, NAS is not suitable for the purposes of running mission- and latency-critical applications, as it does not have the needed scalability, secure data transfer, and secure storage that block-based storage does.

Storage Area Network (SAN)

Storage area networks (SANs) are specialized, separate physical infrastructures, created to provide fast, low-latency, secure and reliable communication between the initiators and the targets (that is, the hosts and the storage systems). The storage systems used are professional, specialized storage systems that support the Fibre Channel Protocol and have HBAs to connect to the SAN.

The initiators usually are the servers in the data center because the applications run on them, and therefore they are the consumer of the services of the storage systems. The servers also need to be physically equipped with HBAs to connect to the SAN.

The communication component of the SAN is built by using specialized switches. These switches use the Fibre Channel Protocol for the communication between the initiators and the servers connected to them. The three major participants—the initiators, the targets, and the FC switches—create the SAN fabric. The fabric is not only the sum of the physical components but also the convergence of all the needed processes and services for the FC Protocol to run in this environment.

The FC switches for physical connectivity use fiber optics and special FC transceivers. This creates a very fast infrastructure, as the speeds supported can be 2, 4, 8, 16, 32, or 64Gbps.

The Fibre Channel Protocol (FCP) is the transport protocol used in the SAN. It provides a high-speed, secure, and lossless exchange of data, sent in blocks, in the form of SCSI commands. It is standardized from the Technical Committee T11 of the INCITS, an ANSI-accredited standards committee. Something interesting is that although nowadays the FCP is used to transport the SCSI commands, it is still a transport protocol and can also be used to transport the communication for other protocols, as long as you can encapsulate the data units of another protocol in FC frames. This is not common; however, it is just mentioned here to make a clear difference between the transport, the FCP, and the block-storage protocol, in this case the SCSI protocol.

The FCP was standardized in 1988, with further approval from ANSI in 1994. Cisco Systems entered the SAN market in 2002 with the acquisition of Andiamo Systems, Inc., which is the company that developed the first intelligent multilayer storage switches. The same year, Cisco released the Cisco MDS switches, FC switches running the SAN-OS (Cisco's implementation of FCP).

A SAN, illustrated in Figure 10-7, provides a lot of benefits for data centers:

- Dedicated infrastructure for storage communication

- High performance and low latency

- Secure and lossless

- Lower total cost of ownership (TCO) compared to DAS

- Controlled sharing of the storage resources

- Easier and faster backup

- Up to 16 million devices

- Segments of up to 10 km without extenders

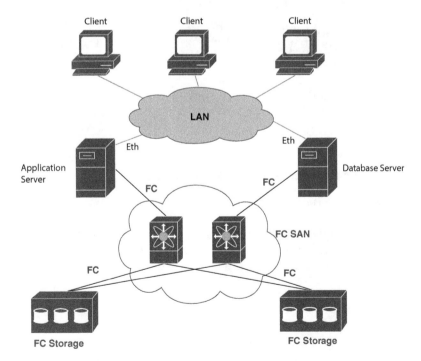

Figure 10-7 *Fibre Channel Storage Area Network*

Fibre Channel Storage Networking

The SAN fabrics are built from the initiators (servers), the targets (storage systems), and the Fibre Channel switches. The SAN fabric uses the Fibre Channel Protocol as a transport, and it is the sum of the physical participants and the convergence of the processes and services of the FCP.

The initiators and the targets to connect to an FC SAN need to use specialized communication adapters designed to process the Fibre Channel Protocol. These adapters, as already mentioned, are called host bus adapters (HBAs). The HBAs process the FCP in their silicone, which provides faster and more secure communication. Figure 10-8 shows a comparison between the stack of an HBA and an NIC.

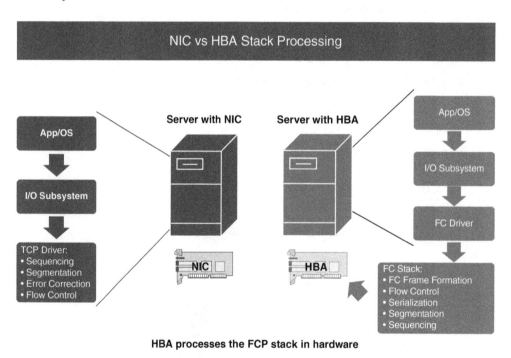

Figure 10-8   *Comparison in the Stack Processing Between an Ethernet NIC and an FC HBA*

The HBAs are similar to the Ethernet network interface cards (NICs) in terms of a function—both are used to provide connectivity to a network environment for the purposes of the communication. However, there is a huge difference in the way they function.

The Ethernet NICs rely on the software drivers in the operating system for protocol-related functions and processing, such as flow control, sequencing, error correction, segmentation, and others.

In comparison, the processing of the Fibre Channel Protocol stack happens in the hardware of the HBA. The SCSI protocol passes the commands to the HBA, where the FCP frames are formed and the physical connectivity is established. This takes the load off the device's CPU and allows for better control.

The communication between the initiator and the target needs to be secure and reliable, as the FC frames carry the data, divided into blocks. It is important that the data is reassembled in the correct order at the destination of the communication and that all the blocks are present. That's why there are multiple mechanisms and stages of FCP communication to take care of that. Figure 10-9 shows the different components of the FCP communication.

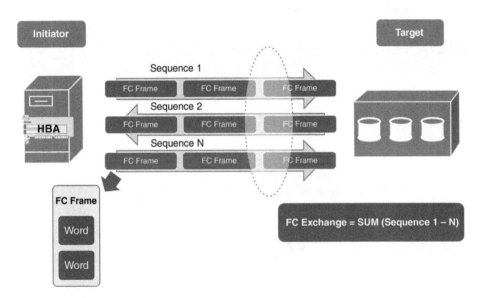

Figure 10-9 *FCP Communication Components*

In the FCP communication, the smallest piece of data transmitted over the FC links is called a word. The size of a word is 32 bits (4 bytes), which is serialized into 40 bits using 8-bit/10-bit encoding. The words form the FC frames. A series of FC frames sent in one direction is called a sequence, and all the sequences that form the whole conversation between an initiator and a target is called an exchange.

For clarity, here are two examples of FCP communication. The first one is a SCSI-FCP read operation, where an initiator requests data stored on the target to be read and sent to it. The second example is of a SCSI-FCP write operation, where an initiator opens communication with a target and sends data to be stored.

The SCSI-FCP read operation, which is illustrated in Figure 10-10, consists of the following steps:

Step 1.   The initiator generates a SCSI read request (**FCP_CMD**). The server notifies the storage system that it wants to read data stored on it.

Step 2.   The HBA of the initiator encapsulates the **SCSI Read** command into an FC frame and sends it to the target. This process is the first sequence (sequence 1) of the whole exchange.

Step 3. The target receives and processes the FC frame. It retrieves the requested data (**FCP_DATA**) from storage and encapsulates the data blocks in FC frames.

Step 4. The target sends the FC frames to the initiator in one sequence (sequence 2).

Step 5. The target generates a status command (**FCP_RSP**) that informs the initiator that the requested data transmission is complete.

Step 6. The target encapsulates the status command in an FC frame and sends it in another sequence (sequence 3).

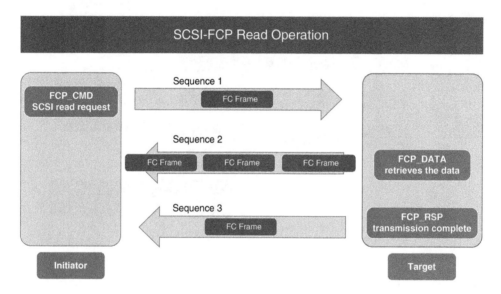

Figure 10-10 *SCSI-FCP Read Operation*

At this point, the I/O operation is complete. The collection of all the three sequences is the entire exchange.

The SCSI-FCP write operation, illustrated in Figure 10-11, consists of the following steps:

Step 1. The initiator node generates a SCSI write request (**FCP_CMD**). The server will notify the storage system that it wants to send data to the storage system.

Step 2. The HBA of the initiator encapsulates the **SCSI-FCP Write** command in an FC frame and sends it to the target in a single sequence (sequence 1).

Step 3. The target node responds with a SCSI write request response (**FCP_XFR_RDY**). The write request response is required for synchronization between the initiator and target.

Step 4. The target response is encapsulated in an FC frame and sent to the initiator in another sequence (sequence 2).

Step 5.   The initiator retrieves the data (**FCP_DATA**) from its upper-layer protocol (ULP) buffers and packages it.

Step 6.   The data is encapsulated in FC frames and sent to the target in a sequence (sequence 3).

Step 7.   The target generates a status command (**FCP_RSP**) to confirm the end of the exchange.

Step 8.   The target encapsulates the status command in an FC frame and sends it as a last sequence of the communication (on the diagram this is sequence 4). All four of these sequences form the entire exchange needed to store data on a storage system.

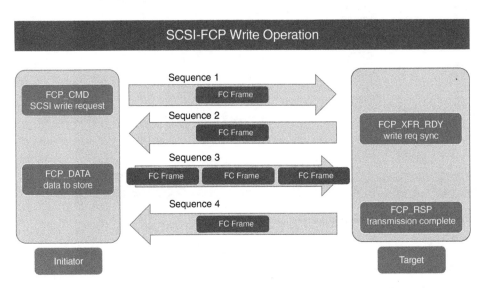

Figure 10-11   *SCSI-FCP Write Operation*

Fibre Channel Topologies

The SAN fabrics are built based on three physical topologies:

■ Point-to-Point

■ FC-AL (Fibre Channel Arbitrated Loop)

■ Switched fabric (SAN)

Figure 10-12 shows the different SAN topologies.

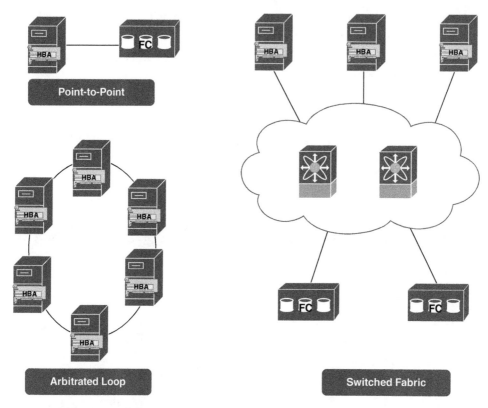

Figure 10-12 *FC SAN Topologies*

Point-to-Point Topology

The point-to-point topology is the smallest and simplest one. It can be qualified as a DAS, as the target is directly connected to the initiator. The initiator and the target are equipped with Fibre Channel HBAs and use fiber optics with FC transceivers for the physical connectivity.

The obvious drawback of this architecture is that the target is dedicated to a single initiator only, meaning that either the resources can be underutilized or they can't match the requirements of the server's workloads. If designed correctly, such a topology might be used for some specific applications requiring more security and control. As this topology lacks scalability, it is not common in the data centers. The topology is shown on Figure 10-13.

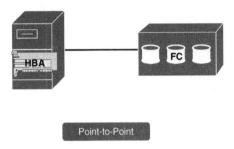

Point-to-Point

Figure 10-13 *Point-to-Point FC SAN Topology*

Arbitrated Loop Topology

The FC-AL (Arbitrated Loop) topology involves physical connectivity in which the initiator and the targets are connected using a ring, or loop, as illustrated in Figure 10-14. In FC-AL, up to 127 devices can participate—a limitation imposed by the FC-AL protocol, which allows up to 127 addresses, as one is reserved for an FC switch in case the loop needs to connect to a SAN fabric. Usually about 12 devices are connected in an FC-AL topology.

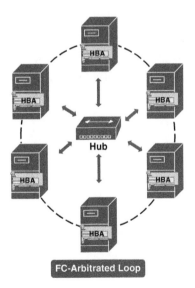

FC-Arbitrated Loop

Figure 10-14 *FC-AL SAN Topology*

The devices can be physically connected to each other through the HBAs in a loop topology. In this setup, if a device's HBA malfunctions, the ring is broken and there is no communication. To overcome this limitation, you can use a fiber channel hub. As it is a passive device (unlike an FC switch), it does not process the communication but instead (in case of a failed HBA) preserves the physical connectivity for the rest of the participants in the loop.

In the FC Protocol, the ports are assigned different roles, based on which participant they belong to and what they connect to. The ports, which are used to connect to an FC-AL, are assigned the role of NL_ports, which stands for Node Loop ports.

When there is an FC-AL that connects only NL_ports, meaning it is not connected to an FC switch, this is called a "private arbitrated loop."

When the FC-AL uses a hub, and one of the ports is connected to an FC switch, which is called an FL_port (Fabric Loop port), this topology is usually referred to as a "public arbitrated loop."

The performance of the arbitrated loop is affected by the type of communication defined by the physical connectivity in a ring—only two of the participants can speak at a time. This introduces very high latencies.

Another drawback is the lack of redundancy in a private loop topology, as the failure of a node will bring down the whole loop.

Switched Fabric Topology

The switched fabric, also known as the SAN fabric, is the physical topology most used in a data center because it is extremely flexible and scalable (see Figure 10-15). Another reason is that the price of FC switches has come down significantly over the last several years. Yet another reason is that in its implementation of the FC protocol, Cisco added an additional construct called a virtual SAN (VSAN) that allows SAN fabrics to be built using fewer physical components and at the same time preserving the level of isolation and separation between them.

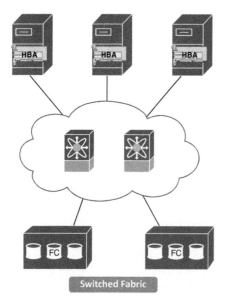

Figure 10-15 *Switched Fabric Topology*

Internet Small Computer System Interface (iSCSI)

The Internet Small Computer System Interface is a transport protocol that allows SCSI communication between two nodes over IP-based networks. However, as you'll remember, the SCSI protocol uses block-based storage communication (that is, the data is divided into blocks and communicated). For this purpose, iSCSI uses TCP for secure and reliable communication. iSCSI encapsulates the SCSI commands in TCP segments, which are then put in IP packets and routed through the network to the destination. As the iSCSI uses the IP networks, which are less expensive than separate, dedicated SAN fabrics, it allows for cost-optimization in the data centers.

iSCSI is implemented either through software-based drivers or in the hardware of the NICs, and it is capable of discovering iSCSI nodes and booting from an iSCSI storage system.

The iSCSI protocol supports IPsec for secure connectivity as well as authentication.

Because iSCSI allows for the communication between hosts that use the SCSI protocol over a network, using TCP as a transport, there are some additional concepts and characteristics to allow for the encapsulation and de-encapsulation of that traffic.

The network entities in the iSCSI communication are as follows:

- **iSCSI initiator:** This is the server/host that wants to use the resources of a storage system

- **iSCSI target:** A storage system that can communicate using the iSCSI protocol

Each iSCSI network entity contains an iSCSI node, which can be either an initiator or a target. The iSCSI node is identified by an iSCSI node name.

The iSCSI node needs to be capable of utilizing the IP network that's connected to the iSCSI network entity to which it belongs. For this, the so called "network portal" is used. This component has network access, supports TCP/IP, and is identified by an IP address. Usually this is the network adapter, which can also be a wireless one.

Here, you can clearly see the different layers of processing data with iSCSI. The iSCSI node takes care of the mapping and encapsulation between the SCSI protocol and the underlying TCP transport protocol. The iSCSI node can be considered an overlay virtual component on the top of the network portal. The concept is shown on Figure 10-16.

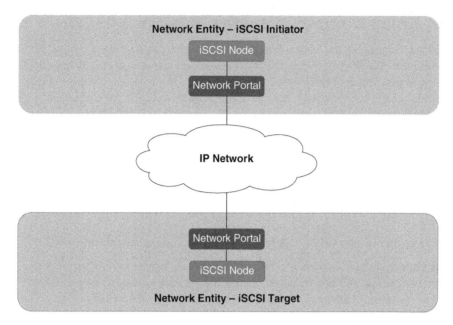

Figure 10-16 *iSCSI Concepts*

The iSCSI nodes use specific addressing known as iSCSI node names. The size of the node names can be up to 255 bytes. They need to use UTF-8 encoding in a human-readable string. They are used for target discovery and for login and authorization purposes.

The iSCSI node names are available in three formats:

- iSCSI Qualified Name (IQN), defined in RFC 3720, is one of the most popular types of iSCSI addressing. The fields in an IQN carry the following information:

    - It always starts with "iqn".

    - The date the domain was acquired (in yyyy-mm format)

    - The reversed domain name of the authority

    - An option prefix of ":".

    - A text-based identifier defined by the naming authority

- Extended Unique Identifier (EUI), which consists of the following information:

    - It always starts with "eui".

    - A 64-bit address.

- T11 Network Address Authority (NAA), which has the following structure:

    - It starts with "naa".

    - A 64- or 128-bit identifier.

Figure 10-17 compares the different types of iSCSI node names.

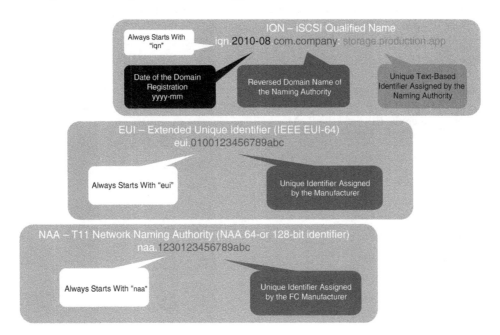

Figure 10-17 *iSCSI Node Names*

It is important to remember that the iSCSI communication relies on IP-based network communication, which means that the iSCSI initiator or target first has to be capable of communicating in the network; only then can iSCSI communication be established. That's why the major components that are always needed are the IP address/hostname of the iSCSI network entity, the port number for the iSCSI communication (3260 to be allowed), the iSCSI node name, and an additional CHAP secret, if there is one.

NVM Express and NVM Express over Fabrics

The storage devices are usually tape drives or hard drives, and the SCSI protocol is used for communication with them. The hard drives are slow mechanical devices with spinning parts, plates, and magnetic heads for reading and writing. This makes access to the stored data slow. That's why in the architecture of the computer there is a cascading approach as to how the data is read and fed into the CPU. RAM is volatile memory, which means that the content of this memory will disappear when it is without power. RAM is significantly faster than the hard drives. It is managed by the CPU, and it is used to read chunks of data from hard drives and to keep it there for the consumption by the CPU. RAM is very fast, but the CPU is still faster; that's why there are additional layers of memory called cache memory, which read from the RAM and pass it in the direction of the CPU. Thus, the data feed is optimized, but still the characteristics of the hard drive affect the performance of the computers.

Solid-state drives (SSDs) were developed later. These are hard drives, but instead of being electromechanical devices with spinning components, they are based on flash memory. The SSDs are much faster because they are just like RAM, but they are considered a non-volatile memory, which means that the data will be preserved even after the power is off. At the beginning, SSDs, which replaced HDDs, used the SCSI protocol for communication. This meant that there had to be a SCSI controller to manage them and also to communicate with the CPU, and the same message-based communication was still in place. Figure 10-18 illustrates the SCSI SSD communication and compares it to the communication between the CPU and the RAM.

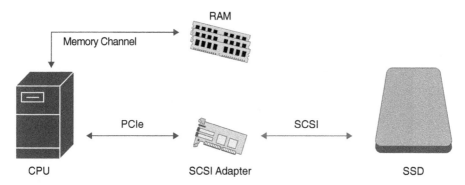

Figure 10-18   *SCSI SSD*

To overcome this challenge, the Non-Volatile Memory Express (NVMe) was developed, also known as the Non-Volatile Memory Host Controller Interface Specification (NVMHCIS). The NVMe is a standard or specification that defines how the non-volatile media (NAND flash memory, in the form of SSDs and M.2 cards) can be accessed over the PCIe bus using memory semantics—said in a different way, how the flash memory storage to be treated as memory, just like the RAM, and the SCSI controller and protocol can become obsolete. Figure 10-19 illustrates the NVMe concept.

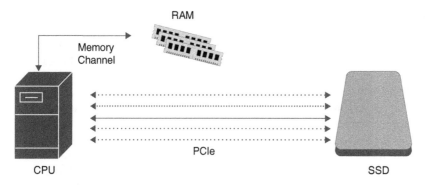

Figure 10-19   *NVMe Concept*

NVMe has been designed from the ground up and brings significant advantages:

■ Very low latency.

■ Larger number of queues for commands communication (65,535 queues).

■ Each queue supports 65,535 commands.

■ Simpler command set (the CPU talks natively to the storage).

■ No adapter needed.

For the sake of the comparison, with the SCSI protocol and a SATA controller, there is support for one queue and up to 32 commands per queue. With the SSD there are 65535 queues each supporting 65535 commands.. This shows the huge difference and impact of the NVMe as a technology, especially in the data center, where the constantly increasing workloads demand an increase in the resources, including the storage devices and the communication with them.

Cisco Unified Computing System (UCS) C-series rack and B-series blade servers support NVMe-capable flash storage, which is best suited for applications requiring ultra-high performance and very low latency. This is achieved by using non-oversubscribed PCIe lanes as a connection between the multicore CPUs in the servers and the NVMe flash storage, bringing the storage as close as possible to the CPU.

The NVMe brings a huge improvement in the performance of the local storage, but in the data centers the data is stored on storage systems, as it needs to be accessed by different applications running on different servers. The adoption of SSDs as a technology also changed the DC storage systems. Now there are storage systems whose drives are only SSDs, also called all-flash arrays. For such storage systems to be able to communicate with the servers and to bring the benefits of the flash-based storage, Non-Volatile Memory Express over Fabrics (NVMe-oF) was developed. It specifies how a transport protocol can be used to extend the NVMe communication between a host and a storage system over a network. The first specification of this kind was NVMe over Fibre Channel (FC-NVMe) from 2017. Since then, the supported transport protocols for the NVMe-oF are as follows (see Figure 10-20):

■ Fibre Channel (FC-NVMe)

■ TCP (NVMe/TCP)

■ Ethernet/RDMA over Converged Ethernet (RoCE)

■ InfiniBand (NVMe/IB)

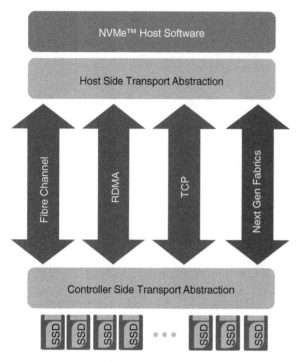

Figure 10-20 *NVMe Concept*

The NVMe-oF uses the same idea as iSCSI, where the SCSI commands are encapsulated in IP packets and TCP is the transport protocol, or Fibre Channel, where FCP is used to transport the SCSI commands.

Fibre Channel is the preferred transport protocol for connecting all-flash arrays in the data centers because of its secure, fast, scalable, and plug-and-play architecture. FC-NVMe offers the best of Fibre Channel and NVMe. You get the improved performance of NVMe along with the flexibility and scalability of the shared storage architecture.

FC-NVMe is supported by the Cisco MDS switches. Here are some of the advantages:

- **Multiprotocol support:** NVMe and SCSI are supported over FC, FCoE, and FCIP.

- **No hardware changes:** No hardware changes are needed to support NVMe, just a software upgrade of NX-OS.

- **Superior architecture:** Cisco MDS 9700 Series switches have superior architecture that can help customers build their mission-critical data centers. Their fully redundant components, non-oversubscribed and nonblocking architecture, automatic isolation of failure domains, and exceptional capability to detect and automatically recover from SAN congestion are a few of the top attributes that make these switches the best choice for high-demand storage infrastructures that support NVMe-capable workloads.

■ **Integrated storage traffic visibility and analytics:** The 32Gbps products in the Cisco MDS 9000 family of switches offer Cisco SAN Telemetry Streaming, which can be combined with the FC-NVMe traffic with just a nondisruptive software-only upgrade.

■ **Strong ecosystem:** Cisco UCS C-series rack servers with Broadcom (Emulex) and Cavium (QLogic) HBAs.

Cisco MDS Product Overview

Cisco Systems is one of the major vendors of SAN infrastructures nowadays. Its journey in the world of the storage communications starts back in 2002, when it acquired Andiamo Systems, Inc. Based on the company's multilayer storage switches, later that year Cisco released its line of FC switches—the Cisco MDS family of switches. The Cisco MDS switches were running a special operating system called the SAN-OS, which was Cisco's implementation of the Fibre Channel Protocol, based on the standard, but also expanded with some unique features such as the virtual SANs (VSANs). The SAN-OS provided support for multiprotocol and multitransport with a rich set of intelligent network and storage services as well as integrated management applications for efficient storage network administration. There was support not only for the Fibre Channel Protocol but also advanced features such as Fibre Channel Protocol port channels, Fibre Channel over IP (FCIP), Inter-VSAN Routing (IVR), Cisco Discovery Protocol, FICON for IBM Mainframes, and more.

Additionally, in the SAN-OS, and later in the NX-OS, there was interoperability support for when the Cisco MDS FC switches would be deployed in a multivendor environment. There were three interoperability modes supporting the specifics of Brocade, McData, and FCP standards based Fibre Channel switches.

The SAN-OS was running on and managing the purpose-built Cisco MDS switches. There were three separate management tools and options.

The SAN-OS provided a command line interface (CLI), which allowed administrators to connect to the FC switch via a terminal emulator supporting Telnet and SSH. The alternative to the CLI was, and still is, the Device Manager. Figure 10-21 shows screenshots from the Device Managers from different models of Cisco MDS switches.

Device Manager is a graphical user interface (GUI) that supports switch provisioning and provides a graphical representation of the linecard and supervisor modules, ports, power supplies, and so on. Here are some of the features supported:

■ Configuring physical Fibre Channel interfaces

■ Configuring virtual Fibre Channel interfaces

■ Configuring FCoE features

■ Configuring zones for multiple VSANs

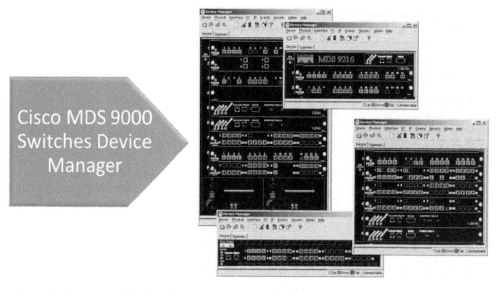

Figure 10-21 *Cisco Device Manager*

■ Managing ports, port channels, trunking, and oversubscription

■ Managing Simple Network Management Protocol Version 3 (SNMPv3) security access to switches

■ Managing command line interface (CLI) security access to the switch

■ Managing alarms, events, and notifications

■ Saving and copying configuration files and software images

■ Viewing the hardware configuration

■ Viewing the chassis, module, port status, and statistics

The tool for discovering, provisioning, configuring, monitoring, and troubleshooting SAN fabrics built with the Cisco MDS and Nexus switches was the Cisco Fabric Manager. Figure 10-22 shows a screenshot from the Cisco Fabric Manager.

Some of the main features were the following:

■ **Discovery:** Cisco Discovery Protocol, Fibre Channel Generic Services (FC-GS), Fabric Shortest Path First (FSPF), and Small Computer System Interface 3 (SCSI-3) for discovery of devices and interconnects on one or more fabrics.

■ **Automation:** Configuration checking, performing successful fabric merges, and resolving configuration inconsistencies automatically. Zone configuration with wizards, Inter-VSAN routing (IVR), FC Port Channels, Fibre Channel over IP (FCIP) tunnels, and IP access control lists (ACLs), and Configuration Analysis Tool.

■ **Monitoring and reporting:** Real-time statistics and historical performance monitoring and reporting as well as visibility into the entire Cisco storage network through Cisco Fabric Manager server federation.

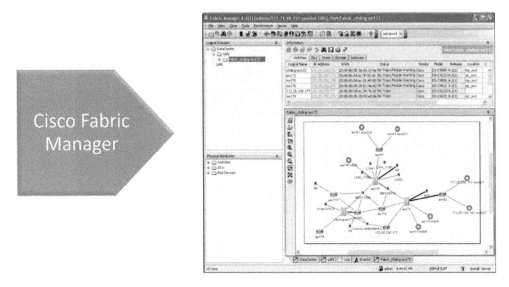

Figure 10-22 *Cisco Fabric Manager*

Later, with the development of the data center technologies, Cisco released the Nexus family of switches. These switches support not only Ethernet environments but also the Fibre Channel over Ethernet (FCoE) protocol. As the FCoE allows FC communication over Ethernet networks, this provided support and flexibility for using different designs in the data centers and led to optimization in the access layer by using Cisco Nexus switches for both Ethernet and SAN communication. This duality in the nature of the Cisco Nexus switches required a new operating system that could support both Ethernet and FC communication. As a result, the NX-OS was released. It is a modular operating system used on the Cisco Nexus and MDS switches. Based on the SAN-OS, the NX-OS module was developed, which is responsible for storage communication.

These developments also affected the Cisco Fabric Manager. As the Cisco MDS and Nexus switches were working together in the new converged designs for the data center infrastructures, there was a need for a provisioning, management, monitoring, and troubleshooting application that could support both the Ethernet and the SAN infrastructures. Thus, the Cisco Fabric Manager evolved as the foundation for the Cisco Data Center Network Manager (DCNM), a management solution for all NX-OS network deployments spanning multitenant, multifabric LAN fabrics, SAN fabrics, and IP Fabric for Media (IPFM) networking in the data center powered by Cisco.

Here are some of the major features supported:

- Fabric management for multiple types of LAN solutions, including VXLAN-EVPN, Cisco Fabric Path, and traditional three-tier LAN deployments

- Day-0 POAP for rapid policy-based bootstrapping of fabric infrastructure

- Auto-detection of unprovisioned switches for use in the Fabric Builder

- Smart topology views showing virtual port channels (vPCs) and virtual device contexts for Cisco Nexus networks (topology views include VXLAN search)

- Resource pooling, such as IP addresses and VXLAN segment IDs to be allocated on a per-fabric basis

- Role-based access control (RBAC) within the fabric to separate administrative tasks between functional domains

- SAN Telemetry function (optional, licensed feature)

- Port monitoring (PMon) configuration

- Historical trend data for SAN Inter-Switch Links (ISLs)

- Integrated device manager

- End-to-end storage topology view from client to LUN

- Storage networking health color-coding on topology views

- Storage bandwidth

- Storage enclosure and VM visibility

- Web-based zoning and IVR zoning configuration

- SAN host path redundancy feature

- Slow-drain analysis features

- Integration and discovery for popular storage LUN manufacturers

- End-to-end flow visualization

- Fabric bootstrap: day-0 provisioning

- Dashboards for a custom summary view of LAN and SAN domains and topology groups

Figure 10-23 shows a screenshot from the topology view of the Cisco DCNM.

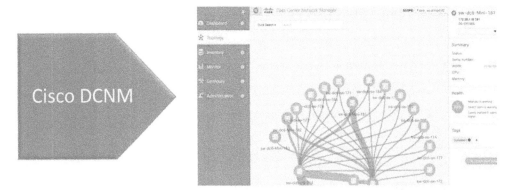

Figure 10-23 *Cisco DCNM*

Cisco MDS 9000 multilayer SAN switches are designed based on the switched fabric flexible hardware architecture. This is combined with the use of hardware buffers, queues, and a virtual output queueing technique with a central arbiter to allow for cutthrough speeds, avoidance of head-of-line blocking, security, stability, and scalability.

Here are some of the important benefits of the Cisco MDS 9000 series SAN switches:

■ **Industry-leading scalability:** Up to 768 line-rate 32G Fibre Channel ports to deliver both scale and performance.

■ **Deep visibility:** Built-in hardware-based analytics enable faster troubleshooting and resolution.

■ **Flexibility:** Multiprotocol support, support for 32Gbps Fibre Channel, and readiness for 64Gbps Fibre Channel, 40G Fibre Channel over Ethernet (FCoE), and Non-Volatile Memory Express (NVMe) over fabric.

Figure 10-24 shows the Cisco MDS 9000 series of switches.

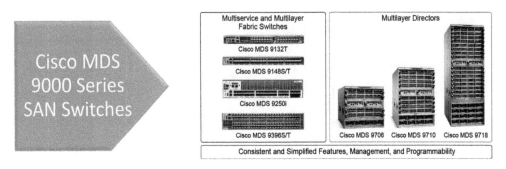

Figure 10-24 *Cisco MDS 9000 Series SAN Switches*

Here are the current Cisco MDS 9000 switches:

- Cisco MDS 9718 Multilayer Director

- Cisco MDS 9710 Multilayer Director

- Cisco MDS 9706 Multilayer Director

- Cisco MDS 9250i Multiservice Fabric Switch

- Cisco MDS 9396T Multilayer Fabric Switch

- Cisco MDS 9396S Multilayer Fabric Switch

- Cisco MDS 9148T Multilayer Fabric Switch

- Cisco MDS 9148S Multilayer Fabric Switch

- Cisco MDS 9132T Multilayer Fabric Switch

Cisco MDS 9700 Series 64Gbps Ready Directors

The Cisco MDS 9700 Multilayer Director switches have a modular architecture. In this architecture is the flexibility of different numbers of slots for the linecards, fabric modules, and supervisor modules. Figure 10-25 illustrates the Cisco MDS 9700 models and major modules and benefits.

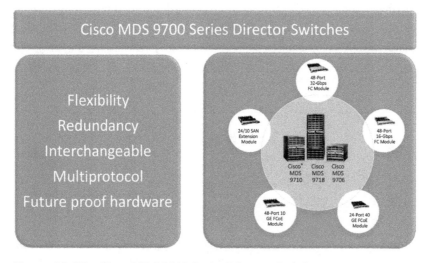

Figure 10-25 *Cisco MDS 9700 Series Director Switches*

The family of the Cisco MDS 9700 directors, shown in Figure 10-26, includes the following platforms:

■ Cisco MDS 9718 is an 18-slot chassis with 16 linecard slots and up to 16 power supplies. It's the biggest one, occupying 26RU.

■ Cisco MDS 9710 is a 10-slot chassis with eight linecard slots and up to eight power supplies. The middle-sized chassis is 14RU.

■ Cisco MDS 9706 is a six-slot chassis with four linecard slots and up to four power supplies. It is 9RU.

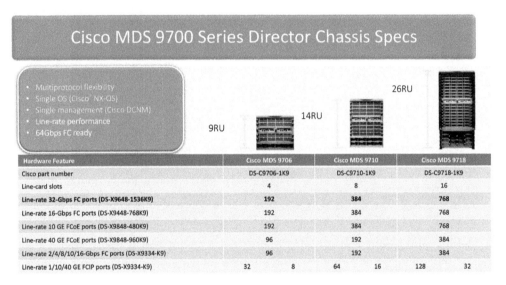

Hardware Feature	Cisco MDS 9706		Cisco MDS 9710		Cisco MDS 9718	
Cisco part number	DS-C9706-1K9		DS-C9710-1K9		DS-C9718-1K9	
Line-card slots	4		8		16	
Line-rate 32-Gbps FC ports (DS-X9648-1536K9)	**192**		**384**		**768**	
Line-rate 16-Gbps FC ports (DS-X9448-768K9)	192		384		768	
Line-rate 10 GE FCoE ports (DS-X9848-480K9)	192		384		768	
Line-rate 40 GE FCoE ports (DS-X9848-960K9)	96		192		384	
Line-rate 2/4/8/10/16-Gbps FC ports (DS-X9334-K9)	96		192		384	
Line-rate 1/10/40 GE FCIP ports (DS-X9334-K9)	32	8	64	16	128	32

Figure 10-26 *Linecard Options and Scalability per Cisco MDS 9700 Director Chassis*

Each of the director chassis supports up to two Supervisor modules. These modules support the management and control planes or provide the management and processes needed for the switches' operation. Using two supervisors provides redundancy.

In the Cisco MDS 9700 Directors, the physical switching of the frames happens in the crossbar fabric modules, also called just "fabric" modules. Each of the chassis has six slots for fabric modules. Depending on the needs, there can be a different number of fabrics installed in these slots, thus controlling the switching capacities. The minimum number of fabric modules per chassis is three for the purposes of supporting a minimum redundant configuration.

The linecards are line rate and support 48' 32Gbps or 48' 16Gbps FC ports, 48' 10Gbps FCoE ports, or 24' 40Gbps FCoE ports.

Cisco MDS 9000 Series 32Gbps Fabric Switches

Here's a list of the Cisco MDS 32Gbps switches (see Figure 10-27):

- **Cisco MDS 9132T:** 16′ fixed FC ports operating at speeds of 4/8/16/32Gbps and a slot for an additional module, which adds another 16 FC ports operating at the same speeds
- **Cisco MDS 9148T:** 48′ fixed FC ports operating at speeds of 4/8/16/32Gbps
- **Cisco MDS 9396T:** 96′ fixed FC ports operating at speeds of 4/8/16/32Gbps

Cisco MDS 9132T	Cisco MDS 9148T	Cisco MDS 9396T
Semi-modular 1RU chassis; configurable to 8, 16, 24 or 32 ports	Fixed 1RU chassis; configurable to 24, 32, 40 or 48 ports	Fixed 2RU chassis; configurable to 48, 64, 80 or 96 ports
16x4/8/16/32-Gbps Fibre channel (line rate) base switch 16x4/8/16/32-Gbps Fibre channel (line rate) expansion module	48x4/8/16/32-Gbps Fibre channel (line rate) fixed switch	96x4/8/16/32-Gbps Fibre channel (line rate) fixed switch

Figure 10-27   *Cisco MDS 9000 Series 32Gbps Fabric Switches*

All of these 32Gbps Fabric Cisco MDS switches support the following features:

- Integrated hardware-based SAN Analytics
- Autozone feature
- NVMe/FC ready
- Virtual machine awareness
- Extended BB_Credits (up to 8270 per port or 8300 per port group)
- Native on-switch REST API and Python interpreter
- FC Trustsec Link encryption
- Power-On Auto Provisioning (POAP) and intelligent diagnostics
- Cisco In-Service Software Upgrade (ISSU) and Downgrade (ISSD)

- Redundant hot-swappable power supplies and fan trays

- Anti-counterfeit technology with secure boot

- Multiple power supplies

- Multiple fans for cooling

Cisco MDS 9000 Series 16Gbps Fabric Switches

The two 16Gbps fabric switches are the Cisco MDS 9148S and Cisco MDS 9396S switches, which are listed in Figure 10-28. They are intended to be used in the SAN access layer of the design, as they provide a huge amount of low-cost ports. Some of the major benefits of using them are as follows:

- The Cisco MDS 9148S switch provides up to 48 fixed FC ports capable of speeds of 2, 4, 8, and 16Gbps, and the Cisco MDS 9396S switch provides up to 96 autosensing Fibre Channel ports that are capable of speeds of 2, 4, 8, 10, and 16Gbps of dedicated bandwidth for each port. The 16Gbps Cisco MDS 9148S and Cisco MDS 9396S are the first generation of NVMe-ready Fibre Channel 1RU and 2RU switches.

- The Cisco MDS 9396S switch offers more buffer-to-buffer credits and support for more VSANs, making it an excellent choice for standalone small and midsize business (SMB) Fibre Channel networks.

- Support for an N-Port Virtualization (NPV) node or an N-Port ID Virtualization (NPIV) core connecting legacy Fibre Channel switches or multiprotocol Nexus NPV switches.

- High-availability - the Cisco MDS 9148S and Cisco MDS 9396S switches support In-Service Software Upgrades (ISSU). This means that Cisco NX-OS Software can be upgraded while the Fibre Channel ports carry traffic.

- The Cisco MDS 9148S and Cisco MDS 9396S switches include dual redundant hot-swappable power supplies and fan trays, port channels for Inter-Switch Link (ISL) resiliency, and F-port channeling for resiliency on uplinks from a switch operating in NPV mode.

- Hardware-based slow port detection and recovery provide enhanced performance and monitoring capability.

- The Cisco MDS 9148S and Cisco MDS 9396S switches offer built-in storage network management and SAN plug-and-play capabilities. All features are available through a command line interface (CLI) or Cisco Prime DCNM for SAN Essentials Edition, a centralized management tool. Cisco DCNM task-based wizards simplify management of single or multiple switches and fabrics. For virtual infrastructures, it manages the entire path: from the virtual machine and switch to the physical storage.

- The Cisco MDS 9148S and Cisco MDS 9396S switches also support PowerOn Auto Provisioning (POAP) to automate software image upgrades and configuration file installation on newly deployed switches. Additionally, they provide intelligent diagnostics, protocol decoding, network analysis tools, and Cisco Call Home for added reliability, faster problem resolution, and reduced service costs.

- The switches offer support for virtual SAN (VSAN) technology for hardware-enforced, isolated environments within a physical fabric. They offer access control lists (ACLs) for hardware-based, intelligent frame processing. Advanced traffic management features, such as fabric-wide quality of service (QoS) and Inter-VSAN Routing (IVR), are included in the optional Cisco MDS 9000 Family Enterprise Package. QoS prioritizes application data traffic for better and more predictable network service. Zone-based QoS simplifies configuration and administration by using the familiar zoning concept. IVR facilitates resource sharing across VSANs without compromising scalability, reliability, availability, and network security.

Cisco MDS 9000 Series 16-Gbps Fabric Switches

Cisco MDS 9148S	Cisco MDS 9396S
Fixed 1RU chassis; configurable to 12, 24, 36, or 48 ports enabled	Fixed 2RU chassis; configurable to 48, 60, 72, 84, or 96 ports enabled
48 x 2/4/8/16- Gbps Fibre Channel (line rate)	96 x 2/4/8/10/16- Gbps Fibre Channel (line rate)

Figure 10-28   *Cisco MDS 9000 Series 16Gbps Fabric Switches*

Cisco MDS 9250i Multiservice Fabric Switch

The Cisco MDS 9250i Multiservice Fabric switch is optimized to support not only the processing of the Fibre Channel Protocol but also other transports for the Fibre Channel frames, such as the Fibre Channel over IP (FCIP) and Fibre Channel over Ethernet (FcoE). In this way, the Cisco MDS 9250i allows for the deployment of high-performance SAN extensions, distributed intelligent fabric services, and cost-effective multiprotocol connectivity for multivendor and multiprotocol systems and mainframe environments. Figure 10-29 shows the front of the Cisco MDS 9250i multiservice fabric switch and the major characteristics.

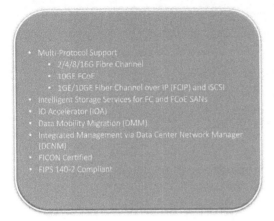

Cisco MDS 9250i Multiservice Fabric Switches

- Multi-Protocol Support
  - 2/4/8/16G Fibre Channel
  - 10GE FCoE
  - 1GE/10GE Fiber Channel over IP (FCIP) and iSCSI
- Intelligent Storage Services for FC and FCoE SANs
- IO Accelerator (IOA)
- Data Mobility Migration (DMM)
- Integrated Management via Data Center Network Manager (DCNM)
- FICON Certified
- FIPS 140-2 Compliant

Figure 10-29   *Cisco MDS 9250i Multiservice Fabric Switch*

The Cisco MDS 9250i Multiservice Fabric switch is equipped with 40 channel ports operating at speeds of 2, 4, 8, and 16Gbps. There are two 1/10-Gigabit Ethernet ports on the IP storage services built-in module that support the FCIP communication. Another eight 10-Gigabit Ethernet ports are used for the FcoE communication. All of this fits within a small fixed 2RU form factor. The Cisco SAN Extension over IP application package license is enabled as standard on the two fixed 1/10-Gigabit Ethernet IP storage services ports, enabling features such as FCIP and compression on the switch without the need for additional licenses. Also, using the eight 10-Gigabit Ethernet FcoE ports, the Cisco MDS 9250i platform attaches to directly connected FcoE and Fibre Channel storage devices and supports multitiered unified network fabric connectivity directly over FcoE.

Here are some of the unique advantages of the Cisco MDS 9250i Multiservice Fabric switch:

- Intelligent application services engine. The Cisco MDS 9250i includes as standard a single application services engine that enables the included Cisco SAN Extension over IP software solution package to run on the two fixed 1/10-Gigabit Ethernet storage services ports.

- Remote SAN extension with high-performance FCIP:

  - Enables backup, remote replication, and other disaster-recovery services over WAN links using open-standards FCIP tunneling.

  - Hardware-based compression, hardware-based encryption, FCIP write acceleration, and FCIP tape read and write acceleration. Up to 16 virtual Inter-Switch Link (ISL) connections are provided on the two 1/10-Gigabit Ethernet ports through tunneling.

  - Support for all the Cisco MDS 9000 family enhanced capabilities, including VSANs, IVR, advanced traffic management, and network security across remote connections.

- iSCSI connectivity to Ethernet-attached servers:

  - Extends the Fibre Channel SAN-based storage to Ethernet-attached servers.

  - Increases storage utilization and availability.

- Mainframe connectivity services:

  - Support for FICON environments, including cascaded FICON fabrics, VSAN-enabled intermix of mainframe and open systems environments, and N-port ID Virtualization (NPIV) for mainframe Linux partitions.

  - IBM Control Unit Port (CUP) support enables in-band management of Cisco MDS 9200 Series switches from the mainframe management console.

  - FICON tape acceleration reduces latency effects for FICON channel extension over FCIP for FICON tape read and write operations to mainframe physical or virtual tape.

  - Support for the IBM Extended Remote Copy (XRC) Acceleration feature, which enables acceleration of dynamic updates for IBM z/OS Global Mirror (formerly known as XRC).

- Cisco Data Mobility Manager (DMM). This fabric-based data migration solution transfers block data, without disruption, across heterogeneous storage volumes and across distances, whether the host is online or offline.

- Support for extended security such as RADIUS and TACACS+, FC-SP, SFTP, SSH protocol, SNMPv3 implementing AES, VSANs, hardware-enforced zoning, ACLs, and per-VSAN RBAC.

- Support for IPv6 as mandated by the U.S. Department of Defense, Japan, and China. IPv6 support is provided for FCIP, iSCSI, and management traffic routed both in band and out of band.

- FIPS 140-2 compliant as mandated by the U.S. federal government.

Summary

This chapter covers the different storage connectivity options in the data center, the different storage communication and transport protocols, and the Cisco MDS 9000 family of Fibre Channel switches. The following information was also covered:

- The requirements for more complex storage infrastructures in the data centers are dictated by the requirements of the applications.

- The communication between the host and the storage device uses block-based and file-based storage communication protocols, which in turn use different transport protocols.

- File-based protocols send the information as files.

- Block-based protocols send the data divided in blocks.

- The Network File System (NFS) is a file-based storage protocol based on the client/server architecture and supported on Linux/Unix systems.

- SMB/CIFS is also a file-based storage protocol supported on the Microsoft Windows Server and desktop operating systems. Using the Samba server, CIFS is also supported on Linux/Unix systems.

- SCSI is a block-based storage protocol. The major participants are the initiator, which is the server, and the target, which is the storage device/system. SCSI uses specific addressing called a Logical Unit Number.

- There are different network storage system designs, depending on the complexity of the infrastructure and the selected storage protocols.

- DAS is when the storage system is directly attached to the host and it's available only to it or through it.

- NAS is when the storage is reachable through a network environment, usually used in data centers where file-based storage communication is implemented.

- SANs are separate physical infrastructures built to provide isolated and secure communication for block-based storage.

- Fibre Channel storage networking is the transport protocol for the SANs.

- In FCP communication, the initiators and the targets connect to the FC switches using specialized communication adapters called HBAs.

- Historically, different FCP topologies have evolved.

- The FCP topologies are point-to-point, arbitrated loop, and switched fabric.

- The point-to-point topology involves DAS connectivity that uses the FCP and HBAs.

- The arbitrated topology is based on ring-type communication. It is limited to 127 devices.

- It is better to use a hub in an arbitrated loop topology to avoid disruptions because of HBA failures.

- The switched fabric topology is also known as a SAN. It is built by using FC switches to create a communication environment for the initiators and the targets.

- The iSCSI protocol transports the SCSI protocol commands over an IP network by encapsulating the data in IP packets. The TCP is responsible for the secure transmission.

- The NVMe standard allows the NAND flash storage devices to communicate without the limitations of the SCSI protocol and to be accessed as memory.

- NVMe over Fabric allows the NVMe storage devices to be accessed by initiators over different communication infrastructures.

- Cisco Systems is one of the major vendors of storage network equipment.

- The Cisco MDS 9000 family of switches includes the Cisco Fibre Channel switches.

- The Cisco MDS 9700 switches are director-class, modular chassis-based devices.

- The Cisco MDS 9000 16Gbps and 32Gbps switches are suitable for the SAN access layer.

- The Cisco MDS 9250i multiservice switch supports different storage communication protocols such as FCP, FCIP, FCoE, and iSCSI, allowing for the implementation of complex and flexible storage communication.

Reference

"Storage Area Networking," https://www.cisco.com/c/en/us/products/storage-networking/index.html

Chapter 11

Fibre Channel Protocol Fundamentals

The previous chapter discussed the building blocks of storage in the data center. The need for scalability and flexibility led to the use of specialized storage infrastructures called storage area networks (SANs). The transport protocol is the Fibre Channel Protocol (FCP). The name comes from the British English spelling and the fact that the storage networks on which the FCP operates are built using fiber optical physical connectivity between the initiators, the targets, and the FC switches. In the SAN, the FCP runs on all the layers of the data center stack—from the physical layer, up to the applications that utilize the storage systems. In this chapter, you will get acquainted with the FCP layered model, the components operating on the different layers, and the relationship between them, such as the FC port types, the physical and logical addressing, and the routing of the FC frames. When you think of storage communication, and specifically the type that happens over the FCP, the most important aspect is the reliable and secure transmission of the FC frames. To understand how this happens in the FCP, we will look at the connections established at the different levels to create the secure transmission environment and the processes that control it.

Fibre Channel Layered Model

In the networking world, a layered model is often used to describe a complex relationship that affects multiple levels with different functions. One such model is the Open Systems Interconnection (OSI) model, which describes the communications between computing systems. Another layered model that describes the internetworking between computing systems is the 4-layer TCP/IP model.

In the same way, the FCP is described and defined by using a layered model. The FCP consists of five layers, which are illustrated in Figure 11-1:

- **FC-4 Upper Layer Protocol (ULP) mapping:** Responsible for the protocol mapping. Identifies which ULP is encapsulated into a protocol data unit (PDU) for delivery to the FC-2 layer. The major ULP using the FCP is the SCSI protocol. There are others, including the Internet Protocol (IP), that are also defined in the standard.

■ **FC-3 Common Services:** The common services for the advanced FCP services, such as striping (multiple node ports transmitting), hunt groups (multiple node ports receiving), multicast, encryption, and redundancy algorithms.

■ **FC-2 Signaling:** This is the layer where the transport mechanism exists. The following functions, defined by the standard, happen at this layer:

  ■ **Ordered Set:** A 4-byte transmission word that contains important operations for the frames, such as Start-of-Frame (SOF) and End-of-Frame (EOF), as well as the so-called primitive signals, such as Idle and Receiver Ready (R_RDY), which control when the transmitting side will start to send frames and such.

  ■ **FC Frame:** The block of communication in the FCP. There are two types of FC frames: the Data frame and the Link_control frames. The Data frame contains the ULP data blocks that have to be carried to the destination. The Link_control frames are the Acknowledge (ACK) and the Link_response frames. The FC frames start with a 4-byte start of frame (SOF) field, followed by a 24-byte Frame header, the Data field (2112 bytes), and the CRC Error check field, and they end with the 4-byte end of frame (EOF) field.

  ■ **Sequence:** A sequence of frames sent in one direction. Each frame in that sequence has a unique sequence number, as the frames have to arrive in the same order in which they were sent. This is because the data is divided into blocks and encapsulated in the FC frames. If the frames arrive out of order, the data will be lost. Besides the data sequences, which exchange the data blocks, there are also the primitive sequences. They are used to indicate the condition of a port. They are supported by the protocol standard Primitive Sequences are Offline (OLS), Not Operational (NOS), Link Reset (LR), and Link Reset Response (LRR).

  ■ **Exchange:** All the sequences in one conversation between an initiator and a target.

  ■ **Protocol:** The protocols for the FCP services. Here are the protocols running on this layer:

    ■ **Primitive Sequencing Protocol:** Responsible for the exchange of primitive sequences.

    ■ **Fabric Login Protocol:** How the initiator or the target connect to the switched fabric and what information is exchanged.

    ■ **Port Login Protocol:** Responsible for the exchange of the service parameters and capabilities between two ports.

    ■ **Data Transfer Protocol:** Used for transferring data to the ULPs.

    ■ **Port Logout Protocol:** Used to disconnect a port from another port and to free resources.

- **Flow control:** The mechanism at FC-2 responsible for controlling the speed at which the FC frames are exchanged between two ports and for avoiding dropped frames.

- **FC-1 encoding:** Defines the rules for the serial encoding and decoding of the data to be transmitted over the fiber. The 8b/10b encoding means that each 8 bits of data are put in a 10-bit transmission character. This is related to how the signals are transmitted over the physical media and the clock synchronization for this serial communication. These details go beyond the scope of the discussion in this chapter. The 8b/10b encoding is used on links with speeds of 1, 2, 4, and 8Gbps. For the faster links, with speeds of 10 and 16Gbps, the encoding used is 64b/66b. The 32, 64, and 128Gbps links use the 256b/257b encoding. The faster links are backward compatible with the slower links with the 8b/10b encoding.

- **FC-0 physical layer:** Defines the characteristics of the physical connectivity, including the fiber optics, transceivers, and electrical signals.

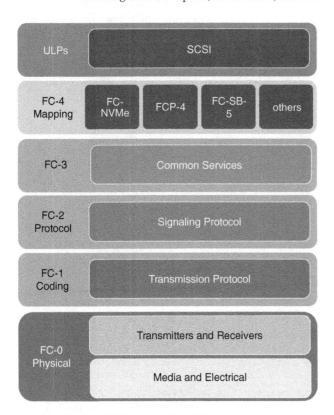

Figure 11-1 *FCP Layered Model*

Fibre Channel Protocol Port Types

The FC switched fabric includes three participants: the initiator, the target, and the FC switch. The initiator and the target are end devices, or *nodes*, that connect to the FC switches that build the switched fabric. All of the participants connect to each other through physical ports. In the FCP world, these ports are assigned different roles, depending on which participant they belong to, what they are connected to, and what communication is allowed through them. The assigned role defines the port type.

Here are the main FC port types (see Figure 11-2):

- **N_Port:** This stands for "node port." This is the port of the HBA that is installed on an initiator or a target node. The N_Port represents a node. A node can have more than one N_Port.

- **F_Port:** The "fabric port" is a port on the FC switch that connects to an N_Port. The F_Port is the point where the end node, initiator, or target connects to the fabric. In standard connectivity, one N_Port always connects to one F_Port. Later will be mentioned some virtualized FC port types, but they will be discussed in more detail when we discuss the topics NPV/NPIV and FCoE.

- **E_Port:** The "expansion port" describes a port on the fabric switch that connects to another fabric switch, thus expanding the switched fabric. The E_Port to E_Port links are called Inter-Switch Links (ISLs).

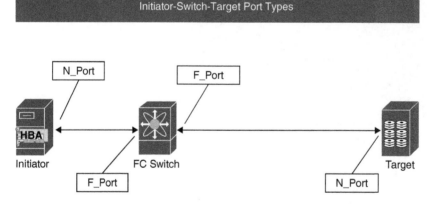

Figure 11-2   *Main FC Port Types*

After that, we have the FC-AL topology, where the devices are connected in a loop directly to each other, or through an FC hub. Here are the FC port types for this connectivity (see Figure 11-3):

- **L_Port:** This is the "loop port," which supports the arbitrated loop (AL) topology functions.

- **NL_Port:** This is a "node loop port," which connects to an FC hub in an AL topology.

- **FL_Port:** This is the "fabric loop port," which is an FC port on a switch and is used to connect an FC-AL to the FC switched fabric.

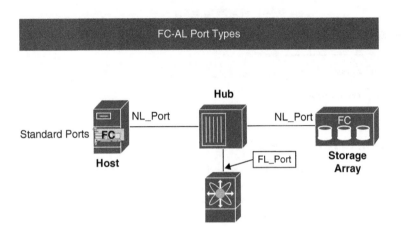

Figure 11-3 *FC-AL Port Types*

Additionally, you can encounter the Fx_Port and the Nx_Port, which are ports that can function as either F_Port/FL_Port or as N_Port/NL_Port, respectively.

When the FCP connectivity communicates over some other transport infrastructure, such as an IP network, the physical connectivity is not native FC. In this situation, virtual FC interfaces, or overlays, are created that are assigned the needed port types and connect to each other using the FCP mechanisms. As illustrated in Figure 11-4, these virtual FC port types are as follows:

- **VF_Port:** The "virtual fabric port" is used as an overlay port on a switch when the communication goes through an Ethernet port. The VF_Port is mapped to the underlying physical port.

- **VN_Port:** This is the "virtual node port," which is the overly FC port, mapped to a physical Ethernet interface in an end node. The VF_Port and the VN_Port are used in FCoE and FCIP communication.

Some additional port types will be discussed later in this chapter.

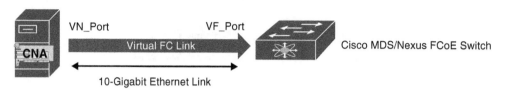

Figure 11-4   *Virtual FC Port Types*

Fibre Channel Physical Addressing

Two types of physical addresses are used in the Fibre Channel Protocol. The World Wide Names (WWNs), also known as World Wide Identifiers (WWIDs), are the physical addresses used in FCP communication. The WWNs are similar in concept to the Media Access Control (MAC) addresses in the Ethernet communication.

WWNs have two main types (see Figure 11-5):

■ **Port World Wide Name (pWWN/WWPN):** This address uniquely identifies one FC port. On one FC device there will be as many WWPNs as the number of FC ports. For example, if an HBA has one FC port, then there will be one WWPN, which will identify that FC port. If there are two FC interfaces, there will be two WWPNs— one for each FC interface. Of course, the FC interface can be virtual, so there will be a WWPN to the virtual FC interface as well.

■ **Node World Wide Name (nWWN/WWNN):** This is the physical address that uniquely identifies an FC device. It can be an HBA or an FC switch. This means that an HBA with one FC port will have one WWNN for itself and one WWPN for the FC port. If there are two FC ports on the HBA, there will be one WWNN for the HBA as an FC device and a WWPN for each of the FC ports.

It is important to know that the WWNNs and the WWPNs have exactly the same format. Because each physical address is used to uniquely identify an FC port or FC device, it has to be different and unique. There are rules for how these addresses are generated and assigned. As they are physical addresses, the FC components come with these addresses already burned in. However, they can be changed, just like the MAC addresses in the Ethernet devices. In this case, it's important that the addresses are unique! An overlap between a WWPN and a WWNN or another WWPN will break the FC communication.

This is very important when you work with the Cisco Unified Computing System, because the WWNNs and the WWPNs have to be created by you when FCoE is used. That's why in the Cisco UCS, WWPN and WWNN address pools are used, which requires careful design and planning.

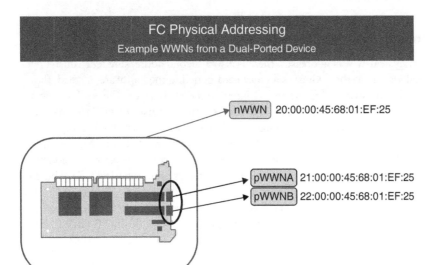

Figure 11-5   *WWNNs and WWPNs*

As already mentioned, both the WWNNs and the WWPNs have the same structure:

■ The size is 64 or 128 bits (the most commonly used are 128-bit WWNNs).

■ They are allocated to the manufacturer by the IEEE.

■ They are hard-coded in the silicone of each FC device.

The structure of a WWN is either 8 or 16 bytes, as the specific format and length are defined by the Network Address Authority (NAA) bits. Then there is the organizationally unique identifier (OUI) of the manufacturer, in addition to other vendor-specific information.

The most common WWN format you will work with in the data center has the following characteristics:

■ A size of 16 bytes (128 bits).

■ The first 2 bytes, which include the NAA nibble and three additional nibbles, can be separated roughly as follows:

■ **10:00:** The NAA value of 1 followed by three 0s. Usually assigned to HBAs.

■ **2x:xx:** The NAA has a value of 2, but here the difference is that the other three nibbles, marked with x's, can be used by the vendor.

■ **5x:xx:** Usually the WWNs assigned to vendors of storage equipment start with 5 as the NAA value.

Fibre Channel IDs

Besides the physical WWN addresses, there is also a second addressing mechanism. It can be called logical, as the addresses are not hard-coded in the hardware; instead, they are generated by the switched fabric and assigned to the FC devices. These addresses are called Fibre Channel IDs (FCIDs) and are used for the purposes of FCP routing and frame transmission. An analogy can be made with the IP addresses in the LAN networks. Used for the same purpose, they are also generated in the network; the differences are that the two addressing schemes are used by different protocols and that the IP addresses are either manually assigned by the network administrators or automatically distributed by DHCP servers. The addressing is defined in the FC-FS-3 standard, where the FCID is referred to as an "address identifier" and has a size of 24 bits. The address identifier, or the FCID, is divided into three 8-bit parts that allow the location of the FC node to be uniquely specified. Here are the three parts (see Figure 11-6):

■ **Domain_ID:** When the switch fabric is created by having one or more FC switches to connect, interact together, and achieve convergence, it becomes one whole entity. As it consists of multiple switches, and each switch has multiple ports, an identifier for each of the switches inside the switched fabric is needed. This is the domain ID—a unique ID assigned to the switch based on a specific mechanism. In general, the switches (if it's a single-switch fabric, there will be a single domain ID), when first connected, establish links between each other and elect a principal switch. The principal switch becomes responsible for the domain IDs selected by the switches in the fabric being unique. Therefore, each switch in an FC fabric has a unique domain ID. Theoretically, there can be up to 239 domain IDs in a switched fabric, as the hex values for the Domain_ID are in the range of 01 to EF, but in reality the most Domain_IDs (switches) operating in a fabric achieved by Cisco is just 100 switches making up the FC switched fabric. Domain_IDs 00 and F0–FF are reserved for the switch fabric services.

■ **Area_ID:** Used to identify groups of N_Ports within a domain (switch). Areas are also used to uniquely identify fabric-attached arbitrated loops. Also, the Area_ID part can be used to encode specific vendor information for components that have specific behavior. Allowed values are in the range of 00–FF (hex).

■ **Port_ID:** Identifies an N_Port in a domain/switch. It can also be said that it specifies which F_Port is connected to the N_Port. This is also referred to as the F_Port:N_Port identifier; as in the FCP, one N_Port can be connected to only one F_Port.

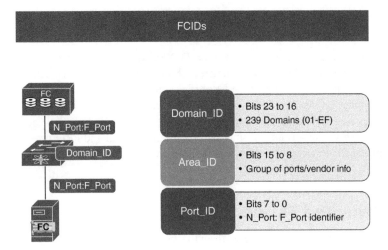

Figure 11-6 *FCID Structure*

When the N_Port establishes a successful link to the F_Port (the fabric switch), which is a successful login to the fabric (FLOGI process, which will be covered later), the N_Port uses an initial FCID of 0x000000 to request an FCID assigned to it. The address manager service, which runs on the switch, generates the FCID, as it uses the switch's Domain_ID, the Area_ID for the switch, and the Port_ID to identify the F_Port: N_Port for the device.

The FCP services use FCIDs as well. These FCIDs are referred to as the well-known addresses. They cannot be used for anything other than their assigned and reserved service. Table 11-1 provides well-known addresses for some of the FCP services.

Table 11-1 *FCP Service Addresses*

Service	Address
Broadcast Alias	0xFFFFFF
Fabric Login Server	0xFFFFFE
Fabric Controller	0xFFFFFD
Name Server	0xFFFFFC
Time Server	0xFFFFFB
Management Server	0xFFFFFA
QoS Facilitator	0xFFFFF9
Alias Server	0xFFFFF8
Key Distribution Server	0xFFFFF7
Clock Synchronization Server	0xFFFFF6
Multicast Server	0xFFFFF5

The well-known addresses are the highest 16 addresses in the 24-bit address space for the FCIDs.

An essential service is the Fibre Channel Name Server (FCNS), also known as just the name server. This server runs in a distributed manner; each FC switch runs its own name server and synchronizes the database with the rest of the switches in the fabric. The FCNS database exchanges information for which WWPNs and WWNNs use which FCIDs, which services are supported, what connectivity is used, which VSAN the device belongs to, and so on. This is important information used by the PLOGI and PRLI processes as well as other FCP services. The information in the FCNS is also very useful for monitoring and troubleshooting the switched fabric.

Building the Switched Fabric

The process of building a switched fabric involves the initial establishment of the links between the devices in the switched fabric, the exchange of information and the negotiations, which happen at the different levels, and the convergence of the different processes and services involved. Besides the establishment of the physical links, where the initial negotiation at the physical level occurs (the exchange of electrical signals to negotiate the pure electrical side of the link), there are multiple similar processes that happen at different levels and aim to build successful relations at these levels between the participants. These negotiations are the Fabric Login (FLOGI) process, the Port Login (PLOGI) process, and the Process Login (PRLI) process and are collectively known as the device login (see Figure 11-7):

- **FLOGI:** Here, the N_Port logs in to the F_Port to which it is connected.

- **PLOGI:** Then, the N_Port logs in to the N_Port with which it will communicate.

- **PRLI:** Finally, the PRLI process ensures that the two N_Ports exchange the needed information regarding the supported ULPs for successful communication between the target and initiator.

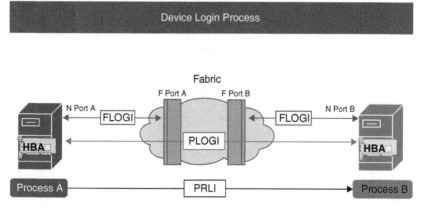

Figure 11-7   *Device Login Processes*

For all these negotiations and exchanges of information to be possible, as well as for the switched fabric to be managed, multiple services run in the FCP, as defined in the FC-SW-6 specification:

- FCNS (Fibre Channel Name Server)

- Login Service

- Address Manager

- Alias Service

- Management Server

- Key Distribution Service

- Time Server

- Fabric Controller

FLOGI Process

After the N_Port and the F_Port are physically connected, the negotiations at the physical layer are successful, and the electrical parameters are in sync, the link negotiation and the registration to the fabric start. This is the FLOGI process, which can be described as the initial bootstrap process that occurs when an N_Port is connected to an F_Port. The FLOGI process is used by the N_Port to discover whether a fabric is present and what its capabilities are as well as to register to it. The fabric uses FLOGI to get the information for the node and assign it an FCID. Once the FLOGI process is successful, the N_Port can start the next process of attempting to communicate with other N_Ports (that is, the PLOGI process).

The steps of the FLOGI process are as follows:

1. The F_Port and the N_Port will reset the link between them, as shown in Figure 11-8. The goal is for the link initialization to start from fresh and for both parties to verify the exchanged parameters and information for this link establishment. This happens by exchanging the **LR** and **LRR** commands.

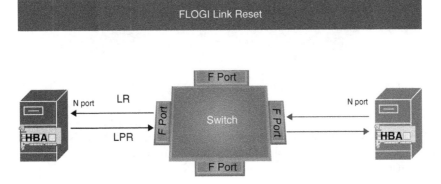

Figure 11-8 *FLOGI Link Reset*

2. After the link is initialized, as shown in Figure 11-9, it will be active and IDLE fill words will flow in both directions on the link. The N_Port will use a source FCID (SID) of 0x000000, as at this time it does not have an FCID assigned by the address manager.

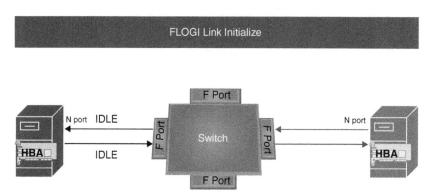

Figure 11-9   *FLOGI Link Initialize*

3. The N_Port will send a FLOGI **link services** command to the switch login server using the well-known address 0xFFFFFE. The N_Port will include its Node name, N_Port name, or the WWNN and the WWPN it uses as well as its service parameters.

4. The login server sends an ACC response frame, as shown in Figure 11-10, that contains the N_Port address in the Destination FCID (DID) field.

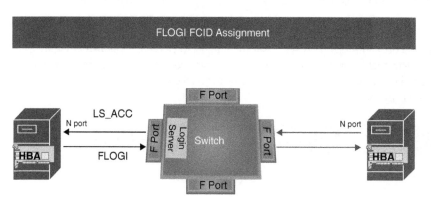

Figure 11-10   *FLOGI FCID Assignment*

5. After an FCID, the N_Port logs in to the fabric name server at the address 0xFFFFFC. The N_Port transmits its service parameters, such as the number of buffer credits it supports, its maximum payload size, and the supported Classes of Services (CoSs).

6. The name server responds with an LS_ACC frame, shown in Figure 11-11, that acknowledges the information is registered. After that comes the next login process—the port login between two N_Ports, when the initiator prepares to communicate with a specific target.

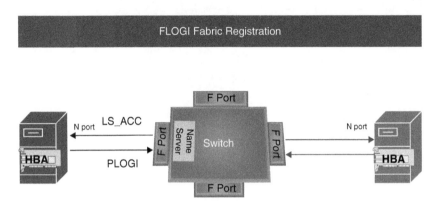

Figure 11-11 *FLOGI Fabric Registration*

To verify a successful FLOGI on Cisco MDS switches, the command **show flogi database** can be used on the command-line interface (CLI), as demonstrated in Figure 11-12. This command provides in the output the information for the N_Ports that performed the successful FLOGI. Which WWNN and WWPNs are used, to which F_Port is connected, and to which VSAN belongs the communication of an N_Port. This is a simple and effective way to find out which node is connected to which switch port.

Verify FLOGI process in the Cisco MDS CLI

```
mds-9100-a# show flogi database
---------------------------------------------------------------------------
INTERFACE      VSAN   FCID        PORT NAME           NODE NAME
---------------------------------------------------------------------------
fc1/1          1      0x3f0000    21:00:00:24:ff:19:c7:30 20:00:00:24:ff:19:c7:30

Total number of flogi = 1.
```

Figure 11-12 *Verify the FLOGI Process*

The same information can also be seen in the Cisco MDS switch graphical user interface (GUI), which is the Device Manager (see Figure 11-13). When you select the FC-enabled interfaces from the menu, you will be taken to a new window where the FLOGI database entries can be seen.

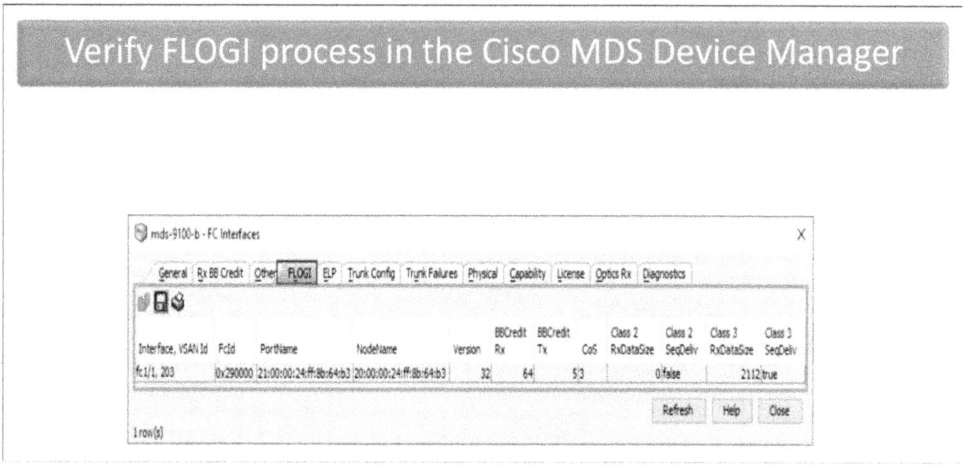

Figure 11-13   *Verify the FLOGI Process in the Cisco MDS Device Manager*

One of the results of the FLOGI process is that the N_Port will be assigned an FCID, and the FCID is also provided in the output of the command.

All the information for the N_Port is also registered in the FCNS. In the CLI, the command to verify this, and also to get information for the N_Ports (or end devices) connected or registered to the switch fabric (not limited to the local switch), is **show fcns database**. In the output of this command, we can see information for the vendor of the end node and its capabilities (is it an initiator or a target?).

```
Cisco-MDS-Switch# show fcns database

VSAN 100:
-------------------------------------------------------------------------
FCID        TYPE  PWWN                    (VENDOR)     FC4-TYPE:FEATURE
-------------------------------------------------------------------------
0x2b273b    N     21:00:c4:19:b4:12:d8:24              scsi-fcp:init
0x4e0041    N     50:06:00:a0:98:cc:c3:0e  (NetApp)    scsi-fcp:target
0x4e0061    N     50:06:00:a0:98:cc:c3:ea  (NetApp)    scsi-fcp:target


Total number of entries = 3
```

From the Cisco MDs Device Manager, you can select the Name Server option under the FC options to check the FCNS database. In a new window will open the Name Server database, as shown in Figure 11-14.

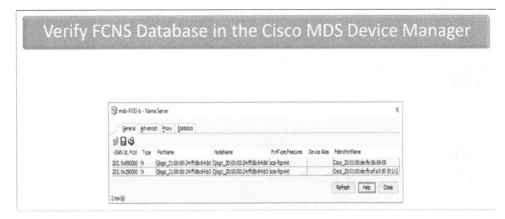

Figure 11-14 *Verifying the FCNS Database in the Cisco MDS Device Manager*

PLOGI Process

After a successful FLOGI process, the N_Port can communicate in the switched fabric. This means sending FC frames to another FC node. That other FC node (either an initiator or target) is connected to the fabric through an N_Port as well. As you already know, FCP is a protocol that is focused on the secure and reliable transmission of the frames. That's why, for the N_Port to be allowed to communicate with a destination N_Port, it needs to establish and negotiate a connection to it. This is known as the port login (PLOGI). The PLOGI must be completed successfully before the nodes can perform a ULP operation.

The steps in the PLOGI process are as follows:

1. The initiator N_Port sends a PLOGI frame that contains its operating parameters in the payload (see Figure 11-15).

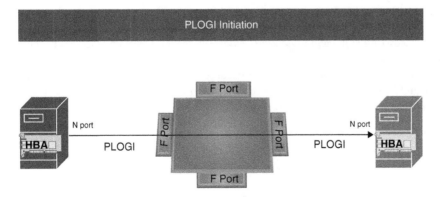

Figure 11-15 *PLOGI Initiation*

2. The target N_Port responds with an ACC frame that specifies the target N_Port operating parameters (see Figure 11-16).

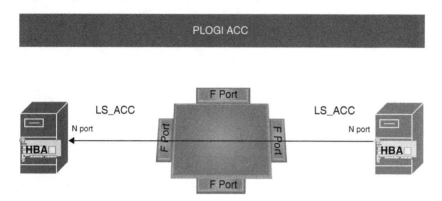

Figure 11-16 *PLOGI ACC*

The number of N_Ports an N_Port is logged in to depends on the communication requirements of this N_Port. It can be connected to a single N_Port or multiple N_Ports at the same time.

After the FLOGI and PLOGI processes are complete, the N_Port can use the following ELS commands to query and verify the fabric and port parameters without performing the PLOGI process and thus forcing a logout of the current session:

- **ADISC:** The address discovery is used to confirm the address of another port or to discover whether the other port has a hard-coded address.

- **FDISC:** Fabric discovery (discover the Fabric Service parameters).

- **PDISC:** Port discovery is used to verify the service parameters of another N_Port.

Process Login

After the successful FLOGI and PLOGI processes, the N_Ports have knowledge of their capabilities and operating parameters. The next step is the PRLI process, which is used to establish a session between two FC-4-level logical processes. It is executed by the PRLI command and allows one or more images of the N_Port to be related to another N_Port. Thus, an image pair is created, or a specific communication between ULPs is negotiated.

The steps of the PRLI process are as follows:

1. The initiator N_Port sends a PRLI frame with the information for its ULP support (see Figure 11-17).

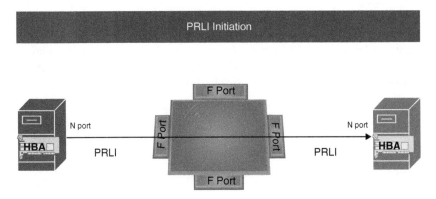

Figure 11-17   *PRLI Initiation*

2. The target N_Port responds with an ACC frame (see Figure 11-18). It contains the information for the ULP support at the target. At this point, a channel has been successfully opened and communication takes place. The relationship between the initiator process and the target process is known as an image pair.

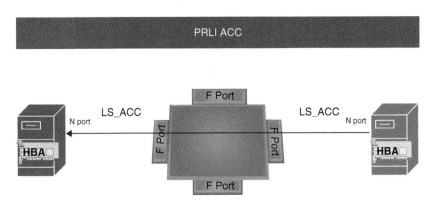

Figure 11-18   *PRLI ACC*

3. At the end of the data exchange, the initiator sends a PRLO frame.

4. The target responds with an ACC frame, and the image pair is then terminated. For a new communication to happen, a new image pair needs to be established.

Fibre Channel Flow Control

One of the major goals for the FC Protocol communication is to create a secure and reliable environment that allows all the FC frames to be received at the destination and to be received in the correct order. You saw how the whole FC switched fabric converges as well as how steps are in place at the different levels and on each link hop to make sure the environment is stable and that the devices communicating are compatible, support the needed FC classes of service and ULPs mapping, and so on. One very important component in the way the FC protocol communicates is the mechanism utilized to control the flow of FC frames in a transmission between two FC ports.

The FCP uses a very strict flow control mechanism based on two major components:

- The size of buffers to store received FC frames on each FC port. These buffers are called BB_Credits, or buffer-to-buffer credits.

- The receiving side always being in control of the transmission.

These two components are the foundation of credit-based flow control, which creates a lossless environment and supports huge traffic loads.

During the link initialization, the FC ports negotiate the electrical parameters, the speeds, and the serialization, but they also exchange information about their capabilities, such as the size of the memory buffers, which are used to store the FC frames received at the port. Once the link is established, each FC port knows the size of the BB_Credits of the port to which it is connected. There are two types of BB_Credits: the BB_Credit_TX and the BB_Credit_RX. The former defines how many FC frames can be stored at the port for transmission, and the latter defines how many frames the port can receive and store before processing. This means that the FC port knows the maximum number of FC frames the connected FC port can receive and store before it can start processing them.

When FC frames have to be transmitted, the transmitting port (Tx_Port), which already knows the size of the BB_Credit_RX at the receiving side (the Rx_Port), will have a variable that has this value. If the other port has reported a BB_Credit_RX size of 64, the Tx_Port will store that value in the BB_Credit_RX variable. The Tx_Port knows that the Rx_Port has space to store four FC frames without the risk of them being dropped due to a busy port that cannot process them.

Now that the Tx_Port knows how many FC frames to send to the Rx_Port, to be able to control the number of frames sent, it also sets another variable, BB_Credit_CNT, to zero.

The Tx_Port is ready to start sending frames, but it cannot because transmission in the FCP is controlled by the receiving side. This means that the Rx_Port must notify the Tx_Port that it is ready to receive the frames. This happens when the Rx_Port sends a receive ready notification (R_RDY) to the transmitting port. The R_RDY notification means that the BB_Credit buffers at the Rx_Port are empty, and it is ready to receive and process the FC frames. Figure 11-19 illustrates the credit-based flow control.

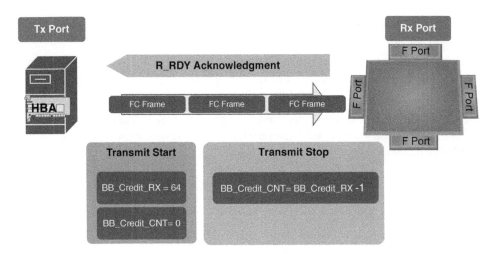

Figure 11-19   *Credit-Based Flow Control*

Once the Tx_Port receives the R_RDY notification, it starts to send frames. With every frame sent, the BB_Credit_CNT value is incremented by one until it reaches the value of BB_Credit_RX minus one. Then the Tx_Port stops sending FC frames, resets the value of the BB_Credit_CNT, and waits for the R_RDY to start transmitting again.

Just as the FCP secures the communication at many levels (like with the login processes, where there is a login between an F_Port and an N_Port), in the same way the flow control is not limited only between two directly connected ports, such as the connections between an N_Port and an F_Port, or between two E_Ports, but extends on the next level of communication—between the two N_Ports of the initiator and the target. At that level, there is another variable called the EE_Credits, which is the end-to-end flow control credits. In the same manner as the buffer-to-buffer flow control, the transmitting N_Port also sets a variable called EE_Credit_CNT initially to zero and then increments it during the transmission.

Additionally, the Cisco MDS switches implement an architecture based on using internal buffer queues and a central arbiter—a component that monitors and controls the switching of the FC frames internally in the switch. It allows an FC frame to be sent to the crossbar fabric in order to be switched in hardware to the egress switch port only when it has received an acknowledgment that the port has enough free resources to store and process the frame.

As you can see, there are various levels of flow control that make the FC communication secure and reliable.

Fabric Shortest Path First

The FC Protocol uses Fabric Shortest Path First (FSPF) to provide the routing functions. This protocol establishes communication with the other switches in the switched fabric using a Hello protocol. The Hello protocol is also used for the FC switches to exchange the FSPF parameters and capabilities.

The FSPF protocol maintains a distributed topology database with the needed functionality to keep it synchronized among the switches in the fabric, including the routing updates.

The FSPF protocol implements a path computation mechanism to calculate and build the routing topology in a way in which the fastest route will be used to avoid the occurrence of loops. It bases the calculation on the following:

- **Link cost:** Depending on the speed of the link, a cost value is assigned. It ranges from 1 to 65535. For example, a link operating at 1Gbps will have a link cost of 1000. If a link operates at 2Gbps, the link cost will be 500.

- **Number of hops between the destination and the source switch:** Each hop represents a node on the path of the Fibre Channel frame.

- **Link state:** Either up or down. A link in down state is excluded from the topology. The FSPF maintains a Link State Database that is populated with Link State Records (LSRs). The standard defines one type of LSR—the Switch Link Record. This record contains the information for the connectivity of each switch in the fabric.

- **Path cost:** The path cost is calculated based on the link cost and the number of hops for the available routes with active state links. The route with the lowest path cost is considered the fastest, although it might not be the route with the least number of hops and is selected by the FSPF for use in the communication between the two specific switches.

- **Avoidance of the occurrence of communication loops:** Runs only on Inter-Switch Links (ISLs) formed from E_Ports and TE_Ports.

- **Per-VSAN instance:** The FSPF runs per VSAN, which means that there is a separate instance of the protocol for each VSAN, and there is also a separate FSPF database set maintained for each VSAN.

Basically, the FSPF is a routing protocol that calculates the routes between the Domain_IDs in a fabric. Each switch has a unique Domain_ID in a switched fabric. In this way, the FSPF gains knowledge for building a database of how each pair of domain IDs, or each pair of switches, can reach each other in the fastest and most secure way. If you remember, the first field of the FCID is the Domain_ID of the switch, which is connected to an N_Port. The FC frame also contains the SID and DID fields, which contain the Source FCID of the N_Port sending the frames as well as the Destination FCID of the destination N_Port, which is the target of that communication. When the source switch receives the FC frame, it looks in the frame header—more specifically, in the DID. From the destination FCID, it looks at the Domain_ID part. Once it knows the destination of the switch, it needs to find a way to reach it (or a route to it), which it can look up in the routing database created by the FSPF protocol. It selects the route with the lowest path cost, calculated by FSPF, and forwards the FC frame to the next hop switch on the path. The FSPF path selection is based on the cost, as illustrated in Figure 11-20.

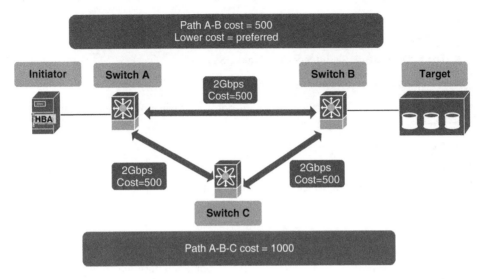

Figure 11-20   *FSPF Path Cost*

Summary

This chapter covered the Fibre Channel Protocol fundamentals, physical and logical addressing, the relationship between ports, the flow control at different levels, and routing in FCP. It also provided some examples from the CLI and the GUI of Cisco MDS switches, in addition to the following information:

- The Fibre Channel Protocol operation is represented by a five-layer model.

- FC-4 is the ULP mapping layer.

- FC-3 runs the protocol's common services, such as multicast, encryption, and so on.

- FC-2 is the signaling layer, which is responsible for the FC frames, the ordered sets, the sequencing, the exchange, the FCP services' protocols, and the flow control.

- FC-1 is where the encoding happens.

- FC-0 is the physical layer, and it covers the electrical signals and the media.

- The ports in the FCP have different roles, depending on what device they belong to and what other port and device they connect to.

- The ports on the end devices, such as initiators and targets, are called N_Ports (node ports).

- F_Port, a fabric port, is the FC port on the FC switch to which an N_Port connects.

- E_Ports, or expansion ports, are the switch ports that connect to other switches, thus expanding the switched fabric.

- The E_Ports create the Inter-Switch Links (ISLs).

- NL_Ports are used to connect in an FC-AL topology.

- The VF_Port and VN_Port are virtual FC ports used when physical communication is realized over Ethernet networks.

- The WWNs are the physical addresses in the FCP.

- There are two types of WWNs: the WWPN identifies an FC port, and the WWNN identifies an FC device, which can have one or more FC ports.

- The FCID is the logical addressing used in the FC routing and communication.

- The FCID consists of three fields that identify the location of the end device: the domain ID, which identifies the switch, the area ID, which identifies the group of ports, and the port ID, which identifies the combination between an N_Port and F_Port.

- FLOGI is the process of an N_Port connecting to and registering with a switched fabric.

- PLOGI is the process that allows an N_Port to establish communication with another N_Port.

- PRLI is the process that allows a successful negotiation at the process level between the initiator and the target.

- Two directly connected ports use a credit-based flow control.

- The communication between two N_Ports uses a similar flow control based on end-to-end credits.

- The Cisco MDS switches have a specific architecture that guarantees internal flow control that's managed by a central arbiter.

- FSPF is a routing protocol that builds the routing topology based on the costs of the links, their state, and the number of hops.

Reference

"Storage Area Networking," https://www.cisco.com/c/en/us/products/storage-networking/index.html

Chapter 12

Describing VSANs and Fibre Channel Zoning

The SANs in the data centers are built to secure the communication between the servers (or the workloads running on the servers) and the storage systems. This is a very sensitive communication, because if data is lost, it is lost forever. If the data is not received in the correct order, it cannot be reassembled correctly, which means it's lost in this case as well. Then there is also the challenge of which initiators are allowed to communicate with which targets. To solve these challenges, the Fibre Channel Protocol (FCP) implements the use of Fibre Channel zones (or zoning). You will learn about this security mechanism in this chapter.

Another challenge is the size and the complexity of the SANs. The FC switches and the needed equipment are not cheap, and the more devices that are in use, the more expensive the SAN. Also, management, monitoring, and troubleshooting become more complicated. To solve these issues, Cisco in its implementation of the Fibre Channel Protocol provides a new feature called a virtual SAN (VSAN).

Because VSANs divide the physical SAN, and because the FC zoning is a mechanism that exists per SAN, both topics are covered in this chapter. It's important to understand the relationship between them, as it affects the communication between the initiators and the targets.

VSAN Overview

It's very common to use the analogy of Ethernet's VLANs when explaining FC VSANs. Certainly, there are a lot of similarities between the two, but do not forget that these are features of two very different communication protocols, so there are some fundamental differences.

So, what is a VSAN, and why do you need it in the data center?

To answer this question, you have to look back at the beginning of the SANs, before
Cisco introduced this feature in the FC Protocol (later adopted to some degree by
Brocade as well). Traditionally, as there was the need to keep the communication within
a SAN protected, under control, and reliable, the approach used was to build multiple
separate physical SANs, each of them dedicated to the specific storage communication
between a set of servers, running an application or a set of common applications, and the
storage system or systems used only by these servers. For example, let's assume that the
servers used by the HR department are running the HR applications and databases. They
will use a dedicated set of storage systems only for their data. The HR servers and the HR
storage systems will be connected to each other with a physical dedicated SAN, built by
Fibre Channel switches. This means that the SAN will be able to communicate only with
the specified servers and storage systems, for the simple reason that only they are physically connected to the SAN. Traditionally, this is how we achieved the fabric isolation
and separation between the needs of different groups, workloads, and so on. Just imagine
how you would need multiple, separate, dedicated, physical SANs, servicing the needs of
other departments, groups, and applications in an organization. Usually, an organization
has multiple different departments and types of applications, with different functionality. Therefore, there was a lot of Fibre Channel equipment, installed and connected in
separate SANs, to meet the requirements for separation and isolation between the fabrics.
That was expensive. Extremely expensive! Another issue was that these Fibre Channel
infrastructures had to be monitored and maintained. These operations were complicated
and difficult. This was also known as a siloed approach (that is, creating multiple SAN
silos), as shown in Figure 12-1

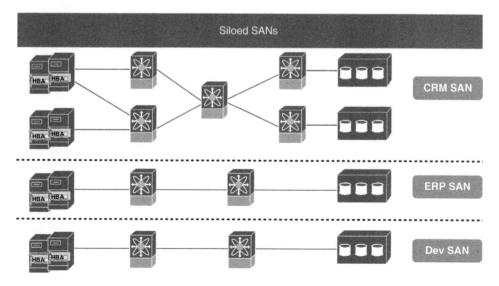

Figure 12-1   *Traditional Siloed Approach with Separate SANs*

The solution came from Cisco: the idea and functionality implemented in their version of
the Fibre Channel Protocol was that the physical SAN could be virtualized, following the

analogy with VLANs that the communication in an infrastructure can be separated and isolated in different groups. However, because this is the Fibre Channel Protocol, there was the need for this separation to be stricter compared to that with VLANs. With the VLANs, based on the VLAN ID the traffic is tagged with, the communication can happen only where this tag is allowed. However, at the same time, it's very easy to allow communication between devices that communicate in different VLANs. This behavior is not acceptable in Fibre Channel communication. That's why the VSAN isolation is implemented in the hardware of the Cisco MDS switches, at the level of the physical Fibre Channel ports. When a Fibre Channel frame enters the Cisco MDS switch through an F_Port, it is tagged with the appropriate VSAN tag in the hardware. Then it can be communicated only through ports, which belong to the same VSAN. Basically, the VSANs do exactly as their name states—they divide the physical Fibre Channel switched fabric, composed of one or more switches, into multiple SANs, but they are virtual. The initiators and the targets can communicate only with other end nodes that belong to the same VSAN. It is not allowed for devices from different VSANs to communicate to each other. Actually, there is a functionality called Inter-VSAN Routing (IVR) that can allow such a communication, but it needs to be specifically configured, and that configuration is complex. In other words, you cannot allow the communication between devices from different VSANs by accident. The traffic isolation implemented with the usage of the VSANs is a huge advantage, as it allows fewer Fibre Channel switches to be used and at the same time have the flexibility and scalability needed by the organization. Figure 12-2 shows the benefits of a VSAN through traffic isolation.

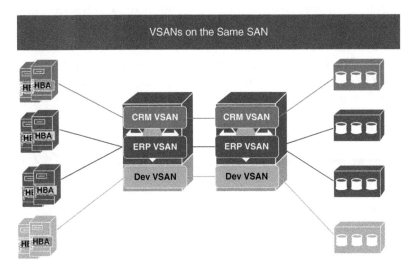

Figure 12-2 *Virtual SANs*

Each VSAN has an ID. The ID is a number in the range 1 to 4094. There are some VSAN IDs that are reserved. VSAN 1 is the default VSAN, and it can be used. It just exists by default and cannot be deleted.

There is the special VSAN 4094, which is used by the system to isolate orphaned FC ports. Orphaned FC ports on the switch are those that belonged to a VSAN, but the VSAN was deleted. These ports cannot automatically move to VSAN 1, as there might be a configuration or end devices connected to them that would cause miscommunication or loss of data. That's why such ports are automatically put in VSAN 4094 and are isolated, which means they can't communicate with any other ports. This leaves the range of user-assigned VSAN IDs from 2 to 4093. However, there is a little bit more to this. Table 12-1 shows which VSAN IDs can be assigned by the administrators and which are reserved.

Table 12-1   *VSAN IDs Allocation*

VSAN IDs	System Reserved	Usage
1	Yes	Default VSAN for all ports
2–4078 and 4080–4093	No	User-configurable
4079	Yes	Exchange Virtual Fabrics Protocol (EVFP)
4094	Yes	Isolated VSAN for orphaned ports

Here are some other attributes of a VSAN:

- **Name:** The name must be unique for each VSAN. A string of up to 32 characters can be used for management purposes. If a name is not configured, the system takes the string VSAN and adds the number as a four-digit string. For example, the system will provide a VSAN with an ID of 11 with the name VSAN0011.

- **State:** The state can be active or suspended. Active state means that the VSAN is configured and enabled, which also enables the Fibre Channel Protocol services for the VSAN. The suspended state specifies that the VSAN is created but it's not enabled.

- **Operational state:** This can be up or down.

- **Load-balancing scheme:** This is the load-balancing scheme used for path selection. It can be based on the source-destination FCID (**src-dst-id**) or the default one, which is based on using the combination of source and destination FCIDs together with the originator exchange ID (OX ID), presented as **src-id/dst-id/oxid**. It means that the communication between a specific source and destination for a specific exchange (or conversation) will take the same path.

The VSAN's goal is to mimic a SAN, and because of that most FCP services run per VSAN. There are separate per-VSAN instances running for some of the FCP services, and other services will use separate databases for each VSAN. No matter the approach, the FCP services must be configured and managed per VSAN. These services are the zone server, principal switch selection and domain ID distribution, management server, and name server.

This being the case, the SAN is not limited only to the theoretical maximum of 239 domain IDs, as each VSAN is a separate virtual SAN, and there is now a theoretical maximum of 239 domain IDs per VSAN. Each switch will have a unique domain ID in each VSAN. This domain ID is unique within the VSAN among the other switches that also communicate in the same VSAN. The principal switch selection service will select one of the switches for a VSAN to become the principal as well as control the domain ID distribution within the VSAN. So, the domain IDs are now limited to 239 per VSAN, and within the VSAN, each of the switches must have a unique domain ID. Because multiple VSANs can be created on a switch, this means there will be a separate domain ID for each of the VSANs. Can the domain ID of a specific switch have the same value for all the VSANs that exist on the switch? It can, if this is configured manually, but this doesn't mean that this domain ID is the same! The domain IDs, even using the same value, are separate and independent between the VSANs. The other important point is that a switch can be elected to be the principal switch for one VSAN but not for another. It is not mandatory that the same switch be the principal for all the VSANs that exist on it. It can be the principal switch for one VSAN and not the principal switch for another.

The E_Ports are the Fibre Channel ports that connect the SAN switches to each other. They expand the switched fabric. The VSANs have a new E_Port mode called the TE_Port. When a port is in E_Port mode, it will allow communication only for the traffic of the VSAN to which it belongs. Also, this means that the other E_Port to which it is connected must also belong to the same VSAN. Otherwise, there will not be communication, and even though the two ports come up, they will stay isolated. If there is a need to carry traffic for multiple VSANs across the E-to-E_Port link, VSAN trunking must be enabled, and the ports will be in TE_Port mode, which stands for trunking E_Ports. The configuration must be the same on both sides of the TE_Ports, and they have to allow communication for the same VSANs. Figure 12-3 illustrates VSAN trunking.

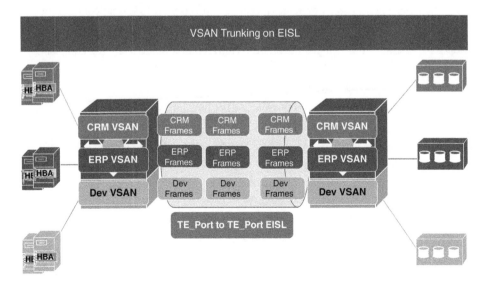

Figure 12-3 *VSANs Trunking*

The same applies if the F_Port of the switch is connected to an NPV switch, and there is the need to carry the communication for multiple VSANs. The F_Port will become a TF_Port (trunking), and the NP_Port on the NPV switch will become TNP_Port (also trunking). The same rules apply in this situation as well; the same VSANs need to be allowed on both sides.

In summary, the VSANs have the following qualities:

- They are equal to SANs, with their own routing, zoning, naming, and addressing.

- They limit the unicast, multicast, and broadcast traffic.

- They are transparent for the initiators and targets, as the membership is defined on the F_Ports.

- An end node can belong only to a single VSAN.

- The membership is enforced on every F_Port and E_Port through which the frames travel.

VSAN Configuration

The configuration examples provided are for a Cisco MDS switch. To configure, modify, or delete a VSAN, you have to be in configuration mode. Keep in mind that even though the useable range of VSAN IDs is large, the switches support only 256 VSANs at the same time.

The steps to create and configure a VSAN are as follows:

Step 1.   Connect to the command line interface (CLI) of the switch using a terminal client and the SSH or Telnet protocol. If this is your first time configuring the switch, you will connect through the console port of the switch.

Step 2.   Log in to the switch and enter the configuration mode using the command config:

```
mds-9200-a# config
```

Enter configuration commands, one per line. End with **Crtl+Z.**

```
mds-9200-a(config)#
```

Step 3.   To be able to create or modify a VSAN, you need to do it from the VSAN database. You enter it using the **vsan database** command:

```
mds-9200-a(config)# vsan database
mds-9200-a(config-vsan-db)#
```

Step 4.   You must create a VSAN with an ID using the **vsan** *X* command:

```
mds-9200-a(config-vsan-db)# vsan 20
mds-9200-a(config-vsan-db)#
```

Step 5. If you don't want to go with the name the system generates, use the command **vsan** *X* **name** *ABC* to set the preferred name:

```
mds-9200-a(config-vsan-db)# vsan 20 name Sales
mds-9200-a(config-vsan-db)#
```

Step 6. Use the **show vsan** command to verify that the VSAN is created:

```
mds-9200-a(config-vsan-db)# sh vsan
vsan 1 information
          name:VSAN0001  state:active
          interoperability mode:default
          loadbalancing:src-id/dst-id/oxid
          operational state:down

vsan 20 information
          name:Sales  state:active
          interoperability mode:default
          loadbalancing:src-id/dst-id/oxid
          operational state:down
```

Step 7. Using the **vsan** *X* **?** command, you can get a list of options that can be used for further configuring the VSAN. The settings that can be changed are the load-balancing mechanism, the operational state, and the interoperability mode. The latter is used when the Cisco MDS switch needs to communicate with switches from other vendors that do not support the standard Fibre Channel Protocol specifications.

```
mds-9200-a(config-vsan-db)# vsan 20 ?
  <CR>
  -                Range separator
  interface        Add interfaces to vsan
  interop          Interoperability mode value
  loadbalancing    Configure loadbalancing scheme
  name             Assign a name to vsan
  suspend          Suspend vsan

mds-9200-a(config-vsan-db)#
```

At this point, you have created a VSAN and assigned it an ID and a name. You also checked the load-balancing mechanism in use and whether the VSAN was created. The next step is to assign interfaces that will communicate with it or belong to it.

Step 8. To assign interfaces to a VSAN, use the **vsan** *X* **interface fc**X/Y command. With the **?** option, you can see the different supported interfaces on the switch that can be assigned:

```
mds-9200-a(config-vsan-db)# vsan 20 interface ?
  fc               Fiber Channel interface
  fv               Fiber Channel Virtualization interface
  port-channel     Port Channel interface
```

```
vfc                 Virtual FC interface
vfc-port-channel    Virtual FC port-channel interface

mds-9200-a(config-vsan-db)#
```

Then assign the interface, like so:

```
mds-9200-a(config-vsan-db)# vsan 20 interface fc1/20
mds-9200-a(config-vsan-db)#
```

Step 9.   To verify which interfaces belong to the VSAN, use the **show vsan X membership** command:

```
mds-9200-a(config-vsan-db)# show vsan 20 membership
vsan 20 interfaces:
    fc1/20

mds-9200-a(config-vsan-db)#
```

To verify which interfaces belong to which VSAN, use the **show vsan membership** command without specifying a VSAN ID:

```
mds-9200-a(config)# sh vsan membership
vsan 1 interfaces:
    fc1/1              fc1/2              fc1/3           fc1/4
    output omitted
    fc1/38             fc1/39             fc1/40

vsan 20 interfaces:
    fc1/20

vsan 4079(evfp_isolated_vsan) interfaces:


vsan 4094(isolated_vsan) interfaces:


mds-9200-a(config)#
```

From the output, you can see that interface fc1/20 belongs to VSAN 20 and the rest of the interfaces on the switch belong to the default VSAN (VSAN 1). There are no interfaces in the isolated VSAN (VSAN 4094). This step ends the sequence of commands for creating a VSAN, assigning interfaces to it, and verifying the correct configuration.

To delete a VSAN, use the **no vsan X** command (you have to be in the VSAN database to execute it):

```
mds-9200-a(config)# no vsan 20
                        ^
% Invalid command at '^' marker.
```

```
mds-9200-a(config)# vsan database
mds-9200-a(config-vsan-db)# no vsan 20
Do you want to continue? (y/n) y
mds-9200-a(config-vsan-db)#
```

After you confirm the deletion, the VSAN will be removed from the switch, and you can verify this with the **show vsan** command:

```
mds-9200-a(config-vsan-db)# show vsan
vsan 1 information
        name:VSAN0001  state:active
        interoperability mode:default
        loadbalancing:src-id/dst-id/oxid
        operational state:down


vsan 4079:evfp_isolated_vsan


vsan 4094:isolated_vsan


mds-9200-a(config-vsan-db)#
```

You can see that there is no more VSAN 20 on the switch. But, what happened to the interface that was assigned to it? When you check the membership of the interfaces, as shown in Example 12-1, you will see that interface 1/20 now belongs to VSAN 4094 (the isolated VSAN). Therefore, it cannot communicate with any other interface, and it is isolated to avoid any wrong configuration being introduced into the default VSAN (VSAN 1).

Example 12-1 *Interface Belonging to the Isolated VSAN 4094*

```
mds-9200-a(config-vsan-db)# show vsan membership
vsan 1 interfaces:
    fc1/1           fc1/2           fc1/3           fc1/4
    output omitted
    fc1/38          fc1/39          fc1/40


vsan 4079(evfp_isolated_vsan) interfaces:



vsan 4094(isolated_vsan) interfaces:
    fc1/20


mds-9200-a(config-vsan-db)#
```

This is done to force you to check the configuration. If you are sure there is nothing potentially dangerous in the configuration of an interface, you can manually add it to another VSAN. In this case, there is only one VSAN, the default one, and the interface will be manually assigned to it:

```
mds-9200-a(config-vsan-db)# vsan 1 interface fc1/20
mds-9200-a(config-vsan-db)#
```

Example 12-2 shows how to verify that the interface is no longer under the isolated VSAN.

Example 12-2   *No Isolated Interfaces in VSAN 4094*

```
mds-9200-a(config-vsan-db)# show vsan membership
vsan 1 interfaces:
    fc1/1           fc1/2           fc1/3           fc1/4
    output omitted
    fc1/37          fc1/38          fc1/39          fc1/40

vsan 4079(evfp_isolated_vsan) interfaces:



vsan 4094(isolated_vsan) interfaces:



mds-9200-a(config-vsan-db)#
```

The interfaces operating as F_Ports allow the communication of the VSAN to which they belong. By default, this is VSAN 1. They can allow the communication of the traffic for multiple VSANs when trunking is enabled for the interface. This means that the interface will operate in TF_Port mode and will allow the port to process frames with tags from multiple VSANs. The trunking F_Ports can be used when a non-NPV switch is connected to an NPV switch. Both N_Port Virtualization (NPV) and N_Port ID Virtualization (NPIV) are explained in Chapter 13, "Storage Virtualization." That's why this chapter focuses on configuring the trunking on the E_Ports, which form the ISL link between two Fibre Channel switches.

The ports that interconnect two Fibre Channel switches operate as E_Ports. The link that is formed by them is called an Inter-Switch Link (ISL). The E_Port allows the communication for a single VSAN. If you need to allow the communication of multiple VSANs between two Fibre Channel switches, trunking on the E_Ports must be enabled. The E_Ports become Trunking Extension ports (TE_Ports). When the trunking is enabled for an ISL, the link becomes Extended Inter-Switch Link (EISL).

The default setting for the trunk mode is enabled on all Fibre Channel interfaces (E, F, FL, Fx, ST, and SD) on non-NPV switches. On the NPV switches, the trunk mode is disabled by default. You can configure trunk mode as on (enabled), off (disabled), or auto (automatic). The trunk mode configuration at the two ends of an ISL, between two switches, determines the trunking state of the link and the port modes at both ends. Table 12-2 provides information for the possible combinations.

Table 12-2 *Trunk Mode Between Two E_Ports*

Switch A	Switch B	Port Mode	Trunking State
On	On or Auto	TE_Port	Trunking (EISL)
Off	Auto, On, or Off	E_Port	No trunking (ISL)
Auto	Auto	E_Port	No trunking (ISL)

To configure the ISL, the two Fibre Channel interfaces need to be connected to each other and configured to operate in E_Port mode. Example 12-3 provides an example of such a configuration.

Example 12-3 *Configuring Port Mode E*

```
mds-9100-a# conf t
Enter configuration commands, one per line.  End with CNTL/Z.
mds-9100-a(config)# interface fc1/2
mds-9100-a(config-if)# switchport mode ?
  E     E mode
  F     F mode
  Fx    Fx mode
  NP    NP port mode for N-Port Virtualizer (NPV) only
  SD    SD mode
  auto  Auto mode

mds-9100-a(config-if)# switchport mode E
```

Then you can check the state of the port, as shown in Example 12-4.

Example 12-4 *Verifying the State of an Interface*

```
mds-9100-a(config-if)# show interface fc1/2
fc1/2 is down (Administratively down)
    Hardware is Fibre Channel, SFP is short wave laser w/o OFC (SN)
    Port WWN is 20:02:00:de:fb:ce:d9:00
    Admin port mode is E, trunk mode is on
```

```
    snmp link state traps are enabled
    Port vsan is 1
    Receive data field Size is 2112
    Beacon is turned off
    Logical type is Unknown(0)
    5 minutes input rate 0 bits/sec,0 bytes/sec, 0 frames/sec
    5 minutes output rate 0 bits/sec,0 bytes/sec, 0 frames/sec
      1 frames input,132 bytes
        0 discards,0 errors
        0 invalid CRC/FCS,0 unknown class
        0 too long,0 too short
      1 frames output,132 bytes
        0 discards,0 errors
      0 input OLS,0  LRR,0 NOS,0 loop inits
      0 output OLS,0 LRR, 0 NOS, 0 loop inits
    Last clearing of "show interface" counters :  never

mds-9100-a(config-if)#
```

The port is down, as it is not enabled yet. The other side also needs to be configured and enabled for the ports to come up and operational.

From the output you can see that the port is in E mode and that the trunking is on, which is the default setting.

There is also another very interesting piece of information that is provided in this output—the port VSAN is 1, which means that the interface belongs to VSAN 1 at this moment. However, there is no information about which VSANs are allowed if the interface trunk mode is enabled. This can be checked with the following command:

```
mds-9100-a(config-if)# sh int fc1/1 trunk vsan
fc1/1 is not trunking
mds-9100-a(config-if)#
```

The trunk mode is set to on, but the interface is not trunking because it is not enabled; it didn't create an ISL and negotiate the trunking with the opposite port.

When the same configuration is performed on the other switch and the two E_Ports are enabled, the output will be different, as shown in Example 12-5.

Example 12-5 *Verify ISL Trunking and an Isolated VSAN 999*

```
mds-9100-a(config-if)# sh int fc1/2
fc1/2 is trunking
    Hardware is Fibre Channel, SFP is short wave laser w/o OFC (SN)
    Port WWN is 20:02:00:de:fb:ce:d9:00
    Peer port WWN is 20:02:00:de:fb:56:6d:a0
    Admin port mode is E, trunk mode is on
    snmp link state traps are enabled
    Port mode is TE
    Port vsan is 1
    Admin Speed is auto max 32 Gbps
    Operating Speed is 16 Gbps
    Rate mode is dedicated
    Port flow-control is R_RDY

    Transmit B2B Credit is 64
    Receive B2B Credit is 500
    B2B State Change: Admin(on), Oper(up), Negotiated Value(14)
    Receive data field Size is 2112
    Beacon is turned off
    Logical type is core
    Trunk vsans (admin allowed and active) (1,999)
    Trunk vsans (up)                       (1)
    Trunk vsans (isolated)                 (999)
    Trunk vsans (initializing)             ()

    Last clearing of "show interface" counters :  never

mds-9100-a(config-if)#
```

From this output you can see that the ISL is up and trunking, which means Extended Inter-Switch Link (EISL). The port operates in TE mode. This means that the two ports negotiated the trunking because it is set to on by default on both sides.

Regarding the trunking, there is also the important information of which VSANs are allowed to communicate over the EISL. By default, all the VSANs that exist on a Fibre Channel switch are allowed on the EISL, but the same VSANs must also exist on the other switch. Otherwise, as you can see from the output, the VSANs that do not exist on the two switches will become isolated, or the frames tagged in these VSANs will not be allowed to traverse the link. In the example, VSAN 999 is isolated, as it exists only on one of the switches. That's why only VSAN 1 is allowed over this EISL.

When the same VSAN is created on the other switch, the situation will change, and the output in Example 12-6 shows that VSAN 999 is now up and trunking on the link as well.

Example 12-6   *All VSANs Trunking*

```
mds-9100-a(config-if)# sh int fc1/2
fc1/2 is trunking
    Hardware is Fibre Channel, SFP is short wave laser w/o OFC (SN)
    Port WWN is 20:02:00:de:fb:ce:d9:00
    Peer port WWN is 20:02:00:de:fb:56:6d:a0
    Admin port mode is E, trunk mode is on
    snmp link state traps are enabled
    Port mode is TE
    Port vsan is 1
    Admin Speed is auto max 32 Gbps
    Operating Speed is 16 Gbps
    Rate mode is dedicated
    Port flow-control is R_RDY

    Transmit B2B Credit is 64
    Receive B2B Credit is 500
    B2B State Change: Admin(on), Oper(up), Negotiated Value(14)
    Receive data field Size is 2112
    Beacon is turned off
    Logical type is core
    Trunk vsans (admin allowed and active) (1,999)
    Trunk vsans (up)                       (1,999)
    Trunk vsans (isolated)                 ()
    Trunk vsans (initializing)             ()
--More--
```

There is an option to define which VSANs will be allowed over a specific port.

It is very important to remember that when a VSAN is allowed to communicate over an ISL or EISL, it is not so much about connecting two VSANs but rather merging them and extending the switched fabric. This means that now the services for that VSAN will extend over these two (or more) switches.

Another important note is that the examples and explanations are given using a two-switch setup, but this does not limit the number of switches that connect together to extend the fabric to two. If you remember from previous discussions, the theoretical limit of switches forming a switched fabric is 249.

Fibre Channel Zoning

The concept of using zones and zoning is the basic security mechanism in the Fibre Channel Protocol standard. With the many different types of servers and storage devices on the network, the need for security is crucial. For example, if a host were to access a disk that another host is using, potentially with a different operating system, then the data on the disk could become corrupted. The zoning provides security within a single fabric, whether physical or logical, by restricting and controlling the access between initiators and targets. The zoning is very similar to the access control list (ACL) mechanism used in the IT as a whole, as the zones are sets of explicit rules that specify which initiator will be allowed to access the resources of which target. Think of an environment in which you have an explicit deny for any communication, and then by using these rules, you can allow very specific communication. In the previous section we discussed VSANs, but here it is important to note that the zoning is per switched fabric, and because the VSANs are logical switched fabrics, the zoning is created and executed on a per-VSAN basis. This also means that the zoning configuration in one VSAN has nothing to do with the zoning configuration in another VSAN. Here, you can see that the Cisco implementation of the Fibre Channel Protocol actually allows for using two layers to virtualize the physical SAN and to control the communication in more detail. These layers are the VSANs and the zoning.

The goals and benefits of the zoning can be summarized as follows:

- Zoning provides a means of restricting visibility and connectivity among devices that share the same SAN fabric.

- The primary goal is to prevent certain devices from accessing other fabric devices.

- Zoning provides basic device security.

Understanding zoning correctly is important for creating and deploying stable switched fabrics. Oftentimes the "limitations" of the zoning are discussed, with the idea that it is supposed to provide other functions such as load balancing (bandwidth allocation) or redundancy.

Zoning was designed to be a simple and effective security mechanism only! It prevents devices from communicating with other unauthorized devices. That's it—nothing more, nothing less.

Because of that, I do not like to discuss the "limitations" of the zoning mechanism. Instead, I focus on what it is and how it can be used. When one understands what zoning is, how it is implemented and operates, what its options are, and how to configure and manage it, then the switched fabric is stable and secure.

The specific rules of engagement for the zones are as follows (see Figure 12-4):

- The zoning is mandatory in a Fibre Channel switched fabric. It is not optional.

- Until an initiator and a target belong to a zone, they cannot see each other.

- The zone is a mapping between initiators and targets.

- A zone can have one member, no members at all, or multiple members.

- Zones can be overlapping, which means that an initiator or a target can be a member of multiple different zones.

- The zoning configuration is per VSAN.

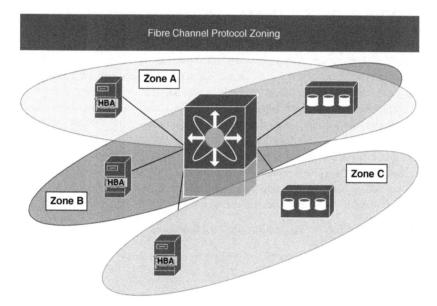

Figure 12-4   *Fibre Channel Zones*

The zoning access control is enforced in two ways:

- **Hard zoning**

   - Enforced as access control lists (ACLs) in the hardware of the Fibre Channel port.

   - The ACL rules are applied to the whole data path, which means that these limitations are applied in the hardware of every switch port on the path.

   - The initiator cannot communicate with a wrong target.

   - This is the default mode of operation on Cisco Fibre Channel switches. No need to be changed to soft zoning.

- **Soft zoning**

   - Software-based limitations enforced by the name server.

   - The name server responds to discovery queries only with the devices that are in the zones of the requester.

   - The initiator can access a target, if the FCID is known.

   - Soft zoning is not recommended.

The soft zoning is based on a mechanism that relies on the information the name server returns to the end devices, when they log in to the fabric and try to discover it. Then the FCNS returns a list of the devices that can be accessed by the end device. These are the devices that are configured to be in the same zones with the end device that requested this information. In other words, the end device will know only of the devices that the name server told it about. Then it will be able to communicate with them, as it knows their addresses from the information in the FCNS response. This means that if the FCID of a different target becomes known to this end device, regardless of whether or not that FCID was in the response from the name server, communication will be possible because there is nothing else on the path to apply the limitations in the zoning configuration.

This is the major reason why soft zoning is not recommended.

With hard zoning, the control is total, as the limitations in the zoning configuration are applied to each of the ports on the communication path between an initiator and a target. They are applied in the silicone of the ports and are enforced on each frame of the communication.

Zoning Configuration

The configuration of the zoning on the Cisco MDS and Nexus switches is specific to Cisco's implementation of the Fibre Channel Protocol, and even though it is based on the Fibre Channel Protocol standard, there's still the need to have a more flexible approach that also considers features such as the VSANs—something that did not exist on other FCP-capable switches until recently.

The zone is a list of members. The members can communicate with each other. Because the zone is an ACL with permit statements, when members are added, the system generates the needed amount of permit rules to cover all the possible communication between the members. The formula to calculate the number of ACL entries based on the number of members (n) is $n*(n-1)$. This means that if there are eight initiators and one target, the number of ACLs the switch will have to generate is 72! This is a huge number, and a lot of the resources of the switch will be consumed. At the same time, if you have a zone that has one initiator and one target as members, you can easily find out by using the same formula that the number of ACLs needed is two! If you take the first example of eight initiators and one target and convert that zone into eight separate one-to-one zones, one for each initiator, with the target belonging to all of them, then you will have two ACLs per zone, with eight zones, for a total of 16 ACLs. This is a significantly smaller number than 72. Also, in that zone with eight initiators and one target, most of these permissions will be controlling the communication between initiators, which is a waste of resources. That's why it is always recommended to have multiple one-to-one zones, then a few zones, but each with multiple members. It is also true that in data centers with a huge number of initiators and targets, this approach can be an administrator's nightmare. To help solve this challenge, Cisco has implemented a feature called Smart Zoning, but it's not covered in this book.

Here are the two main approaches to creating zones:

- **Multi-initiator, single target:** The addresses of multiple initiators and the address of a single target are placed in the same zone. Multiple devices (initiators) are able to access the same target. The drawback is that each such zone generates more ACLs, which results in more hardware resources being used.

- **Single-initiator, single target:** The address of a single initiator and the address of a single target are placed in the same zone. A single device (initiator) is able to access a single target. This results in optimal hardware resource utilization, but it's an administrator's nightmare in environments with a huge number of end nodes.

The members are added using one of the following identities:

- WWN address (usually the WWPN).

- FCID.

- IP address (iSCSI).

- Symbolic node name.

- Device alias or Fibre Channel alias. (The Cisco MDS switches have the option to specify an alias (an administrator-friendly name) that maps to the WWPN of the end node.)

When the needed zones are created, they are combined into a group, which is called a *zoneset*. On a switch there can be multiple zonesets, each containing different zones with different configuration. The group of all the zonesets that exist on a switch is called a *full zoneset*. Figure 12-5 illustrates the difference between a full zoneset and an active zoneset.

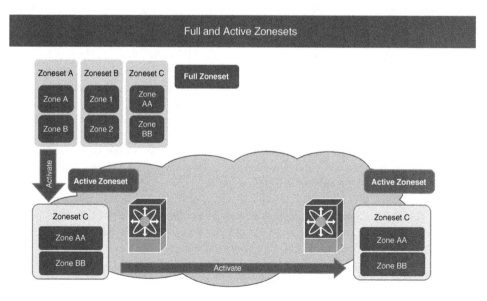

Figure 12-5 *Fibre Channel Full and Active Zonesets*

The next step is to enforce one of the zonesets. This is called "activating a zoneset." A copy of this zoneset is created that is read-only; in other words, it cannot be modified. The copy is sent to all the switches that have ports belonging to the same VSAN. The ACL rules from the zones in this zoneset are applied to the silicone of the ports on the switches. Only one zoneset can be active per VSAN.

When there is a need to modify the active zoneset, changes are made in the original zoneset (that is, the one that was activated). As you'll remember, the active zoneset is a copy, which means that for the changes to be enforced, a new activation is required. Then the modified zoneset will be activated, and the currently active one will be deactivated.

This also means that if one zoneset has been activated and then you activate another zoneset, the same thing will happen—the currently active zoneset will be deactivated and the new one will become active.

To configure the zoning, your first task is to create the needed zones, and for that you need to know the identities of the members you want to add to the zones. You will be working with VSAN 999, and to find the initiators and targets in it, you use the **sh fcns data vsan 999** command, as shown in Example 12-7.

Example 12-7 *Output from the FCNS Command for a Specific VSAN*

```
mds-9200-a(config)# sh fcns data vsan 999


VSAN 999:

-----------------------------------------------------------------------
FCID        TYPE  PWWN                     (VENDOR)      FC4-TYPE:FEATURE
-----------------------------------------------------------------------
0x0c0000    N     21:00:f4:e9:d4:58:d7:88                scsi-fcp:init
0x360000    N     21:00:00:11:0d:40:af:00                scsi-fcp:target


Total number of entries = 2
mds-9200-a(config)#
```

There is one initiator and one target in this VSAN.

You can check the current zoning configuration as follows:

```
mds-9200-a(config)# show zone vsan 999
Zone not present
mds-9200-a(config)# show zoneset vsan 999
Zoneset not present
mds-9200-a(config)#
```

There is no zoning-related configuration for VSAN 999. This also means that the initiator and the target cannot see each other and communicate.

Once you make sure you have the correct initiator and target, the next step is to create a zone. You will have to specify a name for the zone as well as the VSAN to which it will belong:

```
mds-9200-a(config)# zone name Zone999 vsan 999
mds-9200-a(config-zone)#
```

This will take you into the zone configuration submode. Here you can add the members. The identity options for adding members are shown in the output of Example 12-8.

Example 12-8 *Different Options to Define the Member*

```
mds-9200-a(config-zone)# member ?
  device-alias       Add device-alias member to zone
  domain-id          Add member based on domain-id,port-number
  fcalias            Add fcalias to zone
  fcid               Add FCID member to zone
  fwwn               Add Fabric Port WWN member to zone
  interface          Add member based on interface
  ip-address         Add IP address member to zone
  pwwn               Add Port WWN member to zone
  symbolic-nodename  Add Symbolic Node Name member to zone
```

Based on the output of the **show fcns database vsan 999** command, the WWPNs are known for the initiator and the target. They will be added as members of this zone:

```
mds-9200-a(config-zone)# member pwwn 21:00:f4:e9:d4:58:d7:88
mds-9200-a(config-zone)# member pwwn 21:00:00:11:0d:40:af:00
mds-9200-a(config-zone)#
```

Verify that the zone is created with the **show zone vsan X** command:

```
mds-9200-a(config-zone)# show zone vsan 999
zone name Zone999 vsan 999
  pwwn 21:00:f4:e9:d4:58:d7:88
  pwwn 21:00:00:11:0d:40:af:00
mds-9200-a(config-zone)#
```

At this stage, a zone has been created. In order for you to work with it, it needs to become a member of a zoneset; even if there is only a single zone, it still needs to be in a zoneset. When a zoneset is created, a name and the VSAN need to be specified:

```
mds-9200-a(config)# zoneset name ZoneSet999 vsan 999
mds-9200-a(config-zoneset)#
```

Now you can add the zone as a member of the zoneset:

```
mds-9200-a(config-zoneset)# member Zone999
mds-9200-a(config-zoneset)#
```

Next, verify that the zoneset is created and the zone is a member of it:

```
mds-9200-a(config)# sh zoneset vsan 999
zoneset name ZoneSet999 vsan 999
  zone name Zone999 vsan 999
    pwwn 21:00:f4:e9:d4:58:d7:88
    pwwn 21:00:00:11:0d:40:af:00
mds-9200-a(config)#
```

So far, a zone has been created and members have been added to it. Then, this zone was added as a member of the newly created zoneset. However, is it active in the VSAN? To check, use the following command:

```
mds-9200-a(config)# show zoneset active vsan 999
Zoneset not present
mds-9200-a(config)#
```

There is no currently active zoneset for VSAN 999. To activate the zoneset you just created, use the following command:

```
mds-9200-a(config)# zoneset activate name ZoneSet999 vsan 999
Zoneset activation initiated. check zone status
mds-9200-a(config)# 2021 Oct  9 17:40:51 mds-9200-a %ZONE-2-ZS_ZONE_
SET_ACTIVATED: %$VSAN 999%$ Zoneset ZoneSet999 activated

mds-9200-a(config)#
```

The switch also informs you that the zoneset was activated. Now, let's verify it on both the switches that communicate in VSAN 999 (see Example 12-9).

Example 12-9   *Zoning Verification on Both Switches*

```
mds-9200-a(config)# sh zoneset active vsan 999
zoneset name ZoneSet999 vsan 999
  zone name Zone999 vsan 999
  * fcid 0x0c0000 [pwwn 21:00:f4:e9:d4:58:d7:88]
  * fcid 0x360000 [pwwn 21:00:00:11:0d:40:af:00]
mds-9200-a(config)#



mds-9100-a(config)# sh zoneset active vsan 999
zoneset name ZoneSet999 vsan 999
  zone name Zone999 vsan 999
  * fcid 0x0c0000 [pwwn 21:00:f4:e9:d4:58:d7:88]
  * fcid 0x360000 [pwwn 21:00:00:11:0d:40:af:00]
mds-9100-a(config)#
```

From this output, you can come to a few conclusions:

- The zoneset is active on the switch mds-9200-a.

- The zoneset was copied and then sent to and enforced on the switch mds-9100-a, regardless that no zoning configuration was performed on it.

- On the mds-9100-a switch, the full zoneset is empty, as no zoning configuration was performed on it. It only has a copy of the zoneset that was activated on the other switch.

    ```
    mds-9100-a(config)# sh zoneset vsan 999
    Zoneset not present
    mds-9100-a(config)#
    ```

- An asterisk (*) appears in front of the members in the zone in the active zoneset, which means that the members are connected and online in the VSAN and the zone. They will be able to communicate with each other.

This is the flow of configuring zoning on the Cisco MDS/Nexus switches. The configuration was performed in basic zone mode for VSAN 999.

To see the attributes and settings for the zoning in a VSAN, use the **sh zone status vsan 999** command, as shown in Example 12-10.

Example 12-10   *Verifying the Status of a Zone*

```
mds-9200-a(config)# sh zone status vsan 999
VSAN: 999 default-zone: deny distribute: active only Interop: default
    mode: basic merge-control: allow
    session:  none
    hard-zoning: enabled broadcast: unsupported
    smart-zoning: disabled
    rscn-format: fabric-address
    activation overwrite control: disabled
Default zone:
    qos: none broadcast: unsupported ronly: unsupported
Full Zoning Database :
    DB size: 236 bytes
    Zonesets:  1 Zones: 1 Aliases: 0
Active Zoning Database :
    DB Size: 64 bytes
    Name: ZoneSet999 Zonesets: 1 Zones: 1
Current Total Zone DB Usage: 300 / 2097152 bytes (0 % used)
Pending (Session) DB size:
    Full DB Copy size: n/a
    Active DB Copy size: n/a
SFC size: 300 / 2097152 bytes (0 % used)
Status: Activation completed at 17:40:51 UTC Oct  9 2021

mds-9200-a(config)#
```

When the zoning for a VSAN is set to basic mode, the configuration can be made simultaneously from any switch in this VSAN. Also, it can simultaneously be activated in different zonesets from different switches. This can cause a serious misconfiguration, which can also lead to a loss of data.

To avoid such a situation and to address full zoneset database consistency across the switches, you can use enhanced zone mode. In this mode, you perform all configurations within a single configuration session. When a session begins, the switch advertises a lock to all switches in the entire fabric for the specific VSAN. The lock does not allow any zoning configuration for this VSAN to be performed on any other switch in the same VSAN. Once you have finished with the configuration and are sure it is correct, you need to perform a commit with the **zone commit vsan** command. The commit will write the configuration to the local full zoneset database and will synchronize it with the rest of the switches. This approach ensures consistency within the fabric.

In basic zoning, even with distribute full enabled, it is possible that the full zone database is different among switches. With enhanced zoning, it is not possible to change only the local full zoning database, as shown in Figure 12-6.

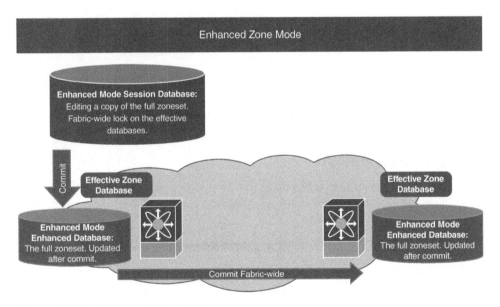

Figure 12-6   *Enhanced Zone Mode*

To change the zone mode, use the **zone mode enhanced vsan 999** command, as shown in Example 12-11.

Example 12-11   *Enabling Enhanced Zoning for a Specific VSAN*

```
mds-9200-a(config)# zone mode enhanced vsan 999
WARNING: This command would distribute the zoning database of this switch throughout
  the fabric. Do you want to continue? (y/n) [n] y
Set zoning mode command initiated. Check zone status
mds-9200-a(config)# 2021 Oct  9 18:09:23 mds-9200-a %ZONE-2-ZS_ZONE_SET_ACTIVATED:
  %$VSAN 999%$ Zoneset ZoneSet999 activated
2021 Oct  9 18:09:23 mds-9200-a %ZONE-2-ZS_POLICY_CHANGE: %$VSAN 999%$ Default zon-
  ing policy changed to deny
```

You can verify this using the command shown in Example 12-12.

Example 12-12   *Verify the Enhanced Zoning*

```
mds-9200-a(config)# sh zone status vsan 999
VSAN: 999 default-zone: deny distribute: full Interop: default
    mode: enhanced merge-control: allow
    session:  none
    hard-zoning: enabled broadcast: unsupported
    smart-zoning: disabled
    rscn-format: fabric-address
    activation overwrite control: disabled
SFC size: 0 / 2097152 bytes (0 % used)
Status: Set zoning mode complete at 18:09:23 UTC Oct  9 2021
```

Zoning Management

When managing the zoning configuration, you need to be aware of some additional guidelines, options, and recommendations. Therefore, before working on the zoning configuration, consider the following:

- Zone membership is based primarily on WWNs or FCIDs.

- Multiple zones can be members of a zoneset.

- The zonesets are created per VSAN.

- Each VSAN can have multiple zonesets, but only one zoneset can be active at any given time.

- When you create a zoneset, that zoneset becomes a part of the full zoneset.

- When a zoneset is activated, a copy of the zoneset from the full zoneset is used to enforce zoning, and it's called the active zoneset.

- An active zoneset cannot be modified.

- A zone that is part of an active zoneset is called an active zone.

- You can modify the full zoneset even if a zoneset with the same name is active. The changes do not take effect until the zoneset is activated with the **zoneset activate name** command.

- During the activation, the active zoneset is stored in the persistent configuration. This process allows the switch to preserve the active zoneset information across switch resets. There is no need to use the **copy running-config startup-config** command to store the active zoneset. However, you need to save the running configuration of the switch to store the full zoneset.

- All other switches in the fabric receive the active zoneset so they can enforce zoning in their respective switches.

- An FCID or N_Port that is not part of the active zoneset belongs to the default zone. The default zone information is not distributed to other switches.

- If one zoneset is active and you activate another zoneset, the currently active zoneset is automatically deactivated. You do not need to explicitly deactivate the currently active zoneset before activating a new zoneset.

Two types of zones are supported on the Cisco MDS switches. Up until now, we have discussed the regular zones. The other type is the default zone.

The default zone always exists for each VSAN on the Cisco Fibre Channel switches. All the end devices that connect to a VSAN and are not added to a zone are automatically put in the default zone. As the zoning is a security mechanism to allow communication between specific initiators and targets, adding them automatically to a zone might pose a significant risk. That's why the communication policy inside the default zone is set to "deny" by default. This means that every end node in the default zone will be isolated.

At this point, the logical question is, why is the default zone needed if the devices will still be isolated until they become members to a zone? The answer is related to the design and scale of your SAN infrastructure. If you are dealing with a significantly small infrastructure and just a couple of initiators and a target, for example, you can set the policy for the default zone to "allow," and the communication of all the devices connected to your switched fabric will be automatically allowed.

This is still a very risky approach, and it is recommended that you create a specific zoning configuration, no matter how small your environment is. Also, you should always set the default zone policy to deny.

Another interesting feature of the Cisco MDS zoning configuration is that you can control exactly what access the initiators will have to the target in a zone. By default, when an initiator and a target belong to a zone, and it is active, the initiator has read and write access. It can retrieve data from the storage system, and it can send data to be stored. But there might be a situation where you want a certain initiator (or initiators) to only be able to read data from a target. Then you will put the initiator(s) in a zone and will set the zone as read-only with the command **attribute read-only** in the zone configuration mode, as shown here:

```
mds-9200-a(config)# zone name Zone999 vsan 999
mds-9200-a(config-zone)# attribute read-only
mds-9200-a(config-zone)#
```

This command can also be used with the default zone.

As already mentioned, the zones belong to a VSAN, or each VSAN has its own zoning configuration. Also, if a VSAN with the same VSAN ID exists on two Fibre Channel switches and they are not connected to each other, these two VSANs are actually separate, different VSANs, regardless of whether you see the same VSAN ID. This also means that each of the VSANs will have its own zoning configuration—one or multiple zonesets with one or multiple zones per zoneset. It is interesting to see what happens when a link is created between these two switches, because then the two separate VSANs with the same VSAN ID will connect and will become one VSAN. In other words, a zone merge will occur between the zone servers of the two VSANs. This is the process where two zone servers need to compare the zones present in each of the VSANs and make sure the zones and the zonesets are the same (that is, the zones have the same members). The question here might be, why do the zone members have to be the same? Or, why do the zones have be the same? The answer is, because the zoning is a security feature, and the goal is always to be in control. Also, there's a risk that suddenly allowing this communication that is not supposed to happen will result in merging together all the zones from the two VSANs, which can lead to serious consequences. Figure 12-7 illustrates the zone merge.

So, the zone merge will happen when the two switches are connected with a link. If the link is an ISL, which means that a single VSAN is allowed to communicate, the zone merge will happen only for this VSAN.

If the switches are connected with an EISL, allowing multiple VSANs, the zone merge will occur for each of the VSANs. Some VSANs might merge their zones successfully, but for others there might be different zoning configurations and the merge will fail. These VSANs will become isolated, and no traffic will be allowed to cross the EISL for these VSANs.

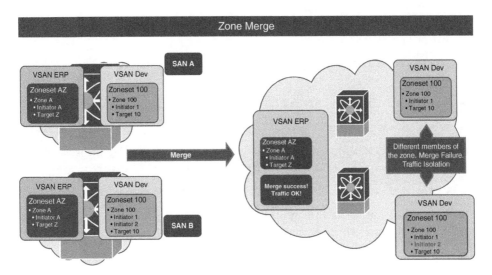

Figure 12-7   *Fibre Channel Zone Merges*

To recover from a zone merge failure, you basically have three options, all of them manual:

■ Import the full zoneset from one switch to the other.

■ Export the full zoneset from one switch to the other.

■ Manually fix the differences in the zoning configuration.

To import or export the full zoneset, the command is **zoneset {distribute | export | import interface** { **fc** *slot-number* | **fcip** *interface-number* | **port-channel** *port-number*}} **vsan** *vsan-id*.

Summary

This chapter covers the Fibre Channel Protocol zoning and the Cisco-developed virtual SAN feature, which allow for the secure and flexible management and control of SANs and for overcoming the limitations in the protocol for scalable and virtualized data center environments. In this chapter, you learned about the following:

■ The VSAN is a feature developed by Cisco and introduced in its implementation of the Fibre Channel Protocol on Cisco MDS switches.

■ A VSAN allows a physical SAN to be virtualized.

■ VSAN traffic isolation is deployed in the hardware of the Fibre Channel ports on the Cisco MDS switches.

- The adoption of a VSAN allows you to better utilize your SANs and avoid having separate physical siloed SANs.

- The VSAN has a name, ID, operational and administrative states, and a load-balancing scheme.

- VSAN 1 is the default VSAN and cannot be deleted, but it can be suspended.

- VSAN 4094 is the isolated VSAN.

- When a VSAN is deleted, the ports that belonged to it are moved to the isolated VSAN to avoid introducing a dangerous configuration.

- VSAN IDs 2–4078 and 4080–4093 can be used for VSAN assignment.

- An ISL allows a single VSAN. When multiple VSANs are allowed, the ISL becomes an EISL and the E_Ports become trunking E_Ports.

- The traffic for a VSAN is tagged in the Fibre Channel Protocol frames.

- To configure a VSAN, you must enter the VSAN database from the switch configuration mode.

- Once a VSAN is created, the next step is to assign ports to become members.

- To check which ports are members of which VSAN, use the **show vsan membership** command.

- The command **show vsan** gives information for the VSANs existing on the current switch.

- Trunking is enabled by default.

- In order for a link to become trunking, it must have the same configuration on both sides.

- If a VSAN is not allowed on one of the sides of a trunking link, it becomes isolated.

- Fibre Channel zoning is a security mechanism that controls which initiators are allowed to access which targets.

- The Fibre Channel zoning configuration is mandatory because the Fibre Channel Protocol will not allow any communication without it.

- Fibre Channel zoning is created per VSAN, and it is only locally significant for the VSAN.

- When Fibre Channel zoning is configured, you first create zones and then add members to them. Then you combine them into zonesets. The last step is to apply one of these sets, and it becomes the active zoneset.

- All the zonesets on a switch for a VSAN form the full zoneset for this VSAN.

- Only a copy of the zoneset that is activated is distributed among the switches that communicate in the same VSAN.

- The full zoneset can be distributed among the switches in a VSAN.

- Changes are made in the full zoneset. Changes cannot be made in the active zoneset.

- Members are added to a zone based on different identity values, such as WWNs, FCID, device alias, and so on.

- It's recommended to use multiple "one initiator–one target" zones.

- In basic mode zoning, the configuration can be changed at the same time from different switches and activated. This can lead to misconfiguration.

- In enhanced zone mode, when you start to change the configuration of a full zoneset, the configuration session lock is applied to all the switches for the specific VSAN.

- Once the changes are complete, you must commit them in order for them to be implemented in the configuration of the switch and distributed to the rest of the switches.

- The command attribute read-only means the initiators are only allowed read access to the targets in a zone.

- Initially, all the devices belong to a default zone.

- By default, the internal communication policy for the default zone is deny.

- During zone merges, the full zonesets on the merging switched fabrics must be the same; otherwise, the merge will fail.

- To recover from a merge fail, you can import one of the full zonesets to the other fabric, export it, or manually fix the configuration.

Reference

"Storage Area Networking (SAN)," https://www.cisco.com/c/en/us/products/storage-networking/index.html

Chapter 13

Storage Virtualization

When a storage area network (SAN) is designed and built, scalability and reliability are fundamental. The Fibre Channel standards, as defined by the ANSI T11 committee, impose some limitation; for example, the maximum theoretical supported number of domain IDs is 239 per fabric or VSAN. As each Fibre Channel switch is identified by a single domain ID, this limitation also puts a theoretical upper limit on the number of switches per fabric. This directly affects the scalability of the SAN.

Cisco has validated stable and reliable performance in a fabric with up to 100 domain IDs (that is, switches), while other vendors have tested 40 or do not specify a number. As a result, the practical maximum number of switches per fabric is 80, if the fabric is built with Cisco MDS/Nexus switches. Also, the number 100 is far from the theoretical maximum of 239. Figure 13-1 illustrates the scalability challenge with the SAN infrastructures in the data center.

When you think about the different physical designs for the SAN in the data center, you must take into account that the blade switches and the top-of-rack access layer switches that are running the Fibre Channel protocol consume domain IDs as well. Additionally, even if you run the Fibre Channel communication over Ethernet, meaning that you use FCoE, the switches will still consume domain IDs.

As data centers grow, the number of devices in a converged fabric increases, and the operational and management issues become more complex. In fact, the whole data center design becomes more complex. This means that having a limitation such as the maximum number of supported domain IDs is not good for the future growth and the adoption of the SAN.

Another challenge is the growing virtualization in the data center. The need to utilize resources at maximum capacity and the added need for flexibility makes virtualization a de facto standard requirement for data center design.

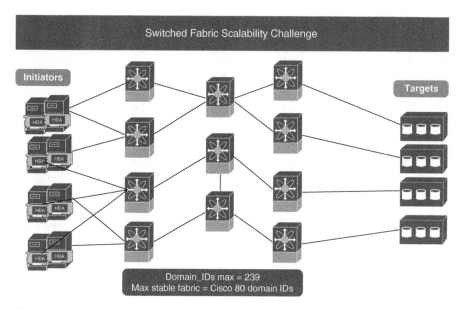

Figure 13-1   *Domain ID Scalability Challenge*

To respond to these challenges, storage virtualization technologies are used, such as running the storage switch in N_Port Virtualization (NPV) mode and using the N_Port ID Virtualization (NPIV) feature.

In this chapter, you will learn about the fundamentals of storage virtualization technologies, what you can use them for, which Cisco devices support them, and how to configure and verify them.

And one very important item of note: N_Port ID Virtualization (NPIV) is a feature on the Cisco MDS/Nexus switches. You either enable it or disable it; it's not disruptive for the operation of the switch. On the other hand, N_Port Virtualization (NPV) is a mode in which the switch operates. Changing between the Fibre Channel switching mode and the Fibre Channel NPV mode *is* disruptive. The configuration must be saved before changing the mode, and the switch will go through a restart. From a designer's perspective and also from the perspective of data center monitoring and support, such a change needs to be planned for and executed during a maintenance window.

Cisco Fibre Channel NPIV Feature

The first of the two storage virtualization technologies that will be discussed is the NPIV feature. What exactly is the challenge and why do you need to know about it?

In a typical physical design, there is a server, or the initiator, that connects to a Fibre Channel switch through its host bus adapter (HBA). There is a physical link between the HBA Fibre Channel port and a Fibre Channel port on the switch. You already know about the N_Port to F_Port connectivity. So, there is a single physical N_Port connected to a single physical F_Port. And the Fibre Channel processes run as follows:

1. **FLOGI:** The N_Port logs in to the F_Port to which it is connected.

2. **PLOGI:** Then the N_Port logs in to the N_Port with which it will communicate.

3. **PRLI:** The two N_Ports exchange the needed information for the supported upper-layer protocols (ULPs) to ensure the target and the initiator can successfully communicate.

If you look at the Fibre Channel ID (FCID), you have the domain ID of the switch to which the server is connected and the port ID. If you remember, the port ID is a unique N_Port-to-F_Port reference between physical ports.

However, in the data center there is now a lot of virtualization. Actually, when it comes to the servers, it is all virtualization, with some minor exceptions when there are specific requirements by the application to run on a bare-metal server, or in other words, to use its own dedicated physical server.

In the case of virtualization, on the top of the physical server you run a specialized operating system, called a hypervisor, that creates virtual images of the physical resources, and then you utilize them to create protected, isolated environments called virtual machines (VMs) to run your applications in.

Let's go back to the example from the beginning of this section and now add virtualization to the server. This means that the communication of multiple different VMs, running on top of it, will go through a single physical N_Port to the F_Port. Fine, but is this going to be possible, as now there are multiple N_Ports that would like to log in to the fabric and get their unique FCIDs? The domain ID will be the same (the area ID is not taken into account), and the port ID will be the same as well, because all of these virtual N_Ports communicate through the same physical N_Port. Figure 13-2 illustrates the N_Port challenge in a virtualized environment.

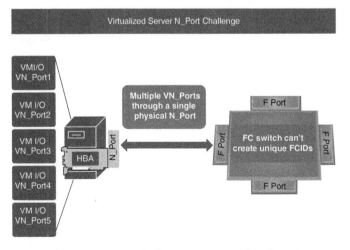

Figure 13-2 *N_Port Challenge in a Virtualized Environment*

To solve this problem, N-Port ID Virtualization (NPIV) was developed (see Figure 13-3). It allows the switch to assign multiple N-Port IDs or FCIDs to a single Fibre Channel host connection (N-Port). This is possible because, on the server side, the NPIV-capable HBA creates and assigns multiple virtual N_Ports to the VMs, and the virtual N_Ports have unique World Wide Port Name (WWPNs) addresses and communicate through the same physical N_Port. Because of that, the switch will see multiple different WWPNs, which will allow it to create multiple different N_Port-to-F_Port references. Based on that, the switch will be able to generate and assign the needed unique FCIDs even if the traffic for all the VMs goes through the same physical N_Port.

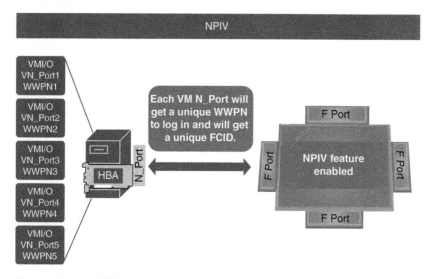

Figure 13-3 *NPIV*

The device login process starts normally, with an initial FLOGI. Then for all subsequent logins, the fabric discovery (FDISC) login process is used.

The NPIV feature is available in the NX-OS and is supported on the following Cisco data center switches:

- Cisco MDS 9250i

- Cisco MDS 9396T 32Gbps 96-Port Fibre Channel Switch

- Cisco MDS 9148T 32Gbps 48-Port Fibre Channel Switch

- Cisco MDS 9148S 16G Multilayer Fabric Switch

- Cisco MDS 9148 Multilayer Fabric Switch

- Cisco MDS 9706 Multilayer Director

- Cisco MDS 9710 Multilayer Director

- Cisco MDS 9718 Multilayer Director

- Cisco UCS 6332-16UP Fabric Interconnect

- Cisco UCS 6324 Fabric Interconnect

- Cisco UCS 6454 Fabric Interconnect

- Cisco UCS 64108 Fabric Interconnect

Support for the NPIV feature on the various Cisco data center products dynamically changes. For the latest information, check the data sheets of the products on the Cisco Systems website.

As mentioned, NPIV is a feature, which means it can be enabled or disabled on the switch in a nondisruptive manner. By default, on the Cisco switches that support it, this feature is disabled, as shown in Example 13-1.

Example 13-1 *NPIV Feature Default State*

```
mds-9100-a# sh feature | include npiv
npiv                 1          disabled
mds-9100-a#
```

The command to enable this feature in the Cisco NX-OS is global. First, you must go into the configuration mode and then to enable NPIV, use the **feature** command, as shown in Example 13-2.

Example 13-2 *Enabling NPIV*

```
mds-9100-a# configure terminal
Enter configuration commands, one per line.  End with CNTL/Z.

mds-9100-a(config)# feature npiv
mds-9100-a(config)#
```

To verify that the NPIV feature is enabled, use the same **show feature** command as before (see Example 13-3).

Example 13-3 *Verifying NPIV Is Enabled*

```
mds-9100-a(config)# sh feature | include npiv
npiv                 1          enabled
mds-9100-a(config)#
```

Cisco Fibre Channel NPV Mode

The Fibre Channel NPV is another SAN virtualization option available in the data center. It solves the challenge due to the limit on the domain IDs that can be used in a SAN fabric. The NPV is a mode in which a Fibre Channel switch operates. In this mode, the Fibre Channel switch does not run most of the Fibre Channel protocol services. It does not run the fabric login server, the Fibre Channel Name Server (FCNS) service, Fibre Channel Shortest Path First (FSPF), zoning, and so on. Because of that, the switch, which operates in NPV mode, does not actually log in to the switched fabric but appears to it as an end device, which allows for communication of multiple N_Ports through the physical Fibre Channel port that connects to the Fibre Channel switch, which operates in Fibre Channel switching mode. A bit of terminology is needed here to make the explanation clear. The switch, which operates in NPV mode, is called an NPV Edge switch. It connects to a switch that operates in Fibre Channel switching mode, which means that it is part of the switched fabric. This switch is an NPV Core switch. It runs all the Fibre Channel protocol services and is part of the switched fabric. As such, it consumes a domain ID for each of the VSANs that exist on it. It also has the NPIV feature enabled in order to service the communication of the multiple N_Ports that comes from the NPV edge switch.

So, the NPV Edge switch is accepted as an end node, as it does not run the needed Fibre Channel protocol services and does not log in to the fabric. However, from the perspective of the initiators and the targets, the real end nodes that connect to it, it is still a Fibre Channel switch. There is still the communication between the N_Ports of the servers and the storage systems as well as the F_Ports (the Fibre Channel ports on the NPV Edge switch) to which the nodes connect. Figure 13-4 shows the NPV Core-Edge topology.

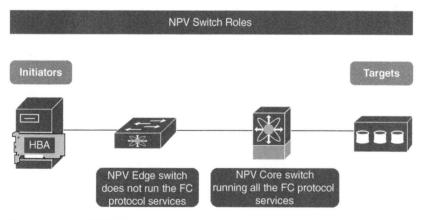

Figure 13-4 *NPV Edge and Core Switches*

The Fibre Channel ports on the NPV Edge switch facing the nodes are operating as
F_Ports, but the switch itself, as it does not run the needed services, and especially the
FLOGI and the FCNS services, can't support the FLOGI requests from the N_Ports.
However, the NPV Core switch, as it is running the needed services and is part of the
switched fabric, can perform the FLOGI. It can also generate and assign the needed
FCIDs, as it has the NPIV enabled. The link between the end nodes and the NPV Core
switch happens as the F_Ports on the NPV Edge switch are mapped to the Fibre Channel
ports that connect to the NPV Core switch. The NPV Edge switch does not switch the
Fibre Channel frames from the nodes to the core switch, but it proxies them to the Fibre
Channel port connected to the NPV Core switch. That's why this port operates as the
NP_Port, which stands for Node Proxy Port. And why do you need to have the NPIV
feature enabled on the NPV Core switch? Because, just like with the virtualized server
connected to the Fibre Channel switch, the NPV Edge switch will present multiple N_
Ports communicating through the NP_Port. In this way, the NPV Core switch will solve
the same challenge and will be capable of assigning multiple different FCIDs. The NPV
port roles are shown in Figure 13-5.

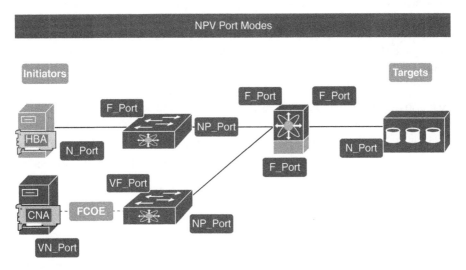

Figure 13-5 *NPV Ports*

The NPV Edge switches support the F_ and VF_Ports for the connectivity of the end
nodes. The latter are used when there is no native Fibre Channel physical connectivity,
and a protocol such as the FCoE is used to carry the Fibre Channel frames over Ethernet
connectivity. And because the FCoE protocol was mentioned, it is important to make
another note here. Sometimes there is a bit of confusion because of the impression that
the terms FCoE and NPV are interchangeable. They are not. NPV refers to the mode in
which the switch operates from the perspective of the Fibre Channel protocol. FCoE
is a way of encapsulating the Fibre Channel frames in Ethernet frames to be capable
of transmitting them over an Ethernet network. It's important to realize that the FCoE

switch might operate in Fibre Channel switching mode or in NPV mode, if supported. As a quick summary, the NPV Edge switch has these characteristics:

- It appears as an end node (initiator/target) to the NPV Core switch.

- It does not consume SAN resources, such as domain IDs.

- It does not participate in the switched fabric.

- It does not run the main Fibre Channel protocol services.

- The NPV Core switch provides the needed Fibre Channel protocol services.

- It appears as a switched fabric switch to the initiators and targets connected to it; that is, it appears as F_Ports.

For the purposes of keeping the explanation simple up until now, the link between the NPV Edge and Core switches was explained as one between an NP_Port and an F_Port. In the data center it is very rare to have a single link between two network devices, as this represents a bottleneck and also a single point for a failure. That's why usually there are multiple links between the NPV Edge and Core switches. Depending on the NPV Edge device, there are different approaches for how the F_Ports are mapped to the available NP_Ports. Usually this happens automatically, as the switch tries to map every new F_Port to the NP_Port, which is either the next one, using a round-robin mechanism, or the NP_Port, which is least busy.

There is also the option to use manual mapping through a traffic map, which is a component from the configuration. This allows the administrator to manually configure which F_Ports will communicate upstream through which NP_Ports.

The NPV mode of operation is supported on the following Cisco Data Center switches:

- Cisco MDS 9396T 32Gbps 96-Port Fibre Channel Switch

- Cisco MDS 9250i Multiservice Fabric Switch

- Cisco MDS 9132T 32Gbps 32-Port Fibre Channel Switch

- Cisco MDS 9148 Multilayer Fabric Switch

- Cisco MDS 9148S 16G Multilayer Fabric Switch

- Cisco MDS 9148T 32Gbps 48-Port Fibre Channel Switch

- Cisco Nexus 9300-GX Series

- Cisco Nexus 9300-FX Series (not the 24-port FX and EX)

- Cisco Nexus 9300-FX2 Series

- Cisco UCS 6332-16UP Fabric Interconnect

- Cisco UCS 6324 Fabric Interconnect

- Cisco UCS 6454 Fabric Interconnect

- Cisco UCS 64108 Fabric Interconnect

Like the configuration of the NPV Edge switch, this is enabled as a feature of NX-OS. However, do not forget that by enabling this "feature," you actually change the mode, and the switch will need to be reloaded to start operating in the new mode. That's why you should first check whether or not the feature is enabled (see Example 13-4).

Example 13-4 *Verifying the NPV Feature State*

```
mds-9100-a(config)# sh feature | include npv
Feature Name         Instance State
-------------------- -------- -----
npv                  1        disabled
mds-9100-a(config)#
```

The second step is to enable the NPV (see Example 13-5). This will be disruptive, as the NX-OS will warn you.

Example 13-5 *Enabling the NPV Feature*

```
mds-9100-a(config)# feature npv
Verify that boot variables are set and the changes are saved. Changing to npv mode
  erases the current configuration and reboots the switch in npv mode. Do you want
  to continue? (y/n):
```

After you confirm that you want to continue, the switch will reload itself, which takes a couple of minutes.

On the upstream Fibre Channel switch (the NPV Core switch), the NPIV feature needs to be enabled (see Example 13-6).

Example 13-6 *Enabling NPIV on the NPV Core Switch*

```
mds-9200-a# sh feature | i npiv
npiv                 1        disabled

mds-9200-a# conf t
Enter configuration commands, one per line.  End with CNTL/Z.
mds-9200-a(config)# feature npiv

mds-9200-a(config)# sh feature | i npiv
npiv                 1        enabled
mds-9200-a(config)#
```

The next step on the NPV Edge switch is to configure the NP ports (see Example 13-7).

Example 13-7   *Configuring the NP Ports on the NPV Edge Switch*

```
mds-9100-a(config)# int fc1/2-3
mds-9100-a(config-if)# shutdown
mds-9100-a(config-if)# switchport mode NP
mds-9100-a(config-if)# no shut
mds-9100-a(config-if)#
```

You also need to configure the ports to which connect the end node in F mode (see Example 13-8).

Example 13-8   *End-Node-Facing Ports on the NPV Edge Switch*

```
mds-9100-a(config)#  int fc1/1
mds-9100-a(config-if)# shut
mds-9100-a(config-if)# switchport mode F
mds-9100-a(config-if)# no shut
mds-9100-a(config-if)# exit
```

On the NPV Core switch, the ports that connect to the NP ports have to be configured as F_Ports (see Example 13-9).

Example 13-9   *Configuring the NPV Core Switch Ports Connecting to the NPV Edge Switch*

```
mds-9200-a(config)# sh npiv status
NPIV is enabled
mds-9200-a(config)# int fc1/2-3
mds-9200-a(config-if)# shutdown
mds-9200-a(config-if)# switchport mode F
mds-9200-a(config-if)# no shut
mds-9200-a(config-if)#
```

Then, the ports will come up on the Core switch, as shown in Example 13-10.

Example 13-10 *NPV Core Switch Ports Status*

```
mds-9200-a(config-if)# show interface brief

---------------------------------------------------------------------------

Interface  Vsan  Admin  Admin   Status   SFP   Oper  Oper   Port     Logical
                 Mode   Trunk                  Mode  Speed  Channel  Type
                        Mode                         (Gbps)
---------------------------------------------------------------------------

fc1/1      1     auto   on      down     swl   --    --     --       --
fc1/2      1     F      on      up       swl   F     16     --       edge

fc1/3      1     F      on      up       swl   F     16     --       edge
```

The same will happen on the NPV Edge switch, as shown in Example 13-11.

Example 13-11 *NPV Edge Switch Ports Status*

```
mds-9100-a(config-if)# show interface brief

---------------------------------------------------------------------------

Interface  Vsan  Admin  Admin   Status   SFP   Oper  Oper   Port     Logical
                 Mode   Trunk                  Mode  Speed  Channel  Type
                        Mode                         (Gbps)
---------------------------------------------------------------------------

fc1/1      1     F      off     up       swl   F     16     --       edge

fc1/2      1     NP     off     up       swl   NP    16     --       core

fc1/3      1     NP     off     up       swl   NP    16     --       core
```

The output of the **show interface brief** command shows that the interface connected to the initiator operates in F mode and is up and that the interfaces connected to the NPV Core switch are operating in NP mode and are also up.

By using the command **show npv status** on the Edge switch, you can check the mode of operation for the external interfaces and the initiator-facing ones (see Example 13-12).

Example 13-12   *NPV Status on the Edge Switch*

```
mds-9100-a(config-if)# sh npv status

npiv is disabled

disruptive load balancing is disabled

External Interfaces:
====================
  Interface:  fc1/2, VSAN:     1, FCID: 0x0a0600, State: Up
  Interface:  fc1/3, VSAN:     1, FCID: 0x0a0500, State: Up

  Number of External Interfaces: 2

Server Interfaces:
==================
  Interface:  fc1/1, VSAN:     1, State: Up

  Number of Server Interfaces: 1
```

On the NPV core switch, you can check the FLOGI and FCNS databases to make sure the NPV Edge switch logged in to the switched fabric as an NPV device and also that the server connected to it was capable to successfully log in to the fabric through the NPV Core switch (see Example 13-13).

Example 13-13   *Verify Successful Fabric Login on the NPV Core Switch*

```
mds-9200-a(config-if)# show flogi database
--------------------------------------------------------------------------------
INTERFACE       VSAN    FCID       PORT NAME              NODE NAME
--------------------------------------------------------------------------------
fc1/2           1       0x0a0600   20:02:00:de:fb:ce:d9:00 20:01:00:de:fb:ce:d9:01
fc1/2           1       0x0a0601   21:00:f4:e9:d4:58:d7:88 20:00:f4:e9:d4:58:d7:88
fc1/3           1       0x0a0500   20:03:00:de:fb:ce:d9:00 20:01:00:de:fb:ce:d9:01

Total number of flogi = 3.

mds-9200-a(config-if)# sh fcns database
```

```
VSAN 1:

-----------------------------------------------------------------------

FCID        TYPE  PWWN                      (VENDOR)     FC4-TYPE:FEATURE

-----------------------------------------------------------------------

0x0a0500    N     20:03:00:de:fb:ce:d9:00  (Cisco)      npv

0x0a0600    N     20:02:00:de:fb:ce:d9:00  (Cisco)      npv

0x0a0601    N     21:00:f4:e9:d4:58:d7:88               scsi-fcp:init


Total number of entries = 3

mds-9200-a(config-if)#
```

Back on the Edge switch, you can see that the **show npv** command has a couple of useful options (see Example 13-14).

Example 13-14 *The show npv Command Options*

```
mds-9100-a(config-if)# show npv ?

*** No matching command found in current mode, matching in (exec) mode ***

  external-interface-usage  Show external interface usage by server interfaces

  flogi-table               Show information about FLOGI sessions

  internal                  Show internal NPV information

  status                    Show NPV status

  traffic-map               Show information about Traffic Map
```

The **flogi-table** option provides information for the end nodes that reached the Core switches through the Edge switch in order to log in to the fabric. It also shows the mapping between the F_Port and the NP_Port (see Example 13-15).

Example 13-15 *Verifying End Nodes FLOGI on the Edge Switch*

```
mds-9100-a(config-if)# sh npv flogi-table

-----------------------------------------------------------------------

SERVER                                                        EXTERNAL

INTERFACE VSAN FCID      PORT NAME            NODE NAME        INTERFACE

-----------------------------------------------------------------------

fc1/1      1   0x0a0601 21:00:f4:e9:d4:58:d7:88 20:00:f4:e9:d4:58:d7:88 fc1/2


Total number of flogi = 1.


mds-9100-a(config-if)#


mds-9100-a(config-if)# sh npv external-interface-usage ?

*** No matching command found in current mode, matching in (exec) mode ***
```

```
>                   Redirect it to a file
>>                  Redirect it to a file in append mode
server-interface  Show external interface usage by a server interface
|                   Pipe command output to filter
```

The option **external-interface-usage** shows the mapping between the server interface and the upstream interface. It also allows you to search based on a specific server interface (that is, F_Port), as shown in Example 13-16.

Example 13-16   *Server-Facing Port to Egress Port Mapping on the Edge Switch*

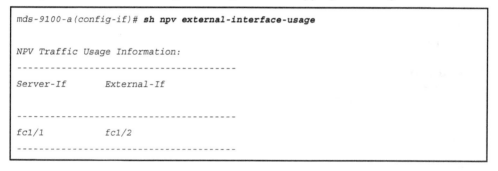

```
mds-9100-a(config-if)# sh npv external-interface-usage

NPV Traffic Usage Information:
----------------------------------------
Server-If      External-If


----------------------------------------
fc1/1          fc1/2
----------------------------------------
```

As you can see, there are enough tools to provide the needed information for the status and the operation of both the Core and Edge NPV switches, as well as the communication of the connected end nodes. Here are some of the benefits of NPV mode:

■ Increased scalability and flexibility, as no domain IDs are consumed.

■ Simplified configuration on the NPV Edge switches, as they do not participate in the SAN fabric. The configuration is limited to configuring the interfaces, the VSANs, and traffic maps, if needed.

■ Simplified troubleshooting, as the Fibre Channel protocol-related configuration is created only on the NPV Core switches and the other switches operating in Fibre Channel switching mode.

■ Simplified troubleshooting on the NPV Edge switches, as less configuration is needed.

■ The NPV Edge switches utilize less resources, which allows for better and more reliable operation. Especially if these are Ethernet switches on which you run FCoE, the resources will be freed to support other services.

Summary

This chapter reviewed the Fibre Channel protocol features, which allow for the use of storage virtualization technologies to overcome limitations in the protocol for scalable and virtualized data center environments. In this chapter you learned about the following:

- The scalability of the SAN is limited by the theoretical maximum of 239 domain IDs per fabric, which can be translated to a maximum number of 239 switches.

- The biggest stable switched fabric is achieved by Cisco with 80 domain IDs.

- A virtualized physical server also has the challenge to log in the VMs in the switched fabric, due to the requirement for a unique N_Port-to-F_Port reference for the generation of an FCID.

- The N_Port ID Virtualization (NPIV) feature solves the virtual server challenge.

- NPIV-capable HBAs are capable of using a separate WWPN for the N_Ports of the VMs.

- The NPIV allows the switch to see a unique N_Port for each VM communicating through a single physical N_Port.

- The NPIV is a feature, and it is nondisruptive to enable it.

- The command on the Cisco MDS switches is **feature npiv**.

- N_Port Virtualization (NPV) mode solved the challenge of limited domain IDs in a switched fabric.

- In NPV mode, the switch does not consume a domain ID.

- The switch that runs in NPV mode is called an NPV Edge switch.

- The NPV Edge switch does not run the core Fibre Channel protocol services and does not log in to the switched fabric.

- The NPV Edge switch connects to an upstream Fibre Channel switch with the Fibre Channel protocol services running.

- The NPV Edge switch proxies the communication of the end nodes to the NPV Core switch, where they can log in to the switched fabric.

- The end nodes still accept the NPV Edge switch as a Fibre Channel fabric switch and connect to F_Ports on it.

- The NPV mode is transparent for the end nodes.

- Inside the NPV Edge switch, the traffic entering through F_Ports cannot be processed and is mapped to the ports, which connect to the upstream NPV Core switch. These are the NP_Ports, or node proxy ports.

- The NPIV feature must be enabled on the NPV Core switch.

- NPV is a mode in which the edge switch operates, and it is disruptive to enable it.

- The NPV mode is enabled with the command **feature npv**.

- The command **show npv** allows one to gain valuable information on the status of the NPV mode running on the switch, including the NP_Ports, F_Ports, the mapping between them, and more.

Reference

"Storage Area Networking (SAN)," https://www.cisco.com/c/en/us/products/storage-networking/index.htmlCisco MDS NX-OS Configuration Limits - https://www.cisco.com/c/en/us/td/docs/dcn/mds9000/sw/9x/configuration/configuration-limits/cisco-mds-9000-nx-os-configuration-limits-9x.html

Chapter 14

Describing Data Center Ethernet Enhancements

The previous chapters discussed storage area networks (SANs) and the requirements for a secure and reliable environment that can support the communication between initiators and targets. The Fibre Channel Protocol (FCP) is selected to be the transport for this type of communication exactly because it is built to create a secure and reliable transmission. The credit-based flow control in the FCP, which is controlled by the receiving side, is the basis of the reliable, secure, and lossless transmission of the FC frames. The FCP runs on specially designed Fibre Channel switches, such as the Cisco MDS family, which provides the needed capacities and resources to support it. Building and maintaining the SANs is expensive and does not always provide the needed flexibility and scalability at the required cost. That's why we've developed other ways to carry the Fibre Channel frames over other infrastructures using less reliable protocols such as the Ethernet protocol. Fibre Channel over Ethernet (FCoE) is one such protocol, which uses as a transport the Ethernet protocol and carries the Fibre Channel frames over the local area networks in the data centers. The FCoE protocol will be discussed in the next chapter. However, before we discuss the protocol, it is important to understand how the Ethernet LANs were modified to support the highly demanding communication of the Fibre Channel Protocol.

This chapter will cover the IEEE Data Center Bridging extensions, which add the needed functionality and features to the Ethernet protocol to allow for secure and reliable transmissions over the Fibre Channel frames.

These enhancements might have been developed for the needs of the FCoE protocol, but nowadays, based on them and the resulting reliable Ethernet infrastructure, new protocols for accessing data between devices are supported, such as RoCE, which stands for Rapid Direct Memory Access over Converged Ethernet. This is a very new protocol, and Cisco Systems has announced that certain models of the Nexus 9000 switches will support it. This technology will be adopted in data centers in the near future.

IEEE Data Center Bridging

The IEEE 802.1 working group developed a collection of extensions to the Ethernet protocol that are designed to improve Ethernet networking in order to support also the Fibre Channel Protocol's lossless communication, thus creating converged, enhanced Ethernet networks, also known as unified fabrics. The unified fabrics allow for the different traffic types to share the common Ethernet infrastructure. This collection of extensions is better known as Data Center Bridging (DCB).

The Cisco DCB architecture is based on the IEEE 802.1 DCB, with some further improvements. The IEEE DCB includes the following standards to enable FCoE transport of inherently lossless traffic over an infrastructure that is inherently susceptible to loss, as is Ethernet communication:

- **IEEE 802.1Qbb Priority Flow Control (PFC):** Lossless delivery for selected types of traffic, based on their priority.

- **IEEE 802.1Qaz Enhanced Transmission Selection (ETS):** Bandwidth management and priority selection.

- **IEEE 802.1Qaz Data Center Bridging Exchange (DCBX):** Protocol for exchanging parameters between DCB devices. An extension of the Link Layer Discovery Protocol (LLDP).

- **IEEE 802.1Qau Quantized Congestion Notification (QCN):** Enables congestion awareness, control, and avoidance. Its use is optional.

The IEEE 802.1AB LLDP is also worth mentioning, as the DCBX protocol uses it as a means to communicate and negotiate FCoE capabilities between the participating devices. The DCBX protocol uses specific LLDP type, length, value (TLV) parameters to pack the FCoE parameters, and LLDP is used for the exchange. Because of that, even though LLDP is not mentioned in the preceding list of DCB specifications, it needs to be enabled, as it is used by the DCBX protocol.

Priority Flow Control

In the Fibre Channel Protocol communication, the flow control is achieved by the buffer-to-buffer credit-based mechanism, where the receiving side is in control of the transmission. The Tx side does not start sending until it gets the R_RDY acknowledgment from the Rx side. After that, the Tx side transmits until it reaches the maximum credits it knows are available at the receiving side. In this way, the transmission is lossless because a Fibre Channel frame is always transmitted when both sides know there are enough resources for the frame to be stored and processed. The FCP credit-based flow control is illustrated on Figure 14-1.

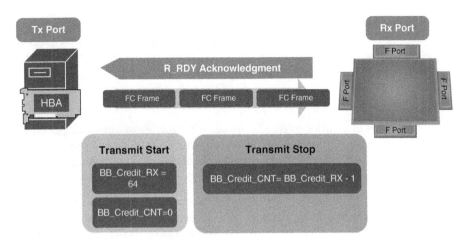

Figure 14-1 *Credit-Based Flow Control in the Fibre Channel Protocol*

In the SAN, the only communication that takes place is the Fibre Channel Protocol communication. Over a link between an N-Port and an F_Port, there is only communication to or from the initiator, and it is only block-based data. In other words, the link is not divided by different types of communication. It is dedicated to this communication.

In Ethernet, a mechanism known as the IEEE 802.3X defines the native flow control at the level of the link. It allows when Ethernet frames can be transmitted over a link, and in the case of congestion, the receiving side can send a pause frame instructing the transmitting side to stop sending frames, as there are no resources to store and process them. This means the receiving side makes a decision to send a pause frame based on its available buffers. When the resources are available again, the receiving side sends another pause frame to notify the Tx side that it can now start transmitting again. This is illustrated on Figure 14-2.

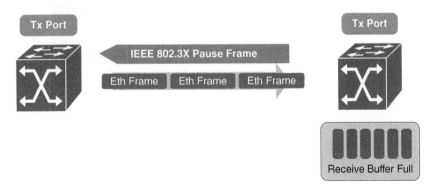

Figure 14-2 *IEEE 802.3X Link-Level Flow Control Using a Pause Frame*

Although the 802.3X pause frame mechanism is not the same, it is very similar to the Fibre Channel protocol flow control. In both cases, the receiving side notifies the transmitting side, and a decision is made based on the availability of resources at the receiving side. In both situations, it is assumed that the link is dedicated only to one type of communication. With both the FCP flow control and the 802.3X pause frame mechanism, all the communication over the link will be stopped.

The challenge comes in using a converged Ethernet infrastructure to carry multiple types of traffic. Over the same link will be different types of Ethernet communication as well as FCoE data communication. If only the native flow control mechanisms are relied on, all the traffic will be disrupted.

To solve these issues, IEEE 802.1Qbb Priority Flow Control (PFC) was developed (see Figure 14-3). It uses the fact that in Ethernet environments, traffic is divided into different VLANs, and for each VLAN, you can set a different class of service (CoS) value in the VLAN tag. So, the IEEE 802.1p CoS and IEEE 802.1Q VLAN specifications can be used to allow traffic over the shared link to be divided and marked with different CoS values, based on which different priorities will be assigned. This also allows the pause frame to be used, not at link level, but to stop only traffic for a specific priority!

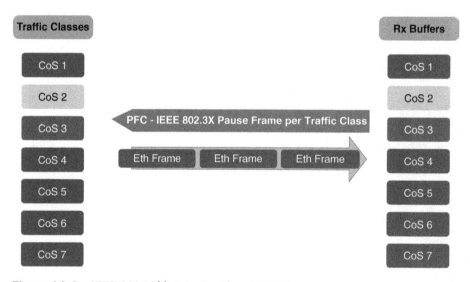

Figure 14-3   *IEEE 802.1Qbb Priority Flow Control*

In summary, the PFC enables lossless behavior for the Layer 2 flows on an Ethernet segment as follows:

■ Dividing the communication into separate VLANs.

■ Assigning CoS values for the traffic in each VLAN.

■ Setting different priorities for the different CoS values.

- Defining which CoS values will be used for the pause control mechanism.

- Using the IEEE 802.3X pause control frames to communicate buffer availability to the sender.

- When the receive buffer of CoS is full, the PFC on the switch sends a pause for this class of traffic to prevent dropped frames.

- PFC emulates the Fibre Channel buffer-to-buffer credits.

If you implement PFC on the DCB link, you can create eight distinct virtual link types on the physical link, with the option of any of these links being paused and restarted independently, as shown in Figure 14-3. Not every type of traffic needs to be controlled with a pause frame. The Fibre Channel traffic, which is carried by the FCoE protocol, cannot be dropped. That's why in the Cisco switches and converged network adapters (CNAs), which support the unified fabric, the CoS value of 3 is reserved for FCoE communication, and the pause frame control mechanism is always used for that traffic. On the other hand, the rest of the traffic, which is Ethernet communication, might not need to utilize the same mechanism, as it relies on the upper protocols' mechanisms for secure communication, such as the TCP protocol.

The switches negotiate PFC capability with the connected CNA or DCB switch by default using the DCBX protocol. Then the PFC is enabled and link-level flow control remains disabled, regardless of its configuration settings. If the PFC negotiation fails, you can force PFC to be enabled on the interface, or you can enable IEEE 802.3X link-level flow control, which is a flow-control scheme within full-duplex Ethernet networks. If you do not enable PFC on an interface, you can enable the IEEE 802.3X link-level pause, which is disabled by default.

Enhanced Transmission Selection

The PFC solves the challenges of marking and controlling which traffic can be stopped with a pause frame to avoid dropped frames, but on the same unified link, which has a certain bandwidth, different types of traffic are still flowing, and there is the need for a mechanism to manage that bandwidth. IEEE 802.1Qaz Enhanced Transmission Selection (ETS) is a specification of a network scheduling algorithm that allows different bandwidth to be allocated based on the different traffic classes. The standard allocates bandwidth for the traffic classes, but if the bandwidth is not utilized for a specific class, the algorithm allows the unused bandwidth to be given to another traffic class that needs more for a certain period of time. This borrowing of unused pipe capacity provides the flexibility to support traffic that is bursty by nature. At the same time, the minimum bandwidth for each traffic class is guaranteed. This means that if a traffic class is loaning some of its bandwidth to another traffic class and suddenly needs it back, that bandwidth will be immediately returned to cover its needs.

The ETS defines two types of classes: the bandwidth allocation classes and the strict-priority classes. This allows for time-sensitive or low-latency traffic to be assigned strict priorities and not to be affected by the bandwidth-sharing mechanism.

In summary, the IEEE 802.1Qaz ETS, shown in Figure 14-4, allows for the following:

- **Bandwidth allocation and sharing:** Enables intelligent sharing of bandwidth between traffic classes. Each traffic class is guaranteed a minimum bandwidth, but if that bandwidth is not used, it is shared among the other traffic classes until it is needed again.

- **Traffic class management:** Uses strict-priority traffic classes, which guarantees compliance with special requirements, and solves the challenge of bursty traffic.

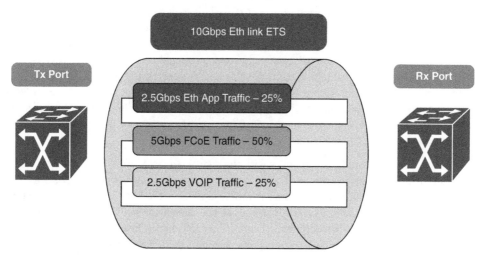

Figure 14-4   *IEEE 802.1Qaz Enhanced Transmission Selection*

DCBX Protocol

The PFC and the ETS provide the means to divide, mark, and control the traffic and the bandwidth used, but there is still the need for these parameters and capabilities to be exchanged and negotiated between the devices in the converged infrastructure. The devices need to support the same standards. They need to be enabled. There is the need to exchange information about which CoS value is assigned to which traffic class. What is the priority for that class, and will the pause frame be used for it?

The converged, expanded Ethernet fabric consists of switches that support the DCB extensions to allow communication over the Ethernet infrastructure of both Ethernet and FCoE (or similar) traffic. Connected to the converged Ethernet infrastructure, also called a unified fabric, are end devices that support multiple different types of communication as well as non-DCB Ethernet switches. Because of that, two challenges need to be solved in such environments:

- Define the borders of the unified fabric, or identify which devices, switches, and end devices support the converged infrastructure and which do not.

- Exchange information about DCB support and capabilities between the devices in the unified fabric

To achieve that, the IEEE 802 working group specified the IEEE 802.1Qaz Data Center Bridging Exchange (DCBX) protocol (see Figure 14-5), which takes care of the exchange and negotiation of the following items:

- Traffic classes

- Drop/no drop policy (PFC)

- Priority groups in ETS

- Logical link-down

- Applications such as FCoE

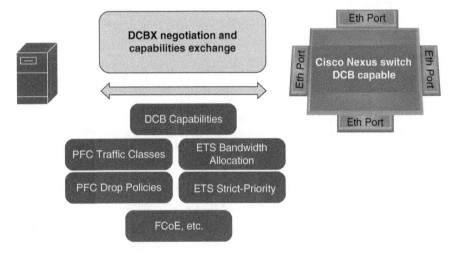

Figure 14-5   *IEEE 802.1Qaz DCBX*

The DCBX utilizes the IEEE 802.1AB LLDP as the transport protocol to communicate between the two devices. The DCBX communication consists of request and acknowledgment messages, as the information is encoded as TLV parameters.

When the devices, switches, and CNAs are connected to each other and the interfaces are enabled, the Cisco switches immediately try to initiate DCBX communication with the other devices. In case the other devices also support the DCB, the DCBX negotiations continue. In the LLDP TLVs, the parameters for the PFC, ETS, and the rest of the required information are exchanged to create a lossless environment for communication.

Summary

This chapter reviewed the standards known as the Data Center Bridging extensions, which allow an Ethernet infrastructure to be converted into a lossless environment for combined communication of both Ethernet and FCoE traffic. In this chapter you learned about the following:

- The IEEE Data Center Bridging extensions were developed by the IEEE 802 working group.

- The adoption of the DCB standards in an Ethernet infrastructure create a converged, enhanced Ethernet, or unified fabric.

- The unified fabric allows for the communication of Ethernet frames and FCoE frames over the same medium.

- The IEEE 802.1Qbb Priority Flow Control enables the traffic to be divided into different types, marked with different class of service values for the different priorities, and to use the pause frame to avoid drops for specific priorities.

- The FCoE traffic in the Cisco unified fabric is marked with a CoS value of 3, and by default it's applied a no drop policy (that is, the IEEE 802.3X Pause frame mechanism is used).

- The IEEE 802.1Qaz Enhanced Transmission Selection is a network scheduling algorithm that allows the bandwidth to manage in a flexible way based on strict-priority queues and bandwidth queues, thus maximizing bandwidth utilization and guaranteeing minimum bandwidth at the same time.

- The IEEE 802.1Qaz Data Center Bridging Exchange is a protocol that exchanges and negotiates the DCB support and capabilities among the connected devices.

- The DCBX uses the LLDP TLVs to exchange information in the request and acknowledge messages.

- The DCBX identifies the boundaries of the unified fabric as well.

References

"Storage Area Networking," https://www.cisco.com/c/en/us/products/storage-networking/index.html

"Unified Fabric White Paper—Fibre Channel over Ethernet (FCoE)," https://www.cisco.com/c/en/us/td/docs/solutions/Enterprise/Data_Center/UF_FCoE_final.html

Cisco Nexus switches design and configuration guides: https://www.cisco.com/c/en/us/support/switches/index.html

Chapter 15

Describing FCoE

This chapter covers the Cisco Unified Fabric and the protocol it uses for storage communication—Fibre Channel over Ethernet (FCoE). You will learn what the Cisco Unified Fabric is, why it is needed, and what its building components are. This chapter also focuses on the architecture and operation of FCoE and the adapters that support this protocol, and some configuration examples are provided as well.

Cisco Unified Fabric

Historically, data centers have always had two separate major communication infrastructures: the local area network (LAN) and the storage area network (SAN).

The LAN infrastructure provides connectivity between the users and the applications running on the servers, and between the various applications in the data center, such as databases, application front ends, and so on. LAN infrastructures are used for the communication between computers using different network protocols. The most popular ones nowadays are the protocols in the Open System Interconnection (OSI) layer. The components of a LAN are the switches and routers, which build the infrastructure itself, and the computers connected to them. The computers need to have a network interface card (NIC), which is the LAN I/O interface used to connect and communicate on the network. The NICs support the communication of the OSI model protocols, and they operate at different speeds, starting with 10/100/1000Mbps and reaching 10/40Gbps and even 100Gbps with the latest Cisco adapters.

The LAN infrastructure is usually consolidated, which in this case means that, usually, unless there are security or compliance requirements, the LAN is one infrastructure, although it might be segmented at the different layers of the OSI model through the use of VLANs, routing, and security access-control lists. It can grow and it has different physical layers, but it stays one infrastructure.

There are also SAN infrastructures in the data center. SANs, as already covered in the previous chapters, are used for the communication between the servers and the storage systems. The servers and the storage systems need to be equipped with I/O controllers that support the communication of the Fibre Channel Protocol. These controllers are called host bus adapters (HBAs) and can communicate at speeds of 1/4/8/16 and 32Gbps. The SAN infrastructures are built by using Cisco MDS switches, which are specialized switches supporting the communication of the Fibre Channel Protocol. Historically, before Cisco entered the SAN market, the only security mechanism supported for isolating the communication was zoning. However, this mechanism was not enough, as it didn't support true segmentation, and this led to the need for building multiple separate physical SAN infrastructures to separate and secure the data communication between different applications and their storage.

Cisco's implementation of the Fibre Channel Protocol introduced the concept of virtual SANs (VSANs), which allowed for consolidating multiple separate physical SAN infrastructures, and on the top of a single SAN, separate virtual SANs, totally isolated from each other, could be created. This led to significant savings when organizations had to plan for and deploy storage infrastructures in their data centers. However, there was still the issue of having the two separate major infrastructures, the LAN and the SAN, each built with different types of devices, requiring the servers to have both NICs and HBAs. When specialized cabling is added into the budget, the cost becomes significant, especially with the price of the small form-factor pluggable (SFP) transceivers used for Fibre Channel Protocol connectivity. The SAN in general is much more expensive to be built compared to the cost of a LAN infrastructure. Figure 15-1 illustrates separate LAN and SAN infrastructures in the data center.

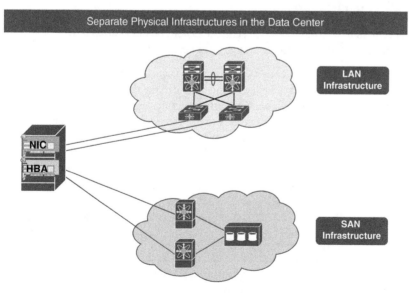

Figure 15-1 *Separate LAN and SAN Infrastructures*

To overcome these challenges and to offer a more flexible way of designing and deploying the needed communication infrastructures in the data center, Cisco came up with a new approach by introducing the creation of a consolidated I/O infrastructure, better known as the Cisco Unified Fabric. The idea is that the cheaper LAN infrastructure can be modified, using the Data Center Bridging enhancements, to create a lossless environment that allows the use of overlay encapsulation for the secure communication of the Fibre Channel Protocol frames. The Fibre Channel frames are encapsulated in Ethernet frames and sent over the Cisco Unified Fabric switches to the storage systems. The Cisco switches that support the FCoE protocol, and thus the Cisco Unified Fabric, include some of the Cisco Nexus and MDS switches as well as some of the Cisco Nexus 2000 fabric extenders. At the time this chapter was written, the list of Cisco switch models that support FCoE was constantly changing, so my advice would be to go and check with the Cisco product documentation for the latest information. Figure 15-2 illustrates the Cisco Unified Fabric.

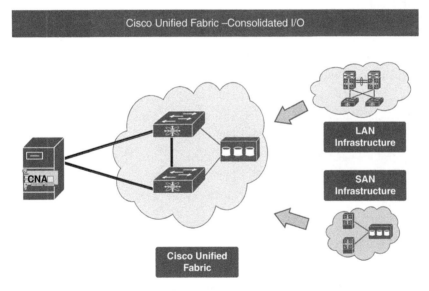

Figure 15-2 *Cisco Unified Fabric*

In the Cisco Unified Fabric, the servers must use a different I/O controller that supports both the Ethernet and the FCoE protocols. These adapters are called converged adapters. The Cisco converged adapters offer extended capabilities compared to the ones offered by Broadcom and Emulex and are called Cisco virtual interface cards (VICs). The FCoE adapters are discussed in a dedicated section later in this chapter.

With the FCoE adapter, the server connects to the FCoE-capable switches with Ethernet cabling and also allows for FCoE communication over the same cheaper cabling. Although the FCoE standard does not impose any specific minimum bandwidth for the link, Cisco requires at least 10Gbps of bandwidth in order to support FCoE in a reliable manner.

The Cisco Unified Fabric provides the following benefits and flexibility in the data center:

- Reduced number of SAN switches.

- Reduced number of I/O adapters in the servers. Instead of separate NICs and HBAs, now converged adapters are used.

- Reduced cost of the cabling, as there are fewer or no native Fibre Channel links, which means less-expensive Fibre Channel Protocol transceivers.

- Significant savings in the amount of power per rack when FCoE is employed.

- Significant savings on power because less cooling is needed to compensate for the heat produced.

- Better cable management.

- Optimized device administration, as fewer devices are managed.

- Optimized troubleshooting, as fewer devices are involved in the communication path.

- Storage administrators manage their fabrics in the same manner they always have, as the FCoE does not change the Fibre Channel Protocol model.

- FCoE maps the Fibre Channel traffic onto lossless Ethernet. This results in performance benefits over technologies that require a gateway.

- FCoE is an extension of Fibre Channel onto the lossless Ethernet fabric.

FCoE Architecture

The FCoE is a transport protocol defined by the American National Standards Institute (ANSI) T11 committee. It has the needed functionality and enhancements to create a lossless environment and to carry the FC frames encapsulated into Ethernet frames. In the FCoE protocol, the lower layers of the Fibre Channel Protocol are replaced with unified fabric I/O consolidation over Ethernet. These are the layers that take care of the encapsulation and de-encapsulation as well as the lossless transmission over Ethernet. The upper-layer Fibre Channel Protocol services, such as domain IDs, Fabric Shortest Path First (FSPF), Fibre Channel Name Server (FCNS), fabric login (FLOGI), zoning, and so on, stay the same as in the Fibre Channel world, because it is the Fibre Channel protocol that operates at these layers. Figure 15-3 shows which layers are changed.

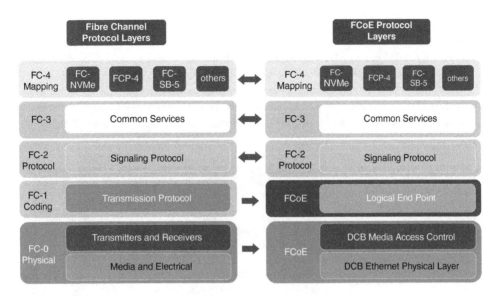

Figure 15-3   *FCoE Protocol Layers*

In the Fibre Channel Protocol operation, the FC frame is created in the hardware of the HBA, which is the FC-2 layer responsible for the framing and flow control. Afterward, the FC frame is passed to the FC-1 layer to be encoded with the needed serialization in place and transmitted over the native FC link. In the case of the Unified Fabric, there is no native FC link but rather an Ethernet link. That's why after the FC frame is formed in the HBA part of the converged adapter, it is passed to the FCoE Logical End Point (LEP). The FCoE LEP is a new component that is responsible for taking the FC frame and encapsulating it in an Ethernet frame, with all the needed information required by the Data Center Bridging Exchange (DCBX) enhancements for the secure transmission of the new Ethernet frame, which is contained inside an FC frame. This new Ethernet frame has some special characteristics. Because the standard FC frame is up to 2112 bytes in size, and the standard Ethernet frame is usually 1500 bytes, without any overhead from encryption or something similar, the maximum transmission unit (MTU) for the FCoE communication must either be set to the default for the FCoE protocol (2240 bytes) or, if the switch does not allow defining such a size, just be allowed to use jumbo frames, which is sufficient enough (see Figure 15-4).

Figure 15-4 shows that the FC frame is inside the Ethernet frame, and there are not any changes made to the original FC frame. It is encapsulated just by adding the needed FCoE header and the Ethernet header. No manipulations are allowed to be performed on the FC frame, as this will invalidate it. This also means that the FC header still has the source and destination FCIDs needed for the FC protocol communication. Do not forget that from the perspective of the Fibre Channel Protocol, the FCoE protocol is just a different cable/transport mechanism. The FCoE header contains control info. The Ethernet header contains important information such as the Ethertype, as the value for the FCoE protocol is 0x8906. This value notifies the switch that inside this Ethernet frame is a Fibre Channel Protocol frame. Additionally, in the Ethernet header is the 802.1Q VLAN tag.

This is important because it defines to which VLAN the FCoE traffic will belong. In Cisco's implementation of the FCoE, dedicated VLANs are used for its traffic, which allows the needed priority flow control and no-drop policies to be applied. And last but not least, in the Ethernet header are the source and destination MAC addresses, as the FCoE frame is basically an Ethernet frame that will be transported over an Ethernet infra-structure. The formation of the MAC address and how it maps to the FCID in the servers' converged adapter is a function of the FCoE Initialization Protocol (FIP), which takes care of the negotiations before any FCoE communication can happen.

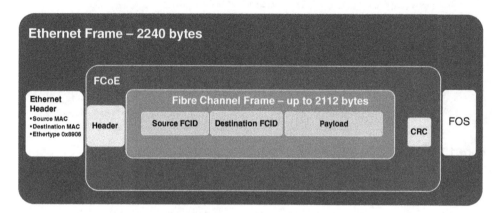

Figure 15-4   *FC Frame Encapsulation in FCoE*

In the FCoE communication are two roles (or participating elements): the FCoE Ethernet nodes (ENodes) and the Fibre Channel Forwarders (FCFs).

An FCF is an Ethernet switch that also supports the FCoE protocol. When a switch sup-ports the FCoE protocol and is also an FCF, it means that this switch is composed of two switches: an Ethernet switch with the Ethernet physical ports and a Fibre Channel switch (or a component that can run and process the Fibre Channel protocol frames). This means that this component runs all the needed Fibre Channel Protocol services, just like any other physical standalone Fibre Channel switch. That's why the FCF, shown in Figure 15-5, can process the Fibre Channel Protocol logins, services, and frames.

When an FCoE frame enters the FCF, it is processed as an Ethernet frame, as it enters through a physical Ethernet port. Based on the Ethertype, the switch knows that it is an FCoE frame, and it must be sent to the FCoE LEP, where it is de-encapsulated. The remaining FC frame is then processed based on the rules of the Fibre Channel Protocol. Once it is processed, either it will be sent as a native FC frame through an egress native FC port, if the FCF also has native FC connectivity, or it will be encapsulated again in an Ethernet FCoE frame if it is supposed to leave through the Ethernet egress port.

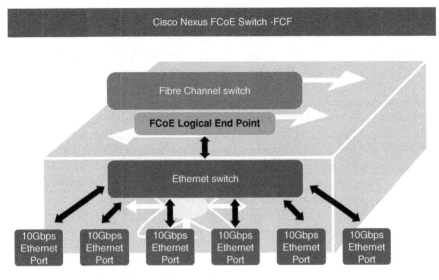

Figure 15-5 *Fibre Channel Forwarder*

The servers are equipped with converged networks adapters (CNAs) in the Cisco Unified Fabric. This allows them to be physically connected to an Ethernet port of a switch with native Ethernet connectivity but over that link to carry both their Ethernet communication as well as their storage communication using the FCoE protocol, in case the switch is FCoE capable. The hardware of the CNA, shown in Figure 15-6, is very different from the traditional NICs and HBAs. For external physical connectivity, the CNA uses 10Gbps or faster Ethernet ports, but inside, facing the server, separate NICs and HBAs are built in. The OS of the server communicates with the CNA and sees the separate HBAs and NICs through the PCIe bus.

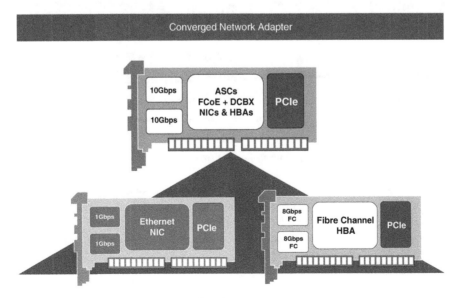

Figure 15-6 *Converged Network Adapter*

The NICs in the CNA natively use the Ethernet physical egress ports. The situation is more complex with the Fibre Channel Protocol communication.

The HBAs in the CNA cannot communicate directly using the physical Ethernet ports. That's why there is a specialized ASIC, or silicone, that performs the function of the FCoE LEP. The HBAs are acting as native FC ports, but as there are no physical FC ports, the HBAs are presented as virtual Fibre Channel (VFC) ports. Through the ASIC, the VFCs use the physical external ports for FCoE communication. By the way, it is the same on the FCF side—because the FC switching component is behind the physical Ethernet ports, the FC ports are virtual (VFCs) and act just like the physical FC ports. Therefore, you have the standard Fibre Channel Protocol communication with the Fibre Channel ports, with the appropriate port roles assigned, with the only difference that these are virtual ports, and the roles are also presented as virtual to provide the information that these roles are assigned to virtual FC interfaces. As with the Fibre Channel Protocol port modes, the virtual ones are as follows (see Figure 15-7):

- **Virtual Node ports (VN):** The VFC on the CAN of the server.

- **Virtual Fabric port (VF):** The FCF VFC ports to the VN ports are connected.

- **Virtual Expansion ports (VE):** The FCF VFC connect to another FCF VFC.

- **Virtual Node Proxy port (VNP):** When the FCF operates as NPV edge switch (that is, when it is not running the FC Protocol services).

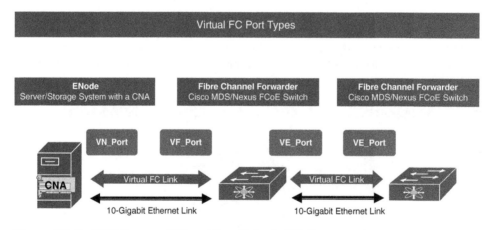

Figure 15-7   *VFC Ports and Virtual Port Roles in FCoE*

The VN port communicates with the VF port at the side of the switch in the same way as in a SAN infrastructure the N_Port will connect and communicate with the F_Port on the FC switch. The difference is that because there is no native FC physical connectivity, the negotiations and the login processes will be performed by the FCoE Initialization Protocol (FIP).

The VE ports connect multiple FCoE switches over the physical Ethernet connectivity, just like with the native FC communication.

Therefore, the ENodes can be defined as a combination of the VFC, operating in VN mode, and the FCoE LEP on the CNA. In the same way, the FCF is the combination of the FCoE LEP on the switch and the FC protocol component, represented by VFC ports, operating in VF or VE mode, and all the Fibre Channel protocol services.

As the VFC ports are Fibre Channel ports, when they communicate, they use FCIDs. However, because the Fibre Channel frames are encapsulated in Ethernet frames to be transported, as the Ethernet frames use MAC addresses, this brings up the issue of what MAC address to use for the FCoE communication of a specific VFC that will allow a direct mapping between the FCID and the MAC address to be created in the FCoE LEP. As the MAC addresses are 48 bits and the FCIDs are 24 bits, a direct mapping is not possible. That's why there needs to be a component added to the value of the FCID. This is called the Fibre Channel MAC Address Prefix (FC-MAP), which has a size of 24 bits, and it represents the first part of the MAC address. The second part is the 24-bit FCID of the VFC. In this way, there is a unique 48-bit MAC address used for the communication of this specific VFC. This also means that each VFC on the CAN will have its own unique MAC address, as each will have its own unique FCID. The FC-MAP is a value set on the FCF switch, and the default value is 0E.FC.00. As you'll remember from the previous chapters, the FCID in the Fibre Channel Protocol communication is created and assigned by the Fibre Channel switch, after a successful fabric login from the end node. With the FCoE protocol, the FCID is also created on the FC switch; in this case, it's the FCF switch. This means that both values that form the MAC address for the FCoE communication are provided by the FCF switch, or the fabric. This method of creating and assigning a MAC address is called a Fabric Provided MAC Address (FPMA) and shown in Figure 15-8. Based on the FC-BB-5 definition, there is a range of 256 FC-MAP values that can be used. In environments where there might be overlapping FCIDs, or for other purposes, administrators can create and use up to 256 different pools of MAC addresses.

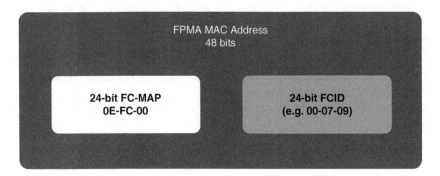

Figure 15-8   *FPMA MAC Address for the FCoE*

With the FPMA approach and the FCoE protocol there is one challenge. For the VFC to log in to the fabric, it needs to be capable of communicating over the Ethernet infrastructure using the FCoE protocol. However, for this to happen, a MAC address is needed, and the MAC address can be created by the fabric after a successful fabric login. Therefore, without an FCID there is no a MAC address, and without a MAC address there is no FCID. To solve this challenge, and others, there is one additional protocol that communicates before the FCoE protocol, and that is the FCoE Initialization Protocol.

FCoE Initialization Protocol

The FCoE Initialization Protocol (FIP) is defined by the T11 FC-BB-5 standard as the control plane component of the FCoE protocol. The FCoE protocol is the other component from that standard, and it is defined as the data plane. This means that FIP is responsible for exchanging the needed information, performing the needed negotiations, and maintaining the information exchange between the connected devices in order to create and maintain an environment that allows the operation of the FCoE protocol (in other words, it allows the exchange of FCoE Ethernet frames).

The FCF and the end node are capable of differentiating between the FIP and the FCoE communication based on the Ethertype value. The FIP Ethertype value is 0x8914.

The FIP sequence of operations, shown in Figure 15-9, is as follows:

1. **FIP VLAN discovery:** The FCoE VLAN used by all other FIP protocols and the FCoE communication is discovered. The FIP uses the native VLAN to discover the FCoE VLAN. The FIP VLAN discovery protocol is the only FIP running on the native VLAN. The rest of the FIP and FCoE communication happens in the discovered FCoE VLANs.

2. **FIP FCF discovery:** When an FCoE-capable device is connected to the network, it announces itself by sending a Discovery Solicitation Message. The Ethertype in these frames is set to 0x8914 to indicate this is an FIP communication. If it's connected to an FCF, it receives the discovery message and responds with a solicited advertisement. In the response message is the FCF FC-MAP value. The Ethertype is still FIP.

3. **FCoE virtual link instantiation:** The FIP carries the needed fabric login (FLOGI), fabric discovery (FDISC), and logout (LOGO). The result is that the VFC port is assigned an FCID and a MAC address for the subsequent FCoE communication. The Ethertype is still FIP.

4. **FCoE virtual link maintenance:** After the previous step, all the needed information has been exchanged between the devices and the needed negotiations have taken place. The devices can communicate using the FCoE protocol to carry FC frames. Therefore, the FCoE protocol is operating at this stage. In the meantime, the FIP continues to regularly exchange control information between the devices to maintain the virtual link between the VN and the VF ports. The Ethertype is FCoE.

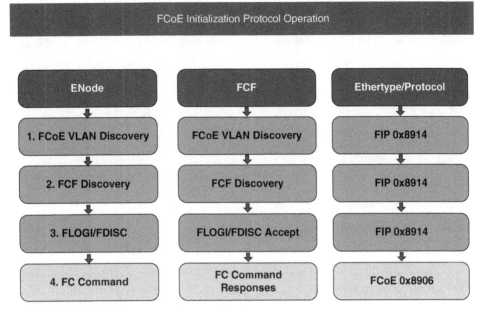

Figure 15-9 *FIP Operation*

During the first stage of the process, the devices communicate with each other with the goal of the CNA reporting that it is FCoE capable and finding the FCoE VLAN, which is used by the FIP. This happens as the CNA, using the Ethernet burnt-in address (BIA) as a source MAC address, sends a solicitation to the All-FCF-MACs multicast address to which all the FCFs listen. The Ethertype of the multicast solicitation frame is set to the FIP value of 0x8914.

This communication happens in the native VLAN, and the FIP VLAN discovery is the only stage that happens in it. The subsequent communication of the FIP takes place in the FCoE VLAN used by the chosen FCF.

In the FC-BB-5 standard, the FIP VLAN discovery protocol is described as optional. This means that if it is not used, the FCoE VLAN will default to VLAN 1002, and it might not be the FCoE VLAN used by the Unified Fabric. That's why Cisco strongly recommends that the FIP VLAN discovery protocol be used.

Once the FCoE VLAN discovery finishes by providing information for the FCoE VLAN, it then starts the next stage, where the FIP FCF discovery protocol takes place. It uses the FCoE VLANs, and the goal is to find the FCFs and to start negotiations with them. For this purpose, the CNA sends a multicast solicitation, the ALL-ENode-MACs multicast MAC address. This message will identify the VF-Port-Capable FCF MACs. One such multicast solicitation will be sent to each of the FCoE VLANs discovered in the previous phase.

Upon receiving the multicast solicitation frame, the FCF will respond with a unicast advertisement. It will contain the first 24 bits of the FPMA; this is the FC-MAP value configured on the FCF. The other information contained in the FCF advertisement is as follows:

- FIP timeout values

- FCF priority

- Fabric name (the WWNN of the fabric)

- FCF MAC address

- Switch name

- Switch capabilities

Based on that information, the CAN will decide which FCF to communicate with. For this decision, the CAN considers the FCF priority and the FCF MAS address.

The third phase will be to establish the virtual link between the VN and the VF port. The ENode, or the host, will send FLOGI frames to the FCID of FF:FF:FE. This is a well-known address for the fabric login communication. The Ethertype of the FCoE frames will still be FIP.

The FCF will assign an FCID for the host and will respond to the FLOGI request. With this, an FPMA MAC address will be created for the subsequent FCoE communication, and the virtual link will be established.

This concludes the work of the FIP for negotiating and establishing the environment for the FCoE communication. The subsequent frames will have the FCoE Ethertype. The FIP will continue to communicate in the background with the goal of maintaining the virtual link.

FCoE Configuration

The FCoE protocol is currently supported on the following Cisco switches:

- Cisco MDS 9700 Series multilayer directors

- Cisco MDS 9500 Series multilayer directors

- Cisco MDS 9250i multilayer switches

- Cisco Nexus 7700 Series switches

- Cisco Nexus 7700 Series switches

- Cisco Nexus 2000 FEXs

- Cisco UCS

The "References" section provides the links to the data sheets of the Cisco switches and linecards that support the FCoE protocol.

The Cisco Nexus 5000, Cisco Nexus 5500, and the Cisco Nexus 6000 Series switches supported the FCoE. These models are end of sale and soon will no longer be supported. The Cisco Nexus 6000 switches also have end of life status. For these reasons, they are not covered in this section.

The sample configuration of the FCoE communication in this chapter refers to a Cisco Nexus 7000/7700 switch with an F-linecard.

The FCoE is a licensed feature in the Cisco NX-OS. The needed license is described in the Cisco NX-OS licensing guide. In the "References" section is the link to the guide on the Cisco website.

The Nexus 7000/7700 switches do not have native Fibre Channel ports. They support FCoE only through Ethernet ports. This means they cannot bridge between an FCoE Ethernet infrastructure and a native Fibre Channel Switch fabric.

The storage VDC is a virtual Fibre Channel switch inside the Cisco Nexus 7000/7700 switches. It is the FCF that will own the VFC ports and will communicate with the FCoE LEP. Only one storage VDC can exist on a switch. All of the subsequent FCoE configuration and processing will happen in the storage VDC or will be linked to it.

The Ethernet interfaces used for the FCoE communication come in one of two types, depending on how they are utilized by the storage VDC: dedicated or shared. The dedicated Ethernet ports will be used only to carry the VLANs for the FCoE communication, while the shared interfaces will be shared between the storage VDC and a data VDC. This means that both data VLANs and the FCoE VLANs will be carried through these interfaces.

Switch Preparation for FCoE

Some steps are needed to prepare the Cisco Nexus 7000/7700 switches for FCoE communication and configuration.

The FCoE feature set needs to be enabled first. This happens when you are in the default VDC of the switch:

```
switch# configure terminal
switch(config)# install feature-set fcoe
```

The LLDP feature needs to be enabled for the DCBX protocol communication:

```
switch(config)# feature lldp
```

Also, it's a best practice to enable the LACP feature:

```
switch(config)# feature lacp
```

The next step is to enable the system quality of service (QoS), which supports the FCoE communication. Without this step, the storage VDC creation will fail later:

```
switch(config)# system qos
switch(config-sys-qos)# service-policy type
 network-qos default-nq-7e-policy
```

Prepare the physical Ethernet interfaces that will be used for the FCoE communication. They will need to allow the communication of multiple VLANs (one of them will be the FCoE VLAN) and to be configured as edge ports in order for the Spanning Tree Protocol not to block them:

```
switch(config)# interface eth 2/1-10
switch(config-if)# switchport mode trunk
switch(config-if)# spanning-tree port type edge trunk
switch(config-if)# no shutdown
```

Finally, save the configuration. It is always a good idea to save the configuration:

```
switch(config-sys-qos)# copy running-config startup-config
```

With this, the switch is prepared for the needed FCoE configuration.

Storage VDC

The storage VDC is a virtual Fibre Channel switch inside the Cisco Nexus 7000/7700 switches. It is the FCF, which will own the VFC ports and will communicate with the FCoE LEP. All of the subsequent FCoE configuration and processing will happen in the storage VDC or will be linked to it.

The first step is to create the storage VDC. Creating the storage VDC and assigning resources to it happen in the admin VDC:

```
switch# configure terminal
switch(config)# vdc fcoe-vdc type storage
switch(config-vdc)#
```

Now that the storage VDC with the name fcoe-vdc is created, the next step is to specify which Ethernet physical ports will be used for the FCoE communication. In this example, the first five interfaces are allocated as dedicated and the second five will be shared:

```
switch(config-vdc)# allocate interface ethernet 2/1-5
switch(config-vdc)# allocate shared interface ethernet 2/6-10
```

The other resource that needs to be assigned is a VLAN or a range of VLANs that will be used to carry the FCoE traffic:

```
switch(config-vdc)# allocate fcoe-vlan-range 10-20 from vdc switch
```

VSANs and FCoE VLANs

As you know, the Fibre Channel communication happens in VSANs. With the FCoE protocol, when the FCoE communication for a specific VSAN is carried over the Ethernet infrastructure, there is a dedicated VLAN to which this traffic is mapped. Then the traffic for this VLAN is treated with high priority, which also means that a no-drop policy is applied to it and the pause frame is used during the communication. So, the next logical step in the configuration of the FCoE communication will be to create the VSAN or VSANs and to map them to the dedicated VLANs. In the previous step in the admin VDC, VLAN IDs were allocated that will be used by the storage VDC for the FCoE communication. In the following steps, in the storage VDC, you will create a VSAN and will map it to an FCoE VLAN.

Go to the storage VDC:

```
switch(config)# switchto vdc fcoe_vdc
```

Create the VSAN:

```
switch-fcoe_vdc# configure terminal
switch-fcoe_vdc(config)# vsan database
switch- fcoe_vdc(config-vsan-db)#vsan 10
```

Map the traffic of this VSAN to an FCoE VLAN:

```
switch- fcoe_vdc(config-vsan-db)#vlan 10
switch- fcoe_vdc(config-vlan)#fcoe vsan 10
switch- fcoe_vdc(config-vlan)exit
```

Virtual Fibre Channel Interfaces

Now that the environment is prepared, the next step will be to create the VFC, specify which Ethernet interface will be used for its communication, assign it to a VSAN, and specify the mode of operation.

Create the VFC in the storage VDC:

```
switch-fcoe_vdc# configure terminal
switch-fcoe_vdc(config)#interface vfc 10
```

Specify the port mode. You can specify two port modes (E or F), depending on the device that is connected to the Ethernet port through which the VFC will communicate. The default port mode is F:

```
switch-fcoe_vdc(config-if)# switchport mode f
```

The next step is to bind the VFC to a physical Ethernet port for the FCoE traffic:

```
switch-fcoe_vdc(config-if)# bind interface ethernet 2/10
```

Just like with the native FC ports, the VFC also needs to be assigned to a VSAN:

```
switch-fcoe_vdc(config)# vsan database
switch- fcoe_vdc(config-vsan-db)#vsan 10 interface vfc 10
```

FCoE Verification

As the final steps, you need to verify the interface status:

```
switch-fcoe_vdc# show interface vfc 10

vfc10 is up
Bound interface is Ethernet2/10
Hardware is Virtual Fibre Channel
Port WWN is 20:02:00:0d:ec:3d:16:13
Port WWN is 20:02:00:0d:ec:3d:16:13
snmp link state traps are enabled
Port WWN is 20:02:00:0d:ec:3d:16:13
APort WWN is 20:02:00:0d:ec:3d:16:13
snmp link state traps are enabled
Port mode is F, FCID is 0x390100
Port vsan is 10
1 minute input rate 0 bits/sec, 0 bytes/sec, 0 frames/sec
1 minute output rate 0 bits/sec, 0 bytes/sec, 0 frames/sec
0 frames input, 0 bytes 0 discards, 0 errors
0 frames output, 0 bytes 0 discards, 0 errors
Interface last changed at Wed Jan 6 01:42:11 2021
```

Also, verify the FCoE capability:

```
switch# show fcoe
Global FCF details
        FCF-MAC is 00:0d:ec:3d:16:13
        FC-MAP is 0e:fc:00
        FCF Priority is 128
        FKA Advertisement period for FCF is 8 seconds
```

Finally, verify the FCoE configuration for a specific Ethernet interface:

```
switch# show interface ethernet 2/10 fcoe
Ethernet2/10 is FCoE UP
    Vfc10 is Up
        FCID is 0x390100
        PWWN is 20:02:00:0d:ec:3d:16:13
        MAC addr is 00:c0:cc:0a:15:16
```

Summary

This chapter described the FCoE protocol, the Unified Fabric created by it, and the FCoE Initialization Protocol (FIP), and it also provided an example of an FCoE-related configuration on the Cisco Nexus 7000 switches. In this chapter, you also learned about the following:

- The Cisco Unified Fabric is a consolidated I/O infrastructure that allows Fibre Channel protocol frames to be carried over an Ethernet infrastructure.

- The Cisco Unified Fabric optimizes the utilization of the resources and minimizes the cost of the infrastructure.

- The FCoE is a protocol defined by the ANSI T11 committee.

- The FCoE protocol allows Fibre Channel frames to be encapsulated intact inside Ethernet frames and to be sent for communication over the Ethernet infrastructure.

- The DCBX extensions allow the Ethernet infrastructure to become lossless and secure for FCoE communication.

- The minimum link bandwidth must be 10Gbps to support FCoE.

- The hosts are equipped with specialized communication controllers called converged networks adapters (CNAs).

- The CNA combines the functionality of NICs and HBAs.

- The network switch that supports the FCoE actually is two switches in one: a physical Ethernet switch and inside a Fibre Channel protocol entity, responsible for processing to the FC.

- The FCoE switches that process the FCoE are called Fibre Channel forwarders.

- The MAC address used for FCoE communication by the CAN is a fabric-provided MAC address (FPMA), which consists of two parts: the FC-MAP and the FCID.

- The FC-MAP is a 3-byte value configured on the FCF. The default value is 0E-FC-00.

- The FC-MAP has a range of 256 values.

- FIP is the control plane protocol for the FCoE.

- FIP discovers the FCoE VLAN.

- FIP then discovers the FCF.

- Finally, FIP performs the FLOGI/FDISC operation in order to establish the virtual FC link.

- In this way, FIP supports the creation of the FPMA MAC address for subsequent communication.

- On Cisco Nexus 7000 switches, the FCF entity is the storage VDC.

- Only a single storage VDC can exist on a Cisco Nexus 7000 switch.

- To create the storage VDC, you must first install the FCoE feature set and then enable the system QoS for FCoE.

- The resources that need to be assigned to the storage VDC are the FCoE VLANs and the physical Ethernet ports that will service the FCoE traffic.

- Ethernet ports can be dedicated to or shared by the storage VDC.

- Once the storage VDC is created, the VSAN must be created and mapped to an FCoE VLAN.

- Next, the VFC interfaces need to be created.

- For each VFC interface, you must configure which VSAN it will belong to, which mode it will operate in, and which physical Ethernet port it will communicate through.

- Once the configuration is done, it needs to be verified with the appropriate commands.

References

"Storage Area Networking," https://www.cisco.com/c/en/us/products/storage-networking/index.html

"Unified Fabric White Paper—Fibre Channel over Ethernet (FCoE)," https://www.cisco.com/c/en/us/td/docs/solutions/Enterprise/Data_Center/UF_FCoE_final.html

Design and configuration guides for Cisco Nexus switches: https://www.cisco.com/c/en/us/support/switches/index.html

"Cisco NX-OS Licensing Guide," https://www.cisco.com/c/en/us/td/docs/switches/datacenter/sw/nx-os/licensing/guide/b_Cisco_NX-OS_Licensing_Guide.htmlCisco Nexus 2000 FEXs supporting FCoE - https://www.cisco.com/c/en/us/products/switches/nexus-2000-series-fabric-extenders/models-comparison.html#~tab-10g

Chapter 16

Describing Cisco UCS Components

This chapter covers the Cisco Unified Computing System (UCS). The Cisco UCS is Cisco's innovative approach to the compute component in the data center. It is a complex integrated solution to address multiple challenges and consists of multiple components. You will get acquainted with the different physical components of the Cisco UCS and the different generations of the integrated system. You will take a closer look at the different compute nodes and their technical characteristics. You will learn which can operate in a standalone mode and which operate as an integrated component of the Cisco UCS. Additionally, we will take a look of the Cisco HyperFlex system as an example of a fully integrated infrastructure for the data center.

Cisco UCS Components

As discussed in previous chapters, data centers are built using different components that represent the physical infrastructure, the layers of operating systems and virtualization, and the different software and applications that provide the needed services, as well as the components used to build and manage the needed level of security and to monitor and respond to issues in the environment at different levels, in addition to the procedures in place to define the smooth operation and disaster recovery. In other words, a data center has multiple building blocks. In the previous chapters, the focus was on the major infrastructure components for building the base of a data center (that is, the network, the storage, and the compute components). Figure 16-1 illustrates the Cisco UCS and HyperFlex, which comprise the Cisco compute component of the data center.

Cisco Unified Computing System and Cisco HyperFlex

Figure 16-1 *Cisco UCS and HyperFlex*

Cisco Systems has been in the network and storage business for a very long time, and somewhere around 2008 it entered the server market with the Cisco Unified Computing System (UCS). It was and still remains a revolutionary, next-generation, highly integrated platform for providing the needed computing resources, together with their communication and storage needs, in a flexible way that allows for the optimal utilization of the hardware computing resources through hardware abstraction.

You will investigate how exactly the hardware abstraction happens and what the benefits are in the next chapter, where Cisco UCS management is discussed. However, to be able to understand the Cisco UCS better, first you will learn about the different physical components of the Cisco UCS and how they connect to each other. You will also learn about the whole physical topology of the Cisco UCS as well as the standalone Cisco UCS servers and their benefits and applications.

Based on the Cisco UCS, Cisco Systems has developed Cisco HyperFlex. It is a hyper-converged application-centric solution that integrates not only the hardware and the management of the Cisco UCS but goes further and creates the needed environment for the virtualization supporting containers. It also includes the needed storage and communication.

Before we can dig deeper into the Cisco UCS hardware abstraction or Cisco HyperFlex, you will need to learn about the physical components that make up the Cisco UCS, as illustrated in Figure 16-2.

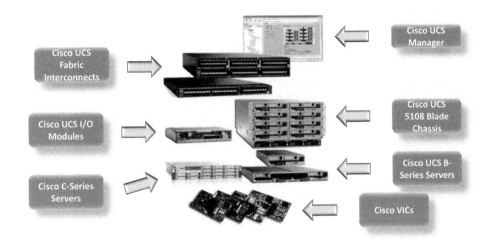

Figure 16-2   *Cisco UCS Components*

The Cisco UCS consists of the following components:

■ **Cisco UCS Manager (UCSM):** This application manages and monitors all the components of the Cisco UCS. In the last generation of the Cisco UCS, the UCS-X, the Cisco UCS Manager is replaced by the Cisco Intersight Managed Mode (IMM).

■ **Cisco UCS Fabric Interconnects (FIs):** The communication devices responsible for the physical connectivity of the Cisco UCS to the LAN and SAN infrastructures. An additional important function is that the Cisco UCS Manager runs on them.

■ **Cisco UCS 5108 Blade Chassis:** The chassis that houses the servers with a blade physical form factor and the I/O modules (IOMs). It provides the connectivity, power supply, and cooling for the blade servers. The new chassis (the UCS X9508), the new blade servers, and their management are discussed in a separate topic.

■ **CISCO I/O Modules (IOMs):** These are the connectivity modules, also known as Fabric Extenders (FEX). They are installed in the blade chassis and provide for the physical connectivity of the servers and the chassis up to the Fabric Interconnects.

■ **Cisco UCS B-series servers:** The Cisco B-series servers are servers that have a smaller physical form factor. This is the blade form factor, and that's why they are usually called blade servers. The Cisco B-series servers are installed in the Cisco UCS blade chassis.

- **Cisco UCS C-series servers:** The Cisco C-series servers are designed as rack-mount servers. They can be either a component of the Cisco UCS, under the management of the Cisco UCSM, or they can be used in the standalone mode, where they are managed by their own Cisco Integrated Management Controller (CIMC).

- **Cisco virtual interface cards (VICs):** The Cisco VIC is a purpose-built converged network adapter to be used in the Cisco UCS servers. It allows for Ethernet, FC, or FCoE communication but also supports the Cisco VM-FEX technology, which allows for the network connectivity awareness and management up to the level of the virtual machines.

These are the major components that build a Cisco Unified Computing System. The whole system appears as one component in front of the rest of the data center components.

All Cisco UCS blade servers come with Cisco UCS Manager capability. Cisco UCS with Cisco UCS Manager provides the following:

- Embedded integration of LAN, SAN, and management

- Auto-discovery, with automatic recognition and configuration of blades

- Local (and optionally global) server profiles and templates for policy-driven server provisioning

The Cisco UCS components are connected and managed in a specific way, as the resulting integrated system is known as a Cisco UCS domain (see Figure 16-3). The Cisco UCS domain consists of two Cisco UCS Fabric Interconnects, which fulfill two roles:

- **Communication:** All the servers' communication to and from the data center goes through them. Upstream, facing the data center LAN and SAN infrastructures, the Cisco UCS Fabric Interconnects provide the connectivity for both the Ethernet data communication and the storage communication. The storage communication can be based on block or file storage protocols; as for the block-based communication, the supported options cover the FC, FCoE, and the iSCSI protocols. The Fabric Interconnects connect upstream to the LAN and SAN infrastructures. And, downstream, the FIs are responsible for the connectivity to the servers. Inside the Cisco UCS, all the communication is based on Ethernet. There is only Ethernet physical connectivity from the Fabric Interconnects down to the servers. That's why the servers are equipped with converged network adapters, which externally use Ethernet connectivity but also support FCoE communication between them and the Fabric Interconnects.

- **Management:** The Cisco UCS Manager application, which takes care of the discovery, provisioning, configuration, and management of the Cisco UCS servers, runs on the Fabric Interconnects. Additionally, the Fabric Interconnects provide a separate out-of-band dedicated interface to connect to the management network in your data center.

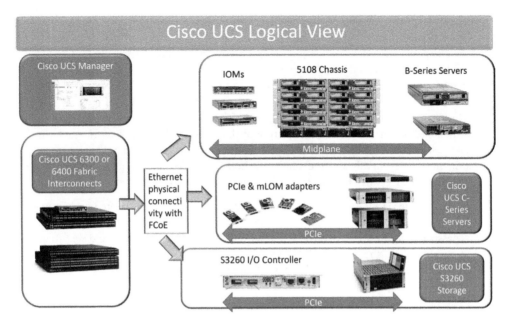

Figure 16-3 *Cisco UCS Logical View*

In a Cisco UCS domain, the two Fabric Interconnects are connected to each other with a special link, called the cluster link. By bringing in the cluster link, you create a cluster; the link is used for configuration synchronization and the exchange of state information between the two Fabric Interconnects. In this way, if one of them becomes unresponsive, the other takes care of the management. However, keep in mind that this applies to the management application (that is, on which of them the management application will run in active mode). When it comes to processing the data communication from the servers, the two Fabric Interconnects are both active. This is another way of adding redundancy and reliability.

South from the Fabric Interconnects are the Cisco UCS servers. There are two types of servers: the B-series and C-series servers (that is, the blade and rack servers). The C-series servers are equipped with their own power supplies, cooling, and communication adapters. Therefore, when the C-series servers are part of a Cisco UCS domain, they are connected directly to the Fabric Interconnects. There are other supported connectivity options between the C-series servers and the Fabric Interconnects that involve the use of special Cisco 2000 Fabric Extenders (FEXs).

The B-series servers are installed in the Cisco UCS 5108 blade chassis. The blade chassis takes care for the redundant power supply, cooling, and connectivity. For the connectivity, the chassis has installed the Cisco UCS 2000/2200/2300/2400 FEXs, or I/O Modules (IOMs). The series represents the generation of the Cisco UCS FEX. For example, the Cisco UCS 2000 FEXs are the first generation and are no longer sold or supported. The Cisco UCS 2200 FEXs are the second generation and are to be used with the second generation of the Fabric Interconnects and such.

The IOMs, or FEXs, are not switches. This means they do not perform L2 lookups as any other Ethernet switch, so there's no processing of the Ethernet frames. The IOMs are communication devices that physically connect the uplinks between the FI and the blade chassis with the servers installed in the blade chassis. This happens through mapping of the server-facing (internal) ports to the uplink (external) ports of the IOM. Depending on the model of the IOM/FEX, there's a different number of internal ports. They are hard-pinned to the slots in which the blade servers are installed. This is a huge advantage, as it means the communication of the servers will always have to reach the Fabric Interconnects, and they will be the first networking-capable devices to process the Ethernet frames. In this way, the number of hops in the communication between the servers inside the UCS will be kept to a minimum.

But here's one very important thing: the Fabric Interconnects can operate in two modes when it comes to Ethernet processing. The default mode is end host mode, which again is passive. In it, the servers' traffic is pinned (mapped) to an uplink port and sent to an upstream switch, and there the Ethernet frame is processed. This is because in this mode the Fabric Interconnects do not learn MAC addresses from the LAN infrastructure. Therefore, the upstream network switch will have the knowledge of where to switch to the Ethernet frame from the Cisco UCS server. But the Fabric Interconnects in this mode still learn MAC addresses on their server ports. These are the Ethernet ports that connect to the Cisco UCS IOMs in the blade chassis, or to the C-series servers connected directly to them. In this way, if two Cisco UCS servers want to communicate with each other, and communicate through the same FI, this traffic will be switched locally, without exiting the FI, and without the burden of additional network processing hops, as the IOMs are passive devices.

The second mode of operation for the Fabric Interconnects is the switching mode, where, with some minor limitations, they operate as network switches.

Note that previously, the terms Fabric Extender (FEX) and I/O Module (IOM) have been used interchangeably. In general, from Cisco's perspective, they mean the same thing, but historically they are used for different things. For example, the Cisco Nexus 2000/2200/2300 FEXs are standalone devices, intended to increase the port density when they are connected to upstream Nexus 5500, 5600, 6000, 7000, 7700, or 9000 Series switches. They belong to the LAN component of the data center, and their role is to extend the access layer. The Cisco UCS FEXs/IOMs devices are installed in the blade chassis (they do not have their own power supply or cooling) for the purpose of providing connectivity for the blade servers. As it is true that they operate the same way as the Nexus 2K FEXs, they are different devices with different application.

Now we reach the blade servers. As already mentioned, they are installed in the server slots of the blade chassis, which has a total of eight server slots. The blade servers come in two physical forms: half-width and full-width servers. The half-width blade server occupies one server slot on the chassis. If equipped only with half-width blade servers, the chassis can accommodate up to eight servers. The full-width blade servers occupy two horizontal slots in that chassis, for a maximum of four full-width servers per chassis.

The B-series servers are equipped with a blade connector, which connects the server to the chassis in the slot. The blade connector provides the power to the server, enables the management communication, and also communicates with the server's converged network adapter. With that said, there are two major types of communication for the blade server:

- **The data plane communication:** This includes both the LAN and SAN communication. It happens through the converged adapter or in the Cisco UCS, also called a mezzanine adapter. The mezzanine adapter provides the server separate NICs and HBAs, and externally it has only 10Gbps or higher Ethernet interfaces and supports FCoE for the FC communication.

- **The management plane communication:** Every Cisco server is equipped with separate, autonomous management hardware. It is called the Cisco Integrated Management Controller (CIMC) and it has its own CPU, memory, flash storage, and network interface. When the server is part of a Cisco UCS domain, the CIMC is under the control of the Cisco UCSM, or put a different way, you as an administrator connect to the Cisco UCSM and work from there. The UCSM is responsible for communicating with the CIM and pushing down configurations and commands and retrieving back status and monitoring information. When you work with a C-series server, and it operates in standalone mode, there is no Cisco UCSM. You connect directly to the server's CIMC in order to manage and configure it.

Both the management and data plane communication on the B-series server go through the blade connecter, using separate paths of communication through the blade chassis midplane, and through the chassis' IOMs to reach the Fabric Interconnects.

With all of that said, it is very important to understand that Cisco UCS's physical connectivity creates the underlying communication infrastructure. This infrastructure is available for the communication needs of the servers. How it will be used by each of the servers is a matter of configuration in the Cisco UCSM and relates to the hardware abstraction principle on which the Cisco UCS is based, discussed in the chapter "Describing Cisco UCS Abstraction".

Cisco UCS Fabric Interconnect Product Overview

The Cisco Fabric Interconnect is a core part of Cisco UCS. Here's an overview of Cisco UCS Fabric Interconnect:

- Provides the management and communication backbone

- Supports Unified Fabric:

  - Provides LAN and SAN connectivity for all servers within the domain

  - Includes unified ports with support for Ethernet, Fibre Channel over Ethernet (FCoE), and Fibre Channel

- Comprises a fixed number of unified ports with optional expansion modules

The Cisco UCS Fabric Interconnects are now in their fourth generation. The Cisco UCS 6100 Fabric Interconnects were the first generation. They are no longer supported or sold.

The second generation is the Cisco UCS 6248UP and Cisco 6296UP Fabric Interconnects, which are shown in Figure 16-4.

Cisco UCS 6200 Fabric Interconnects

Cisco UCS 6248UP: 1-RU

Cisco UCS 6296UP: 2-RU

Figure 16-4   *Cisco UCS 6200 Fabric Interconnects*

They offer line-rate, low-latency, lossless 10-Gigabit Ethernet, FCoE, and Fibre Channel functions. Cisco UCS 6200 Series Fabric Interconnects provide LAN and SAN connectivity for all blades within their domain. Cisco UCS 6200 Series uses a cut-through networking architecture, supporting deterministic, low-latency, line-rate 10-Gigabit Ethernet on all ports, a switching capacity of 2 terabits (Tb), and a bandwidth of 320-Gbps per chassis, independent of packet size and enabled services.

The Cisco UCS 6248UP 48-Port Fabric Interconnect is a one-rack-unit (1-RU) 10-Gigabit Ethernet, FCoE, and Fibre Channel switch offering up to 960-Gbps of throughput and up to 48 ports. The switch has 32 1Gbps and 10Gbps fixed Ethernet, FCoE, and Fibre Channel ports and one expansion slot.

The Cisco UCS 6296UP 96-Port Fabric Interconnect is a 2-RU 10-Gigabit Ethernet, FCoE, and native Fibre Channel switch offering up to 1920-Gbps of throughput and up to 96 ports. The switch has 48 1Gbps and 10Gbps fixed Ethernet, FCoE, and Fibre Channel ports and three expansion slots.

The third generation is the Cisco 6300 Fabric Interconnects, shown in Figure 16-5. They provide the following:

- Support for Ethernet, FCoE, or FC
- Up to 2.56-Tbps throughput
- Up to 32× 40-Gbps ports

Cisco UCS 6300 Fabric Interconnects

Figure 16-5 *Cisco UCS 6300 Fabric Interconnects*

The Cisco UCS 6324 Fabric Interconnect extends the Cisco UCS architecture into environments with requirements for smaller domains. Providing the same unified server and networking capabilities as in the full-scale Cisco UCS solution, Cisco UCS 6324 Fabric Interconnect embeds the connectivity within the Cisco UCS 5108 blade server chassis to provide a smaller domain of up to 20 servers.

Cisco UCS 6324 Fabric Interconnect provides the management, LAN, and storage connectivity for the Cisco UCS 5108 blade server chassis and direct-connect rack-mount servers. It provides the same full-featured Cisco UCS management capabilities and XML application programming interface (API) as the full-scale Cisco UCS solution, in addition to integrating with Cisco UCS Central Software and Cisco UCS Director.

From a networking perspective, Cisco UCS 6324 Fabric Interconnect uses a cut-through architecture, supporting deterministic, low-latency, line-rate 10-Gigabit Ethernet on all ports, switching capacity of up to 500-Gbps, and 80-Gbps uplink bandwidth for each chassis, independent of packet size and enabled services. Sixteen 10Gbps links connect to the servers, providing a 20-Gbps link from each Cisco UCS 6324 Fabric Interconnect to each server. The product family supports Cisco low-latency, lossless 10-Gigabit Ethernet unified network fabric capabilities, which increase the reliability, efficiency, and scalability of Ethernet networks. The Fabric Interconnect supports multiple traffic classes over a lossless Ethernet fabric from the blade through the Fabric Interconnect.

The Cisco UCS 6400 Fabric Interconnects, shown in Figure 16-6, comprise the fourth and latest generation:

- 54 or 108 ports
- Up to 7.64-Tbps of throughput
- 1/10/25/40/100-Gbps Ethernet or FCoE
- 8 or 16 unified ports, which support either 10/25-Gbps Ethernet communication or can operate as native FC ports at speeds of 8/16/32-Gbps.

Figure 16-6 *Cisco UCS 6400 Fabric Interconnects*

The Cisco UCS 6454 Fabric Interconnect is a core part of Cisco UCS, providing network connectivity and management capabilities for the system. Cisco UCS 6454 Fabric Interconnect offers line-rate, low-latency, lossless 10-, 25-, 40-, and 100-Gigabit Ethernet, FCoE, and Fibre Channel functions.

The Cisco UCS Fabric Interconnects provide the management and communication backbone for Cisco UCS B-series blade servers, Cisco UCS 5108 B-series server chassis, Cisco UCS Managed C-series rack-mount servers, and Cisco UCS S-series storage servers. All servers attached to the Cisco UCS Fabric Interconnect become part of a single, highly available management domain. In addition, by supporting a unified fabric, Cisco UCS provides LAN and SAN connectivity for all servers within its domain.

From a networking perspective, Cisco UCS 6454 Fabric Interconnect uses a cut-through architecture, supporting deterministic, low-latency, line-rate 10-, 25-, 40-, and 100-Gigabit Ethernet ports, a switching capacity of 3.82-Tbps (terabits per second), and 320-Gbps bandwidth between Cisco UCS 6454 Fabric Interconnect and the Cisco UCS 2208XP I/O module per Cisco UCS 5108 blade server chassis, independent of packet size and enabled services. The product family supports Cisco low-latency, lossless 10-, 25-, 40-, and 100-Gigabit Ethernet unified network fabric capabilities, which increase the reliability, efficiency, and scalability of Ethernet networks. The Fabric Interconnect supports multiple traffic classes over a lossless Ethernet fabric from the server through the Fabric Interconnect.

The Cisco UCS Fabric Interconnect comes with a fixed number of ports. You can optionally install expansion modules that allow you to have a greater number of unified ports.

Cisco UCS Blade Chassis

The Cisco UCS 5108 chassis incorporates unified fabric; integrated, embedded management; and Fabric Extender technology. It uses fewer physical components, has no need for independent management, and enables greater energy efficiency than traditional blade server chassis. This simplicity eliminates the need for dedicated chassis management and blade switches, reduces cabling, and enables Cisco UCS to scale to 20 chassis without adding complexity.

The Cisco UCS 5108 blade server chassis is the first blade server chassis offering by Cisco and is 6-RU. The chassis can mount in an industry-standard 19-inch (48-cm) rack and uses standard front-to-back cooling.

At the front of the chassis, shown in Figure 16-7, are the server slots. It can accommodate up to eight half-width or four full-width Cisco UCS B-Series blade server form factors within the same chassis.

Cisco UCS 5108 Blade Chassis Front View

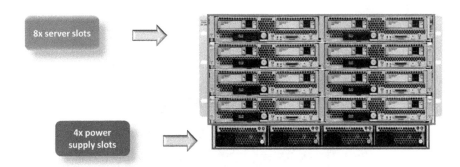

Figure 16-7   *Cisco UCS 5108 Blade Chassis (Front)*

Also, at the front are installed the power supplies. The Cisco UCS 5108 blade server chassis supports up to four fully modular PSUs that are hot-swappable under certain power redundancy configurations.

The power management and redundancy modes are as follows:

■ **Non-redundant:** Cisco UCS Manager turns on the minimum number of power supplies needed and balances the load between them. If any additional PSUs are installed, Cisco UCS Manager sets them to a "turned-off" state. If the power to any PSU is disrupted, the system may experience an interruption in service until Cisco UCS Manager can activate a new PSU and rebalance the load.

■ **N+1:** The total number of PSUs to satisfy non-redundancy, plus one additional PSU for redundancy, are turned on and equally share the power load for the chassis. If any additional PSUs are installed, Cisco UCS Manager sets them to a "turned-off" state. If the power to any PSU is disrupted, Cisco UCS Manager can recover without an interruption in service.

■ **Grid:** Two power sources are turned on, or the chassis requires greater than N+1 redundancy. If one source fails (which causes a loss of power to one or two PSUs), the surviving PSUs on the other power circuit continue to provide power to the chassis.

The power policy is a global policy that specifies the redundancy for power supplies in all chassis in the Cisco UCS domain. This policy is also known as the PSU policy.

At the back, as shown in Figure 16-8, are installed the FEXs for the uplink connectivity to the Fabric Interconnects and the fan modules.

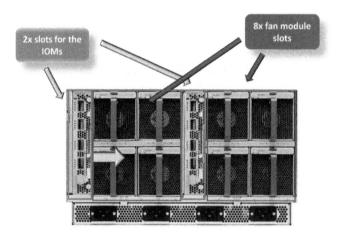

Figure 16-8   *Cisco UCS 5108 Blade Chassis (Back)*

As the blade servers use passive colling, which means that they do not have their own cooling, the fan modules of the chassis take care of the cooling of the chassis, the servers, the power supplies, and the FEX modules. The chassis has a total of eight slots for fan modules to provide the needed redundant cooling capacity.

In the chassis are also installed the FEX modules. They are installed at the back of the chassis because there are two slots for the two FEX modules. To build a Cisco UCS cluster, you need to have two Fabric Interconnects. The cluster link between them does not carry any data communication, because each of the Fabric Interconnects is a separate data path. This is very important because, upstream, the Cisco UCS connects to two different infrastructures—the LAN and the SAN. Each of them has different design requirements for supporting redundancy and increased reliability. A very important principle is always to have two physically separate paths between the initiator and the target. In the LAN infrastructure the approach is almost the opposite—the goal is to interconnect as much as possible and then leave it to the switching and routing protocols as well as to technologies such as port channels and virtual port channels (VPCs) to take care of the redundancy. However, inside the Cisco UCS, it is one and the same physical connectivity, over which communication to both the LAN and the SAN occurs. And this also means that there must be a way for the internal Cisco UCS infrastructure to support the redundancy design for both the LAN and SAN. As the LAN is more flexible, the challenge is to be compliant with the more restrictive design of the SAN infrastructure. That's why, inside the Cisco UCS, it is important to preserve two physically separate paths of communication. Because of that, there are two Cisco UCS FEXs per chassis: one for the communication path through each of the Fabric Interconnects. Put in a different way, each UCS FEX connects to only one UCS Fabric Interconnect.

Cisco IOM Product Overview

Cisco UCS 2200 Series Fabric Extenders, shown in Figure 16-9, bring the unified fabric into the blade server enclosure, providing multiple 10-Gigabit Ethernet connections between blade servers and the Fabric Interconnect, simplifying diagnostics, cabling, and management. This series is a second-generation I/O module (IOM) that shares the same form factor as the IOM of the first-generation Cisco UCS 2100 Series Fabric Extenders, and it is backward-compatible with the shipping Cisco UCS 5108 Blade Server Chassis.

Figure 16-9 *Cisco UCS 2200/2300/2400 Fabric Extenders*

Cisco UCS 2200 Series extends the I/O fabric between Cisco UCS 6200 Series Fabric Interconnects and the Cisco UCS 5100 Series blade server chassis, enabling a lossless and deterministic FCoE fabric to connect all blades and chassis. Because the Fabric Extender is similar to a distributed line card, it does not perform switching and is managed as an extension of the Fabric Interconnects. This approach removes switching from the chassis, reducing overall infrastructure complexity and enabling Cisco UCS to scale to many chassis without multiplying the number of switches needed, reducing total cost of ownership (TCO) and allowing all chassis to be managed as a single, highly available management domain.

Cisco UCS 2200 Series also manages the chassis environment (the power supply, fans, and blades) along with the Fabric Interconnect. Therefore, separate chassis management modules are not required. Cisco UCS 2200 Series Fabric Extenders fit into the back of the Cisco UCS 5100 Series chassis. Each Cisco UCS 5100 Series chassis can support up to two Fabric Extenders, allowing increased capacity and redundancy.

The Cisco UCS 2204XP Fabric Extender has four 10-Gigabit Ethernet, FCoE-capable, SFP+ ports that connect the blade chassis to the Fabric Interconnect. Each Cisco UCS 2204XP has 16 10-Gigabit Ethernet ports connected through the midplane to each half-width slot in the chassis. Typically configured in pairs for redundancy, two Fabric Extenders provide up to 80-Gbps of I/O to the chassis.

The Cisco UCS 2208XP Fabric Extender has eight 10-Gigabit Ethernet, FCoE-capable, Enhanced Small Form-Factor Pluggable (SFP+) ports that connect the blade chassis to the Fabric Interconnect. Each Cisco UCS 2208XP has 32 10-Gigabit Ethernet ports connected through the midplane to each half-width slot in the chassis. Typically configured in pairs for redundancy, two Fabric Extenders provide up to 160-Gbps of I/O to the chassis.

The Cisco UCS 2304 Fabric Extender has four 40-Gigabit Ethernet, FCoE-capable, Quad Small Form-Factor Pluggable (QSFP+) ports that connect the blade chassis to the Fabric Interconnect. Each Cisco UCS 2304 can provide one 40-Gigabit Ethernet port connected through the midplane to each half-width slot in the chassis, giving it a total eight 40G interfaces to the compute. Typically configured in pairs for redundancy, two Fabric Extenders provide up to 320-Gbps of I/O to the chassis.

The Cisco UCS 2408 Fabric Extender has eight 25-Gigabit Ethernet, FCoE-capable, Small Form-Factor Pluggable (SFP28) ports that connect the blade chassis to the Fabric Interconnect. Each Cisco UCS 2408 provides 10-Gigabit Ethernet ports connected through the midplane to each half-width slot in the chassis, giving it a total 32 10G interfaces to UCS blades. Typically configured in pairs for redundancy, two Fabric Extenders provide up to 400Gbps of I/O from FI 6400 series to 5108 chassis.

Cisco UCS B-Series Servers

The Cisco UCS B-Series blade servers have also gone through multiple generations. At the time of writing this chapter, the current generations available are the fifth (M5) and the sixth (M6).

The Cisco UCS servers either have a two-CPU socket mainboard or a four-CPU socket mainboard. To distinguish between them and also to get more information quickly, you need to know the naming convention. For example, Cisco UCS B200 M5 means that this is a blade server (B). If the server name starts with a C, it means that it's a C-series rack mount server. The first digit, which is 2, gives you the information for the number of CPU sockets on the mainboard. This digit can be either 2 or 4 (the latter is for specifying a four-CPU socket mainboard). The M5 at the end of the model's name specifies that this is a fifth-generation server.

Here are the current Cisco B-series servers:

- Cisco UCS B200 M5 blade server

- Cisco UCS B200 M6 blade server

- Cisco UCS B480 M5 blade server

The Cisco UCS blade servers come in full-width and half-width physical sizes. The full-width size takes up two slots in a Cisco UCS 5108 chassis and the half-width size occupies a single slot.

Half-Width Blade Servers

Half-width blade servers take up half of a Cisco UCS B-Series server chassis width, which is one blade server slot. The Cisco UCS B200 M5 and B200 M6 are half-width servers (see Figure 16-10).

Figure 16-10   *Cisco UCS B200 M5 and B200 M6*

The Cisco UCS B200 M5 blade server has the following features:

- Up to two second-generation Intel Xeon Scalable and Intel Xeon Scalable processors with up to 28 cores per CPU.

- Twenty-four DIMM slots for industry-standard DDR4 memory at speeds up to 2933 MHz, with up to 3TB of total memory when using 128GB DIMMs. Up to 12 DIMM slots ready for Intel Optane DC Persistent Memory to accommodate up to 6TB of Intel Optane DC Persistent Memory.

- Modular LAN On Motherboard (mLOM) card with Cisco UCS Virtual Interface Card (VIC) 1440 or 1340, a two-port, 40-Gigabit Ethernet (GE), Fibre Channel over Ethernet (FCoE) capable mLOM mezzanine adapter.

- Optional rear mezzanine VIC with two 40-Gbps unified I/O ports or two sets of 4× 10-Gbps unified I/O ports, delivering 80-Gbps to the server; adapts to either 10 or 40-Gbps fabric connections.

- Two optional, hot-pluggable, hard disk drives (HDDs), solid-state drives (SSDs), or Nonvolatile Memory Express (NVMe) 2.5-inch drives with a choice of enterprise-class RAID (redundant array of independent disks) or pass-through controllers.

- Support for optional SD Card or M.2 SATA drives for flexible boot and local storage capabilities.

- Support for up to two optional GPUs.

- Support for one rear storage mezzanine card.

- Support for one 16GB internal flash USB drive.

The Cisco UCS B200 M6 offers the following features:

- Up to two third-generation Intel Xeon Scalable Processors (with up to 40 cores per socket)

- Memory:

    - 32 DIMM slots (16 DIMMs per CPU socket)

    - 3200 MHz DDR4 memory, plus other speeds, depending on the CPU installed

    - 32× DDR4 DIMMs for up to 8TB of capacity using 256GB DIMMs, or

    - 16× DDR4 DIMMs + 16× Intel Optane persistent memory modules for up to 12TB of memory

- Cisco UCS Virtual Interface Card (VIC) 1440 modular LAN On Motherboard (mLOM)

- Two mezzanine card adapters:

    - One rear slot for the VIC (Cisco UCS VIC 1480 or port expander)

    - One front dedicated slot for a Cisco FlexStorage RAID controller, Cisco FlexStorage passthrough, or Cisco M.2 RAID controller

- Up to two SATA/NVMe disk drives or up to four M.2 drives

Full-Width Blade Server

A full-width blade server, shown in Figure 16-11, takes up the full width of a Cisco UCS B-Series server chassis, which means it takes two horizontal server slots in the chassis.

Figure 16-11   *Cisco UCS B480 M5 Full-Width Blade Server*

The Cisco UCS B480 M5 blade server is the only currently offered full-width blade server, and it has the following characteristics:

- Four new second-generation Intel Xeon scalable CPUs (up to 28 cores per socket)
- Four existing Intel Xeon scalable CPUs (up to 28 cores per socket)
- Support for higher-density DDR4 memory, from 6TB (128G DDR4 DIMMs) to 12TB (256G DDR4 DIMMs)
- Memory speed increase from 2666 MHz to 2933 MHz
- Intel Optane DC Persistent Memory Modules (DCPMMs): 128G, 256G, and 512G1
- Up to 18TB using 24× 256G DDR4 DIMMs and 24× 512G Intel Optane DC Persistent Memory Modules
- Cisco FlexStorage storage subsystem
- Five mezzanine adapters and support for up to four NVIDIA GPUs
- Cisco UCS Virtual Interface Card (VIC) 1340 modular LAN On Motherboard (mLOM) and upcoming fourth-generation VIC mLOM
- Internal Secure Digital (SD) and M.2 boot options

Only one CPU is required for normal system operation. If only one CPU is installed, the CPU must go into the first socket. The CPUs must be identical on the same blade server but can be mixed between blade servers in the same chassis. Also, depending on which CPU sockets, different memory configurations are supported.

Cisco UCS C-Series Servers and the Cisco IMC Supervisor

Cisco UCS C-Series rack servers deliver unified computing in a rack-mount form factor. The Cisco UCS C-Series rack server family offers an entry point into unified computing. Cisco UCS C-Series rack servers offer the flexibility of standalone management or can be integrated as part of a Cisco UCS managed environment.

The Cisco UCS C-Series rack servers, shown in Figure 16-12, from the fifth generation (M5) are as follows:

- Cisco UCS C220 M5 rack server

- Cisco UCS C240 M5 rack server

- Cisco UCS C480 M5 rack servers

- Cisco UCS C480 ML M5 rack servers

- Cisco UCS C4200 Series rack server chassis

- Cisco UCS C125 M5 rack server node

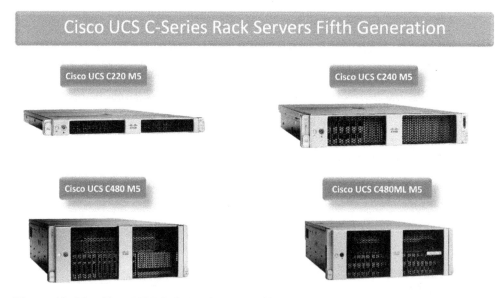

Figure 16-12   *Cisco UCS C-Series Servers Fifth Generation*

The Cisco UCS C-series offers various models that can address different workload challenges through a balance of processing, memory, I/O, and internal storage resources.

When used with Cisco UCS Manager, Cisco UCS C-Series servers bring the power and automation of unified computing to enterprise applications, including Cisco

SingleConnect technology. Cisco SingleConnect unifies LAN, SAN, and systems management into one simplified link for rack servers, blade servers, and virtual machines. This technology reduces the number of network adapters, cables, and switches needed, radically simplifies the network, and reduces complexity.

Cisco UCS Manager uses service profiles, templates, and policy-based management to enable rapid deployment and to help ensure deployment consistency. It also enables end-to-end server visibility, management, and control in both virtualized and bare-metal environments.

Cisco UCS C-Series M5 servers are Cisco Intersight ready. Cisco Intersight is a new cloud-based management platform that uses analytics to deliver proactive automation and support. By combining intelligence with automated actions, you can reduce costs dramatically and resolve issues more quickly.

The Cisco UCS C220 M5 rack server is among the most versatile, general-purpose, enterprise infrastructure and application servers in the industry. It is a high-density two-socket rack server that delivers exceptional performance and efficiency for a wide range of workloads, including virtualization, collaboration, and bare-metal applications.

The Cisco UCS C220 M5 server extends the capabilities of the Cisco UCS portfolio in a 1RU form factor. It incorporates Intel Xeon Scalable processors, which support up to 20% more cores per socket, twice the memory capacity, 20% greater storage density, and five times more PCIe NVMe SSDs compared to the previous generation of servers. These improvements deliver significant performance and efficiency gains that will improve your application performance.

The Cisco UCS C220 M5 delivers outstanding levels of expandability and performance in a compact package that includes the following:

- Latest (second-generation) Intel Xeon Scalable CPUs, with up to 28 cores per socket
- Support for first-generation Intel Xeon Scalable CPUs, with up to 28 cores per socket
- Up to 24 DDR4 DIMMs for improved performance
- Support for the Intel Optane DC Persistent Memory (128G, 256G, 512G)
- Up to 10 Small-Form-Factor (SFF) 2.5-inch drives or four Large-Form-Factor (LFF) 3.5-inch drives (77TB storage capacity with all NVMe PCIe SSDs)
- Support for a 12-Gbps SAS modular RAID controller in a dedicated slot, leaving the remaining PCIe Generation 3.0 slots available for other expansion cards
- Modular LAN-On-Motherboard (mLOM) slot that can be used to install a Cisco UCS Virtual Interface Card (VIC) without consuming a PCIe slot
- Dual embedded Intel x550 10GBASE-T LAN-On-Motherboard (LOM) ports

The Cisco UCS C240 M5 rack server is a two-socket, 2RU rack server that offers industry-leading performance and expandability. It supports a wide range of storage and I/O-intensive infrastructure workloads, from big data and analytics to collaboration.

The C240 M5 delivers outstanding levels of storage expandability with exceptional performance and includes the following:

- The latest (second-generation) Intel Xeon Scalable CPUs, with up to 28 cores per socket

- Support for the Intel Optane DC Persistent Memory (128G, 256G, 512G)

- Up to 24 DDR4 DIMMs for improved performance, including higher-density DDR4 DIMMs

- Up to 26 hot-swappable Small-Form-Factor (SFF) 2.5-inch drives, including two rear hot-swappable SFF drives (up to 10 support NVMe PCIe SSDs on the NVMe-optimized chassis version) or 12 Large-Form-Factor (LFF) 3.5-inch drives plus two rear hot-swappable SFF drives

- Support for 12-Gbps SAS modular RAID controller in a dedicated slot, leaving the remaining PCIe Generation 3.0 slots available for other expansion cards

- Modular LAN-On-Motherboard (mLOM) slot that can be used to install a Cisco UCS Virtual Interface Card (VIC) without consuming a PCIe slot, supporting dual 10 or 40-Gbps network connectivity

- Dual embedded Intel x550 10GBASE-T LAN-On-Motherboard (LOM) ports

- Modular M.2 or Secure Digital (SD) cards that can be used for boot

The Cisco UCS C480 M5 rack server is a storage- and I/O-optimized enterprise-class rack server that delivers industry-leading performance for in-memory databases, big data analytics, virtualization, and bare-metal applications. The C480 M5 comes in a 4RU form-factor and has the following characteristics:

- Four new second-generation Intel Xeon Scalable CPUs (up to 28 cores per socket)

- Four existing Intel Xeon Scalable CPUs (up to 28 cores per socket)

- Support for two-or four-processor configurations

- Support for the Intel Optane DC Persistent Memory (128G, 256G, 512G)

- Support for higher-density DDR4 memory, from 6TB (128G DDR4 DIMMs) to 12TB (256G DDR4 DIMMs)

- Memory speed increase from 2666 MHz to 2933 MHz

- Intel Optane DC Persistent Memory Modules (DCPMM): 128G, 256G, and 512G1

- Up to 18TB using 24× 256G DDR4 DIMMs and 24× 512G Intel Optane DC Persistent Memory Modules

- Up to four GPUs (two-CPU configuration) or six GPUs (four-CPU configuration) with offerings from NVIDIA and AMD

- Twelve PCI Express (PCIe) 3.0 slots

    - Six x8 full-height, full length slots

    - Six x16 full-height, full length slots

- Flexible storage options with support up to 32 Small-Form-Factor (SFF) 2.5-inch, SAS, SATA, and PCIe NVMe disk drives

- Cisco 12Gbps SAS modular RAID controller in a dedicated slot

- Internal Secure Digital (SD) and M.2 boot options

- Dual embedded 10-Gigabit Ethernet LAN-On-Motherboard (LOM) ports

The Cisco UCS C480 ML M5 rack server is a purpose-built server for deep learning. It is storage- and I/O-optimized to deliver performance for training models. It comes in a 4RU form factor and offers these capabilities:

- Eight NVIDIA SXM2 V100 32G modules with NVLink interconnect.

- The latest Intel Xeon Scalable processors with up to 28 cores per socket and support for two processor configurations. It supports both first- and second-generation Intel Xeon Scalable CPUs.

- 2933MHz DDR4 memory and 24 DIMM slots for up to 7.5TB of total memory

- Support for the Intel Optane DC Persistent Memory (128G, 256G, and 512G)

- Memory speed increase from 2666 MHz to 2933 MHz

- Intel Optane DC Persistent Memory Modules (DCPMM): 128G, 256G, and 512G[1]

- Up to 7.5TB using 12× 128G DDR4 DIMMs and 12× 512G Intel Optane DC Persistent Memory Modules

- Four PCI Express (PCIe) 3.0 slots for 100G UCS VIC 1495

- Flexible storage options with support for up to 24 Small-Form-Factor (SFF) 2.5-inch, SAS/SATA solid-state disks (SSDs) and hard-disk drives (HDDs)

- Up to six PCIe NVMe disk drives

- One Cisco 12-Gbps SAS modular RAID controller in a dedicated slot

- M.2 boot options

- Dual embedded 10-Gigabit Ethernet LAN-On-Motherboard (LOM) ports

Figure 16-13 shows the Cisco UCS C4200 rack server and the C125 M5 rack server node.

Figure 16-13 *Cisco UCS C4200 Series Rack Server and the C125 M5 Rack Server Node*

The C4200 chassis extends the capabilities of the Cisco UCS portfolio in a two-rack-unit (2RU) form factor supporting up to four Cisco UCS C125 M5 rack server nodes. The latest update includes support for AMD EPYC 2 (Rome) 7002 processors. The AMD EPYC 2 processors have higher core density (up to 64 cores) and higher performance with an enhanced AMD Zen 2 core design. The existing AMD EPYC 7001 processors will continue to be offered for flexibility of customer choice. Both CPU types deliver significant performance and efficiency gains in a compact form factor that will improve your application performance while saving space. The C4200 and C125 M5 nodes deliver outstanding levels of capability and performance in a highly compact package, with the following features:

- AMD EPYC 7002 (Rome) series processors with up to 64 cores per socket, and AMD EPYC 7001 (Naples) series processors with up to 32 cores per socket

- Up to 1TB of DRAM using 16 64GB DDR4 DIMMs for two-socket CPU configuration (eight DIMMs/memory channels per CPU)

- 3200MHz 16G/32G/64G DIMMs for AMD EPYC 7002 (Rome) CPUs, and 2666MHz 16G/32G/64G DIMMs of AMD EPYC 7001 (Naples) CPUs

- Over 45TB of storage, with up to six Small-Form-Factor (SFF) 2.5-inch direct-attached drives per node

  - Either six direct-attached SAS/SATA drives or two NVMe plus four SAS/SATA drives

- Optional dual SD cards or M.2 modular storage for increased storage or boot drive capacity

- Support for the Cisco 12-G 9460-8i PCIe SAS RAID controller with 2GB Flash-Backed Write Cache (FBWC)

- Support for the Cisco 12-G 9400-8i PCIe SAS controller for use with external disk arrays

- OCP 2.0 network mezzanine slot supporting speeds up to 100Gbps

- Support for Cisco's fourth-generation PCIe Virtual Interface Card (VIC)

The sixth-generation (M6) Cisco UCS C-Series rack servers, shown in Figure 16-14, are as follows:

- Cisco UCS C220 M6 rack server

- Cisco UCS C225 M6 rack server

- Cisco UCS C240 M6 rack server

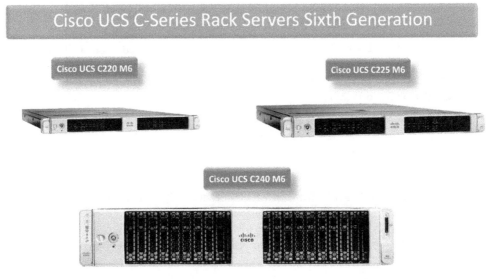

Figure 16-14   *Cisco UCS C-Series Sixth-Generation Rack Servers*

The Cisco UCS C220 M6 rack server extends the capabilities of the Cisco UCS rack server portfolio. It incorporates the third-generation Intel Xeon Scalable processors with more than 40% more cores per socket and 33% more memory versus the previous generation. These improvements deliver up to 40% more performance that will improve your application performance. The Cisco UCS C220 M6 rack server delivers outstanding levels of expandability and performance. It offers the following features:

- Up to two third-generation Intel Xeon Scalable processors (with up to 40 cores per socket)

- Memory:

  - 32 DIMM slots (16 DIMMs per CPU socket)

- 3200 MHz DDR4 memory plus other speeds, depending on the CPU installed

- 32× DDR4 DIMMs for up to 4TB of capacity using 128 GB DIMMs, or

- 16× DDR4 DIMMs + 16x Intel Optane persistent memory modules for up to 10TB of memory

■ Up to three PCIe 4.0 slots plus a modular LAN On Motherboard (mLOM) slot

■ Support for Cisco UCS VIC 1400 Series adapters as well as third-party options

■ Up to 10 SAS/SATA or NVMe disk drives

■ RAID controller options available

■ M.2 boot options

■ Up to 960 GB with optional hardware RAID

■ Up to two GPUs supported

The C225 M6 rack server is single socket optimized. All I/O is tied to one CPU and its 128 PCIe lanes. Since each server supports up to 2TB and 64 cores per socket, many customers find that one CPU server now meets their needs. This can reduce software licensing and support costs leading to a better TCO.

The technical characteristics of the C225 M6 server are as follows:

■ One or two third-generation AMD EPYC CPUs, with up to 64 cores per socket

■ Memory:

- 32 DIMM slots (16 DIMMs per CPU socket), 3200 MHz DDR4

- Up to 4TB of capacity

■ Up to 10 Small-Form-Factor (SFF) front-loading hot-pluggable drives (NVMe/SAS/ SATA)

■ Up to three PCIe 4.0 slots

■ Support for 1400 Series VIC and OCP 3.0 network cards

■ RAID controller and GPU options available

■ Internal dual M.2 drive options

The Cisco UCS C240 M6 server extends the capabilities of the Cisco UCS rack server portfolio with third-generation Intel Xeon Scalable processors supporting more than 43% more cores per socket and 33% more memory when compared with the previous generation. This provides up to 40% more performance than the M5 generation for your most demanding applications. It is well-suited for a wide range of storage and I/O-intensive applications such as big data analytics, databases, collaboration, virtualization, consolidation, and high-performance computing in its two-socket, 2RU form factor, as it offers the following features:

- Up to two third-generation Intel Xeon Scalable processors (with up to 40 cores per socket)

- Memory:

    - 32 DIMM slots (16 DIMMs per CPU socket)

    - 3200 MHz DDR4 memory plus other speeds, depending on the CPU installed

    - 32× DDR4 DIMMs for up to 8TB of capacity using 256GB DIMMs, or

    - 16× DDR4 DIMMs + 16× Intel Optane persistent memory modules for up to 12TB of memory

- Up to eight PCIe 4.0 slots plus modular LAN On Motherboard (mLOM) slot

- Support for Cisco UCS VIC 1400 Series adapters as well as third-party options

- Up to 28 SAS/SATA/NVMe disk drives

    - RAID controller options available

    - M.2 boot options

    - Up to 960 GB with optional hardware RAID

- Support for up to five GPUs

Cisco UCS S-Series Storage Server

The Cisco UCS S3260 storage server, shown in Figure 16-15, is a modular, high-density, high-availability, dual-node storage-optimized server that is well-suited for service providers, enterprises, and industry-specific environments. It provides dense, cost-effective storage to address your ever-growing data needs. Designed for a new class of data-intensive workloads, it is simple to deploy and excellent for applications for big data, data protection, software-defined storage environments, scale-out unstructured data repositories, media streaming, and content distribution.

Figure 16-15   *Cisco UCS S3260 Storage Server*

The Cisco UCS S3260 server is based on a chassis, which supports two compute nodes, each based on the second-generation Intel Xeon Scalable processor. The compute nodes provide the computing power. The supported local storage is up to 1080TB in a compact four-rack-unit (4RU) form factor. The drives can be configured with enterprise-class RAID (redundant array of independent disks) redundancy or with a pass-through host bus adapter (HBA) controller. Network connectivity is provided with dual-port up-to-40Gbps nodes in each server, with expanded unified I/O capabilities for data migration between network-attached storage (NAS) and SAN environments. This storage-optimized server comfortably fits in a standard 32-inch-depth rack, such as the Cisco R 42610 rack.

The following are the product highlights:

- Dual two-socket server nodes based on Intel Xeon Scalable processors. The M5 server node supports the following processors: 4214, 5218, 5220, 6238, 6240, 6262V, 4210R, 4214R, 5218R, 5220R, 6226R, and 6230R.

- Up to 48 cores per server node.

- Up to 1.5TB of DDR4 memory per M5 server node.

- Support for high-performance NVMe and flash memory.

- Up to 12.8TB NVMe for an M5 server node.

- Massive 1080TB data storage capacity that easily scales to petabytes with Cisco UCS Manager software.

- Supported drives:

    - Up to 56 top-accessible, hot-swappable 3.5-inch, 2, 4, 6, 8, 10, 12, 14, 16, or 18TB 7200-RPM NL-SAS hard-disk drives (HDDs).

- Up to 28 top-accessible, hot-swappable 800GB, 1.6TB, or 3.2TB SAS solid-state drives (SSDs).

- Up to two rear-accessible, hot-swappable, 2.5-inch, 240GB or 480GB SATA or 1.6TB SSDs per server node.

- Policy-based storage management framework for zero-touch capacity on demand.

- Dual-port 40Gbps system I/O controllers.

- PCIe Slot based with choice of Cisco UCS VIC 1455 Quad Port 10/25G, Cisco UCS VIC 1495 Dual Port 40/100G, or third-party Ethernet and FC adapters.

- Unified I/O for Ethernet or Fibre Channel to existing NAS or SAN storage environments.

- Support for Cisco bidirectional transceivers, with 40Gbps connectivity over existing 10Gbps cabling infrastructure.

- I/O expansion module:

    - Dual x8 Peripheral Component Interconnect Express (PCIe) half-height, half-width slots for third-party add-in cards. (Note: This is available with M5 and M4 server node and uses server bay 1.)

    - Choice of I/O Ethernet and Fibre Channel options: 1-, 10- or 40-Gigabit Ethernet or 16-Gbps Fibre Channel

- NVMe SSD options of 1.6, 3.2, or 6.4TB

- Application acceleration with support for NVIDIA T4 16GB GPU

Cisco UCS management provides enhanced storage management functions for the Cisco UCS S3260 and all Cisco UCS servers. Storage profiles give you flexibility in defining the number of storage disks and the roles and uses of those disks and other storage parameters. You can select and configure the disks to be used for storage by a virtual drive.

A logical collection of physical disks is called a disk group, and a disk group configuration policy defines the way in which a disk group is created and configured. A disk group can be partitioned into virtual drives. Each virtual drive appears as an individual physical device to the operating system. The policy specifies the RAID level for each disk group. It also specifies either manual or automatic selection of disks for the disk group and the roles for the disks. This feature allows optimization of the storage resources without additional overhead and licensing costs. The RAID storage controller characteristics are as follows:

- M5 server node:

    - Dual-chip RAID controller based on LSI 3316 ROC with 4GB RAID cache per chip and Supercap

    - Controller support for RAID 0, 1, 5, 10, 50, and 60 and JBOD mode, providing enterprise-class data protection for all drives installed in the system

- Pass-through controller:

  - Dual-chip pass-through controller with LSI IOC 3316 using LSI IT firmware

Cisco HyperFlex Data Platform

Hyperconverged infrastructure (HCI) combines compute, virtualization, storage, and networking in a single cluster. Starting with as few as three nodes, users can easily scale out to match computing and storage resource needs. Hyperconvergence brings cloudlike simplicity on-premises and within a single, easily managed platform.

Nowadays, the organizations must meet the challenges of growing data center requirements because of a wider set of application deployment models:

- **Traditional enterprise applications:** Monolithic components are transitioning to a more scalable, cloud-like model (for example, components such as presentation layers).

- **Big data and analytics:** Require scale-out architectures with large amounts of high-performance storage. Data scientists need massive amounts of GPU acceleration for artificial intelligence and machine learning processes.

- **Cloud-native architectures:** Based on microservices, cloud-native architectures require both virtualized and container-based deployment. Developers are creating these applications so they can run across multiple clouds with automatic deployment and scaling.

Building and integrating data center infrastructures that meet these versatile requirements is complex, challenging, and takes a lot of resources. Reducing this complexity is the only way to support existing and new applications, ensure service delivery, maintain control over data, and attain necessary performance. This makes the hyperconverged solutions the right answer because they deliver the compute, networking, storage, virtualization, and container support as one integrated and tested solution.

The Cisco HyperFlex System, shown in Figure 16-16, is an adaptive, hyperconverged system built on the foundation of the Cisco UCS. It meets the requirements for the different application deployments by supporting multicloud environments.

Cisco HyperFlex HX-Series servers combine software-defined networking and computing with the next-generation Cisco HyperFlex HX data platform.

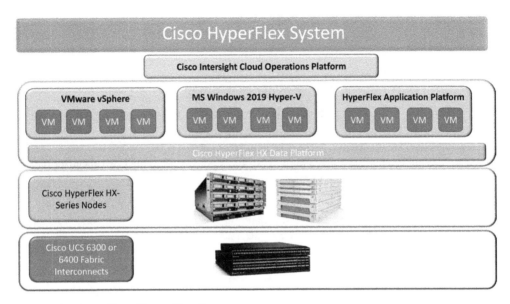

Figure 16-16 *Cisco HyperFlex System*

With hybrid or all-flash memory storage configurations and a choice of management tools, Cisco HyperFlex systems are deployed as a pre-integrated cluster with a unified pool of resources that you can quickly provision, adapt, scale, and manage to efficiently power your applications and your business.

The Cisco HyperFlex platform is faster to deploy, simpler to manage, easier to scale, and ready to provide a unified pool of resources to power your business applications. You harness these resources with your choice of centralized management tools: Cisco Intersight cloud-based Management as a Service (covered in Chapter 21, "Cloud Computing"), Cisco HyperFlex Connect, Microsoft System Center Virtual Machine Manager, Hyper-V Manager, or a VMware vSphere plug-in. Cisco HyperFlex systems integrate into the data center you have today without creating an island of IT resources. You can deploy Cisco HyperFlex systems wherever you need them—from central data center environments to remote locations and edge-computing environments.

Cisco HyperFlex systems are based on Cisco UCS M5 rack servers. Based on Intel Xeon Scalable processors, these fifth-generation servers have faster processors, more cores, and faster and larger-capacity memory than previous-generation servers. In addition, they are ready for Intel 3D XPoint nonvolatile memory, which can be used as both storage and system memory, increasing your virtual server configuration options and flexibility for applications.

- Cisco HyperFlex HX240c M5/M6

- Cisco HyperFlex HX240c M5/M6 All Flash

- Cisco HyperFlex HX240c M5 HX240c M5 LFF

- Cisco HyperFlex HX220c M5/M6

- Cisco HyperFlex HX220c M5/M6 All Flash

- Cisco HyperFlex HX220c M5/M6 All NVMe

Physically, the system is delivered as a cluster of three or more of Cisco HyperFlex HX240c M5, HX240c M5 All Flash, HX240c M5 LFF, HX220c M5, HX220c M5 All Flash, or HX220c M5 All NVMe nodes that are integrated into a single system by a pair of Cisco UCS 6300 or 6400 Series Fabric Interconnects. The HX240c M5 node is excellent for high-capacity clusters, and the HX240c M5 All Flash node is excellent for high-performance, high-capacity clusters.

The Cisco HX240c M5 node is excellent for balanced-capacity clusters. The HX240c M5 LFF node delivers high-capacity clusters, and the HX240c M5 All Flash node is excellent for balanced-performance and capacity clusters. Each node configuration includes the following:

- Memory (up to 3TB of memory supported)

- Storage:

  - All-flash memory, all-NVMe, or hybrid storage configurations (combination of HDDs and SSDs)

  - Cisco 12Gbps modular SAS host bus adapter (HBA) with internal SAS connectivity

    M.2 SATA SSD drive for boot

    Data platform logging drive

  - M.2 boot drive for VMware vSphere

- One Cisco UCS VIC

- Cisco UCS service profile templates for automated cluster configuration

- Software:

  - Cisco HyperFlex HX Data Platform software (software subscription)

  - VMware vSphere ESXi 6.0 software preinstalled (ESXi 6.5 supported but not pre-installed)

Cisco HyperFlex nodes can be deployed with various Cisco UCS B-series blade servers and C-series rack servers to create a hybrid cluster. With a single point of connectivity and management, you can easily scale your cluster to support more workloads and deliver the performance, bandwidth, and low latency your users and applications need.

Cisco UCS X-Series Modular System

The Cisco UCS X-Series Modular system, shown in Figure 16-17, is the latest generation of the Cisco UCS. Here are the major new features:

- The system operates in Intersight Managed Mode (IMM), as it is managed from the Cisco Intersight.

- The new Cisco UCS X9508 chassis has a midplane-free design. The I/O connectivity for the X9508 chassis is accomplished via frontloading, with vertically oriented compute nodes intersecting with horizontally oriented I/O connectivity modules in the rear of the chassis.

- Cisco UCS 9108 Intelligent Fabric modules provide connectivity to the upstream Cisco UCS 6400 Fabric Interconnects.

- Cisco UCS X210c M6 compute nodes – blade servers designed for the new chassis.

The new Cisco UCS X9508 chassis provides a new and adaptable substitute for the first generation of the UCS chassis. It is designed to be expandable in the future. As proof of this, the X-Fabric slots are intended for future use. It has optimized cooling flows to support reliable operation for longer times. The major features are as follows:

- A seven-rack-unit (7RU) chassis has 8× front-facing flexible slots. These can house a combination of compute nodes and a pool of future I/O resources, which may include GPU accelerators, disk storage, and nonvolatile memory.

- 2× Cisco UCS 9108 Intelligent Fabric Modules (IFMs) at the top of the chassis that connect the chassis to upstream Cisco UCS 6400 Series Fabric Interconnects. Each IFM has the following features:

  - Up to 100Gbps of unified fabric connectivity per compute node.

  - 8× 25-Gbps SFP28 uplink ports. The unified fabric carries management traffic to the Cisco Intersight cloud-operations platform, Fibre Channel over Ethernet (FCoE) traffic, and production Ethernet traffic to the fabric interconnects.

  - At the bottom are slots, ready to house future I/O modules that can flexibly connect the compute modules with I/O devices. This connectivity is called "Cisco UCS X-Fabric technology" because X is a variable that can evolve with new technology developments.

  - Six 2800W power supply units (PSUs) provide 54V power to the chassis with N, N+1, and N+N redundancy. A higher voltage allows efficient power delivery with less copper and reduced power loss.

- Efficient, 4×100mm, dual counter-rotating fans deliver industry-leading airflow and power efficiency. Optimized thermal algorithms enable different cooling modes to best support the network environment. Cooling is modular so that future enhancements can potentially handle open- or closed-loop liquid cooling to support even higher-power processors.

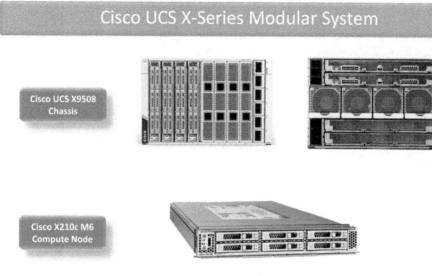

Figure 16-17 *Cisco UCS X-Series Modular System*

The chassis supports up to eight Cisco UCS X210c M6 compute nodes. These are newly designed Cisco UCS blade servers, specifically for the Cisco UCS X9508 chassis. The main features are as follows:

- **CPU:** Up to 2× third-generation Intel Xeon Scalable processors with up to 40 cores per processor and 1.5MB Level 3 cache per core.

- **Memory:** Up to 32× 256GB DDR4-3200 DIMMs for up to 8TB of main memory. Configuring up to 16× 512GB Intel Optane persistent memory DIMMs can yield up to 12TB of memory.

- **Storage:** Up to six hot-pluggable solid-state drives (SSDs) or Non-Volatile Memory Express (NVMe) 2.5-inch drives with a choice of enterprise-class RAID (redundant array of independent disks) or passthrough controllers with four lanes each of PCIe Gen 4 connectivity and up to two M.2 SATA drives for flexible boot and local storage capabilities.

- **mLOM virtual interface card:** The Cisco UCS Virtual Interface Card (VIC) 14425 can occupy the server's modular LAN On Motherboard (mLOM) slot, enabling up to 50-Gbps of unified fabric connectivity to each of the chassis Intelligent Fabric Modules (IFMs) for 100-Gbps connectivity per server.

- **Optional mezzanine virtual interface card:** Cisco UCS Virtual Interface Card (VIC) 14825 can occupy the server's mezzanine slot at the bottom of the chassis. This card's I/O connectors link to Cisco UCS X-Fabric Technology, which is planned for future I/O expansion. An included bridge card extends this VIC's 2× 50Gbps of network connections through IFM connectors, bringing the total bandwidth to 100Gbps per fabric—for a total of 200Gbps per server.

■ **Security:** The server supports an optional Trusted Platform Module (TPM). Additional features include a secure boot FPGA and ACT2 anti-counterfeit provisions.

Summary

This chapter described the components of the Cisco UCS and HyperFlex system. In this chapter, you learned about the following:

■ The Cisco Unified Computing System (UCS) is a complex, highly integrated solution for the compute component of the data center.

■ The Cisco UCS Manager provides the management functionality and runs on the Cisco Fabric Interconnects.

■ The northbound Cisco Fabric Interconnects connect the Cisco UCS to the LAN and SAN infrastructures of the data center.

■ The servers always communicate through the Fabric Interconnects.

■ The physical connectivity inside the Cisco UCS is based on Ethernet physical links and the use of the FCoE protocol for storage communication.

■ The servers are equipped with converged network adapters, called mezzanine cards, that support converged communication.

■ The B-series servers are the blade servers.

■ The B-series servers are installed in the Cisco UCS 5108 blade chassis.

■ The blade chassis provides eight slots for the servers and takes care of their cooling and power supply needs.

■ The Cisco UCS 2200/2300/2400 FEXs are installed in the blade chassis. They connect the chassis to the Fabric Interconnects.

■ Half-width blade servers, such as the Cisco UCS B200 M5 and B200 M6, occupy a single slot in the chassis.

■ The Cisco UCS B480 M5 is a full-width blade server, as it occupies two horizontal slots in the chassis.

■ The C-series servers are rack-mountable servers that can operate as a part of the Cisco UCS or as standalone servers.

■ When operating in standalone mode, the C-series servers are managed through the Cisco Integrated Management Controller (CIMC) directly.

■ The CIMC is separate autonomous hardware that provides out-of-band management access to the Cisco servers.

- The Cisco UCS C4200 rack server is a chassis itself, as the memory and CPUs are separated on the so-called compute nodes. This allows you to increase or decrease the computing capacity based on your needs.

- The Cisco UCS S3260 is a rack mount server that's optimized to be a storage server, with the support of a massive amount of local storage.

- The Cisco HyperFlex integrated platform is Cisco's hyper-converged solution based on the Cisco UCS. It consists of the compute, communication, storage, virtualization, and container components to provide an integrated solution for the needs of the hybrid cloud, data analytics, and cloud-native applications based on microservices.

- The latest generation of the Cisco UCS is the Cisco UCS X-Series Modular platform.

- The Cisco UCS-X platform consists of the new Cisco X9508 chassis and the new X210c compute nodes.

Reference

"Cisco Servers – Unified Computing System (UCS)," https://www.cisco.com/c/en/us/products/servers-unified-computing/index.html

Chapter 17

Describing Cisco UCS Abstraction

This chapter discusses the Cisco Unified Computing System (UCS) abstraction. The Cisco UCS is a complex system that consists of different physical components covered in the previous chapter, such as the B- and C-series servers, which provide the computing resources, the Cisco 5108 blade chassis, the IOMs (FEXs) for the physical connectivity of the servers, and the Fabric Interconnects, which connects the Cisco UCS with the other components of the data center and is the platform on which the Cisco UCS Manager application runs. Therefore, you can see that there are various components with different functions that, through integration and centralized management, operate as a single entity. And on top of this is the major benefit of using the Cisco UCS—the ability to abstract the servers from the physical environment, to improve the utilization of the computing resources, and to provide redundancy and flexibility. The abstraction in the Cisco UCS is achieved by using two components to create a server—the physical server node and the associated service profile. Only when the two are associated with each other in a one-to-one relationship is there a server that can be used. The service profile is the logical component created in the Cisco UCS Manager by the administrator, and it describes the server. With other words, it contains all the needed configurations, the identity values used by the server, and the communication to the data center LAN and SAN. Then, when the service profile is associated with the physical server node, either a B- or C-series server, the two components create a server that can be used for further installation of the operating system (OS) and the applications. In this chapter, you will be acquainted with the Cisco UCS Manager, the server environment, the global policies, or how the Cisco UCS Manager discovers the hardware it will manage. Then you will learn about the server identities and how they are abstracted in the Cisco UCS. You will look into what exactly a service profile and a service profile template are, what policies can be used in them, and how to configure them in the Cisco UCS Manager. At the end of this chapter, you will learn about a centralized management application that allows you to oversee multiple Cisco UCS domains from a single pane of glass.

Cisco UCS Manager Overview

In the Cisco UCS, the Cisco UCS Manager (UCSM) is the application that takes care of the discovery of the physical components of the system, creates and applies the configuration, and monitors and reports on any changes and issues. It runs on the two Fabric Interconnects that form the Cisco UCS cluster. A single UCS cluster is under the management of one Cisco UCSM, and this combination is called a Cisco UCS domain. To be more precise, a Cisco UCS domain represents a pair of Cisco UCS Fabric Interconnects, connected through the cluster link to create a Cisco UCS cluster, under the management of a single Cisco UCSM. In a single Cisco UCS domain, a Cisco UCSM instance can manage up to 160 B- and C-series servers.

The two Fabric Interconnects in a Cisco UCS cluster operate in a high-availability and redundant mode. When it comes to the data communication of the servers, or the data plane, the two Fabric Interconnects are active (that is, they both process the data communication or provide active data paths). At the level of the management and control planes, they operate in an active-standby manner. This means that after the Fabric Interconnects have booted up, there is a negotiation between the two, based on which is determined to be the primary one. On the primary Fabric Interconnect, the management and control applications and services run in active mode; on the other Fabric Interconnect (the subordinate), they run in standby mode. The active instances will be distributed between the two for load balancing. The cluster link is used to synchronize configuration and state information between the active and standby instances of the applications and services. But what are these applications and services that run on the Fabric Interconnects?

The following software resides and runs on the Fabric Interconnects:

- **Cisco Nexus OS (NX-OS):** NX-OS consists of two files:

    - **Kickstart image file:** This is the Linux kernel of the operating system.

    - **System image file:** This file contains all the applicable modules of the Nexus OS for the hardware platform on which it is used. Let's not forget that Cisco uses the Nexus OS on a variety of devices—the Cisco Nexus and MDS switches as well as on the Cisco UCS Fabric Interconnects.

- **Cisco UCS Manager application-** an XML application that manages the Cisco UCS.

So far, you know that a Cisco UCS domain consists of two Fabric Interconnects running in a redundant mode, also known as a Cisco UCS cluster. On both Fabric Interconnects the NX-OS is loaded and the services needed for the Cisco UCS are up and running in a load-balancing and redundant mode. This means that there will be a single active instance for each service and one standby. Which service will be active on which Fabric Interconnect, regardless of whether it's the primary or the subordinate, is decided during the negotiations at the start. The primary Fabric Interconnect is the one on which the Cisco UCSM instance runs in active mode. The other is the subordinate Fabric Interconnect because on that one the Cisco UCSM application runs in standby (passive) mode. It will receive configuration and state updates from the primary Fabric Interconnect and then update itself. The following points are important to remember:

- The primary/subordinate mode of operation of the Fabric Interconnects applies only to the management and control planes and does not affect the data plane operation, which is always active through both Fabric Interconnects.

- The primary/standby mode of the Fabric Interconnects is defined by the active instance of the Cisco UCSM application. The rest of the processes, which also run in active/standby mode, are distributed between the two Fabric Interconnects for better utilization of the resources and for load-balancing their consumption. This means that on the subordinate Fabric Interconnect will be processes running in active mode, and their standby instances will be on the active Fabric Interconnect.

Figure 17-1 illustrates the Cisco UCS management components.

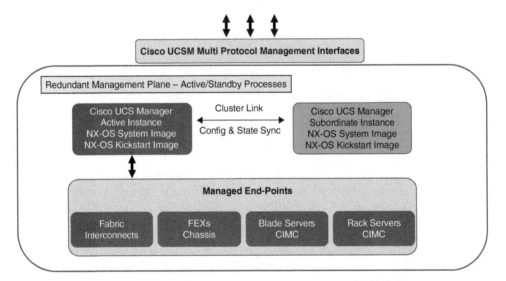

Figure 17-1   *Cisco UCS Primary/Subordinate Cluster with Nexus OS and the Cisco UCSM Application*

The Cisco UCSM is an XML application. It is based on an XML scheme that represents the hierarchical structure of the logical and physical components of the Cisco UCS. This allows for each of these components to be addressed and for the related configuration and information to be applied to them. All the configuration and state information is stored in the Cisco UCSM database in XML format. The physical components under Cisco UCSM management are called managed endpoints, and they include the following:

- **The switch elements:** The Fabric Interconnects, the Cisco FEXs, the switch modules and ports for the Fabric Interconnects

- **The chassis elements:** The chassis management controller (CMC), the chassis I/O modules (IOMs), and the chassis power and fan modules.

■ **Managed server endpoints:** The servers and their components, such as the disks, mezzanine adapters, the BIOS, the Cisco Integrated Management Controller (CIMC), and so on

Figure 17-2 illustrates the Cisco UCS Manager interfaces.

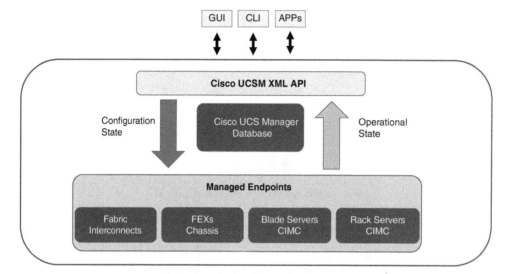

Figure 17-2   *Cisco UCSM Application Interfaces*

The Cisco UCSM, which is the central point for the management and configuration of the whole Cisco UCS domain, sits between the administrator and the server system. The administrator, or other applications and systems, can communicate with the Cisco UCSM through the available management interfaces:

■ **Cisco GUI:** The graphical user interface initially was based on Java, and an additional client application was used to access it, but with the latest versions of the Cisco UCSM, starting with major version 4, the GUI is based on HTML5 and only a browser is needed.

■ **Cisco CLI:** The command line interface to access the Cisco UCSM

■ **Third-party access:** Using the Cisco UCS XML application programming interface (API), third-party applications can connect to the system.

All the management access—whether you are using the GUI or the CLI, or it's an application trying to communicate—goes through the Cisco UCSM XML API. This means your actions will be converted into XML and sent to the appropriate managed endpoint as a configuration request, and the operational state will be communicated back.

The operational state communicates information for the managed endpoint. This consists of not only the state of the component but also monitoring and reporting information.

The Cisco UCSM supports widely used industry-standard protocols such as the following:

- Serial over LAN

- KVM over IP

- SNMP

- SMASH CLP

- CIM XML

- IPMI

It also supports the following Cisco features for monitoring and reporting:

- **Call Home:** This feature automates the notifications and even creates Cisco TAC cases based on physical issues occurring within the system.

- **Cisco UCSM XML API:** With the XML API, the Cisco UCSM can be integrated with third-party monitoring and reporting tools.

- **Cisco GUI and CLI:** The monitoring and reporting information is available in the GUI and CLI of the UCSM as well.

The Cisco UCSM GUI, shown in Figure 17-3, consists of two major elements: the navigational pane, where you traverse the XML hierarchical tree, and the content pane. Once you select a component, either physical or logical, you will see in the content pane to the right all the related information and options.

Additionally, the buttons in the top-right corner allow you to access the quick links, help, administrative session properties, and "about" information as well as to exit.

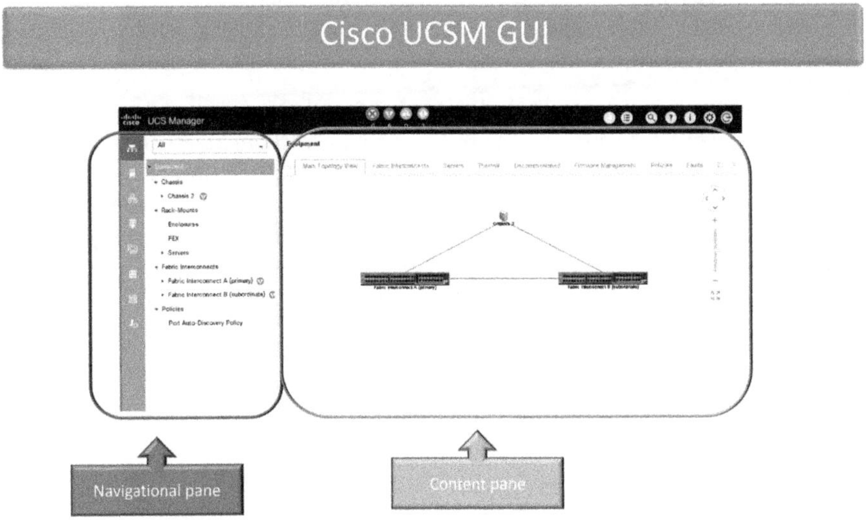

Figure 17-3 *Cisco UCSM GUI*

Another convenient feature, located at the middle top of the GUI, is quick information regarding the critical, major, and minor faults and warning messages (see Figure 17-4). By clicking one of these icons, you will be taken to the appropriate page containing information about what is happening with the system.

Figure 17-4   *Cisco UCSM GUI Faults*

The navigational pane is divided into eight tabs. The Equipment tab, shown in Figure 17-5, is where you can access all the physical components of the Cisco UCS. This is where you can get information for and access to the Fabric Interconnects, the chassis and its components, and the servers and their components.

The Equipment tab points only to physical components and policies related to the hardware discovery, power redundancy, fan control, and so on. You can access the topology view for the UCS domain in a separate tab for the Fabric Interconnects, the B- and C-series servers' hardware, the firmware management policies, thermal information, decommissioned servers, and so on. The information you can gather from the Equipment tab is important for understanding the physical connectivity and the resources in the UCS domain. The Equipment tab is where you can monitor the discovery process and configure policies related to it.

Figure 17-5 *Cisco UCSM Equipment Tab*

The UCS Manager is responsible for managing, pushing configurations to, and monitoring the hardware components of a Cisco UCS domain. To be capable of doing this, the UCS Manager needs to know what is connected and how. The process of learning and acquiring this information is called discovery. In the discovery process, the UCS Manager, which runs on the Fabric Interconnects, communicates with the control and management components from the underlying hardware. These are the Chassis Management Controllers (CMC) on the IOMs, the Cisco Integrated Management Controllers (CIMC) on the B- and C-series servers, and, in the case of C-series servers' integration through Cisco Nexus 2000 FEXs, their CMCs as well. The whole process of discovery starts when the UCS Manager finds Fabric Interconnect ports that are configured as server ports. This means that servers are connected to these ports. The UCS Manager establishes communication with the CMCs from the IOMs. The CMCs, as they are the management and control components of the IOMs in the server chassis, have already gathered the following information for the hardware in the chassis:

■ Thermal sensors

■ Fans status

■ Power supplies (status and temperature)

■ Servers

For the servers' discovery, the CMCs of the IOMs connect through dedicated management interfaces in the mid-plane of the chassis to the CIMCs of the servers. The CIMCs communicate all the information for the hardware of the server and its status to the CMC. This means that when the UCS Manager starts to communicate with the CMCs, they already have all the information for the hardware in the chassis, including the servers. Thus, the UCS Manager can build a topology and gather the information for the available hardware resources and their connectivity.

Here are some of the available hardware-related policies:

- Global policies include the following (see Figure 17-6):

  - **Chassis/FEX Discovery Policy:** Defines the minimum number of links that must exist between a Fabric Interconnect and an FEX in order for the FEX and the equipment behind it to be discovered.

  - **Rack Server Discovery Policy:** Discovery of the C-series servers.

  - **Rack Management Communication Policy:** How the changes are to be applied to the C-series server—either immediately or after acknowledgment from the administrator.

  - **Power Policy:** Defines the power redundancy. Depending on the setting, there might be requirements for the number of power supplies in the chassis.

  - **Fan Control Policy:** Controls the fan speed to optimize power consumption and noise levels.

  - **MAC Address Table Aging:** Configures how long a MAC address will remain in the MAC address table.

  - **Global Power Allocation Policy:** Specifies the power capping policies (how much power is allowed per server) to apply to the servers in a chassis.

  - **Info Policy:** Enables the information policy to display the uplink switches to which the Fabric Interconnects are connected. By default, this is disabled.

  - **Global Power Profiling Policy:** Defines how the power cap values for the servers are calculated.

  - **Hardware Change Discovery Policy:** Any change in the server hardware component will raise a critical "hardware inventory mismatch" fault.

- **Autoconfig Policies:** Used to automate the deployment of the newly discovered servers in production. If such a policy exists, the new server will be checked against a set of requirements (a qualification policy). If the server's hardware matches the qualification policy, it will be associated with a service profile and can be used immediately.

- **Server Inheritance Policies:** Used to automate the generation of a service profile based on the hardware of the server. In this situation, the hardware identity values of the server are used, and the service profile can be used only with this server.

Figure 17-6 *Cisco UCSM Equipment Tab – Global Policies*

■ **Server Discovery Policies:** These define the behavior of the UCS Manager when a new server is discovered.

■ **SEL Policy:** A configuration that allows you to export the system event logs from the hardware.

The next tab is the Servers tab, shown in Figure 17-7. The Equipment tab is the only one that shows information for the physical equipment. The Servers tab provides all the logical configuration and state information related to the servers. Here is where you can create a service profile or look at the available one. Also, you can create service profile templates and all the policies related to the servers, such as the boot policy or the BIOS policy. In the Cisco UCS Manager, anything created for a specific aspect of the server configuration is called a policy. That's why in the Servers tab there is a separate section for all the policies that can be created and used in a service profile. These include not only the forementioned BIOS and boot policies, but also maintenance, memory, scrub, power, adapter, and many more policies. In general, the Cisco UCS Manager is so granular that you can create a policy for any specific piece of configuration you can think of. This allows for extreme flexibility when it comes to the configuration of the servers in your data center. At first glance this might not look very important, but when you start solving the challenges in a real data center, you will appreciate this flexibility.

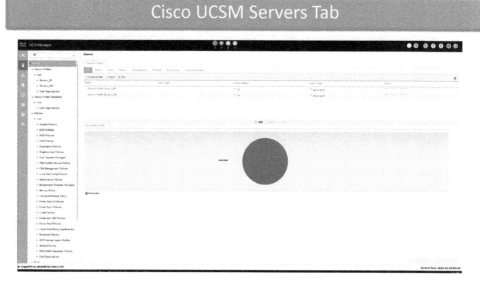

Figure 17-7 *Cisco UCSM Servers Tab*

The LAN tab, shown in Figure 17-8, is where you perform all the configurations related to the network connectivity of the Cisco UCS as a whole and the network connectivity of the servers in particular. Here, under the LAN Cloud option, you create the VLANs in which all the server communication will occur, and you configure the communication of directly attached network devices under the Appliances section. In this tab, you also create the specific configuration for the servers' communication.

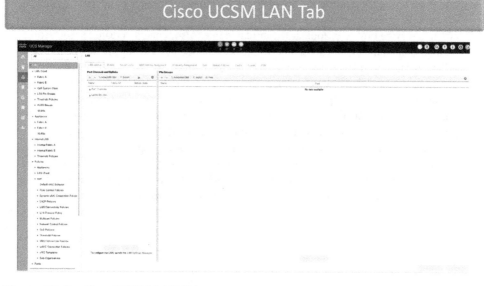

Figure 17-8 *Cisco UCSM LAN Tab*

The fourth tab is the SAN tab (see Figure 17-9). In the SAN tab, you create all the logical configuration related to the storage communication of the servers. This is about the Fibre Channel–based communication of the servers. All of the needed policies, identity pools, VSANs, and HBA adapters' configuration is created and managed in this tab—both for Cisco UCS communication with the data center SAN and with directly attached FC storage appliances.

Figure 17-9   *Cisco UCSM SAN Tab*

The VM tab, shown in Figure 17-10, allows for the integration of the Cisco UCS Manager with the VMware and Microsoft hypervisors to reach up to the level of the virtual machines.

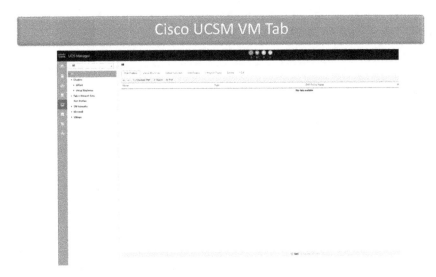

Figure 17-10   *Cisco UCSM VM Tab*

The Storage tab, shown in Figure 17-11, allows for the creation of local storage profiles and policies for the provisioning of the local storage.

Figure 17-11   *Cisco UCSM Storage Tab*

The Chassis tab, shown in Figure 17-12, is a new one. It allows the DC administrators to focus on tasks specific to the management of multiple chassis in a Cisco UCS domain. In one place, you can create and manage all the needed policies for the chassis of the blade servers.

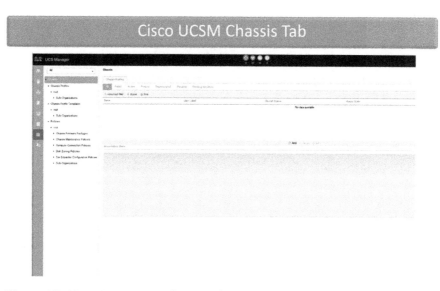

Figure 17-12   *Cisco UCSM Chassis Tab*

The Admin tab, shown in Figure 17-13, is where all the configuration related to the administration of, monitoring of, and access to the Cisco UCS is configured. Here you can access the faults, events, and audit logs. You can also configure the authentication and authorization, which can be based on creating a database of local users or using external authentication, authorization, and accounting (AAA) servers such as a Microsoft Windows Active Directory (AD).

Figure 17-13   *Cisco UCSM Admin Tab*

Exploring the Cisco UCS Server Environment

The Cisco UCS uses hardware abstraction to provide flexibility, better utilization of resources, and redundancy for the servers. The abstraction is achieved by decoupling the server's hardware from the server's configuration that defines its behavior. To put it another way, the Cisco UCS cluster is built as a physical infrastructure. This is the understructure, just like the road infrastructure. There are multiple roads to take you from point A to point B. Which road you take depends on the requirements for your trip (how fast do you want to get there? are there tolls on the road?), on the availability, and on the traffic of the roads on a specific route. But these conditions change for your car and trip; the infrastructure is not affected by the parameters of your trip. Here it is similar—the physical infrastructure is built and available after the physical components of the Cisco UCS are installed (their cabling and the initial configuration) and the cluster is brought up. Of course, this includes the configuration of connectivity to the LAN and SAN of the data center. But, to explain this, first you need to get acquainted with the physical infrastructure and some of the connectivity options when the UCS cluster is built.

In order to keep things clear and simple, our explanation will focus on a Cisco UCS cluster that consists of a pair of Fabric Interconnects, a blade chassis, and B-series servers in the chassis.

A pair of Fabric Interconnects is a requirement for a Cisco UCS cluster. A topology with a single Fabric Interconnect is allowed for lab and test purposes, as it does not provide redundancy. The two Fabric Interconnects must be connected to each other only using the dedicated cluster ports, which are marked with L1 and L2 (L1 connects to L1, and L2 connects to L2). This is all you must do for the cluster link—connect the cluster port. The system will automatically detect the link and configure a port channel using the two physical links. This happens transparently.

Additionally, there is the management plane. On each Fabric Interconnect is a dedicated Ethernet port for management communication. They must be connected to the management switches. Each port is assigned an IP address from the management network. There is one additional IP address from the management network, called the cluster IP address. It is assigned to the active instance of the Cisco UCSM and floats between the Fabric Interconnects, depending on which one of them is running the active instance. The management plane has a separate physical path of communication from the data plane. Further discussion in this chapter will focus on the data plane communication, as it is important for understanding the hardware abstraction in the Cisco UCS.

When it comes to the data plane connectivity of the Cisco UCS, you have external connectivity to the LAN and SAN infrastructures of the data center and internal connectivity to the system, starting from the Fabric Interconnects and going down to the servers.

The external connectivity to the LAN infrastructure is created by linking the Ethernet ports of the Fabric Interconnects to the upstream LAN switches. Based on best practices, and in order to achieve redundancy, each Fabric Interconnect can be connected to a pair of upstream LAN switches. Technologies such as port channels or vPCs can be used for adding additional redundancy and load balancing. For the Cisco UCSM to know that through these specific Ethernet ports the Cisco UCS is connected to the LAN infrastructure, the ports need to be configured as such. This happens by selecting the port on the Fabric Interconnect and assigning it the Uplink Port role.

Creating and configuring the connectivity to the SAN infrastructure is similar, but there are some differences. Again, you have to select ports to connect to the SAN. This time there are some requirements and some options. The major choice that needs to be made, depending on the design of your data center, is which storage communication protocol to use. The options are iSCSI, NFS, CIFS/SMB, FC, and FCoE. For the iSCSI, NFS, and CIFS/SMB options, there is no need for any additional upstream connectivity other than the LAN connectivity, as these protocols are using Ethernet and IP connectivity to carry the storage communication.

For the FCoE connectivity, the Ethernet uplink ports need to be configured as FCoE Uplink ports or as Unified ports, depending on whether you will use dedicated Ethernet links for the storage communication or you will use the same Ethernet links for both Ethernet and FCoE traffic.

In both cases, you must consider the SAN design best practices, which require each server to be connected to two separate physical SAN infrastructures. As all the server's data plane communication goes through the Fabric Interconnects, this means that each of them can be connected to only one SAN, as they will become an extension of the SANs down to the server.

The same design considerations apply if you want to connect the Cisco UCS to the SANs using native Fibre Channel connectivity. For this, you must use dedicated FC ports. Once again, each Fabric Interconnect connects to a single SAN (no cross-connects like in LAN connectivity). As discussed Chapter 11, "Fibre Channel Protocol Fundamentals," the redundancy is achieved in a different way than in the LAN infrastructure. The FC ports must be assigned the Fiber Channel Uplink ports role.

Figure 17-14 illustrates the internal and external physical connectivity of Cisco UCS.

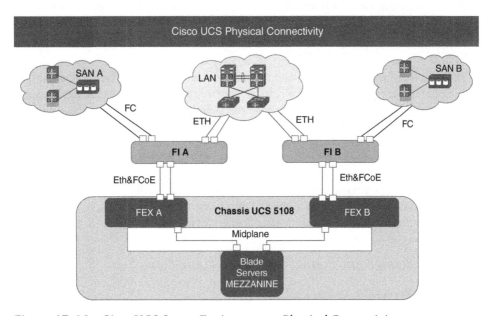

Figure 17-14   *Cisco UCS Server Environment – Physical Connectivity*

Once external connectivity, or upstream connectivity to the other elements of the data center, is created, it is important to understand how the internal connectivity is realized so that you know what is available to the servers to consume.

As already mentioned, the servers' communication always goes through the Fabric Interconnects. Here we will explain the physical internal connectivity of the Cisco UCS starting with the Fabric Interconnects and moving down to the servers.

In each Cisco UCS 5108 blade chassis are two FEXs that connect to the Fabric Interconnects externally, thus securing the blade chassis' outside connectivity. Each FEX connects to only one of the Fabric Interconnects. This allows for the separation of the physical infrastructure to be maintained down to the level of the physical server. This is Ethernet connectivity, as the Ethernet links are shared to carry the management and control communication, the Ethernet data communication of the servers, as well as their storage communication using the FCoE protocol. That's why these links operate at speeds of 10, 25, and 40Gbps.

The number of links between the FEX and the Fabric Interconnect define the total bandwidth of the connectivity of the chassis using that path. This is the available communication capacity to the servers in that chassis for this path. The other FEX is connected to the other Fabric Interconnect in the same way. This ensures the blade chassis has two paths of communication: one through Fabric Interconnect A and the other through Fabric Interconnect B. Both paths are active and available.

Another important point is that the FEXs do not perform Layer 2 switching for the data plane communication. This results in one hop less of processing the server communications. This makes transmission faster, and it decreases latency. This is possible because, instead of the standard Layer 2 switching, inside the FEX is a mapping between the external ports and the internal ports.

The FEX is connected to the midplane of the blade chassis. The midplane is a passive component that provides multiple electrical lanes for the signal, hard wiring the different components as required. Also connected to the midplane are the blade servers when they are installed in the chassis; this is done through a special blade connector. Therefore, the midplane provides the internal physical connectivity at the lowest physical layer. Think of the midplane as the physical network cabling. This physical connectivity is utilized by the internal ports on the FEX, from one side, and the mezzanine adapter of the server. The FEX has dedicated internal ports for each server slot in the chassis. Once installed in the blade chassis, these ports are connected to the midplane and are available to the server slots. How much of the internal FEX data connectivity will be utilized by a blade server depends on two things:

- The supported connectivity by the mezzanine adapter in the server

- The number of mezzanine adapters in the servers

The mezzanine adapter in the blade server is installed in a specific slot, which provides for the physical connectivity in both directions:

- **External:** The mezzanine adapter, through the mezzanine slot and the blade connector, is connected to lanes from the midplane. For each mezzanine slot, half of the lanes of the midplane are hard-wired to one of the FEXs, and the other half lead to the other FEX. If we look at the Cisco UCS 1380 mezzanine adapter, shown in Figure 17-15, we see that it has two 40-Gbps ports, as each connects to one of the available paths through the midplane to one of the FEXs. Each of the 40-Gbps ports can be divided into four 10-Gbps ports. Depending on the capabilities of the installed FEXs, the server can have up to 40-Gbps available bandwidth for each path.

■ **Internal:** Again, through the mezzanine slot, the adapter is connected to the PCIe bus of the server. Through the PCIe bus, the OS is capable of seeing and utilizing the vHBAs and the vNICs on the mezzanine adapter. The Cisco virtual interface cards utilize a programmable silicon that allows you to program (or create) multiple NICs and HBAs for the purposes of the OS on the server and for providing redundant connectivity and load balancing. These logical adapters are called vNICs and vHBAs, but these are not the vNICs and vHBAs from the VMware ESXi hypervisor. Take note that although the terminology is the same, these are two different vNICs and vHBAs. Let's try to clarify it a bit more: as you know, the VMware ESXi creates a virtual image of the physical hardware, and after that the virtualized resources are utilized to create the isolated spaces, which are called virtual machines. In the case of networking, the ESXi hypervisor creates a virtual image of the network interface card that it sees on the server and names it a vmNIC. Afterward, when a VM is created, a logical network adaptor is created, named vNIC, which connects to a virtual switch, which in turn is connected to a vmNIC for the external connectivity of the ESXi host and the VMs. In the case of using a Cisco VIC, the Cisco vNIC will be seen as a "physical" network adaptor by the ESXi and will be created. Therefore, the Cisco VIC vNIC is equal to a VMware ESXi vmNIC. This is important for you to understand to avoid further confusion.

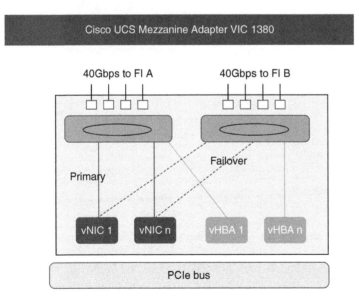

Figure 17-15 *Cisco UCS Mezzanine Adapter, VIC 1380*

To summarize, starting with the Cisco VIC in the server and going through the midplane and the two FEXs, and reaching the two Fabric Interconnects, two communication paths are available for each server. These paths are physically separated, and their bandwidth depends on the capabilities of the hardware used, such as FEXs and mezzanine adapters. However, this is the physical infrastructure for the communication of each server. What and how much of it a server will utilize depends on how you configure it in the Cisco UCS Manager by using a service profile. Before we can explain the service profiles, which allow us to abstract the hardware resources of the Cisco UCS, you will need to understand the challenge of the static hardware servers.

Identity and Resource Pools for Hardware Abstraction

The Cisco UCS abstraction of the hardware and how it affects the server's identity is illustrated in Figure 17-16.

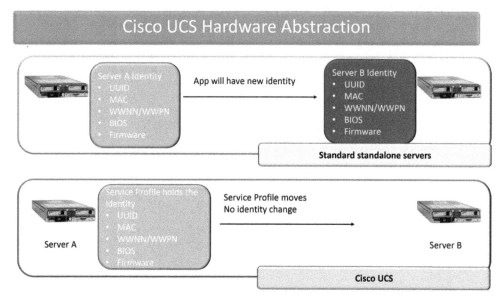

Figure 17-16 *Cisco UCSM Hardware Abstraction*

Each physical server has an identity that uniquely identifies it for the purposes of network and storage communication, and the operating system. This identity is used for security purposes and for licensing. As such, it is tightly connected to the behavior of the applications running on the server. The result is that the applications are stuck to the identity of the server. If something happens with the server, such as a hardware failure or an upgrade, this identity changes. This can affect the applications in different ways, from needing a slight reconfiguration to needing to be reinstalled with a new configuration. This is usually disruptive and affects the provided services. These identity values are the UUID of the server, the MAC addresses used for the network communication, the WWPN and WWNN addresses for the Fibre Channel communication, and the BIOS and firmware settings.

With the Cisco UCS, this challenge is solved through hardware abstraction, which is achieved by removing the identity and configuration of the server from the physical hardware. All of the identity information and the needed configuration for the server is contained in a logical object created in the Cisco UCS Manager, called a service profile. When the service profile is associated with a physical server, the identity and configuration are applied to it. If the service profile is disassociated, the identity stays with the service profile, and it will be used on the physical server to which the service profile is associated. This mobility of the server identity and configuration, achieved through the decoupling from the physical hardware via the use of service profiles, allows the physical server to be used only as the provider of the needed hardware resources. As long as a physical server has the needed hardware resources, as required by the service profile, it can be used. It does not matter which one is the physical server—the first, second, or the fifth one in the blade chassis—or whether it's going to be on the same chassis or on another chassis from the same Cisco UCS domain.

The identity values can be manually configured for each service profile. To avoid overlapping values, you can use identity resource pools, which can be created in the Cisco UCSM, and from them the service profiles can consume identity values.

Each computer, whether it's a server, desktop computer, or laptop, has a unique identifier that is burned into the BIOS. This is called a universally unique identifier (UUID). UUIDs are 128-bit identifiers with the following characteristics:

- They are standardized serial numbers that identify a particular server.

- The servers have hardware UUIDs stored in the system BIOS.

- UUIDs are used for licensing purposes.

- The UUIDs can be manually or automatically assigned in the Cisco UCSM.

When the UUID is assigned manually, the whole 128-bit value needs to be entered. For automating the assignment, you can use a UUID pool. When a UUID pool is created (see Figure 17-17), the Cisco UCSM follows some rules:

- The Cisco UCSM divides the 128-bit UUID into two pieces: a 64-bit prefix and a 64-bit suffix pool.

- To create a UUID, you take the prefix and a value from the suffix pool. This results in a unique ID.

- Cisco recommends using the same 24-bit organizationally unique identifier (OUI) across all the identity pools.

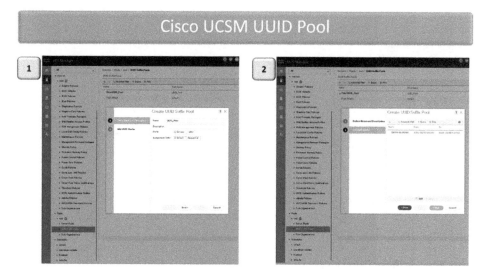

Figure 17-17 *Cisco UCSM UUID Pool*

For the network communication, you use physical network addresses called Media Access Control (MAC) addresses. The MAC address uniquely identifies a network interface and has a 48-bit value. In the Cisco UCS, the MAC address is assigned to the vNIC, which is visible to the operating system (OS). Just like with the UUIDs, the MAC address value can be configured manually in the service profile, or you can use a MAC pool from which to derive the value (see Figure 17-18). Cisco recommends using a Cisco OUI of 00:25:B5 as the first 24 bits of the MAC address.

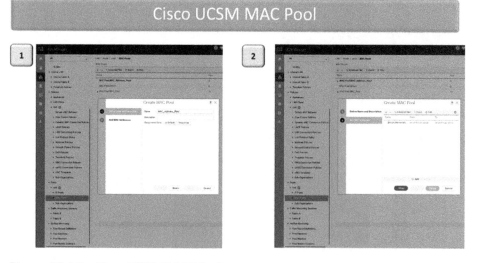

Figure 17-18 *Cisco UCSM MAC Pool*

The World Wide Node Name (WWNN) and the World Wide Port Name (WWPN) addresses are the physical addresses used in the Fibre Channel protocol communication. Both have the same structure and a size of 64 bits, but it is important to remember that they identify different things in the communication. The WWNN uniquely identifies the device. Usually, it is the HBA of the server, but in the Cisco UCS, as the HBAs are created in the silicon of the mezzanine adapter, and are virtualized, the WWNN will represent the server. The WWPN identifies an FC port in the storage communication. In the Cisco UCS, a WWPN will uniquely identify a vHBA from the mezzanine adapter. Again, just like with the previously described types of identities, the WWNN and WWPNs can be set manually in the service profile, or you can use WWNN pools and WWPN pools (see Figure 17-19). In both approaches, special attention has to be paid to the values used. The WWNN must be a different value from the WWPN—especially when the WWNN and WWPN ranges of values are configured in the pools. If they overlap, the Cisco UCSM will fail to associate the service profile with the server, as it will assign first the WWNN value. When it tries to assign the WWPNs, if there is an overlap with the WWNNs, it will stop the procedure with a failure message.

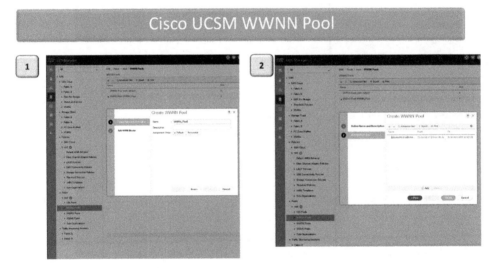

Figure 17-19 *Cisco UCSM WWNN Pool*

Besides the identity resource pools, which can also be referred to as logical resource pools since they are created by the Cisco UCS administrator and the values are generated, there is one other type of pool in the Cisco UCSM: the server pool. The server pool is also referred to as a physical pool because it is used to group and classify the existing physical servers in a Cisco UCS domain, based on their hardware characteristics, such as model and type of the CPU, number of cores, minimum and maximum memory, mezzanine adapters, and so on. Server pools allow you to utilize in full the mobility of the service profiles. When a server pool is specified in a service profile, the physical server will be taken from it. In case of a failure, the service profile can get another physical server from the same pool, and it will provide the required hardware, as based on this it was included in the server pool.

A physical server can belong to a server pool only when it is not associated with a service profile. It can also belong to multiple server pools, as long as it matches the requirements for the hardware (see Figure 17-20). The moment that a service profile is associated with a physical server, then it becomes unavailable in the pool, or pools, to which it belongs.

Figure 17-20   *Cisco UCSM Server Pools*

There are two options for how a server can be added to a server pool:

- **Manual:** The administrator manually adds the server to one or multiple server pools.

- **Automated:** This is done using a server pool policy, which has an empty server pool and a qualification policy. The qualification policy is a set of hardware requirements. When a physical server is discovered by the UCSM, its hardware is checked against the qualification policy. If it matches the requirements, it will be added to the empty server pool.

Service Profiles and Service Profile Templates

In the Cisco UCS, the server consists of two components:

- **Compute node:** This is the physical server, which provides the needed computing resources, such as CPUs, memory, local storage, and mezzanine adapters for physical connectivity.

■ **Service profile:** This is the logical construct created in the Cisco UCSM that defines the following items related to the server:

■ **Identity:** The combination of UUID, MAC addresses, and WWNN and WWPN addresses.

■ **Connectivity:** This defines the number of vNICs and vHBAs that will be connected to the available communication paths and used by the server in an active manner.

■ **Policies:** These are the pieces of the service profile that define the specific configuration and behavior related to the server and its components.

When a service profile, shown in Figure 17-21, is associated with a compute node, the result is a server that can be used. Without a service profile, the physical server cannot be used in the Cisco UCS. Also, there is a 1:1 relationship between the service profile and the compute node. At any given time, a service profile can be associated only with a single server, and a compute node can be associated only with a single service profile. This also means that for each physical server used in the Cisco UCS, a service profile is needed.

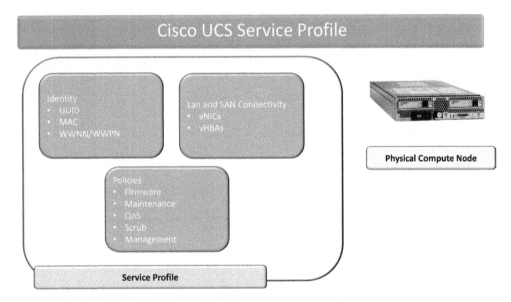

Figure 17-21 *Cisco UCS Service Profile*

During the association process, the Cisco UCSM pushes the service profile down to the CIMC of the server, together with the instruction to apply the configuration to the compute node. Then the CIMC reboots the server, as it needs the server to boot from a specialized operating system that resides in the storage of the CIMC that's designed to take all the configuration from the service profile and apply it to the correct components of the server. Once this process has finished, the compute node is rebooted again. After the second reboot, the association of the service profile with the server has finished, all the needed configuration and identity values are applied to the server, and the server is ready for the installation of the operating system (a bare-metal OS or a virtualization hypervisor).

When the service profile is disassociated from the compute node, the same process is followed, but this time the configuration is reset to the default values, and the identity values are removed. The identity values always stay with the service profile, and when the service profile is associated with another server, the identity is applied to the new compute node.

The one challenge with the service profiles is that a service profile is needed for every server. To optimize the process of creating the needed amount of service profiles, especially when they are to be similar, you can use a service profile template.

The service profile template is a special type of service profile that is used to generate multiple service profiles at once. They will be similar, which means they will have the same configuration and policies, but each will have a unique identity. For example, all the generated service profiles will have the same BIOS configuration policy, the same vNICs and vHBAs, but each vNIC and vHBA will have a unique physical address. Because of this, during the process of creating multiple service profiles from a service profile template, you will need to get multiple unique identity values. This is achieved by using identity resource pools.

There are two types of service profile templates (detailed next), and it's important to know the difference between them, as this affects the service profiles generated from them (see Figure 17-22):

- **Initial template:** Service profiles are created from an initial template; they inherit all the properties of the template. Any changes to the initial template do not automatically propagate to the bound service profiles.

- **Updating template:** The service profiles created from an updating template inherit all the properties of the template and remain connected to the template. Any changes to the template automatically update the service profiles created from the template.

To create a service profile template, you must start the wizard, which is located in the Servers tab. It is similar to the Service Profile Wizard, as the major difference is that you have to set the type at the start.

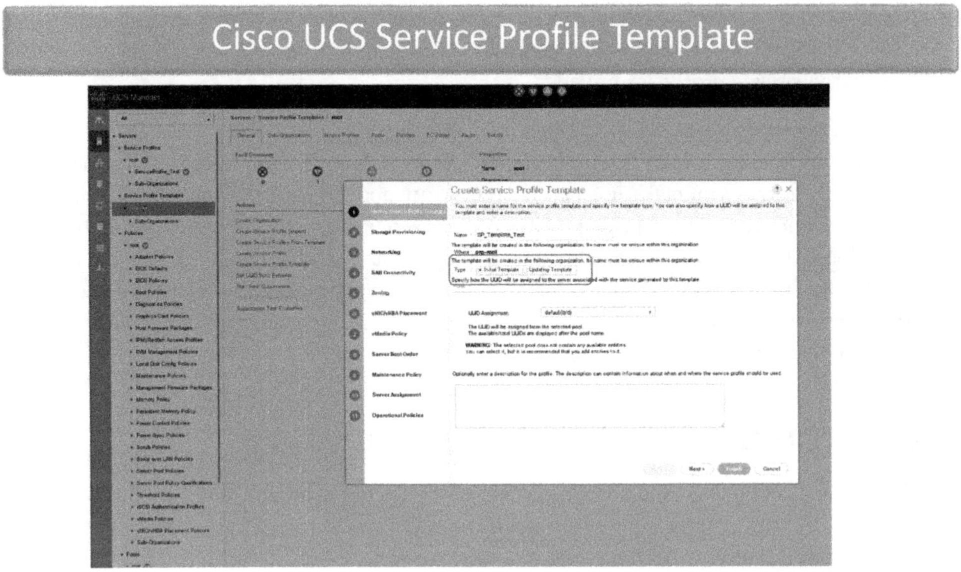

Figure 17-22 *Cisco UCS Service Profile Template Wizard*

Cisco UCS Polices for Use in Service Profiles

The policies in the Cisco UCSM service profile define the configuration of the different physical components of the server as well as the behavior of the server. That's why they can be divided into two categories:

- Configuration policies
- Operational policies

Examples of configuration policies are the QoS policies— they are applied to the configuration of the vNICs and the vHBAs, and are used to configure how the traffic will be handled. Another example is the boot policy, which configures the boot order, and so on.

Operational policies are the BIOS policy, power control policy, scrub policy, maintenance policy, and so on.

Some policies are specific and need a little bit more explanation. The scrub policy defines what happens with the BIOS configuration and with the data on the local storage during a disassociation of the service profile. It allows the administrator to instruct the system to erase the local data and reset the BIOS to the default settings.

If the physical server needs to run specific versions of the firmware for specific components, a firmware policy can be used with the service profile. It can specify which versions of the firmware are needed. Then, during the association process, the system will first check the versions of the firmware currently running on the compute node, and based on the information from the firmware policy, it will retrieve the needed versions from the Fabric Interconnects and perform the upgrades before the rest of the configuration in the service profile is applied.

One extremely important policy is the maintenance policy, and Cisco strongly recommends that you always use it with every service profile. The maintenance policy defines when the changes you make in a service profile are applied to the compute node. It affects the behavior of a service profile already associated with a compute node. In this situation there are certain changes that can require the use of a specialized OS from the CIMC that applies these changes. As this will be disruptive to the operation of the server, the maintenance policy allows you to define whether such changes will be applied after the administrator's acknowledgment or immediately.

Cisco UCS Service Profile Configuration

The service profile is a logical object in the Cisco UCSM that is created by the administrator. To create a service profile, the administrator needs to start the Service Profile Wizard. It is located at the Servers tab, under the Service Profiles option. The wizard, shown in Figure 17-23, consists of 11 pages (or steps), as per the current version of the Cisco UCSM. Each step allows you to focus on a certain aspect of the server's configuration.

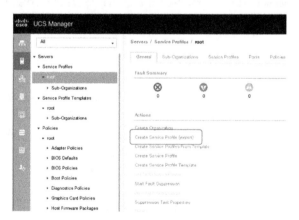

Figure 17-23   *Cisco UCS Service Profile Wizard Start*

At the first step, you have to specify a name for the service profile. Here it is important to note that the names in the Cisco UCSM are important to be unique for the same type of objects. As the UCSM is an XML-based application, it refers to the objects using their names, and if two objects have different names, they are different for the UCSM, no matter what their content is, even if it is the same. That's why it's important to use unique names.

After a name for the service profile is specified, the next thing to do is to specify the UUID that will be used for the server (see Figure 17-24). There are three options:

- **Hardware Default:** The service profile will not provide a UUID value. Instead, it will use the UUID in the BIOS. This means this service profile will not be mobile.

- **Manual Using OUI:** Allows the administrator to enter a UUID value manually.

- **Domain Pools:** Select a UUID pool from which a UUID value will be taken. If the administrator hasn't created UUID pools in advance, there is a link that allows a UUID pool to be created without exiting the Service Profile Wizard.

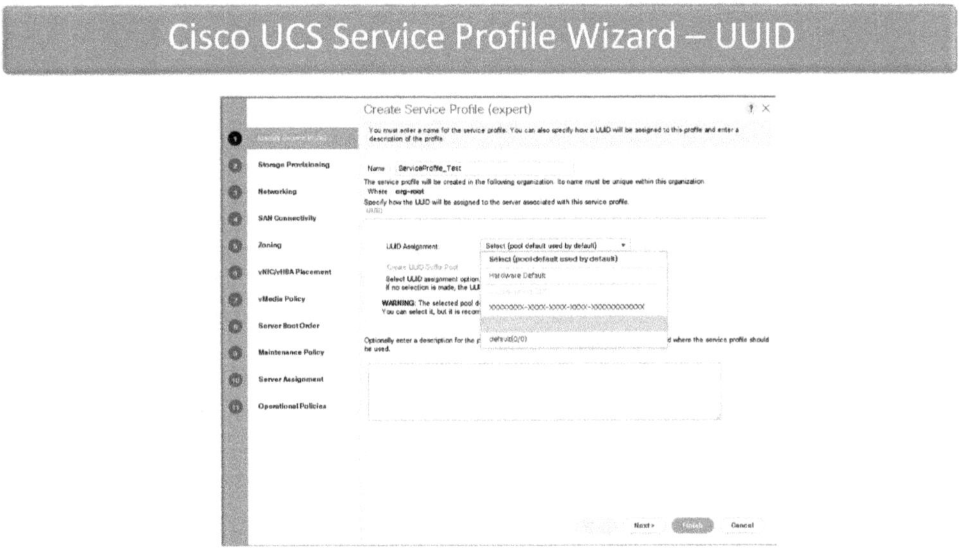

Figure 17-24   *Cisco UCS Service Profile Wizard – Identity Service Profile*

The second step is for storage-related configuration (see Figure 17-25). Here you can select or create a storage profile that defines the number of storage disks, roles, and the use of these disks, and other storage parameters. With it you can configure multiple virtual drives and select the physical drives used by a virtual drive. Additionally, you can configure the local disk configuration policy, which defines the local RAID controller and disks configuration.

Cisco UCS Service Profile Wizard – Storage Provisioning

Figure 17-25 *Cisco UCS Service Profile Wizard – Storage Provisioning*

The third step is for networking (see Figure 17-26). The vNICs that will be used by the server are created and configured here. You have to switch to Expert mode to be able to add vNICs. A vNIC can use one communication path at a time. You have to specify a name for the vNIC, which will be the method to acquire a MAC address value, as the options are to create it manually or use a MAC address pool. You have to select through which Fabric Interconnect this vNIC will communicate, A or B, and whether you want to enable the hardware-based failover. The vNICs in the Cisco UCS are capable of switching the paths of communication in case of a failure in the hardware. This is extremely fast switching, and it practically cannot be detected.

The next thing that needs to be defined is which VLANs are allowed to communicate through this vNIC. Optionally, you can configure the MTU size, a QoS policy, and some other operational policies.

The SAN Connectivity step, shown in Figure 17-27, allows you to create and configure the vHBAs that will be used by the server to communicate with the SAN infrastructures. Just like with the network configuration, you have to switch to Expert mode to be able to add vHBAs. There is no hardware failover supported for the vHBAs because of the design standards for the SANs; that's why, if you need to have redundancy, it is strongly recommended that you have at least one vHBA per communication path.

Once the WWNN assignment method is selected, manually or from a WWNN address pool, you can add the vHBA.

For the vHBA you have to specify a name, the WWPN assignment method, which fabric path will be used (A or B), which VSAN, the QoS, and so on.

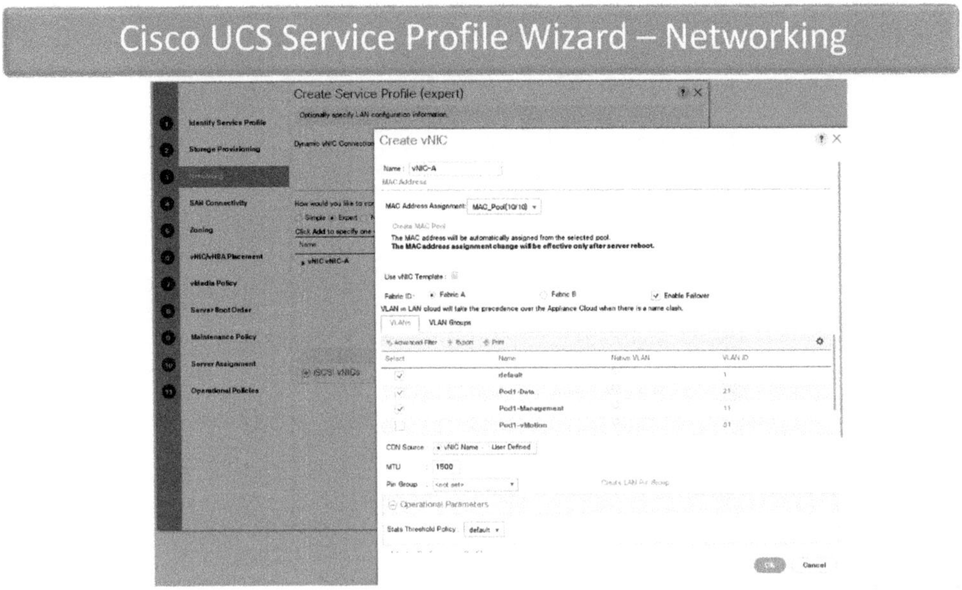

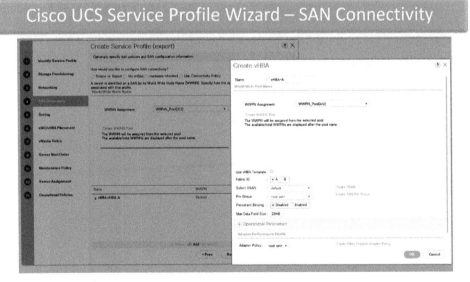

Figure 17-26   *Cisco UCS Service Profile Wizard – Networking and vNIC Creation*

Figure 17-27   *Cisco UCS Service Profile Wizard – SAN Connectivity and vHBA Creation*

The Zoning step, shown in Figure 17-28, allows you to create a Fibre Channel zoning configuration that will apply to the vHBAs of the server.

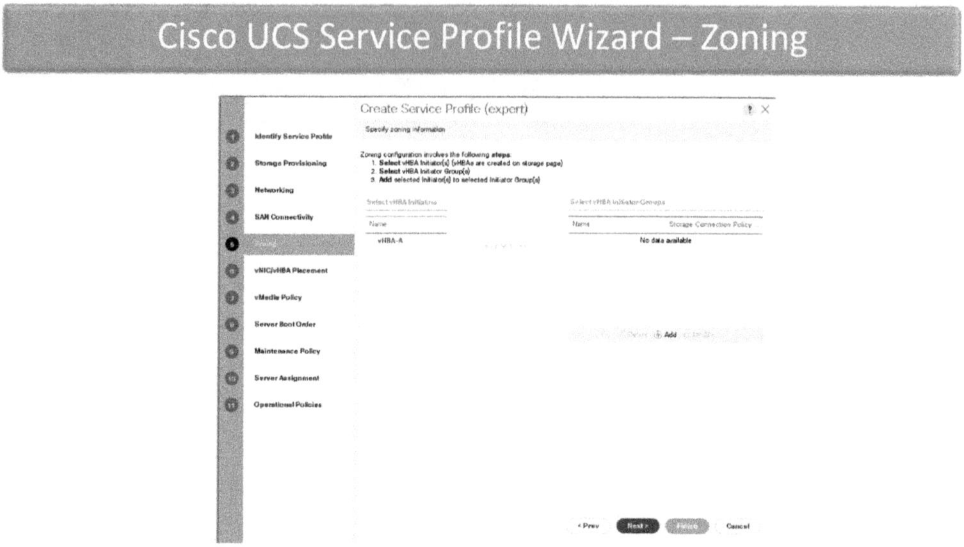

Cisco UCS Service Profile Wizard – Zoning

Figure 17-28   *Cisco UCS Service Profile Wizard – Zoning*

The vNIC/vHBA Placement step, shown in Figure 17-29, allows you to manually change which lane on the midplane will be used by which vNIC and vHBA. The general recommendation is to let the system make this decision, but in case of issues, you can change it here.

Cisco UCS Service Profile Wizard – vNIC/vHBA Placement

Figure 17-29   *Cisco UCS Service Profile Wizard – vNIC/vHBA Placement*

If you need to map a specific image to the server, you can create a vMedia policy in the vMedia Policy step of the wizard (see Figure 17-30). The supported protocols are NFS, CFS, HTTP, and HTTPS, as the software image can be mapped as a CDD or an HDD.

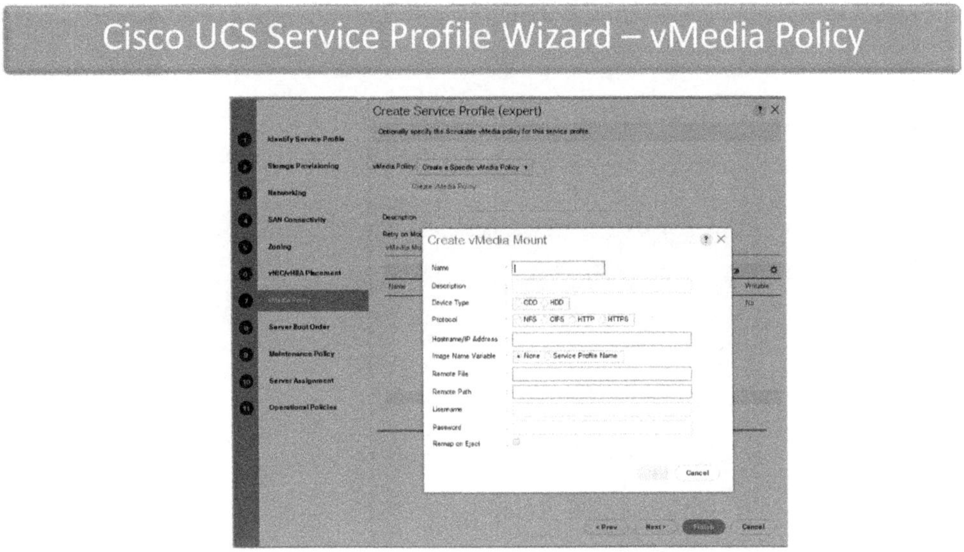

Cisco UCS Service Profile Wizard – vMedia Policy

Figure 17-30   *Cisco UCS Service Profile Wizard – vMedia Policy*

The Server Boot Order step, shown in Figure 17-31, allows you to create the boot order for the server. Here you can specify the local and remote boot devices and their order. You can select a remote network-based boot, over the vNIC or an iSCSI vNIC, or specify a boot from a specific storage system over the vHBA.

Cisco UCS Service Profile Wizard – Server Boot Order

Figure 17-31   *Cisco UCS Service Profile Wizard – Server Boot Order*

The next step allows for the selection of a maintenance policy (see Figure 17-32). If there isn't one, you can create a new one. The maintenance policy, a highly recommended component, allows you to specify when any disruptive changes in the service profile will be applied to the server: immediately, after acknowledgment from the administrator, or scheduled.

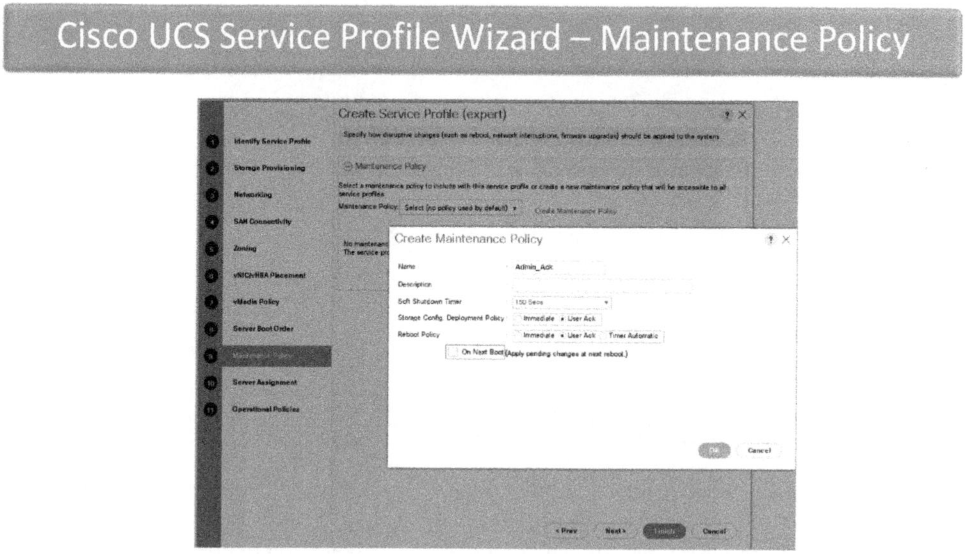

Cisco UCS Service Profile Wizard – Maintenance Policy

Figure 17-32   *Cisco UCS Service Profile Wizard – Maintenance Policy*

The Server Assignment step, shown in Figure 17-33, is where you can select the physical server that will be used by the service profile. It is not mandatory to select a server at this point. You can just skip this step and assign a physical server later. The other options here are to select from the existing server and to select a server pool.

Cisco UCS Service Profile Wizard – Server Assignment

Figure 17-33   *Cisco UCS Service Profile Wizard – Server Assignment*

Another important option at this step is to select whether you need to use a firmware management policy. With it, you can specify the versions of the firmware for the different components of the server, such as BIOS, mezzanine adapter, and so on.

The last step, shown in Figure 17-34, is where you specify the operational policies. Here you can select or create a custom configuration for the following items:

- BIOS

- External IPM/Redfish Management Configuration

- Management IP Address

- Monitoring Configuration (Thresholds)

- Power Control Policy Configuration

- Scrub Policy

- KVM Management Policy

- Graphics Card Policy

- Persistent Memory Policy

Figure 17-34   *Cisco UCS Service Profile Wizard – Operational Policies*

Once you click the Finish button, the service profile will be created. The system will warn you of any conflicting situations. The service profile will appear under the appropriate area in Service Profiles, and you can make changes (see Figure 17-35).

Figure 17-35   *Cisco UCS Service Profile General Information*

At this point the service profile can be associated with a physical server, if such was not selected during the wizard.

In the FSM tab you can see information for the association or disassociation processes, as well as any firmware upgrades.

Cisco UCS Central Overview

A Cisco UCS Manager can control, manage, configure, and monitor the servers that belong to a single Cisco UCS domain, which means that these are the servers connected to the pair of Fabric Interconnects that run the instance of the Cisco UCSM. If you have other UCS domains, you have to take care and perform the needed configuration on each Cisco UCS Manager separately. It is true that you can export and import configurations between the Cisco UCS Managers, but this is a manual process that's prone to errors. To solve this challenge and to provide a single pane of glass for all of your UCS domains, Cisco has developed Cisco UCS Central. It can extend the capabilities and concepts of Cisco UCS Manager to enable the streamlined management of up to 10,000 servers across hundreds of sites from a single user interface. It is an HTML5 application that can manage multiple Cisco UCS Manager applications (see Figure 17-36).

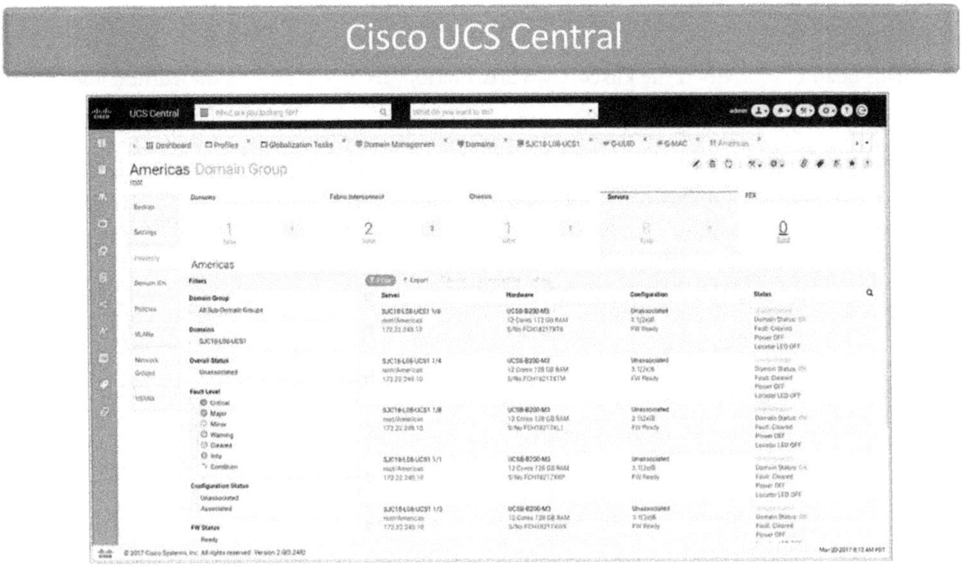

Figure 17-36   *Cisco UCS Central*

Here are some of the capabilities at a global level:

- Centralized inventory and health status information for all Cisco UCS components for a definitive view of the entire infrastructure

- An API-based integration into higher-level data center management frameworks

- Global service profiles and templates that extend the power of policy-based management introduced in Cisco UCS Manager well beyond the boundary of a single Cisco UCS domain

- A centralized keyboard, video, and mouse (KVM) manager to launch KVM sessions anywhere in the Cisco UCS environment from a single pane

- Centralized, policy-based firmware upgrades that can be applied globally or selectively through automated schedules or as business workloads demand

- Global administrative policies that enable both global and local management of Cisco UCS domains, help ensure consistency and standardization across domains, and eliminate any configuration drift typically experienced after servers are initially deployed

- Hardware compatibility reports that retrieve the latest compatibility information from Cisco.com and compare that to your managed configuration to help ensure that current or future firmware is compatible with deployed operating system and driver versions

- Global ID pooling and multidomain ID visibility to eliminate identifier conflicts

Summary

This chapter described the Cisco UCS abstraction. In this chapter, you learned about the following:

- The Cisco Unified Computing System (UCS) is a complex system that builds a physical compute infrastructure and deploys abstraction from the hardware by separating the server into two components—the physical compute node and the logical object of the service profile.

- The Cisco UCS Manager (UCSM) provides management and runs on the Cisco Fabric Interconnects.

- An instance of the Cisco UCSM runs on each of the Fabric Interconnects.

- On one of the Fabric Interconnects, the Cisco UCSM runs in active mode; on the other, it runs in stand-by mode.

- The Fabric Interconnect on which the UCSM is active is called the primary Fabric Interconnect.

- The other Fabric Interconnect is the subordinate.

- The software that runs on the Fabric Interconnect consists of three files: the kickstart and system image files of NX-OS and the UCSM application.

- The Cisco UCSM is the management point for the UCS administrator.

- The UCSM communicates with the management end points in the UCS.

- The management end points in the UCS are the Fabric Interconnects, the chassis elements, the blade and rack servers, and their components.

- The Cisco UCSM is an XML application and, as such, is based on an XML schema.

- The Cisco UCSM has an API interface to which you can connect in three ways: via the GUI, via the CLI (in a programmatic way), and using third-party tools and applications.

- The Cisco UCSM supports multiple monitoring and reporting protocols.

- The Cisco UCSM GUI is divided into navigation and content panes.

- The navigation pane is divided into eight tabs.

- The Equipment tab provides information for the physical equipment and policies.

- The discovery process starts from the CMCs in the FEXs, which gather information from the servers and provide it to the UCSM.

- The Servers tab is for the logical objects related to the servers—policies and service profiles.

- The Networking tab is for the connectivity of the system to the LAN and any specific network policies.

- The SAN tab is for the SAN communication and storage policies.

- The VM tab allows for integration with hypervisors and visibility to the level of the virtual machines.

- The Storage tab is for creating storage profiles and policies.

- The Chassis tab is for information, profiles, and policies related to the chassis.

- The Admin tab is for monitoring, reporting, administering the system, and controlling administrative access to the UCS.

- A UCS domain consists of a pair of Fabric Interconnects connected as a cluster through the dedicated cluster ports and the servers and chassis connected to that pair.

- The cluster link is used to synchronize configuration and state information.

- Server communication always goes through the Fabric Interconnects.

- Physical connectivity depends on the mezzanine adapters in the servers, the models of the FEXs in the chassis, and the number of links between an FEX and a Fabric Interconnect.

- An FEX can be connected to only one of the Fabric Interconnects.

- The ports on the Fabric Interconnects connected to FEXs are configured as server ports.

- The links between the Fabric Interconnects and the FEXs are Ethernet.

- These links are used for the data, management, and storage communication of the servers.

- The ports of the Fabric Interconnects that connect to the upstream LAN infrastructure are configured as uplink ports.

- The FC ports that connect to the SAN infrastructures are configured as Fibre Channel uplink ports.

- The identity of a server is formed from the unique values for the UUID, MAC addresses, and WWPN and WWNN addresses.

- In the Cisco UCSM, the identity of the server does not depend on the hardware values provided by the physical server; instead, they are generated and stored in the service profile.

- The service profile contains all the identity and configuration information for the server.

- To avoid overlaps and to automate the assignment of identity values to the service profiles, you use identity resource pools.

- There are UUID, MAC address, and WWNN and WWPN address pools.

- They are also called logical resource pools, as the values in them are created by the administrator.

- The physical resource pools are the server pools.

- The server pools are used to group the physical servers that are not associated to a service profile based on their hardware characteristics.

- The combination of the physical resources of a compute node and a service profile creates a server in the Cisco UCS.

- The relationship is 1:1, as at any moment one SP can be used by a single server, and a single SP can be associated with only one server at a time.

- Each physical server needs a service profile to be used.

- To automate the creation of multiple service profiles, you can use service profile templates.

- The type of a service profile template is either initial or updating, depending on if the template is used only to generate a service profile or if a bond is preserved between them.

- Configuration and operational policies in the service profile define the behavior of the server and how the different components will be configured.

- The service profile is created using a wizard.

- The Service Profile Configuration Wizard consists of 11 steps that allow for the configuration of the server's identity, network and SAN communication, zoning, vNIC/vHBA placement, maintenance and operational policies, boot order, vMedia mapping, and server assignment.

- One UCS Manager can manage one UCS domain. To manage multiple UCS domains, or UCS Managers, you can use the Cisco UCS Central application.

  This application allows for centralized management of up to 10,000 servers and global service profiles and pools.

Reference

"Cisco Servers – Unified Computing System (UCS)," https://www.cisco.com/c/en/us/products/servers-unified-computing/index.html

Chapter 18

Server Virtualization

Servers are often underutilized in nonvirtualized environments because each application or service is assigned to only one physical server, resulting in unused resources available on each server that cannot be redistributed. Underutilization directly impacts both operational and capital expenditures by increasing the number of servers required. Every extra server requires additional physical space, power, and cooling systems. As the number of servers grows, management challenges also increase.

Virtualization abstracts dedicated, physical resources that can be allocated to specific tasks. Types of virtualization include storage, application, desktop, server, and networking. Key components of server virtualization are physical infrastructure or host, virtual machine, and server virtualization software/hypervisor. Server virtualization enables multiple operating systems and applications to run on a single physical server or host as highly efficient virtual machines. Virtual machines are tightly isolated software containers with an operating system and application inside.

In this chapter, we will be discussing the key components of server virtualization, including the virtual machine and its components, types of hypervisors, VMware vSphere architecture, VMware ESXi, and VMware vCenter Server Appliance installation procedure.

Virtual Machine

A virtual machine (VM) is a software computer that, like a physical computer, runs an operating system and applications. The virtual machine is composed of a set of specification and configuration files and is backed by the physical resources of a host. One or more virtual "guest" machines run on a physical "host" machine. Each virtual machine runs its own operating system and functions separately from the other VMs, even when they are all running on the same host. Every virtual machine has virtual devices that provide the same functionality as physical hardware and have additional benefits in terms of portability, manageability, and security.

Virtual machines are easy to manage and maintain, and they offer several advantages over physical machines:

- Multiple VMs can run on a single physical host, allowing more efficient use of resources and saving physical space, time, and management costs.

- From a security perspective, VMs provide security similar to traditional physical server environments. VMs that share the same host are completely isolated from each other.

- Virtual machines support legacy applications, reducing the cost of migrating to a new operating system.

- VMs can be easily moved between physical hosts, providing optimum performance, maintenance, and resource optimization options. Recovery is much faster with VMs than with physical servers. Other hosts in the virtualized infrastructure can take over VMs from the failed host and have less downtime.

While virtual machines have several advantages over physical machines, there are also some potential disadvantages:

- Running multiple virtual machines on one physical machine can result in unstable performance if infrastructure requirements are not met.

- The failure of a critical hardware component of the physical host such as the motherboard or power supply can bring down all the VMs that reside on the affected host.

Virtual Machine Components

A VM is a logical container that holds all the resources an operating system requires for normal operation, such as a graphics adapter, memory, processor, networking, and so on. Virtual machine hardware specifications vary according to the physical resources available, such as memory and CPU capacity of the host. Other virtual machine hardware specifications such as network interface cards (NICs) and disk controllers do not depend on the physical host.

Figure 18-1 shows the components and capabilities of a vSphere 7.0.1, which has a Version 18 VM format.

CPU and memory are typically the two resources that strongly affect VM performance. The number of vCPUs assigned to a VM depends on the logical cores present in the ESXi host and the license that is purchased. Virtual random access memory (vRAM) creates many virtual address spaces and allows the ESXi host to allocate the virtual address space to any licensed VM. Virtual memory for each VM is protected from other VMs. The operating system detects the resources assigned to the VM as though they are physical resources.

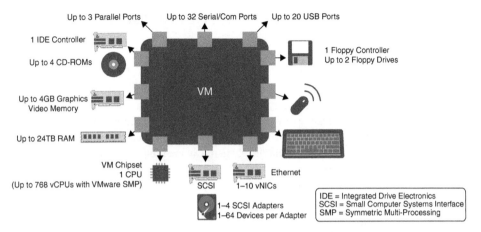

Figure 18-1 *Virtual Machine Components*

Datastores/virtual disks are storage containers for files. Datastores are where the host places virtual disk files and other VM files. Datastores hide the specifics of physical storage devices and provide a uniform model for storing VM files. They could be located on a local server hard drive or across the network on a SAN. Different types of controllers, including Integrated Drive Electronics (IDE), floppy, and Small Computer Systems Interface (SCSI), let the VM mount one or more types of disks and drives. These controllers do not require any physical counterparts.

vNICs facilitate communication between virtual machines on the same host, between virtual machines on different hosts, and between other virtual and physical machines. While configuring a virtual machine, you can add the vNICs along with the adapter type specification. The adapter type used typically depends on the type of guest operating system and applications installed. Selecting a wrong adapter type can result in low networking performance or the inability of the guest operating system to properly detect the virtualized hardware. Following are some network adapters that might be available for your VM.

- **Vlance:** This adapter is also called PCnet32, supports 32-bit legacy guest operating systems, and offers 10Mbps speeds.

- **E1000:** This adapter supports various guest operating systems, including Windows XP and later and Linux versions 2.4.19 and later.

- **E1000E:** This is the default adapter for Windows 8 and Windows Server 2012.

- **VMXNET:** This adapter provides significantly better performance than Vlance.

- **VMXNET2 (Enhanced):** This adapter provides high-performance features commonly used on modern networks, such as jumbo frames and hardware offloads.

- **VMXNET3:** This adapter offers all the features available in VMXNET2 and adds several new features such as IPv6 offloads.

■ **Flexible:** This adapter can function as either a Vlance or a VMXNET adapter, depending on which driver initializes it.

Virtual Machine Files

A virtual machine consists of several types of files you store on a supported storage device. The key files that make up a virtual machine are the configuration file, virtual disk file, NVRAM setting file, and the log file. For VMware virtual machines, the virtual machine settings can be configured via the vSphere Client. Table 18-1 lists the VMware virtual machine file types.

Table 18-1   *VMware Virtual Machine Files*

File	Usage	Description
.vmx	vmname.vmx	Virtual machine configuration file
.vmxf	vmname.vmxf	Additional virtual machine configuration files
.vmdk	vmname.vmdk	Virtual disk characteristics
-flat.vmdk	vmname-flat.vmdk	Virtual machine data disk
.nvram	vmname.nvram or nvram	Virtual machine BIOS or EFI configuration
.vmsd	vmname.vmsd	Virtual machine snapshots
.vmsn	vmname.vmsn	Virtual machine snapshot data file
.vswp	vmname.vswp	Virtual machine swap file
.vmss	vmname.vmss	Virtual machine suspend file
.log	vmware.log	Current virtual machine log file
-#.log	vmware-#.log (where # is a number starting with 1)	Old virtual machine log files

Additional files are created when you perform certain tasks with the virtual machine:

■ A .hlog file is a log file used by vCenter Server to keep track of virtual machine files that must be removed after a certain operation completes.

■ A .vmtx file is created when you convert a virtual machine to a template. The .vmtx file replaces the virtual machine configuration (.vmx) file.

Note   Every vendor has different file types that make up a virtual machine.

Virtual Machine vs. Container

Before comparing virtual machines with containers, let's first look at what a container is and what its main components are. A container is a unit of lightweight, executable software that packages application code and its dependencies in a standardized way. This packaging allows an application to be mobile and executed across different locations.

The container image contains all the information for the container to run, such as application code, operating system, and other dependencies (for example, libraries). There are multiple container image formats, with the most common of them being the Open Container Initiative (OCI). The container engine pulls the container images from a repository and runs them. There are a number of container engines, such as Docker, RKT, and LXD. Container engines can run on any container host (such as a laptop), on a datacenter physical server, or in the public cloud. The container is a container image that has been initiated or executed by the container engine.

Containers are often compared to VMs, as they are both portable single units of packaged compute; however, they solve different problems. Whereas VMs aim to abstract an operating system from the physical server, containers aim to create an environment for application code to be executed in. Similar to how VM hypervisors virtualize the hardware to host multiple isolated operating systems, the container engine virtualizes the operating system to host multiple isolated applications. Containers are naturally smaller in size compared to VMs, as they are purposely built to run applications and they package only the absolute minimum amount of data and executables required. Containers have introduced the concept of immutability, as they do not need to be updated or patched, as with virtual machines. Any updates require an existing container to be destroyed and replaced with a new one.

Figure 18-2 compares a virtual machine with a container.

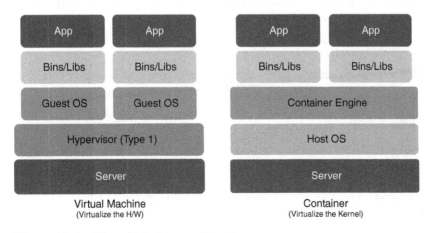

Figure 18-2   *Virtual Machine vs. Container*

Hypervisor

A hypervisor is a function that abstracts (that is, isolates) operating systems and applications from the underlying hardware. A hypervisor enables multiple operating systems to share a single hardware host machine. Whereas each operating system appears to have the dedicated use of the host's processor, memory, and other resources, the hypervisor controls and allocates only needed resources to each operating system and ensures that the operating systems (VMs) do not disrupt each other.

The two types of hypervisors are Type 1 and Type 2, as detailed next:

- **Type 1:** A Type 1 hypervisor runs over a bare-metal x86 hardware architecture, as an operating system does, but it also enables other operating systems to run on it. VMs are installed in the virtualization software. Resources that are available to the VMs are maximized, and potential bugs and security vulnerabilities of the host operating system are avoided.

  Here are some of the common types of Type 1 hypervisors on the market today:

  - VMware ESXi

  - KVM

  - Microsoft Hyper-V

  - Citrix XenServer

- **Type 2:** A Type 2 hypervisor runs on an operating system (OS) as a hosted environment. The OS can be running on either a PC or a server. Virtualization software is installed on the OS, and VMs are then deployed on the virtualization software. The benefit of a Type 2 hypervisor is that a single host (PC/server) can be used for everyday requirements in addition to virtualization needs. The downside of the Type 2 hypervisor is that the host OS uses up some resources that could be assigned to the VMs. Type 1 hypervisors have direct access to hardware and, hence, provide better performance than Type 2 hypervisors, which run on an OS.

  Here are some of the common types of Type 2 hypervisors on the market today:

  - VMware Workstation Pro/VMware Fusion

  - Windows Virtual PC

  - Parallels Desktop

  - Oracle VM VirtualBox

Figure 18-3 illustrates the difference in the deployment of Type 1 and Type 2 hypervisors.

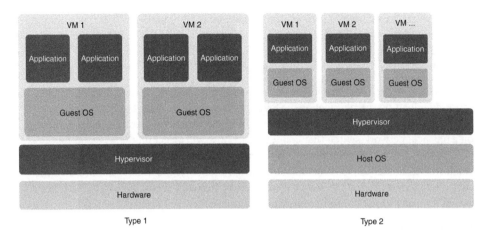

Figure 18-3 *Type 1 vs Type 2 Hypervisor*

Virtual Switch

A virtual switch (vSwitch) is a software application that connects VMs with both virtual and physical networks. The functionality of a virtual switch is quite similar to that of an Ethernet switch, with added security controls provided specifically for virtual environments. A vSwitch does more than just forward data packets; it intelligently directs the communication on a network by checking data packets before forwarding them to a destination.

Virtual switches are usually embedded into installed hypervisor software and provide the connectivity that each VM requires. A virtual switch is completely virtual and can connect to a Physical NIC. Figure 18-4 illustrates typical vSwitch connectivity.

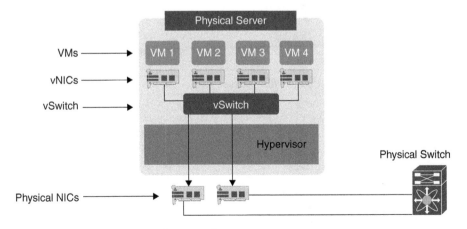

Figure 18-4 *Virtual Switch (vSwitch)*

Since physical host network adapters are usually limited in number, it is not possible to assign individual physical NICs to each VM for network connectivity. VMs are usually assigned one or more vNICs, which are attached to a vSwitch. The physical NICs act as uplink ports to the vSwitch for network access.

There are, however, a few challenges in using vSwitches. vSwitches create an additional processing load on the physical host. vSwitches lack familiar management options such as SSH and do not support all the features of a physical switch. Configuration performed on a physical network switch that connects to a host will affect all the VMs on that host. If the VM is moved between hosts, a different configuration on the network switch port connected to the target host can impact it. In a VM environment, if you shut down the switch port connected to the server, it impacts the network access for all the VMs and causes a greater impact to the production environment.

VMware vSphere virtual switches are discussed in detail in Chapter 7, "Describing Network Virtualization."

VMware vSphere

VMware vSphere is the name of VMware's server virtualization product suite. It was formerly known as VMware Infrastructure, and it consists of ESXi, a Type 1 hypervisor, vCenter Server, vSphere Client, and a few other important features that are not easily replicated on a physical infrastructure, such as vSphere vMotion and vSphere High Availability, to ensure virtual servers are up and running. Figure 18-5 shows the VMware vSphere components.

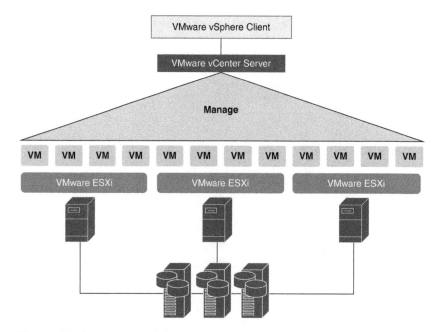

Figure 18-5   *VMware vSphere Components*

VMware ESXi

VMware ESXi (Elastic Sky X Integrated) is a Type 1 hypervisor that installs directly on the physical server. VMware ESXi is based on the VMkernel operating system, which interfaces with agents that run on top of it. With direct access to and control of underlying resources, VMware ESXi effectively abstracts the CPU, storage, memory, and networking resources of the physical host into multiple virtual machines. This means that applications running in virtual machines can access these resources without direct access to the underlying hardware. Through the ESXi, you run the VMs, install operating systems, run applications, and configure the VMs. Admins can configure VMware ESXi using its console or a vSphere Client. An ESXi 7.0 host can support up to 1024 VMs.

VMware vCenter Server

VMware vCenter Server is an advanced server management software that provides a centralized platform for controlling vSphere environments. It enables you to deploy, manage, monitor, automate, and secure a virtual infrastructure in a centralized fashion. You can install vCenter Server on a Windows virtual machine or physical server, or you can deploy the vCenter Server Appliance, which is a preconfigured Linux-based VM based on Photon OS with an embedded PostgreSQL database optimized for running vCenter Server and the associated services.

vCenter Server requires an extra license and serves as a focal point for management of ESXi hosts and their respective virtual machines. It correlates traffic between hosts for functionalities that span more than a single host, such as vSphere vMotion, vSphere Distributed Switch (vDS), vSphere Fault Tolerance, vSphere High Availability, and so on. Failure of a vCenter Server does not stop production traffic or affect VMs operation, but features like central management of ESXi hosts, vSphere High Availability, vSphere Distributed Switch, vSphere DRS, and vSphere vMotion are not available until the vCenter Server is restored. It is always recommended to have a redundant vCenter deployment. vCenter version 7.0 can manage up to 2500 ESXi hosts per vCenter Server and can have 45,000 registered VMs with 40,000 powered-on VMs.

VMware vSphere Client

vSphere Client is a lightweight HTML5-based GUI component for the vCenter Server that allows you to connect to a vCenter Server system for managing vSphere environments and is included with vCenter Server. As of vSphere 7.0, the vSphere Web Client (flash-based GUI) has been deprecated and the vSphere Client is the primary interface for connecting to and managing vCenter Server instances.

The VMware vSphere environment supports integration with Active Directory (AD) as the identity source, which simplifies user management. Therefore, when users log in to the vSphere Client, they can use their domain credentials. This approach allows administrators to define user roles for users with different permissions (administrator, read-only, and so on) that can then be used to access and manage all systems connected to the AD database. Depending on the access permissions configured, the user can access some of the virtualized environment or the entire environment using vSphere Client. For example, users can connect to the consoles of the VMs but not be able to start or stop those VMs, or change the parameters of the underlying host. Users also use one set of credentials to access multiple systems or devices. This allows administrators to create user accounts, change user permissions, or disable user accounts via a central location (AD database) and not on each system/device separately. Figure 18-6 shows the GUI interface of vSphere Client.

Figure 18-6   *vSphere Client*

vSphere vMotion

The vSphere vMotion feature migrates a live, running VM from one physical server to another with zero downtime and continuous service availability. This capability is possible across vSwitches, clusters, and even clouds. The entire process takes less than two seconds on a gigabit Ethernet network. The vMotion feature enables you to perform hardware maintenance without scheduling downtime or disrupting business operations. You can also move virtual machines away from failing or underperforming servers using vMotion. It is a powerful tool for maintenance or resource distribution situations, but it is not designed for disaster recovery. If a physical host fails, the VMs running on the host go offline until another host recovers the VMs. Figure 18-7 shows the vSphere vMotion feature in action.

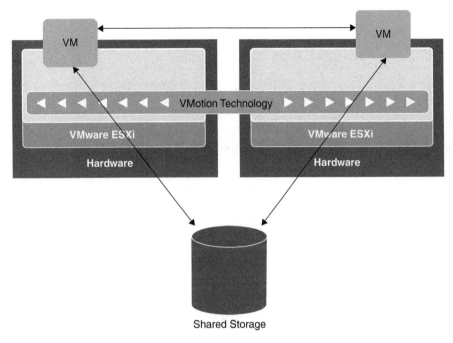

Figure 18-7   *vSphere vMotion*

vSphere High Availability

The vSphere High Availability (HA) feature automatically restarts a VM on the same physical server or a different physical server within an ESXi cluster without manual intervention when a guest operating system or hardware failure is detected. When you create a vSphere HA cluster, a single host is automatically elected as the primary host. The primary host communicates with vCenter Server and monitors the state of all protected virtual machines and the state of the secondary hosts. The primary host monitors the network and datastore's heartbeat from the secondary hosts and if doesn't detect both the heartbeats (that is, if the secondary host lost both network connectivity and connectivity to its datastore), it restarts the virtual machines of the failed host on other ESXi hosts in the cluster. Because the feature allows for fast recovery from a failed state without much overhead, it is the most common resiliency option used in the vSphere environment. Figure 18-8 shows vSphere High Availability in action.

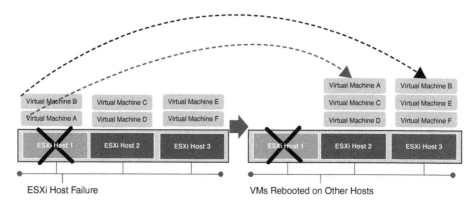

Figure 18-8   *vSphere High Availability*

vSphere Fault Tolerance

The vSphere Fault Tolerance (FT) feature allows a protected virtual machine, called the primary VM, to survive the failure of a host with zero downtime. It creates and maintains an identical virtual machine, called the secondary VM, that runs on another host and is continuously available to replace the failed primary VM if the host running the primary VM fails. The primary VM is continuously replicated to the secondary VM using the VMware Fast Checkpointing system so that the secondary VM can take over at any point, thereby providing fault-tolerant protection. If the host running the secondary VM fails, it is also immediately replaced. Although vSphere FT provides zero downtime, unlike vSphere HA, this option is not used very often due to synchronization limitations and overhead.

Figure 18-9 shows how VMware Fast Checkpointing synchronizes the primary and secondary VMs by following the changes on the primary VM and mirroring them to the secondary VM.

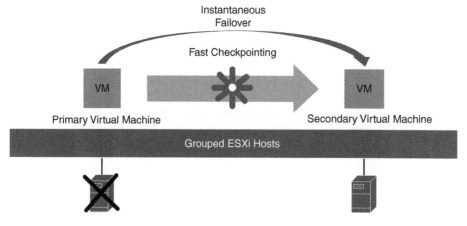

Figure 18-9   *vSphere Fault Tolerance*

vSphere DRS

The VMware vSphere Distributed Resource Scheduler (DRS) feature ensures that VMs and their applications are always getting the compute resources they need to run efficiently. vSphere DRS provides resource management capabilities like load balancing and virtual machine placement across the available hosts in an ESXi cluster to provide optimum performance. Migrating the VMs is done automatically using the underlying vMotion feature. If usage of the resources on a current host exceeds the defined limit, one or more of the VMs are relocated to other hosts to prevent degraded performance. If you need to perform an upgrade on one of the hosts in the group, vSphere DRS allows you to automatically migrate all VMs to other hosts once it is placed into maintenance mode without service disruption. Figure 18-10 shows how vSphere DRS helps dynamically balance VM workloads across resource pools.

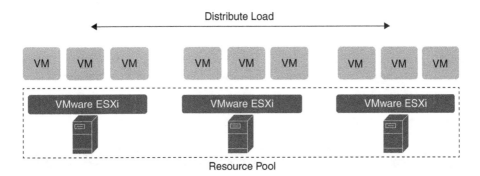

Figure 18-10   *vSphere DRS*

vSphere DPM

The VMware vSphere Distributed Power Management (DPM) feature reduces power consumption in the datacenter by powering hosts on and off based on cluster resource utilization. vSphere DPM monitors the cumulative demand of all virtual machines in the cluster and migrates the VMs to as few of the hosts as possible and then powers off the remaining hosts. Migrating the VMs is done automatically using the underlying vMotion feature. Wake-up protocols are used to restart the standby host if more resources are needed. Figure 18-11 depicts vSphere DPM consolidating VM workloads to reduce power consumption.

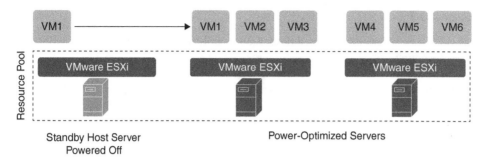

Figure 18-11 *vSphere DPM*

VMware ESXi Installation

In this section, we look at the steps required to install VMware ESXi hypervisor Version 6.7 on a Cisco UCS C-Series server. The steps to install ESXi hypervisor Version 7.0 are exactly the same.

Step 1. Log in to the KVM (keyboard, video, mouse) Console of the server and activate virtual devices (**Virtual Media, Activate Virtual Devices**), as shown in Figure 18-12.

Figure 18-12 *Activating Virtual Devices*

Step 2. Map the drive where the ISO image of the ESXi hypervisor is located to the virtual CD/DVD device on the KVM Console (**Virtual Media, Map CD/ DVD**, *locate the ISO*, **Map Drive**), as shown in Figures 18-13 and 18-14.

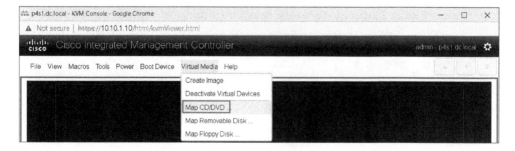

Figure 18-13 *Mapping the ESXi Hypervisor ISO Image (1)*

Figure 18-14   *Mapping the ESXi Hypervisor ISO Image (2)*

Step 3.   Reset the system and enter the boot menu by pressing **F6** when Cisco BIOS screen with the Cisco logo appears (**Power, Reset System (warm boot)**, *press F6 on Cisco BIOS screen)*, as shown in Figures 18-15 and 18-16.

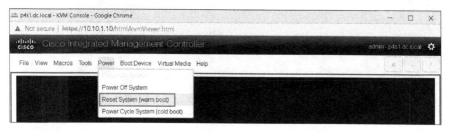

Figure 18-15   *Rebooting the Server*

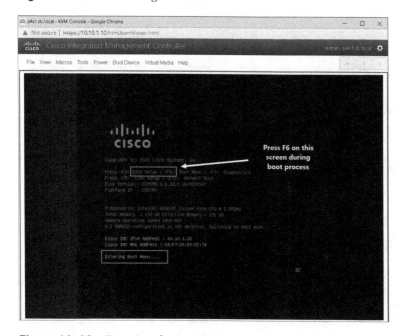

Figure 18-16   *Entering the Boot Menu*

Step 4.   Choose **Cisco vKVM-Mapped vDVD1.24** as the boot device and press **Enter** (see Figure 18-17). Then select the VMware ESXi Installer from the VMware ESXi boot menu (see Figure 18-18).

Figure 18-17   *Selecting vKVM-Mapped vDVD as the Boot Device*

Figure 18-18   *Selecting the ESXi Installer*

Step 5. Once the installer loads, press **Enter** to begin the installation (see Figure 18-19). On the End User License Agreement (EULA) page, press **F11** to proceed (see Figure 18-20).

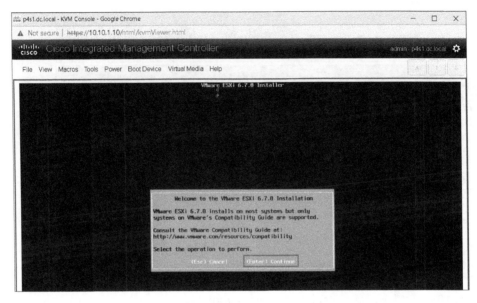

Figure 18-19 *Beginning the ESXi Installation*

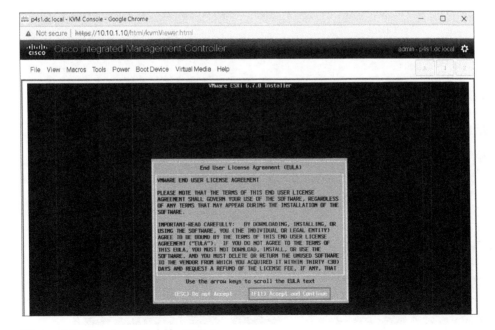

Figure 18-20 *Accepting the EULA*

Step 6.   Choose a disk (local or remote) where you want to install the ESXi hypervisor (see Figure 18-21).

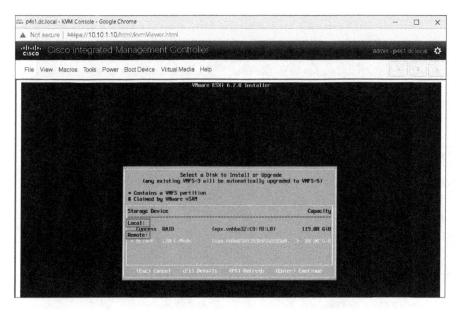

Figure 18-21   *Choosing a Disk for ESXi Installation*

Step 7.   Choose a keyboard layout (see Figure 18-22) and set the root password for the ESXi host (see Figure 18-23), which will be used to log in to the ESXi host later.

Figure 18-22   *Choosing a Keyboard Layout*

Figure 18-23   *Setting the Root Password for ESXi Hypervisor*

Step 8.   Press **F11** to confirm the installation of the ESXi hypervisor (see Figure 18-24). Once the installation is complete, press **Enter** to reboot the server (see Figure 18-25). The completed installation initiates a CD-ROM eject call, which unmounts the virtual ESXi ISO image we mapped earlier in Step 2.

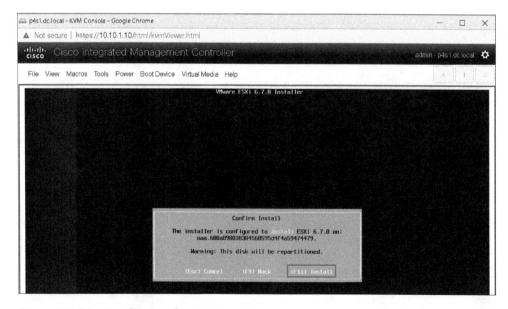

Figure 18-24   *Confirming the ESXi Installation*

Figure 18-25 *Rebooting the Server After the ESXi Hypervisor Is Installed*

Step 9.   Once the reboot has completed, you will see the VMware ESXi home screen (see Figure 18-26). This completes the ESXi installation on the server. Before you can connect to the HTTP management of the newly installed ESXi hypervisor, you need to configure its management network and connectivity options. There are two ways to configure a management IP address on an ESXi hypervisor: via DHCP automatic IP assignment or via static IP configuration.

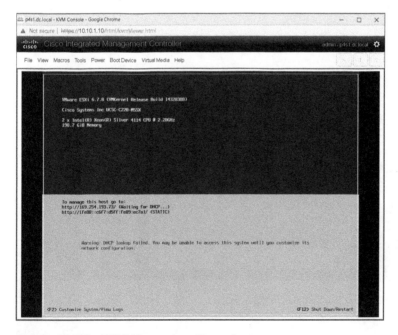

Figure 18-26 *ESXi Hypervisor Home Screen*

Step 10. To configure the management IP address statically, press **F2** and log in using the root password to go to the System Customization menu (see Figure 18-27). In the System Customization menu, select **Configure Management Network** and press **Enter** (see Figure 18-28).

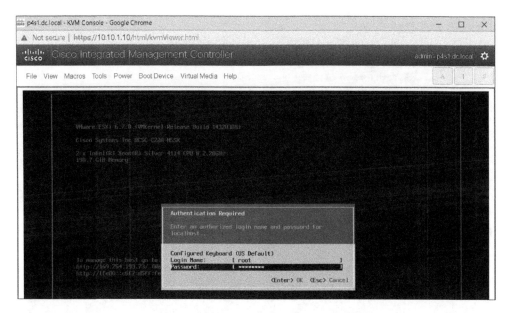

Figure 18-27 *Authenticating with Root Credentials for the System Customization Menu*

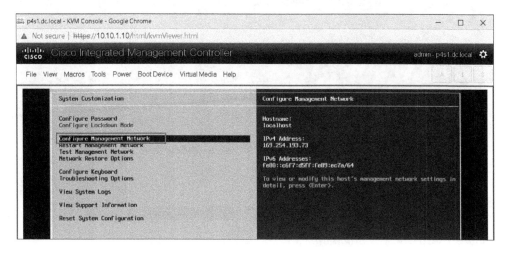

Figure 18-28 *System Customization Menu*

Step 11. Here, you can select which network adapter will be used for management network connectivity as well as what VLAN it will be on. Also, you can configure the static IP address along with the gateway for the management interface (see Figures 18-29 and 18-30).

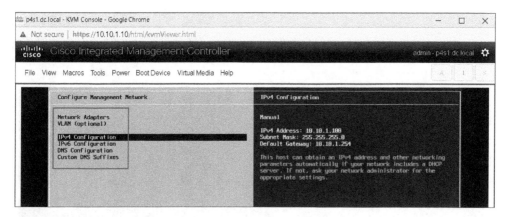

Figure 18-29   *Management Network Configuration Menu*

Figure 18-30   *IPv4 Configuration for ESXi Management Network*

Step 12. SSH access to the ESXi hypervisor can be enabled from **Troubleshooting Options** under the System Customization menu (see Figure 18-31).

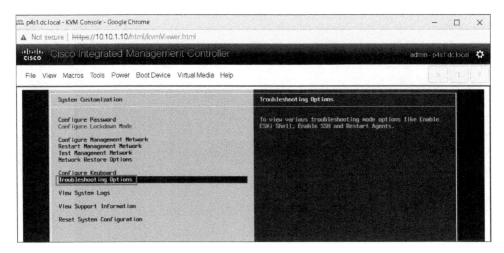

Figure 18-31   *Troubleshooting Options for ESXi Hypervisor*

Step 13.   Once you configure the management network, you can connect to the ESXi hypervisor at https://<Management IP of the ESXi Server> (see Figures 18-32 and 18-33).

Figure 18-32   *ESXi Hypervisor Login Page*

Figure 18-33   *ESXi Hypervisor Home Page*

VMware vCenter Installation

In this section, we look at the steps required to install vCenter Server Appliance Version 6.7 on the previously installed ESXi host and add the host to the vCenter Server. The steps to install vCenter Server Appliance Version 7.0 are exactly the same.

Step 1.   Locate the vCenter Server Appliance ISO image and then double-click the **installer.exe** file located under the **vcsa-ui-installer\<*operating system folder*>** folder. Once the installer window opens, click **Install** (see Figure 18-34).

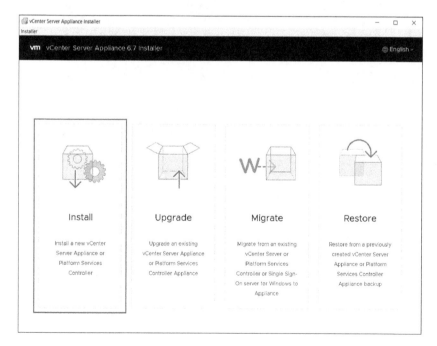

Figure 18-34   *Beginning vCenter Server Appliance Installation*

Step 2.   In the **Introduction** step, shown in Figure 18-35, read the instructions and click **Next.**

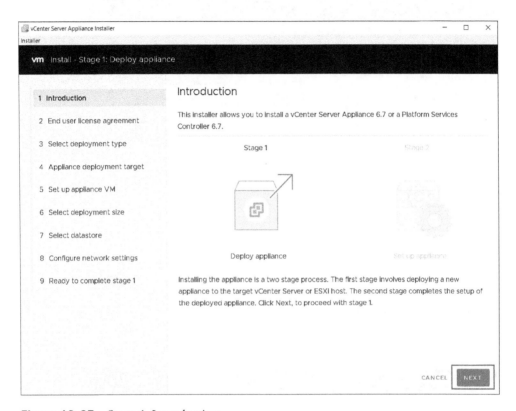

Figure 18-35   *Stage 1: Introduction*

Step 3.   In the **End user license agreement** step, shown in Figure 18-36, accept the license agreement and click **Next.**

Step 4.   In the **Select deployment type** step, shown in Figure 18-37, select **Embedded Platform Services Controller** and click **Next.** The External Platform Services Controller deployment model is deprecated.

Figure 18-36   *Stage 1: EULA*

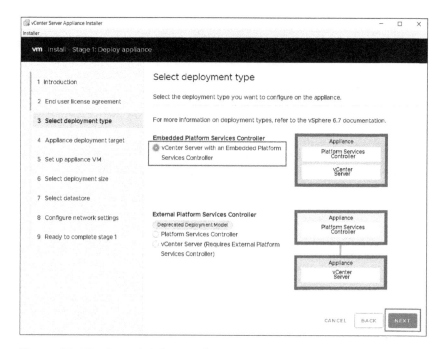

Figure 18-37   *Stage 1: Select Deployment Type*

Step 5.   In the **Appliance deployment target** step, shown in Figure 18-38, enter the details of your ESXi host where you want the vCenter Server Appliance VM to run and then click **Next.** Here we will give the details of the ESXi host installed in the previous section.

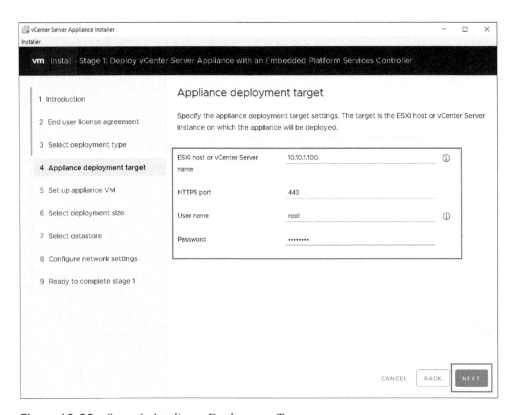

Figure 18-38   *Stage 1: Appliance Deployment Target*

Step 6.   In the **Set up appliance VM** step, shown in Figure 18-39, enter the name and set the root password for the vCenter Server Appliance and then click **Next.**

Step 7.   In the **Select deployment size** step, shown in Figure 18-40, select the deployment size as per your organization's requirements and click **Next.**

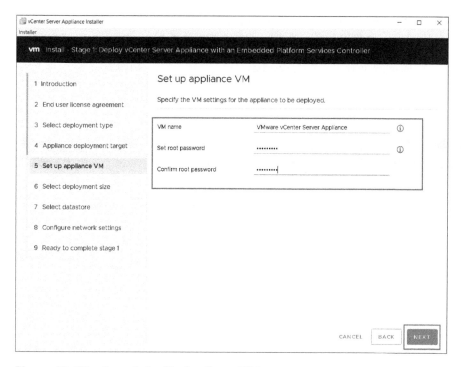

Figure 18-39   *Stage 1: Set Up Appliance VM*

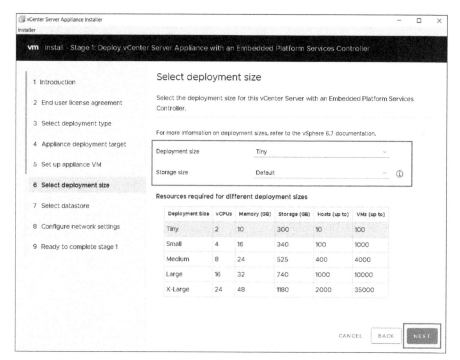

Figure 18-40   *Stage 1: Select Deployment Size*

Step 8.   In the **Select datastore** step, shown in Figure 18-41, select the appropriate datastore connected to the ESXi host and click **Next.**

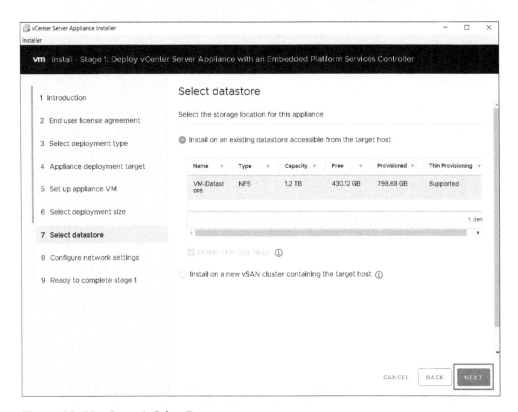

Figure 18-41   *Stage 1: Select Datastore*

Step 9.   In the **Configure network settings** step, shown in Figure 18-42, fill in the network settings such as the fully qualified domain name (FQDN), IP address, subnet mask, default gateway, and DNS server details for the vCenter Server appliance and click **Next.**

Step 10.   In the **Ready to complete stage 1** step, shown in Figure 18-43, review the configuration and click **Finish.** In stage 1, the vCenter Server Appliance is deployed (see Figure 18-44). Once the server is deployed, click **Continue** to move to stage 2, where we will set up the vCenter Server Appliance deployed in Step 1 (see Figure 18-45).

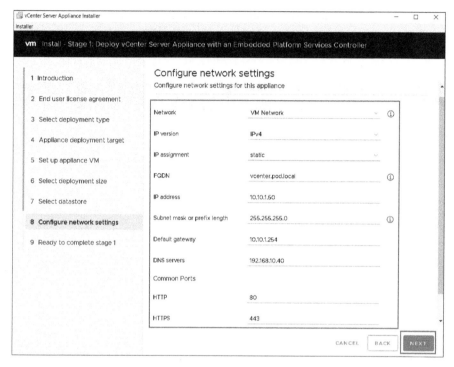

Figure 18-42   *Stage 1: Configure Network Settings*

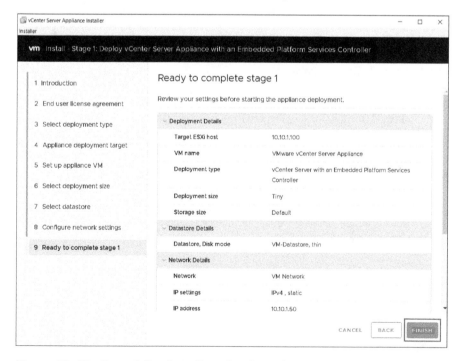

Figure 18-43   *Stage 1: Ready to Complete Stage 1*

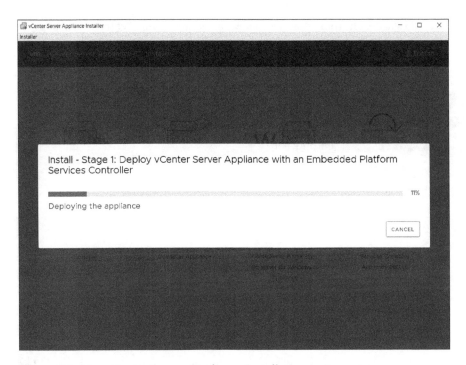

Figure 18-44   *vCenter Server Appliance Installation in Progress*

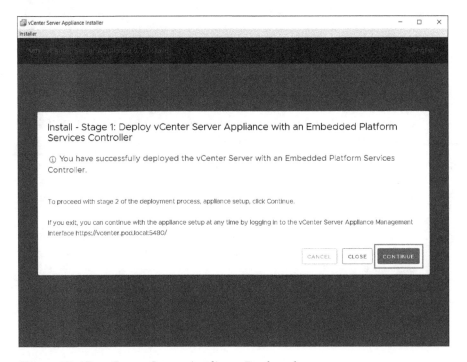

Figure 18-45   *vCenter Server Appliance Deployed*

Step 11.   In stage 2's **Introduction** step, shown in Figure 18-46, read the instructions and click **Next**.

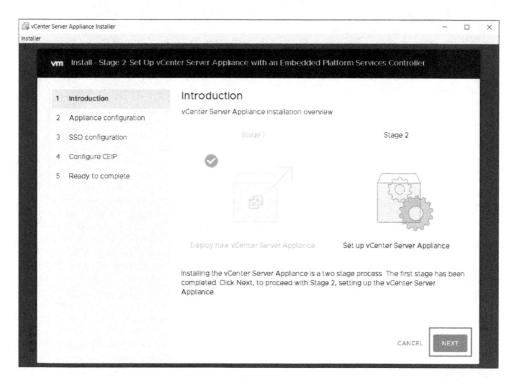

Figure 18-46   *Stage 2: Introduction*

Step 12.   In stage 2's **Appliance configuration** step, shown in Figure 18-47, choose the appropriate options for time synchronization mode and SSH access. In this example, we will let the vCenter server synchronize time with the ESXi host and will keep the SSH access to the vCenter Server disabled.

Step 13.   In stage 2's **SSO configuration** step, shown in Figure 18-48, you can either create a new SSO domain or join an existing SSO domain. In this example, we will create an SSO domain named vsphere.local and configure the SSO username and password to log in to the vCenter Server Appliance using SSO.

Step 14.   In stage 2's **Configure CEIP** step, shown in Figure 18-49, you can join the VMware's Customer Experience Improvement Program as per your preference.

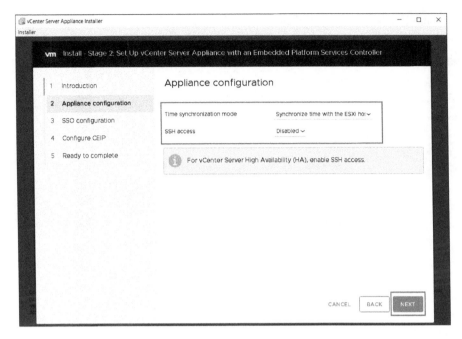

Figure 18-47   *Stage 2: Appliance Configuration*

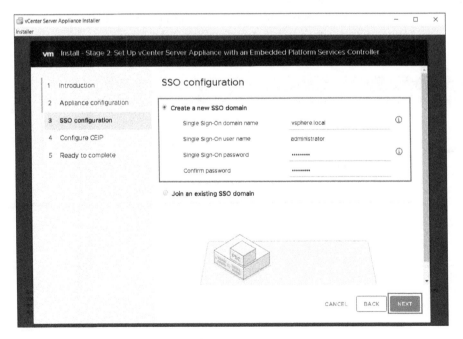

Figure 18-48   *Stage 2: SSO Configuration*

Figure 18-49   *Stage 2: Configure CEIP*

Step 15.   In stage 2's **Ready to complete** step, shown in Figures 18-50, 18-51, and 18-52, review the configuration and click **Finish** to complete the installation. This completes the vCenter Server Appliance installation.

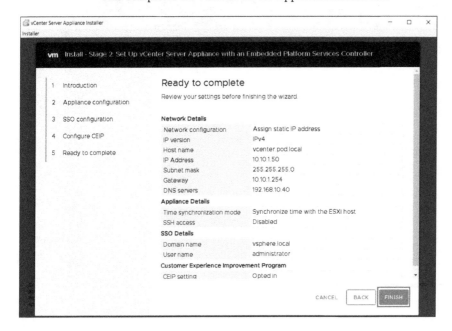

Figure 18-50   *Stage 2: Ready to Complete*

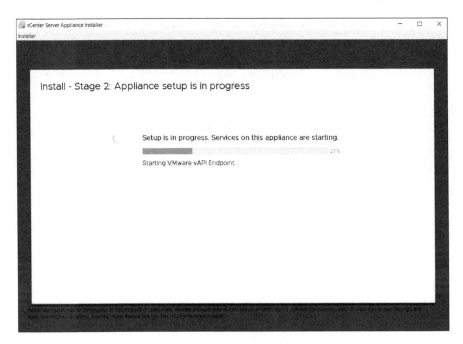

Figure 18-51   *vCenter Server Appliance Setup in Progress*

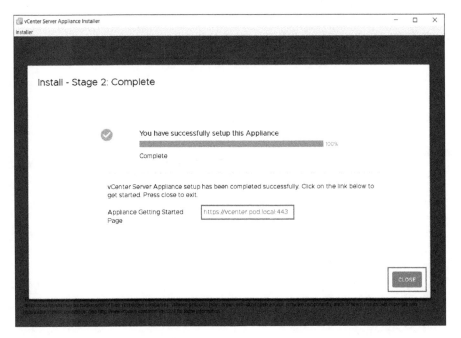

Figure 18-52   *vCenter Server Appliance Setup Complete*

Step 16. Once the installation is complete, you can log in to the vCenter Server using the link https://vcenter.pod.local:443, as per the configuration we did in Step 9. Click the **LAUNCH VSPHERE CLIENT(HTML5)** button and log in using the SSO credentials configured in Step 13 (see Figures 18-53, 18-54, and 18-55).

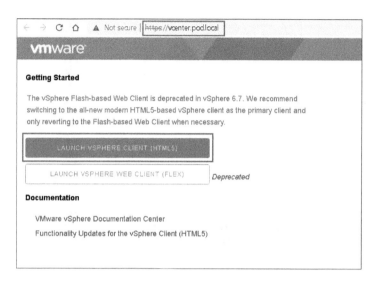

Figure 18-53 *Launching the vSphere Client*

Figure 18-54 *Logging in to the vCenter Server Appliance Using SSO Credentials*

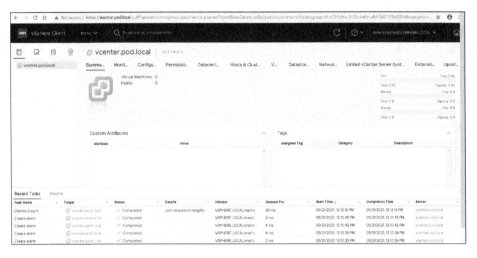

Figure 18-55   *vCenter Server Appliance Home Page*

Step 17.   Once the vCenter Server is up and running, you can add hosts to the vCenter Server to manage them. These hosts can be segmented by their location (vCenter sub-unit known as *data center*) and group (data center sub-unit known as *cluster*). In this example, we will add the same ESXi host where the vCenter Server Appliance is hosted. Right-click vCenter **vcenter.pod.local** in the left pane and choose **New Datacenter** (see Figure 18-56). Provide a name for the data center and click **OK** (see Figure 18-57).

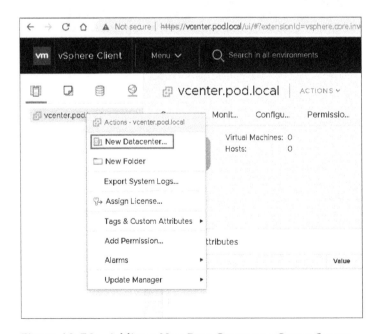

Figure 18-56   *Adding a New Data Center on vCenter Server*

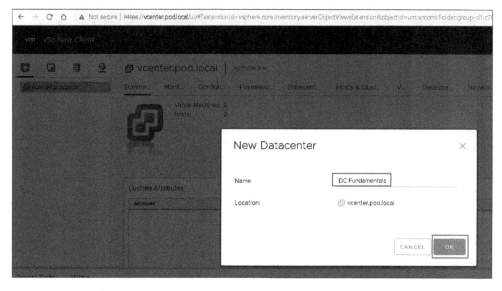

Figure 18-57 *Naming the New Data Center*

Step 18.   Right-click the newly created data center and choose **Add Host** (see
Figure 18-58).

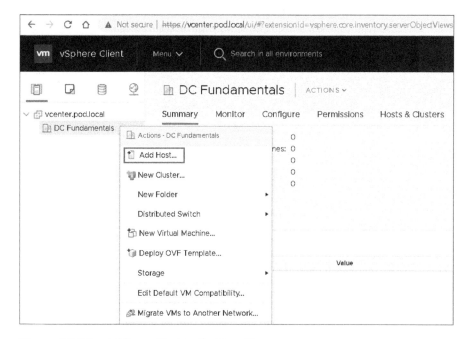

Figure 18-58 *Adding a Host to the Data Center*

Step 19.   In the Add Host Wizard's **Name and location** step, shown in Figure 18-59, provide the IP address of the host you want to add. In this example, we will add the ESXi host configured in the previous example.

Figure 18-59   *Name and Location of the Host*

Step 20.   In the Add Host Wizard's **Connection settings** step, shown in Figure 18-60, enter the root login credentials of the ESXi host and click **Next**.

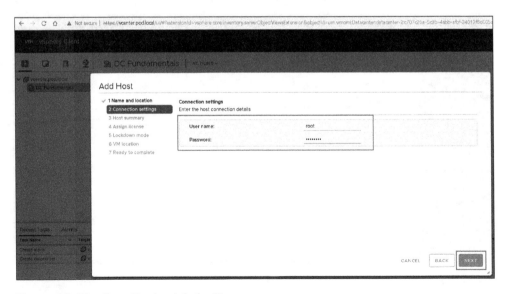

Figure 18-60   *Root Credentials for Host*

Step 21. In the Add Host Wizard's **Host summary** step, shown in Figure 18-61, review the host details and click **Next**.

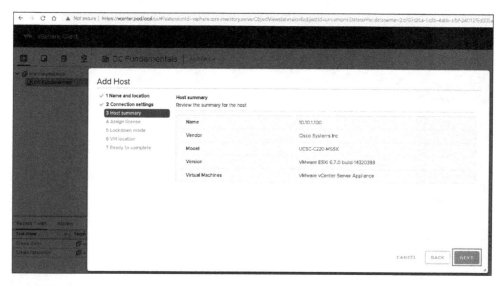

Figure 18-61 *Host Summary*

Step 22. In the Add Host Wizard's **Assign license** step, shown in Figure 18-62, assign the appropriate license. For this example, we will use the evaluation license.

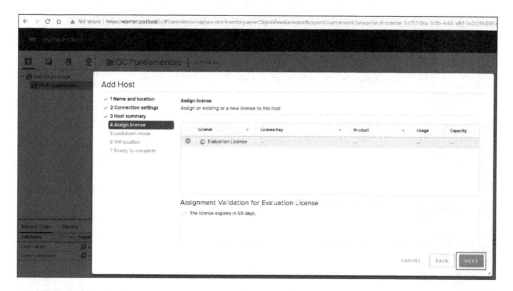

Figure 18-62 *Assigning a License to the Host*

Step 23. In the Add Host Wizard's **Lockdown mode** step, shown in Figure 18-63, choose the appropriate lockdown mode. Lockdown mode prevents remote users from logging directly in to the host. For this example, we will keep it disabled.

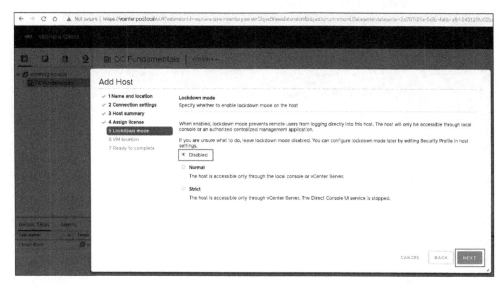

Figure 18-63 *Configuring Lockdown Mode for the Host*

Step 24. In the Add Host Wizard's **VM location** step, shown in Figure 18-64, choose the data center where you want the VM to be located and click **Next**.

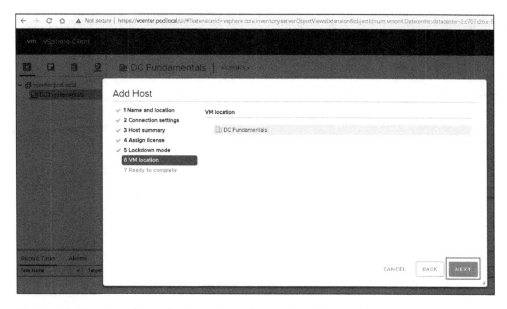

Figure 18-64 *Specifying the Data Center for the Host VM*

Step 25. In the Add Host Wizard's **Ready to complete** step, shown in Figures 18-65 and 18-66, review the information and click **Finish**. Verify that the ESXi host has been added successfully and that the vCenter virtual machine shows underneath the ESXi host.

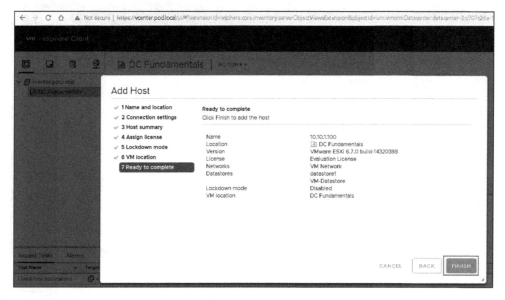

Figure 18-65 *Verifying Host Details Before Adding the Host*

Figure 18-66 *Host Successfully Added to vCenter Server*

This completes the VMware vCenter Server Appliance installation.

Summary

This chapter discusses server virtualization components such as the virtual machine, hypervisor, virtual switch, VMware vSphere product suite, and VMware ESXi as well as vCenter Server Appliance installation, including the following points:

■ Servers are often underutilized, and virtualization provides better performance and efficiency from the existing computing resources using hardware abstraction.

■ A virtual machine is a software computer that uses abstracted resources via virtualization software and can run an operating system and applications just like a physical computer.

■ A virtual machine consists of components such as vCPU, vRAM, vNICs and so on, and it is typically stored on the physical host's datastore/virtual disk as a set of files.

■ A hypervisor is virtualization software that hosts virtual machines by abstracting resources from the physical hardware to allocate to VMs.

■ There are two types of hypervisor: Type 1 runs on bare-metal x86 hardware architecture, and Type 2 runs on an operating system as a hosted environment.

■ A virtual switch (vSwitch) is a software application that connects VMs with both virtual and physical networks.

■ VMware vSphere is VMware's server virtualization product suite consisting of ESXi (a Type 1 hypervisor), vCenter Server, vSphere Client, and a few other important features.

■ VMware vCenter Server is server management software that enables you to manage the vSphere environment from a centralized location.

■ The vSphere vMotion feature enables the migration of live, running VMs from one physical server to another with zero downtime and continuous service availability.

■ The vSphere High Availability feature can automatically restart a failed VM on alternative host servers to reduce application downtime.

■ The vSphere Fault Tolerance feature allows a protected VM, called the primary VM, to survive the failure of a host with zero downtime.

■ The vSphere Distributed Resource Scheduler (DRS) is the resource-scheduling and load-balancing solution for vSphere environments. It ensures that VMs and their applications always get the compute resources they need to run efficiently.

■ The VMware vSphere Distributed Power Management (DPM) feature is part of VMware's DRS feature and provides power savings during periods of low resource utilization by migrating VMs onto fewer hosts and powering off unneeded ESXi hosts.

References

"VMware Infrastructure Architecture Overview" (White Paper), https://www.vmware.com/pdf/vi_architecture_wp.pdf

"VMware vSphere Documentation," https://docs.vmware.com/en/VMware-vSphere/index.html

Relevant Cisco Live sessions: http://www.ciscolive.com

Chapter 19

Using APIs

Each application provides one or more services. Depending on the logic of the service, the application architecture, and the processes, the different components will have to communicate with each other. The applications will have to connect to other applications to exchange data, and there will be requests for data and responses with the needed information. Because the applications are different, the communication, interfaces, and data formats need to be standardized.

The APIs specify these sets of requirements, defining how the applications can connect to each other and exchange data.

This chapter covers application programming interfaces (APIs) and the different protocols, data formats, and methods.

Common Programmability Protocols and Methods

In this chapter, we discuss APIs from the perspective of their application in the automation of the data center components. It is nothing new for the applications to have APIs for the interaction between them, based on the logic of the services they provide. It is very common for an application to communicate with a database application, for example. But it is a fairly new approach to try to automate the provisioning and the operation of the data center components. The need for automation became increasingly obvious with the adoption of the cloud. As it is one of the fundamental requirements for a private cloud to have the needed orchestration and automation in the data center, the ability to connect to its components in a programmatic manner became crucial.

This approach requires the use of standard protocols, data formats, and access methods for programmatic communication with the network, compute, and storage devices.

An API is a set of definitions, functions, and procedures that enable the communication between devices, applications, or services. Each API, as shown in Figure 19-1, must define which functions or endpoints to call, which data to provide as parameters, which data to expect as outputs, which data formats are supported by the endpoint for the data encoding, and what authentication is required. An API exposes internal functions to the outside world, allowing external applications to utilize functionality within the application.

Operationally, when an API is used, the communication consists of calls sent from one application to another. For these calls to be successful, the target application must understand the calls and accept them as commands.

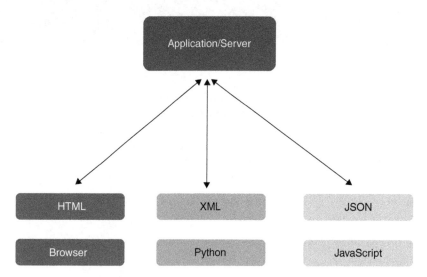

Figure 19-1   *APIs Example*

The two most used API types are the remote procedure call (RPC) API and the REST API.

The RPC API is based on remote procedure calls sent by the client to an application (see Figure 19-2). The call contains parameters and represents a remote function call, as it triggers an action on the application. The application responds with a message, and then the client continues the execution. With the RPC API, the following must be considered:

- **Authentication:** Authentication is necessary based on how secure the communication environment is.

- **Latency and overhead:** These aspects depend on the transport and the load of the application.

- **Error handling:** Errors are handled by the application and error messages are sent to the client.

The RPC API is an approach to (or architecture for) building an API, not a protocol. Because of this, many different protocols use it.

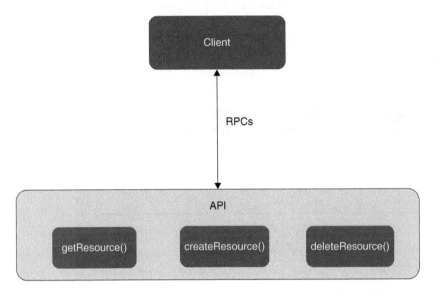

Figure 19-2   *RPC API Architecture*

The REST API is another style of building APIs (see Figure 19-3). The REST API is based on HTTP and uses the HTTP methods GET, PUT, and DELETE as its operations. With the REST API, the application transfers a representation of the state of the objects defined in the call by the client. The objects are the resources in this client/server architecture and are identified by a URL/URI. There are six specific characteristics of the REST API architecture:

- **Stateless:** No client context needs to be stored on the application side. The client request contains all the required information.

- **Cacheable:** On the web, HTTP responses can be cached. This results in caching being used to overcome issues such as latency. That is why the REST API responses need to contain information about whether they are cacheable.

- **Client/server:** A standard application architecture nowadays that allows for the decoupling of the client and the server components of an application. This allows for an independent evolution of each of the components and more flexibility for the ecosystem of the services.

- **Layered:** The architecture must support multiple layers of functions, such as load balancers, firewalls, proxy and cache servers in a transparent manner for the client.

■ **Uniform interface:** The representation of the resources provided to the client by the server must contain enough information for the client to be able to work with them. However, it is not mandatory that the internal representation of the resources be the same.

■ **Code on demand:** This is an optional characteristic that defines the ability of the server to temporarily extend the execution of code to the client, such as running JavaScript or Java applets.

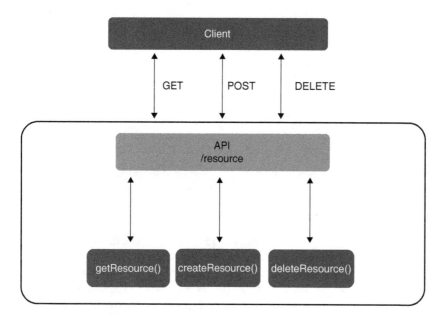

Figure 19-3   *REST API Architecture*

Based on the constraints of the REST API architecture, the RESTful API leverages HTTP to define operations over the exposed resources. Based on the representations of the resources and on which resource an HTTP method is used, the result can be different. For example, if the method GET is used on a collection resource such as /users, the response will contain the URIs of all the users, but if the same method is used on a member resource, such as the user "John" (/users/john), the response will contain a representation of the user John or all the attributes that define this object.

Here are the main HTTP methods:

■ **GET:** Requests a representation of a specific object.

■ **POST:** Requests the resource to process the representation sent. Used to modify a resource.

■ **DELETE:** Requests a resource state to be deleted.

- **PUT:** Creates or updates a resource state based on the representation in the request.

- **HEAD:** Like GET, this method requests the representation of a resource, but without the data enclosed in the response body.

- **PATCH:** Requests the resource state to be partially modified.

Additional methods are available, but they are not discussed in this chapter.

Also contained in the HTTP response bodies are status codes. The HTTP status codes are grouped as follows:

- **Informational (1xx):** Indicates the request has been received and processed by the server.

- **Success (2xx):** Indicates a successful operation. Here are some of the most commonly used codes:

  - **200 (OK):** Standard response for a successful HTTP request.

  - **201 (Created):** The request has been received and the resource created.

  - **204 (No content):** The request has been received and successfully processed, but the response body is empty.

- **Redirection (3xx):** The resource is either moved permanently and the requests will be redirected to a different URI (**301**) or the resource is found under a different URI temporarily (**302**).

- **Client error (4xx):** Specifies an error condition because of an issue with the client request. Here are some of the most commonly used codes:

  - **400 (Bad request):** The request has bad syntax, routing, size and cannot be processed.

  - **401 (Unauthorized):** An issue occurred with the user authentication or authorization.

  - **403 (Forbidden):** A valid request was received, the server refused to process it due to insufficient permissions to the resource.

  - **404 (Not found):** There is no matching resource at the specified URI.

- **Server error (5xx):** Error messages generated because of an issue on the server side. Here are some of the most commonly used codes:

  - **500 (Internal Server Error):** A generic error message indicating an issue occurred on the server, and there is no specific explanation of the problem.

  - **501 (Not Implemented):** The server does not support the requested function.

  - **503 (Service Unavailable):** The service or the server is not available because of a system crash, power failure, and so on.

The traditional implementation of the APIs presented a lot of challenges, as they were developed initially to take care of the communication between applications and not for the purpose of automating the components of the data center. It was very difficult to try to translate the command line interface (CLI), as it is unstructured text, not intended to be consumed by the machines but by humans. This led to the adoption of a model-based approach for creating device APIs.

The data models specify how the different components of the data center devices are described as objects and how configurations can be created and applied to these objects. This allows the whole API framework to be built based on this model-driven approach (see Figure 19-4). The data models for the specific devices, YANG for the network devices (such as the Cisco Nexus switches and Cisco ACI), and a management information tree (MIT) for the Cisco UCS are the base layers in the API framework.

The next layer of the framework contains the transport protocols used for communication with devices. This depends on the implementation, but some examples are HTTP/S, SSH, TLS. The transport protocols are also used to provide the authentication services for access through the API.

The encoding layer defines the data formats to be used in the communication with the device. The most commonly used are JSON, YAML, and XML.

The final layer contains the network configuration protocols, such as NETCONF, RESTCONF, and gRPC.

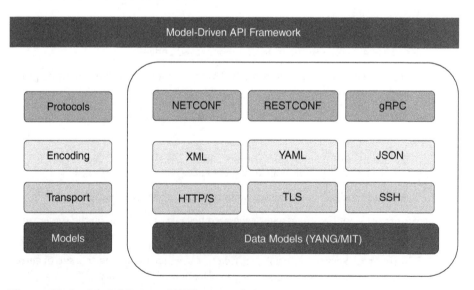

Figure 19-4   *Model-Driven API Framework*

The data model used with the Cisco network devices in the data center is the YANG data model (see Figure 19-5). YANG is a data-modeling language used to describe configuration and operational data, remote procedure calls, and notifications for network devices. It provides the definitions for the data sent over network configuration and management protocols such as NETCONF and RESTCONF. Because YANG, is protocol independent, it can be converted to any encoding format, such as XML, JSON or YAML.

YANG creates a hierarchical data model consisting of namespaces with modules containing the definitions and the configurations for the objects. Cisco sticks to the open source and open standards approach, and that's why the YANG implementation consists of two major namespaces: the YANG OpenConfig and the YANG native. Under the YANG OpenConfig are vendor-agnostic configuration and management models. This allows Cisco to adopt standards-based configuration and management of the network devices and components in the data center. The features specific only for the Cisco network devices are under the YANG native models. This allows for the precise configuration and management of advanced features and functionality.

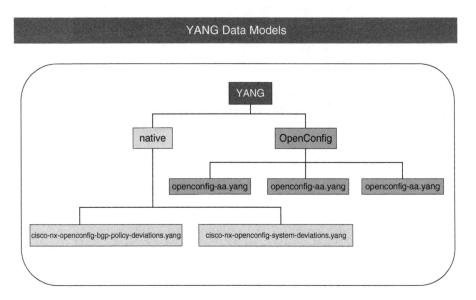

Figure 19-5 *YANG Data Model*

When data is exchanged, it must be understandable by both sides of the exchange. This means we will first need to agree on the rules of how the data will be structured, how it will look, and what the constraints will be, before it can be transferred. In other words, what are the syntax and grammatical rules? These rules are organized and standardized as sets called data formats. That is why the data formats are part of the APIs. The most common are JavaScript Object Notation (JSON), eXtensible Markup Language (XML), and the YAML Ain't Markup Language (YAML).

Each of the data formats has different semantics and syntax. One will use spaces, and others will use commas, quotation marks, and so on. However, the common thing between them is the concept of an object. This is the element that will be manipulated and described with multiple attributes. Usually, the attributes are defined by using **key:value** pairs. The **key** is the name of the attribute and is positioned on the left side of the pair. The **value** component defines the attribute state. Because **key:value** pairs are used to describe objects, it is important to know the syntax for the different data formats in order to notate them.

JSON is a data format for transmitting data between web services. It is simpler and more compact compared to XML. JSON is faster for humans to code in, and because it is better suited for object-oriented systems, it is widely used with scripting platforms.

JSON is platform independent and language independent. There are parsers and libraries for JSON in many different programming languages.

JSON is also plaintext and human readable. The JSON text format is syntactically identical to the code for crating JavaScript objects. It uses a hierarchical structure with nested values. JSON can use arrays, and there are no end tags and reserved words.

As shown in the example in Figure 19-6, JSON uses curly braces to define a new object. The objects appear in quotes, and the **key:value** pairs are separated using a colon.

JSON Example

```
{
    "user": {
        "name": "George",
        "email": "George@company.com",
        "location": "Alabama",
        "title": "IT Administrator"
    }
}
```

Figure 19-6   *JSON Example*

XML is another data format. It is a markup, human-readable format created to structure, store, and transport information. The first version of XML was defined back in 1998, and it looks very similar to the HTML.

Here are some of XML's characteristics:

■ It stores data in plaintext.

■ It is human readable.

- Its code is similar to HTML.

- There's no predefined document structure.

- The content is wrapped in tags.

- There are no predefined tags.

- Parsing and processing the data requires additional software configuration.

XML uses tags in the following format: <tag></tag>. The tags are used to define both the objects and the **key:value** pairs. The tag can be considered the key in the pair, as the value will be enclosed between the opening and the closing tags. As shown in the example in Figure 19-7, the key is <name> and the value is George. The object being described is a user, and between the opening and the closing tags for the user object are all the attributes describing this object.

XML Example

```
<?xml version="1.0" encoding="UTF-8" ?>
<user>
  <name>George</name>
  <email>George@company.com</email>
  <location>Alabama</location>
  <title>IT Administrator</title>
</user>
```

Figure 19-7 *XML Example*

YAML has a very minimalistic syntax, as shown in Figure 19-8. It was designed to be easier for humans to work with. It's becoming more and more popular because it is not only more convenient for humans but also easy for programs to use as well.

The **key:value** pairs are separated by colons, but in the syntax of YAML, the use of whitespace is very important. Whitespace is used for indentation levels, and it defines the structure of the objects and the YAML file. For example, all the data inside an object must have the same indentation level.

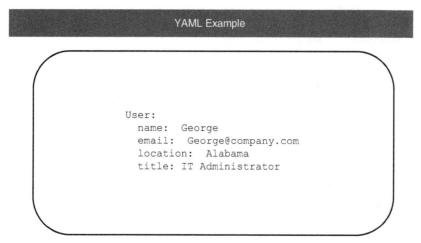

YAML Example

```
User:
  name:  George
  email:  George@company.com
  location:  Alabama
  title: IT Administrator
```

Figure 19-8   *YAML Example*

NETCONF is a network management protocol used to configure network devices using an XML management interface for configuration data and protocol messages. It is defined in RFC 4741 and revised in RFC 6241 by IETF. It uses XML-encoded messages for both the configuration data and as protocol messages over a secured transport protocol. NETCONF uses SSH or TLS as the secure transport protocol.

Four layers are defined for the NETCONF protocol:

- **Content layer:** Configuration and notification data

- **Operations layer:** Set of operations to retrieve and manipulate configuration data

- **Messages layer:** Provides the mechanism of encoding RPC and messages

- **Secure Transport layer:** Secure transport for the communication of the NETCONF protocol

The NETCONF protocol also defines and uses objects called datastores. A datastore is a complete set of configurations needed by a network device to get from its initial default configuration state to a required operational configuration state. Explained in a different way, each network device has a running configuration, which resides in the memory and is lost during a reset or power failure. This is referred to as the running configuration. The configuration used during the boot of the device and stored in the permanent memory is called the startup configuration. With NETCONF, the datastores use a similar approach to the device configuration. There's the "running" datastore, which holds the complete configuration currently running on the device, just like the running configuration you are used to working with on network devices. The second type of datastore is the startup, which holds the complete configuration used during the boot of the device. An additional datastore is called the candidate datastore. It creates an environment in which configuration operations are executed and configuration changes are made without affecting the running configuration. After a commit operation, the candidate configuration will be pushed to the running configuration of the device. There are also other datastores; the datastores that exist on a device are reported as capabilities by the device during the start of the NETCONF sessions.

The NETCONF protocol operations allow for retrieving, copying, configuring, and deleting datastores and for exchanging state and operational information. The operations are encoded in XML and use the YANG data models.

During the message exchanges, RPCs with three tags are used: <rpc>, <rpc-reply>, and <notification>, depending on the type of the message.

Here are the base NETCONF operations:

- **<get>**: Retrieve the running configuration and the device state data
- **<get-config>**: Retrieve all or part of a configuration datastore
- **<edit-config>**: Edit a configuration datastore
- **<copy-config>**: Copy one configuration datastore to another
- **<delete-config>**: Delete a configuration datastore
- **<lock>**: Lock a configuration datastore
- **<unlock>**: Unlock a configuration datastore
- **<close-session>**: Gracefully disconnect a NETCONF session
- **<kill-session>**: Forcefully terminate a NETCONF session

RESTCONF is an HTTP-based protocol and can be described as a subset of the NETCONF protocol, which provides a programmatic interface to allow access to the configuration and state data, data-model-specific RPC operations, and event notifications. It is defined in RFC 8040 by the IETF.

The NETCONF protocol defines a set of operations to support the basic CRUD (create, read, update, delete) approach and the use of datastores with the YANG data models.

RESTCONF uses HTTP methods to support CRUD operations on datastores based on YANG-defined data.

Here are the RESTCONF characteristics:

- YANG data models
- HTTP/S transport
- HTTP methods
- Subset of NETCONF
- XML and JSON encoding

The supported operations are based on HTTP and include GET, POST, PUT, PATCH, and DELETE.

Configuring Cisco NX-OS with APIs

Cisco NX-OS is a very flexible operating system powering most of the Cisco devices in the data center. Because nowadays there is the need to implement automation and orchestration through programmability, as well as to provide better support for integration with monitoring and third-party solutions, Cisco NX-OS is bundled with open source software to provide the needed support and openness.

The principles and concepts behind automation and orchestration in Cisco data center devices throughout the lifecycle are covered in Chapter 20, "Automating the Data Center." Here you will get acquainted with the Cisco NX-OS programmability options.

The Cisco NX-OS software stack is built based on the Cisco Open NX-OS model-driven programmability (MDP) architecture (see Figure 19-9). It is an object-oriented software framework aimed at developing management systems. At the base of the MDP architecture is the object model, which is used to represent the components, configurations, operational states, and features of the devices.

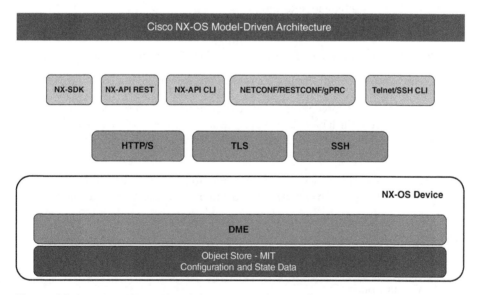

Figure 19-9 *Cisco NX-OS Model-Driven Programmability Architecture*

In the MDP architecture, the goal is to abstract the physical device and to represent its components using a data model, such as the YANG data model. This allows the device's components and features to be accessed and configured through APIs, thus achieving automation and supporting the needed levels of orchestration. The component from the

Cisco NX-OS MDP responsible for looking into the hardware and software features, based on the YANG OpenConfig and native models to create this representation, called a management information tree (MIT), is the data management engine (DME). The DME creates the hierarchical namespaces populated with objects representing the underlying components. It is part of the APIs, as it exposes the MIT to the external clients, applications, and administrator automation tools in different ways.

As a result, Cisco NX-OS offers the following automation and programmability framework:

- **NX-API REST:** Provides support for RESTful API calls.

- **NX-API CLI:** Provides support for embedding Cisco NX-OS CLI commands for execution on the switch. The transport protocol is HTTP/S, and the commands need to be structured using the JSON or XML data format.

- **Network configuration protocols:** Provide support for NETCONF, RESTCONF, and gRPC for configuration and management.

- **Cisco NX-OS Software Development Kit (NX-SDK):** A C++ abstraction and plug-in library layer that streamlines access to infrastructure for automation and custom application creation. The programming languages supported with the NX-SDK are C++, Python, and Go.

- **NX-Toolkit –** A set of Python libraries that supports basic configuration of Cisco devices running the NX-OS.

- **Onboard Python –** A built-in Python interpreter available in the NX-OS.

- **Embedded Event Manager (EEM) –** A feature that allows real-time detection of events and triggering of certain actions. The EEM is available in Cisco IOS and NX-OS.

The NX-API REST and CLI are backed by a built-in web server, called NGINX, which is the endpoint for HTTP communication. It responds to HTTP requests and is used by both the NX-API CLI and the NX-API REST.

The NX-API CLI extends the Cisco NX-OS CLI outside of the device and allows administrators to use a programmatic approach for configuration. The API communicates through the NGINX web server using the HTTP/S protocols as a transport. This interface does not provide a big difference when it comes to optimizing the configuration and achieving better automation, as you still have to work with a single device to use the CLI commands, encode them in JSON or XML, and then to push them to the device. However, this API allows administrators to examine and learn the MIT, the different programmatic operations, integrations, and so on.

The NX-API REST is a RESTful programmatic interface. The configuration and state data for the objects is stored in the MIT. The NX-API REST has access to the MIT. When the configuration is pushed to the MIT, the DME validates and rejects any incorrect values.

It is said that the DME operates in forgiving mode during the validation process, because if there are values missing for the attributes of objects in the MIT, instead of rejecting the whole configuration, the DME will use default values.

The Cisco NX-OS devices offer a unique option to run Python scripts directly on them. This is achieved by embedding a native Python execution engine that supports the use of a dynamic Python interpreter on the device. This is known as onboard Python. It can be used to automate CLI commands and generate syslogs for event-based activities. It can be used together with the Embedded Event Manager (EEM) and the scheduler. To start it, simply type **python** in the CLI and press **Enter**.

Cisco NX-OS devices come with a preinstalled Python module called "cisco." It can be used with three core methods:

- **cli():** Returns the raw output of the CLI commands, including control and special characters

- **clip():** Prints the output of the CLI commands directly to stdout and returns nothing to Python

- **clid():** Returns a dictionary of attribute key:value pairs for CLI commands that support JSON

The Embedded Event Manager (EEM) consists of three components:

- **Event statements:** The events that will be monitored.

- **Action statement:** The actions to be taken when an event occurs. Actions include sending an email and disabling an interface.

- **Policies:** A combination of an event and the associated actions to troubleshoot and recover.

This structure allows the EEM to be used to monitor and react when specific events occur according to the actions specified. Additionally, it can be used with a scheduler and integrated with the onboard Python interpreter.

Exploring the Cisco UCS Manager XML API Management Information Tree

The Cisco UCS Manager is an application that manages the Cisco compute. It is an XML application that is built around an HTTP-based XML API. From one side, the administrators and third-party applications communicate with the Cisco UCSM through the XML API for configuration and monitoring purposes. The API also supports integrations with third-party hardware and software.

From another side, the XML API exposes the representation of the underlying physical and logical resources. These resources are abstracted and represented as objects with the needed attributes to describe them by the DME in an MIT. In Figure 19-10, we can see a similar approach to the Cisco NX-OS APIs.

Each of the objects in the hierarchical structure of the MIT is described with attributes that represent the configuration and the state.

The managed objects in the MIT have unique distinguished names (DNs), which describe the object and its location in the tree.

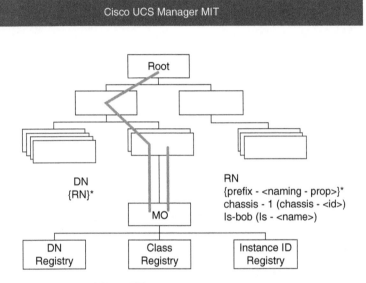

Figure 19-10   *Cisco UCSM MIT*

The DME centrally stores and manages the information model, which is a user-level process that runs on the Fabric Interconnects. When a user initiates an administrative change to a Cisco UCS component (for example, applying a service profile to a server), the DME first applies that change to the information model and then applies the change to the actual managed endpoint.

The Cisco UCS Manager XML API supports operations on a single object or an object hierarchy. An API call can initiate changes to attributes of one or more objects such as physical hardware, policies, and other configurable components. The API operates in forgiving mode. Missing attributes are replaced with applicable default values that are maintained in the internal DME.

To examine the MIT, you can use the built-in Cisco UCSM and CIMC-managed object browser. It's called Visore (see Figure 19-11) and can be accessed at the following URL: http://<UCSM/CIMC-IP-Address>/visore.html.

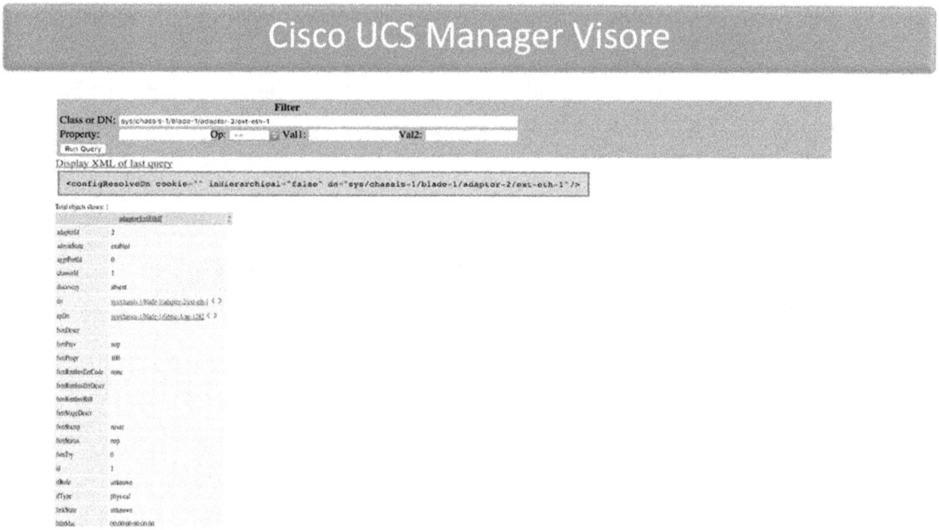

Figure 19-11 *Cisco UCSM Visore*

Visore uses the Cisco UCS XML API to query the DME for information on the managed objects. For each object, you can see all its information, including child and parent objects, to which class it belongs, and more. A pink background color is used for the fields that display the managed object instances and the class name. The property names have a green background, and the values are in yellow.

There is also a reference to the Cisco UCS Manager information model on the Cisco DevNet site, which can be accessed and researched for free at the following URL:

https://developer.cisco.com/site/ucs-mim-ref-api-picker/

Cisco UCS PowerTool suite is a set of PowerShell modules that helps automate all aspects of Cisco UCS Manager. It also helps automate server, network, storage, and hypervisor management. Cisco UCS PowerTool suite enables easy integration with existing IT management processes and tools. The PowerTool cmdlets work on the Cisco UCS MIT. The cmdlets can be used to execute, read, create, modify, and delete operations on all the UCS managed objects (MOs) in the MIT. Cisco UCS PowerTool 2.0 also provides support for Microsoft's Desired State Configuration (DSC).

An additional functionality, which helps administrators understand the MIT and how to use it with the Cisco UCS PowerTool, is the ability to convert actions in the UCS Manager GUI into DSC configuration code. This functionality is provided by the ConvertTo-UcsDSCConfig cmdlet.

The Cisco UCS Python SDK is a Python module that helps automate all aspects of Cisco UCS management, including server, network, storage, and hypervisor management, similar to Cisco UCS PowerTool. Just like Cisco UCS PowerTool, the Cisco UCS Python SDK also performs similar functions on the Cisco UCS Manager MIT in that it creates, modifies, and deletes managed objects in the tree.

Summary

This chapter describes the Cisco UCS abstraction. In this chapter you learned about the following:

- An API is a set of definitions, functions, and procedures to enable communication between devices, applications, and services.

- The RPC API is an architecture based on remote procedure calls sent by the client to an application.

- The REST API is an architecture based on HTTP and uses the HTTP methods GET, PUT, and DELETE for its operations.

- HTTP uses methods to define the operations and status codes for the results.

- Data models specify how the different components of the data center devices are described as objects and how the configurations can be created and applied to these objects.

- The data model used with the Cisco network devices in the data center is the YANG data model.

- YANG is a data modeling language.

- YANG OpenConfig has vendor-agnostic configuration and management models.

- YANG native models are vendor-proprietary features models.

- The data formats for encoding are JSON, XML, and YAML.

- NETCONF is a network management protocol used to configure network devices.

- RESTCONF is an HTTP-based protocol and a subset of NETCONF for configuring and managing network devices.

- Cisco NX-OS offers NX-API REST, NX-API CLI, NX-SDK, NX-Toolkit, onboard Python, and EEM.

- The Cisco UCSM APIs support the model-driven framework based on an MIT.

- Cisco UCSM Visore allows the MIT to be examined.

- Cisco UCS PowerTool is a set of PowerShell modules to help automate the Cisco UCSM.

- The Cisco UCS Python SDK is a Python module that helps automate the Cisco UCSM.

Reference

The Cisco Data Center Dev Center: https://developer.cisco.com/site/data-center/

Chapter 20

Automating the Data Center

The data center is home to the applications that provide needed services. There are multiple different components, starting with the physical characteristics of the premises, such as the power supply and cooling, going through the infrastructure components, such as the compute, network, and storage building blocks, and moving up through the application stack to the operating systems, virtualization, microservices, and everything else that's needed to create the redundant environment for our applications to run in and offer services. Multiple different professionals are involved in the designing and creation of a data center, and it continues to evolve and change over time. It is obvious that building and operating a data center is a complex effort. That is why one of the most important goals has always been to optimize and simplify this effort. The way this can happen when it comes to the data center infrastructure and the whole application stack is through automation. In Chapter 19, "Using APIs," we discussed APIs and the model-driven API framework with the data formats and network configuration protocols such as NETCONF and RESTCONF. These tools and standards are used in the automation. In this chapter, we discuss the need for automation, what automation and orchestration are, Infrastructure as Code, and some of the toolsets supported with the Cisco data center solutions. The focus will be on the data center infrastructure components—the network, storage, and compute.

Automation Basics

The data center infrastructure components consist of multiple separate devices that need to be interconnected and configured for initial deployment. Afterward, they need full configuration in order to achieve the needed levels of integration. Then, when we start to use them—or, in other words, to operate them—we have to monitor and troubleshoot them in order to maintain a stable and redundant environment for our applications. This effort requires multiple different administrators to plan, configure, and monitor multiple separate devices. Each needs to be accessed, to perform the initial configuration, and then fully configured to make sure it operates as designed.

Troubleshooting is another huge challenge in the data center. We all know about the big support teams that are maintained by the vendors, their partners, and customers. This is because when it comes to troubleshooting, a simple workflow is followed—define the problem, find out the root cause for the problem, and apply a fix. Although this is a simplified view of the process, which involves many more steps and much more effort, we will use it to demonstrate the challenges of troubleshooting in a modern data center. Now, to define the problem, engineers need to take multiple steps to isolate which device (or devices) is affected. Is it a feature that runs on a single device? Is it a global running process? For this to happen, even with the use of complex monitoring systems, multiple devices still need to be accessed separately, endless logs need to be examined, and configurations need to be checked. And the interesting thing is that in most cases, the issue is a result of human intervention. A human-induced error results in a wrong configuration, broken process, or disruption in the infrastructure that might even affect the availability of the services. There are two huge challenges when it comes to troubleshooting—how to make sure the correct configuration is applied to the correct devices at scale, and how to be proactive in preventing failures due to such errors.

These challenges accompany the whole operations lifecycle of the data center solutions. The lifecycle, shown in Figure 20-1, is usually represented by days:

- **Day 0:** Onboarding of the device in the infrastructure, which includes the very initial basic setup.

- **Day 1:** Configuration and operation. This is the stage at which the full configuration is applied, depending on the solution from which the device is part of. The device becomes fully operational as a component of the infrastructure.

- **Day 2:** Monitoring and troubleshooting. The device is operational and is being monitored to identify and fix any issues.

- **Day N:** Optimization and upgrade. This stage includes all the activities related to the optimization of the configuration, the solution, and the maintenance, such as applying patches and software upgrades.

Going through all the stages, from Day 0 to Day N, requires the administrators to access each device separately, perform the initial setup, and make sure that each device has the basic needed connectivity. Then, on each device separately, they need to create the full configuration, test it, and then operate, monitor, and troubleshoot, again on a per-device basis.

The solution to these challenges is automation, which is the idea of using a wide range of technologies and methods to minimize human intervention. With automation, the goal is to be able to work with multiple devices and configurations, as we want to have predictable results and avoid any issues created by human error. We want to have faster results, and the data centers need to be agile, as the services require changes to be implemented quickly in the data center.

Automation is achieved through the ability to connect to the devices in a programmatic way, using the APIs and the model-driven framework. This allows the administrator to create the needed configuration, using a supported programming language, test it, and then to send it for execution on the device through the API. This allows the administrator to send the configuration to multiple devices simultaneously. And this is just one example. Another use case is when another application uses the APIs to connect to other devices to make the needed configurations and changes.

The automation goes hand-in-hand with another concept in the data center—orchestration. Orchestration is the ability, through automation, to manage and configure entire infrastructures or data centers, up to the level of the application. To do so, the orchestration uses workflows, which specify the exact sequence of tasks to be executed on the devices with the needed actions to be performed in order to manage the resources of the data center. The tasks in the workflows are automated pieces of actions, as each is executed on a specific device. An example would be to configure interfaces on a switch or to create a virtual machine. Then, the tasks are put in the correct order of execution, depending which component needs to exist before the creation of another. This is how the workflows are created and then automatically executed.

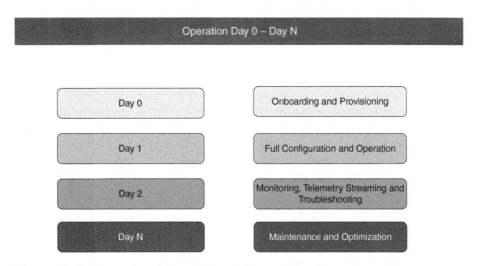

Figure 20-1   *Operations Lifecycle Day 0 Through Day N*

The automation and orchestration can be implemented in a data center at different levels. We can have some limited automation, affecting some components of the infrastructure and certain functionality, or we can have automation and orchestration that are fully implemented, allowing for provisioning of resources up to the level of deploying applications. In this last scenario, this is the level of automation required from a data center that will offer cloud services. The adoption of the automation and orchestration affects each of the operations lifecycle stages. Depending on the technologies in use, we can have automation and orchestration that will automate the initial provisioning of the devices on Day 0, or to orchestrate the full configuration and creation of virtual resources on Day 1. The automation can also be a component of Day 2, to facilitate proactive monitoring and troubleshooting approaches, or in the maintenance and optimization of Day N, by automatically applying patches or updates, increasing or decreasing resources, or moving workloads between the infrastructures to optimize their utilization.

One example of the benefits of using automation and orchestration in a data center component is software-defined networking (SDN). This approach uses the idea of separating the control and management plane processes to a dedicated SDN controller and leaving to the physical switches only the task of maintaining the data plane (that is, to switch the Ethernet frames). The administrators will connect only to the SDN controller, which is usually an application that is capable of orchestrating, monitoring, and managing the switches in an automated manner, and this is where all the configurations will be created. Then, these configurations will be pushed to the correct devices. The control plane processes, such as routing protocols, will be running on the SDN controller, and as the result of their operation, they will be pushed only to the devices that require this information. Therefore, the resources of the data plane devices are utilized better, as they do not have to run such processes any more, and only the devices that need them receive the appropriate configuration. At the same time, the SDN controller will collect streaming telemetry and other monitoring information, analyze it, and present it to the administrators. Depending on the SDN solution, as there are a few on the market, the system can take proactive measures to mitigate certain issues, or it can limit itself only to notifications for certain events.

Maybe one of the best examples of a solution for the data center networking component is the Cisco Application Centric Infrastructure (ACI). You already know about ACI from the first chapters of this book, but from the perspective of discussing automation and the orchestration, which are the main principles in the core of the SDN concept, Cisco ACI goes several steps further, as it utilizes a new approach to networking, looking from the perspective of the communication needs of the application.

Automation and Orchestration Technologies

Various automation and orchestration technologies and tools can be used in the data center. Different approaches can be used during the various operations lifecycle stages, depending on the data center infrastructure and its capabilities.

Cisco POAP

One technology for automating the initial provisioning during Day 0 is Cisco PowerOn Auto Provisioning (POAP). It is supported in Cisco NX-OS and allows the processes of configuring and upgrading devices to be automated. This significantly reduces the manual tasks related to the deployment of networking and storage communication infrastructures in the data center.

The POAP feature is enabled by default, and for its successful operation it needs to have the following components in the network (Figure 20-2):

■ **DHCP server:** Used to assign IP addressing information (IP address, gateway, DNS)

- **TFTP server:** Contains the configuration scripts

- **Software images repositories:** One or more servers containing software images

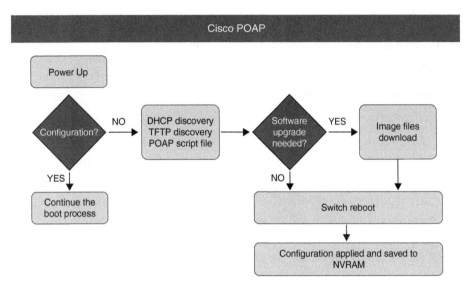

Figure 20-2 *Cisco POAP Process*

The POAP process starts with booting up the switch. If the switch has a configuration, it is loaded, and then the switch goes into normal operation. However, if there is no configuration, by default, the switch will enter POAP mode. Then the following will occur:

- **DHCP discovery:** The switch will send a DHCP request through the management interface.

- **DHCP response:** The DHCP server will reply with the needed IP addressing configuration and with information about the IP address of the TFTP server and the configuration script filename.

- **TFTP server communication:** The switch will connect to the TFTP server and download the configuration script file. It will execute the file.

- **Software images (kickstart and system image files) download:** If the configuration script file specifies that the switch has to upgrade its software image files, it will download the images, install them, and reboot the switch.

- **Configuration file application:** After the successful installation of the software images and the rebooting of the switch, the configuration file will be applied to the configuration of the switch.

- **Normal operation:** At this point, the POAP process has finished. The switch runs the required version of the software, has the needed configuration applied, and is functioning as expected.

The POAP configuration script file is developed in Python, and Cisco provides a reference one that can be modified and reused. The configuration script file contains the following information:

- A procedure to retrieve the serial number of the device

- A procedure to define the software image's version

- A procedure to download and install the software image files

- A procedure to get the configuration file and copy it to the startup configuration file

- A procedure to reboot the switch

The reference POAP configuration script file for the Cisco Nexus 9000 switches can be found at https://github.com/datacenter/nexus9000/blob/master/nx-os/poap/poap.py.

Cisco POAP is a great example of automation and orchestration that fits in Day 0 and can be used to perform the provisioning of the devices in the infrastructure and to automate the process of upgrading the operating system.

Cisco NX-OS Scheduler

The scheduler is another feature in Cisco NX-OS that adds to the automation technologies in the data center. The scheduler can be used to run tasks automatically, without any intervention from the administrator, who can set them for periodic execution or to run at a specific time. This is extremely convenient when it comes to automating tasks such as creating backups, saving configurations, pushing a notification, and so on.

There are two main components to the scheduler (see Figure 20-3):

- **Job:** This is the task that needs to be performed. There can be multiple jobs.

- **Schedule:** When and how many times a job is to be executed:

  - **Periodic mode:** This defines a recurring execution, at daily, weekly, monthly, or delta intervals.

  - **One-time mode:** This specifies a one-time execution.

When you're working with the scheduler, it is important to keep in mind that if a feature you intend to use as a job requires a specific license, you have to check whether the license is present on the switch. Otherwise, if the scheduler attempts to execute the job and the license is not present, the job will fail. The other limitation is that if the command to be executed is interactive, the job will fail again.

For job creation, you use the standard command from the CLI. You also have the flexibility to use variables. Some of the variables are predefined in the system, such as *TIMESTAMP*, but you can also define a variable with the command **cli var** *name*.

The scheduler is a feature for automating tasks on a per-device basis. It needs to be configured and executed on each device.

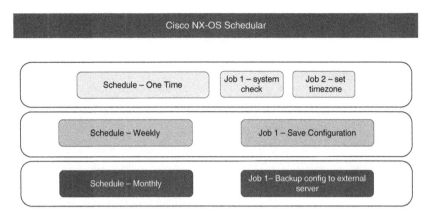

Figure 20-3 *Cisco NX-OS Scheduler*

Cisco EEM

The Cisco Embedded Event Manager (EEM) is one extremely flexible tool for automating the behavior of a Cisco NX-OS device. It allows you to configure events that will trigger one or more actions.

A Cisco EEM policy consists of three components:

- **Event:** What will trigger the policy? Various events can start the execution of the EEM policy, including the following:

  - **Memory:** Triggers an event if memory thresholds are crossed.

  - **Counter:** Triggers an event if counter thresholds are crossed.

  - **Module:** An event is triggered if the selected module enters a specific state.

  - **None:** No event; describes a manual run of the EEM policy.

  - **CLI:** When a specific command is executed in the CLI, the policy is triggered.

- **Action:** What will happen when the event that triggers the policy occurs. This can be one or more actions, including the following:

  - Execute a command in the CLI.

  - Generate a notification using SNMP or Call Home.

  - Generate a syslog entry.

  - Shut down a module or an interface.

  - Reload the device.

  - Use the default action for the system policy.

- **Applet:** This is the configuration construct of the EEM that links events with actions.

The applet is used to create an EEM policy in the CLI. There is also the option to create a policy with a script in virtual shell and then copy it to the device and activate it.

Infrastructure as Code

With the growing need for more agility in the data center came the idea of changing the way we look at the configuration of the infrastructure by looking at it as code. By creating definitions of the desired infrastructure and then applying them to the needed devices and components, we can create the needed environment in our data centers much faster. Infrastructure as Code (IaC) is this process, and it uses machine-readable definitions to orchestrate the infrastructure.

One of the best examples of why such an approach is needed is to look at the flow of the DevOps. In a very simplified way, three major teams are involved in the DevOps—the developers, the testers, and the operations team. The developers have the task of developing an application. For this purpose, they set up an environment in the data center infrastructure using some servers running in the needed software environment, with the needed security, network, and storage connectivity. After the application is developed in this environment, it needs to be tested. However, in order for the results from the testing to be valid and to find any real issues, the application needs to be run in an environment that is the same as the development environment. The third stage is when the application needs to be deployed into production. The production environment also needs to be the same as the development and testing environments in order to be sure the application will behave as planned during the development and testing phases. An operations team is usually responsible for setting these environments, and they need to be able to quickly replicate the same environment—for development, then testing, and finally production—and they might have to be able to scale it. That's why defining the state and configuration of the environment as a machine code makes the process easier and faster and helps reduce the risk of human-induced errors. Also, it guarantees that the environment will be the same. This is guaranteed by a characteristic of the IaC called idempotence, which means that certain mathematical or computer operations can be applied multiple times with the same result. Put in a different way, the idempotence of the IaC approach guarantees that every time the same configuration is applied, the result will be the same.

There are two approaches with the IaC:

- **Declarative:** This approach is also known as functional, as it focuses on what the configuration should be by defining a desired state, and the system performs the needed actions to get to this state.

- **Imperative:** This is a procedural approach that focuses on how to achieve the needed configuration state by defining the specific commands needed to achieve the desired configuration.

Examples of IaC tools include Chef, Puppet, Ansible, Terraform, and PowerShell DSC. We will take a look at some of these tools that are supported by Cisco NX-OS.

Cisco NX-OS and Puppet

Note   Use of the terms "master" and "slave" is ONLY in association with the official terminology used in industry specifications and standards, and in no way diminishes Pearson's commitment to promoting diversity, equity, and inclusion, and challenging, countering and/or combating bias and stereotyping in the global population of the learners we serve.

Cisco NX-OS supports integration with Puppet, an automation IaC tool developed by Puppet, Inc., in 2005. The main product is Puppet Enterprise. There is also open source Puppet software, which is convenient for small infrastructures consisting of several devices. For medium-to-big infrastructures it's recommended to use Puppet Enterprise. Cisco NX-OS has a native Puppet agent that can communicate with the Puppet master server.

Puppet uses a declarative approach. The Puppet Domain Specific Language (DSL) is used to create manifests, which are Puppet programs where the states that need to be achieved by the devices are defined. As with any of the declarative IaC tools, the specific commands to create the configuration to achieve the desired state are not used.

From an operational perspective, there are two components—the Puppet master and the Puppet agent. The Puppet agent is installed on the end device. It collects information for the device and communicates it to the Puppet master. Based on this information, the Puppet master will have the knowledge of the IP address and hardware-specific information as well as the supported device-specific commands. After a manifest is created, and based on the information from the agent, Puppet will determine which commands are needed for the device to get to the desired state, as described in the manifest.

Here's the workflow of the operation:

- The agent sends information to the Puppet master.
- A graph is built with the resources and interdependencies based on the information from all the agents in the infrastructure. This allows the Puppet master to decide on the order of the execution of the manifests.
- On the Puppet master, the manifests will be compiled into programs.
- The appropriate program is sent to each of the agents, and the state of the device is configured based on the instructions.
- The agent will send the master a report of the changes and any errors that might have occurred.

In the Cisco data center infrastructure offerings, Puppet is supported on Cisco Nexus 9000, 7000, 5000, 3000 switches and the Cisco UCS. The appropriate Puppet agents need to be installed. For the Nexus switches, this is done in the bash or guest shell. For the Cisco UCS, the Puppet modules are built with Ruby and the Cisco UCS Python SDK.

Cisco NX-OS and Ansible

Another IaC platform is Ansible. Created by Michael DeHaan and acquired by Red Hat in 2015, Ansible is an open source, agentless tool for software provisioning, configuration management, and application deployment. The operation of Ansible is interesting and different from tools like Puppet, which require agents. With Ansible, there are no agents on the managed devices. Instead, the Ansible control node connects to the managed device via SSH and then installs and runs modules to execute the needed tasks temporarily. At the end, the processes are terminated, and no processes are left running. This approach makes it a lighter option for the end devices and does not consume resources before and after.

Ansible uses a declarative approach by defining the desired state of the managed device. The tasks are organized in playbooks, which are executed against the managed nodes. When it comes to the nodes, the control node(s) have the task of managing the target nodes. The control nodes are only supported on Linux at this time. The managed nodes, or the target nodes, are described in inventory files in order for the control node to know how to connect. One requirement for the managed nodes is to have Python installed. The control nodes use a push model, which means they initiate the communication with the target nodes.

Regarding the logical components of Ansible, we have the following:

- **Playbooks:** Lists of tasks to be performed on the target nodes, written in YAML.

- **Inventory files:** Define the target nodes, as we can organize them hierarchically using groups.

- **Templates:** Generate configurations using the information from the inventory files. This helps with generating faster configuration for larger environments.

- **Roles:** Allow specific, commonly used tasks with properties to be organized into a role and then reused.

There is support for Ansible in Cisco NX-OS, which makes it a very convenient tool for network automation, configuration management, orchestration, and deployment for the Cisco Nexus switches and the Cisco UCS.

Red Hat Ansible Automation Platform, with the automation controller (formerly Ansible Tower), allows the IT and DevOps teams to define, operate, manage, and control access to the automation tasks at a centralized place. For up to 10 users, Ansible is free to use and test, and it offers a web UI and REST API.

Cisco NX-OS and Terraform

Terraform is IaC software created by HashiCorp. It uses a declarative approach to describe the desired state of the devices in configuration files. Then the configuration files are organized into an execution plan. The plan contains all the needed information regarding the devices and how to reach the desired state. Before a Terraform plan can be executed, it needs to be confirmed.

The configuration files are created using a proprietary syntax called HashiCorp Configuration Language (HCL).

The Terraform configuration file works with resources as the fundamental construct. The resources are organized in blocks. A resource block describes an infrastructure object, along with the needed characteristics and the intent.

The target infrastructure is defined as providers, which contain the target IP address, URL, credentials, and so on. HashiCorp maintains and continues to grow a huge list of official providers; there is support for such external resources as AWS, Microsoft Azure, Google Cloud Platform, OpenStack, VMware vSphere, and others.

Cisco Systems is an official provider for HashiCorp, and the Terraform software can be used for automation and integration of the Cisco Data Center, Cloud, Security, Enterprise products.

Cisco NX-OS and Python

Python is a high-level, interpreted, general-purpose language. It supports object-oriented, structured, and functional programming. Because it was designed to be extensible, it is suitable for a wide variety of tasks in various fields (science, IT, and so on). This makes it especially good for automating data center infrastructures.

The only thing needed for a Python script to be executed is a Python interpreter. It is installed natively on Cisco NX-OS. In the recent past, there was a requirement for the Cisco Nexus switches to use Python v2.7, but this limitation is no longer valid. Cisco NX-OS supports all the latest Python releases. In addition to the Python interpreter in Cisco NX-OS, for the Cisco UCS Manager there is the Cisco UCS Python software development kit (SDK), which provides support for the automation of all aspects of the Cisco UCS.

Support for Python on the Cisco data center devices allows for the following:

- Running scripts on the Cisco devices
- Accessing the CLI
- Integrating with POAP
- Integrating with EEM
- Managing the configurations
- Performing tasks at different stages of device deployment and operation

Support for Python is a feature that allows for the integration of the Cisco data center devices and solutions with automation and orchestration systems. Because of the open source nature, there's enormous support for extensions and ease of use.

Choosing the Automation Toolset

After all the different automation and orchestration tools we've looked at, selecting one can be difficult. Which one you will use depends on a wide variety of parameters:

- What are the devices you want to automate?

- What tasks do you want to automate?

- What are the capabilities of the devices?

- Do you need to use a scalable approach?

- What automation and orchestration systems are already in use?

There might be other questions that need answers as well; it all depends on the specific situation, infrastructure, and capabilities. But in any situation, to be able to make the correct choice for your needs, you need to know the capabilities of your devices and what they support.

The Cisco data center devices, such as the Cisco Nexus and MDS switches and the Cisco UCS, run Cisco NX-OS. It contains open source software (OSS) and commercial technologies that provide automation, orchestration, programmability, monitoring, and compliance support. Additionally, there are tools and SDKs to extend the support for automation, programmability, orchestration, proactive monitoring, and troubleshooting.

Table 20-1 summarizes the types of support for automation and orchestration during the various operations stages.

Table 20-1   *Tools for the Different Operational Stages*

Operations Stage	Tools
APIs	NX-API
Open interfaces	Bash, guest shell, Python, Broadcom shell
Provisioning	POAP, PXE
Configuration management	NETCONF, RESTCONF, gRPC
Infrastructure-as-Code	Ansible, Terraform, Chef, Puppet
Event management	EEM, Call Home

You will need to have a deeper knowledge and understanding of the different automation tools and platforms. This chapter is only intended to give you a glimpse and a starting point into the world of automation and is not meant to be an extensive guide. That's why it is strongly recommended that you continue your education in the field of data center automation. The official Cisco training material and books from Cisco Press can help you in your journey.

Summary

This chapter describes the basics of data center automation and orchestration. In this chapter you learned about the following:

- The need to reduce human-induced errors and to optimize provisioning, configuration, and monitoring of the data center infrastructures. This requires automation.

- Automation is based on a programmatic approach.

- Orchestration is when automated workflows of tasks are created to provision and manage resources across the data center infrastructures.

- The operations lifecycle is usually described using Days 0 to N.

- Day 0 is the initial provisioning of the device in the infrastructure.

- Day 1 is the full configuration, and the device goes into normal operation.

- Day 2 is monitoring and troubleshooting.

- Day N is maintenance and optimization.

- Automation and orchestration can be used in each of the operation lifecycle stages.

- Software-defined networking is an approach to automating the provisioning, configuration, and management of the network infrastructure by using an SDN controller, which runs the management and control planes, and using the switches only to run the data plane.

- Cisco ACI is an example of an advanced automated network infrastructure based on the SDN principle.

- Cisco POAP is a tool that can be used for provisioning devices in the infrastructure on Day 0.

- The Cisco NX-OS Scheduler is an automation toll per device. It allows us to schedule the execution of jobs without the need for human intervention.

- Cisco EEM allows us to manage the behavior of a device when specific events occur.

- Infrastructure as Code is a process that uses machine-readable definitions to automate and orchestrate the configuration of the data center infrastructure.

- Puppet is a declarative IaC software.

- Ansible is an agentless declarative IaC software from Red Hat.

- HashiCorp Terraform is declarative IaC software that manages external resources, called "providers," with its own syntax, called HCL.

- Python is a high-level, interpreted, multipurpose language that is supported on Cisco data center devices natively, as the Python interpreter is installed in the Cisco NX-OS.

- To choose the correct toolset, you must know the capabilities of the different automation tools and also what your devices support.

Reference

The Cisco Data Center Dev Center: https://developer.cisco.com/site/data-center/

Chapter 21

Cloud Computing

The book so far has covered the different components of the data center, how they integrate and interact with each other, and how the utilization of the resources is maximized through abstraction and virtualization, with the sole purpose of creating the environment in which the applications will run. This whole stack—starting with the physical infrastructure, building through the operating systems, the required middleware, up to the applications—is the de facto data center.

It is particularly important to understand the driving mechanisms for the evolution of the data center. This will clarify the current stage of data center development—cloud computing, or "the cloud."

This chapter discusses cloud computing, its definitions and components, the different deployment models, and the services provided. As there are a lot of cloud service providers and vendors of different cloud-oriented products and technologies, the cloud terminology is often diluted and misused based on marketing needs and stories. That's why the cloud discussion here will be based on the definition of cloud by the National Institute for Standards and Technology (NIST). We believe that this approach will allow readers to understand and build a solid foundation of cloud computing concepts.

Cloud Computing Overview

In any discussion of cloud computing, it's important to start from the beginning and understand the power that drives the changes and technological advancements in data centers and the technology as a whole.

The ancient Greek philosopher Heraclitus had the following to say: "Everything changes and nothing remains still." Change is the only constant in human life. And, as the world changes, so do the requirements for companies to develop their business, for organizations to continue their operations, and so on. This leads to the services offered by different entities that address the need to continuously change and evolve, stay up to date, and satisfy the needs of businesses or organizations.

So how does this change affect data centers, and what is the link to cloud computing?

The services are provided by applications. The applications run on top of servers, virtualized or bare metal, which require operating systems and additional software to create the environment for the applications. The applications have to be accessible by the end users and administrators, and at the same time the applications have to be capable of communicating with the databases, which are other applications running on servers, with operating systems, and responsible for the data being organized and stored within a specific structure. Therefore, there is the need for communication, which is provided by the networks in the data centers. The Cisco ACI is one such example, and it's covered in Chapter 8, "Describing Cisco ACI," and Chapter 9, "Operating ACI," of this book. All the data needs to be stored somewhere, and this is where the storage infrastructures and the storage systems are involved. Also, all these components need to be secured and monitored because they are the components that build the data center. Said in a different way, these components, working together, provide the needed computing resources for the applications to run.

The aforementioned leads us to the conclusion that what will change, and what is changing, is how the computing resources provided by the data centers are utilized, managed, and consumed! And this is the next step in the evolution of the data centers, and it is known as "cloud computing." Cloud computing is an approach in which the computing resources are utilized in a way where their consumption can be measured, automated, accessible, and managed.

One especially important clarification needs to be made: what are the "computing resources"? The cloud resources are not only the resources of the server or virtual machine required to run the applications. They also include the resources we need for communication, as the network and security devices, being physical or virtual, also use CPUs, memory, operating systems, and so on. The storage infrastructures and systems also need CPUs, memory, and operating systems. Therefore, the term "computing resources," from the perspective of defining and describing cloud computing, includes any and all hardware and software resources in the data center.

Three important documents were created by the computer security division at the Information Technology Laboratory at NIST. These documents provided the first definition of "cloud computing" and its components:

- NIST Special Publication 800-145: The NIST Definition of Cloud Computing (September, 2011)

- NIST Special Publication 800-144: Guidelines on Security and Privacy in Public Cloud Computing (December, 2011)

- NIST Special Publication 800-146: Cloud Computing Synopsis and Recommendations (May, 2012)

Cloud Computing Definition

The NIST defines cloud computing as follows (see Figure 21-1):

"Cloud computing is a model for enabling ubiquitous, convenient, on-demand network access to a shared pool of configurable computing resources (for example, networks, servers, storage, applications, and services) that can be rapidly provisioned and released with minimal management effort or service provider interaction. This cloud model is composed of five essential characteristics, three service models, and four deployment models."

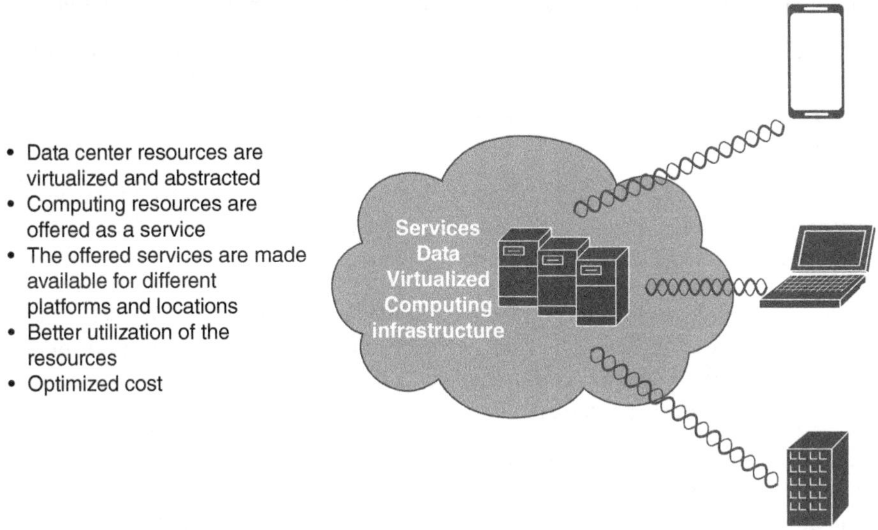

- Data center resources are virtualized and abstracted
- Computing resources are offered as a service
- The offered services are made available for different platforms and locations
- Better utilization of the resources
- Optimized cost

Figure 21-1   *Cloud Computing Overview*

This definition specifies a flexible, highly automated approach to how the computing resources of a data center, or multiple data centers, can be consumed and rented to external or internal users. The five essential characteristics describe in detail the requirements for such an environment. Based on that, the consumer of the resources does not need to bother with where exactly the resources are and how they are managed. This is done by the cloud service provider, the owner of the data centers. Also, the cloud service provider is responsible to build the infrastructures with the needed redundancy, reliability, and scalability. The required automation and orchestration need to be in place to allow the computing resources to be provisioned and made available transparently for the end user.

Nowadays, users are highly mobile. That is why these resources, which are called "cloud services," must be accessible, which happens through network connectivity. Access through the Internet or through protected lines is essential, as the user has to be capable to connect from anywhere and on any device. The computer resources offered cover the whole variety in the application stack—from providing compute in the form of virtual machines, even dedicated physical servers, going through platforms, up to the application resources that run in the cloud.

The cloud approach offers advantages for both the cloud users and the cloud service providers.

For the end user, some of the benefits include the following:

- The end user does not need to build and maintain a data center.

- The computing resources are available when needed.

- Scalability is not an issue. The resources scale based on the needs of the consumer.

- Redundancy and reliability. Usually, the consumer needs to design and deploy solutions to achieve the needed service uptime and to prevent loss of data. With the cloud, there are solutions integrated with the infrastructure at different levels and are optional.

- Optimizing expenses. The cloud services are offered and consumed based on the pay-as-you-go model, which means that the end user pays only for the resources used and only for the amount of time they are used.

The cloud offers a way for the user to plan for and to manage costs. The expenses shift from capital expenses (CAPEX), which are needed if the infrastructure needs to be purchased and deployed, to operational expenses (OPEX) due to the way in which the cloud services are offered, measured, and paid for.

The CAPEX for building a data center includes not only the budget to buy the needed equipment, but also the real estate (the premises can be rented or bought), expenses for the redundant power supplies and cooling (which is a huge expense), and the budget for the needed services to design, deploy, operate, and maintain the entire infrastructure. In the process, it is common to have unexpected expenses, which are exceedingly difficult to plan for. Also, it is hard to plan for future releases of the applications, additional services needed, and additional resources that need to be added to the data center. Also, experts are needed to operate and maintain the data center, including all its components, up to the level of the applications. And these teams need to go through continuous education, as the technologies evolve and change. In such a situation, a small- to medium-sized company that needs to run its applications, but does not want to invest in building the needed infrastructure, can benefit from the cloud services, as it will be able to plan in advance, to upsize or downsize resources, and to rely on the mechanisms deployed by the cloud service providers for redundancy and reliability based on service level agreements (SLAs). And it is not only small- to medium-sized companies that can benefit from using cloud services. Take Netflix for example—a huge content streaming company. Netflix started out using its own resources, but the need to support massive scale and optimize costs cause, Netflix to move to the Amazon Web Services (AWS) cloud. This allows Netflix to support more than 200 million members in more than 190 countries worldwide, resulting in more than 125 million hours of TV shows and movies watched every day!

The cloud service providers benefit from this approach in a variety of ways:

- The cloud computing approach allows the owners of data centers to achieve huge and efficient utilization of the resources. When the resources can be managed in such a way, the costs for maintaining the data center and expanding its resources are optimized as well.

- This approach allows for increased profits and at the same time an expansion in the services offered.

- The aggregation of customer demand brings another way of better utilizing resources.

- Through the adoption of orchestration and automation, which are mandatory when building a cloud, the processes of operating and maintaining the data centers are highly optimized, the results are repeatable, and the outcomes are predictable. This leads to better usage of the computing and human resources.

The three biggest cloud service providers are

- Amazon Web Services (AWS)

- Microsoft Azure

- Google Cloud Platform (GCP)

They offer a huge variety of cloud services, covering all the levels of the data center, including infrastructure services such as VMs and storage as well as platform services such as containers, microservices, and databases, and application services.

Cloud Computing Characteristics

The cloud computing characteristics define the requirements for a data center to offer cloud services. The NIST came up with five essential characteristics for the cloud computing:

- On-demand self-service

- Broad network access

- Resource pooling

- Rapid elasticity

- Measured service

All five essential characteristics are important, and they separate the cloud services offering from a hosting or colocation service.

On-Demand Self-Service

The NIST defines on-demand self-service as follows (see Figure 21-2):

"A consumer can unilaterally provision computing capabilities, such as server time and network storage, as needed automatically without requiring human interaction with each service provider."

This definition immediately sets a requirement for the data center to have the needed level of automation and orchestration, which will allow the user to access the cloud portal and select a service and provision it, without waiting for administrators from the provider to set it up. A simple example is how a user can open Outlook.com or Gmail.com and select an offered service, such as registering and creating a personal email account. Then, without waiting for any interaction with an employee from the provider, the account will be created and available almost immediately.

On-demand self-service: A consumer can unilaterally provision computing capabilities, such as server time and network storage, as needed, automatically, without requiring any human interaction with each service provider.

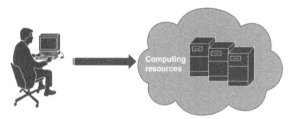

Figure 21-2   *On-Demand Self-Service Essential Characteristic*

Measured Service

When the services are used, it is important for both the service provider and the user to know what was consumed and how it was consumed, what resources were utilized, and how the consumption changes in time (see Figure 21-3). This also applies to the access bandwidth and the quantity of data transported. This is important because the charges are calculated based on what was consumed and for how long. It is also important for the end user, as they can downsize or upsize the resources they use, based on the cost, the need for resources, and so on. Another aspect is that service providers can analyze the data for consumption and trends in order to plan for expanding the capacities of their data centers, as the ability to scale is important for the needs of the customers.

Measured service: Cloud systems automatically control and optimize resource use by leveraging a metering capability at some level of abstraction appropriate to the type of service; for example, storage, processing, bandwidth, and active user accounts. Resource usage can be monitored, controlled, and reported, providing transparency for both the provider and consumer.

Figure 21-3   *Measured Services Essential Characteristic*

Resource Pooling

Service providers rent their computing resources in an automated manner. They also have to be capable of supporting multiple users simultaneously, and there must be enough resources available for the customers.

At the same time, the resources used by the customers are the resources of the data centers, which are not unlimited. To solve this situation, the NIST defines the resource pooling characteristic (see Figure 21-4). It describes the need for the utilization of the resources to be most effective. This requirement also means that the resources' utilization will become more flexible as well. The virtualized resources provided from a physical server have to be available to multiple users, as a single user might not utilize them all. And this becomes even more effective when we scale it to the level of a data center and beyond. The end user does not know on which exact physical resources their workloads are running—and does not need to know this information, as long as the resources are available and the services are up and running and accessible.

For the purposes of compliance and to stay close to the customers, the cloud service providers use the approach of dividing their resources into regions, countries, continents, and so on.

Resource pooling: The computing resources of the provider are pooled to serve multiple consumers using a multitenant model with different physical and virtual resources that are dynamically assigned and reassigned according to consumer demand.

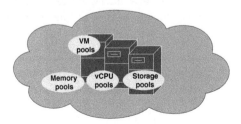

Figure 21-4   *Resource Pooling Essential Characteristic*

Rapid Elasticity

When resources are not being used by an end user, they need to go back into the pools to be available for new provisioning. This is the rapid elasticity characteristic (see Figure 21-5), and it creates the impression that the cloud resources are infinite. However, the more important aspect is that when the resources are managed in such an elastic manner, the cloud providers are capable of supporting horizontal and vertical scaling of the capacities, to support the needs of the users. As an example, some businesses see spikes in the services they offer during certain periods of the year. For these time slots, the companies will need more resources to keep their services up and running, and during the rest of the year, these resources will be idle. If these companies were to buy and build their own infrastructure, the cost would be too high for something that's used for a short period of time. By using cloud resources, these companies can be developing and testing their services, using far fewer resources, while during the peak hours, days, weeks, they can automatically, or manually, scale up and down. In this way, they will be capable of providing only the needed resources, and thus expenses will be optimized.

Rapid elasticity: Capabilities can be elastically provisioned and released, in some cases automatically, to scale rapidly outward and commensurately inward with demand. To the consumer, the capabilities available for provisioning often appear unlimited and can be appropriated in any quantity at any time.

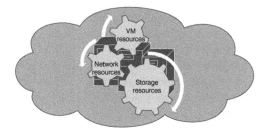

Figure 21-5 *Rapid Elasticity Essential Characteristic*

Broad Network Access

Although the cloud computing resources can be made available, they also need to be accessible. In order for users to start consuming the cloud services, they need to be able to access them. And the access needs to be supported from a variety of end-user platforms, such as laptops, desktops, tablets, and mobile phones, running various operating systems.

Because the cloud services are usually available remotely, and because the users are highly mobile, the access to these services needs to be protected (see Figure 21-6). Once the necessary secured access is provided, the services can be consumed over different private and public networks.

Broad network access: Capabilities are available over the network and accessed through standard mechanisms that promote use by heterogeneous thin or thick client platforms (for example, mobile phones, tablets, laptops, and workstations).

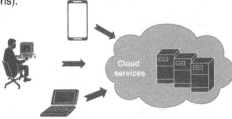

Figure 21-6 *Broad Network Access Essential Characteristic*

Cloud Computing Services

Cloud computing is about offering available computing resources to consumers (businesses, organizations, and people) in the form of services. The NIST has defined three types of services (see Figure 21-7) that can be used as a reference:

■ Infrastructure as a Service (IaaS)

■ Platform as a Service (PaaS)

■ Software as a Service (SaaS)

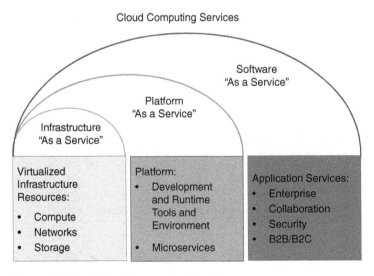

Figure 21-7 *Cloud Computing Services*

With the huge variety of services offered nowadays, the boundaries between them are becoming blurred. That's why the term Everything as a Service (XaaS) can be used, even though it is not defined officially by the NIST.

The important point here is the "as a service" approach. When cloud services are offered "as a service," the customer can plan their costs, as the services are metered. Having multiple different cost models provides flexibility in the way services are offered.

The relationship between the cloud provider and the cloud customer has additional parameters that can influence the cost. The most important parameter is the scope of responsibility of the provider and the customer. Depending on the category of services, the responsibilities of the provider can be limited only to the physical and virtual layers, and the customer is responsible for everything else, or the provider can be responsible for the whole application stack, as is the case of SaaS.

Infrastructure as a Service (IaaS)

Infrastructure as a Service, shown in Figure 21-8, is when the consumed services can be defined as "infrastructure." These are the resources of servers (in this case, usually virtualized), but there are special cases where even dedicated physical servers are offered. Other infrastructure services are storage, communication, and so on.

With IaaS, as the customer uses VMs or storage, the provider is responsible for the underlying infrastructure as well as the reliability, compliance, and availability of the resources. The customer is responsible for any software or data used or stored on top of the resources. For example, if the customer decides to use a virtual server, which is a VM, the provider is responsible for providing and securing the resources up to the level of the virtual machine; from there, the operating system and installed applications are the responsibility of the customer, including the needed measures to be taken to safeguard the data. Some IaaS offerings also include the operating system, but this is more for convenience, as the customer is still responsible for maintaining and operating it.

NIST defines IaaS as follows "The capability provided to the consumer is to provision processing, storage, networks, and other fundamental computing resources where the consumer is able to deploy and run arbitrary software, which can include operating systems and applications. The consumer does not manage or control the underlying cloud infrastructure but has control over operating systems, storage, and deployed applications; and possibly limited control of select networking components (e.g., host firewalls)."

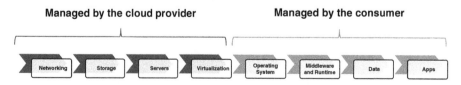

Figure 21-8 *IaaS NIST Definition and Responsibilities Demarcation*

Here are some examples of IaaS:

- Amazon EC2 (virtual servers in the cloud)
- Amazon Simple Storage Service (S3, storage services)
- Microsoft Azure VMs
- Microsoft Azure Storage
- GCP Compute Engine
- GCP Cloud Storage

Platform as a Service (PaaS)

Platform as a Service, shown in Figure 21-9, goes a step further, as the customer is capable of ordering not only the needed virtualized infrastructure, but also the needed software environment and communication, in a way that creates a "platform," ready for the deployment of the customer's data and applications.

This also shifts the responsibilities, as now the cloud provider is responsible for the whole environment, the access, the communication, the needed middleware, and the runtime. The customer has to deploy the application, which will provide services, or the data if the PaaS is a cloud database or data warehouse. The customer has to patch and update the software under their control, define the access control, and back up the data.

NIST defines PaaS as follows "The capability provided to the consumer is to deploy onto the cloud infrastructure consumer-created or acquired applications created using programming languages, libraries, services, and tools supported by the provider. The consumer does not manage or control the underlying cloud infrastructure including network, servers, operating systems, or storage, but has control over the deployed applications and possibly configuration settings for the application-hosting environment."

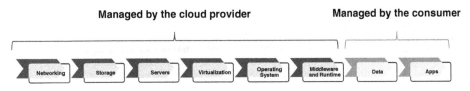

Figure 21-9 *PaaS NIST Definition and Responsibilities Demarcation*

Here are some examples of PaaS:

- GCP App Engine
- AWS Lambda
- Amazon Aurora

- Amazon Elastic Container Service (ECS)

- Azure App Service

- Azure Kubernetes Service

- Azure Cosmos DB

One interesting Platform as a Service that's offered by all the three major cloud service providers (that is, AWS, Azure, and GCP) is microservices. With GCP App Engine, AWS Lambda, and Azure App Service, the consumer can provision the whole environment in which to directly publish their application. But this application is still more or less a traditional monolithic application. Microservices comprise a new architectural and design approach for creating applications, as the applications are divided into separate processes, and only the process needed to service a user request will run and then stop afterward. This approach provides the benefit of extremely efficient utilization of the resources, as there is no need to run all the processes of the applications and to keep them idle waiting for the next request. The cloud providers have created and offer such environments where the customers can utilize this approach.

Software as a Service (SaaS)

Software as a Service, shown in Figure 21-10, means that the provider is running an application (or a suite of applications) that offers some services. The consumer can just subscribe to use these services. Usually, the application runs in the provider's environment, but sometimes there might be a small executable piece that must be downloaded on the customer's side. The SaaS offerings are extremely popular and are not limited only to the big cloud providers.

When it comes to SaaS responsibilities, the provider is responsible for the underlying infrastructure, connectivity, reliability, storage, security, runtime, middleware, and applications. The provider also has to make sure the services are compliant and available.

NIST defines SaaS as follows "The capability provided to the consumer is to use the provider's applications running on a cloud infrastructure. The applications are accessible from various client devices through either a thin client interface, such as a web browser (e.g., web-based email), or a program interface. The consumer does not manage or control the underlying cloud infrastructure including network, servers, operating systems, storage, or even individual application capabilities, with the possible exception of limited user-specific application configuration settings."

Managed by the cloud provider

Figure 21-10   *SaaS NIST Definition and Responsibilities Demarcation*

The list of SaaS offerings is exceedingly long, but here are just a few:

- Salesforce

- Google Apps

- Dropbox

- Box

- Microsoft Office 365

- Netflix

- Cisco WebEx

- Cisco Meraki

- Cisco Umbrella

- Cisco Duo

Cloud Computing Components

So far, we've covered the definition of cloud computing, the essential characteristics to create a cloud environment, and the three common types of cloud services. Cloud services provide an automated way of renting the computing resources of the underlying physical and virtualized infrastructure, which is the data center. To create the cloud environments, cloud providers need to build multiple data centers, geographically separated, to secure the needed reliability and availability of the resources.

To understand what changes in the data center and why, it is important to understand the relationship between the cloud and the consumer and how it develops.

The providers want to utilize the resources of their data centers better and increase their profits. For that purpose, they need to make the resources available, and they have to be able to manage these resources in a flexible way. They must adopt the needed levels of virtualization and abstraction, organize the resources into pools, and allow for flexible and quick provisioning of resources and their release. This can happen when orchestration is used to dynamically manage resources and automate usage. For this to happen, different tools and approaches are employed. Programs called orchestrators can coordinate the different components of the data center, such as storage, compute, and network, by supporting the required abstraction to bring up the virtualized environment. Additional automation through application programming interfaces (APIs) can be used for deploying containers, microservices, runtime environments, and the needed applications. Automation, orchestration, and APIs in the data center were discussed in Chapter 19, "Using APIs," and Chapter 20, "Automating the Data Center."

Once the data center has achieved the needed levels of automation and orchestration, the resources need to be made available to the consumers. The providers create service offerings.

These offerings define what resources can be used, the cost model, the licensing, and additional dependencies on other resources. These offerings not only have technical aspects but also financial. This means that to create the offerings, providers need tools that can simulate both the technical and business logic. Special applications called catalogs are used for this. The catalogs can communicate through APIs with the orchestrators and the other management and automation frameworks of the data center to gain access to the resources, which are exposed and grouped into different services. In the catalog is information for the technical services supported by the orchestrators; then service offerings can be created with the rest of the attributes—cost model, budgets, time restrictions, regional restrictions, reporting, chain of approval, and so on.

Once the service offerings are ready in the catalogs, they need to be presented to the customers. For this, applications called portals are used. The portals are intended to provide the needed interface for the consumers to access and work with the cloud resources.

This whole relationship can be seen in Figure 21-11, which presents the cloud solution framework. These are the separate components that build the cloud environment.

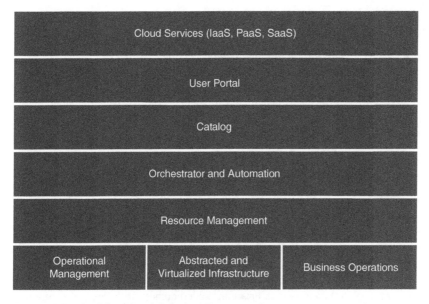

Figure 21-11 *The Cloud Solution Framework*

The virtualized multitenant environment includes the underlying infrastructure. Resource management is responsible for the pooling of resources, their usage, and their release. The business services provide the business and financial logic for the catalog application to create the service offerings. The front portals work together with the catalogs, orchestration, and automation to make the service offerings available to the customers. Operational management covers the monitoring, reporting, and access control services.

The data centers, being a major part of a cloud environment, have certain architecture and components that form the "cloud operating system" or the "cloud stack."

To map the cloud solution framework to the data center in a more technical way, Figure 21-12 shows the cloud solution architecture.

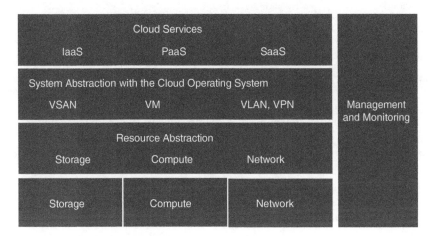

Figure 21-12   *The Cloud System Architecture*

At the bottom of Figure 21-12 is the physical infrastructure, which provides the resources for the needed abstraction and virtualization. The virtualization is created on the top of the physical servers, network communication, storage infrastructure, and systems. The virtualization extends even outside single data centers for the purposes of redundancy and high availability.

The next step is the system abstraction. This is when, with the help of automation and orchestration, the virtualized resources are abstracted to be separated from the dependencies on the specific systems and then organized into pools.

This creates the foundation on which the catalogs will be created and the services, such as IaaS, PaaS, and SaaS, will be offered and published to the portals.

The terms *catalog*, *portal*, and *orchestrator* are used in this discussion for clarity. They describe certain major functions that are fundamental for the cloud computing. These functions can be implemented in separate applications, or they can be combined within a few applications, even on a single one. It all depends on the size of the cloud that needs to be created and the services to be offered.

These principles are used by the big three cloud providers—AWS, Azure, and GCP—with their own implementations and automation. On their portals you can find further documentation on the specific approach used to build their cloud environments.

Cloud Deployment Models

The NIST defines four cloud deployment models based on ownership and who is consuming the resources:

- Private cloud
- Public cloud
- Hybrid cloud
- Community cloud

When the NIST's definition was created, only these four types of clouds were defined based on the technologies and customer needs at the time. Nowadays, with technology developments and the need for services, there are also the multicloud and government cloud types.

Private Cloud

The NIST defines the private cloud as follows (see Figure 21-13):

"The cloud infrastructure is provisioned for exclusive use by a single organization comprising multiple consumers (e.g., business units). It may be owned, managed, and operated by the organization, a third party, or some combination of them, and it may exist on or off premises."

This describes the data center(s) of a company or organization. The infrastructure is owned by that company or organization and is intended to be used for internal purposes in its relationship with its partners and customers.

In the infrastructure, the needed automation, orchestration, catalog, and portal functions will be implemented to allow for the management of the resources and the creation of catalogs and service offerings, which will be published either internally or externally in a protected manner.

The services made available to the employees, partners, and customers will be provided only by the data centers of that company. It is the responsibility of the company's IT teams to deploy, operate, and maintain the cloud environment.

Here are some of the advantages of a private cloud:

- **Ownership of all resources:** The resources are provided by the infrastructure of the company or organization, which allows for the full control and management of the resources. The resources are not usually shared with other cloud users. This excludes the access provided to the partners and the customers of the company.

- **Control of change management:** The organization controls the change management procedures, which define how changes in the configuration, patches, and updates will be applied.

■ **Compliance:** The organization or the company, depending on its activities and the region or country in which it resides and operates, might be subject to laws or regulations. Owning the resources makes compliance easier.

■ **Information control:** Control of information is important for companies, as it prevents information theft or ransomware attacks. If a company controls its own cloud, all the way down to the hardware and premises, it can control the level of IT and physical security. In certain situations, this can be required.

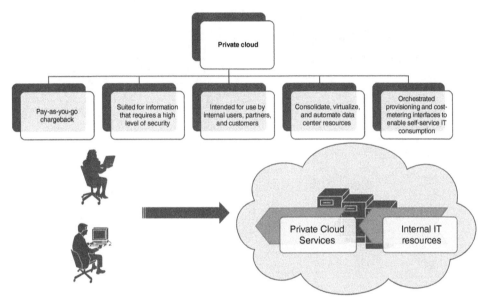

Figure 21-13 *Private Cloud Characteristics*

Here are some of the disadvantages of using a private cloud:

■ **Big capital expenses:** When the company operates its own data center, it incurs the capital expense for building and deploying the infrastructure and the cloud environment.

■ **Operational expenses:** Operational expenses remain, as there are electricity bills, cooling expenses, human resources expenses as well as expense for ongoing training of the personnel.

■ **Scalability:** The scalability capacities are limited, as it means additional investment in hardware, software, and people.

■ **Infrastructure upgrades:** Due to the technology developments and changing requirements facing companies, the hardware needs to be upgraded on a regular basis, which adds to the expenses of running a private cloud.

Public Cloud

The NIST defines the public cloud as follows (see Figure 21-14):

"The cloud infrastructure is provisioned for open use by the general public. It may be owned, managed, and operated by a business, academic, or government organization, or some combination of them. It exists on the premises of the cloud provider."

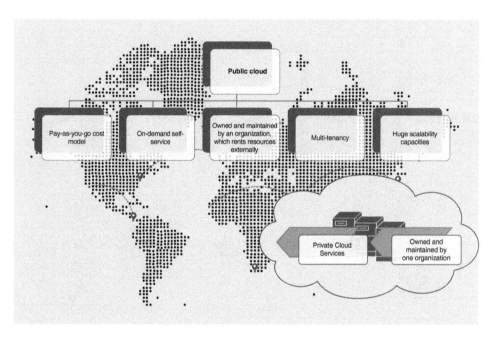

Figure 21-14   *Public Cloud Characteristics*

These are cloud environments created with the goal of providing resources to external entities. We already mentioned the three big public clouds: AWS, Azure, and GCP. The infrastructure is owned and managed by an entity, and usually the resources are rented for profit. The public cloud providers build multiple data centers, in different geographical locations, with the goal of being close to the consumers, to achieve the needed reliability and redundancy and to be compliant with any local regulations or laws.

Another aspect, which has been the subject of heated discussions since the beginning, is the security of the information. Because the consumers are not in control of the underlying infrastructure, which also includes the storage systems, security is the responsibility of the cloud providers. They must take the needed measures to protect the data when it resides on their storage infrastructure (data at rest) but also provide means for the customers to protect their data on the wire (data in transit). The way consumer data is handled is also a subject of different laws and regulations. Even when the public cloud providers have taken the needed measures and have deployed solutions to take care of the customers' data, there's still the need for external proof. That's why public cloud providers are subject to constant audit processes from external regulatory and standard-ization bodies.

Here are some of the benefits of using a public cloud:

- Self-service
- Pay-as-you-go billing
- No capital expenses
- Scalability
- Reliability and redundancy
- Huge variety of services

Drawbacks can include the following:

- Lack of full control of the infrastructure
- Lack of physical control
- Cost, which might be more than the cost of running a data center on premises
- Limitations imposed by certain laws and regulations

Hybrid Cloud

Companies and organizations differ in size, activities, and needs. Because of that, when an application or workload needs to be deployed, the different requirements and possible solutions need to be considered. For some companies, a specific workload might be more cost effective to run on premises on its own equipment. In other situations, that same company might be better off running certain workloads in a public cloud. For example, consider a DevOps process. DevOps is a set of procedures and tools as well as a mental-ity for how the work of the development teams and operations teams should be orga-nized, where a product of the development team can be easily tested and then deployed in a production environment. This means the operations teams need to be capable of cre-ating and re-creating the same environment used first in the development, then in testing, and finally for deployment in production. However, there's one additional important dif-ference: the production environment, unlike the development and testing environments, has to be capable of scaling!

The process of building a specific environment in a private data center can be time- and resource-consuming. It requires planning. In some situations, additional equipment needs to be acquired, and resources are needed to set up that equipment and configure it. In other words, this process usually takes time. And when it comes to scaling, the process is the same, unless it was taken into account from the beginning, but this is rarely the case.

If the company is required to run these workloads in-house, the task becomes complicated. The company will have to build these environments in its own data center and deal with the scalability challenges.

The opposite can also be true: the company can build the development and testing environments, but it isn't cost-effective to run the production environment with the needed scale.

Also, the company might develop a solution that's idle, or at least working at a minimum capacity, for most of the year, and then for a specific short period of time, the solution requires massive computing resources. How does one justify a multimillion-dollar budget for equipment that will be used for only one month (or less) of the year?

In such situations, companies can benefit from combining the resources of their private clouds and a public cloud. This is known as a hybrid cloud (see Figure 21-15), which is defined as follows:

"The cloud infrastructure is a composition of two or more distinct cloud infrastructures (private, community, or public) that remain unique entities, but are bound together by standardized or proprietary technology that enables data and application portability (e.g., cloud bursting for load balancing between clouds)."

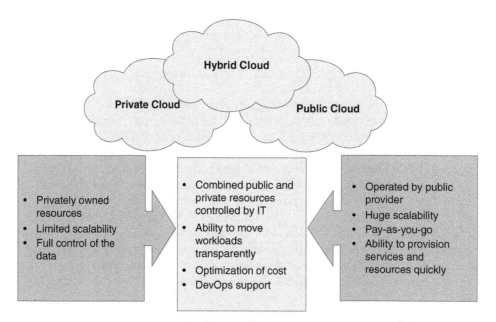

Figure 21-15 *Hybrid Cloud Characteristics*

An important detail of a hybrid cloud is that a communication technology must be used to allow for the seamless moving of the workloads between the clouds. This communication needs to be protected, and different approaches can be used—from private leased lines to solutions based on virtual private networks (VPNs), to the latest approach, which uses software-defined connectivity with overlay networks.

As of late, the industry has adopted the use of the term multicloud, which is an upgrade of the hybrid cloud, as it demands integration between the private clouds of a customer with a minimum of two public clouds. Currently the hybrid cloud has the widest adoption, as companies are starting to move in the direction of multicloud.

The major benefit of using hybrid and multicloud is that the consumer can dynamically decide which environment offers the best combination of price, resources, and protection for each workload. This allows the workloads to be moved between the clouds in a transparent way for the end user.

Community Cloud

The community cloud is a specific type of collaboration, or resource sharing, between the private clouds of organizations or companies in a specific industry or field. The needed level of integration between these clouds allows only the participating organizations to have access. As per the official definition, a community cloud is defined as follows (see Figure 21-16):

"The cloud infrastructure is provisioned for exclusive use by a specific community of consumers from organizations that have shared concerns (e.g., mission, security requirements, policy, and compliance considerations). It may be owned, managed, and operated by one or more of the organizations in the community, a third party, or some combination of them, and it may exist on or off premises."

Examples for community clouds:
- Open Cloud Consortium BCC
- Healthcare services under regulation
- Financial services under regulation

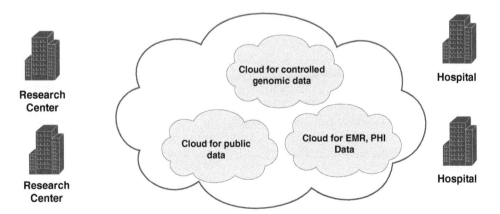

Figure 21-16 *Community Cloud Characteristics*

As you can tell from the definition, maintaining and operating the integration and resources among the clouds that share these resources is a shared responsibility. It must be stressed that the resources are not available publicly.

Community clouds are created because of a specific need to share resources, but the data shared is heavily regulated and needs to stay compliant. Examples of areas where community clouds are applicable are science research, healthcare, and insurance.

Government Clouds

Various countries and their governments have certain requirements when it comes to working with their information and their agencies. In these situations, a public cloud can be an obstacle, as the public environment might not adhere to the governmental requirements. For these use cases, some of the public cloud providers, such as AWS and Azure, have created totally isolated clouds, dedicated to the needs of some governments. The government clouds operate using separate data centers that do not have any connectivity to public clouds.

Here are some examples of government clouds:

- **AWS GovCloud (U.S.):** Specifically for the U.S. government, agencies, and state authorities

- **Azure Government:** Specifically for the U.S. government, agencies, and state authorities

- **Azure Germany:** A dedicated cloud for German data-handling regulations

- **Azure China 21Vianet:** A dedicated cloud, located in China, that's compliant with the Chinese government's regulations and operated by 21Vianet

Cisco Intersight

Cisco Intersight is an SaaS cloud operations platform that provides automation and orchestration to support the lifecycle management of a private cloud. It is a modular platform, allowing only the needed services to be used. As Cisco Intersight is an SaaS platform, it runs in the Cisco cloud, which makes it accessible from everywhere. The data center infrastructure is connected to Cisco Intersight and is managed and maintained from there. The IT departments can add multiple data centers, as this will simplify operations and monitoring. Cisco Intersight offers services to manage the whole cloud stack—from the underlying physical infrastructure, all the way up to the application level (see Figure 21-17).

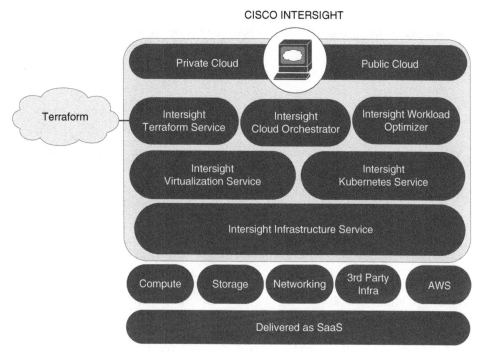

Figure 21-17   *Cisco Intersight*

The Intersight Infrastructure Service supports an advanced infrastructure—Cisco UCS servers, Cisco HyperFlex integrated platforms, and Hitachi and PureStorage storage solutions. The Intersight Virtualization Service and the Intersight Assist appliance provide support for VMware virtualization and the ability to pool resources. Intersight Assist also adds support for third-party hardware and software.

Furthermore, the Intersight Kubernetes Service allows Kubernetes clusters to be configured and provisioned from the cloud. With the underlying infrastructure and the virtualization being under the management of Intersight and the Intersight Kubernetes Service, IT departments can deploy and run containerized workloads in local data centers and public clouds.

The Cisco Intersight Workload Optimizer helps IT departments solve the challenges of underutilized on-premises infrastructure, public cloud overprovisioning, and cost overruns, optimizing the approach to troubleshooting and monitoring, which leads to saved time cycles, in the multicloud. Support for more than 50 common platforms and public clouds provides real-time, full-stack visibility across your applications and infrastructure. This allows for optimal distribution of workloads across private and public clouds. Here are some of the capabilities of the Intersight Workload Optimizer:

■ Manage resource allocation and workload placement in all your infrastructure environments, in a single pane of glass, for supply and demand across the combined private and public clouds

- Optimize cloud costs with automated selection of instances, reserved instances (RIs), relational databases, and storage tiers based on workload consumption and optimal costs

- Lower the risk for migrations to and from the cloud with a data-driven scenario modeling engine

- Dynamically scale, delete, and purchase the right cloud resources to ensure performance at the lowest cost

- Continuously optimize workload placement and cut overprovisioning based on utilization trends

- Scale Kubernetes container limits/requests up or down

- Monitor and recommend Kubernetes clusters scaling up or down

- Support modeling what-if scenarios based on the real-time environment for the Kubernetes clusters

Cisco Intersight Cloud Orchestrator is a powerful tool. It allows IT departments to create and execute complex workflows that can provision environments in the data centers. The Intersight Cloud Orchestrator converts a data center into a private cloud. It includes a library with predefined and custom tasks for the setup and provisioning of the underlying compute, storage, networking, and virtualized infrastructures. The Workflow Designer, shown in Figure 21-18, offers a graphical user interface (GUI) to create, validate, execute, and manage the workflows. Additionally, there are some sample workflows for provisioning storage, compute, network, and virtualization.

Figure 21-18 *Workflow Designer in the Intersight Orchestrator*

Last, but not least, is the Intersight Terraform Service, shown in Figure 21-19, which integrates the Terraform Cloud with Cisco Intersight and provides support for Infrastructure as Code, an important component for any DevOps organization.

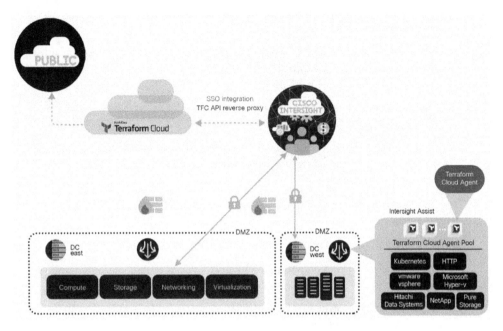

Figure 21-19 *Cisco Intersight Service for HashiCorp Terraform*

Because HashiCorp Terraform is supported in all the major public cloud providers, and the DevOps teams can use it for automated provisioning of resources in the cloud, its adoption in private clouds has been a challenge, as there was the need to deploy additional Terraform agents on premises, change firewall rules and access, and so on. With the integration of the Terraform Cloud with Cisco Intersight, the adoption of Terraform has become seamless and natural. Cisco Intersight already manages the private cloud, so the automation extends from the public clouds used by your organization to the data centers, thus forming a successful, transparent multicloud.

Summary

This chapter covered cloud computing, based on the NIST definition, by looking at the essential characteristics of a cloud, the different deployment models, and the types of cloud services. Additionally, this chapter reviewed the Cisco Intersight cloud platform. Here are some other important points covered in this chapter:

■ The NIST was the first standardization body to provide a definition for cloud computing, or "the cloud."

- Cloud computing is an approach for better utilizing and consuming the computing resources of a data center (or multiple data centers) through orchestration and automation.

- The NIST has defined five essential characteristics, three types of services, and four cloud deployment models.

- The cloud environment must possess the following characteristics: on-demand self-service, measured service, broad network access, resource pooling, and rapid elasticity.

- The three types of cloud services are Infrastructure as a Service, Platform as a Service, and Software as a Service.

- The difference between the cloud services comes down to what computing resources the customer uses and where the demarcation is between the provider's responsibilities and the customer's.

- Cloud solution components include virtualized infrastructure, orchestrator, catalog, and portal.

- There are three cloud deployment models: private, public, and hybrid.

- The private cloud is the organization's own data center with the needed levels of automation and orchestration.

- The public cloud is owned by an organization that provides services in cloud-like manner to external consumers for profit.

- The hybrid cloud is a combination of private and public clouds with the needed level of integration to allow workloads to easily move between the clouds.

- The ability to integrate multiple public and private clouds, as well as cloud services from other companies, has created what's called the "multicloud."

- The Cisco Intersight is an SaaS cloud operations platform and a suite of multiple services allowing for the management, provisioning, orchestrating, automating, deploying, and monitoring of resources across multiple private and public clouds, thus providing companies with the ability to create multiclouds.

- The Intersight Infrastructure Service manages compute, storage, and network infrastructures.

- The Intersight Virtualization Services integrates VMware virtualization.

- The Intersight Kubernetes Service centralizes and automates the management and provisioning of containerized workloads.

- The Intersight Workload Optimizer automates the management of workloads to utilize the resources in the optimal way.

- The Intersight Cloud Orchestrator allows for creating and working with workflows to coordinate resources in the multicloud.

- The Intersight Terraform Service integrates the HashiCorp Terraform Cloud to support Infrastructure as Code automation for the purposes of DevOps processes.

References

NIST Special Publication 800-144: Guidelines on Security and Privacy in Public Cloud Computing, https://nvlpubs.nist.gov/nistpubs/Legacy/SP/nistspecialpublication800-144.pdf

NIST Special Publication 800-145: The NIST Definition of Cloud Computing, https://nvlpubs.nist.gov/nistpubs/Legacy/SP/nistspecialpublication800-145.pdf

NIST Special Publication 800-146: Cloud Computing Synopsis and Recommendations: Recommendations of the National Institute of Standards and Technology, https://nvlpubs.nist.gov/nistpubs/Legacy/SP/nistspecialpublication800-146.pdf

Netflix on AWS: https://aws.amazon.com/solutions/case-studies/netflix/

Azure for the U.S. Government: https://azure.microsoft.com/en-us/global-infrastructure/government/

Azure Germany: https://docs.microsoft.com/en-us/azure/germany/germany-welcome

Azure China 21Vianet: https://docs.microsoft.com/en-us/azure/china/overview-operations#:~:text=Microsoft%20Azure%20operated%20by%2021Vianet%20(Azure%20China)%20is%20a%20physically,Center%20Co.%2C%20Ltd

AWS GovCloud (U.S.): https://aws.amazon.com/govcloud-us/?whats-new-ess.sort-by=item.additionalFields.postDateTime&whats-new-ess.sort-order=desc

Index

D

E

F

M

S

Photo courtesy of Cisco

Register Your Product at ciscopress.com/register

Access additional benefits and **save 35%** on your next purchase

- Automatically receive a coupon for 35% off your next purchase, valid for 30 days. Look for your code in your Cisco Press cart or the Manage Codes section of your account page.

- Download available product updates.

- Access bonus material if available.*

- Check the box to hear from us and receive exclusive offers on new editions and related products.

Registration benefits vary by product. Benefits will be listed on your account page under Registered Products.

Learning Solutions for Self-Paced Study, Enterprise, and the Classroom

Cisco Press is the Cisco Systems authorized book publisher of Cisco networking technology, Cisco certification self-study, and Cisco Networking Academy Program materials.

At ciscopress.com, you can:

- Shop our books, eBooks, practice tests, software, and video courses
- Sign up to receive special offers
- Access thousands of free chapters and video lessons

Visit **ciscopress.com/community** to connect with Cisco Press

Addison-Wesley · Adobe Press · Cisco Press · Microsoft Press · Pearson IT Certification · Que · Sams · Peachpit Press